ROUTLEDGE HANDBOOK OF BANKING AND FINANCE IN ASIA

The *Routledge Handbook of Banking and Finance in Asia* brings together leading scholars, policy-makers, and practitioners to provide a comprehensive and cutting-edge guide to Asia's financial institutions, markets, and systems.

Part I provides a country-by-country overview of banking and finance in East, Southeast, and South Asia, including examples from China, Japan, Hong Kong, India, and Singapore.

Part II contains thematic chapters, covering topics such as commercial banking, development banking, infrastructure finance, stock markets, insurance, and sovereign wealth funds. It also includes examinations of banking regulation and supervision, and analyses of macroprudential regulation, capital flow management measures, and monetary policy. Finally, it provides new insights into topical issues such as SME, green, and Islamic finance.

This handbook is an essential resource for scholars and students of Asian economics and finance and for professionals working in financial markets in Asia.

Ulrich Volz is Head of the Department of Economics and Reader in Economics at SOAS University of London, UK, and Senior Research Fellow at the German Development Institute, Germany.

Peter J. Morgan is Senior Consulting Economist and Co-chair of Research at the Asian Development Bank Institute, Japan.

Naoyuki Yoshino is Dean and CEO of the Asian Development Bank Institute and Emeritus Professor of Economics at Keio University, Japan.

ROUTLEDGE HANDBOOK OF BANKING AND FINANCE IN ASIA

Edited by Ulrich Volz, Peter J. Morgan, and Naoyuki Yoshino

CO-PUBLICATION OF THE ASIAN DEVELOPMENT
BANK INSTITUTE AND ROUTLEDGE

Routledge
Taylor & Francis Group
www.routledge.com

ADBInstitute

First published 2019
by Routledge
2 Park Square, Milton Park, Abingdon, Oxon OX14 4RN

and by Routledge
52 Vanderbilt Avenue, New York, NY 10017

First issued in paperback 2020

Routledge is an imprint of the Taylor & Francis Group, an informa business

The views in this publication do not necessarily reflect the views and
policies of the Asian Development Bank (ADB) Institute, its Advisory
Council, ADB's Board of Governors, or the governments of ADB members.

The ADB Institute (ADBI) does not guarantee the accuracy of the
data included in this publication and accepts no responsibility for any
consequence of their use.

By making any designation of or reference to a particular territory or
geographic area, or by using the term "country" or other geographical
names in this publication, ADBI does not intend to make any judgments as
to the legal or other status of any territory or area.

Kasumigaseki Building 8F
3–2–5, Kasumigaseki, Chiyoda-ku
Tokyo 100–6008, Japan

www.adbi.org

British Library Cataloguing-in-Publication Data
A catalogue record for this book is available from the British Library

Library of Congress Cataloging-in-Publication Data
Names: Volz, Ulrich, 1977– editor. | Morgan, Peter J., 1951– editor. |
Yoshino, Naoyuki, 1950– editor.
Title: Routledge handbook of banking and finance in Asia/edited by
Ulrich Volz, Peter J. Morgan and Naoyuki Yoshino.
Description: Abingdon, Oxon ; New York, NY : Routledge, 2019. |
Includes bibliographical references and index.
Identifiers: LCCN 2018027456 (print) | LCCN 2018029165 (ebook) |
ISBN 9781315543222 (Ebook) | ISBN 9781134862078 (Adobe Reader) |
ISBN 9781134862146 (ePub) | ISBN 9781134862214 (Mobipocket
Encrypted) | ISBN 9781138685406 (hardback)
Subjects: LCSH: Banks and banking – Asia. | Finance – Asia.
Classification: LCC HG3252 (ebook) | LCC HG3252. R68 2019 (print) |
DDC 332.1095 – dc23
LC record available at https://lccn.loc.gov/2018027456

ISBN 13: 978–0–367–58048–3 (pbk)
ISBN 13: 978–1–138–68540–6 (hbk)

Typeset in Bembo
by Apex CoVantage, LLC

CONTENTS

Contents

FIGURES

TABLES

BOX

CONTRIBUTORS

Joshua Aizenman, Robert R. and Katheryn A. Dockson Chair in Economics and International Relations, Department of Economics, University of Southern California

Iwan J. Azis, Adjunct Professor at Charles H. Dyson School of Applied Economics and Management, Cornell University; Professor of Economics, Faculty of Economics and Business, University of Indonesia

Jonathan A. Batten, CIMB Chair Professor of Banking and Finance, School of Economics, Finance and Banking, Universiti Utara Malaysia

Pornpinun Chantapacdepong, Assistant Director, Monetary Policy Group, Bank of Thailand

Hwee Kwan Chow, Professor of Economics and Statistics, School of Economics, Singapore Management University

Nestor Aldave Espenilla Jr., Governor, Bangko Sentral ng Pilipinas

Hans Genberg, Executive Director, The South East Asian Central Banks (SEACEN) Research and Training Centre

Kiseok Hong, Professor of Economics, Department of Economics, Ewha Womans University

Hiro Ito, Department Chair and Professor of Economics, Department of Economics, Portland State University

Takatoshi Ito, Professor of International and Public Affairs, School of International and Public Affairs, Columbia University

Yothin Jinjarak, Associate Professor School of Economics and Finance, Victoria University of Wellington

Akbar Komijani, Deputy Governor, Central Bank of the Islamic Republic of Iran

W. Jean J. Kwon, Edwin A. G. Manton Endowed Chair Professor in International Insurance and Risk Management, School of Risk Management, Peter J. Tobin College of Business, St. John's University, New York

Choong Lyol Lee, Dean and Professor, College of Business and Economics, Korea University at Sejong Campus

Jong-Wha Lee, Professor of Economics, Department of Economics and Director of the Asiatic Research Institute, Korea University

Igor Lončarski, Associate Professor of Finance, Faculty of Economics, University of Ljubljana

Rakesh Mohan, Senior Fellow, Jackson Institute for Global Affairs, Yale University; Distinguished Fellow, Brookings India

Peter J. Morgan, Senior Consulting Economist and Co-chair of Research, Asian Development Bank Institute

Shinichi Nakabayashi, Director for Administration, Management, and Coordination, Asian Development Bank Institute

Vikram Nehru, Distinguished Practitioner-in-Residence, Johns Hopkins University School of Advanced International Studies

Cyn-Young Park, Director for Regional Cooperation and Integration, Economic Research and Regional Cooperation Department, Asian Development Bank

Sai Fan Pei, Associate Professor of Quantitative Finance, Lee Kong Chian School of Business, Singapore Management University

Partha Ray, Professor of Economics, Indian Institute of Management, Calcutta

Shubhomoy Ray, Managing Director and CEO, Finnacle Capital Advisors

Andrew Sheng, Distinguished Fellow of Asia Global Institute, University of Hong Kong; Chief Adviser to the China Banking Regulatory Commission

Ilhyock Shim, Special Adviser on International Financial Stability Policy, Monetary and Economic Department, Bank for International Settlements

Sukudhew Singh, Deputy Governor, Central Bank of Malaysia

Péter G. Szilágyi, Associate Professor, Department of Economics and Business, Central European University

Farhad Taghizadeh-Hesary, Assistant Professor of Economics, School of Economics, Keio University

Damian Tobin, Lecturer in Chinese Business and Management, School of Finance and Management, SOAS University of London

Ulrich Volz, Head of Department of Economics and Reader in Economics, SOAS University of London; Senior Research Fellow, German Development Institute

Quan-Hoang Vuong, Senior Research Fellow, Centre Emile Bernheim, Universite Libre de Bruxelles

Naoyuki Yoshino, Dean and CEO, Asian Development Bank Institute

Michael J. Zamorski, Chief Executive of Compliance and Regulatory Affairs, Beal Bank

ACKNOWLEDGMENTS

The editors are grateful to Pornpinun Chantapacdepong for helping to organize an authors' workshop at ADBI and for commenting on several chapters, Ainslie Smith for coordinating the formatting of chapters, Muriel Ordonez and Jera Lego for publication management, Long Q. Trinh for research assistance, and Ayako Kudo for secretarial support. The editors would also like to thank all contributors for their chapters.

ABBREVIATIONS

ABF	Asian Bond Fund
ABMF	Asian Bond Market Forum
ABMI	Asian Bond Markets Initiative
ACU	Asian currency unit
ADB	Asian Development Bank
ADM	Asian dollar market
AE	advanced economy
AEC	ASEAN Economic Community
AFC	Asian financial crisis
AIIB	Asian Infrastructure Investment Bank
AMC	asset management company
AMLATFPUAA	Anti-Money Laundering, Anti-Terrorism Financing and Proceeds of Unlawful Activities Act
ASEAN	Association of Southeast Asian Nations
ASEAN+3	Association of Southeast Asian Nations plus the People's Republic of China, Japan, and the Republic of Korea
ASM	Asia SME Finance Monitor
ATS	automated trading services
AUM	assets under management
BAP	Bankers Association of the Philippines
BAPINDO	Indonesian Development Bank
BCBS	Basel Committee on Banking Supervision
BCP	Basel Core Principles
BDFI	bilateral development finance institution
BI	Bank Indonesia
BIS	Bank for International Settlements
BNM	Bank Negara Malaysia
BoJ	Bank of Japan
BOT	Bank of Thailand
BSP	Bangko Sentral ng Pilipinas
CAR	capital adequacy ratio

CB	central bank
CBA	Central Bank of Malaysia Act
CBLO	collateralized borrowing and lending obligation
CBP	Central Bank of the Philippines
CCIL	Clearing Corporation of India Limited
CCP	Communist Party of China
CDB	China Development Bank
CDS	credit default swap
CFM	capital flow management measure
CFWC	Central Financial Work Commission
CGIF	Credit Guarantee and Investment Facility
CIC	China Investment Corporation
CIRC	China Insurance Regulatory Commission
CIS	Commonwealth of Independent States
CLI	China Life Insurance
CMIC	Capital Markets Integrity Corporation
CMU	Central Money Markets Unit
CP	core principles
CPF	Central Provident Fund
CRD	Credit Risk Database
C-ROSS	China Risk Oriented Solvency System
CSRC	China Securities Regulatory Commission
DBJ	Development Bank of Japan
DBU	domestic banking unit
DFI	development finance institution
DOF	Department of Finance
D-SIB	domestic systemically important bank
ECA	export credit agency
EME	emerging market economy
EMEAP	Executives' Meeting of East Asia-Pacific Central Banks
EMP	exchange market pressure
EPF	Employees Provident Fund of Malaysia
EXIM	Export-Import
FDI	foreign direct investment
FIEA	Financial Instruments and Exchange Act
FII	foreign institutional investor
FILP	Fiscal Investment and Loan Program
FOCB	foreign-owned commercial bank
FPI	foreign portfolio investment
FSA	Financial Services Act, Financial Services Agency
FSAP	Financial Sector Assessment Program
FSC	Financial Stability Committee
FSCC	Financial Stability Coordination Council
FSEC	Financial Stability Executive Committee
FSF	Financial Sector Forum
FSPB	Financial Services Professional Board
FSRG	Financial Sector Review Group
FSSN	financial system safety net

FTV	financing-to-value ratio
FX	foreign exchange
GB	government bond
GDP	gross domestic product
GFC	global financial crisis
GIC	Government Investment Corporation
GIC	General Insurance Corporation
GNI	gross national income
GNPA	gross non-performing assets
GPIF	Government Pension Investment Fund in Japan
G7	Group of Seven
G20	Group of Twenty
G-SIBs	global systemically important banks
HIT	hometown investment trust
HKEX	Hong Kong Exchanges and Clearing Limited
HKMA	Hong Kong Monetary Authority
HNWI	high net worth individual
HNX	Hanoi Stock Exchange
HOSE	Ho Chi Minh Stock Exchange
IBK	Industrial Bank of Korea
IBRD	International Bank for Reconstruction and Development
IC	Insurance Commission
IDB	Islamic Development Bank
IFC	international financial center
IFSA	Islamic Financial Services Act
IFSB	Islamic Financial Services Board
IMF	International Monetary Fund
IPO	initial public offering
IR	international reserves
IT	information technology
JBIC	Japan Bank for International Cooperation
JFC	Japan Finance Corporation
JFG	Japan Federation of Credit Guarantee Corporations
JGB	Japanese Government Bond
JSCB	joint-stock commercial bank
KOSPI	Korea Composite Stock Price Index
KYC	know your customer
LCY	local currency
LIC	life insurance corporation
LPS	Lembaga Penjamin Simpanan
LTV	loan-to-value
M&A	mergers and acquisitions
MADB	Myanmar Agricultural Development Bank
MAS	Monetary Authority of Singapore
MDB	multilateral development bank
MF	mutual fund
MFI	microfinance institution
MGS	Malaysian Government Securities

MoA	memorandum of agreement
MoF	Ministry of Finance
MPM	macroprudential measure
MSE	Manila Stock Exchange
MSME	micro, small, and medium-sized enterprise
NBFC	non-banking financial company
NBFI	non-bank financial institution
NCB	National Credit Bureau
NDB	national development bank
NeDB	New Development Bank
NGO	non-governmental organization
NIM	net interest margin
NPL	non-performing loan
NSE	National Stock Exchange
OCBC	Oversea-Chinese Banking Corporation
OECD	Organisation for Economic Co-operation and Development
OJK	Otoritas Jasa Keuangan (Financial Services Authority of Indonesia)
OSE	Osaka Exchange
PBC	People's Bank of China
PCF	People's Credit Fund
PDEx	Philippine Dealing and Exchange Corporation
PDIC	Philippine Deposit Insurance Corporation
PIDM	Malaysian Deposit Insurance Corporation
POS	point of sale
POSB	Post Office Savings Bank
PPP	public-private partnership
PRC	People's Republic of China
PSE	Philippine Stock Exchange
PSEI	Philippine Composite Index
RBC	risk-based capital
RBI	Reserve Bank of India
RCS	Registrars of Cooperative Societies
ROA	return on assets
ROE	return on equity
RP	repurchase agreement
RPT	related party transaction
RRB	Regional Rural Bank
RTGS	real-time gross settlement system
SBFC	Small Business Finance Corporation
SBP	State Bank of Pakistan
SBV	State Bank of Vietnam
SC	Securities Commission
SCSC	State Council Securities Commission
SEBI	Securities and Exchange Board of India
SEC	Securities and Exchange Commission
SFC	Securities and Futures Commission
SFI	specialized financial institution
SGS	Singapore Government Securities

SGX	Singapore Exchange
SIB	systemically important bank
SIFC	Small Industry Finance Corporation
SIFO	Small Industry Finance Office
SLI	Samsung Life Insurance
SMEs	small and medium-sized enterprises
SML	special mention loan
SOCB	state-owned commercial bank
SRC	Securities Regulation Code
SWF	sovereign wealth fund
SWIFT	Society for Worldwide Interbank Financial Telecommunication
TFB	Trust Fund Bureau
TSE	Tokyo Stock Exchange
UK	United Kingdom
UOB	United Overseas Bank
US	United States
VCF	venture capital fund
VSD	Viet Nam Securities Depository Center
VSM	Viet Nam Stock Market
WTO	World Trade Organization

1

INTRODUCTION

Characteristics of Asian financial systems in comparative perspective

Peter J. Morgan, Ulrich Volz, and Naoyuki Yoshino

Asia has become the most dynamic economic area in the world economy, and this dynamism is reflected in the developments that are taking place in the banking and financial systems of Asian economies. The chapters in this handbook aim to provide an overview of the developments and trends that have taken place in Asian banking and finance, and of the challenges ahead.

The financial sector in Asia has generally performed well in supporting the growth process, as shown by Asia's unmatched growth record. Nonetheless, maintaining a strong growth path and meeting the needs of savers and investors in the coming decades will provide many new challenges to Asia's financial sector. These include the need to fund investments in infrastructure and human capital, support the development of innovation and the emergence of new enterprises, promote financial inclusion, accommodate the aging of Asian populations, and support green growth. Maintaining economic and financial stability in a world subject to external shocks and volatile capital flows provides another set of major challenges. This chapter aims to provide comparative perspectives on the previous and current situation of financial market development in the Asian economies covered in this book, including aspects such as financial inclusion and capital market openness.

Current situation of financial development, capital market openness, and financial inclusion

This section provides broad measures of financial development in Asia, including market size, capital market openness, and financial inclusion. Of course, there are many other dimensions that are covered in more detail in the individual chapters.

Overall financial size

Table 1.1 provides a snapshot of the overall level of financial development in many Asian economies in 2015, as measured by the share of bank credit, bonds, and stocks in gross domestic product (GDP).[1] Clearly there is a huge range of development, from low-income economies with relatively rudimentary financial systems to sophisticated financial centers such as Hong Kong, China; Japan; and Singapore. The mix of funding by source also varies significantly, as the share of funding from bonds and stocks tends to rise with the level of per capita income and

Table 1.1 Total finance as percentage of GDP, 2015

Economy	Bank Credit	Bonds	Stocks	Total
Bangladesh	41.0	NA	24.9	65.9
Brunei Darussalam	40.1	NA	0.0	40.1
Cambodia	56.5	NA	NA	56.5
People's Republic of China	140.4	62.6	64.1	267.2
Hong Kong, China	212.2	NA	1,029.1	1,241.3
India	50.2	32.4	42.0	124.7
Indonesia	31.5	24.6	71.5	127.6
Japan	102.6	208.1	85.9	396.6
Republic of Korea	136.6	140.3	99.8	376.7
Lao PDR	18.9	NA	NA	18.9
Malaysia	119.6	108.7	26.3	254.6
Mongolia	55.2	NA	24.9	80.0
Myanmar	16.0	NA	4.0	20.0
Nepal	56.7	NA	26.5	83.1
Pakistan	14.9	35.8	27.1	77.8
Philippines	39.5	50.5	25.2	115.2
Singapore	127.9	97.5	88.4	313.9
Sri Lanka	27.5	11.5	29.3	68.3
Thailand	114.6	77.7	97.7	290.1
Viet Nam	102.8	24.2	53.6	180.5

Notes: Bank credit calculated from bank deposit to GDP and bank credit to bank deposit ratio. Lao PDR data for 2010. GDP = gross domestic product. Lao PDR = Lao People's Democratic Republic. NA = not available.

Source: World Bank Financial Development Index Database.

financial sophistication. Highly financially developed economies tend to show overall financing ratios of over 300% of GDP, including Hong Kong, China; Japan; the Republic of Korea; and Singapore. Total financing in economies with intermediate level of financial development range from 100% to 300% of GDP, including the People's Republic of China (PRC), India, Indonesia, Malaysia, the Philippines, Thailand, and Viet Nam. The other economies have overall financing levels less than 100% of GDP.

To be sure, total financing is only a crude measure of financial development and may be biased by factors such as excessive lending by the banking sector. To address this issue, Svirydzenka (2016) developed a composite measure of financial development which aggregates scores for six measures of how deep, accessible, and efficient are financial institutions and financial markets, respectively. The scores range from zero to one. Figures 1.1a, 1.1b, and 1.1c show the movements of the index from 1980 to 2014 for countries with latest scores in the range of 0–0.25 (low), 0.25–0.5 (medium), and 0.5–1.0 (high), respectively.

Overall, the results in Figures 1.1a–c match up fairly well with the crude measures of financial development in Table 1.1. All of the economies with gross financing over 300% of GDP also have composite financial development scores over 0.5. So do Malaysia and Thailand, which is not too surprising given that their gross financing levels were only slightly below 300%. Similarly, aside from Malaysia, Thailand, and Viet Nam, all of the economies with gross financing between 100% and 300% of GDP scored in the medium range of 0.25–0.5 for the composite financial development indicator, including the PRC, India, Indonesia, and the Philippines, and Viet Nam's score was only a shade below the cutoff level.[2]

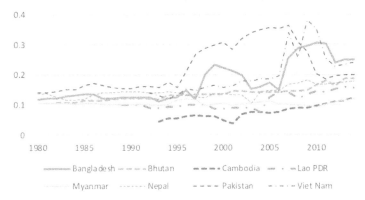

Figure 1.1a   Composite measure of financial development: economies with current score of 0–0.25 (low development)

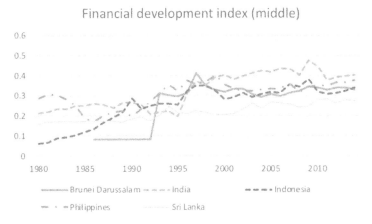

Figure 1.1b   Composite measure of financial development: economies with current score of 0.25–0.5 (medium development)

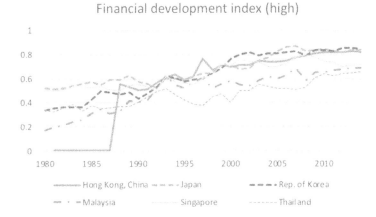

Figure 1.1c   Composite measure of financial development: economies with current score of 0.5–1.0 (high development)

Note: Lao PDR = Lao People's Democratic Republic.

Source: Svirydzenka (2016).

Banking sector development

Within the financial sector as a whole, the banking sector tends to develop first, and the importance of the banking sector in Asian finance is well known. Table 1.1 shows that the banking sector has the largest share of aggregate finance in all economies, except Hong Kong, China; Indonesia; Japan; the Republic of Korea; Pakistan; the Philippines; and Sri Lanka. Table 1.2 shows the development of the banking sector over time in Asian economies. The share of bank credit in GDP in most economies has shown a steady uptrend, with the highest levels being reached in the PRC; Hong Kong, China; Japan; the Republic of Korea; Malaysia; Singapore; Thailand; and Viet Nam (all over 100% of GDP). However, Japan's level fell sharply from earlier levels, reflecting the collapse of the financial bubble of the 1980s. Lending in Indonesia, Malaysia, and Thailand also fell after the Asian financial crisis of 1997, although no such effect was seen in the Republic of Korea. Lending ratios were stable if erratic in Pakistan and Sri Lanka.

Bond markets

Bond markets have developed more slowly and unevenly in Asian economies, reflecting difficulties related to the concept of "original sin" regarding local currency bonds and the risks associated with issuing bonds in foreign currencies that were highlighted painfully during the Asian financial crisis of 1997. However, bond markets have now achieved substantial development in some economies. Table 1.3 breaks down the current level of Asian debt by major class

Table 1.2 Banking sector development in Asia (bank credit as percentage of GDP)

Economy	1990	2000	2005	2010	2015
Bangladesh	NA	22.7	31.1	35.6	41.0
Brunei Darussalam	NA	66.6	39.7	40.7	40.1
Cambodia	NA	5.9	8.2	25.0	56.5
PRC	75.9	107.4	109.7	119.7	140.4
Hong Kong, China	NA	148.0	138.8	163.8	212.2
India	24.1	26.6	35.3	44.1	50.2
Indonesia	38.0	17.7	22.7	22.3	31.5
Japan	167.6	186.5	94.5	101.5	102.6
Republic of Korea	43.2	66.1	78.7	91.4	136.6
Lao PDR	0.5	6.7	5.8	18.9	NA
Malaysia	76.8	122.8	101.8	101.7	119.6
Mongolia	NA	6.5	24.9	36.6	55.2
Myanmar	3.3	8.2	4.0	3.9	16.0
Nepal	11.7	27.7	26.5	51.2	56.7
Pakistan	23.4	21.0	27.1	21.0	14.9
Philippines	16.6	35.7	25.2	27.8	39.5
Singapore	74.0	93.6	88.4	90.9	127.9
Sri Lanka	17.7	27.0	29.3	20.8	27.5
Thailand	72.3	116.6	97.7	92.2	114.6
Viet Nam	NA	30.4	53.6	100.0	102.8

Notes: Calculated from bank deposit to GDP and bank credit to bank deposit ratio. Lao PDR = Lao People's Democratic Republic. NA = not available. PRC = People's Republic of China.

Source: World Bank Financial Development Index Database.

Table 1.3 Bond market development in Asia (outstanding debt as percentage of GDP, 2015)

Economy	Gov't Bond LCY	Corp Bond, LCY	Gov't Bond FCY	Corp Bond FCY	Total
PRC	38.3	20.6	0.3	3.5	62.6
India	30.9	0.0	0.0	1.5	32.4
Indonesia	13.0	2.2	5.6	3.8	24.6
Japan	187.6	14.9	1.2	4.4	208.1
Republic of Korea	52.6	76.6	2.4	8.8	140.3
Malaysia	52.7	41.5	3.4	11.2	108.7
Pakistan	33.9	0.0	1.9	0.0	35.8
Philippines	29.6	6.1	10.3	4.5	50.5
Singapore	44.9	34.3	0.0	18.3	97.5
Sri Lanka	NA	0.0	8.7	2.9	11.5
Taipei,China	32.9	28.4	0.0	2.6	63.8
Thailand	54.8	18.4	0.7	3.8	77.7
Viet Nam	21.6	0.8	1.5	0.3	24.2

Notes: FCY = foreign currency debt. LCY = local currency debt. NA = not available. PRC = People's Republic of China.

Sources: Data for the PRC, Indonesia, Japan, Republic of Korea, Malaysia, Philippines, Singapore, Thailand, and Viet Nam are from ADB's Asian Bond Online Database; data for other countries are from BIS's debt statistics and World Bank Development Indicators (GDP at current price).

of issuer and currency of issuance. Japan, the Republic of Korea, Malaysia, and Singapore have the highest levels of total debt, consistent with the overall high level of financial development. Economies with intermediate levels of debt include the PRC; the Philippines; Taipei,China; and Thailand. For all economies except the Republic of Korea, Sri Lanka and Taipei,China, local currency government debt makes up by far the largest share of total debt. This partly reflects expenditures for funding large-scale buildups of foreign exchange reserves in some economies. Excluding Sri Lanka, the share of foreign currency debt in the total is relatively small, only about 12% of the total. Only the PRC, the Republic of Korea, Malaysia, Singapore, and Taipei,China have well-developed corporate bond markets.

Stock markets

Table 1.4 shows, as percent of GDP, the evolution of stock market capitalization of Asian economies. Most have shown rapid development since 1990, except for some more mature markets such as Japan and Malaysia. As with other financial development indicators, the ratios are highest for Hong Kong, China; Japan; Malaysia; and Singapore. Hong Kong, China has by far the largest market capitalization, partly reflecting the listing of shares of PRC companies on the "H share" index. Market capitalization ratios are generally lower in South Asia, with India having the most developed market.

Financial openness

Along with economic and financial development, financial systems tend to become more open as well (i.e., restrictions on capital accounts tend to be eased). However, capital account regimes can become more restrictive as well, particularly if countries experience shocks from episodes of rapid capital inflows or outflows.

Table 1.4 Stock market capitalization (percentage of GDP)

Economy	1990	2000	2005	2010	2015
Bangladesh	NA	3.42	4.63	26.30	24.90
PRC	NA	38.09	19.19	63.79	64.14
Hong Kong, China	105.39	356.55	526.93	1,086.34	1,029.13
Indonesia	4.39	26.52	25.65	39.88	42.02
India	9.66	34.15	56.58	89.58	71.5
Republic of Korea	43.76	44.10	67.01	92.34	85.85
Japan	113.30	80.44	84.75	64.61	99.79
Malaysia	99.05	134.60	126.48	141.80	129.01
Mongolia	NA	3.10	1.43	10.92	5.13
Nepal	NA	10.50	13.53	33.98	55.98
Pakistan	6.29	8.77	41.41	19.28	24.46
Philippines	18.89	39.14	33.38	62.05	84.51
Singapore	98.69	179.07	187.18	246.13	227.69
Sri Lanka	7.89	7.75	19.05	25.74	26.30
Thailand	25.77	33.03	63.76	69.06	95.85
Viet Nam	NA	NA	0.61	23.36	24.94

Notes: PRC = People's Republic of China. NA = not available.

Sources: All data collected from the World Bank Financial Development Index database, except data for Bangladesh, Sri Lanka, Mongolia, Nepal, and Pakistan in 2015; Bangladesh in 2015, Dhaka Stock Exchange Ltd. for market capitalization; Mongolia in 2015, Mongolian stock exchange for market capitalization; Nepal in 2015, Nepal stock exchange for market capitalization; Pakistan in 2015, Pakistan Stock Exchange Ltd. for market capitalization; WDI for GDP and exchange rate for these five markets.

Financial openness is not easy to measure, and there are two broad approaches to doing so: de jure and de facto. De jure measures assess the restrictiveness of published laws and regulations regarding foreign exchange and capital account transactions. These are typically based on the IMF's *Annual Report on Exchange Arrangements and Exchange Restrictions* (IMF 2016). Examples of this approach include Quinn (2003) and the Chinn-Ito Index (Chinn and Ito 2006). The Chinn-Ito Index is compiled by evaluating four major categories of restrictions on external accounts: (1) the presence of a multiple exchange rate regime, (2) the presence of restrictions on current account transactions, (3) the presence of restrictions on capital account transactions, and (4) the presence of a requirement of the surrender of export proceeds. The index score ranges from −1.9 (fully closed) to +2.3 (fully open).

Figure 1.2 shows the values of the Chinn-Ito Index for Asian economies in 2015. The data show a wide range, with roughly half of the economies having relatively closed accounts, about one quarter of economies with partially closed accounts, and about one quarter with relatively open accounts. Hong Kong, China; Japan; and Singapore are rated as fully open, consistent with their status as regional financial centers, while both the PRC and India have maintained relatively low ratings of −1.19 (i.e., fully closed). In general, financial openness is positively correlated with other measures of financial development, although there are significant exceptions, such as Cambodia and Malaysia.

However, it is widely recognized that de jure measures may not reliably capture the effective degree of capital market openness, since application and enforcement of rules may vary widely, and details of regulations not captured in the index may have significant implications for market openness. For example, both the PRC and India regulate inflows by foreign institutional investors, but the PRC has established strict quotas, while India has no quotas.

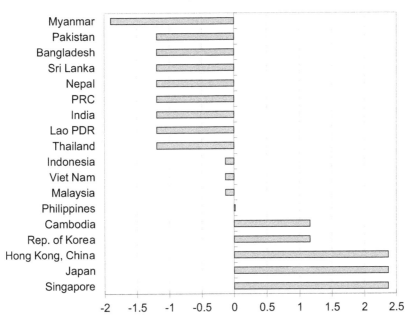

Figure 1.2 Chinn–Ito indices for Asian economies, 2015

Notes: Lao PDR = Lao People's Democratic Republic. PRC = People's Republic of China.

Source: Chinn and Ito (2006).

The alternative approach is to measure the de facto capital market openness based on estimates of actual capital flows. One of the main sources in this regard is Lane and Milesi-Ferretti (2007), who estimated ratios to GDP of gross external assets and liabilities for 145 countries for 1970–2004. The essential idea was that a higher level of external assets and liabilities (relative to GDP or some other measure) indicated the effective openness of capital markets. However, there are many difficulties with this approach.

Beck and Demirgüç-Kunt (2009) examined a number of globalization indicators, including the ratio to GDP of international debt securities outstanding; net issuance of international debt securities, loans from non-resident banks, and remittances; and the ratio of offshore deposits to bank deposits. However, only the level of outstanding international debt securities showed a clear and consistent correlation with income levels. Figure 1.3 shows the ratio of international debt securities to GDP for some major Asian economies. The distribution of values is broadly similar to that of the Chinn–Ito de jure index, with Hong Kong, China and Singapore being the most open and the PRC, India, Pakistan, and Thailand being relatively closed. However, there are some notable exceptions as well. The Philippines and Sri Lanka have relatively high shares, while Japan and the Republic of Korea have relatively low shares. In the case of the latter, this partly reflects the fact that they have relatively little need to tap foreign currency markets.

Financial inclusion

Financial inclusion, that is, access to finance, is receiving increasing attention as having the potential to contribute to economic and financial development while at the same time fostering more inclusive growth and greater income equality. Leaders of the G20 countries have

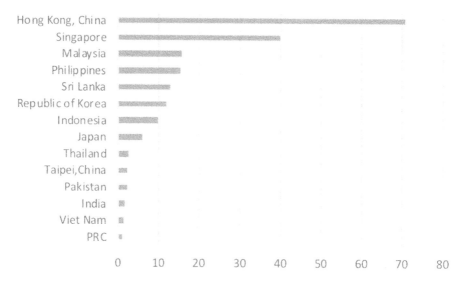

Figure 1.3 Ratio of international debt securities to GDP

Notes: GDP = gross domestic product. PRC = People's Republic of China.

Sources: Data from the BIS's international debt securities database (www.bis.org/statistics/secstats.htm) and the IMF World Economic Outlook database (www.imf.org/external/pubs/ft/weo/2017/01/weodata/index.aspx).

approved the Financial Inclusion Action Plan and established the Global Partnership for Financial Inclusion to promote the financial access agenda. The Asia-Pacific Economic Cooperation (APEC) finance ministers' process has a dedicated forum looking at financial inclusion issues. The implementation of the Association of Southeast Asian Nations (ASEAN) Framework on Equitable Economic Development has made the promotion of financial inclusion a key objective (ASEAN 2014). Reflecting the importance of financial inclusion, the Asian Development Bank has approved 121 projects (amounting to USD 2.59 billion as of 2012) to support microfinance in countries in Asia and the Pacific (ADB 2012). Many individual Asian economies have adopted strategies on financial inclusion as an important part of their overall strategies to achieve inclusive growth.[3]

However, there is still much to achieve. One key indicator of household access to finance is the percentage of adults who have an individual or joint account at a formal financial institution such as a bank, credit union, cooperative, post office, or microfinance institution, or with a mobile money provider. According to the most recent Global Findex database for 2014, the total number of adults without accounts is about two billion. East Asia and the Pacific and South Asia combined account for 55% of the world's unbanked adults, mainly in India and the PRC (Demirgüç-Kunt et al. 2015).

One of the main measures of financial inclusion is the percentage of adults with accounts at a formal financial institution. Account holdings tend to rise with per capita GDP, as would be expected, but there is still huge variation across countries (Figure 1.4). The large variation implies that other factors besides income play important roles, including overall financial development, financial system structure, regulatory, institutional, social, and geographic

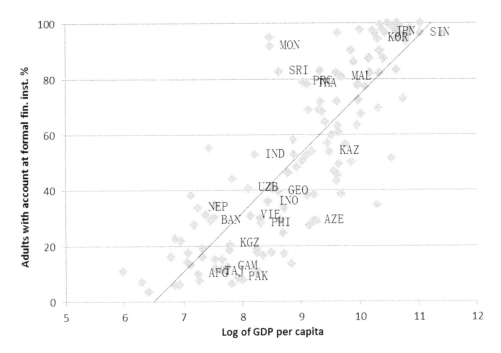

Figure 1.4 Relation of per capita GDP to deposit penetration for adults, 2014

Note: GDP = gross domestic product.

Source: World Bank Global Findex Survey (www.worldbank.org/en/programs/globalfindex).

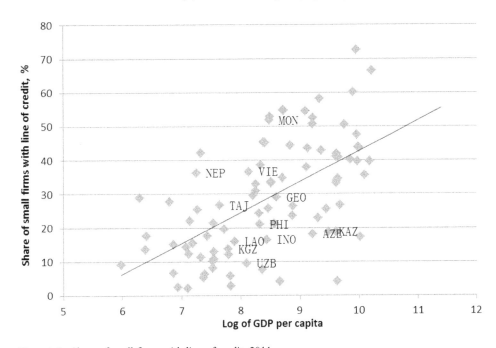

Figure 1.5 Share of small firms with line of credit, 2011

Source: World Bank Global Findex Survey (www.worldbank.org/en/programs/globalfindex).

factors. The majority of Asian economies (for which data are available) have penetration shares of less than 55%.

Figure 1.5 shows a fairly strong relationship between per capita GDP and the share of small firms with a line of credit overall, but, again, the pattern among emerging Asian economies shows a high degree of variation. Data are available for considerably fewer countries than in the case of household financial access. Central and West Asian economies, Indonesia, the Lao PDR, and the Philippines stand out as having relatively low financing for small and medium-sized enterprises (SMEs).

Outline of the book and outlook

The preceding overview is of course only cursory, but the following chapters will provide much more in-depth perspectives of the state of banking and finance in Asian economies. The first part of the handbook comprises country chapters for the following economies: the PRC; Hong Kong, China; India; Indonesia; Japan; the Republic of Korea; Malaysia; the Philippines; Singapore; Thailand; and Viet Nam. The second part of the handbook comprises thematic chapters addressing a range of important issues: commercial banking in Asia; development banking; the development of Asian bond and stock markets; the role of institutional investors and sovereign wealth funds; trends in the insurance sector; the importance and challenges of infrastructure finance; household financial inclusion; SME finance; monetary policy and central banking in Asia; macroprudential regulation and capital flow management; international capital flows and exchange rate policies; financial integration in Asia; banking regulation and supervision in Asia; the development of green finance in Asia; and recent trends in Islamic banking and finance in Asia.

Finance and banking have clearly played an important role in the development of Asian economies. But the people in many Asian countries have also experienced the significant cost of financial crises that resulted from financial excesses and speculation related to insufficient or inappropriate financial and macroprudential regulation and badly managed capital account liberalization. Public policy and financial regulation need to ensure that financial institutions adapt to the changing needs of firms and households in dynamic economies, and that the financial sector supports the development of the real economy instead of serving primarily its own interest. As discussed in several chapters of this handbook, a lot of progress has been made in developing the capacities of financial authorities and regulatory and supervisory frameworks in response to lessons from crises at home and abroad. There has also been an increase in international cooperation both on a regional and global level as Asian financial sectors have opened up and become increasingly interconnected. Safeguarding financial stability will be a continuing challenge.

Together, policy-makers and the financial sector will also have to continue efforts in promoting financial inclusion, supporting innovation activity, channeling investments into sustainable infrastructure and human capital, developing insurance and pension solutions for aging Asian populations, and aligning finance with sustainable development. All of these activities will be crucial to help Asian societies fully develop their potential.

Notes

1 Other aspects of financial development, such as the insurance sector, are covered in their respective individual chapters.
2 Bangladesh, Pakistan, and Viet Nam had higher financial development scores in some earlier years, but these proved not to be sustainable.
3 See Chapter 20 for a more detailed discussion of financial inclusion in Asia.

References

Asian Development Bank (ADB). 2012. *Technical Assistance Report. Improving Financial Inclusion in Asia and the Pacific.* Manila: Asian Development Bank.

Association of Southeast Asian Nations (ASEAN). 2014. *The ASEAN Framework for Equitable Economic Development.* Jakarta, Indonesia: ASEAN Secretariat. www.asean.org/news/item/the-asean-framework-for-equitable-economic-development

Beck, T., and A. Demirgüç-Kunt. 2009. Financial Institutions and Markets Across Countries and over Time – Data and Analysis. Policy Research Working Paper. Working Paper WPS4943. Washington, DC: World Bank.

Chinn, M., and H. Ito. 2006. What Matters for Financial Development? Capital Controls, Institutions, and Interactions. *Journal of Development Economics* 81(1): 163–192.

Demirgüç-Kunt, A., L. Klapper, D. Singer, and P. Oudheusden. 2015. The Global Findex Database 2014: Measuring Financial Inclusion Around the World. Policy Research Working Paper 7255. Washington, DC: World Bank.

International Monetary Fund. 2016. *Annual Report on Exchange Arrangements and Exchange Restrictions.* Washington, DC: International Monetary Fund.

Lane, P.R., and G.M. Milesi-Ferretti. 2007. The External Wealth of Nations Mark II: Revised and Extended Estimates of Foreign Assets and Liabilities, 1970–2004. *Journal of International Economics* 73(November): 223–250.

Quinn, D. 2003. Capital Account Liberalization and Financial Globalization, 1890–1999: A Synoptic View. *International Journal of Finance and Economics* 8(3): 189–204.

Svirydzenka, K. 2016. Introducing a New Broad-based Index of Financial Development. IMF Working Paper WP/16/5. Washington, DC: International Monetary Fund. www.imf.org/external/pubs/ft/wp/2016/wp1605.pdf

PART I

Country chapters

2

THE DEVELOPMENT AND TRANSFORMATION OF THE FINANCIAL SYSTEM IN THE PEOPLE'S REPUBLIC OF CHINA

Damian Tobin and Ulrich Volz

Introduction

After close to two decades of financial sector reform, the financial system in the People's Republic of China (PRC) is now a participant in the global financial system in a way that other large Asian economies such as Japan and India have never been. Its banks and insurance companies rank among the world's largest. According to a new composite index of financial development constructed by the International Monetary Fund (IMF), the PRC has witnessed significant development since the early 1980s (Figure 2.1). Yet despite remarkable growth, the PRC's policy-makers continue to grapple with questions over how to best to make the financial system serve the real economy. As pointed out by Justin Lin,

> there is a mismatch between China's real economy and the financial system. The country's real economy is largely comprised of farmers, small and medium-sized businesses, and yet the financial sector is dominated by big banks that prefer to deal with big companies.
>
> *(quoted from Tsai 2015: 1)*

Access to credit continues to be a major constraint facing small and medium-sized enterprises (SMEs). According to a 2012 survey in 15 provinces, 57.5% of SMEs had obtained funding through informal credit markets (Li and Hu 2013). Many rural counties lack access to adequate banking services, and private enterprises face punitively high interest rates.

Despite the rapid financial development since the 1990s, the PRC's financial system continues to be dominated by bank lending (Figures 2.2 and 2.3). Although non-bank financial institutions have increased in importance, regulatory reforms have not eliminated the credit expansion impetus of large commercial banks, while the effectiveness of capital-based constraints and administrative measures is far below potential. Instead the financial system is becoming increasingly interconnected. Banks have not only become important players in bond and equity markets, but they are also closely linked with the rapid growth of off-balance-sheet finance. Importantly, through a combination of interbank funding activities, wealth management products and shadow banking/gray capital market activities, large state-owned banks have

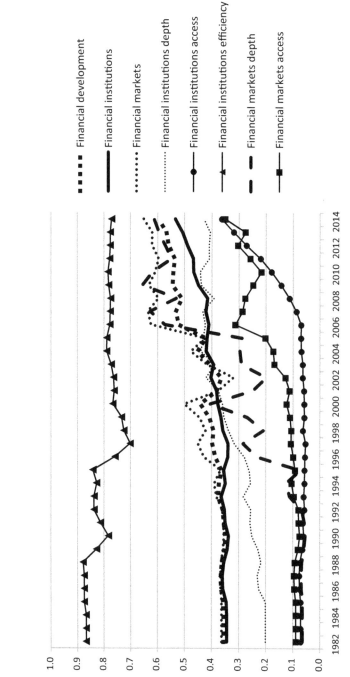

Figure 2.1 New IMF measures of financial development for the People's Republic of China, 1982–2014

Note: IMF = International Monetary Fund.

Source: Compiled by authors with data from Svirydzenka (2016).

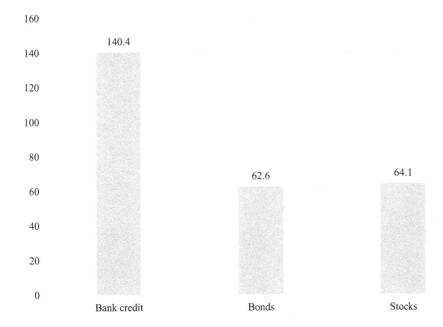

Figure 2.2   Total finance as percentage of GDP, 2015

Note: GDP = gross domestic product.

Source: Compiled by authors with data from the World Bank Financial Development Index database.

become important sources of liquidity provision to both smaller commercial banks and a range of non-bank financial institutions. Recent estimates put the size of the PRC's shadow banking system at 138% of gross domestic product (GDP) for May 2017 (Shih 2017).

An unintended consequence of these developments is that the PRC's state-run financial system has become more complex and more interconnected. In exploring how this occurred, the remainder of this chapter is structured as follows: the next section provides a brief overview of the PRC's financial governance framework. This is followed by outlines of the development of the PRC's banking sector, equities markets, and bond markets. Then a brief overview of the rapidly developing fintech market is given, which is followed by a short outline of exchange rate management and the opening of the PRC's financial sector. The chapter concludes by briefly touching on current developments and challenges.

Financial governance framework

The People's Bank of China (PBC) was created in 1948 under the leadership of the Ministry of Finance (MoF). With the "socialist transformation" of the Chinese economy along the model of the Soviet Union's centrally planned economy in 1951, the PRC introduced a mono-bank financial system. The PBC became essentially the country's sole financial institution (besides credit cooperatives operating at the township level).[1] In 1979, the PBC was separated from the MoF and granted the authority of a central bank. Over time it developed into the regulator and supervisor for the entire financial system, including banking, securities, and insurance. As these sectors developed, the PRC adopted a sector-based regulatory model in the early 1990s, with dedicated regulators for banking, securities and insurance (Huang 2010). In 1992, the State

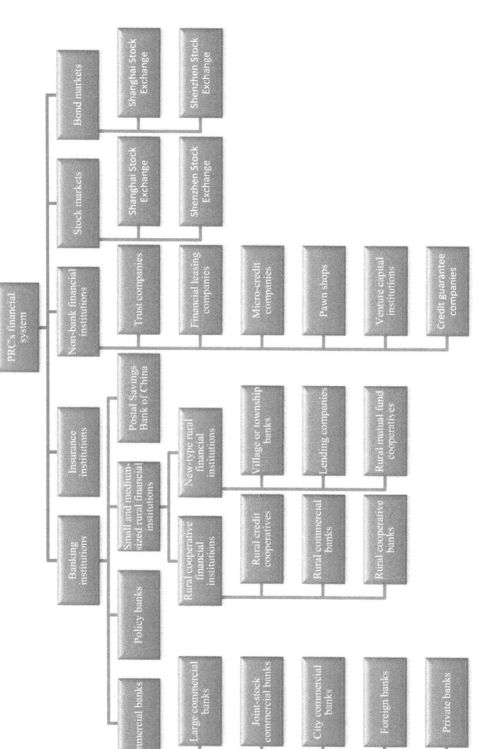

Figure 2.3 Overview of the PRC's financial system

Note: PRC = People's Republic of China.

Council Securities Commission (SCSC) and the China Securities Regulatory Commission (CSRC) were tasked with supervising and regulating the issuance and trading of securities on the stock exchanges. The SCSC was subsequently integrated into the CSRC, which in 1998 became the singular authority to regulate the securities market. The same year, the China Insurance Regulatory Commission (CIRC) was established to exercise oversight over the insurance sector.

In 1998, the Central Financial Work Commission (CFWC) was created in response to the Asian financial crisis. Although the crisis did not directly affect the PRC, which at the time still maintained tight capital controls, the Communist Party of China (CCP) realized the danger of financial crisis and hence sought to exert greater control over the financial sector (Heilmann 2005). The CFWC was created to this end, with direct and exclusive reporting responsibility to the CCP's Central Committee (Pistor 2012). The CFWC was abolished in 2002 and in 2003 the newly established China Banking Regulatory Commission (CBRC) assumed responsibilities for banking regulation from the PBC and the CFWC.

With a central bank charged with monetary and exchange rate policies and three specialized supervisory agencies – collectively referred to as Yihang Sanhui ("one bank, three commissions") – the PRC thus adopted a formal governance regime for its financial sector that resembled the regulatory structure found in many developed Western market economies at the time (Huang 2010; Pistor 2012). The PBC and the three regulatory authorities are subordinate to the State Council. In practice, the PBC retained an important role in banking supervision and maintained a powerful voice in strategic discussions over the direction of financial reforms (Pistor 2012).

Strategic decisions on financial sector reforms have been taken by the Leading Group for Financial and Economic Affairs, a body under the CCP Central Committee that was established by the CCP Politburo Standing Committee in 1980. It is led by either the CCP general secretary or the premier of the State Council and is generally considered the most powerful entity in matters of economic and financial governance. Decisions on the strategic direction of financial market reforms have been also set by the National Financial Work Conference. Its participants have included high-ranking government officials, central bankers, and regulators from the national and provincial level, as well as representatives from the headquarters and provincial branches of all major banks, insurance firms, and non-bank financial firms (Lardy 1998).

Following the fifth National Financial Work Conference in July 2017, President Xi Jinping announced the creation of a cabinet-level committee to coordinate financial oversight to overcome the fragmentation of financial regulation (Bloomberg 2017). He also announced a bigger role for the PBC in managing financial market risks. The new Financial Stability and Development Committee, which is headed by the vice premier, was established under the State Council in November 2017. The committee's office will be based at the PBC. Its remit is to supervise the PRC's monetary policy and financial regulation. It will have the authority to supervise and interrogate financial regulators and local governments (SCMP 2017a). A further change to the regulatory structure was proposed in March 2018 at the National People's Congress, including a merger of the CBRC and the CIRC, and a transfer of greater responsibilities for drafting key regulations and prudential oversight to the PBC.

An important element of financial governance in the PRC has been the control of state ownership of publicly owned financial institutions. The MoF and Central Hui Jin Investment Ltd. (Hui Jin) have been the two most important state entities with large ownership stakes in the financial sector (Pistor 2012). Hui Jin was established in 2003 with a mandate to "to exercise the rights and the obligations as an investor in major state-owned financial enterprises, on behalf of the State" (Hui Jin 2018).[2]

Pistor (2012) highlights that formal governance structures for the financial sector have been effectively superseded by informal governance structures which are controlled by the CCP. In particular, she points to the role of the CCP Central Organization Department, which not only appoints senior executives of the PRC's regulatory authorities (PBC, CBRC, CSRC, CIRC) but also those of all major financial institutions.

Evolution of the banking sector

The start of reform of the PRC's mono-banking system coincided with major upheavals in international finance. These included the collapse of the Bretton Woods system in 1973, an increase in competition from non-bank financial institutions, and the emergence of global money center banks. Figure 2.4 provides a summary of major reforms in the PRC's financial system since 1978. In many ways these have mirrored developments in international banking. In 1979, the PRC established or re-opened three state-owned commercial banks (SOCBs): the Agricultural Bank of China, the Bank of China, and the Construction Bank of China. In 1984 a fourth SOCB was established: the Industrial and Commercial Bank of China. By the mid-1990s these large specialized SOCBs – often referred to as the "big four" – accounted for over 60% of the PRC's banking assets. These subsequently restructured along these lines of modern corporations, launched initial public offerings (IPOs), appointed non-executive directors, and sold minority shareholding to foreign banks (Sun and Tobin 2005).

The first joint-stock banks were formed in the early 1980s. This was followed in 1994 by the establishment of three specialized "policy" banks: the Agricultural Development Bank of China, the China Development Bank, and the Export-Import Bank of China. Whereas joint-stock banks were characterized by smaller state shareholding and faced a greater risk of bankruptcy, the specific objective of the three policy banks was to reduce the commercial banks' role in financing development projects (Lin and Zhang 2009). Since 2013, the loan books of the joint stock and smaller city commercial banks have grown considerably as the SOCBs reduced their loan growth. While this indicates a gradual erosion of the dominance of the SOCBs, smaller banks continue to face a funding constraint as they do not enjoy the nationwide deposit raising networks of the SOCBs. As a result they became more reliant on interbank funding (BIS 2016). Another notable feature has been the reorganization and restructuring of the China Post and Savings Bank. This has allowed it to engage in commercial lending since 2007, a move that saw it evolve into the country's fifth largest banking organization (Tobin 2012).

A distinguishing feature of the PRC's banking reforms is the low presence of foreign banks. This contrasts sharply with other transitional economies, such as Hungary and Poland, where foreign banking assets accounted for more than half of total banking assets after a decade of reform (Bonin, Hasan, and Wachtel 2010: 856). Even after the relaxation of geographical restrictions on their operations after 2006 and restrictions on local incorporation in 2007, the market share of foreign banks was just 2.1% in 2008 (Table 2.1). By 2015, some 37 solely funded foreign banks with 306 branches and subsidiaries were locally incorporated. Their growth continues to face considerable restrictions including the requirement to allocate CNY 100 million (around USD 16 million) in freely convertible currencies transferred from the parent bank and the treatment of capital injections as foreign direct investments. Consequently, the presence of foreign banks remains low, at just 1.3% of assets in 2015. In an effort to reverse this decline, the requirement to allocate a certain amount of freely convertible currency was relaxed in 2015 (Xinhua 2014).

While foreign banks have had a relatively low domestic presence, the PRC's banks have been increasing their international activities, becoming an increasingly important source of

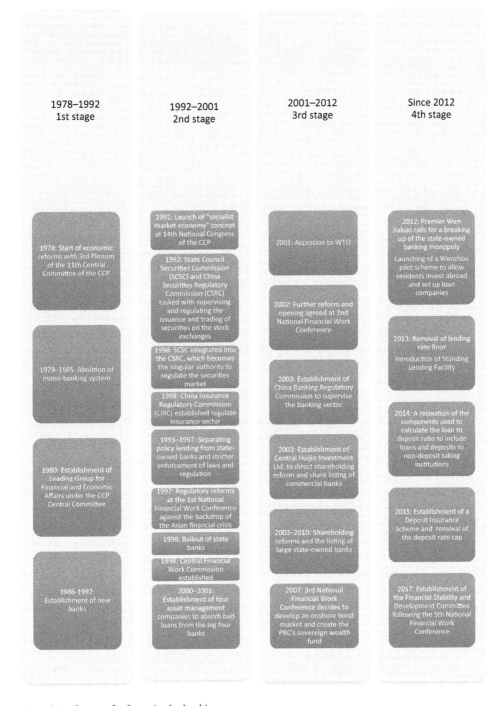

1978–1992
1st stage

1978: Start of economic reforms with 3rd Plenum of the 11th Central Committee of the CCP

1978–1985: Abolition of mono-banking system

1980: Establishment of Leading Group for Financial and Economic Affairs under the CCP Central Committee

1986-1992: Establishment of new banks

1992–2001
2nd stage

1992: Launch of "socialist market economy" concept at 14th National Congress of the CCP

1992: State Council Securities Commission (SCSC) and China Securities Regulatory Commission (CSRC) tasked with supervising and regulating the issuance and trading of securities on the stock exchanges

1998: SCSC integrated into the CSRC, which becomes the singular authority to regulate the securities market

1998: China Insurance Regulatory Commission (CIRC) established regulate insurance sector

1993–1997: Separating policy lending from state-owned banks and stricter enforcement of laws and regulation

1997: Regulatory reforms at the 1st National Financial Work Conference against the backdrop of the Asian financial crisis

1998: Bailout of state banks

1998: Central Financial Work Commission established

2000-2001: Establishment of four asset management companies to absorb bad loans from the big four banks

2001–2012
3rd stage

2001: Accession to WTO

2002: Further reform and opening agreed at 2nd National Financial Work Conference

2003: Establishment of China Banking Regulatory Commission to supervise the banking sector

2003: Establishment of Central Huijin Investment Ltd. to direct shareholding reform and share listing of commercial banks

2003–2010: Shareholding reforms and the listing of large state-owned banks

2007: 3rd National Financial Work Conference decides to develop an onshore bond market and create the PRC's sovereign wealth fund

Since 2012
4th stage

2012: Premier Wen Jiabao calls for a breaking up of the state-owned banking monopoly

Launching of a Wenzhou pilot scheme to allow residents invest abroad and set up loan companies

2013: Removal of lending rate floor

Introduction of Standing Lending Facility

2014: A relaxation of the components used to calculate the loan to deposit ratio to include loans and deposits to non-deposit taking institutions

2015: Establishment of a Deposit Insurance Scheme and removal of the deposit rate cap

2017: Establishment of the Financial Stability and Development Committee following the 5th National Financial Work Conference

Figure 2.4 Stages of reforms in the banking sector

Notes: CCP = Communist Party of China. WTO = World Trade Organization.

Source: Compiled by the authors, drawing partly on Okazaki (2017: 305).

Table 2.1 Market share (by assets) of major banking institutions (2003–2015)

	2003	2005	2008	2010	2013	2015
SOCBs	57.9	56.1	51.6	49.2	43.3	39.2
Joint-stock banks	10.7	11.9	14.0	15.6	17.8	18.5
City commercial banks	5.3	5.4	6.5	8.2	10.0	11.4
Rural commercial banks	–	–	–	2.9	5.6	7.6
Rural credit coops	9.6	8.4	8.3	6.7	5.7	4.3
Foreign banks	1.5	1.9	2.1	1.8	1.7	1.3
Postal savings bank	3.2	3.7	3.5	3.7	4.1	4.2

Note: SOCBs = state-owned commercial banks.

Source: Compiled by authors with data from the CSRC Annual Report (2015).

international credit. By the end of 2015, their cross-border assets accounted for some USD 722 billion, making them the tenth largest creditor in the international banking system and a significant supplier of US dollar credit (BIS 2016). However, unlike other larger international creditors like the UK, Japan, and Germany, the PRC is a net debtor in the international financial system. This is partly to do with the unique role of Hong Kong, China, where the PRC's banks have listed subsidiaries on the Hong Kong Stock Exchange and operate the market in renminbi deposit accounts and bonds (Tobin 2016). Consequently, the cross-border liabilities of mainland banks amounted to USD 944 billion at the end of 2015, a significant proportion (USD 320 billion) of which related to the market value of the banks' traded equity in Hong Kong, China (BIS 2016).

Non-performing loans, stock market listings, and deferred structural reforms

A combination of poor lending practices and limited experience in managing risk meant that by the end of the 1990s the non-performing loan (NPL) ratio of the PRC's state banks stood at 33%. The PRC responded by launching a bank bailout and establishing four state-owned asset management companies (AMCs) to absorb almost CNY 1.4 trillion in bad loans.[3] This was followed by the international listing of three of the four large SOCBs between 2005 and 2006. The fourth bank, the Agricultural Bank of China, was listed in 2010. By the end of 2017, 39 banks were listed on the stock markets, usually in Shanghai and Hong Kong. The advantage of this incremental transactional approach to reform, which involved integrating international best practices and investments where appropriate, was that it did not seek to immediately replicate international banking models (Pistor 2009). Its drawback was that it left intact the Leninist-type control structures, which were conducive to centralized regulation but ultimately failed to improve the allocation of capital (Heilmann 2005). A lack of structural reforms in the financial sector also contributed to the buildup of macroeconomic imbalances (Ito and Volz 2013).

The costs of deferring structural reforms became apparent following the 2008–2009 fiscal stimulus. This was not strictly a "fiscal" stimulus, since most of it consisted of bank loans and local government investment rather than central government expenditure. Bank managers had little autonomy to resist government lending priorities, and they knew that based on experience they would be rescued (Goodstadt 2011). Much of this lending went to local government "financing platforms." These were technically prohibited as they involved, albeit indirectly, local government borrowing (Figure 2.5). By the end of 2010, there were 6,576 of these

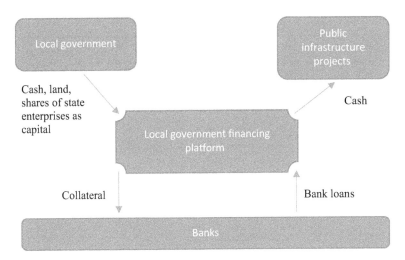

Figure 2.5 Typical structure of a local government funding platform

Source: Compiled by authors based on IMF (Lu and Sun 2013: 4).

platforms, a majority of which operated at the county level, and their debt balances accounted for 46.4% of local government debt (NAO 2011). Their connection to the banking system meant that local government debt became a source of risk for bank balance sheets. Bank finance is the main source of debt funding for local government, accounting for some 78% of loans in 2012 (NAO 2013).

The emergence and growth of shadow banking

Trust and investment companies first played a role in responding to the pressing need to finance local development in the early 1980s. The unprecedented decision of the PBC in 1994 to restrict lending to the MoF for the budget deficit was also a factor in driving the increase in the proportion of off-balance-sheet finance (Lardy 1998). The term came to represent a pejorative film for all non-bank financial intermediation after 2008, thus obscuring the true nature of risk and usefulness as a source of non-bank funding for small firms (Tsai 2015). The PBC's acknowledgment that state-owned banks had participated in creating large amounts of off-balance-sheet liquidity also led the PBC to adopting a wider monetary aggregate, namely, total social financing (Table 2.2). This was designed to capture the discrepancy between the growth in total liquidity growth and bank lending. Between 2002 and 2010, the average annual growth of the all-system aggregate was 27.8%, while the average annual growth of bank loans was 18.4% (PBC 2011).

The growth in off-balance-sheet lending partly reflected a structural change in the funding of bank liabilities. The PRC's large banks had long benefited from fixed interest rates and a surplus of deposits over loans as the PBC purchased foreign exchange from banks (Sun 2015). The post-financial crisis reduction in the role of FDI in capital formation, which fell from a pre-financial crisis of 6.8% for the years 2005–2007 to 3.0% for the years 2011–2016 (UNCTAD 2017), placed pressure on domestic sources of bank funding. This saw banks turn to off-balance-sheet wealth management products (WMPs) to fund their activities. WMPs are financial products that offer higher returns than conventional equity or deposit accounts. Large SOCBs can purchase WMPs from smaller banks in return for funding. SOCBs can also

Table 2.2 The components of total social financing

On balance sheet	Off balance sheet
Renminbi loans by financial institutions	Entrusted loans (in which the bank acts as a loan intermediary)
Foreign currency denominated loans	Trust loans (involving the repackaging and sale of loans as wealth management products)
Stock markets and net financing of corporate bonds	Undiscounted bankers' acceptances (a form of off-balance-sheet bank draft guaranteed by the bank)
Others, e.g., micro financing	

Source: Compiled by authors.

issue their own WMPs to fund interbank lending to smaller banks. While most do not carry an explicit guarantee, their systematic importance in the financial system has earned them a level of public confidence. This is illustrated in data from the BIS, which indicated that approximately 40% of WMP asset portfolios were invested in bond markets with a further 16% invested in money market instruments (BIS 2017).

A second consequence of the growth in shadow banking has been the emergence of a discrepancy between bank lending and liquidity growth. From 2008 onwards, bank lending started to outpace the growth in the broad money supply (Figure 2.6). In 2011, the PBC acknowledged that bank lending was no longer particularly useful in explaining the growth in M2 and that "all-system" or total social financing now played a more important role in supporting economic growth (PBC, Monetary Policy Report, Q1 2011). A further change in this relationship occurred in 2016 and 2017, as the growth in the broad money supply and lending to non-financial began to slow in response to government policy, while total social financing continued to expand faster (Figure 2.7). This indicated the continuing channeling of funds off-balance sheet into poorly performing state enterprises and funding platforms.

Interest rate reforms, deposit insurance, and bank diversity

The removal of the lending interest rate cap in July 2013 represented a new chapter in the PRC's financial reforms. It also necessitated a more complex monetary framework. In 2013, the PBC introduced a standing lending facility to meet large-scale demand for long-term liquidity and short-term liquidity operations to facilitate repurchase operations with shorter-term maturities (Sun 2015). The reforms, which began with a widening of interest rate margins in the 1990s, sought to give banks greater flexibility in the pricing of risk but limit competition by retaining control over deposit rates. On the deposit side, banks were required to match the official deposit rate until 2004, when the lower limit was removed.

In July 2014 the CBRC relaxed its stance on the components used to calculate banks' loan-to-deposit ratios – a move that effectively allowed banks to expand liquidity. To protect against competition leading to a greater frequency of bank failures, a scheme was implemented in May 2015 that stipulated depositors could receive up to CNY 500,000 in compensation if a bank were to collapse. Finally, in October 2015 it was announced that the deposit rate cap would be lifted, effectively allowing deposit-taking institutions to compete for deposit funds.

While interest rate reform and deposit insurance offered market-based incentives for new entrants, the PRC's efforts to improve the diversity of financial relied on a combination of administrative measures, policy guidelines, and pilot schemes. A lack of diversity carries economic and social costs. One study found that rural financial services did not satisfy the diverse

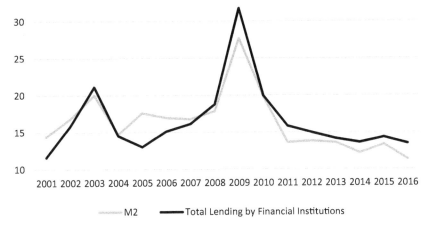

Figure 2.6   Growth in broad money supply vs. bank credit (in percentage)

Source: Compiled by authors using the PBC's Monetary Statistics.

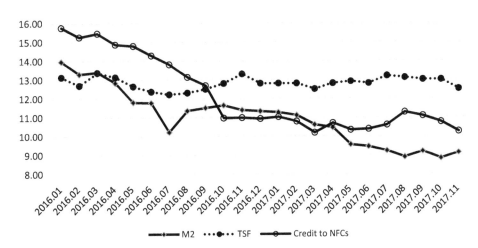

Figure 2.7   Year-on-year growth (percentage) in credit to non-financial corporations, total social financing, and M2

Notes: NFCs = non-financial corporations. TSF = total social financing.

Source: Compiled by authors using the PBC's Monetary Statistics.

public demand for more sophisticated banking services, with many provinces lacking even basic
banking services (PBC 2010). It further noted that three western provinces had more than 50
counties that were classified as "unbanked." The Rural Household Survey (PBC 2014) found
that only 27% of demand for loans from the PRC's rural dwellers is met, compared to 40% in
urban areas. Since 2011, the PBC has set differentiated favorable reserve requirements for lending related to agricultural and rural financial services (Sun 2015). The restructuring and expansion of rural financial institutions has also continued, and by end-2016 the PRC had 1,114 rural
commercial banks and 1,443 township banks.

Foreign-owned and pilot private banks have also played a role in promoting financial diversity
in the rural sector, albeit within the constraints of capital controls. By 2015, foreign banks had a

presence in 69 cities in 27 provinces, with 17% of outlets located in the northeast, middle, and west of the PRC (PBC 2016). By the end of 2015, the PRC had also launched five private pilot banks, which were mostly located in eastern provinces and municipalities such as Zhejiang, Tianjin, Shanghai, Wenzhou, and Qianhai. Their location indicates that they are mainly targeted at the PRC's growing private sector. However, they are highly reliant on non-deposit funding sources. Deposits represented just 30.6% of their funding (PBC 2016). The pilot private banks had a loan book totaling CNY 23.6 billion. This represented just a fraction (0.023%) of total loans.

Stock markets and financial centers

The emergence of Shanghai and Shenzhen as the PRC's main onshore financial centers can be traced to policies based on *equity developmentalism* that both municipalities followed (Green 2004). This involved the use of a range of policy tools to boost trading volumes and attract new listings. While Shanghai has benefited from the location of foreign banks and the listing of large SOEs, Shenzhen's cost advantage has made it attractive for small and medium-sized enterprises and venture capital. Recently both cities have benefited from national-level policies promoting pilot free trade zones (FTZs) and Stock Connect schemes. FTZs allow controlled offshore currency trading, while the Stock Connect schemes allow approved overseas investors to purchase domestic shares via Hong Kong's offshore financial market. Shanghai was the first to benefit from this in 2014, and the scheme was extended to Shenzhen in 2016. The developments have seen Shanghai and Shenzhen emerge as the world's sixth and 20th largest financial centers, respectively, by 2017 (Yeandle 2017).

Rapid development has also left unresolved challenges. Both the traded capitalization and ratio of stock finance to loans remain low (Table 2.3). The majority of the 3,052 companies listed at the end of 2016 were SOEs (Table 2.3). Trading patterns remain highly erratic (Figure 2.8). The average turnover ratio of shares on the Shanghai stock market was some 388% in 2015, while the market had a price-earnings ratio of 17.6%. High turnover and valuations imply that market activity has been driven by a small group of individual shareholders who own comparatively small portions of total equity. By 2015 the number of accounts had grown to over 214 million, but the ratio of new to existing accounts remains volatile (Table 2.4). The diffuse nature of shareholders mitigates the possibility of a credible takeover threat.

Table 2.3 Selected measures of the role of the PRC's stock markets (1990–2015)

Year	Number of listed companies	Market capitalization (CNY billion)	Ratio of stock financing to loans	Market capitalization to GDP (%)	Traded market capitalization to GDP (%)
1990	10	–	–	–	–
1992	53	104.8	–	3.9	–
1993	183	353.1	4.96	10.2	2.5
1995	323	347.4	1.27	5.9	1.6
2000	1,088	4,809.1	11.5	48	16.2
2005	1,381	3,243.0	2.05	18.0	5.8
2010	2,063	26,542.2	11.3	67.0	48.5
2015	2,827	53,130.4	7.09	78.5	61.8
2016	3,052	50,824.5	15.3	68.3	52.8

Notes: GDP = gross domestic product. PRC = People's Republic of China.

Source: Compiled by the authors with data from the People's Bank of China and China Securities and Regulatory Commission.

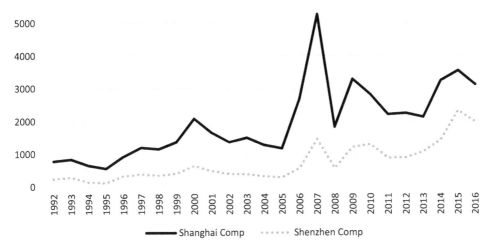

Figure 2.8 Shanghai and Shenzhen composite indices annual closing level (1992–2016)

Source: Compiled by authors with data from PBC Financial Stability Reports, various years.

Table 2.4 Selected indicators of share ownership

Year	Ratio tradable to total shares	Average turnover ratio Shanghai market	Total share accounts ('000s)	Ratio of new share accounts to total accounts
1993	27.8	–	7,776.7	72.1
1995	35.5	528.7	12,424.7	14.8
2000	35.7	492.9	58,011.3	22.7
2003	35.4	250.7	69,926.6	2.0
2005	32.8	274.4	73,360.7	1.6
2008	37.2	392.5	104,490.9	−32.9
2009	62.0	499.4	120,376.9	13.2
2010	72.7	197.6	133,910.4	10.1
2015	78.6	388.5	214,775.7	33.8

Source: Compiled by the authors with data from the China Securities and Regulatory Commission.

The potential of both Shanghai and Shenzhen to offer a more sophisticated range of financial products is also hindered by a lack of a fully convertible renminbi (RMB) and capital controls. Notwithstanding these drawbacks, there are some salient aspects of the PRC's shareholding reforms. As will be discussed below, concessions on overseas access and foreign share ownership have seen domestic PRC shares added to the Morgan Stanley Emerging Markets Index (MSCI), while the split share reform has provided a politically acceptable way of reducing the proportion of non-traded shares. In the absence of full capital account liberalization, Hong Kong, China has provided a safe channel to facilitate the entrance of foreign via quota-based allocations.

From "one-third privatization" to the "split share reform"

At the outset of the PRC's stock market development, at least two-thirds of the capital of most of the PRC's listed firms was not freely floated on the stock market. Shares owned by the state tend not to be freely traded and explain the difference between the ratio of market capitalization (which includes traded and non-traded shares) to GDP and the ratio for traded shares. The ratio of non-tradable to tradable shares remained just above 30% until 2008. One-third privatization meant that one of the main benefits of privatization for state enterprises (i.e., the achievement of a hard budget constraint) was not realized (Sun 2003). Shares of listed SOEs were divided into three categories, usually about one-third each. These were tradable shares which were sold to the public; legal person shares – typically held by a state-owned parent company and in principle non-tradable; and non-tradeable shares held by the state. Tradeable shares were further divided into A-shares, which were traded in domestic currency, and B-shares designed for foreign investors and traded in foreign currency (US dollars in Shanghai). The separation from the more liquid domestic market meant that B-shares tended to have lower valuations and small trading volumes, and by 2016 there were just 100 listed B-shares.

Efforts to reform the overhang of non-tradable shares were often frustrated by market volatility as individual investors feared that the market would be flooded with low-quality A-shares. Efforts to float non-tradable A-shares in 2001 led to a significant collapse in the Shanghai and Shenzhen composite indices (Figure 2.8). It also resulted in a more gradual approach to the pricing of non-traded shares. Beginning in 2002, foreign investors – who are licensed by the CSRC – were permitted to purchase and sell tradable A-shares through the Qualified Foreign Institutional Investor (QFII) scheme and non-tradable shares via a series of reforms to the mergers and acquisitions rules during 2002–2004 (Lee 2008). By the time the split share reform was launched on a trial basis in September 2005, foreign investors had two tracks through which they could purchase domestic shares. The split share reform ameliorated many of the agency costs of small information and control disadvantaged tradable shareholders that plagued earlier reform efforts, by allowing for negotiation between tradable and non-tradable shareholders to determine the appropriate compensation level (Yeh et al. 2009). Its overall effect was a rapid change from one-third to two-thirds privatization, and by 2015 the ratio of tradable to non-tradable shares stood at 78%.

Overseas holdings of the PRC equity remain low, accounting for around 1.3% of total market capitalization at end of 2016. The absence of a feasible way of allowing foreign participation in domestic markets also represented a significant obstacle to efforts to have the PRC's tradable A-shares included in the MSCI. Inclusion has the potential to increase the demand for A-shares but also requires exchanges to reach certain thresholds of accessibility, transparency, and liquidity. In June 2017, it was announced that 222 eligible A-share stocks (a weighting of around 0.7% of the MSCI index in 2018) would be admitted to MSCI index beginning in May 2018, with access provided through the Hong Kong-based Stock Connect scheme (SCMP 2017b). The decision opens the possibility of an increased weighting subject to future market reforms.

Hong Kong and the northbound and southbound routes

Listing on Hong Kong-provided state enterprises with a means of raising funds and bonding themselves to higher corporate governance standards (Tobin and Sun 2009). Between 1993 and 2017, some 229 PRC enterprises listed H-shares on Hong Kong's stock exchange. Other state enterprises incorporated subsidiaries in Hong Kong and were listed as "red chips." The first PRC SOEs to list in Hong Kong, China in 1993 were mostly industrial enterprises, and did so at a time when the PRC markets were in their infancy. In the 2000s all of the PRC's big four state-owned banks were listed in Hong Kong, China. More recently Hong Kong's stock exchange has been used by smaller provincial level banks such as Harbin Bank, the Bank of Zhengzhou, and the Bank of Tianjin as a way of mitigating domestic funding constraints.

Hong Kong, China's role has also evolved to allow foreign investors a route into the A-share market (the northbound route) and domestic PRC investors an option to invest in Hong Kong, China shares (the southbound route) via the stock connect scheme. Both routes are subject to daily quotas and restrictions on beneficial ownership. Hong Kong, China has also offered a useful platform to expand on the qualified investors scheme. In December 2011, a pilot program was launched to allow fund management companies approved as Renminbi Qualified Foreign Institutional Investors (RQFII) to use their renminbi funds raised in Hong Kong, China to invest in domestic securities markets. This mitigates against the prospect of capital outflows. In 2013 the scheme was extended to London. While the initial QFII scheme was viewed as a watershed reform, its extension to include renminbi raised in Hong Kong, China is indicative of the cautious quota-based approach to allowing foreign capital into the PRC's financial centers and the dilemma faced by the PRC in implementing capital account reforms.

Bond markets

Domestic government and corporate bonds are traded on the country's two stock exchanges (mainly Shanghai), OTC and, most importantly, in the interbank bond market. The exchange-based market is an order-driven market. Its participants include securities companies, insurance companies, securities investment funds, trust and investment companies, credit cooperatives, other non-financial institutional investors, and individual investors. As mentioned earlier, bonds have also become a major component of WMPs. Banks often use securities companies to manage the proceeds of WMPs, while securities companies themselves often use repo agreements to sustain bond prices (BIS 2017). Capital account controls and a limited pool of offshore renminbi liquidity have meant relatively few international issues of government bonds. Their relative scarcity has meant that such bonds tend to be highly sought after. Nevertheless, liquid markets for government debt are a prerequisite for foreign residents to hold part of a government debt and exercise their judgment on the solvency of the country concerned (Noyer 2015). As the following section shows, a combination of domestic market opening and capital account controls have created a trade-off between the onshore and offshore markets.

Much of the early growth of the PRC's bond markets was motivated by the demands that financing economic growth placed on central and local government. Bond issues by the MoF climbed steeply after 1997 as part of a fiscal stimulus plan designed to prevent sharp economic contraction in an environment characterized by long-lasting deflation (1996–2003). This feature was again apparent following the 2008–2009 fiscal stimulus, with local governments making use of funding platforms to issue debt (see above). What stood out about these funding platforms was that they were effectively bonds in all but name in the sense that they were set up to finance specific projects, mostly infrastructure related.

The PRC's corporate bond market remains largely restricted to state corporations. Corporate bond issues fell sharply in the early 1990s, but have started to rise again in recent years. For much of the 2000s the market was heavily dominated by government securities. Since 2015 the paying down of foreign currency loans has witnessed the increasing issue of domestic bonds as corporations restructure their debts. The scope for corporate bonds has expanded since 2005 when firms were allowed issue short-term commercial paper for the first time. By 2014 short-term financing bills accounted for 4.1% of bond issues (PBC 2015). As of June 2017, the government bond market had reached a total volume of CNY 37,159 billion or 47% of GDP, while the corporate bond market stood at CNY 14,771 billion or 19% of GDP (Figure 2.9).

The offshore market has long had a far smaller pool of liquidity to draw on than the onshore market. Renminbi-denominated (Dim Sum) bonds issued in Hong Kong, China provided a

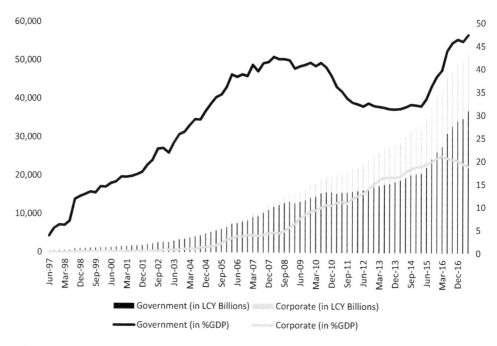

Figure 2.9   Development of the PRC's local currency bond market in CNY billion (left axis) and as share of GDP (right axis)

Notes: GDP = gross domestic product. LCY = local currency.

Source: Compiled by authors with data from AsianBondsOnline.

short-term solution to this. A renminbi devaluation and a decline in offshore renminbi deposits served to highlight the limited settlement options and renminbi liquidity of the offshore market. Capital controls made it difficult for domestic Chinese issuers to repay offshore bonds. Consequently, renminbi Dim Sum bond issues in Hong Kong, China fell from CNY 300 billion in 2014 to CNY 130 billion in 2016 (SCMP 2017c). A liberalization of access restrictions for foreign financial institutions in 2016 made it easier for them to participate in the onshore market. That said, just as in the case of equities, international investors accounted for only 1.2% of the onshore bond market at the end of 2016 (SCMP 2017c). 2016 also saw the first offshore renminbi sovereign bond issued by the MoF outside the PRC on the London Stock Exchange. Other countries such as Poland have issued so-called Panda Bonds, which are denominated in renminbi. Tight control over settlement, normally conducted through overseas PRC state-owned banks, indicates that the market for these bonds remain short of a fully liquid market for government debt.

Fintech

The PRC's financial technology (or fintech) industry (i.e., the application of internet-based technology within the financial services industry) has been flourishing. As of January 2018, 8 of the 28 global fintech companies with a valuation exceeding USD 1 billion are from the PRC, and 9 when including Hong Kong, China (TechCrunch 2018). The rise of fintech in the PRC has benefited from an underdeveloped banking sector. It also benefited from an initial light-touch approach regarding regulation and a technophile population with 772 million internet users, 98% of whom use mobile devices (CNNIC 2018). Arguably, fintech companies in the PRC have also benefited from effective protection that limits the scope of foreign tech companies to operate in the PRC.

Fintech in the PRC comprises seven areas: payments and e-wallets; supply chain and consumer finance; peer-to-peer (P2P) lending platforms; online funds; online insurance; personal finance management; and online brokerage (Mittal and Lloyd 2016). The PRC leads the world in many of these areas. Notably, it has developed the world's biggest markets for digital payments and online lending (The Economist 2017).

Mobile payments have grown rapidly in the PRC (Figure 2.10). In 2016, Chinese consumers spent CNY 157.55 trillion (USD 22.8 trillion) via mobile payment platforms, compared to only USD 112 billion in the US (Wang and Dollar 2018). Estimates suggest that mobile payment transactions reached almost CNY 200 trillion in 2017. In 2016, over 90% of mobile payments were made with apps developed by Alibaba's Alipay (54%) and Tencent's TenPay (37%), the PRC's two leading fintech firms (Wang and Dollar 2018).

Online lending in the PRC is dominated by peer-to-peer (P2P) lending, which has been developing in the PRC since around 2010. In 2017, the transaction volume of P2P lending reached CNY 2.8 trillion (Figure 2.11). P2P online platforms connect borrowers directly with lenders (or investors), who can get higher returns than the bank interest rate. The number of P2P lending platforms increased rapidly from about 200 in 2012 to a peak of almost 3,500 in November 2015. Given that P2P lending operated in a regulatory vacuum until 2016, it is not surprising that the market included a large number of rogue schemes. By the end of 2015, more than a third of all P2P platforms were considered "problem platforms" that had either stopped

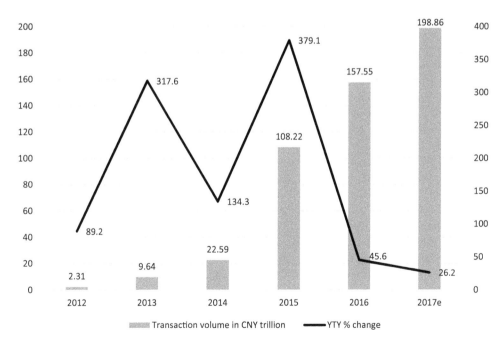

Figure 2.10 Transaction volume in the PRC's mobile payments business (CNY trillion) and year-to-year percentage change (right axis), 2012–2017

Note: YTY = year-on-year.

Source: Compiled by authors with PBOC data used by Wang and Dollar (2018).

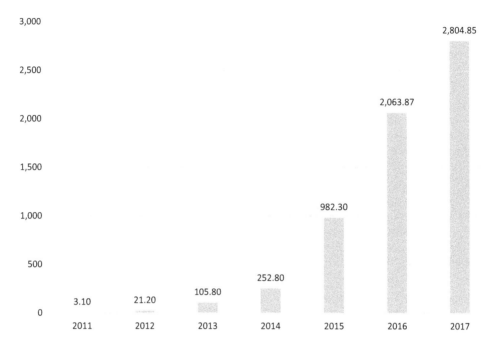

Figure 2.11 Transaction volume of P2P online lending platforms (CNY billion), 2011–2017

Note: P2P = peer-to-peer.

Source: Compiled by authors with data from Wang Dai Zhi Jia used by Wang and Dollar (2018).

repayments, were investigated by the police, or whose operators had disappeared with lenders' money (Chorzempa 2016). The most prominent P2P Ponzi scheme was the supposed P2P platform Ezubao, which attracted USD 7.6 billion from nearly one million lenders in only 18 months before it was found out that 95% of its borrowers were fake (Wang and Dollar 2018).

In April 2016, a "rectification campaign" was launched to "probe legal compliance and limit risks in Internet finance," followed by the introduction of comprehensive CBRC regulation in August 2016 imposing caps on P2P borrowing and prohibiting P2P platforms to act as financial intermediaries (Chorzempa 2017). The CBRC regulation also caps the size of online loans at CNY 1 million for individuals and CNY 5 million for companies, requires lenders to use a custodian bank, and forbids platforms to guarantee the principal or the interest on loans they facilitate (Wang and Dollar 2018). Since the introduction of regulation of P2P lending, the number of P2P platforms has fallen significantly, to fewer than 2,000 by the end of 2017. Despite the market consolidation, the transaction volume has continued to increase at a rapid pace, to CNY 2,805 billion (USD 442 billion) at the end of 2017. The PRC therefore accounts for about three-quarters of global online lending (PWC 2017b).

Exchange rate management and financial opening

The renminbi exchange rate has been tightly managed by the PBC (Figure 2.12). In January 1994, the PRC unified its dual exchange rates, devalued the renminbi by 33% overnight and pegged it to the US dollar at 8.7. From August 1994 onwards, the renminbi gradually appreciated against the dollar until May 1995. It was then kept firmly at CNY 8.3/USD until

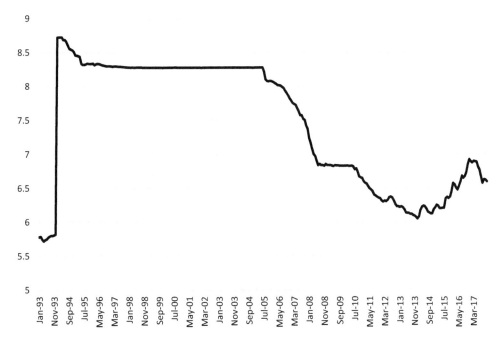

Figure 2.12 CNY/USD exchange rate, January 1993–December 2017

Source: Compiled by the authors with data from the Pacific Economic Exchange Rate Service.

July 2005, when the PBC allowed for a modest appreciation against the dollar of 2.1% and announced that it would adopt "a managed floating exchange rate regime based on market supply and demand with reference to a basket of currencies" (PBC 2005). The renminbi was subsequently allowed to strengthen, not least in response to massive pressure from the US and other major trading partners who complained about "currency manipulation."

In July 2008, in the face of the global financial crisis, the PBC effectively reinstalled the dollar peg, this time at CNY 6.8/USD. In June 2010, the peg was abandoned and the PRC returned to a strategy of increasing currency flexibility, with a gradual widening of daily trading bands. The renminbi continued to strengthen up to a high of CNY 6.1/USD in January 2014. Net capital outflows since mid-2014 caused the renminbi to depreciate up to the end of 2016. Various reasons were behind this, including the slowdown of the PRC economy and doubts about the country's future growth prospects; a growing importance of outward direct investments by the PRC's firms; the PRC's firms' repayments of their dollar-denominated debt; and capital flight. The PBC responded by tightening capital controls and by heavily intervening in the foreign exchange market to strengthen the renminbi. As a result, the PRC's foreign exchange reserves declined by nearly USD 1 trillion from a peak of USD 3.99 trillion in June 2014 to USD 2.998 trillion in January 2017. The PRC's foreign exchange reserves had built up rapidly since the early 2000s (Figure 2.13) on the back of large and growing capital account surpluses and recurrent foreign exchange intervention aimed at keeping the renminbi competitive.

Throughout, the PRC authorities have maintained tight capital controls, which enabled the PBC to manage the exchange rate while at the same time allowing a reasonable degree of monetary policy independence (Reade and Volz 2012). Capital controls have also permitted the government to keep a tight grip on the financial sector. The PRC has taken cautious steps in liberalizing cross-border financial flows since the early 2000s. Commercial credit inflow and

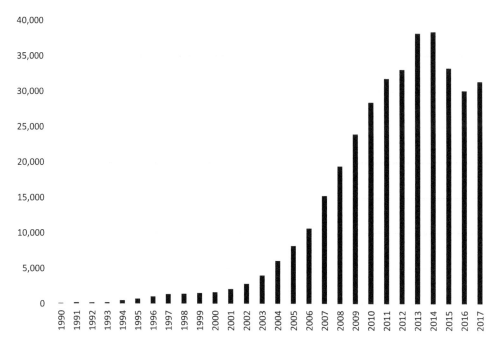

Figure 2.13 The PRC's foreign exchange reserves (in USD 100 million), 1990–2017

Source: Compiled by the authors with data from the State Administration of Foreign Exchange.

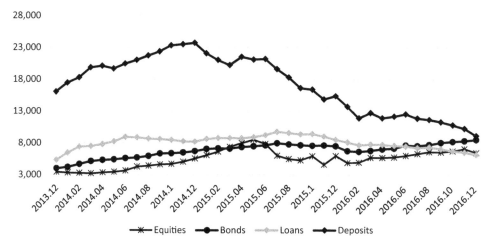

Figure 2.14 Domestic renminbi financial assets held by overseas entities, 2013–2016 (CNY 100 million)

Source: Compiled by authors with data from the PBOC's Monetary Statistics.

outflow restrictions were lifted in 2013. However, the slow pace of domestic financial reform and the continued presence of widespread capital controls have been an impediment to the internationalization of the renminbi, a goal that the PRC has pursued since 2009 (Volz 2014). Figure 2.14 shows that while foreign holdings of domestic financial assets such as equities, bonds, and loans have remained low for the reasons described earlier, the PRC did succeed in creating a large pool of offshore renminbi. Currency devaluation and capital controls have seen a substantial reduction in this since 2014. As previous sections indicated, this reduction may have a knock-on effect on the prospects for increasing the overseas holdings of equities and bonds.

Conclusion

The PRC has come a long way in developing its financial system. The PRC's "big four" banks (ICBC, CCB, ABC, and BOC) are now the four largest banks in the world by assets, while another 14 PRC banks make it into the top 100 largest banks (Mehmood 2017). Her bond market is the third largest after the US and Japan. China has also become the world's leading nation in the area of fintech, with the biggest market for digital payment and online lending. Moreover, the PRC's efforts to promote the renminbi as an international currency have already resulted in the inclusion of the renminbi in the International Monetary Fund's Special Drawing Rights basket. While this reflects the incredible growth and development success, caution is warranted. Indeed, the rise of the PRC's banks is somewhat reminiscent of the rise of Japanese banking institutions, which in 1989 entirely occupied the list of the 10 largest banks in the world (Chicago Tribune 1989). For Japan, the rapid expansion and internationalization of its financial system proved a challenging and costly experience. The current PRC leadership has started to deal with these challenges. While it remains committed to the goal of establishing Shanghai as a global financial center and develop the renminbi into a truly global currency, it has become increasingly conscious of the dilemmas posed by an open capital account.

Going forward, the PRC faces major challenges in terms of financial stability emanating from its enormous level of debt and the enormous size of its shadow financial system (e.g., Song and Xiong 2018). An optimal scenario for the PRC policy-makers is a managed unwinding of counterparty obligations involving the restructuring and diversification of corporate debt alongside the creation of a more diverse financial system. Debt restructuring also increases the urgency of corporate governance reform in financial markets. Weak governance continues to present a significant limitation on restructuring as banks face significant governance obstacles in monitoring repayment. In the medium term, the financial sector also faces the challenge of how to achieve better alignment with the goals of sustainable development. At present, the vast majority of lending and investment does not sufficiently take into account environmental and climate risk (UNEP 2017; Volz 2018). These challenges are part of a broader need to align the interests of society and the financial sector. While they are in no way unique, for the PRC these challenges are arguably intensified by the transition process and the need to accommodate the needs of an increasingly affluent society.

Acknowledgments

This study was written as part of an ESRC-NSFC grant on "Developing financial systems to support sustainable growth in China – The role of innovation, diversity and financial regulation" (RC grant reference ES/P005241/1). We thank Peter Morgan for very helpful comments and suggestions. A longer version is available as Tobin and Volz (2018).

Notes

1 Over time, a number of banks were established but later abandoned or integrated into the PBC, including the Agricultural Cooperative Bank (established in 1951) and the Agricultural Bank of China (ABC; established in 1955).

2　Hui Jin was initially a subsidiary of the State Administration for Foreign Exchange (SAFE), the administrative agency of the PBC responsible for foreign exchange management. In 2007 the MoF acquired all shares in Hui Jin from the PBC, which was compensated with specially issued treasury bonds. The MoF then injected the shares in Hui Jin into China Investment Corporation (CIC), the PRC's new sovereign wealth fund, which was created the same year. Hui Jin has since been a wholly owned subsidiary of CIC. Hui Jin's shareholder rights are exercised by the State Council.

3　One AMC was created for each of the big four commercial state-owned banks: China Great Wall Asset Management for the Agricultural Bank of China, China Orient Asset Management for the Bank of China, China Huarong Asset Management for the Industrial and Commercial Bank of China, and China Cinda Asset Management for the China Construction Bank.

References

Bank for International Settlements (BIS). 2017. From Wealth Management Products to the Bond Market. *Bank for International Settlements Quarterly Review* 2017(March): 13.

BIS. 2016. International Business of Banks in China. *Bank for International Settlements Quarterly Review* 2016(June): 7–8.

Bloomberg. 2017. Five Takeaways from China's Weekend Meeting on Financial Regulation. *Bloomberg News*, 16 July. www.bloomberg.com/news/articles/2017-07-16/five-takeaways-from-china-s-weekend-meet-on-financial-regulation

Bonin, J. P., I. Hasan, and P. Wachtel. 2010. Banking in Transition Countries. In *The Oxford Handbook of Banking*, edited by A. N. Berger, P. Molyneux, and J.O.S. Wilson. Oxford: Oxford University Press, pp. 844–867.

Chicago Tribune. 1989. For the First Time, the 10 Largest Banks in the World Are All Japanese, 26 July. articles. chicagotribune.com/1989-07-26/business/8902200323_1_largest-banks-dai-ichi-kangyo-bank-japan

Chorzempa, M. 2016. P2P Series Part 1: Peering into China's Growing Peer-to-Peer Lending Market. *China Economy Watch*, 27 June. https://piie.com/blogs/china-economic-watch/p2p-series-part-1-peering-chinas-growing-peer-peer-lending-market#_ftn2

Chorzempa, M. 2017. P2P Series Part 3: China's Online Lending Consolidates as Market Grows. *China Economy Watch*, 12 October. https://piie.com/blogs/china-economic-watch/p2p-series-part-3-chinas-online-lending-consolidates-market-grows

China Internet Network Information Center (CNNIC). 2018. 第41次中国互联网络发展状况统计报告 [The 41st China Statistical Report on Internet Development]. Beijing: China Internet Network Information Center.

Goodstadt, L. F. 2011. *Reluctant Regulators: How the West Created and How China Survived the Global Financial Crisis*. Hong Kong, China: Hong Kong University Press.

Green, S. 2004. *The Development of China's Stock Market, 1984–2002: Equity Politics and Market Institutions*. London: Routledge Curzon.

Heilmann, S. 2005. Regulatory Innovation by Leninist Means: Communist Party Supervision in China's Financial Industry. *China Quarterly* 181(March): 1–21.

Huang, H. 2010. Institutional Structure of Financial Regulation in China: Lessons from the Global Financial Crisis. *Journal of Corporate Law Studies* 10(1): 219–254.

Hui, Jin. 2018. About Us. Central Huijin Investment Ltd. www.huijin-inv.cn/wps/portal/!ut/p/a0/04_Sj9CPykssy0xPLMnMz0vMAfGjzOL9DMwMDJ2DDbwMfB3dDBwtDFx9_Y29jPx9TfULsh0VARptofo!/

Ito, H., and U. Volz. 2013. China and Global Imbalances from a View of Sectorial Reforms. *Review of International Economics* 21(1): 57–71.

Lardy, N. R. 1998. *China's Unfinished Economic Revolution*. Washington, DC: The Brookings Institution Press.

Lee, S.L.J. 2008. From Non-Tradable to Tradable Shares: Split Share Structure Reform of China's Listed Companies. *Journal of Corporate Law Studies* 8(1): 57–78.

Li, J., and F. Hu. 2013. Zhongguo zhongxiao qiye jinrong jiegou rongzi chengben yu xinzi xindai shichang fazhan. [Financing Structure and Cost of China's SMEs and Development of the Shadow Credit Market.] *Hongguan Jingji Yanjiu* 5: 7–11.

Lin, X., and Y. Zhang. 2009. Bank Ownership Reform and Bank Performance in China. *Journal of Banking and Finance* 33: 20–29.

Lu, Y., and T. Sun. 2013. Local Government Financing Platforms in China: A Fortune or Misfortune? IMF Working Paper No. 13/243. Washington, DC: International Monetary Fund.

Mehmood, J. 2017. The World's 100 Largest Banks. S&P Global Market Intelligence, 11 April. www.snl. com/web/client?auth=inherit#news/article?id=40223698&cdid=A-40223698-11568

Mittal, S., and J. Lloyd. 2016. *The Rise of FinTech in China. Redefining Financial Services.* A Collaborative Report by DBS and EY, DBS Group Research. Singapore: DBS Bank.

NAO. 2013. Audit Results of Nationwide Governmental Debts. Audit Report No. 32. Beijing: National Audit Office.

National Audit Office (NAO). 2011. Audit Findings on China's Local Government Debts. Audit Report No. 35. Beijing: National Audit Office.

National Bureau of Statistics (NBS). 2014. Rural Household Survey 2014, Beijing: National Bureau of Statistics.

Noyer, C. 2015. Spheres of Influence in the International Monetary System. Speech at the 21st Century Conference of Montreal, 8 June. www.bis.org/review/r150713c.htm

Okazaki, K. 2017. Banking System Reform in China: The Challenges to Improving Its Efficiency in Serving the Real Economy. *Asian Economic Policy Review* 12: 303–320.

PBC. 2005. Spokesman of the People's Bank of China on the Reform of the RMB Exchange Rate Regime, 25 July. www.pbc.gov.cn/english/130721/2831443/index.html

PBC. 2010. *China Financial Stability Report 2010: Reform and Development of the Rural Financial System.* Beijing: People's Bank of China.

PBC. 2011–2016. *Monetary Policy Reports*, Various Issues. Beijing: People's Bank of China.

Ping, S. J. 2015. *China MSME Finance Report 2015* (Compact Edition). Beijing: Mintai Institute of Finance and Banking/Central University of Finance and Economics. www.smefinanceforum.org/sites/default/files/post/files/SME-Finance-Annual-Summary-Translation-15.pdf

Pistor, K. 2009. Banking Reform in the Chinese Mirror, Columbia Law and Economics Working Paper No. 354. New York: Columbia University.

Pistor, K. 2012. The Governance of China's Finance. In *Capitalizing China*, edited by J.P.H. Fan and R. Morck. Chicago, IL: University of Chicago Press, pp. 35–60.

PWC. 2017b. Global FinTech Survey China Summary 2017. www.pwccn.com/en/financial-services/publications/fintech/global-fintech-survey-china-summary-jun2017.pdf

Reade, J. J., and U. Volz. 2012. Chinese Monetary Policy and the Dollar Peg. In *The Evolving Role of China in the Global Economy*, edited by J. de Haan and Y.-W. Cheung. Cambridge, MA: MIT Press, pp. 265–299.

Shih, V. 2017. Financial Instability in China: Possible Pathways and Their Likelihood. MERICS China Monitor, 20 October. Berlin: Mercator Institute for China Studies. www.merics.org/sites/default/files/2017-10/191017_merics_ChinaMonitor_42.pdf

Song, Z. M., and W. Xiong. 2018. Risks in China's Financial System. NBER Working Paper No. 24230. Washington, DC: National Bureau of Economic Research.

South China Morning Post (SCMP). 2017a. China's Super Financial Regulator Headed by Vice-premier More Powerful Than Ministries. *South China Morning Post*, 8 November. www.scmp.com/news/china/economy/article/2119001/chinas-super-financial-regulator-headed-vice-premier-more.

South China Morning Post (SCMP). 2017b. MSCI Includes China A-shares in Its Global Benchmark. *South China Morning Post*, 21 June. www.scmp.com/business/companies/article/2099260/msci-includes-chinese-shares-its-global-benchmark

South China Morning Post (SCMP). 2017c. Dim Sum Bond Market Seen Declining Further as China Improves Onshore Access. *South China Morning Post*, 16 February. www.scmp.com/business/money/markets-investing/article/2071454/dim-sum-bond-market-seen-declining-further-china

Sun, G. 2015. *Reforms in China's Monetary Policy*. New York: Palgrave Macmillan.

Sun, L. 2003. *Ownership and Governance of Enterprises: Recent Innovative Developments*. London: Palgrave Macmillan.

Sun, L., and D. Tobin. 2005. International Listing as a Mechanism of Commitment to More Credible Corporate Governance Practices: The Case of the Bank of China (Hong Kong). *Corporate Governance: An International Review* 13(1): 81–91.

Svirydzenka, K. 2016. Introducing a New Broad-based Index of Financial Development. IMF Working Paper No. 16/5. Washington, DC: International Monetary Fund.

TechCrunch. 2018. Crunchbase Unicorn Leaderboards. https://techcrunch.com/unicorn-leaderboard/

The Economist. 2017. In Fintech, China Shows the Way, 25 February. www.economist.com/news/finance-and-economics/21717393-advanced-technology-backward-banks-and-soaring-wealth-make-china-leader

Tobin, D. 2012. The Anglo-Saxon Paradox: Corporate Governance, Best Practices and the Reform Deficit in China's Banking Sector. *Journal of Chinese Economic and Business Studies* 10(2): 147–168.

Tobin, D. 2016. Continuity and Pragmatism: How Chinese State-Owned Banks Adapted to Hong Kong's Free Market (1949–1978). *Journal of Contemporary Asia* 46(2): 267–285.

Tobin, D., and L. Sun. 2009. International Listing as a Means to Mobilize the Benefits of Financial Globalization: Micro-Level Evidence from China. *World Development* 37(4): 825–838.

Tobin, D., and U. Volz. 2018. The Development and Transformation of the People's Republic of China's Financial System. ADBI Working Paper No. 825. Tokyo: Asian Development Bank Institute.

Tsai, K. S. 2015. Financing Small and Medium Enterprises in China: Recent Trends and Prospects beyond Shadow Banking. HKUST IEMS Working Paper No. 2015-24. Hong Kong, China: Hong Kong University of Science and Technology.

United Nation Conference on Trade and Development (UNCTAD). 2017. *World Investment Report 2017.* Geneva: UNCTAD.

United Nation Environment Programme (UNEP). 2017. *Establishing China's Green Financial System: Progress Report 2017.* Geneva: UNEP Inquiry into the Design of a Sustainable Financial System.

Volz, U. 2014. All Politics Is Local: The Renminbi's Prospects as a Future Global Currency. In *The Financial Statecraft of Emerging Powers*, edited by L. Armijo and S. Katada. Houndmills, Basingstoke: Palgrave Macmillan, pp. 103–137.

Volz, U. 2018. Fostering Green Finance for Sustainable Development in Asia. In *Routledge Handbook of Banking and Finance in Asia*, edited by U. Volz, P. Morgan, and N. Yoshino. London and New York: Routledge, ch. 27.

Wang, W., and D. Dollar. 2018. What's Happening with China's Fintech Industry? Order from Chaos, 8 February. www.brookings.edu/blog/order-from-chaos/2018/02/08/whats-happening-with-chinas-fintech-industry/

Xinhua. 2014. China Eases Market Access for Foreign Banks, 20 December. http://europe.chinadaily.com.cn/business/2014-12/20/content_19133286.htm

Yeandle, M. 2017. The Global Financial Centres Index 22. Shenzhen and London: China Development Institute and Z/Yen Partners. www.luxembourgforfinance.com/sites/luxembourgforfinance/files/files/GFCI22_Report.pdf

Yeh, Y.-H., P.-G. Shu, T.-S. Lee, and Y.-H. Su. 2009. Non-Tradable Share Reform and Corporate Governance in the Chinese Stock Market. *Corporate Governance: An International Review* 17: 457–475.

3

FINANCIAL SECTOR IN HONG KONG, CHINA

Andrew Sheng

Introduction

The rise of Hong Kong, China as an important entrepôt and international financial center (IFC) in the 1970s was considered one of the remarkable achievements in Asia (Jao 1997). As a colonial freeport, Hong Kong, China was an important trading center for the People's Republic of China (PRC) since the 1950s. But by 1989, the financial sector (19.5% of GDP) overtook the manufacturing industry (19.3% of GDP) in terms of its contribution to GDP. Although there were apprehensions about the success of Hong Kong, China on reversion to the PRC on 1 July 1997, Hong Kong, China has continued to thrive with the financial sector gaining strength in scale and depth. Hong Kong, China has a well-developed financial system with a significant banking sector (accounting for 39.9% of total financial market size in 2014) and a dynamic equity market (54.2%), followed by a relatively smaller debt securities market (5.9%) (Table 3.1).

Hong Kong, China is one of the leading IFCs but is not yet a global financial center; these two positions are held by New York and London (TheCityUK 2015a; Figure 3.1). In the Asian time zone, Hong Kong, China is considered a leader among the group of vibrant, evolving, and emerging regional hubs, with strong competition from Tokyo, Singapore, Shanghai, and Seoul. Furthermore, in the contest for the PRC business, there is competition from cities such as Shenzhen. Hong Kong, China authorities recognize that there is no room for complacency in maintaining its competitiveness.

This chapter examines the development of Hong Kong, China's financial sector and explores the issues in maintaining its position as a premier IFC. First, the current state of the financial system is reviewed with respect to its global position. Next, its strength is evaluated in its financial governance framework. Following sections examine the domestic and external challenges, such as competition from other IFCs, and the impact of global megatrends, including the disruptive role of financial technology, and at how Hong Kong, China can reinvent itself to enhance its competitiveness by leveraging on its first mover advantage in renminbi business and by leapfrogging other IFCs in adopting financial technology (fintech). Success hinges on the political will to design a holistic roadmap to reinvent Hong Kong, China to stay ahead of the competition.

Table 3.1 Hong Kong, China's financial markets, selected indicators (USD billion)

	2011	2012	2013	2014	*2014 market share*
Stock market capitalization[3] (1)	2,258.0	2,831.9	3,100.8	3,233.0	54.2%
Total debt securities[4] (2)	216.0	260.0	317.1	354.3	5.9%
Bank assets[5] (3)	1,766.3	1,914.8	2,183.2	2,379.6	39.9%
Total market size (1 + 2 + v3)	4,240.3	5,006.7	5,601.1	5,966.9	100.0%
Debt as % of GDP (2) + (3)/GDP	797.7%	828.2%	906.9%	939.8%	
Financial sector a % of GDP (1) + (2) + (3)/GDP	1,706.4%	1,906.6%	2,031.6%	2,051.2%	
Crude leverage ratio (2) + (3)/(1)	87.8%	76.8%	80.6%	84.6%	
Memo: GDP[1]	248.5	262.6	275.7	290.9	
Total external reserves[2]	285.3	317.3	311.1	328.4	

Notes: [1]Data from the World Bank. GDP at market prices (current USD). [2]Data from IMF IFS. Reserves Selected Indicators. [3]Data from WFE. [4]Data from BIS. Includes debt securities issues and amounts outstanding, Q4 data. [5]Data from HKMA Monthly Statistical Bulletin (February 2016; Issue No. 258), Table 1.2 Banking Statistics.

Sources: Bank for International Settlements (BIS) (http://stats.bis.org/statx/srs/table/c3?c=hk&p=20141); HKMA Monthly Statistical Bulletin (www.hkma.gov.hk/eng/market-data-and-statistics/monthly-statistical-bulletin/table.shtml); IMF, International Financial Statistics (http://data.imf.org/regular.aspx?key=60998114); World Bank (http://data.worldbank.org/indicator/NY.GDP.MKTP.CD); World Federation of Exchanges (www.world-exchanges.org/home/index.php/statistics/monthly-reports); author's calculations.

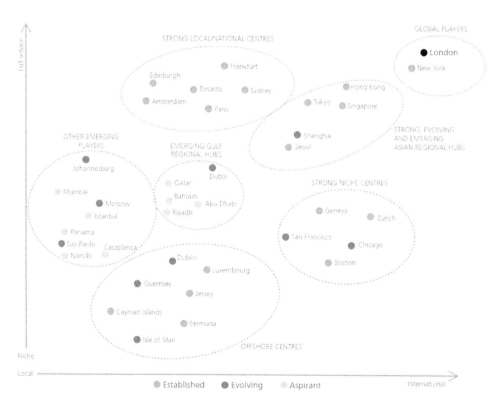

Figure 3.1 Key global financial centers

Source: TheCityUK based on Citi, Oliver Wyman and Z-Yen (https://www.thecityuk.com/research/uks-competitiveness-as-a-global-financial-centre-august-2015/).

Overview of economic and financial system

Between the mid-1950s and the 1990s, the Hong Kong, China economy experienced rapid economic growth in excess of 7% per annum. The World Bank attributed this success to a free market, export-led regime, low taxes, and minimal state intervention (World Bank 1993; Chang 2006). In 1983, there was a crisis in the exchange rate regime, which led to the implementation of the fixed Linked Exchange Rate System at HKD 7.8/USD. By the mid-1990s Hong Kong, China had already shifted most of its manufacturing base to the PRC as its domestic labor costs, rents, and GDP per capita had reached advanced-country levels. On its reversion to the PRC in 1997, Hong Kong, China had already established its leading position as a logistics, trade, and financial center for the PRC and the region. The Asian financial crisis of 1997–1999 was a major shock that caused slow growth, but Hong Kong, China quickly recovered after the US Fed started lowering interest rates and the rest of Asia revived. Between 2003 and 2014, Hong Kong, China enjoyed a period of unprecedented prosperity as the PRC economy took off, while the advanced countries embarked on near zero interest rate policies in the aftermath of the global financial crisis. Capital inflows into Hong Kong, China rose even as property prices and stock prices reached unprecedented heights. In 2015 Hong Kong, China was the world's eighth largest trading economy, with international merchandise trade exceeding USD 1 trillion.

Financial system is well developed, among best in the world

Befitting its status as an IFC, Hong Kong, China has a large and well-developed financial system, but it shares certain characteristics common to other Asian IFCs. The soundness of the financial system was tested during the summer of 2015, when Hong Kong, China's markets functioned in an orderly manner, despite increased volatility in equity and currency markets following the correction in the PRC's A-share market.

Hong Kong, China has played a major role in facilitating cross-border financial transactions in the Asian region, notably in intermediating foreign direct investment (FDI) and portfolio investment flows (Leung and Unteroberdoerster 2008). Its lead in this area comes from the common law tradition, with an independent judiciary and strong rule of law. Over time, the regulatory framework has been strengthened as a result of different crises and experiences. According to the Heritage Foundation, Hong Kong, China has secured the top spot as the world's most free-market economy for 21 years (1995–2015; GovHK 2015a). The low-tax regime, with minimal government intervention; clear, transparent rules; and a well-developed and resilient financial system, has contributed significantly to the attractiveness of Hong Kong, China as an IFC.

The Linked Exchange Rate System is an anchor of financial stability

The stability of the financial system is underpinned by the Exchange Fund, which was established by the currency board regime adopted in October 1983. The fund comprises cumulative revenue from its reserves, reserve deposits from commercial banks, currency issue, and deposits from the government. The Hong Kong Monetary Authority (HKMA) manages the Exchange Fund to maintain currency stability through the Linked Exchange Rate System, which the IMF (IMF 2016) noted has provided an anchor of stability for over 30 years. The system maintains automatic monetary and financial system stability by providing both liquidity and capital to the banking system in case of shocks. The fund provides the backstop for the Deposit Protection Scheme, together with a swap facility with the People's Bank of China of HKD 500 billion.

The total assets of the Exchange Fund reached HKD 3,428.9 billion at end-2015, with appropriate diversification into various asset classes (HKMA 2016b). At end-2014, aside from highly liquid investments such as US treasuries, the portfolio also included USD 80.5 billion in private equity and USD 34.7 billion in real estate (HKMA 2014).

The banking industry is well capitalized and profitable, with low non-performing loans

Banks in Hong Kong, China are well capitalized, profitable, and have very low levels of non-performing loans (Table 3.2), with assets amounting to over 735% of GDP (IMF 2014a). Capital adequacy levels remain sound at around 16.8%, with compliance with the second phase of the Basel III standards by end-2014 (HKMA 2014). As of mid-2015, the banking system comprised 157 licensed banks, 23 restricted license banks, and 21 deposit-taking companies, together with 64 local representative offices of overseas banking institutions. Foreign banks have a strong presence, coming from 36 countries and including 71 out of the world's largest 100 banks (GovHK 2015a). Twenty-seven of the 29 global systemically important banks (G-SIBs) have operations in Hong Kong, China. Banks provide a wide range of retail and wholesale banking business ranging from private banking to investment banking services (GovHK 2015a). Financial inclusion is very high, with 96% of the adult population having a bank account (Table 3.3). The shadow banking industry was relatively small, at about 10% of GDP in 2014, slightly more than that in Singapore (FSB 2015).

Table 3.2 Hong Kong, China's banking sector performance (in percentage)

	2010	2011	2012	2013	2014
Asset quality: all authorized institutions					
As percent of total credit exposures[1]	0.47	0.42	0.39	0.35	0.38
As percent of total loans[1]	0.71	0.63	0.6	0.55	0.55
Overdue >3 months and rescheduled loans	0.58	0.47	0.42	0.36	0.34
Profitability: all authorized institutions					
Return on assets (operating profit)	0.82	0.80	0.84	1.03	0.97
Return on assets (post-tax profit)	0.76	0.72	0.74	1.05	0.82
Net interest margin	1.02	0.98	1.08	1.12	1.14
Cost-to-income ratio	58.1	55.4	54.8	49.1	49.0
Bad debt charge to total assets	0.05	0.07	0.08	0.06	0.06
Liquidity: all authorized institutions					
Loan to deposit ratio (all currencies)	61.6	66.9	67.1	70.3	72.2
Loan to deposit (e) ratio (Hong Kong dollar)	78.1	84.5	79.8	82.1	83.3
Asset quality: surveyed institutions					
Delinquency ratio of residential mortgage loans	0.01	0.01	0.02	0.02	0.03
Delinquency ratio of credit card receivables	0.20	0.19	0.20	0.20	0.20
Capital adequacy: locally incorporated licensed banks					
Equity to assets ratio	8.3	7.9	8.5	8.5	8.8
Capital adequacy ratio (consolidated): All locally incorporated authorized institutions	15.8	15.8	15.7	15.9	16.8

Note: [1]Refers to total outstanding provisions/impairment allowances.

Source: HKMA Annual Report 2014, www.hkma.gov.hk/media/eng/publication-and-research/annual-report/2014/ar2014_E.pdf.

Table 3.3 Hong Kong, China's financial inclusion, selected indicators (2014)

	Hong Kong, China	World
Financial institution account (% age 15+)		
All adults	96.1	60.7
Access to financial institution account (% age 15+)		
Has debit card	69.9	40.1
Use of account in the past year (% age 15+)		
Used an account to receive wages	43.0	17.7
Used an account to receive government transfers	11.8	8.2
Used a financial institution account to pay utility bills	39.8	16.7
Other digital payments in the past year (% age 15+)		
Used a debit card to make payments	50.8	23.2
Used a credit card to make payments	59.3	15.1
Used the internet to pay bills or make purchases	36.3	16.6
Savings in the past year (% age 15+)		
Saved at a financial institution	50.0	27.4
Credit in the past year (% age 15+)		
Borrowed from a financial institution	8.2	10.7

Source: World Bank. The Little Data Book on Financial Inclusion 2015 (www.worldbank.org/content/dam/Worldbank/Research/GlobalFindex/PDF/LDB_Financial_Inclusion_2015.pdf).

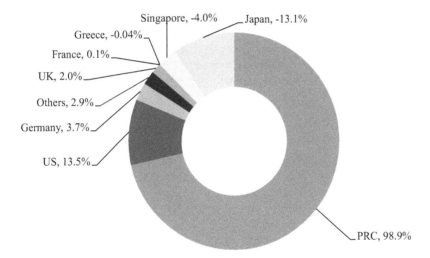

Figure 3.2 External exposure of Hong Kong banks, 2014 (HKD billion)

Notes: PRC = People's Republic of China. UK = United Kingdom. US = United States.

Source: HKMA Annual Report 2014 (www.hkma.gov.hk/media/eng/publication-and-research/annual-report/2014/ar2014_E.pdf).

In the last few years, lending to PRC enterprises has been a dominant source of income, accounting for 98.9% of Hong Kong, China's banks' external exposure in 2014 (Figure 3.2). Due to reversal of foreign exchange (FX) exposure as the yuan began to weaken, the exposure declined sharply to 31.9% by end-June 2015 (HKMA 2015).

Hong Kong, China has strengthened its position as a private banking hub, although Singapore has gained a lead due to its double taxation agreement with Europe and other countries. According to the World Wealth Report 2015, the Asia-Pacific region has the largest population of high net worth individuals (HNWI), with 4.69 million HNWIs holding USD 15.8 trillion of wealth in 2014 (Capgemini 2015). The PRC has a fast-growing HNWI population, with an estimated 890,000 HNWIs holding an estimated USD 4.5 trillion of wealth in 2014 (Capgemini 2015). Research by Knight Frank, a property consultancy, showed that Hong Kong, China is home to 3,854 ultra-HNWIs, with assets exceeding USD 30 million each in 2015, the highest number in Asia and third globally (Knight Frank 2016).

The foreign exchange market is the fifth largest globally

According to the triennial central bank survey conducted by the Bank for International Settlements (BIS) in 2016, Hong Kong, China was the world's fourth largest foreign exchange market in terms of global foreign exchange market turnover by country (BIS 2016). Hong Kong, China places just behind Singapore (third), the US (second), and the UK (first). Hong Kong, China has a mature and active foreign exchange market, due to the absence of exchange controls and its favorable time zone location. Furthermore, according to the BIS' International Banking Statistics (BIS 2015), Hong Kong, China had USD 425 billion in foreign banking assets at end-2014.

The offshore yuan business hub is the world's largest

As the yuan became more internationalized, Hong Kong, China has become a major beneficiary by being home to the world's largest offshore yuan business hub, the world's largest offshore renminbi liquidity pool, and an important center for business with the PRC in terms of inward and outward investments. In Q1 2015, renminbi deposits and outstanding renminbi certificates of deposit totaled CNY 1,061.2 billion, while outstanding yuan bonds issued in Hong Kong, China (called Dim Sum bonds) amounted to CNY 356.2 billion (GovHK 2015a). The issuance of Dim Sum bonds in the first three months of 2015 was almost double the amount issued for the whole of 2014 (CNY 197 billion; Ng 2016).

By August 2016, according to SWIFT data, the renminbi was the fifth global payments currency, accounting for 1.86% of global payments by value, up from number seven and 1.39% in January 2014 (SWIFT 2016). Over 1,800 banks use renminbi for payments with or without the PRC and Hong Kong, China, an annual increase of 12% over June 2015. The renminbi clearing platform in Hong Kong, China has a total of 224 participating banks, of which 199 were branches and subsidiaries of foreign banks and overseas presence of banks in the PRC (GovHK 2015a).

The money market is an important indicator of cost of funds

The Hong Kong, China money market consists primarily of the interbank market, utilized by financial institutions at the wholesale level. The Hong Kong Interbank Offer Rate (HIBOR) is one of the most important indicators of the price of short-term funds in Hong Kong, China. The daily turnover in the interbank market averaged HKD 239 billion in February 2015 (GovHK 2015a). Today, automated trading services (ATS, using algorithmic or computerized trading) have become major traders in the money and foreign exchange markets, with 27 overseas exchanges and market operators authorized as ATS providers in Hong Kong, China at the end of April 2015 (GovHK 2015a).

The success of Hong Kong, China as a financial center hinges on its world-class financial infrastructure. The HKMA has been leading efforts to upgrade its funds transfer and payments system through its real-time gross settlement system (RTGS), installed in June 2013. To further support robust market development, the HKMA launched its Central Money Markets Unit (CMU) Fund Order Routing and Settlement Service in August 2009, as well as the regional clearing of US dollar payments in December 2000 (GovHK 2015a; HKMA 2016a). The CMU was further linked to the euro (April 2003) and yuan (March 2006) RTGS systems (HKMA 2016a). In addition to the stock market and the futures market, there is also an active over-the-counter (OTC) market which is mainly operated and used by professional institutions and trades in swaps, forwards, and options in relation to equities, interest rates, and currencies. These are cleared by OTC Clearing Hong Kong Limited (OTC Clear), a subsidiary of the Hong Kong Exchanges and Clearing Limited (HKEx), since November 2013, and today offers clearing services for inter-dealer interest rate swaps and non-deliverable forwards (GovHK 2015a).

Equity markets are deep, liquid, and efficient, and top in IPOs

Hong Kong, China's major engine of financial development is its dynamic equity market, led by the HKEX, which was demutualized successfully in 2001. Driven by the listing of companies from the PRC, Hong Kong, China's equity market has reached a stock market capitalization of 1,000% of GDP, the seventh largest in the world and fourth largest in the Asia-Pacific region at end-2015 (WFE 2016). New channels for two-way flows between the PRC and Hong Kong, China, such as the Shanghai-Hong Kong Stock Connect scheme in November 2014, enable individuals and institutions with brokerage accounts in either Shanghai or Hong Kong, China to trade stocks in the other market. In addition, the launch of the Mutual Recognition of Funds scheme in July 2015 permits mutual funds in either location to mobilize investments from the other jurisdiction. These initiatives facilitate closer integration of the stock markets and promote greater trading volumes, while increasing market liquidity (IMF 2016). Between 2009 and 2011, Hong Kong, China led the world in total funds raised through initial public offerings (IPOs), surpassing even London and New York (Basic Law 2012). In the fourth quarter of 2015, Hong Kong, China was number one in the world in IPO fund-raising, raising USD 33.5 billion (Ernst and Young 2015). A survey by HKEX revealed that local and foreign investors contributed 39% each to total market turnover in 2014–2015. Institutional investors (both local and foreign) accounted for 51% of total turnover. Principal trading reached a record high growth of 22% in 2014–2015 (HKEX 2016).

Although relatively small, the debt market has grown rapidly

Partly due to the lack of government debt as the government runs a fiscal surplus, Hong Kong, China's debt market is relatively small compared to its banking and equity markets. Nevertheless, debt market growth has been rapid, with total outstanding value of Hong Kong dollar debt securities rising from 8% of GDP in 1994 to 63% in 2014 and 73% by mid-2016. The government bond (GB) program was implemented in 2009 to enlarge the local bond market to meet the needs of domestic pension and insurance funds. The size of the GB program amounted to HKD 200 billion in 2013 (Ng 2016). Hong Kong, China's corporate bond market is the preferred market for bond issuances by domestic and foreign corporations and multinationals due to its well-developed financial infrastructure and ready access to global debt markets. Private sector bonds account for 80% of bond issuances and trading (AsianBondsOnline 2016). In recent years, Hong Kong, China has also focused attention on developing its Islamic finance platform. The first *sukuk* (Islamic bond) under the GB program was successfully issued in September 2014. The USD 1 billion five-year issuance attracted strong demand from global investors. The legislative framework for a new regulatory regime for stored value facilities and retail payment systems was also finalized (HKMA 2014).

The insurance industry has the second highest penetration in the world

Hong Kong, China has one of the most open insurance sectors in the world, with 158 authorized insurers, 72 of which were incorporated in the PRC and 21 other countries as at the end of April 2015 (GovHK 2015a). The insurance sector is mature and well capitalized (IMF 2014a), due to high insurance penetration (total gross premiums as % of GDP) of 16.2% in the first half of 2015 (Ng 2015). Overall, Hong Kong has the second highest insurance penetration rates among advanced markets in 2014 after Taipei,China (Swiss Re 2015). Gross assets amounted to HKD 452 billion as at end-2014. Growth has been underpinned by increasing affluence, an aging population, and growing public awareness on planning for aging healthcare needs.

The introduction of the Mandatory Provident Fund (MPF) in December 2000 represented an important initiative to improve retirement protection for Hong Kong's aging workforce. All employees (other than those who are self-employed or have approved provident or pension schemes) must join this system of privately managed and employment-related schemes, whereby the employee and employer each contributes 5% of the employee's income toward his retirement (GovHK 2015b). In the process, the MPF has also contributed to the deepening of institutional fund management and financial markets for long-term investment, with more than three million MPF holders (Chan 2015). Apart from creating new demands for investment products, MPF also contributes to greater stability in the financial markets. As at end-March 2015, accrued net assets of MPF schemes amounted to HKD 594.8 billion (USD 76.3 billion; GovHK 2015a).

Hong Kong, China is home to one of Asia's biggest asset management centers, ex-Japan

Outside Japan, Hong Kong, China has a vibrant and active asset management industry that actively competes with Singapore for its share of asset management business. According to the 2015 Deloitte Wealth Management Centre ranking, Hong Kong, China was ahead of Singapore, but that depends on the metric used (Deloitte 2015). Hong Kong, China's combined fund management business rose by 10.5% to USD 2.3 trillion in 2014, with another USD 397 billion of assets under management under private banking. As at end-June 2015, there were 2,626 collective investment schemes, including 2,063 unit trusts and mutual funds (HKTDC Research 2016). Although there is intense competition with Singapore, Hong Kong, China had USD 1,648 billion or 1.5% of total global assets under management in 2014 (author's calculation with data from TheCityUK 2015b and SFC 2015). Because of the PRC's growing private equity and venture capital business, Hong Kong, China has developed substantial depth and professional critical mass in its alternative investment business, with Asia's biggest concentration of private equity, hedge funds and specialist fund managers. Hong Kong, China has a leadership role in the PRC's Qualified Foreign Institutional Investors and Qualified Domestic Institutional Investor schemes.

Financial governance framework well institutionalized

To sum up, Hong Kong, China's success as an IFC reflects its world-class business infrastructure and strong regulatory framework. A robust common law system governed by an independent judiciary and an independent anti-corruption agency underpins market confidence in conducting business. A cosmopolitan lifestyle and low tax rates attract the top talent needed to support Hong Kong, China's success as an IFC. Its strong network of international accounting, legal, and other professional services firms makes it an ideal hub as an IFC and as a gateway to the PRC (FSDC 2013).

Hong Kong, China's role as an IFC is underpinned by its robust financial governance framework, the principal regulators being the HKMA, the Securities and Futures Commission (SFC), the Insurance Authority, and the Mandatory Provident Fund Authority (GovHK 2015a). These agencies are represented in the key global regulatory standard-setting authorities, such as the Basel Committee on Banking Supervision and International Organization of Securities Commissions. The IMF (2016) has commended Hong Kong, China for its strong track record in preemptively updating its regulatory standards, addressing systemic risks, and enhancing the loss absorption buffers of financial institutions. These views reaffirmed the May 2014 conclusion of the IMF's Financial System Stability Assessment, which noted that both the HKMA and SFC have an international outlook and staff themselves with international talent in order to discharge their responsibilities in maintaining monetary and financial stability and enhancing Hong Kong, China's IFC reputation (IMF 2014b).

The IMF (2016) has suggested areas for enhancement, including the following:

- In insurance, the IMF supported the authorities' plans for an independent insurance authority and implementation of a risk-based capital regime for insurance companies. Legislation for an independent insurance authority was enacted in July 2015, and an independent Insurance Authority was established in December 2015. The Insurance Authority took over the regulatory functions of the then Office of the Commissioner of Insurance, which was a government department, in June 2017.
- In the securities area, the IMF called for stronger oversight of auditors, enforcement and regulation of securities markets, broker–dealers, and asset managers as their business model changes with new channels connecting Hong Kong, China and the PRC.
- In banking, the IMF encouraged Hong Kong, China to expedite legislation on a comprehensive crisis resolution and recovery plan, given the significant presence of global systemically important institutions.
- The IMF also urged the strengthening of cooperation with bilateral and international regulatory fora to minimize cross-border risks and extra-territorial effects of global regulatory developments.

Emerging challenges to Hong Kong, China's competitive position as an IFC

Despite these favorable achievements to date, most observers also note that there is little room for complacency. The global mega-trends of growing geopolitical tensions, climate change, disruptive technology, and impact of quantitative easing and complex regulatory standards pose significant external and domestic challenges to Hong Kong, China's role as an IFC. On the external front, the PRC's financial reform and liberalization process represents both an opportunity and a challenge to Hong Kong, China in terms of increased competition from Shanghai. An added challenge will be the rise of other Asian financial centers such as Singapore, particularly in challenging Hong Kong, China's role in private banking, FX trade, and renminbi business. At the same time, as Shanghai, Shenzhen, and other PRC cities become more sophisticated in improving domestic financial services, particularly in fintech (such as Alibaba's P2P payments) and also in nurturing home-grown start-ups and technology companies, Hong Kong, China has to step up its capabilities to attract such funding ventures.

The Financial Services Development Council report (FSDC 2013) noted that Singapore had already surpassed Hong Kong, China in terms of FX, fixed income, commodities, alternative investments, and private banking. Furthermore, with a market capitalization of USD 4.5 trillion in 2015, the Shanghai stock market is already larger than Hong Kong, China (USD 3.2 trillion) although it has a fewer number of listed companies (WFE 2016). Also, FX trading in Shanghai far surpasses Hong Kong, China's FX market (Steinbock 2010).

Domestically, Hong Kong, China has been facing a more politicized and polarized society as it struggles to improve the quality of life, such as tackling pollution, air and water quality, affordable housing for the middle-income population and greater demands for jobs for unemployed youth, welfare needs of the aging population, and the growing income and wealth gap. Some, but not all, of such social discontent erupted through the Occupy Central events in September through December 2014. Inability to agree on the necessary political reforms also created uncertainties on the future of political leadership. Indeed, the recent decision by HSBC against relocating its headquarters from London to Hong Kong, China is an important reminder for its citizens to get their act together to further strengthen its competitiveness as a premier IFC in Asia and the world.[1]

Specifically, a study by PwC on Building Better Cities covering 28 cities in the APEC region suggested that although Hong Kong, China ranked first and second, respectively, in terms of economic competitiveness and connectivity (physical and ICT infrastructure), it scored poorly in terms of cultural and social fabric, education, health, and environmental sustainability. These shortcomings pulled down its overall ranking to 11th out of 28 APEC cities (PwC 2015).

The World Economic Forum's Global Competitiveness Report (2015–2016) showed that Hong Kong, China's financial sector finished third, behind New Zealand (No. 1) and Singapore (No. 2) (Table 3.4). While its financial sector remains well developed, with a high level

Table 3.4 The financial trinity (2015)

Key Indicators, 2014	Hong Kong, China	Singapore	Shanghai
Population (millions)	7.3	5.5	24
GDP (USD billions)	289.6	308.1	384
GDP per capita (USD)	39,871	56,319	16,000
Stock market (rank/18, Asia-Pacific)	4th	10th	2nd
Stock market (rank/57, World)	7th	19th	4th
International trade (merchandise, USD billions)	1,125 (8th)	776 (16th)	0.5 (179th)
Foreign exchange reserves (USD billions)	328 (8th)	257 (11th)	3,859 (1st)[1]
International Banking (total cross-border claims)	10th	8th	7th[1]
Foreign exchange market (turnover), 2013	5th	3rd	16th[1]
Global Competitiveness Index, 2015 (rank/140)	7th	2nd	28th[1]
Financial market development (rank/140)	3rd[2]	2nd	54th[1]
Health and primary education (rank/140)	29th	2nd	44th[1]
Technological readiness (rank/140)	8th	5th	74th[1]
Innovation (rank/140)	27th	9th	31st[1]

Key Indicators, 2014	Hong Kong, China	Singapore	Shanghai
Market size (rank/140)	32nd	35th	1st[1]
Infrastructure (rank/140)	1st	2nd	39th[1]
Quality of air transport infrastructure	3rd	1st	51st[1]
Ease of doing business (rank/140)	2nd	1st	58th[1]
No. days to start a business	3	2.5	31.4[1]
No. procedures to start a business	2.5	3	11[1]
Office rent (USD/s.f./year)	262 (1st)	90 (11th)	136 (5th)
Corporate income tax, 2014	16.5	17	25
Individual income tax (max. tax rate, %)	15	20	45
Global start-up ecosystem, 2015 (rank/25)	25th	10th	15th[3]

Notes: [1]The PRC data serves as proxy for Shanghai. [2]Hong Kong, China ranked first (2011–2014). The change in methodology for the Legal Rights Index resulted in Hong Kong, China's drop to third place. [3]Currently ranking does not include Shanghai, but expected to rank in top 15.

Sources: WEF World Competitiveness Report 2015–2016; The World Bank Doing Business 2015 (www.doingbusiness.org/data/exploretopics/paying-taxes); WTO International Trade Statistics 2015 (www.wto.org/english/res_e/statis_e/its2015_e/its2015_e.pdf); IMF (IFS) (http://data.imf.org/regular.aspx?key=60998114); BIS Triennial Central Bank Survey 2013 (www.bis.org/publ/rpfx13fx.pdf); BIS Locational Banking Statistics (http://stats.bis.org/statx/srs/table/a3.1?p=20144&c=); Compass Global Startup Ecosystem Ranking 2015 (http://blog.compass.co/the-2015-global-startup-ecosystem-ranking-is-live/); JLL Global Premium Office Rent Tracker Q1 2016 (www.jll.com/Research/jll-global-premium-office-tracker-2016.pdf?a2c4266e-2c97-435a-a1c3-f80ac4539aa6); author's calculations.

of sophistication, trustworthiness, and stability, and relatively good availability of credit, Hong Kong, China's performance was hampered by a lack of innovation (Schwab 2015).

Some of its competitiveness issues relate to high real estate costs. A Jones Lang LaSalle survey indicated that office space in Hong Kong, China is the most expensive in the world at USD 262 per square foot, surpassing Shanghai (USD 136) and Singapore (USD 90; JLL 2016). According to the World Bank's Ease of Doing Business Ranking, Hong Kong, China ranked fifth out of 189 economies, while Singapore took the top spot (World Bank 2016).

Taking the challenges forward

HKMA Chief Executive Norman Chan (2014) rightly noted that Hong Kong, China should not view the rise of Shanghai and other regional IFCs as a zero-sum game. The 2016–2017 budget showed that the authorities were aware of the challenges and have taken proactive measures to address them. To improve social amenities and living conditions, allocations for healthcare, education, and social welfare were raised to HKD 198 billion, an increase of 80% from a decade ago (Kwok et al. 2016; Tsang 2016). The salaries tax was reduced and the supply of residential and office space supply increased to address inequality and high property prices.

On the issue of whether the link to the US dollar should be retained, most influential analysts consider the status quo should be maintained, while a small minority favored switching to a CNY link.[2] Given the credibility of the present regime, no change to the Linked Exchange Rate System is officially considered on the cards.

To address the challenges of increased competition due to advances in information technology, a HKD 2 billion Innovation and Technology Venture Fund was created to co-invest with private venture capital funds in local technology start-ups (GovHK 2016). Higher tax incentives were given to encourage private investment in research and development (R&D). The budget also sought to develop new channels to promote mutual capital market access between Hong Kong, China and the PRC and attract corporate treasury centers to Hong Kong, China.

Recognizing the long-term opportunities of financial technology (fintech), the government will encourage fintech start-ups, investors, and R&D institutions to locate in Hong Kong, China with a dedicated program to provide support for 150 fintech start-ups over the next five years. Cyber security will be strengthened, and the regulatory authorities will help to foster the setup of dedicated fintech financing platforms.

Success requires a holistic approach

While Hong Kong, China's ongoing policies appear to be steps in the right direction, the reforms remain hampered by the lack of cooperation between the executive and the legislature, as well as the differences in addressing issues that cut across different jurisdictions. For example, efforts to develop the fintech hub pose important questions about how (and by whom) it is to be regulated, given the absence of specific legislation on fintech activities (KPMG 2015). Success in developing fintech also hinges on the availability of the right talents and requires changes in its education policies and the role of universities and business collaboration to nurture more creative thinkers (arts and humanities graduates) to match its current strength in producing math and science talent. Some of these efforts are hampered by the division in public opinion and inability to reach political consensus.

The FSDC 2013 report called for a holistic review to design a comprehensive strategy to position Hong Kong, China as a premier IFC, which merits consideration. More recently, it was suggested that Hong Kong, China should strive to become the center for reinsurance business in East Asia as well as a regional securities (stocks and bonds) market for Asian sovereigns and corporates to raise capital and debt (Lau 2016). These solutions are not new, but the question of political governance will be a stumbling block to quick action in this regard.

There is little doubt that Hong Kong, China remains a vibrant and successful IFC, but many external and internal challenges hamper its ability to meet the competition in a determined and holistic manner. While many policy measures have been introduced, most recently in the 2016–2017 budget to address the emerging challenges, Hong Kong, China needs to move quickly and decisively to reinvent itself to stay ahead of the competition. Time and tide awaits no IFC.

Notes

1 For a detailed discussion of the factors affecting Hong Kong, China's competitive position, see FSDC (2013).
2 For a discussion of the pros and cons of changing the HKD link, see Yam (2012), Tsang and Greenwood (2013); HKMA (2005).

References

Asian Development Bank. 2016. Overview of Hong Kong, China Market Structure. AsianBondsOnline. https://asianbondsonline.adb.org/hongkong/structure/overview.php (accessed 1 August 2016).
Basic Law. 2012. Hong Kong as Asia's World City. In *The Basic Law and Hong Kong – The 15th Anniversary of Reunification with the Motherland*. Hong Kong: Basic Law. www.basiclaw.gov.hk/en/publications/book/15anniversary_reunification_ch3_3.pdf (accessed 3 February 2016).
Bank of International Settlements. 2015. *International Banking Statistics as at End-December 2014*. Basel: Bank of International Settlements. www.bis.org/statistics/rppb1504.htm (accessed 1 August 2016).

Bank of International Settlements. 2016. *Triennial Central Bank Survey of Foreign Exchange and OTC Derivatives Markets in 2016*. Basel: Bank of International Settlements. www.bis.org/statistics/d11_1.pdf (accessed 2 October 2016).

Capgemini. 2015. *World Wealth Report 2015: Regional View*. Paris: Capgemini. www.worldwealthreport. com/reports/wealth/asia_pacific/china (accessed 8 March 2016).

Chan, N. 2014. *The Future of Hong Kong as an International Financial Centre Amidst the Liberalisation of Mainland China's Financial Sector*. Hong Kong: HKMA, 4 August. www.hkma.gov.hk/eng/key-information/insight/20140804.shtml (accessed 20 February 2016).

Chan, D. 2015. *Universal Retirement Protection: The Relevance of MPF in the Debate*. Hong Kong: Mandatory Provident Fund Schemes Authority. www.mpfa.org.hk/eng/main/speeches/files/2015-05-06-Article-e.pdf (accessed 7 March 2016).

Chang, H.J. 2006. *The East Asian Development Experience: The Miracle, the Crisis and the Future*. London: Zed Books.

Deloitte. 2015. *The Deloitte Wealth Management Centre Ranking 2015*. Zurich: Deloitte. https://www2. deloitte.com/content/dam/Deloitte/ch/Documents/financial-services/ch-en-financial-services-the-deloitte-wealth-management-centre-ranking-2015.pdf

Ernst and Young. 2015. *EY Global IPO Trends, 2015 4Q*. London: Ernst and Young. www.ey.com/Publication/vwLUAssets/EY-global-ipo-trends-2015-q4/$FILE/EY-global-ipo-trends-2015-q4.pdf (accessed 20 January 2016).

Financial Services Development Council (FSDC). 2013. *Strengthening Hong Kong as a Leading Global International Financial Centre*. FSDC Research Paper 01. Hong Kong: FSDC. www.fsdc.org.hk/sites/default/files/(REV)%20Strengthening%20Hong%20Kong%20As%20Leading(English).pdf (accessed 29 February 2016).

Financial Services Development Council (FSDC). 2015. *Annual Report 2014–15*. Hong Kong: FSDC. www.fsdc.org.hk/sites/default/files/Annual%20Report-2015%28Eng%20%26%20T%20Chi%29.pdf (accessed 16 November 2015).

Financial Stability Board (FSB). 2015. Exhibit 6: Shadow Banking, OFIs, and Banks as a Percent of GDP. In *Global Shadow Banking Monitoring Report 2015*. Basel: Financial Stability Board, 12 November. www.fsb.org/wp-content/uploads/global-shadow-banking-monitoring-report-2015.pdf (accessed 16 November 2015).

GovHK. 2015a. *Hong Kong: The Facts, Financial Services*. Hong Kong Fact Sheets Series. Hong Kong: Government of Hong Kong Special Administrative Region of the People's Republic of China. www.gov.hk/en/about/abouthk/factsheets/docs/financial_services.pdf (accessed 8 December 2015).

GovHK. 2015b. *Hong Kong: The Facts, Mandatory Provident Fund*. Hong Kong Fact Sheets Series. Hong Kong: Government of Hong Kong Special Administrative Region of the People's Republic of China. www.gov.hk/en/about/abouthk/factsheets/docs/mpf.pdf (accessed 8 December 2015).

GovHK. 2016. *FS Unveils Budget Measures to Respond to New Economic Order*, 24 February. Hong Kong: Government of Hong Kong Special Administrative Region of the People's Republic of China. www.info.gov.hk/gia/general/201602/24/P201602240411.htm (accessed 26 February 2016).

HKEX. 2016. *Cash Market Transaction Survey 2014–15*, February 2016. Hong Kong: HKEX. www.hkex.com.hk/eng/stat/research/Documents/cmts2015.pdf (accessed 20 March 2016).

Hong Kong Monetary Authority (HKMA). 2005. Hong Kong's Linked Exchange Rate System, HKMA Background Brief No. 1, 2nd Edition. www.legco.gov.hk/yr06-07/english/panels/fa/papers/facb1-657-1-e.pdf

HKMA. 2014. *Annual Report 2014*. Hong Kong: HKMA. www.fsdc.org.hk/sites/default/files/Annual%20Report-2015%28Eng%20%26%20T%20Chi%29.pdf (accessed 16 November 2015).

HKMA. 2015. Banking Sector Performance. In *Half-Yearly Monetary and Financial Stability Report*, September 2015, pp. 58–75. Hong Kong: HKMA. www.hkma.gov.hk/media/eng/publication-and-research/research/half-yearly-monetary-and-financial-stability-report/201509/E_Half-yearly_201509.pdf (accessed 18 February 2016).

HKMA. 2016a. *Central Money Markets Unit*, 8 March. Hong Kong: HKMA. www.hkma.gov.hk/eng/key-functions/international-financial-centre/infrastructure/cmu.shtml (accessed 8 March 2016).

HKMA. 2016b. *Exchange Fund Position at End-December 2015*, 22 January. Hong Kong: HKMA. www.hkma.gov.hk/eng/key-information/press-releases/2016/20160122-3.shtml (accessed 8 March 2016).

Hong Kong Trade Development Council (HKTDC) Research. 2016. *Fund Management Industry in Hong Kong*, 14 January. Hong Kong: HKTDC. http://hong-kong-economy-research.hktdc.com/

business-news/article/Hong-Kong-Industry-Profiles/Fund-Management-Industry-in-Hong-Kong/hkip/en/1/1X000000/1X003UUO.htm (accessed 1 August 2016).

International Monetary Fund (IMF). 2014a. *People's Republic of China – Hong Kong Special Administrative Region: Financial Sector Assessment Program, July 2014.* IMF Country Report 14/205. Washington, DC: International Monetary Fund. www.imf.org/external/pubs/ft/scr/2014/cr14207.pdf (accessed 1 February 2016).

International Monetary Fund (IMF). 2014b. *People's Republic of China – Hong Kong Special Administrative Region Financial System Stability Assessment, May 2014.* IMF Country Report 14/130. Washington, DC: International Monetary Fund. www.imf.org/external/pubs/ft/scr/2014/cr14130.pdf (accessed 1 February 2016).

International Monetary Fund (IMF). 2016. *People's Republic of China – Hong Kong Special Administrative Region. 2015 Article IV Consultation – Press Release; Staff Report and Statement by the Executive Director for the People's Republic of China – Hong Kong Special Administrative Region.* Washington, DC: International Monetary Fund. www.imf.org/external/pubs/ft/scr/2016/cr1617.pdf (accessed 25 January 2016).

Jao, Y. C. 1997. *Hong Kong as an International Financial Centre: Evolution, Prospects and Policies.* Hong Kong, China: City University of Hong Kong Press.

JLL. 2016. *The JLL Global Premium Office Rent Tracker, Q1 2016.* Illinois: JLL. www.jll.com/Research/jll-global-premium-office-tracker-2016.pdf?a2c4266e-2c97-435a-a1c3-f80ac4539aa6 (accessed 2 March 2016).

Knight Frank. 2016. *The Wealth Report 2016: The Global Perspective on Prime Property and Investment.* London: Knight Frank. http://content.knightfrank.com/research/83/documents/en/wealth-report-2016-3579.pdf (accessed 20 March 2016).

KPMG. 2015. *Making Hong Kong a FinTech Centre: Innovating Business in Asia,* June 2015. Hong Kong: KPMG. www.kpmg.com/CN/en/IssuesAndInsights/ArticlesPublications/Documents/Making-HK-FinTech-Centre-201506.pdf (accessed 20 February 2016).

Kwok, D., T. Siu, F. Master, C. Baldwin, and J. Pomfret. 2016. Highlights – Hong Kong Budget for Fiscal 2016/17. *Reuters,* 24 February. www.reuters.com/article/hongkong-budget-idUSL3N16239Z (accessed 26 February 2016).

Lau, L.J. 2016. How Hong Kong Can Survive – Even Thrive – Amid a Decline in Demand from Mainland China. *South China Morning Post,* 9 March. www.scmp.com/comment/insight-opinion/article/1922470/how-hong-kong-can-survive-even-thrive-amid-decline-demand (accessed 20 March 2016).

Leung, C., and O. Unteroberdoerster. 2008. Hong Kong SAR as a Financial Center for Asia: Trends and Implications. IMF Working Paper 08/57. Washington, DC: International Monetary Fund. www.imf.org/external/pubs/ft/wp/2008/wp0857.pdf (accessed 27 January 2016).

Ng, G. 2015. *Insurance Industry in Hong Kong.* HKTDC Research, 21 September. Hong Kong: HKTDC. http://hong-kong-economy-research.hktdc.com/business-news/article/Hong-Kong-Industry-Profiles/Insurance-Industry-in-Hong-Kong/hkip/en/1/1X000000/1X003UWM.htm (accessed 18 February 2016).

Ng, G. 2016. *Debt Market Industry in Hong Kong.* HKTDC Research, 15 January. Hong Kong: HKTDC. http://hong-kong-economy-research.hktdc.com/business-news/article/Hong-Kong-Industry-Profiles/Debt-Market-Industry-in-Hong-Kong/hkip/en/1/1X000000/1X003UPT.htm (accessed 18 February 2016).

PwC. 2015. *Building Better Cities: Competitive, Sustainable and Livable Metropolises in APEC (and How to Become One).* APEC 2015 CEO Summit Philippines. www.pwc.com/us/en/apec-ceo-summit/2015/apec-building-better-cities.pdf (accessed 23 November 2015).

Schwab, K. 2015. *The Global Competitiveness Report 2015–2016.* World Economic Forum. Geneva: World Economic Forum. http://www3.weforum.org/docs/gcr/2015-2016/Global_Competitiveness_Report_2015-2016.pdf (accessed 2 February 2016).

Securities and Futures Commission (SFC). 2015. *Fund Management Activities Survey 2014.* Hong Kong: SFC, 21 July. www.sfc.hk/web/EN/files/ER/PDF/2014%20FMAS%20Report_English_20150721_Final.pdf (accessed 21 January 2016).

Steinbock, D. 2010. Shanghai and Hong Kong: China's Emerging Global Financial Hubs. *The Globalist.* www.theglobalist.com/shanghai-and-hong-kong-chinas-emerging-global-financial-hubs/ (accessed 17 February 2016).

SWIFT. 2016. RMB Tracker. *September 2016 Report.* La Hulpe: Society for Worldwide Interbank Financial Telecommunication. www.swift.com/file/32466/download?token=NXRJtZeE (accessed 2 October 2016).

Swiss Re. 2015. Figure 17: Insurance Density and Penetration in Advanced Markets, 2014. In *World Insurance in 2014: Back to Life: 19.* Swiss Re sigma 4/2015. Zurich: Swiss Re. www.tsb.org.tr/images/ Documents/Raporlama/2015/sigma4_2015_en.pdf (accessed 2 February 2016).

TheCityUK. 2015a. *The UK's Competitiveness as a Global Financial Centre.* London: TheCityUK, 3 August. www.thecityuk.com/research/uks-competitiveness-as-a-global-financial-centre-august-2015/ (accessed 7 March 2016).

TheCityUK. 2015b. *UK Fund Management: An Attractive Proposition for International Funds.* London: TheCityUK, 19 November. www.thecityuk.com/assets/2015/Reports-PDF/UK-Fund-Manage ment-An-attractive-proposition-for-international-funds.pdf (accessed 8 January 2016).

Tsang, J. C. 2016. *The 2016–17 Budget.* Speech by the Financial Secretary, the Honorable John C. Tsang Moving the Second Reading of the Appropriation Bill 2016, 24 February. www.budget.gov.hk/2016/ eng/speech.html (accessed 25 February 2016).

Tsang, J., and J. Greenwood. 2013. 30 years on the Hong Kong Dollar's Peg is Still a Star Performer, *South China Morning Post,* 17 October. https://www.scmp.com/comment/insight-opinion/article/1333090/ 30-years-hong-kongs-dollar-peg-still-star-performer

World Bank. 1993. *The East Asian Miracle: Economic and Growth Public Policy.* Public Policy Research Report. New York: Oxford University Press. http://www-wds.worldbank.org/external/default/ WDSContentServer/WDSP/IB/1993/09/01/000009265_3970716142516/Rendered/PDF/multi_ page.pdf (accessed 20 November 2015).

World Bank. 2015. *The Little Data Book on Financial Inclusion 2015.* Washington, DC: World Bank. www.worldbank.org/content/dam/Worldbank/Research/GlobalFindex/PDF/LDB_Financial_Inclu sion_2015.pdf (accessed 18 February 2016).

World Bank. 2016. *Doing Business 2016: Measuring Regulatory Quality and Efficiency.* Washington, DC: World Bank. www.doingbusiness.org/~/media/GIAWB/Doing%20Business/Documents/Annual-Reports/English/DB16-Full-Report.pdf (accessed 18 February 2016).

World Federation of Exchanges (WFE). 2016. *January 2016 Monthly Report.* Paris: World Federation of Exchanges. www.world-exchanges.org/home/index.php/statistics/monthly-reports (accessed 18 February 2016).

Yam, J. 2012. The Future of the Monetary System of Hong Kong. Institute of Global Economics and Finance Working Paper No. 9, Hong Kong, China: The Chinese University of Hong Kong.

4

INDIAN FINANCIAL SECTOR

Structure, trends, and turns

Rakesh Mohan and Partha Ray

Introduction

This chapter covers the Indian financial sector reforms and their evolution from the 1990s to the mid-2010s. As a consequence of successive reforms over the past 25 years, the Indian financial sector has been transformed comprehensively, but the task remains unfinished. Significant progress has been made in making interest and exchange rates largely market determined, though the exchange rate regime remains one of managed float, and some interest rates still remain administered. Considerable depth has been added to the banking sector along with new competition being introduced through new private sector banks, but public sector banks continue to have a dominant share in the market. Contractual savings systems have been improved, but pension funds in India are still in their infancy. Similarly, despite the introduction of new private sector insurance companies, coverage of insurance can expand much further, which would also provide greater depth to the financial markets. The extent of development along all the segments of the financial market has not been uniform. While the equity market is quite developed, technically its domestic investor base remains relatively shallow, and activities in the private debt market are predominantly confined to private placement and continue to be largely limited to blue-chip companies.

Going forward, future areas for development in the Indian financial sector include further reduction of public ownership in banks and insurance companies, expansion of the contractual savings system through more rapid expansion of the insurance and pension systems, greater spread of the equity culture and mutual funds, and development of institutional investors. It is only then that the both the equity and debt markets will display greater breadth as well as depth, along with greater domestic liquidity. At the same time, while reforming the financial sector, Indian authorities need to constantly keep the issues of equity and efficiency in mind.

The ensuing sections of this chapter are devoted to the four broad genres of financial institutions, namely, banking, insurance, the capital market, and India's external sector and opening up of the financial sector. Finally, the non-banking financial companies in India are covered before concluding the chapter.

Over the years, the Indian financial sector has emerged as a substantial segment of the economy, comprising diverse financial institutions and various markets (Figures 4.1 and 4.2).

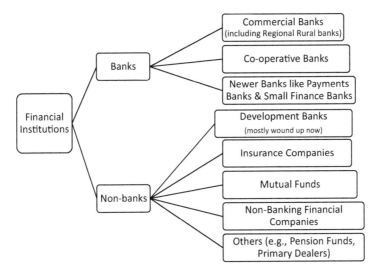

Figure 4.1   Financial institutions in India

Source: Authors.

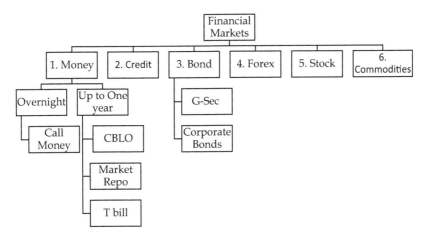

Figure 4.2   Financial markets in India

Notes: CBLO = collateralized borrowing and lending obligations. G–Sec = Government Securities. T bill = Treasury Bill.

Source: Authors.

Banking in India: toward modern competitive banking

Over the years there has been a huge increase in the extent of financial development of the Indian economy. This is reflected in the upward trend in aggregate deposits and credit as a percentage of GDP (Figure 4.3). After the 1990s, all the reform measures led to the emergence of a modern banking sector in India and resulted in improvement in many of the profitability, efficiency, and stability indicators of commercial banking in India (Table 4.1). The new private

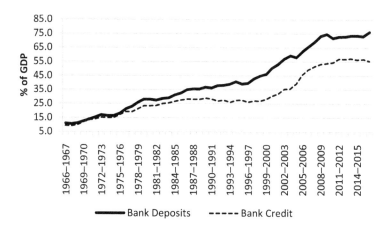

Figure 4.3 Aggregate deposit and credit (as percentage of GDP)

Note: Deposit and Credit refers to those of commercial and cooperative banks taken together. GDP = gross domestic product.

Source: Compiled from Handbook of Statistics on Indian Economy, RBI.

Table 4.1 Select indicators of scheduled commercial banks (excluding regional rural banks)

Year	March 1980	March 1990	March 2000	March 2010	March 2015
No. of Banks	75	75	101	85	91
Credit-Deposit Ratio (%)	63.32	61.64	49.26	73.66	78.31
Investment-Deposit Ratio (%)	31.50	33.58	45.97	36.42	33.59
(Credit + Investment)-Deposit Ratio (%)	94.82	95.22	95.23	110.09	111.90
Ratio of Deposits to Total Liabilities (%)	73.78	70.60	81.08	78.76	78.40
Ratio of Net Interest Margin to Total Assets (%)	NA	3.48	5.24	2.54	2.64
Ratio of Intermediation Cost to Total Assets (%)	NA	4.61	4.79	1.78	1.77
Ratio of Wage Bills to Intermediation Cost (%)	NA	65.68	66.96	55.23	54.26
Ratio of Wage Bills to Total Expense (%)	NA	19.77	19.06	14.85	13.13
Ratio of Operating Profits to Total Assets (%)	NA	0.39	3.21	2.17	2.02
Return on Assets (%)	NA	0.39	1.28	1.05	0.81
Return on Equity (%)	NA	23.37	22.58	14.31	10.42

Note: NA = not available.

Source: Statistical tables relating to banks in India, RBI (various issues).

sector banks, along with the housing finance company HDFC, ushered in the era of retail lending and housing finance in India, starting in the late 1990s (Ahluwalia 1999). Public sector banks followed suit with a lag. This change helped greatly in increasing the demand for automobiles, two-wheelers, and other consumer durables, thereby promoting overall economic growth in the country while also helping in diversifying the asset base of banks. As of March 2016, the Indian commercial banking sector (exclusive of 56 regional rural banks) consisted of 27 public sector banks, 21 private sector banks, and 43 foreign banks; their shares in aggregate assets were around 70%, 24%, and 6%, respectively.

In addition to the country widespread of national commercial banks, both public and private, there is a large presence of ancillary local banking institutions that have had a long history. As at end-March 2016, India's cooperative banking sector comprised 1,574 urban cooperative banks and 93,913 rural cooperative credit institutions, including short-term and long-term credit institutions (RBI 2016). Despite their large numbers, their weight in the Indian banking sector is somewhat meager; illustratively, as per IMF's 2013 *Financial System Stability Assessment Update*, aggregate assets of nearly 98,500 operative credit institutions (of which nearly 98% are rural) stood at nearly INR 6,800 billion (9% of GDP) as against 81 scheduled commercial banks' aggregate assets of nearly INR 60,000 billion (78% of GDP; IMF 2013). A majority of these banks tend to operate in a single state, and they are regulated and supervised by state-specific Registrars of Cooperative Societies (RCS), along with overall oversight by the Reserve Bank of India. Thus, there has been dual control of regulation and supervision of cooperative banks between the state-specific RCSs and the Reserve Bank of India (RBI), which has often been problematic. They have also suffered from governance problems along with the incidence of frequent local political interference, which has hampered the effectiveness of these banks. They have also been slow to modernize.

To strengthen the reach of commercial banks for greater financial inclusion, Regional Rural Banks (RRBs) were established in 1975 as local level banks in different states of India. They are co-owned by the central and state governments and by sponsoring public sector banks. Unlike the cooperative banks, RRBs are structured as commercial banks and were established with a view to developing the rural economy. They were envisaged to create a supplementary channel to the "Cooperative Credit Structure" for enlarging institutional credit extended to the rural and agriculture sectors. While these were vehicles for financial inclusion, their high cost-income ratios and non-performing assets have been causes of concern. Thus, there have been substantial mergers within this sector and the number of RRBs has come down from 196 in 1990 to 56 in 2015.

The Post Office Savings Bank (POSB) has a customer base of about 330 million account holders as of March 2015 (Government of India 2016), thereby contributing significantly to financial inclusion on the deposit side.[1] In assessing financial inclusion in India, observers often understate the spread of formal banking channels by counting only bank accounts and neglecting the coverage of post office accounts. However, the POSB offers only deposit and remittance facilities, not any credit to account holders.

The key elements of financial sector reforms in India include significant reduction of financial repression (including removal of automatic monetization); dismantling of the complex administered interest rate structure to enable the process of price discovery; providing operational and functional autonomy to public sector institutions; preparing the financial system for increasing international competition; opening the external sector in a calibrated manner; and promoting financial stability in the wake of domestic and external shocks (Mohan 2006, 2011c). All these measures were designed to create an efficient, productive, and profitable financial sector. Illustratively, gradual reduction of CRR from 15% to about 4%, and reduction in the SLR[2] from nearly 40% to 21.5% between the early 1990s and the mid-2010s have made a huge improvement to the availability of lendable resources to the banking sector.

This trend has been supported by a number of measures that have been initiated toward inculcating a credit culture through enforcement of creditors' rights and hastening the process of credit recovery. The Securitization and Reconstruction of Financial Assets and Enforcement of Securities Interest Act was passed in 2002, enabling the setting up of debt-recovery tribunals and asset-reconstruction companies. Credit Information Bureaus have been given legal status through passing of the Credit Information Bureau Act in 2005, but these agencies are still in their infancy. Introduction of unique identification for every natural person in the country should potentially be very helpful for the expansion in coverage of these bureaus, thereby leading to reduction in transactions costs for small order lending. Most recently, the Bankruptcy Act was passed by the Indian Parliament in May 2016.

Information technology has also played a key role in this transformative journey of Indian banking. Technology has enabled more effective, lower cost, and real-time delivery of financial services through the establishment of a modern payments system. Setting up of the Indian Financial Network as the communication backbone for the financial sector, and introduction of a real-time gross settlement system and core banking solutions across banks encompassing most of their branches across India, are some of the major technological initiatives implemented. Establishment of the Institute for Development and Research in Banking Technology by the Reserve Bank in 1996 helped greatly in promoting connectivity among all the banks through development of and propagation of common IT standards throughout the system. The new private sector banks, with no legacy issues to constrain them, enthusiastically adopted the new information technology from their inception, thereby also acting as a competitive spur to induce similar adoption by public sector banks.

While experiencing strong balance sheet growth of the banks, commensurate with the impressive growth of the liberalizing Indian economy, the financial health of banks had also improved significantly in terms of both capital adequacy and asset quality (Mohan 2011a). Gross non-performing loans as a percentage of gross advances came down steadily from 15.7% in 1996 to 2.4% in 2009 (Figure 4.4). Notwithstanding recent stress, the capital to risk-weighted assets ratio of scheduled commercial banks in India was 12.7% while Tier-I leverage ratio stood at

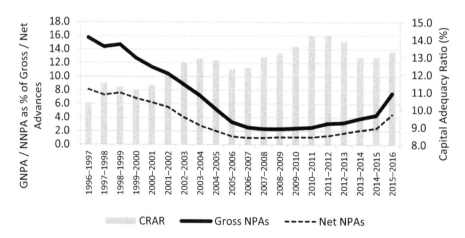

Figure 4.4 Gross and net NPAs of all commercial banks and capital adequacy ratio

Notes:
1. Net NPA is Gross NPA less provisioning for bad loans.
2. Gross Advances = Standard Advances + Gross NPAs.
3. Net Advances = Gross Advances − Provisions for NPA Accounts − deposits insurance and export credit insurance claims received and held pending adjustment − Part payment received and kept in Suspense Account − Balance in Sundries Account in respect of NPA Accounts − Floating Provisions − Provisions in lieu of diminution in the fair value of restructured accounts classified as NPAs − Provisions in lieu of diminution in the fair value of restructured accounts classified as standard assets.
   CRAR = capital to risk-weighted assets ratio. NPA = non-performing asset.

Source: Handbook of Statistics on Indian Economy, RBI.

6.5% in September 2015.[3] These are impressive by standards of comparator economies. While improved capitalization of public sector banks was initially brought about through infusions of funds by government to recapitalize these banks, subsequently public sector banks were allowed to raise funds from the market through equity issuance subject to the maintenance of 51% public ownership (Mohan 2005). Along with divestiture in the public sector banks and their subsequent listing in stock exchanges, a significant number of private sector banks were allowed entry; consequently the share of public sector banks continued to decline gradually in banking business and a private sector bank emerged as the second largest bank in India over the last 10 years or so. In terms of adoption of technology, the share of electronic payments has been increasing continuously.

Monetary policy transmission

With the initiation of reforms and the transition to indirect, market-based instruments of monetary policy in the 1990s, the RBI made conscious efforts to develop an efficient, stable, and liquid money market by creating a favorable policy environment through appropriate institutional changes, instruments, technologies, and market practices. Accordingly, the call money market was developed into primarily an interbank market. Presently the Indian monetary policy framework, "aims at setting the policy (repo) rate. . . . (where) repo rate changes transmit through the money market to alter the interest rates in the financial system."[4] Once the repo rate is announced, the operating framework envisages liquidity management on a day-to-day basis through appropriate actions, which aim at anchoring the operating target – the weighted average call rate – around the repo rate. Over the years, depending on the demand management imperatives, the RBI has used the repo rate as the key instrument of effective control of overnight liquidity.

Money market

The money market is a key component of the banking sector and monetary policy in India. Over the years, the money market has become deep and diverse, with emergence of several segments like collateralized borrowing and lending obligations (CBLO); it experienced significant increase in the level of activity in its various segments.

An important institutional reform was the establishment of the Clearing Corporation of India Limited (CCIL) as a central counterparty to provide guaranteed clearing and settlement functions for transactions in money, G-Secs, foreign exchange, and derivative markets. This led to significant improvement in the market efficiency, transparency, liquidity, and risk management/measurement practices in these markets along with added benefits like reduced settlement and operational risk, savings on settlement costs. CCIL also provides non-guaranteed settlement for rupee interest rate derivatives and cross-currency transactions through the CLS Bank. Further, new innovative instruments, such as collateralized borrowing and lending obligations (CBLO; a tripartite repo between any two financial entities along with CCIL) and market repo were introduced for widening and deepening the money market. These instruments provided avenues for non-banks to manage their short-term liquidity mismatches and facilitated the transformation of the call money market into a pure interbank market (Mohan 2005). Furthermore, issuance norms and maturity profiles of instruments such as commercial paper and certificate of deposits have been modified over time to encourage wider participation.

Emerging issues

Notwithstanding such trends, the Indian banking sector continued to remain predominantly public in nature, with the public sector banks still accounting for more than 70% of total banking sector assets. A recent official report argued for reduction in government shareholding to below 50% to allow more autonomy to banks as well as to create distance between the government and governance of banks (RBI 2014). However, during 2014–2015, despite their substantive share in total assets, public sector banks accounted for only 42% in total profits (RBI 2015), down from 74% in 2003–2004. Are the public sector banks inherently less efficient than the private banks? Or is their less impressive performance an outcome of an inefficient governance structure subject to bureaucratic interference? Do Indian banks continue to suffer from the imperatives of societal concerns and, thus, torn between the dilemmas of efficiency and equity? The fact that the performance of public sector banks had converged to that of the new private sector banks by 2008–2009 before deteriorating subsequently poses a further puzzle, and raises further questions about the determinants of their performance.

The issue of recent deterioration of asset quality in public sector banks has emerged as the key concern surrounding the banking sector today. Earlier, gross non-performing assets (GNPAs) of the Indian banking sector, as a percentage of gross advances, had come down from 15% in 1998 to 3.3% in 2009: since then GNPAs have increased steadily to 9.1% by September 2016. Taking a wider definition, the stressed assets (i.e., gross NPA plus restructured standard assets plus written off accounts) for the banking system as a whole increased from 9.8% in 2012 to 12.3% in September 2016; stressed assets in public sector banks increased from 11.0% to 15.8% during the same period (Mundra 2016; RBI 2016).

Financial inclusion

Financial inclusion has been a concern in India since at least the early part of the last century. The setting up of a postal savings bank, rural and urban cooperative banks, regional rural banks, and the nationalization of banks were all done at different points in time to promote financial inclusion. Despite all the decades of social sector banking and success in spreading the banking network, there has been evidence that poorer sections of the society have not been able to access financial services adequately from the organized financial system (NABARD 2008).[5]

India's approach to financial inclusion has been multi-pronged. One of its major cornerstones is the presence of stipulations on "priority sector lending" by the commercial banks. For this purpose, the priority sector includes the following categories, namely, agriculture; micro, small, and medium-sized enterprises; export credit; education; housing; social infrastructure; renewable energy; and others (like weaker sections of the community). Indian commercial banks are required to lend 40% of their credit to the priority sector. Now foreign banks with 20 branches and above also have to achieve the 40% total within a maximum period of five years over April 2013–March 2018 as per the action plans submitted by them and approved by RBI. Besides, there are sub-targets within this overall 40% target; illustratively, 18% has to be disbursed to agriculture while 7.5% has to be disbursed to the small and medium-sized enterprises. In recent times, introduction of Priority Sector Lending Certificates (PSLCs) have enabled banks to achieve the priority sector lending target and sub-targets by purchase of these instruments in the event of shortfall. Further, commercial banks can also invest the amount of their shortfalls in the Rural Infrastructure Development Fund (RIDF) run by NABARD. The incidence of farmers' suicides has also cast doubt about the efficacy of the formal credit delivery mechanism as well as the limitations of credit disbursals from microfinance institutions

Table 4.2 Outstanding debt of rural household: institutional versus non-institutional sources (in percentage)

Sources of credit	1951	1961	1971	1981	1991	2002	2012*
Non-institutional	**92.8**	**85.2**	**70.8**	**38.7**	**36.0**	**42.9**	**40.2**
Landlords	*3.5*	*0.9*	*8.6*	*4.0*	*4.0*	*1.0*	
Agricultural moneylenders	*25.2*	*45.9*	*23.1*	*8.6*	*7.1*	*10.0*	
Professional moneylenders	*46.4*	*14.9*	*13.8*	*8.3*	*10.5*	*19.6*	
Institutional	**7.2**	**14.8**	**29.2**	**61.3**	**64.0**	**57.1**	**59.8**
of which:							
Government	*3.7*	*5.3*	*6.7*	*4.0*	*6.1*	*2.3*	
Cooperative societies	*3.5*	*9.1*	*20.1*	*28.6*	*21.6*	*27.3*	
Commercial banks	*NA*	*0.4*	*2.2*	*28.0*	*33.7*	*24.5*	
Total	**100.0**	**100.0**	**100.0**	**100.0**	**100.0**	**100.0**	**100.0**

Notes: *There are issues relating to comparability of the constituent groups of data collected under the 59th round of the National Sample Survey (NSS) (for 2002) and 70th round of NSS (for 2012). NA = not available.

Sources: Mohan (2011b) and NSSO (2012).

and self-help groups. The All India Debt and Investment Survey of December 2013 indicated that during 2012–2013, non-institutional sources (i.e., sources of credit other than government, banks, insurance companies, pension funds, financial companies, and so on) continued to play a major role in providing credit to the rural households – about 19% of all rural households obtained credit from non-institutional sources while for urban households it was about 10% by non-institutional agencies (Table 4.2).

There are, of course, two ways of interpreting such trends, and it is difficult to decide whether the glass is half empty or three-quarters full (Mohan 2011b). In fact, the improvement in financial inclusion in the recent past can be associated with the activist stance of the authorities in ensuring financial inclusion. Some the key measures in this regard include opening of no-frills accounts in commercial banks; introduction of a credit card specifically for the farmers' community (Kisan credit card); and engaging business correspondents as intermediaries for providing financial and banking services. A recent major initiative is the Pradhan Mantri Jan-Dhan Yojana (Prime Minister's People Money Scheme). Introduced in August 2014, this scheme has now become synonymous with a National Mission on Financial Inclusion and has envisaged universal access to banking facilities with at least one basic banking account for every household. Apart from accessing basic banking services like credit, insurance, and pension facility, the beneficiaries get a debit card having inbuilt accident insurance cover of INR 100,000. By July 2016, over 230 million new bank accounts were opened and INR 400 billion was deposited under the scheme.[6]

New developments

There are three recent developments with regard to entry of new private sector banks. First, after nearly 10 years of no new banking licenses, licenses were granted in 2015 to two existing financial institutions to become universal commercial banks: IDFC Ltd. (an integrated infrastructure finance company) and Bandhan Financial Services (a large microfinance organization).[7] Two new major types of small and differentiated banks – payments banks and small finance banks – have also emerged as the newest entrants in the Indian financial sector. While payments banks are essentially narrow banks (i.e., without any lending activity), which can raise deposits of up to INR 100,000 and pay interest on these balances just like a savings bank account does, their basic business model is geared toward utilizing newer mobile technology and payment gateways whereby they can enable transfers and remittances through a mobile phone and can issue debit cards and ATM cards usable on ATM networks of all banks. Ever since August 2015 when the RBI issued licenses to 11 entities[8] to establish payments banks, there is speculation whether this would usher in a new era of Indian banking. At the same time, small finance banks are being licensed to further financial inclusion primarily through mobilization of savings as well as supply of credit to small business units (such as small and marginal farmers; micro and small industries; and other unorganized sector entities) through high technology, low cost operations. Small finance banks are similar to regular commercial banks except that their scale of services will be much smaller: 50% of their loans should be of ticket sizes under INR 2.5 million. Small banking licenses have been issued to 10 entities, most of which are successful microfinance institutions. The use of new information technology is expected to propel these new banks in their efforts to enhance financial inclusion.

Many of these developments mark a departure from the past. Unlike the past when only universal banking licenses were issued, now differentiated banking licenses are also being issued. Similarly, although there has been a general policy of not issuing bank licenses to non- financial corporate groups, payments banks licenses were issued to some non-financial corporate groups as well. The justification is that since payments banks are essentially narrow banks not permitted to do any lending, the possibility of conflict of interest arising from intra-group lending is not an issue. Thus, these small but differentiated banks could constitute competitive challenges to the existing commercial banks in terms of access to financial savings or for lending. However, the business model of payments banks may face some challenges since their earning opportunities will be restricted to investments in government securities.

A recent development in this regard has been the announcement of INR 2.11 trillion recapitalization package for the Indian public sector banks on 24 October 2017. In funding this plan, while INR 1.35 trillion is expected to come from the issue of recapitalization bonds, the remaining INR 0.76 trillion will be through budgetary allocation and markets borrowing. Recapitalization bonds were also used for a similar purpose in the mid-1990s. With the stock-piling of non-performing assets with the banking sector and a lackluster credit growth, such a measure for recapitalization has been welcomed by various stakeholders. With the enactment of the Insolvency and Bankruptcy Code in December 2016, such recapitalization efforts along with restructuring the Indian public sector banks could bring about the much-needed change in the Indian financial sector.

At the risk of oversimplification, the following trends in Indian banking can be highlighted. First, while commercial banks have seen an all-around improvement in key financial indicators, particularly in areas of capital adequacy, asset quality and earnings, their recent trends raise some disquieting developments. Second, "the financial results of the co-operative banking structure however, show some degree of vulnerability, though they may not be systemically very large" (RBI 2009). Third, the new entrants in the financial sector, namely, payments banks and small banks, are at this juncture are really unknown unknowns. Finally, while various efforts toward financial inclusion seemed to have borne fruit, there is still much to achieve.

Finally, no contemporary description of the Indian financial sector is complete without an account of the recent demonetization process. Since 8 November 2016, the two largest denomination notes, INR 500 and INR 1,000 (together comprising nearly 86% of currency outstanding) were "demonetised" with an aim to "curb corruption, counterfeiting, the use of high denomination notes for terrorist activities, and especially the accumulation of 'black money,' generated by income that has not been declared to the tax authorities" (Government of India 2017). The Reserve Bank of India (RBI), in its Annual Report for 2016–2017 released on 27 August 2017, revealed that nearly 99% demonetized currency had come back to the banking system. While the process has clearly led to a short-term adverse impact on the small, informal, and cash-intensive sectors in the economy, over the medium term the government expects a cleanup of the system from the menace of black money and/or tax-evaded income. It is also expected to help in leapfrogging the economy to a new digital era of transactions. Admittedly, in the absence of any firm evidence, it may still be early to pronounce any verdict on the efficacy (or its lack) of the demonetization process.[9]

The insurance sector since the 1990s: opening up the doors

As of March 2016, this sector comprised 24 life insurance companies, 28 general insurance companies, and one national reinsurer. Among the life insurers, the Life Insurance Corporation (LIC) as the sole public sector company is the predominant player, still accounting for nearly 73% of total premium. Among the nonlife insurers there are six public sector insurers. In addition to these, there is the sole national reinsurer, General Insurance Corporation of India. Out of 28 nonlife insurance companies, there are five private sector players dealing exclusively in health, personal accident, and travel insurance segments.

With about 360 million policies, India's life insurance sector is perhaps the biggest in the world in terms of number – reflecting India's population size. The size of the general insurance business in India was at INR 964 billion in 2015–2016, or about 0.7% of GDP. In 2015, with a share of 2.2% in the global life insurance business, India has been ranked 10th among the 88 countries in life insurance business (Swiss Re 2016). In nonlife insurance, while vehicle insurance accounted for nearly 40% of the gross direct premiums earned in 2015–2016, penetration of health insurance is rather poor. In fact, despite the absolute size of the insurance sector, penetration in this sector is still too low. While the rate of insurance penetration in the life segment (measured by the ratio of premiums to GDP) of India increased from 2.2% to in 2002 to 4.6% in 2010, it declined thereafter to reach 2.6% in 2014 (Table 4.3). Industry reports tended to indicate that with higher inflation and lower disposable incomes, the overall intention to buy life insurance policies in India has taken a hit (Saraswathy 2015). Interestingly, while India's insurance penetration is comparable to China's 3.2% – similar metrics for the Republic of Korea (at 11.3%) or Thailand (at 5.8%) are much higher (IRDA 2015).

Although the insurance sector initially experienced robust growth (around 31% in new business premiums) in the decade of 2001–2010 after opening up, there has been a slowdown subsequently (KPMG 2012). This sluggish growth brings to the fore various challenges in the Indian insurance business. Though its share in total business has indeed come down, the insurance sector is still dominated by the public sector. In 2014–2015 the share of LIC in total premiums was around 73%, in case of nonlife insurance business, the private and public sector companies have approximately equal share. The share of the life insurance fund as a proportion of changes in gross financial assets of the household sector has gone up significantly and tended to hover around 20% in recent years.

The current issues facing Indian insurance are diverse. The key issue is the need for much greater expansion of insurance services, particularly that of life insurance and health insurance. Apart from the need for greater spread of social protection, the expansion of insurance funds is also essential for the development of capital markets, particularly the corporate debt market which is typically dependent in institutional investors. Other issues include the efficiency and spread of distributional channels, the level of government control, regulatory constraints, and

Table 4.3 Indian insurance sector: key indicators

Year	Life Insurance Sector				NonLife Insurance Sector			
	No. of companies (as on 31 March)	No. of branches (as on 31 March)	Insurance penetration (%) (calendar year)	Insurance density (calendar year)	No. of companies (incl reinsurer) (as on 31 March)	No. of branches (as on 31 March)	Insurance penetration (%) (calendar year)	Insurance density (calendar year)
2000–2001	5	2,199			10			
2001–2002	12	2,306	2.2	9.1	13		0.5	2.4
2002–2003	13	2,445	2.6	11.7	15		0.6	3.0
2003–2004	13	2,612	2.3	12.9	16		0.6	3.5
2004–2005	14	3,001	2.5	15.7	16		0.6	4.0
2005–2006	15	3,865	2.5	18.3	16		0.6	4.4
2006–2007	16	5,373	4.1	33.2	17		0.6	5.2
2007–2008	18	8,913	4.0	40.4	20		0.6	6.2
2008–2009	22	11,815	4.0	41.2	22		0.6	6.2
2009–2010	23	12,018	4.6	47.7	26	6,417	0.6	6.7
2010–2011	23	11,546	4.4	55.7	26	6,660	0.7	8.7
2011–2012	24	11,167	3.4	49.0	28	7,050	0.7	10.0
2012–2013	24	10,285	3.2	42.7	28	8,099	0.8	10.5
2013–2014	24	11,032	3.1	41.0	29	9,872	0.8	11.0
2014–2015	24	11,033	2.6	44.0	29	10,407	0.7	11.0

Note: While insurance penetration is measured as the percentage of insurance premium to GDP, insurance density is calculated as the ratio of premium to population (per capita premium).

Source: Handbook on Indian Insurance Statistics 2014–2015, Insurance Regulatory and Development Authority of India.

consumer education and protection (IMF 2013). Continuance of archaic agent-based distribution channels has led to allegations of mis-selling of insurance products as well as low persistency of insurance policies in India (Government of India 2015). Besides, there is a huge untapped potential in sectors like health insurance.

Capital market: uneven progress in different segments

Table 4.4 reports the resource mobilization by the commercial sector. Interestingly, Indian corporates' recourse to non-bank sources tended to hover between 40% and 55% during the period 2009–2010 through 2015–2016. Both domestic as well as foreign sources are significant in the case of non-bank funding sources. However, in terms of resource mobilization, the Indian capital market has depended heavily on private placement whose costs are found to be much lower (Table 4.5). As far as price discovery is concerned, the capital market reflects the operations of market forces; this is reflected in the movement of yield on 10-year benchmark government security as well as indices in equity market like the NSE Nifty 50 (Figure 4.5).

Bond and/or debt market

The story of the government bond market is intimately interlinked with the evolution of fiscal policy in India. A system of unbridled deficit financing via fixed coupon ad hoc treasury bill market has been transformed into a market-driven auction process in electronic platform by late 1990s. Institutionally, the creation of primary dealers to function as market makers (both in primary and secondary markets) in the government bond market since 1995 was a major development in this sector (Mohan and Ray 2011). With increased volume of transactions, liquidity in this market has increased as well (Table 4.6).

In contrast, the corporate debt market in India has been far less developed. Much of the transactions in this market are concentrated in the bonds of blue-chip corporates and the market is predominantly a private placement market with limited liquidity (Table 4.7). There are several reasons for this. First, large corporates often tend to go abroad for their longer-term borrowing requirements. Second, on the demand side, with the pension and insurance industries being in their infancy, there is a very limited number of institutional investors with limited funds. Third, limited availability of other investors also could have influenced the size of the debt market. While this is in line with international experience, several official committees have looked into this issue, but in terms of ground reality things have not changed substantially. In terms of outturn, the market size at around 15% of GDP is much smaller than bank assets (89% of GDP) and equity markets (80% of GDP).

Equity market

The success story of the Indian equity market has been driven by two major institutions, both established under government auspicious, namely, Securities and Exchange Board of India (SEBI) and the National Stock Exchange (NSE). While SEBI, the securities market regulator, was established in 1988, it was given statutory powers in April 1992 through the SEBI Act, 1992, which set out its basic functions as "to protect the interests of investors in securities and to promote the development of, and to regulate the securities market and for matters connected therewith or incidental thereto." Thus, SEBI is the overall capital market regulator charged with the orderly functioning of the securities market.

Table 4.4 Resource mobilization by the commercial sector in India (INR billion)

	2007–2008	2008–2009	2009–2010	2010–2011	2011–2012	2012–2013	2013–2014	2014–2015	2015–2016
A. Adjusted Non-food Bank Credit	**4,448** (44.1)	**4,211** (47.3)	**4,786** (45.0)	**7,110** (56.9)	**6,773** (55.7)	**6,849** (48.3)	**7,627** (54.0)	**5,850** (45.5)	**7,754** (52.4)
1. Non-food Credit	4,328	4,118	4,670	6,815	6,527	6,335	7,316	5,464	7,024
2. Non-SLR Investment by commercial banks	120	93	117	295	246	514	311	386	731
B. Flow from Non-banks (B1 + B2)	**5,646** (55.9)	**4,686** (52.7)	**5,850** (55.0)	**5,392** (43.1)	**5,383** (44.3)	**7,335** (51.7)	**6,505** (46.0)	**7,005** (54.5)	**7,052** (47.6)
B1. Domestic Sources	**2,552** (25.3)	**2,984** (33.5)	**3,652** (34.3)	**3,011** (24.1)	**3,079** (25.3)	**4,212** (29.7)	**4,302** (30.4)	**4,740** (36.9)	**4,593** (31.0)
1. Public issues by non-financial entities	515	142	320	285	145	119	199	87	378
2. Gross private placements by non-financial entities	682	779	1420	674	558	1,038	1,314	1,277	1,095
3. Net issuance of CPs subscribed to by non-banks	107	56	261	68	36	52	138	558	320
4. Net credit by housing finance companies	418	266	285	428	539	859	737	954	1,145
5. Total gross accommodation by four RBI regulated financial institutions*	223	314	338	400	469	515	436	417	446
6. Systematically important non-deposit taking NBFCs (net of bank credit)	365	768	607	795	912	1,188	1,124	1,046	840
7. LIC's net investment in corporate debt, infrastructure and Social Sector	243	658	422	361	419	441	354	401	369
B2. Foreign Sources	**3,093** (30.6)	**1,702** (19.1)	**2,198** (20.7)	**2,381** (19.0)	**2,304** (19.0)	**3,123** (22.0)	**2,203** (15.6)	**2,265** (17.6)	**2,459** (16.6)
1. External Commercial Borrowings/FCCB	912	380	120	539	421	466	661	14	–388
2. ADR/GDR Issues excluding banks and financial institutions	118	48	151	92	27	10	1	96	0
3. Short-term Credit from abroad	689	–312	349	426	306	1,177	–327	–4	–96
4. Foreign Direct Investment to India	1374	1586	1578	1324	1,550	1,470	1,868	2,159	2,943
C. Total Flow of Resources (A + B)	**10,094** (100.0)	**8,897** (100.0)	**10,636** (100.0)	**12,503** (100.0)	**12,156** (100.0)	**14,184** (100.0)	**14,132** (100.0)	**12,855** (100.0)	**14,806** (100.0)

Notes: *National Bank for Agriculture and Rural Development (NABARD), National Housing Bank (NHB), Small Industries Development Bank of India (SIDBI), and Export-Import Bank on India. Figures within brackets are percentage to total.

Source: Annual Report, RBI (various issues).

Table 4.5 Resources mobilized by corporate sector (public, rights, and private placements): monthly averages (INR billion)

Month	Equity Issues			Debt Issues			Total Resource Mobilization (4 + 7)
	Public	Private Placements	Total (2 + 3)	Public	Private Placements	Total (5 + 6)	
1	2	3	4	5	6	7	8
2010–2011	48.6	46.9	95.4	8.0	182.3	190.3	285.5
2011–2012	10.7	23.2	33.9	29.6	217.7	247.3	281.4
2012–2013	12.9	52.5	65.3	14.2	301.2	315.3	380.6
2013–2014	11.0	50.1	61.2	35.3	230.3	265.5	326.6
2014–2015	8.2	47.9	55.9	7.9	336.9	344.7	400.6
2015–2016 (until December 2015)	23.1	63.4	86.7	20.8	379.3	400.1	486.8

Source: NSE website.

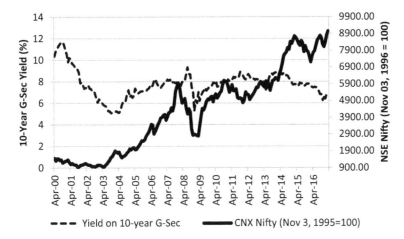

Figure 4.5 Yield on 10-year government security and NSE Nifty

Sources: Bloomberg database, NSE website.

Table 4.6 Turnover in government securities market (face value): weekly average (INR billion)

Year	Central Government Dated Securities	State Government Dated Securities	Treasury bills					RBI
			Cash Management bills	14-Day	91-Day	182-Day	364-Day	
2000–2001	195	1	–	2	3	2	16	6
2001–2002	435	2	–	2	8	1	18	8
2002–2003	496	3	–	–	13	–	16	10
2003–2004	597	6	–	–	19	–	26	8
2004–2005	340	10	–	–	51	–	46	1
2005–2006	218	7	–	–	24	8	41	1
2006–2007	95	5	–	–	13	11	23	1
2007–2008	338	6	–	–	20	10	26	4
2008–2009	752	14	–	–	43	7	18	22
2009–2010	972	29	–	–	105	15	25	20

(Continued)

Table 4.6 (Continued)

Year	Central Government Dated Securities	State Government Dated Securities	Treasury bills					RBI
			Cash Management bills	14-Day	91-Day	182-Day	364-Day	
2010–2011	996	20	38	–		16	21	21
2011–2012	1190	20	23	–	73	20	34	32
2012–2013	2277	46	–	–	96	43	80	34
2013–2014	3086	61	126	–	125	61	118	19
2014–2015	3520	72	28	–	160	56	98	21
2015–2016	3246	123	–	–	185	54	88	45

Source: Database on Indian Economy, RBI.

Table 4.7 Turnover in equity market (INR billion)

Year	BSE	NSE	Bombay Stock Exchange Limited (BSE)				National Stock Exchange of India Limited (NSE)				
	Spot Market	Spot Market	Index Futures	Index Options	Stock Futures	Stock Options	Index Futures	Index Options	Stock Futures	Stock Options	Interest Rate Futures
1990–1991	360	–	–	–	–	–	–	–	–	–	–
1991–1992	718	–	–	–	–	–	–	–	–	–	–
1992–1993	457	–	–	–	–	–	–	–	–	–	–
1993–1994	845	–	–	–	–	–	–	–	–	–	–
1994–1995	677	18	–	–	–	–	–	–	–	–	–
1995–1996	501	673	–	–	–	–	–	–	–	–	–
1996–1997	1,243	2,945	–	–	–	–	–	–	–	–	–
1997–1998	2,076	3,702	–	–	–	–	–	–	–	–	–
1998–1999	3,120	4,145	–	–	–	–	–	–	–	–	–
1999–2000	6,850	8,391	–	–	–	–	–	–	–	–	–
2000–2001	10,000	13,395	17	0	0	0	24	–	–	–	–
2001–2002	3,073	5,132	13	1	5	1	215	38	515	252	–
2002–2003	3,141	6,180	18	0	6	0	440	92	2,865	1,001	–
2003–2004	5,026	10,995	66	0	52	3	5,544	528	13,059	2,172	–
2004–2005	5,187	11,401	136	23	2	0	7,721	1,219	14,840	1,688	–
2005–2006	8,161	15,635	0	0	0	0	15,138	3,385	27,917	1,802	–
2006–2007	9,562	19,453	555	0	35	0	25,396	7,919	38,310	1,938	–
2007–2008	15,789	35,510	2,347	0	76	0	38,207	13,621	75,486	3,591	–
2008–2009	11,001	27,520	118	0	0	0	35,701	37,315	34,796	2,292	–
2009–2010	13,788	41,380	1	1	0	0	39,344	80,279	51,952	5,061	–
2010–2011	11,035	35,774	2	0	0	0	43,568	183,654	54,957	10,303	–
2011–2012	6,670	28,109	1,783	6,183	100	14	35,780	227,200	40,747	9,770	–
2012–2013	5,488	27,083	1,214	70,275	34	102	25,271	227,816	42,239	20,004	–
2013–2014	5,217	28,085	635	90,552	546	461	30,831	277,673	49,492	24,094	302
2014–2015	8,551	43,258	486	201,292	98	1751	41,072	399,227	82,918	32,825	4,215
2015–2016	7,195	41,153	131	43,863	13	743	45,571	489,519	78,286	34,881	5,264

Notes:
1. BSE: Bombay Stock Exchange Limited; NSE: National Stock Exchange of India Limited.
2. Index futures were introduced in June 2000, index options in June 2001, stock options in July 2001 and stock futures in November 2001, both in the BSE and NSE, while interest rate futures were introduced on NSE in June 2003.
3. Notional turnover includes call and put options.
4. The RBI has introduced cash settled interest rate futures on 10-year G-sec on December 5, 2013.

Source: RBI database on the Indian economy.

Figure 4.6 Market capitalization in equity and wholesale debt market segment in NSE (as percentage of GDP)

Source: NSE website.

Though the more traditional stock market, the BSE (formerly known as Bombay Stock Exchange) was established as early as 1875, it was essentially a mutualized exchange and was not modernized. The NSE was established in 1992 as the first demutualized electronic exchange in India. Over time, the NSE emerged as a modern electronic trading platform and took new initiatives to introduce derivative trading in India. Though subsequently, BSE too has modernized, at the current juncture the NSE (and in particular its derivative segment) has the lion's share of the equity market turnover (Table 4.7).

The Indian equity market has witnessed significant improvement since the early 1990s; this is reflected in metrics such as size of the market, liquidity, transparency, stability, and efficiency. The spread of equity shares in the domestic market is, however, still very low, with company shareholdings being dominated by owning family shareholders, usually in excess of 50%. Despite its volatility, India's market capitalization to GDP ratio stood nearly 70% at the end of 2016 but its share of global market capitalization was only 2.3% at the end of 2015 (Figure 4.6). Changes in the regulatory and governance framework have brought about significant improvement in investor confidence over time (RBI 2007).

Mutual funds (MFs): the early reformer

A mutual fund is a mechanism for pooling resources by issuing units to investors and then investing funds in securities, in both equity and debt. The MFs as a group have tended to play a very important role in the Indian capital market. As of March 2016, there were 44 asset management companies in the country with assets under management (AUM) of around INR 13.5 trillion (or 10% of GDP), which though high is far below the level deposits of commercial banks (at about INR 99 trillion or 73% of GDP) (ICRA 2016). In terms of net inflows, the share of private sector MFs far exceeded that of public sector MFs. While the growth in the MF industry has been shared both by debt-oriented schemes as well as equity oriented schemes, MFs in the recent past have shown a preference for debt oriented schemes. Interestingly, the share of retail investors (including retail and high-net-worth individuals) of AUM of the MFs was 48.5% with the rest (51.5%) coming from the institutional investors (includes corporates, banks/Fis, and the FIIs).[10] In a country where direct investments by households in equity and debt markets are meager, MFs have a huge potential to grow.

Pension funds: a late entrant

India, like most developing economies, does not have a universal social security system, and the pension system has largely catered to the organized segment of the labor force and the public sector. While until recently public sector/government employees typically had a threefold structure comprising provident fund, gratuity,[11] and pension schemes, the bulk of the private sector (with the sole exception of the major corporates) had access only to provident funds (i.e., a defined-contribution, fully funded benefit program providing lump sum benefits at the time of retirement). The Employees' Provident Fund is the largest benefit program operating in India. Reflecting this state of affairs, the significance of pension funds in the Indian financial sector has been rather limited. In terms of size, India's pension funds stood at 0.3% of its GDP, as against the People's Republic of China's 1% or Brazil's 13% (OECD 2015).

The pension funds sector has, however, undergone significant reforms. In recognition of the possibility of an unsustainable fiscal burden in the future, the Government of India moved from a defined-benefit pension system to a defined-contribution pension system, called the "New Pension System" in January 2004. While the government constituted an interim regulator, the Interim Pension Fund Regulatory and Development Authority, to regulate the pension sector in 2003, it finally started functioning as a statutory regulator for the New Pension System in 2014. As of March 2016, there were 8.7 million subscribers with AUM amounting to INR 1.18 trillion. Under the present scheme, a subscriber has the option to select any one of eight pension funds, which are primarily floated by public sector banks and/or insurance companies. Considering the fact that India's population is around 1.25 billion, of which the share of the elderly (i.e., 60 years and above) is around 10%, pension funds in India have a large potential both as a social security measure as well as means to providing a depth to the financial markets. Going forward, pension funds will emerge as sources of funds in infrastructure and other projects with long gestation period and for providing depth to the equity market.

The external account and India's financial opening

India has generally incurred a current account deficit that has been financed by foreign direct and portfolio investment and by various kinds of debt flows including external commercial borrowing, portfolio flows, and official borrowing. Significant changes have taken place in the management of the external sector since the early 1990s.

The exchange rate regime moved from a basket-based, pegged exchange rate to a market determined, but managed, exchange rate in 1993, paving the way for current account convertibility in 1994. In line with the substantial liberalization of capital account transactions over time, India's exchange rate arrangement has been classified as "floating" but with a significant degree of capital account management (IMF 2014). While the details of such control are beyond the scope of the present chapter, it needs to be noted that almost all the financial markets witnessed a significant entry of foreign players but at a varied and calibrated pace while recognizing a hierarchy in capital flows – and favoring equity flows over debt flows and foreign direct investment over portfolio investment (Mohan and Kapur 2011). In particular, foreign players have a greater presence in the equity market than the debt market. This calibrated pace of capital account convertibility of the Indian authorities has, however, been seen as slow/conservative in some quarters (Shah and Patnaik 2008).

Development of the foreign exchange market has been a key ingredient of India's external sector. Market participants have been provided with greater flexibility to undertake foreign exchange operations through simplification of procedures and availability of several new instruments. There has also been significant improvement in market infrastructure in terms of trading platforms and settlement mechanisms. As a result of various reform measures, turnover in the foreign exchange market experienced a quantum jump, and the bid-ask spreads have experienced significant declines. Apart from the spot segment, a derivatives segment has also emerged (Figure 4.7). For example, in beginning of May 2016, the spot as well as swap interbank transaction together exceeded USD 8.6 billion. While their presence in different segments of the financial market has added significant depth, they have also contributed to volatility from time to time.

Since 1992, foreign portfolio investors (FPIs) in general and foreign institutional investors (FIIs), in particular, were allowed to invest in both equity and debt instruments.[12] Besides, Indian corporates were allowed to access international capital markets through American depository receipts, global depository receipts, foreign currency convertible bonds, and external commercial borrowings. Over the years, while FIIs have emerged as key players in India's debt, equity, and forex markets, there has been considerable volatility in these flows (Table 4.8).

While there is little restriction on foreign direct investment, excepting print, media, and real estate, there are still some restrictions on FPI. As far as equity is concerned, portfolio investment has virtually unrestricted access as there are aggregate limits on FPI in sovereign as well as corporate debt. These limits have been progressively increased over time. In recent times, Indian authorities have been adopting a policy of channeling FPI into debt instruments of a certain minimum maturity in view of credit and interest rate risks. Besides, the regulatory regime for external borrowing had the following broad components: (1) restrictions on short-term (fewer than three years) borrowing; (2) a loosely monitored overall aggregate limit on foreign currency liability; (3) a discriminatory regime channeling flow into the priority sectors and disallowing flow into sensitive sectors such as real estate; and (4) a cap on the overall cost of borrowing, as a tool to address the adverse selection problem (Padmanabhan 2015).

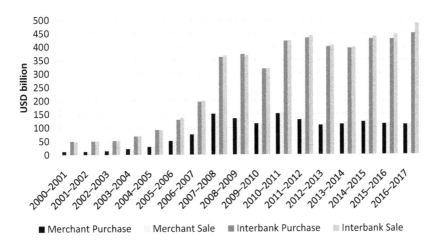

Figure 4.7 Average turnover in foreign exchange market

Table 4.8 Foreign investment in India

Year	Foreign Investment/ Exports (%)	Foreign Investment/ GDP (%)	Net Investments by FII (INR Billion)
1992–1993	3.0	0.2	0
1993–1994	18.7	1.5	55
1994–1995	18.3	1.5	48
1995–1996	14.9	1.3	67
1996–1997	18.0	1.6	74
1997–1998	15.1	1.3	59
1998–1999	7.0	0.6	−7
1999–2000	13.8	1.2	98
2000–2001	14.9	1.5	97
2001–2002	18.2	1.7	83
2002–2003	11.2	1.2	27
2003–2004	23.7	2.6	440
2004–2005	18.0	2.1	414
2005–2006	20.3	2.6	487
2006–2007	23.1	3.1	238
2007–2008	37.3	5.0	626
2008–2009	14.8	2.3	−433
2009–2010	35.9	4.8	1149
2010–2011	23.6	3.5	1108
2011–2012	16.3	2.8	499
2012–2013	17.8	3.0	1406
2013–2014	11.2	1.9	0
2014–2015	24.5	3.8	55
2015–2016	15.5	2.0	48

Source: Database on Indian Economy, RBI.

Non-banking finance companies: checkered trend

Apart from the banks, India has a number of non-banking financial companies (NBFCs). The fundamental difference between banks and NBFCs in India are three: (1) NBFCs cannot accept demand deposits; (2) NBFCs do not form part of the payment and settlement system and cannot issue checks drawn on themselves; and (3) deposit insurance facility is not available to depositors of NBFCs, unlike in the case of banks. The NBFCs include many diverse types of financial institutions from housing finance companies to equipment leasing companies.[13] The diversity among the entities of the NBFC sector is also reflected in attributes such as size and the extent of regulatory oversight. As of March 2016, there were 11,682 NBFCs registered with the RBI, of which 202 were deposit-accepting NBFCs and 11,480 were non-deposit-accepting NBFCs, of which 220 were declared as systemically important (i.e., those with an asset size of INR 1 billion or more).[14] The role of NBFCs are seen from two distinct angles: (1) they have been very useful for sectors/activities that are generally excluded from formal banking activities; and (2) at some regularity some of the deposit-taking NBFCs have been a source of financial irregularity in some localized pockets and raised issues of consumer protection.

Presently all deposit-taking NBFCs and systemically important non-deposit-taking NBFCs are subject to prudential regulations such as capital adequacy requirements and provisioning norms along with reporting requirements.

While a number of types of NBFCs exist, which do not come under the ambit of RBI's regulatory oversight, the incidence of financial irregularity involving some NBFCs had come down and had predominantly been confined to the state/district level.[15] In fact, in the recent past, after a financial scandal involving an NBFC named Saradha (predominantly active in the state of West Bengal) surfaced in 2013, there has been further tightening of norms on deposit-taking NBFCs.

Interestingly, in line with the increasing regulatory control, over the years, while acceptance of deposits by the NBFCs had come down, there has been a spurt in their other activities. The ratio of NBFCs' assets in GDP increased steadily from just 8.4% as on 31 March 2006 to 12.9% as on 31 March 2015; while the ratio of bank assets increased from 75.4% to 96.4% during the same period.

Concluding observations

The following broad trends can be highlighted as key features of the Indian financial sector. As a consequence of successive reforms over the past 25 years, there has been significant progress in making interest and exchange rates largely market determined, though the exchange rate regime remains one of managed float, and some interest rates remain administered. Considerable competition has been introduced in the banking sector through new private sector banks but public sector banks continue to have a dominant share in the market. Contractual savings systems have been improved, but provident and pension funds in India are still in their infancy. Similarly, despite the introduction of new private sector insurance companies, coverage of insurance can expand much further, which would also provide greater depth to the financial markets. The extent of development along all the segments of the financial market has not been uniform. While the equity market is quite developed, activities in the private debt market are predominantly confined to private placement form and continue to be limited to the blue-chip companies. Going forward, the future areas for development in the Indian financial sector include further reduction of public ownership in banks and insurance companies, expansion of the contractual savings system through more rapid expansion of the insurance and pension systems, greater spread of mutual funds, and development of institutional investors. It is only then that the both the equity and debt markets will display greater breadth as well as depth, along with greater domestic liquidity.

Notes

1 Recently the Indian postal department has been given a license to open a payments bank.
2 The proportion of aggregate deposits that a bank has to keep in government and other approved securities.
3 Tier-I leverage ratio is defined as the ratio of Tier-I capital to total assets; total assets include the credit equivalent of off-balance-sheet items.
4 Repo rate is the fixed interest rate at which the RBI provides short-term (overnight) liquidity to banks against the collateral of government and other approved securities under the liquidity adjustment facility (LAF); see RBI website, www.rbi.org.in/scripts/FS_Overview.aspx?fn=2752 (accessed in August 2016).
5 Similar sentiments were echoed in the report of the Committee on Financial Sector Reforms (Government of India, Planning Commission 2009, p. 49), which noted: "Financial sector policies in India have long been driven by the objective of increasing financial inclusion, but the goal of universal inclusion is still a distant dream".
6 www.pmjdy.gov.in/ (accessed in August 2016).
7 More recently (on 5 May 2016), deviating from past practice of stop and go licenses, the RBI released Draft Guidelines for "on tap" Licensing of Universal Banks in the Private Sector.

8 Three of these entities have already surrendered their licenses as of July 2016.
9 The IMF (2017), in its revised forecast of January 2017 noted, "In India, the growth forecast for the current (2016–2017) and next fiscal year were trimmed by 1 percentage point and 0.4 percentage point, respectively, primarily due to the temporary negative consumption shock induced by cash shortages and payment disruptions associated with the recent currency note withdrawal and exchange initiative".
10 The large share of corporate entities in debt mutual funds has perhaps been caused by the prohibition of interest-bearing bank deposits. Further, interest is not permitted in bank deposits of fewer than seven days.
11 Gratuity refers to the lump-sum amount payable to the retiring government servant; a minimum of five years' qualifying service and eligibility to receive service gratuity/pension is essential to get this one-time lump sum benefit.
12 Foreign portfolio investors include asset management companies, pension funds, mutual funds, and investment trusts as nominee companies, incorporated/institutional portfolio managers or their power of attorney holders, university funds, endowment foundations, charitable trusts and charitable societies. The FIIS were allowed to invest in debt instruments subsequently in the financial year 1996–1997.
13 These include (1) asset finance companies (AFCs); (2) loan companies (LCs); (3) investment companies (ICs); (4) infrastructure finance companies (IFCs); (5) core investment companies (CICs); (6) infrastructure debt funds (IDF-NBFCs); (7) NBFC-microfinance institutions (NBFC-MFIs); (8) factoring companies (FCs); (9) mortgage guarantee companies (MGCs); (10) residuary non-banking companies (RNBCs); (11) housing finance companies; (12) mutual benefit companies; and (13) chit fund companies.
14 See the RBI "Master Circulars–Miscellaneous Instructions to NBFC- ND-SI" of 1 July 2015; available at https://rbi.org.in/scripts/BS_ViewMasCirculardetails.aspx?id=9835.
15 A major financial irregularity in this respect involved a leading NBFC conglomerate, Sahara India Pariwar, which was barred by the Securities Market Regulator, SEBI, in 2010 from raising money from the public through optionally fully convertible debentures that SEBI deemed illegal. Subsequently, the CEO of the company was arrested and the Supreme Court of India has directed the company to pay up INR 240 billion. The case is still sub judice.

References

Ahluwalia, M.S. 1999. Reforming India's Financial Sector: An Overview. In *India: A Financial Sector for the Twenty-First Century*, edited by J. Hanson and S. Kathuria. New Delhi: Oxford University Press.
Government of India. 2015. *Report of the Committee to Recommend Measures for Curbing Mis-selling and Rationalising Distribution Incentives in Financial Products* (Chairman: Sumit Bose). New Delhi. http://finmin.nic.in/reports/Final_Report_Committee_on_Incentive_Structure.pdf
Government of India. 2016. *Annual Report: 2015–16 – Department of Posts*. New Delhi. www.indiapost.gov.in/Report/FinalPostAnnualReportEnglish2015-16.pdf
Government of India. 2017. *Economic Survey*. New Delhi. http://indiabudget.nic.in/es2016-17/echapter.pdf (accessed February 2017).
Government of India, Planning Commission. 2009. *A Hundred Small Steps: Report of the Committee on Financial Sector Reforms* (Chairman: Raghuram Rajan). New Delhi: Government of India, Planning Commission.
ICRA. 2016. *Mutual Fund Screener* (for the Quarter Ended March 2016). Gurgaon: ICRA. https://mutualfundindia.com/Images/Research/PdfPaths/7a11b786a2c942b690db34e7c39db743Mutual%20Fund%20Screener%20-%20Mar%202016.pdf
Insurance Regulatory and Development Authority of India (IRDA). 2015. *Handbook on Indian Insurance Statistics: 2014–15*. Hyderabad: IRDA.
International Monetary Fund (IMF). 2013. *India: Financial Sector Assessment Program – Detailed Assessments Report on IAIS Insurance Core Principles*. Washington, DC: International Monetary Fund. www.imf.org/external/pubs/ft/scr/2013/cr13265.pdf
IMF. 2014. *Annual Report on Exchange Arrangements and Exchange Restrictions 2014*. Washington, DC: International Monetary Fund.
IMF. 2017. World Economic Outlook 2017 Update. Washington, DC: International Monetary Fund. www.imf.org/external/pubs/ft/weo/2017/update/01

KPMG. 2012. *Insurance Industry – Road Ahead*. Hyderabad: KPMG. www.kpmg.com/IN/en/IssuesAnd Insights/ArticlesPublications/Documents/Insurance_industry_Road_ahead_FINAL.pdf

Mohan, R. 2005. Financial Sector Reforms in India: Policies and Performance Analysis. *Economic and Political Weekly* 40(12): 1106–1121.

Mohan, R. 2006. *Financial Sector Reforms and Monetary Policy: The Indian Experience*. Paper Presented at the Conference on Economic Policy in Asia at Stanford, Organized by Stanford Center for International Development and Stanford Institute for Economic Policy Research, California, 2 June. www.rakesh mohan.com/docs/RBIBulletinJuly2006-1.pdf

Mohan, R. 2011a. Development of Banking and Financial Markets in India: Restoring Growth While Containing Risk. In *Growth with Financial Stability: Central Banking in an Emerging Market*, by Mohan. New Delhi: Oxford University Press.

Mohan, R. 2011b. Financial Inclusion in India: A Glass Half Empty or Three Quarters Full? In *Growth with Financial Stability: Central Banking in an Emerging Market*, edited by R. Mohan. New Delhi: Oxford University Press.

Mohan, R. 2011c. *Growth with Financial Stability: Central Banking in an Emerging Market*. New Delhi: Oxford University Press.

Mohan, R., and M. Kapur. 2011. Managing the Impossible Trinity: Volatile Capital Flows and Indian Monetary Policy. In *Growth with Financial Stability: Central Banking in an Emerging Market*, edited by R. Mohan. New Delhi: Oxford University Press.

Mohan, R., and P. Ray. 2011. Development of the Indian Debt Market. In *Growth with Financial Stability: Central Banking in an Emerging Market*, edited by R. Mohan. New Delhi: Oxford University Press.

Mundra, S. S. 2016. *Asset Quality Challenges in India: Diagnosis and Prognosis*. Speech by RBI Deputy Governor at the Edelweiss Credit Conclave, Mumbai, 28 April. https://rbi.org.in/Scripts/BS_Speeches-View.aspx?Id=1001

National Bank for Agriculture and Rural Development (NABARD). 2008. *Report of the Committee on Financial Inclusion* (Chairman: C. Rangarajan). Mumbai: NABARD.

National Sample Survey Organization (NSSO). 2012. National Sample Survey 2012. Jammu: National Sample Survey Organization.

OECD. 2015. *Pension Markets in Focus – 2014*. Paris: OECD. www.oecd.org/daf/fin/private-pensions/Pension-Markets-in-Focus-2014.pdf

Padmanabhan, G. 2015. *Is India Ready for Full Capital Account Convertibility?* Speech by Executive Director. Mumbai: Reserve Bank of India, 16 May. www.rbi.org.in/Scripts/BS_SpeechesView.aspx?Id=956

RBI. 2007. *Report on Currency and Finance, 2005–06*. Mumbai: Reserve Bank of India.

RBI. 2009. *India's Financial Sector: An Assessment*. Mumbai: Reserve Bank of India. www.rbi.org.in/scripts/PublicationReportDetails.aspx?ID=544

RBI. 2014. *Report of the Committee to Review Governance of Boards of Banks in India* (Chairman: P.J. Nayak). Mumbai: Reserve Bank of India.

RBI. 2015. *Report on Trend and Progress of Banking in India 2014–15*. Mumbai: Reserve Bank of India. www.rbi.org.in

RBI. 2016. *Financial Stability Report*, December 2016. Mumbai: Reserve Bank of India. www.rbi.org.in (accessed February 2017).

Saraswathy, M. 2015. Insurance Penetration at 10-year Low. *Business Standard*, 25 June.

Shah, A., and I. Patnaik. 2008. Managing Capital Flows: The case of India. National Institute of Public Finance and Policy Working Paper 2008–52. New Delhi: National Institute of Public Finance and Policy.

Swiss Re. 2016. *World Insurance in 2015: Steady Growth Amid Regional Disparities*. Zurich: Swiss Re. www.swissre.com/sigma/382655591.html

5

DEVELOPMENT AND SHORTCOMINGS OF INDONESIA'S FINANCIAL SECTOR

Iwan J. Azis

Introduction

Nothing is surprising when, after going through a major financial crisis like in 1997, efforts have been made to strengthen the financial sector. This has always happened in all crisis-affected countries. Being one of them, Indonesia is no exception. In several areas since the crisis, the country's financial sector has made some improvements. Yet a combination of side effects of a liberalized system, misguided policy, and failure to diversify especially during the period of strong growth and ample liquidity still makes the country vulnerable to external shocks. Boundless complacency prevails due to weaknesses and policy. While the sector has grown steadily, supported by improvements in the regulatory and supervisory work, shortcomings remain.

In this chapter, the development and the structure of Indonesia's financial sector are put in the context of a changing external and domestic environment, from which shortcomings are identified, and risks and uncertainties are highlighted. It is argued that in a liberalized and open financial system, where the financial sector is still small and shallow like in Indonesia, vulnerabilities to external shocks bound to ascend. The sequence of episode is typical: vulnerabilities preceded by a period of massive capital inflows. This time, the surge of inflows is prompted by the ultra-easy money policy in developed economies, while the vulnerabilities are reflected in elevated risks of pro-cyclicality and reversals of capital flows.

Risks in Indonesia are further heightened by the absence of formal financial safety nets until only recently when a draft law was passed by the parliament. Struggling to safeguard financial stability amid growing ineffectiveness of standard monetary policy, policymakers and regulators came up with various initiatives and measures, some of which are controversial.

After discussing the country's structure of financial sector, followed by issues surrounding the regulatory and supervisory framework and the financial sector challenges, in the last section before the summary the chapter focuses on the recent development, externally and domestically, and presents the resulting risks in conjunction with the changing policy and institutional arrangements with respect to crisis management.

Financial structure: banks, non-bank financial institutions, equity market, bond market

The total assets of Indonesia's financial sector are around 75% of GDP, relatively smaller compared to the neighboring Association of Southeast Asian Nations (ASEAN) countries. As in many developing and emerging market economies, the country's financial sector is dominated by the banking sector, which constitutes 80% of the entire financial system (Figure 5.1).

Out of 118 commercial banks (11 of which are Islamic banks), more than 40% are state-owned including regional development banks.[1] Private commercial banks constitute a roughly similar share, and the remaining 15% are foreign banks branches and joint ventures.[2] By the end of 2015, the total assets of commercial banks are recorded at IDR 6,530 trillion (less than USD 500 billion), with a persistently high concentration where 47% of total assets belongs to the top five banks: Bank Mandiri, Bank Rakyat Indonesia, Bank Central Asia, Bank Negara Indonesia, and Bank CIMB Niaga.

Indonesian banks are highly segmented. The formal classification, based on BUKU, is the following:[3] BUKU-1 consists of banks with core capital of less than IDR 1 trillion; BUKU-2 between IDR 1 trillion and IDR 5 trillion; BUKU-3 between IDR 5 trillion and IDR 30 trillion; and BUKU-4 with more than IDR 30 trillion.[4] Those under BUKU-4 can have a wider range of business activities and are allowed to enter into domestic or offshore equity investment with ownership not more than 35%.

The average capital adequacy ratio (CAR) of the banking system is around 20% (some 90% of available capital is tier 1 category), where foreign banks have the highest ratio. Although return on assets (ROA) is still above the average in emerging markets with around 2.7%, banks' net interest margin (NIM) is notoriously high. At 5.3%, it is the highest among ASEAN-6.[5] Table 5.1 displays data per December 2015 of CAR, ROA, NIM, and other indicators for different categories of banks. A high NIM captures the spread between the interest earned on the

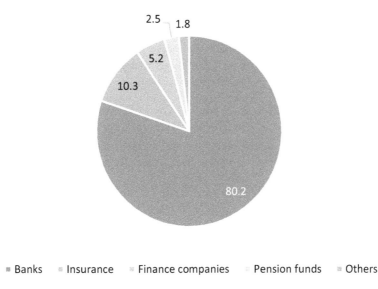

Figure 5.1 Structure of financial system, 2016

Table 5.1 Set of indicators for different categories of banks (as of December 2015)

		Conventional Banks	Forex	Non-Forex	BPD	Mixed	Foreign
ROA	%	2.3	1.8	1.6	2.4	1.0	1.7
Total Asset	IDR billion	6,129,357	2,363,516	193,149	475,696	313,570	473,336
NPL	%	2.5					
CAR	%	21.3	18.1	21.2	20.6	20.4	46.5
LDR	%	92.1	86.9	86.0	92.2	132.8	131.5
NIM	%	5.4	4.9	5.1	6.7	3.4	3.6
BOPO	%	81.5	84.8	86.8	79.6	87.5	92.7
Deposit/ DPK	%	46.0	52.5	84.8	36.4	58.7	31.7
Number of banks		118	39	27	26	12	10

Notes: CAR = capital adequacy ratio. LDR = loan-to-deposit ratio. NIM = net interest margin. NPL = non-performing loan. ROA = return on assets.

Source: Compiled by author.

bank's assets and the interest costs on its liabilities; it is supposed to reflect the asset and liability management. However, NIM in Indonesia is more numerator driven. That is, the persistently high NIM is driven more by the high lending rates.[6]

Also, NIM should not be confused with profitability as banks earn significant income from fees and service charges, none of which are affected by interest margins. Banks' profitability remains good although it has started to decline. A sizeable untapped market and growing number of middle class continue to make the appetite of foreign investors to either acquire banks or set up operations in Indonesia strong.[7] With the commencement of ASEAN Economic Community last year, and the issuance of ASEAN Banking Integration Framework as part of ASEAN Framework Agreement on Services, the opportunity for ASEAN banks to operate in Indonesia is bigger. Realizing the absence of a level playing field and different sizes among banks in ASEAN – the 10 largest belong to Singapore, Malaysia, and Thailand – and considering the current level of Indonesian banks' efficiency, there is a fear of competition asymmetry. This explains why at this stage the Indonesian authorities are still reluctant to allow neighboring banks to come with the strength and speed they wish.[8]

High interest rates translate into bond yields. The Indonesian bond market is largely sovereign and in local currency, as the corporate bond market is still in its infancy. Per December 2015, the outstanding value is recorded at IDR 1,650 trillion or USD 126 billion with the following breakdown: IDR 1,410 trillion government bond and IDR 249 trillion corporate bond (Table 5.2). The bond market is relatively young as it began to grow only since the issuance of recapitalization bond following the 1997 Asian financial crisis (AFC). Several banks receiving such bonds during the crisis, some of them are now foreign owned, continue to hold them, generating interest incomes until today.[9]

The largest holders of bond are banks. Bond holding by corporates (mostly banks) is four times larger than the amount of bonds outstanding. This has an important implication on the link between monetary policy and financial stability. Any changes in yield – hence price of bond – driven by changes in the interest rates would have repercussions on bank's balance sheet (Azis and Shin 2015). Particularly in a high interest rate environment like Indonesia, a

Table 5.2 Assets of non-bank financial institutions (as of December 2015)

	Total
Insurance (IDR billion)	803,715
Gross premium of insurance (IDR billion)	261,087
Pension fund (IDR billion)	206,593
Financing companies (multi finance, venture capital, infrastructure financing companies, SOE financing)	10,576
Others (Indonesia Eximbank, SOE pawnshop, guarantee institutions (IDR billion)	138,652
Capital Market (as of December 2015)	
Number of companies listed	521
Market capitalization (IDR billion)	4,796,800
NAV mutual funds (IDR billion)	268,447
Outstanding of local currency bonds	
– Government bonds (IDR billion)	1,410,000
– Corporate bonds (IDR billion)	249,000
Issuance of local currency bonds	
– Government bonds (IDR billion)	311,790
– Corporate bonds (IDR billion)	62,420
Daily trading (IDR billion)	5,768

Source: Compiled by author.

rate increase may harm the quality of banks' balance sheets and hence financial stability. The situation when net foreign capital inflows turned to net foreign capital outflows in 2015 provides an illustration of this vulnerability (for the turnaround of capital flows, see Azis 2016). Despite the fact that movements of capital have been driven more by the push/supply factors (external), less to do with domestic interest rates, Bank Indonesia (BI) was adamant to keep the outdated thinking of setting high interest rates believing that it could deter outflows. On the one hand, the policy was ineffective; on the other hand, keeping high interest rates caused banks' net worth to deteriorate through falling bond prices.[10] Smaller banks were particularly affected.

Offering highest yields in ASEAN-6, the market has attracted foreign investors especially during the period of ultra-easy money policy including the quantitative easing in advanced economies after the 2008 global financial crisis. Almost 40% of local currency bond in Indonesia is foreign-owned. As this happens while market is shallow and not liquid, any shock that may change investors' perception could easily rattle the market. The episode of taper tantrum in summer 2013 provides a clear example. Compared to the bond market in, say, Malaysia, where foreign ownership is also relatively high but domestic investors' base is large, Indonesia's bond market is more vulnerable to market volatility due to investors' change in perception.

The equity market is also less developed than in other major ASEAN countries. The number of companies listed has not changed much over the years; per December 2015 only 521 companies are listed, with market capitalization around IDR 4,800 trillion or USD 370 billion, less than 50% of the country's GDP. The concentration ratio is high: 50 companies constitute almost three-quarters of total market capitalization. In the case of mutual fund, the net asset value is only less than IDR 270 trillion, albeit growing. The share of foreign ownership, around 60%, is even higher than in the bond market, and it is more volatile.

The asset size of non-bank financial institutions (NBFIs) is recorded at IDR 1,160 trillion (USD 89 billion), where insurance companies and pension fund dominate (around 87%). The remaining NBFI assets belong to financing companies such as multi-finance, venture capital, infrastructure financing companies, pawnshops, Export-Import or Exim Bank, and so forth (see again Table 5.2).

Regulatory and supervisory framework

Fragmented regulatory structure and framework not all in line with international best practices are among the most notable features of Indonesia's financial regulatory and supervision. In such circumstances, a lack of diversity in capital market is expected.

The absence of formal policy about future direction and strategy of the country's banking sector makes it unclear as to what direction the banking industry would take in the long term. Only when such a policy is in place a proper regulatory and supervision can be designed. This prompted the authority to launch the Indonesian Banking Architecture (Arsitektur Perbankan Indonesia, or API).[11] Since then, some improvements have subsequently been made particularly in areas related to the specific strategies for development of rural banks, SMEs including micro enterprises, and in institutional strengthening of rural banks (Bank Perkreditan Rakyat, or BPR) and Shariah banks.[12] The authority sought to build constructive cooperation with the relevant stakeholders in the API programs to generate a sound, strong, and efficient banking industry to secure financial system stability. Obviously, this can be achieved only when backed by a strong regulatory and supervisory work, on which a major institutional change has occurred in Indonesia (Financial Stability Board 2014).

Until 2012–2013, BI was responsible for regulating and supervising banks, while the Capital Market and Financial Institution Supervisory Board (Badan Pengawas Pasar Model or Bapepam-LK) was responsible for non-bank financial institutions and the capital market. Issued in 2011, Law 21 stipulates that the regulatory and supervisory work for the entire financial sector, not just banks, will be transferred to the financial service authority OJK (Otoritas Jasa Keuangan 2016). For non-bank financial institutions and capital market, the actual transfer began at the end of 2012, and for banks at the end of 2013.[13] BI will retain regulatory responsibilities for macroprudential policies. An important reason behind the move was the growing public dissatisfaction with BI's handling of the AFC and the subsequent corruption scandals.

But questions have been raised as to whether OJK will be better prepared to deal with financial crises and be independent from political and other pressures. Another yet more fundamental question is whether separating monetary policy from bank supervision is the optimal and appropriate strategy for Indonesia, especially since there is no global consensus on the optimality of such a strategy.

Nonetheless, the decision has been made. In practice, the transfer of responsibility was not easy; the process has been far from smooth. Lack of accurate data and information about the operations of non-banks and capital market, and uncertainties surrounding the status of staffs responsible for bank regulation and supervision, add to the difficulties. By the end of 2015, some BI staffs who were lent to OJK opted to return to BI. This poses a challenge for OJK to conduct the work more optimally, considering this happens in the midst of growing economic uncertainty. One could only envisage what would have happened if the country's financial sector was hit by a major external shock at the time. Fortunately, that did not happen, and the growth performance of the Indonesian economy was still relatively strong, although a large part of it was due to the primary sector boom driven by the People's Republic of China's (PRC) strong demand. That favorable condition ended in late 2014 when commodity prices continued to fall, the PRC's boom ceased, and capital flows began to reverse (Azis 2016).

Like in many other emerging markets, the focus of the regulatory and supervisory work has been to maintain financial stability, at least on paper, while at the same time insuring that the financial sector is supportive to economic growth. The latter becomes more urgent in the current environment of growth slowdown. In this context, the policy to put a cap on deposit rates by the OJK cannot reflect better the overlap and confusion over the regulatory-cum-supervisory action and monetary policy.

Easing monetary policy in a slowing-growth environment is expected. This would have reflected in a fall of interest rates. However, while BI began to lower the rates only since early 2016, the effects on deposit and lending rates have been limited.[14] OJK tried its own approach to change that by introducing deposit rate caps effective 1 October 2014. The regulation is aimed at alleviating the competition among large banks for term deposits and bring down lending rates.

It is true that in a highly segmented market only a small number of big banks (BUKU-4 category) dominate and become the real movers of the rates. But putting a cap on interest rates could limit banks' ability to adjust to liquidity shocks via interest rate flexibility and reduce bank's ability to mobilize not only large deposits but also small ones. One possible outcome is that banks will resort to keeping more liquidity rather than extending credits. Such a measure also encroaches on BI's policy signals and operations that could distort policy transmissions. The line separating supervisory and regulatory work from monetary policy is blurred. Many wonder whether it represents controls on interest rates since the deposit rates offered are not allowed to go beyond a level that satisfies a pre-determined spread around the BI rate.[15] Is the country's financial system resorting to financial repression?

Still on the effort to stimulate growth, BI introduced reserve requirement averaging to reduce the need for banks to hold high precautionary reserves. This policy is expected to ease the liquidity constraint and deepen the money market. Indeed, the money market in Indonesia is shallow and needs a further boost. In this context, OJK launched the Global Master Repurchase Agreement to help develop the collateralized interbank market.

BI also took another move on its policy rate by replacing the BI Rate with the seven-day (Reverse) Repo Rate effective on 19 August 2016. In the announcement, improving the effectiveness of monetary policy transmission was cited as the primary goal of the change. It is also expected – along with other measures – that it will help support financial market deepening as it will encourage transactions and develop interbank rate structure for 3–12 months. It is unclear, however, how the seven-day repo rate will have any meaningful difference with the previous BI rate in terms of its effectiveness to lower the lending rates, especially that more fundamental reasons for the ineffectiveness have not changed.

On capital market, the Indonesian Capital Market Law was promulgated in 1995, before the AFC.[16] The regulation made no provision for safe havens, implying no exemption and different treatment for sophisticated investors. It was not until 1997 that a set of new rules was introduced, allowing foreign companies considering dual listing or an initial public offering to issue Indonesian depository receipts. One of the biggest regulatory challenges at the moment concerns the possibility that foreign companies will be allowed to be listed on the Jakarta stock exchange. Such development is increasingly inevitable as the ASEAN Economic Community has officially commenced, yet there is no specific regulation to support it so far.

Now that OJK has been designated as the sole institution in charge of bank and non-bank supervision, a consolidated framework for risk-based supervision of banks and non-banks is needed. More importantly, it is imperative for OJK to have the appropriate capacity to implement the consolidated system.

Challenges

Indonesia's financial sector faces fundamental and contemporary challenges. The fundamental ones are generally linked to the underdeveloped stage and shallowness of the sector. Not only the size is small – barely higher than the size of the country's economy – but the dependence on the banking sector is also the highest among the ASEAN-6 countries. Decades of open capital account make such conditions vulnerable to the volatility of capital flows, and clear and robust crisis management protocols were not in place until recently.

In the banking sector, the high cost of intermediation indicated by a low penetration ratio and inefficiency continue to shape the country's capacity to finance investment and consumption. Sources of funds are predominantly short term (more than 90% having one-month maturity), and about half of them are traditional current and savings accounts. The banking system is highly segmented, and the dominant source of banks' funding comes from the deposits of large corporations. Banks of BUKU-4 category alone absorb 60% of the entire banks' current and saving accounts. Small banks, on the contrary, have to rely on higher-cost funding. The interbank and money markets are not functioning optimally, and the policy rate set by the central bank (BI rate) has been also getting less and less effective in influencing the market interest rates.

Another fundamental challenge related to the segmentation is with regards to state-owned and regional development banks that control around half of the entire banking market. Unlike domestic private banks, these banks receive favorable treatments from the government, such as giving them exclusive rights to deposit financial resources from the central/regional government's institutions. This makes their NIM higher than that of other banks. For domestic private banks, conglomeration is growing and becoming more difficult to monitor. One of the major challenges is for the regulators to put a restriction on the practice of financing own affiliated companies. Such a practice is common particularly among big companies belong to the same people or group who also own the banks.

Still another serious challenge concerns financial inclusion. Only slightly more than one third of Indonesia's population 15 years and older has a financial institution account; this is lower than the average proportion in lower-middle-income countries. Of that category, among the poorest 40%, only 22% have an account. For those living in rural areas, the number is less than 30%. What about access to loans? More than 40% of borrowers get the loans from friends and family. Also, in the current age of technology, where the mobile phone has a great potential to reach low-income people in need for financial access, including those in remote areas, the actual number of adults having mobile accounts is only 0.4%, markedly lower than the average number in lower-middle-income countries (2.5%).

Creating innovative programs and putting in place a more supportive regulation to increase the number of population with financial access, especially among the poor, continues to be among the biggest challenges the financial authority must deal with. A low level of financial literacy and weak consumer protection make such a challenge more daunting.

A further concern is the tiny proportion of population (less than 0.4%) that has access to the capital market. As a result, while a booming capital market may help boost the financing for the national economy,[17] the distribution of benefits is likely skewed. This could exacerbate the already worsening income and wealth distribution.

Contemporary challenges also abound. Increased capital inflows following the ultra-easy money policy in advanced economies since the mid-2000s, coupled with excess savings since the AFC, have provided ample liquidity (Azis and Shin 2014; Azis 2014a). Yet this did not translate into a robust growth in productive sector. The actual spending on infrastructure, for example, remains low. At first, the inflows were largely channeled through the banking system (bank-led flows). Banks' external debt soared during the period, causing their balance sheet to expand. Then, as the US quantitative easing policy began in 2009, a new round of massive inflows took place. This time, however, a large amount went to the capital market (debt-led flows) searching for higher yields (Azis 2016). As a result, the proportion of foreign ownership in the capital market surged, reaching around 60% in the equity market and nearly 40% in the bond market.[18]

As discussed in Azis and Yarcia (2015), those massive inflows changed the behaviors of agents. A more risk-taking behavior was clearly detected as most of the excess liquidity was invested not in the businesses or real sector activities but instead in financial assets. As expected, the latter grew more rapidly than the real sector of the economy (financialization). This suggests that there remain problems in the overall investment climate, while yields and returns from investing in financial assets are lucrative and easier to earn. The long-term growth capacity of the economy declines, and employment elasticity falls as a result. It also exacerbates the income inequality since only the high-income and urban-based households are involved in the financial sector. Indeed, without appropriate compensating measures, financial liberalization and free flows of capital in many emerging markets tend to worsen the income inequality (Azis 2015; Naceur and Zhang 2016).

A combination of shallow financial market and open capital account exposes the economy to volatile capital flows, elevating the risks of financial instability. Bank-led flows increase the risk of pro-cyclicality, and debt-led flows make the system vulnerable to flows reversals. The taper tantrum episode of 2013 demonstrates how financial market could easily turn volatile when investors' perception changed and capital flows reversed. A more recent round of volatility that began in 2015 occurred because financial conditions were tightening, as shown by a sharp decline of credit growth. At the same time, the economic growth has been slowing. Heightened competition for funding in the midst of economic slowdown put more strains on the financial sector.

Another serious challenge is the increase of non-performing loans (NPLs). The uptrend began in early 2014 as many companies struggled to repay debts. One estimate suggests that Indonesia's NPLs could reach 3%–4% in 2016 – a steep increase considering it was only 1.8% in 2013. The expected NPLs for SMEs and for mining-related activities could be as high as 8% – the highest level since the 2008 global financial crisis.[19] This forced banks to increase bad loan provisions. The risk of deteriorating credit quality and margin pressure is likely to heighten, given the weak economic environment.[20]

Segmentation also implies different challenges for different category of banks. Local, state-owned, and Shariah banks clearly face a margin pressure. This is not so much the case for foreign banks. The latter are more concerned with issues like uncertainty related to the use of IT data, banking rules, on-shoring requirements, complex and more demanding domestic and international compliance regime. These factors could affect their ability to leverage global operating models.

Given the current slowdown in the economy and uncertainty in global conditions, the most real and immediate challenge for Indonesia's banking sector is to reduce the cost of funds on the one hand and to develop new revenue sources on the other hand.[21] This has to be done while banks must also meet the regulatory compliance framework in line with Basel III (requiring a stronger capital surcharge). They also have to comply with the recent rule that puts a limit (a cap) on the deposit rate. Such a rule was issued by the financial service authority OJK because, as discussed in the preceding section, beginning in 2014 the responsibility for regulating and supervising banks was transferred from the central bank to OJK.

Policy and crisis management

When the prospect of world economy is uncertain, the growth slowdown in the PRC feeds back negatively to other countries and the global growth, the quandary for an emerging market like Indonesia is multitude.

Having relied too much on the PRC's demand for primary commodities, especially coal and palm oil, the impact of a slower PRC expansion has been significant. After years of enjoying a double-digit improvement in the terms of trade spurred by a strong demand and high price of commodities, the trend began to reverse in 2011. The terms of trade have declined by around 8% since then (IMF 2015). For an economy like Indonesia, where major commodities constitute half of all merchandise exports and where the share of commodities sector is around 10% of GDP, the impact of the turnaround is quite severe. Growth is slowing, risks in financial sector are rising, and firms having a large borrowing in foreign currencies are under severe stress.

It is estimated that the country's GDP growth has been about one percentage point lower because of the 8% decline in commodity terms of trade. Through the reduction of imports and by considering the inter-industry linkages, the current account balance improves. On the other hand, a combination of lower oil prices that cut government revenues through a profit-sharing arrangement, spending for subsidies that remain substantial albeit declining, and purchases of other energy sources, has raised the fiscal deficit and narrow the country's fiscal space.

Equally important to understand is the effect of falling prices of commodities on the revenues and profits of producers and exporters. Through multiplier effects, domestic demand and incomes are affected. Declining incentives to invest in commodity sector or the related activities also cause a contraction. A shift of resources including labor and capital (credits) from primary good tradables to non-primary good tradables is an inevitable outcome. In the process, lenders to commodity-related activities have to bear significant losses. Most loans become NPL or special mention loans (SML) as a growing number of companies have to struggle with debt repayment. The problem of high leverage is further exacerbated by the decline of profitability. A slowdown in the overall economic growth puts further pressures on NPL and SML. It also causes lending growth to fall and asset quality to deteriorate.

In response to slower economic growth, BI loosened the monetary policy and relaxed some of its macroprudential policies. It reduced the interest rates and cut the rupiah primary reserve requirement to enable banks to have additional liquidity, lowering the cost of loanable funds. But given weak demand for credit, it is doubtful that the measure could boost lending and growth. To help banks manage liquidity risk, liquidity coverage ratio requirements have been adopted, as well as the requirement for counter-cyclical capital buffer. From the OJK side, a set of measures are also taken, one of which is specifically intended to facilitate loan restructuring for banks that have a relatively strong risk management capacity.

Even with all those measures, however, systemic financial stability risks remain high. Part of the reason is because risks in corporate sector are also increasing. Another reason is the uncertainty over the procedure and legal framework of the financial safety net system.

Many corporates, especially those affected by commodity price falls and a weak rupiah, are facing growing risks of refinancing or default; the latter could create negative spillovers to the banking system and damage confidence.[22] Another concern is increased conglomeration as discussed earlier. The practice of lending to own affiliated companies is common. If left unattended, it could make the risk not only increasing but also systemic. A severe stress is also felt by corporates with high foreign currency leverage. Debt rollover is unavoidable for some of them. Including foreign exchange debt to banks, foreign currency debt was recorded at 20% of GDP in 2016, twice the level in 2010.

For the policy-makers and regulators, managing such difficult conditions is far from easy since the domestic and external environments are no longer benign. To the extent safeguarding the domestic financial stability is the only choice, efforts in this direction should include strengthening the facility for hedging of the foreign exchange debt, requiring foreign exchange hedging by corporates, and limiting external borrowing to only firms with a strong balance sheet or investment grade firms. Improvements in corporate resolution framework and bankruptcy regime are also urgently needed. The oligopolistic market and large connected conglomerates in Indonesia pose systemic risks that could be dealt only with a strong resolution and bankruptcy framework.

Nonetheless, in a bank-dependent economy like Indonesia, vulnerabilities in the banking sector are more important to watch. They are more likely to elevate risks of systemic financial stability. The central bank's lender of last resort function is important in this regard. In a normal condition, the facility related to such a function is available to illiquid but solvent banks able to provide liquid, high-value collateral. In a crisis situation, however, the primary consideration is the potential for systemic impact in addition to solvency and bank's ability to provide collateral.[23]

Yet, a broader framework that includes the deposit insurance scheme, crisis resolution, and the emergency financial facility is more needed. Together with the directives for crisis prevention, such a framework can hold the key to the country's Financial System Safety Net (FSSN). In 2017, a Draft Law of FSSN has been passed by the parliament.[24] It specifies the following tasks and responsibilities of the relevant institutions involved in the operation of the Safety Net: the Ministry of Finance is responsible for drafting legislation for the financial sector and providing funds for crisis resolution, BI is responsible for safeguarding monetary stability, maintaining a sound banking system and ensuring a secure and robust operation of the payment system, and the Indonesian Deposit Insurance Corporation is responsible for guaranteeing bank customer deposits and resolution of problem banks.

Realizing the seriousness of the risk of moral hazard from adopting a government blanket guarantee despite its merit for restoring public confidence in the banking sector during a crisis, the new FSSN Draft Law does not allow such a scheme. Instead, the Indonesian Deposit Insurance Corporation (Lembaga Penjamin Simpanan or LPS) is expected to be in charge of handling the systematically important banks when they are in trouble. This is on top of the LPS basic responsibility to guarantee bank customer deposits. In executing the rescue task, the first step would be to use a private sector-based solution such as selling the bank to other investors or asking bank owners to provide additional capital and so forth. Only if that early step fails to work will the LPS take over the bank. To ensure the effectiveness of crisis resolution, each relevant institution is assigned clear lines of responsibility and accountability, and to avoid high social and economic costs, the new Draft Law prohibits the use of public money (no more bailout approach).

Now that the FSSN Draft Law has been passed, the subsequent revisions of the laws of BI, LPS, and OJK have to be well coordinated to ensure an overall consistency of the legal framework to the new institutional arrangements. More importantly, since LPS is now given a larger task and responsibility in crisis resolution, it is imperative to strengthen its capacity by granting additional instruments and tools, and greater room for raising more funds.

Summary and final remarks

Indonesia's financial sector is typical of that of many lower-middle-income countries. While it has grown steadily and made improvements in some areas, especially after the 1997 crisis, the sector remains small, bank-dependent, having limited inclusion, and highly concentrated. Almost half of banks' total assets belongs to the top five banks, and three quarters of capital market capitalization is owned by less than 10% of all listed companies. The segmented banking sector combined with small and shallow capital market makes the cost of intermediation high, and interbank market and money market not functioning optimally. The regulatory structure and framework are fragmented, not all in line with international best practices. A lot in the supervisory work still needs to be improved.

Banks' excessive reliance on short-term sources of funding and the illiquidity of capital markets lead to high interest rates, NIM, and bond yields; in all three, Indonesia has the highest among major ASEAN countries. Small market coupled with a large ownership of yield-driven foreign investors poses a challenge to financial stability. A minor perturbation that sparks capital outflows could easily rattle the market. Bank-led inflows expose the system to pro-cyclicality risks, and debt-led inflows makes the system vulnerable to flows reversals.

As capital inflows surged since the mid-2000s, vulnerability increased. The subsequent lack of prudent behavior among agents elevated the risks. Another challenge pertains to the consequences of growing conglomeration where lending to own affiliated companies is a common practice. The resulting risk is not only high but also systemic.

The effectiveness of standard monetary policy is limited because of increased financialization driven by ample liquidity from massive capital inflows on the one hand, and high cost of domestic borrowing on the other. As corporates face increased risks of refinancing and default, the difficulty spillovers to the banking system. A close interlink between banks and capital markets (e.g., banks being the largest holders of bonds) also makes the policy choices more complex. It intensifies the trade-off between achieving the conventional growth-price stability and newly added financial stability. This suggests the need for a more effective macroprudential policy to complement the standard macro policy.

Against such a backdrop, recent slowdowns in the economy and elevated risks of financial instability pose a difficult challenge to policy-makers and regulators. Since efforts to ease monetary conditions by using standard monetary policy have failed to translate into lower lending rates, authorities attempt to take a rather drastic – yet controversial – measure: BI abandons completely the policy rate (BI-rate) and replaces it with seven-day repo rate, OJK imposes a cap on deposit rates, risking a return to financial repression. Before the slowdown, when capital inflows were still large, financial stability got the upper hand. As growth is slowing, the pendulum is swinging back to growth-price stability. The recent loosening of macroprudential policy – along with the monetary ease – is a poster-child of the shift. This could be risky because the ingredients of financial instability still remain, if not amplified; low measured-risks can abruptly turn into high real risks.

Amid heightened uncertainty and elevated risks, for eight years since the onset of the global financial crisis there was no formal procedure and protocols with a strong legal support for crisis resolution. Effective financial safety nets were essentially absent. Only in 2016 the FSSN Draft Law has been passed by the parliament, albeit still prompting questions regarding some of the points (e.g., making LPS almost single-handedly deal with troubled banks, vagueness in BI role as the lender of last resort, and prohibiting the use of public money for rescue operations). Also, a new set of legal and institutional adjustments still need to follow the Draft Law.

Curiously, even during that period of uncertainty the government proceeded with a major institutional shift that led to the establishment of OJK. It could be no other than by sheer luck Indonesia did not experience a major shock triggering a crisis at the time. Given the heightened uncertainties and risks, financial authorities would be wise not to push the luck too far.

Notes

1 The ongoing plan is to consolidate through M&A to reduce the number of banks to 60–70 within the next 10 to 15 years. The intended classification is international, national, and specialized or rural banks.

2 Foreign and joint-venture banks focus more on corporate and commercial-loan segments which they are more knowledgeable about and able to leverage on the networks of their principals.

3 The classification was made by Bank Indonesia through Regulation No. 14/26/PBI/2012 on Business Activities and Office Networks Based on Bank Core Capital, entered into force on 2 January 2013. It regulates the permitted business activities, obligations for the amount of credit a bank must grant as productive financing, and establishment/expansion of branch office networks – all based on the amount of Core Capital. BUKU stands for Bank Umumberdasarkan Kegiatan Usaha or Commercial Bank Based on Business Activities).

4 The classification is part of the Indonesian Banking Architecture or API (Arsitektur Perbankan Indonesia) launched in early 2004 as one of the key programs for promoting national economic recovery.

5 At the time of writing, the NIM of one of the state-owned banks, Bank Rakyat Indonesia (BRI), reaches even more than 8%.

6 Early this year, the Financial Services Authority (OJK) announced its plan to push state-owned banks' NIM to 3%–4% in a bid to lower the lending rates.

7 For example, banks from the People's Republic of China and the Republic of Korea are currently screening for targets to gain a foothold in Indonesia, especially for BUKU-1 category that requires more limited capital for expansion and limited banking activity that can perform. Some Japanese banks are also eying at the opportunity.

8 Also, the implementation of services liberalization under AFAS is scheduled to come into effect only in 2020.

9 Some of them are foreign-owned because after taken over by the government through a specially set-up agency called IBRA banks were subsequently sold to the market.

10 In the past, BI's high interest rates policy also posed problems as foreign and domestic institutions, including local governments, tended to hold the BI certificate (SBI) rather than to invest in the real sector. The burden on BI's liability associated with SBI also increased

11 The launching was in early 2004. API provides the outline of the direction and structure of the banking industry for the next 5 to 10 years, aiming at building a sound, strong, and efficient banking industry in order to create financial system stability for promotion of national economic growth. Note also that setting a long-term direction and development strategy for the banking industry has now become a global trend.

12 Shariah banks are banks managed according to Islamic Shariah law where the collection of interest is prohibited, and charging fees for provided services as well as profit sharing replace charging interest on loaned capital.

13 In the process, BI handed over "Book of Bank Indonesia Function Implementation Report in the Sector of Regulation, Licensing and Supervision of Banks" as an overview of how BI implements the function and supervision duties of banks before the transfer took place.

14 After resisting interest rates reduction despite the supply-driven nature of capital flows and no signs of serious inflation, beginning this year BI started to lower the rates. At the time of writing, three rate cuts in a row has been made. Hoping that the move will translate into lower deposit and lending rates, BI also set an upper limit for deposit rates at 50 basis points above BI rate, and set prime lending rates as reference for interest rates on loans. The intended results, however, failed to materialize.

15 Deposit rates offered on deposits up to IDR 2 billion were capped at the maximum LPS-guaranteed rate, and on deposits above IDR 2 billion were capped at certain bps above the BI rate, where the assigned bps depends on the category of banks (based on BUKU).

16 The law does not allow foreign firms to be listed in the country's bourse; cross-border offerings are also prohibited.

17 The development of capital market, at least in the case of government bond, proves also beneficial for financial safety nets. During the 2008 global financial crisis, for example, a significant portion of the fiscal stimulus conducted by the government was funded through government bond (for detailed discussions on this, see Azis 2014b).

18 These figures are far higher than before the crisis, especially that the bond market was virtually non-existent before the AFC.

19 Like in most countries, SMEs are most vulnerable to economic slowdown. Note also that BI requires banks operating in Indonesia to direct at least 20% of their credit portfolio to SMEs by 2018.

20 So far the strategy to ease margin pressure adopted by some banks, especially Shariah and state-owned banks, has been to increase fee-based products and to focus on SMEs and higher yield products.

21 Another immediate yet perennial challenge often voiced by banks is in human resources. Finding people who meet stringent banking requirements is getting more difficult, and the turnover is high (could reach as high as 15%). On the opportunity side, financing infrastructure and maritime development currently being prioritized by the government is expected to be the "new" revenue sources (based on "Indonesian Banking Survey 2015" conducted by PwC Indonesia).

22 Note, however, that many corporates in Indonesia tend to rely on internal cash flows rather than external financing.

23 Before the passage of the new FSSN Draft Law, to resolve liquidity difficulties with systemic impact the emergency financing facility would have been funded by the government through the state budget under the BI Law (Act No. 23 of 1999, amended by Act No. 3 of 2004). The implementing regulations governing the lender of last resort function are Regulation of the Minister of Finance No. 136/PMK.05/2005 dated 30 December 2005 and BI Regulation No. 8/1/2006 dated 3 January 2006. In the new FSSN law, however, no public money can be used. Such a drastic reversal is the result of a bargain in order to get impunity coverage where officials involved in the rescue effort will not be prosecuted.

24 In 2008, the parliament rejected a proposed financial stability law that contained provisions for a crisis management framework, including emergency lending. This has left a vacuum of decision-making framework and procedures to deal with a systemic crisis, especially that the subsequent presidential decree providing the crisis management framework has lapsed. The new Draft Law, approved early this year, specifies the following components of the FSSN: (1) effective bank regulation and supervision; (2) lender of last resort; (3) adequate deposit insurance scheme; and (4) effective mechanism for resolution of crisis.

References

Azis, I.J. 2014a. Asia in a Changing Global Liquidity: Dancing with the System. *The Indonesian Quarterly* 42(2).

Azis, I.J. 2014b. Capital Markets in the Context of Financial Safety Nets. In *Asian Capital Market Development and Integration: Challenges and Opportunities*. Oxford: Oxford University Press.

Azis, I.J. 2015. Integration, Contagion, and Income Distribution. In *Regional Science Matters*, edited by P. Nijkamp, A. Rose, and K. Kourtit. Heidelberg and New York: Springer.

Azis, I.J. 2016. Four-G Episode and the Elevated Risks. *Asia Pacific Economic Literature* 30(2): 3–32.

Azis, I.J., and H. Shin (eds.) 2014. *Global Shock, Asian Vulnerability, and Financial Reform*. Cheltenham, UK: Edward Elgar.

Azis, I.J., and H. Shin. 2015. *Managing Elevated Risk: Global Liquidity, Capital Flows, and Macroprudential Policy – An Asian Perspective*. Singapore: Springer.

Azis, I.J., and D. Yarcia. 2015. How Capital Flows in the Midst of Excess Savings Affect Macrofinancial Vulnerability. *Asian Development Review* 32(2): 115–152.

Financial Stability Board. 2014. *Peer Review of Indonesia Review Report*, February. Basel: Financial Stability Board.

International Monetary Fund (IMF). 2015. *IMF Country Report No. 15/75: Indonesia*. Washington, DC: International Monetary Fund.

Naceur, S., and R. Zhang. 2016. Financial Development, Inequality and Poverty: Some International Evidence. International Monetary Fund Working Paper 16/32. Washington, DC: International Monetary Fund.

Otoritas Jasa Keuangan. 2016. *Booklet Perbankan Indonesia 2016*, 3rd ed. Jakarta: Otoritas Jasa Keuangan.

PwC Indonesia. 2015. *Indonesian Banking Survey 2015*. Jakarta: PwC.

6

JAPAN'S FINANCIAL SYSTEM AND ITS CHALLENGES

Naoyuki Yoshino, Shinichi Nakabayashi, and Peter J. Morgan

Introduction

This chapter discusses post-war economic development of Japan's financial system and the current status of Japanese financial sector issues. Japan has one of the world's most developed and largest financial systems. It served the needs of Japan's economy during the high-growth period of the 1960s and 1970s very well, but has struggled to adapt fully to the era of slow growth following the bursting of the financial bubble in 1989. Compared with other advanced economies, the banking sector is still relatively large, with an excessive number of differentiated institutions. Start-up companies and small and medium-sized enterprises still find it difficult to obtain finance. Key challenges include the need to respond to innovative financial technology ("fintech") and to encourage households to invest in riskier assets.

The next section provides an overview of the Japan's financial sector. Later sections describe the private banking sector; the government financial institutions, which play a decreasing but still major role in the economy; the insurance sector; the stock market; the bond market; and regulation of the financial sector. The final section concludes and describes some remaining challenges.

Overview of Japan's financial sector

Before the bursting of the "bubble economy" at the end of the 1980s, the financial system, along with Japanese management system and employment practices, was considered a key factor behind the country's rapid economic rise. Principal features of that system were (1) high levels of household saving; (2) market segmentation in financial system by function, maturity, region, and source of funding; (3) the predominance of indirect finance and the "main bank" system; and (4) a wide range of government-guided mechanisms to allocate savings and investment and provide stability to Japan's "convoy" system, including direct control over 30% of savings deposits through the postal savings system, regulatory controls, non-market-determined interest rates (by the Ministry of Finance), branch licensing (by the Ministry of Finance), administrative guidance (by various ministries), window guidance (by the Bank of Japan), and, until 1980, restrictions on capital inflows and outflows.

The development and subsequent bursting of the financial and real estate bubble in the 1980s was a defining event for the subsequent development of Japan's financial system. In 1985, the yen's strong rise following the Plaza Accord forced Japan to increase imports in order to reduce its balance of payments surplus. In response, the Bank of Japan eased monetary policy dramatically, leading to the rapid rise of Japanese stock and real estate prices that came to be known as the bubble economy. In this setting, private banks used land as collateral. Inflated land prices raised collateral values and loans increased to the real estate sector, construction companies, and non-bank finance companies. Large corporations were increasingly tapping the capital market and overseas markets, which caused commercial banks, long-term credit banks, and trust banks to lose valued customers. At the same time, they were competing on the basis of size in order to continue collecting deposits. In response to these pressures, their lending exposure to real estate and construction companies and non-banks grew rapidly.

Tight monetary policy and credit regulation were introduced in 1989. The discount rate went up to 6% in 1990 from 2.5% in 1988. The amount of loans from banks to real estate, construction, and non-bank finance companies were restricted. This triggered the collapse of the bubble, which set the stage for a long period of weak growth and gradual restructuring of the financial sector in Japan.

Table 6.1 shows the relative size of the major types of markets in Japan since 2001, including stocks and bonds (direct finance) and bank loans (indirect finance). The total outstanding amount of stocks, bonds, and loans in 2017 reached JPY 2,426 trillion, or 443.9% of GDP – one of the highest levels for advanced economies, and, relative to GDP, an increase of 60% since 2001. The level of loans has been relatively stable, while the size of the stock market fluctuated dramatically as a result of the global financial crisis, and the outstanding amount of bonds doubled over the period, mainly reflecting big increases in issuance of Japanese government bonds (JGBs).

A survey of changes that have occurred in the amount of funds raised from external sources as a percentage of the outstanding balance of financial debts shows that bank borrowings have tended to decrease since the 1980s. In the 2000s, funds raised through the issue of securities have outpaced those obtained through bank borrowings, suggesting that the weight of corporate financing structure has shifted from indirect to direct financing. This tendency to raise funds from external sources is due to the fact that following the liberalization and internationalization of the financial markets since the 1980s, businesses have actively sought to raise funds by selling new shares and bonds on the market. Although at one point the proportion of loan

Table 6.1 Size of loans and capital markets in Japan

	2001		2005		2010		2017	
	JPY trillion	*% GDP*	*JPY trillion*	*% GDP*	*JPY trillion*	*%GDP*	*JPY trillion*	*% GDP*
Stocks	296.8	56.7	539.7	103.0	310.5	62.0	701.0	128.3
Bonds	570.1	109.0	804.7	153.5	894.9	178.9	1,126.5	206.1
Loans	574.0	109.8	497.6	94.9	508.3	101.6	598.5	109.5
Total	1,440.9	275.5	1,842.0	351.4	1,713.7	342.5	2,426.0	443.9

Note: Loans include those from domestically licensed banks, foreign banks, *shinkin* banks, and other financial institutions.

Sources: Japan Exchange Group, Japan Securities Dealers Association, Bank of Japan.

financing rose after the financial crisis of 2008 curtailed the functioning of the capital market, funds raised through the issue of securities have considerably outpaced those obtained through borrowings after the hike in stock prices at the end of 2012. With the growth of emerging markets and the liberalization and abolition of regulations on the issue of debt securities, not only large corporations but also small to–medium-sized companies have come to obtain financing through the capital market. Consequently, financing through the issue of securities is also expected to retain its predominance going forward.

Financial institutions in Japan

Table 6.2 shows the development of total assets of major Japanese financial institutions. Despite the stagnation of Japan's nominal GDP during the period, the ratio of financial institution assets to Japan has increased significantly, reaching about 500% of GDP in 2016. Banks make up about 40% of total assets, but other credit institutions for small businesses and agriculture, forestry, and fisheries also contribute a sizeable share. The size of public financial institutions has shrunk significantly due to various reforms, but still is significant.

Table 6.3 shows the number of banks, amount of capital and the number of branches by the type of financial institutions in Japan. The Japanese banking financial system was segregated in terms of which sectors served large companies and small and medium-sized enterprises (SMEs). For example, city banks are providing nationwide loans to mainly large corporations, while regional banks are providing loans to SMEs in each region. Regarding the number of branch offices, agricultural cooperatives and fishery cooperatives and *shinkin* credit banks have many branch offices. However, the fact that Japan's widely dispersed 24,167 post offices function as collection points for its saving system equals the total number of the branches of regional banks, *shinkin* banks and agriculture cooperatives, showing how the wide-based infrastructure of post offices reaches out to rural areas as well.

Table 6.2 Total assets of major Japanese financial institutions

	2001		2010		2016	
	JPY trillion	*% GDP*	*JPY trillion*	*% GDP*	*JPY trillion*	*% GDP*
Banks	756.3	144.6	821.2	164.1	1075.3	199.7
City Banks	371.3	71.0	419.4	83.8	538.1	99.9
Regional Banks I	204.6	39.1	240.1	48.0	311.8	57.9
Regional Banks II	63.3	12.1	63.0	12.6	74.5	13.8
Foreign Banks	52.6	10.1	32.5	6.5	50.4	9.4
Trust Banks	64.5	12.3	66.2	13.2	100.4	18.6
Financial Institutions for Small Business	185.1	35.4	411.4	82.2	466.0	86.5
Financial Institutions for Agriculture, Forestry, and Fishery	188.0	36.0	227.5	45.5	287.3	52.6
Life Insurance	184.9	35.3	318.3	63.6	375.7	69.8
Nonlife Insurance	30.3	5.8	29.7	5.9	31.3	6.0
Public Financial Institutions	634.2	121.3	288.6	57.7	252.1	46.1
Japan Post Bank	299.6	57.3	194.7	38.9	209.6	38.3
Total	2278.4	435.6	2291.4	457.9	2697.3	499.1

Sources: Data for Japan Post Bank from its annual reports and Bank of Japan before 2006, Bank of Japan, CEIC databank.

Table 6.3 Capital and branch networks and of Japanese financial institutions

Type of Institution	Number of Firms (as of September 2017)	Capital Stock (JPY billion)	Number of Branches
City Banks	5	5,237	2,835
Regional Banks	64	2,595	7,488
Regional Banks II	41	875	3,049
Foreign Banks in Japan	55	NA	NA
Trust Banks	4	949	273
Financial Institutions for Small Business			
Shinkin Banks	264	814	7,370
Credit Cooperatives	150	439	1,679
Labor Credit Association	13	29	639
Financial Institutions for Agriculture, Forestry, and Fishery			
Agriculture Cooperatives	652	NA	8,010
Life Insurance Companies	41	NA	NA
Nonlife Insurance Companies	26	NA	NA
Securities Finance Companies	264	NA	NA
Government Financial Institutions	5	7,100	305
Japan Post Bank	1	3,500	24,167

NA = not available.

Sources: Financial Services Agency (FSA) and Japan Financial News (number of banks), Japan Post Bank Annual Report 2017, Japan Banks Association (capital stock and number of branches).

Composition of Japanese household saving

Households have a range of options when saving. Money can be deposited in a bank or other types of savings institutions or invested in the capital or other markets. Figure 6.1 shows a three-country distribution of financial products held by households. The five types of financial products are (1) cash and deposits, (2) insurance and pensions, (3) securities (excluding stocks), (4) stocks and mutual funds, and (5) others. Japanese still prefer to keep 52% of their savings in the form of cash, time, and savings deposits (at banks and post offices), which is high compared to other countries, such as the US (14%) and Germany (39%). One possible explanation for Japanese preference for time and savings deposits is that banks, and in particular post offices, have vast branch networks and Japanese value this convenience factor.

Since Japanese banks were obligated, until the year 2001, to guarantee 100% return of principal on such deposits, banks bear all risk associated with the reinvestment of deposits. To accommodate more risk-sharing, a wider range of investment opportunities, including investment trusts and various securities-related products should be made available to Japanese households.

Household savings flow directly or indirectly to all of the nine segments of the Japanese financial industry: (1) commercial banks; (2) long-term financial institutions; (3) financial institutions for small businesses; (4) financial institutions for agriculture, forestry and fishery; (5) insurance companies and other intermediaries; (6) securities firms and money market dealers; (7) public banks; (8) public corporations; and (9) other public bodies.

As mentioned earlier, compared to other industrialized countries, there is a high degree of financial intermediation in Japan. The massive amount of household saving that has flowed

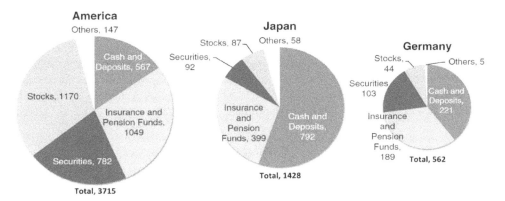

Figure 6.1   International comparison of distribution of personal financial assets, 2016 (percentage of total personal assets)

Source: OECD (2018).

into Japan's banks has been an important source of banks' power over corporate borrowers. Securities markets were relatively underdeveloped and corporations had little recourse from financial intermediation until the 1980s. Large amounts of household saving also flowed to the post office. Since postal savings were channeled into the Ministry of Finance's Trust Fund Bureau, and then into various government-related financial institutions, the government has had significant influence over how a large share of Japan's household savings have been used.

However, a stronger direct link has been forged between households and the securities market with the introduction of such systems as the defined-contribution pension plan in 2001 and the Nippon Individual Saving Account, a small amount investment tax exemption scheme introduced in January 2014. In addition, a broader range of investment trusts and exchange-traded funds, among other factors, are widening options for household investment in financial assets. Going forward, this sector will call for an improvement in the quality of retail sales operations and the greater dissemination and understanding of financial knowledge among Japanese households.

Banking sector

Commercial banks

Private commercial banks can be divided into several categories, based on such factors as their business function or historical background (Table 6.2). The distinction between city banks, regional banks, and member banks of the Second Association of Regional Banks (regional banks II) is not a legal one, but is a customary classification for the purposes of administration and statistics. City banks are large in size, with headquarters in major cities and branches in Tokyo, Osaka, other major cities, and their immediate suburbs. Regional banks are usually based in the principal city of a prefecture and they conduct the majority of their operations within that prefecture and have strong ties with local enterprises and local governments. Like regional banks, regional banks II serve smaller companies and individuals within their immediate geographical regions. As shown in Table 6.3, city banks have 2,835 branches, regional banks 7,488 branches, and regional banks II have 3,049 branches.

From 1999, non-financial institutions began to enter the banking business by establishing new types of banks such as banks specializing in settlements or internet banks, categorized under "other banks." The entry of non-financial institutions into the banking business led to an amendment to the Banking Act concerning regulation of bank shareholders in April 2002: shareholders of more than 5% of a bank's total shares must file with the Financial Services Agency (FSA), and those seeking to hold 20% or more require FSA permission to acquire the shares and are subject to FSA inspection (Japan Bankers Association 2018).

Postal savings

With 24,167 branches and JPY 210 trillion (USD 1.84 trillion) in total assets in 2017 (equal to about 39% of Japan's GDP and making the Japan Post Bank the 13th largest bank in the world; Relbanks 2018). Its vast network provides it with significant advantage, in terms of convenience, vis-à-vis other deposit-taking institutions in Japan.

Ministry of Finance (MoF) branch office guidelines strictly regulated the number of bank branches during the 1960s and 1970s. Since postal offices (and agricultural cooperatives) were regulated by the Ministry of Posts and Telecommunications, rather than MoF, post offices were not subject to MoF constraints on number of branches.

The success of the postal savings system can be attributed to several factors. First, there is the accessibility of locations. The number of post offices far outstrips the number of private bank offices. Second, post offices are very easy to visit. If agricultural farmers or small business employees want to use ordinary banks, it is often joked that they need to wear good clothes and good shoes. However, post office can be accessed in their daily clothes and shoes. Closeness, convenience, and friendliness are the reasons why the post office had attracted many people. Third, there is affordable transaction cost. Postal savings had been operated under the government. Therefore, there was strong trust by many individuals especially in rural regions. Japan has a deposit insurance system which covers both private banks and the postal savings bank. However, during the financial crisis period, many people shifted their deposits from private banks to postal savings due to an image that postal savings are under the government and strongly protected.

In addition to convenience, another factor contributing to the popularity of postal savings is that postal savings offer guaranteed, fixed-rate interest on 10-year savings that can be withdrawn any time after six months. In the past, in an environment of falling interest rates, the popularity of postal savings increased since it was the only institution permitted to offer fixed, long-term returns. City and regional banks were not permitted until recently to offer long rates because that would have put them in direct competition with the long-term credit banks, which rely heavily on long-term debentures for financing. With nearly all rates now being market determined, competition among different types of financial institutions is becoming more and more a function of rates of return, particularly in large cities.

Cost efficiency of postal savings relative to private bank industries is another reason why the Japan Post Bank has been so successful. First, it has economies of scale due to the large number of branch offices in Japan. Second, the post office has economy of scope. Post offices handle three businesses: mail services, postal savings, and postal life insurance.

In view of its large size, the Japan Post Bank was viewed as an unfair source of competition by private banks. This led to its privatization (along with the rest of the Japan Post group). In 2003, the Japan Post was established, replacing the previous Postal Services Agency, and, in 2007, the Japan Post Group was established, including Japan Post Holdings Co., Ltd.; Japan Post Service Co., Ltd.; Japan Post Network Co., Ltd.; Japan Post Bank Co., Ltd.; and Japan

Post Insurance Co., Ltd. In 2015, Japan Post Holdings Co., Ltd. listed on the First Section of the Tokyo Stock Exchange; Japan Post Bank Co., Ltd. listed on the First Section of the Tokyo Stock Exchange; and Japan Post Insurance Co., Ltd. listed on the First Section of the Tokyo Stock Exchange (Japan Post 2018). The initial public offering in 2015 raised about JPY 1.43 trillion, which included shares in Japan Post's banking and insurance units.

Non-bank depositary institutions

As shown in Tables 6.1 and 6.2, Japan has a large number of non-bank depositary institutions aimed at providing credit to small businesses and farmers, including *shinkin* banks, credit cooperatives, labor credit associations, agricultural cooperatives, forestry cooperatives, and fishery cooperatives. These institutions typically serve very local areas. *Shinkin* banks are cooperative regional financial institutions serving SMEs and local residents. Anyone who lives, works, or has an office in the region served by the bank can become a member, although companies with over 300 employees are prohibited from membership. They serve some of the same functions as credit unions but can accept deposit from non-members (inside and outside their area) without limitation and make loans to members that "outgrow" their qualifications (NASB 2017). The national-level financial institution for agricultural, fishery, and forestry cooperatives in Japan is the Norinchukin Bank, one of the world's largest financial institutions, ranked 28th in 2017 (Relbanks 2018).

Government-related financial institutions

There are two types of government-related financial institutions: those that receive funds from the private sector and those that lend to it. The only government financial institution that receives deposits from the private sector is the Japan Post Bank. Eleven government institutions lend to the private sector: two banks and nine special-purpose government finance corporations. The two banks are Development Bank of Japan (DBJ), founded in April 1951, and the Export-Import Bank of Japan (EXIM Bank), founded in December 1950. Japan's nine finance corporations, fully capitalized by the government, are People's Finance Corporation; Housing Loan Corporation; Agriculture, Forestry, and Fisheries Corporation; Small Business Finance Corporation (SBFC); Hokkaido and Tohoku Development Corporation; Japan Finance Corporation for Municipal Enterprises; Small Business Credit Corporation; Environmental Sanitation Business Finance Corporation; and Okinawa Development Finance Corporation.

The two banks are funded primarily by government borrowing and overseas bond issues. DBJ proceeds were primarily for economic development and domestic infrastructure investment, but more recently have been available for environmental improvement and reconstruction following natural disasters such as earthquakes. EXIM Bank proceeds are used to finance private sector exports, imports, and foreign direct investment. In addition to lending, both DBJ and EXIM Bank provide loan guarantees.

The finance corporations are funded principally by the Trust Fund Bureau (TFB) of the Ministry of Finance, with other sources of finance being bond issuance and funding from the General Account and other special accounts of the Japanese government. The high portion of Japan's massive savings that flow into the post office, as well as premiums received by postal life insurance, are entrusted to the TFB. The TFB then allocates these funds to government banks, and various public corporations and public enterprises. Some of the funds are used for purchase of Japanese government bonds or municipal bonds as portfolio asset investments. This system of government collection and allocation of funds is referred to as the Fiscal Investment and Loan Program (FILP).

Fiscal Investment and Loan Program (FILP)

During Japan's high growth period (1955–1973), the growth rate averaged about 10% per annum. As a result of such rapid growth, large corporations and small businesses faced a shortage of investment funds. Japan's capital markets (the stock and bond markets) were underdeveloped so businesses were dependent on loans from private and government banks. Long-term credit banks, trust banks, and government banks provided long-term finance. The government banks were particularly essential for long-term lending in the absence of a mature capital market in Japan. Among the sectors that benefited most from government loans were the sea transport, shipbuilding, electric power sectors, and machinery industries (Ogura and Yoshino 1988). In the late 1950s and early 1960s, most FILP funds flowed to the Electric Power Development Resources Corporation, JDB, the old Japan National Railway Corporation, SBFC, or the EXIM Bank. Over 20% of FILP loans were to industry and technology. After the first oil crisis of 1974, the share of FILP funds allocated to housing increased very rapidly.

The postal savings system and the Fiscal Investment and Loan Program in the Japanese financial system

Figure 6.2 illustrates how postal savings had been utilized. In the Japanese case, the top line applies to the traditional Japanese use of postal savings. In Japan, postal savings and public pension funds are deposited into the FILP program of the Ministry of Finance. The Ministry of Finance allocated these funds through government banks for lending to SMEs, infrastructure, and housing (Cargill and Yoshino 2003). The second type is postal savings to be put into private financial institutions and private financial institutions make loans by use of their own deposits and postal savings. Another way to utilize the postal savings is to make them only be invested into government bonds, which will be called core bank. The third type of postal savings is the post office directly making loans to SMEs or housing, showing the post banks in the sense that the post office became an ordinary bank.

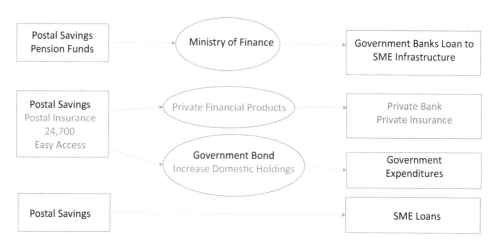

Figure 6.2 Use of postal savings

The Fiscal Investment and Loan Program and Japan's industrial policy

Table 6.4 shows the amount of Japanese disbursement of subsidies and the share allocated to various sectors from 1955 to 2017. Japan has introduced industrial policy where sea transport, coal mining, electric power, shipbuilding, and coal mining were strongly supported by the government. Table 6.4 reveals that agriculture, forestry, and fisheries accounted for over 80% of total subsidies. Of the subsidies provided to non-agricultural industries, the subsidies often directed to weak sectors or declining sectors such as small business, textile, and coal mining. On the other hand, the high technology sector only received a very small number of subsidies, reached a peak of 3.6% in 1974, and declined again to slightly over 1%.

However, government loans are not always welcomed by the private sector. Especially, there is a case of crowding out. The best case of government bank is government bank becomes leading financial institutions, which is called "cow bell effect." Government banks such as development banks and SME banks had lent money to the private sector. Then private banks joined to lend money together with government banks. In other words, government banks became a leader of the direction of loans. In these cases, supply curve shift to the right when government started to lend money. However, a crowding-out case can be observed. For example, if housing loans were too much supplied by the government, private banks cannot lend money to the housing sector. This is the case where government loans to the housing sector crowds out the private loans. It is important that the government loans should not crowd out private loans. Moreover, they should induce private bank loans that could be win-win for both government and private banking industries.

In fact, the earlier FILP system was ended in 2001 and the government banks no longer receive money from the Post Office. Instead, the Post Office invests its money in government bonds and capital markets. The government banks started to receive money from MoF, which issues fiscal investment loan bonds (FILP-bond) to finance their loans. FILP bonds are regarded as government bonds and have the same interest rate as other central government

Table 6.4 Sectoral disbursement of subsidies from the FILP, 1955–2017 (JPY billion)

Year	Sea Transport		Coal Mining		Small Businesses, Textiles, etc.		Agriculture, Forestry and Fisheries		High Technology		Total Subsidies
1955	3.5	5.0%	0.0	0.0%	0.5	0.7%	65.7	93.5%	0.5	0.7%	70.3
1960	1.7	1.8%	5.8	6.0%	2.6	2.7%	86.1	89.0%	0.5	0.5%	96.7
1965	10.1	4.1%	20.1	8.1%	21.8	8.8%	190.1	77.0%	0.8	0.3%	246.9
1970	15.4	2.3%	78.8	11.8%	51.6	7.8%	510.7	76.8%	7.7	1.2%	665.2
1975	15.0	1.1%	61.1	4.5%	129.4	9.6%	1,102.3	81.5%	43.3	3.2%	1,352.2
1980	9.5	0.3%	48.8	1.7%	243.7	8.7%	2,473.8	88.0%	34.6	1.2%	2,811.8

Year	Social Security		Education and Science		Public Projects		Agriculture		Other		Total Subsidies
1990	6,356.4	42.3%	3,436.6	22.9%	2,132.5	14.2%	1,269.2	8.4%	1,833.5	12.2%	15,028.2
2000	9,513.6	46.0%	4,082.1	19.7%	4,243.5	20.5%	1,655.2	8.0%	1,202.5	5.8%	20,696.9
2010	14,863.1	55.6%	5,374.1	20.1%	3,221.7	12.1%	1,265.1	4.7%	1,985.9	7.4%	26,709.9
2017	19,431.3	63.2%	5,105.1	16.6%	2,998.7	9.8%	1,084.1	3.5%	2,103.7	6.8%	30,722.9

Sources: Ogura and Yoshino (2004), Yoshino (forthcoming).

debts obligations. Loans to SMEs and agricultural loans had been consolidated in the Japan Finance Corporation. The DBJ is under the process of privatization. The Housing Loan Corporation has stopped making housing loans and instead began to sell secondary private banks' housing loans to the financial market. Thus, they became a guarantor of housing loans and are not providing direct housing finance anymore.

Insurance sector

Life insurance

Japan's life insurance business is well developed, and in terms of premium payments it ranks second in size after the US as of 2016 (Insurance Information Institute 2018). The number of policies in force for individual insurance was 160.11 million, and the amount of policies in force was JPY 858,604 billion. Of the total amount of policies in force for individual insurance, term insurance ranked top (JPY 252,132 billion, 29.4% of the total), followed by whole life insurance (JPY 167,174 billion, 19.5%), whole life insurance with term rider (JPY 136,835 billion, 15.9%), whole life insurance with variable accumulation rate (JPY 80,667 billion, 9.4%), and endowment insurance (JPY 43,630 billion, 5.1%). Gross annual premium income has trended upward in recent years due to increase in single-premium insurance policies. Gross premium income by type of business had the following results: individual insurance (JPY 25,607 billion), individual annuity insurance (JPY 4,729 billion), group insurance (JPY 1,124 billion), and group annuity insurance (JPY 4,562 billion; Japan Life Insurance Association 2018). As of March 2016, there were 41 member companies of the Life Insurance Association of Japan, including the Japan Post Insurance Co. Ltd. Total assets of Japan Post Insurance were JPY 80.3 trillion as of March 2017 (Japan Post Group 2017), making it the sixth largest insurance company in the world as well as the largest life insurance company in Japan. In the early 20th century, private banks and private insurance companies were reluctant to make contracts with agricultural farmers and small businesses. Therefore, the post office insurance was established in 1916 to provide life insurance to those people who were excluded from private life insurance. However, it turned out that farmers and SME employees were not much different from employees in large companies and government employees, so private life insurance companies started to provide insurance contracts to farmers and small business workers as well. However, the postal life insurance was popular because the reliability of postal offices was well established in Japan. Post office masters were very much respected in the region and there was a relationship of trust between them and the people.

Nonlife insurance

Japan's nonlife insurance sector is also well developed, ranking fourth in size globally after the US, the People's Republic of China, and Germany in terms of size of gross premiums. As of October 2017, a total of 52 general insurance companies were operating in Japan; a total of 30 companies were licensed as domestic insurers, including seven foreign capital domestic insurers, while 22 companies were licensed as foreign insurers. The total of direct premiums, including the savings portion thereof, written in fiscal 2016 was JPY 9,010.1 billion. The total of net premiums written was JPY 8,243.9 billion. By category, the largest net premiums are generated in automobile insurance, followed by fire, miscellaneous casualty, and personal accident (GIAJ 2018).

Stock market

Stock trading has a long history in Japan, as floor trading began at the Tokyo Stock Exchange and the Osaka Stock Exchange in June 1878. The stock trading floors were closed in April 1999 as trading switched to electronic means in order to accelerate the speed and reduce the cost of transactions by member securities companies and seek further efficiency in the Tokyo market. In January 2013, Japan Exchange Group was established, combining all the major stock exchanges and related entities in Japan into one entity, including the Tokyo Stock Exchange, Inc. (TSE) and Osaka Exchange, Inc. (OSE), as well as Japan Exchange Regulation and Japan Securities Clearing Corporation. In July 2013, the cash equity market of the OSE was integrated into the TSE, the self-regulatory operations of OSE were integrated into TSE regulations, and the derivatives clearing operations of the OSE were integrated into the Japan Securities Clearing Corporation. There are also small exchanges in Nagoya, Fukuoka, and Sapporo, but their combined trading volume amounts to only 0.1% of total stock trading in Japan (Japan Exchange Group 2018).

Japan's stock exchanges rank among the world's largest. By equity market capitalization, as of April 2017, Japan's market ranked fourth globally at USD 4.485 trillion, after the New York Stock Exchange, the NASDAQ, and the London Stock Exchange (Statista 2018). Major stock exchanges include the TSE First and Second Sections, JASDAQ[1] and Mothers (for start-up companies). Table 6.5 shows the major statistics for these exchanges.

New developments on corporate governance

The importance of corporate governance is strongly recognized particularly by developed countries in Europe and the US. Basic views on corporate governance are reflected in various principles compiled while securing the effectiveness based on securities exchange regulations, laws on companies and other relevant rules. New measures on corporate governance have also been implemented in Japan.

In June 2013, the Cabinet approved and announced the Japan Revitalization Strategy (revised in 2014). The revised strategy strongly proposed the need to strengthen corporate governance to increase mid-long profitability and productivity of Japanese companies and to pass the fruits of such increase on to the people widely. In response to this proposal, the Council of Experts

Table 6.5 Major statistics of Japanese equities markets (2017)

Market	Trading Volume (billion shares)	Trading Value (JPY trillion)	Market Capitalization (JPY trillion)	Number of Listed Companies
TSE First Section	490.4	683.2	674.2	2,062
TSE Second Section	46.4	12.7	10.1	517
Mothers	19.2	27.4	5.3	247
JASDAQ Standard	28.4	16.0	11.0	707
JASDAQ Growth	3.4	1.9	0.4	41
Total*	587.7	741.3	701.0	3,596

JASDAQ = Japanese Association of Securities Dealers Automated Quotation, TSE = Tokyo Stock Exchange.
*Including others.

Source: Japan Exchange Group (2018).

formed jointly by the Financial Services Agency and the TSE released the exposure draft for the Japan's Corporate Governance Code in December 2014 and called for public comments. Following this draft, the TSE formulated its Corporate Governance Code and began implementing the code in June 2015. This TSE code is based on the existing rules and guidelines of the bourse as well as on the 2004 version of the OECD Principles of Corporate Governance. Meanwhile, following the announcement of the Japanese Revitalization Strategy (2013 version), the Council of Experts established within the Financial Services Agency released the Japanese Version of the Stewardship Code as a code of conduct for institutional investors, and efforts for implementation are underway. It is anticipated that the TSE Code together with the Stewardship Code will drive effective promotion of corporate governance in Japan.

The OECD Principles of Corporate Governance, originally formulated in 1999, went through revisions in 2004 and were released as the updated G20/OECD Principles of Corporate Governance in September 2015. The updated principles reflect enhancements made to the 2014 version of principles and newly include the following key elements: (1) the role of stock markets in supporting good corporate governance, (2) the use of information technology at shareholder meetings, (3) proxy advisors, analysts, brokers, rating agencies and others that provide analysis or advice relevant to decisions by investors or disclose and minimize conflicts of interest that might compromise the integrity of their analysis or advice, (4) stakeholders' access to information, and (5) disclosure of non-financial information. Points of particular attention in the updated principles include the importance of the role of a "Say-on-Pay" system where shareholders convey their opinions on remuneration of board members and the efforts to strengthen functions of the board of directors through (1) having the board apply high ethical standards and (2) regular board evaluations supported by external facilitators as the Responsibilities of the Board. These elements will likely influence future revisions to the TSE Code.

Bond market

Japan's bond market also ranks among the world's largest, thanks mainly to prolific bond issuance by the Japanese government. Bonds are classified into the categories listed in Table 6.6.

Table 6.6 Types of Japanese bonds

---

1. Japanese government bonds: including JGBs, Treasury bills (T-bills), and financing bills (FBs)
2. Local governments bonds (prefectures, municipalities [cities, towns, and villages])
3. Government agency bonds
   a. Japanese government-guaranteed bond
   b. Fiscal Investment and Loan Program (FILP)-agency bond
   c. Government-affiliated corporation bonds
4. Local public corporation bonds
5. Local governments agency bond
6. Corporate bonds
   a. Straight corporate bonds
   b. Asset-backed corporate bonds
   c. Convertible bonds
7. Bank debentures
8. Non-resident bonds (foreign bonds)
   a. Yen-denominated foreign bonds
   b. Asset-backed foreign bonds

Source: Japan Securities Dealers Association.

Public offering of corporate bonds, asset-backed bonds and non-resident bonds (as classified earlier) are subject to disclosure requirements under the Financial Instruments and Exchange Act (FIEA). All other bonds are exempt from FIEA disclosure requirements (ASEAN+3 2016). Figure 6.3 shows that the growth of JGBs has dwarfed all other categories, as their outstanding amount has more than tripled since 1998, while the levels of other categories bonds have largely been stable.

Government bond market

Both the bond dependency ratio (the share of bond issuance, including refinancing, in total government funding) and the balance of outstanding government debt securities remained at a low level until the first half of the 1970s. However, as tax revenues had leveled off due to an economic slowdown that began in the second half of the 1970s, the government had no choice but to issue a large amount of government bonds, and their outstanding balance had increased sharply to JPY 71 trillion at the end of fiscal 1980. As a result, government debt securities had come to carry an increasing weight in the securities market, and the influence of government fiscal policies on the securities market had taken on a growing importance. With a view to improving the market's financial condition, the government adopted a fiscal restructuring policy since 1981. Helped by economic recovery, the government had succeeded in lowering the dependency on deficit financing and in curbing increases in the balance of outstanding public securities in the second half of the 1980s. Since the 1990s, however, the bond dependency ratio has risen sharply due to a contraction of tax revenues caused by a prolonged recession and the implementation of a series of fiscal stimulus packages. As a result, the bond dependency ratio remained high at 36%, and the balance of outstanding government debt securities reached about JPY 944 trillion at the end of 2016.

The ownership of JGBs by private financial institutions, including postal savings (Japan Post Bank) and postal insurance (Japan Post Insurance), has been declining since fiscal 2012. This change is primarily due to the bold quantitative and qualitative monetary easing measures introduced by the Bank of Japan in April 2013. Meanwhile, the Bank of Japan considerably

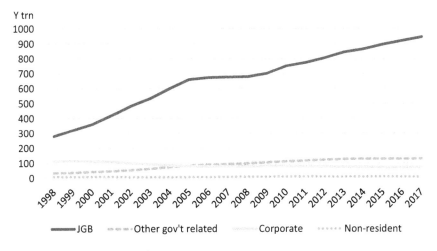

Figure 6.3 Japanese bonds outstanding

Source: Japan Securities Dealers' Association.

increased its percentage of ownership, which exceeded 40% as of September 2017, and has become the highest investor. Public pension funds that used to be stable investors premising their investments on long-term ownership are gradually lowering their percentage of investment in domestic bonds given that the Government Pension Investment Fund made a major change to its distribution of investment assets in October 2014. As a result, the percentage held by public pension funds dropped as low as 4.3% by September 2017 (MoF 2017). The upward trend in percentage ownership of Japanese households that existed since the introduction of JGBs (10-year, variable rate) for individuals in 2002 turned downward after fiscal 2008 due to lower interest rates and other factors. On the contrary, overseas investors continue to maintain a relatively high percentage, 11%, even today after a period of growth in demand for JGBs as safe assets in the light of the sovereign debt crisis in Europe occurred in 2010.

Corporate bond market

The issuance of corporate bonds had long been subject to strict regulation. However, the Commercial Code was amended in 1993 to drastically change the system, and the regulations on the issuance of corporate bonds have been substantially eased. In the case of public offering of corporate bonds, the issuing corporation (issuer) first appoints a lead manager and other underwriters that together constitute an underwriting syndicate, a commissioned company for bondholders or a fiscal agent, and providers of other relevant services and at the same time applies for a credit rating (ASEAN+3 2016).

In contrast to the steady rise of JGBs, the level of corporate bond issuance (including bank debentures) has stagnated, and the outstanding balance has been flat at around JPY 70 trillion in 2015–2017 following a long decline since the collapse of the bubble. This mainly reflected declines in bank debentures due to restructuring by banks. The level of straight bonds has been roughly flat at around JPY 60 trillion since 2009, reflecting limited demand for capital investment due to slow growth of the economy, while the level of convertible bonds and asset-backed bonds has been much smaller, about JPY 500 billion and JPY 300 billion, respectively, since 2017.

Regulation

Japan's Financial Services Agency (FSA) is the main regulatory agency for the financial sector. Its three major objectives are: establishment of stable financial system; protection of users and improvement of use convenience; and establishment of fair and transparent markets (JFSA 2018). The FSA is responsible for protecting deposit insurance holders, insurance policyholders, and securities investors. It is also charged with ensuring smooth operation of the financial system, including inspection and supervision of private financial institutions, including banks, insurance companies and exchanges, and surveillance of securities transactions. Other responsibilities include establishment of rules for trading in markets; establishment of business accounting standards and other rules for corporate finance; supervision of certified public accounts and auditing firms; participation in international fora to set international standards for the financial sector; and surveillance of compliance with rules in financial markets.

The FSA was established as an agency under the Prime Minister's Office in June 1998. Until 1998, regulation of the financial sector was housed primarily in the Banking Bureau, the Securities Bureau, and the Securities and Exchange Surveillance Commission of the Ministry of Finance. However, as a result of the experience of the bubble burst and the ensuing long period of restructuring, it became increasingly recognized that such an arrangement had too many conflicts of interest, and that an independent regulatory agency was needed.

The Bank of Japan (BoJ) also has responsibility for supervising banks. Article 1 of the Bank of Japan Act states that, along with achieving price stability, another purpose of the BoJ is to contribute to financial system stability by ensuring smooth settlement of funds. Financial system stability refers to a situation in which people can lend/borrow or accept/pay money with confidence. A key premise is that financial institutions appropriately manage the risks related to these functions and soundly conduct their business. If financial system stability were to show signs of instability, downside pressure from the financial sector on economic activity might intensify, and an adverse feedback loop between financial and economic activity could emerge. Moreover, the transmission mechanism of monetary policy might be impaired. In this context, financial system stability is also important from the perspective of ensuring price stability (Bank of Japan 2018).

To monitor them, the BoJ conducts on-site examinations by visiting the offices of financial institutions that hold current accounts at the Bank. Also, the BoJ conducts offsite monitoring by analyzing various documents on financial institutions' business activities and by interviewing their executives and staff members. The BoJ can also advise financial institutions to improve their business activities if necessary (Bank of Japan 2018).

If the possibility of systemic risk arising increases despite the BoJ's efforts to identify risks and encourage improvement in financial institutions' business activities from both microprudential and macroprudential perspectives, the BoJ, when necessary, exercises its function as the lender of last resort. If a temporary liquidity shortage at a financial institution results in payment difficulties, the Bank may provisionally provide it with necessary funds. Moreover, the BoJ sometimes has taken extraordinary measures such as purchasing stocks from financial institutions when it was judged necessary to ensure the stability of the financial system (Bank of Japan 2018).

Conclusion

Japan's financial sector has gradually emerged from the trials of the bubble-burst period and the "lost decade," and is generally healthy from a balance sheet perspective. This was demonstrated by the lack of any domestic crisis resulting from the global financial crisis of 2007–2009. It also has a highly developed and sophisticated financial infrastructure. However, profitability is generally low, and growth prospects in the domestic market remain very subdued, primarily due to the aging and outright decline of the population, which is expected to continue for the foreseeable future. Returns on assets, especially bonds, have fallen to very low and even negative rates, hardly an attractive picture for investors. Japanese financial institutions need to look abroad for higher sources of growth. At the same time, they continue to have high cost bases, and these are under increasing threat from new developments in financial technology (fintech).

As noted earlier, a large share of Japan's household assets is tied up in low-risk, principal-guaranteed deposits. This constrains an adequate supply of risk-taking capital in the Japanese economy. A larger share of household asset portfolios needs to be allocated to investment trusts and securities investment. One way to accomplish this would be to allow the postal savings and agricultural cooperatives to sell a full range of financial products. The extensive network of the postal system would then provide convenient access to a variety of competing financial products, including those offered by various private financial institutions.

Also, new financial products such as trust funds and investment trusts should be expanded. These products carry risks, which can be transferred to individuals rather than keeping them in private banks. Much more competition among financial products will create many more channels for financial intermediaries. In order to create much more competition in the financial products, various financial products were allowed to be sold through nationwide post offices and agricultural cooperatives and so forth.

Japanese financial institutions, including banks and insurance companies typically invested large shares of their portfolio in JGBs. However, as mentioned earlier, the supply of JGBs has diminished markedly due to the Bank of Japan' large-scale purchases of them as part of its quantitative easing program. Also, following the introduction of the Bank of Japan's negative interest rate policy, Japanese government bonds in 2016 up to 18 years maturity had negative interest rates, which made it difficult for financial institutions, including Japan Post Bank and Japan Post Insurance, and their holdings have gradually declined, to invest in government bonds. This has mainly been offset by increased investment in foreign securities. However, this introduces greater foreign exchange risk into the portfolios of Japanese institutional investors, an issue of particular concern for insurers and pension funds whose liabilities are basically in yen terms.

Looking toward the future, Japanese banks are facing challenging and difficulties in a changing environment. Development of the fintech companies had started companies' transactions by electronic methods which will reduce transactions' accounts traditional banks. Major investment of government bonds will not achieve a high rate of return for Japanese financial institutions. Competition will become more severe. Large nationwide branch networks will face challenges too. Most financial transactions will be made by mobile phones and internet in the near future, which will make it costly to maintain large branch office networks.

Note

1 Short for "Japanese Association of Securities Dealers Automated Quotation" System.

References

ASEAN+3. 2016. *ASEAN+3 Bond Market Guide 2016: Japan*. Manila: Asian Development Bank. www.adb.org/sites/default/files/publication/198591/asean3-bond-market-guide-2016-jpn.pdf

Bank of Japan. 2018. *The Bank of Japan's Business for Ensuring Financial System Stability*. Tokyo: Bank of Japan. www.boj.or.jp/en/about/outline/data/foboj08.pdf

Cargill, T., and N. Yoshino (2003). *Postal Savings and Fiscal Investment in Japan*. Oxford: Oxford University Press.

General Insurance Association of Japan (GIAJ). 2018. *General Insurance in Japan Fact Book 2016–2017*. Tokyo: General Insurance Association of Japan. www.sonpo.or.jp/en/publication/pdf/fb2017e.pdf

Insurance Information Institute. 2018. *World Insurance Marketplace*. www.iii.org/publications/insurance-handbook/economic-and-financial-data/world-insurance-marketplace

Japan Bankers Association. 2018. *Financial Institutions in Japan*. Tokyo: Japan Bankers Association. www.zenginkyo.or.jp/en/banks/financial-institutions/

Japan Exchange Group. 2018. *Corporate Information*. Tokyo: Japan Exchange Group. www.jpx.co.jp/english/corporate/jpx-profile/index.html

Japan Financial Services Agency (JFSA). 2018. *Financial Services Agency*. Tokyo: Japan Financial Services Agency.

Japan Life Insurance Association. 2018. *Life Insurance Fact Book 2016*. Tokyo: Japan Life Insurance Association. www.seiho.or.jp/english/statistics/trend/

Japan Post Group. 2017. *Japan Post Group Annual Report 2017*. Tokyo: Japan Post Group. www.japanpost.jp/en/ir/library/disclosure/2017/pdf/all.pdf (accessed 29 March 2018).

Japan Post Group. 2018. *History*. Tokyo: Japan Post Group. www.japanpost.jp/en/corporate/changes/

Ministry of Finance. 2017. *Japanese Government Bonds*. Tokyo: Ministry of Finance. www.mof.go.jp/english/jgbs/publication/newsletter/jgb2017_12e.pdf

National Association of Shinkin Banks (NASB). 2017. *What Are Shinkin Banks* (in Japanese). Tokyo: The National Association of Shinkin Banks. www.shinkin.org/shinkin/index.html (accessed 4 December 2017).

Ogura, S., and N. Yoshino. 1988. The Tax System and the Fiscal Investment and Loan Program. In *Industrial Policy of Japan*, edited by R. Komiya, N. Okuno, and K. Suzumura. Tokyo, Japan: Academic Press, pp. 121–153.

Ogura, S., and N. Yoshino. 2004. The Tax System and the Fiscal Investment Loan Program. In *The Japanese Economy: Technology, Foreign Investment and Competition Policies*, edited by P. Drysdale and L. Gower. London and New York: Routledge, pp. 142–156.

Organisation for Economic Co-operation and Development (OECD). 2018. *Household Financial Assets.* Paris: OECD. https://data.oecd.org/hha/household-financial-assets.htm

Relbanks. 2018. www.relbanks.com/worlds-top-banks/assets (accessed 27 March 2018).

Statista. 2018. Largest Exchanges Worldwide as of April 2017, by Equity Market Capitalization (in Billion US Dollars). Hamburg, Germany: Statista. www.statista.com/statistics/264661/domestic-market-capitalization-worldwide-top-10/ (accessed 28 March 2018).

Yoshino, N. forthcoming. Postal Savings and Financial Inclusion in Japan. In *Postal Savings: Reaching Everyone in Asia*, edited by N. Yoshino and M. Helble. Tokyo: Asian Development Bank Institute.

7

BANKING AND FINANCE IN THE REPUBLIC OF KOREA

Kiseok Hong and Jong-Wha Lee

Introduction

The financial sector of the Republic of Korea has continued strong growth over the past decades. The Republic of Korea's financial sector contributed to the country's rapid economic growth by successfully mobilizing domestic resources and channeling them to productive activities. Also, there has been continuous progress toward marketization and liberalization. Despite the significant improvements, when it was hit by two major financial crises in 1997–1998 and 2008, the Republic of Korea's financial system showed significant weaknesses and susceptibility to external shocks.

Over the past decades, the government implemented various restructuring and reform measures to remove the structural weaknesses in the financial sector and improve financial policy and regulatory frameworks. As a result, market participants have developed a heightened appreciation of financial risks and greater emphasis on the efficiency of resource allocation. However, gains of structural reforms have not yet been fully materialized, and there are new shocks and challenges arising to deal with. This chapter reviews the development of the Republic of Korea's financial sector, assesses the structural changes since the 1997–1998 crisis, and examines the major challenges ahead.

Structure and development of the financial sector

Overview

The financial sector of the Republic of Korea has continually expanded in size while simultaneously going through important compositional changes. In accordance with the trend of financial deepening, the total assets of the financial sector have grown faster than GDP. As Table 7.1 shows, the ratio of aggregate financial sector assets to GDP increased from 212% in 2006 to 292% in 2015, which is higher than the average of other East Asian and Southeast Asian economies. Another clear pattern in the Republic of Korea's financial sector development is the diminishing share of banks. Although it was still the most important source of funding for corporations and households, the banking sector accounted for only 58.1% of total financial sector assets in 2015, substantially lower than 72.5% in 2006. The flip side of this was strong

Table 7.1 Total assets of the Republic of Korea's financial institutions

	2006		2010		2015	
	KRW trillion	*%*	*KRW trillion*	*%*	*KRW trillion*	*%*
Banks						
Domestic banks	1,394.2	68.0	1,840.8	61.9	2,398.8	52.7
Foreign bank branches	92.0	4.5	161.6	5.4	247.1	5.4
Non-bank Depository Institutions						
Mutual savings bank	50.8	2.5	86.8	2.9	40.2	0.9
Credit unions	26.3	1.3	47.8	1.6	63.0	1.4
Mutual banking entities					330.8	7.3
Merchant banking corporations	1.2	0.1	1.8	0.1	1.2	0.0
Other Financial Institutions						
Financing companies	67.8	3.3	120.8	4.1	189.8	4.2
Life insurance	265.8	13.0	408.5	13.7	691.0	15.2
Nonlife insurance	55.8	2.7	99.0	3.3	212.4	4.7
Securities companies	92.9	4.5	199.8	6.7	366.3	8.1
Futures companies	1.3	0.1	1.8	0.1	3.4	0.1
Asset management companies	2.1	0.1	3.7	0.1	5.0	0.1
Total	2,050.1	100	2,972.3	100	4,549.0	100
% of GDP	212		235		292	

Source: Financial Supervisory Service (http://fisis.fss.or.kr/fss/fsi).

growth of the non-banking sector including insurance companies and asset management companies. The Republic of Korea has one of the highest insurance penetration rates, exceeded only by three economies (Taipei,China; Hong Kong, China; and South Africa), and ranks 8th in terms of the total premium volume (Swiss Re 2015). An aging population and lack of public safety net may be responsible for this. The expansion of asset management companies can be associated with the rapid growth of the mutual funds market. According to a recent report by Investment Company Institute (2016), net assets of all mutual funds in the Republic of Korea were USD 343.3 billion at end-2015, the 13th largest in the world. Also, the Republic of Korea has the second largest number of mutual funds in operation, after Luxembourg. However, the high number of mutual funds in the Republic of Korea partly reflects over-flourishing of minor funds which may hamper efficiency in asset management.

The patterns in Table 7.1 suggest that direct financial markets are becoming increasingly important in the Republic of Korea. Table 7.2 shows the development of direct financial markets in detail. In the money market, commercial paper and repurchase agreements (RP) account for the largest share, with their collective value growing by more than 200% between 2000 and 2014. Also, RPs play a key role in the monetary policy as the Bank of Korea uses RP transactions (mostly with seven-day maturities) in steering the overnight call rate — used in the adjustment of temporary surpluses or shortages of funds by financial institutions — around the target policy rate. Short-term government securities with maturity less than one year are not available in the Republic of Korea. In the capital market, market capitalization of listed stocks has more than sextupled since 2000, with the ratio of total market cap to GDP reaching 90% in 2014. The bond market exhibits a similar pattern. The stock market return, as measured by annual percentage changes in the Korea Composite Stock Price Index (KOSPI), was 8.3% on

Table 7.2 The Republic of Korea's capital market

	2000		2010		2014	
	KRW trillion	*%*	*KRW trillion*	*%*	*KRW trillion*	*%*
Money Market[1]	*138.8*	*100*	*267.6*	*100*	*338.9*	*100*
Call	16.1	11.6	22.5	8.4	17.9	5.3
RP	26.1	18.8	76.9	28.7	104.0	30.7
CP	44.7	32.2	80.9	30.2	119.4	35.2
CD	14.2	10.2	44.5	16.6	20.1	5.9
Cover bills	11.2	8.1	1.6	0.6	1.3	0.4
Monetary stabilization bonds (short-term)	26.5	19.1	41.1	15.4	55.2	16.3
Asset backed short-term bond					21.0	6.2
	KRW trillion		KRW trillion		KRW trillion	
Capital Market	614.2		2,352.0		2,791.5	
Stocks[2]	217.1		1,236.8		1,335.3	
Bonds[1]	398.2		1,074.1		1,401.0	

CP = commercial papers, CD = certificate of deposit, RP = repurchase agreement.

Notes: [1]period end balance, [2]market capitalization.

Source: Bank of Korea, Korea Exchange.

average during the 2000–2015 period. Foreign ownership of stocks and bonds has been stable around the average of 32% and 6.5%, respectively, since 2010 (Financial Supervisory Service, various years).

However, the development of capital markets did not directly translate into corresponding changes in corporate financing. As can be seen in Figure 7.1, the ratio of direct financing (bonds and equities) to indirect financing (loans) for non-financial corporations has been roughly stable since 2003. Also, the ratio is far lower than that of more advanced economies. This suggest that, while large corporations may be turning to direct financing through bonds and stocks, the overall corporate sector is still largely dependent on loans from banks and non-bank financial institutions. This pattern is not fully consistent with the view that banks and capital markets provide different financial services and that the relative importance of banks and capital markets naturally changes as economies develop (Demirgüç-Kunt, Feyen, and Levine 2013). Banks are believed to be more effective in financing standardized and lower-risk projects, while capital markets have comparative advantages in financing higher-risk, longer-run projects. As a result, banks can play a greater role in the early stage of economic development but the role of capital markets becomes more important as economies mature. In the Republic of Korea, the evidence is rather weak, with the share of banks remaining relatively stable in corporate finance.

The source-of-funds data reveal that the expansion of the capital market can be attributed mostly to the development of the government sector. The rapid expansion of government debt directly contributed to the growth of the Republic of Korea's bond market. Government debt increased persistently since the Asian financial crisis, from 12% of GDP in 1997 to 36% of GDP in 2015. The trend was initiated by government-led structural reforms during the Asian crisis under which public funds were raised and injected into troubled financial institutions. In subsequent years, other factors – such as construction of large-scale social overhead capital (SOC)

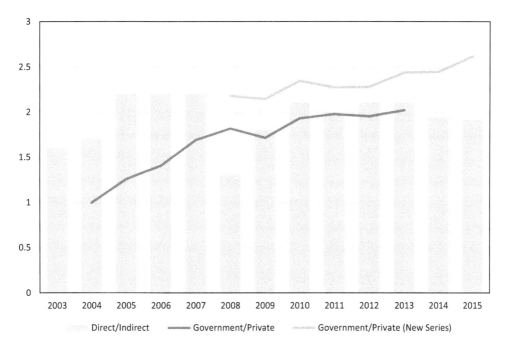

Figure 7.1   The development of the capital market

Notes: Direct/Indirect: the ratio of direct financing (bonds and equities) to indirect financing (loans) for non-financial corporations.

Government/Private: the ratio of government bonds to corporate bonds.
Government/Private (New Series): a new series of the ratio government bonds to corporate bonds.

Source: Bank of Korea, Flow of Funds.

projects and public rental housing units, regional development policies, and the expansionary fiscal stance[1] following the 2008 global crisis – contributed to the trend of government debt expansion. As the growth of government bonds exceeded that of corporate bonds, the proportion of government bonds in total outstanding bond issued increased continuously from 13% in 2004 to about 20% in 2013.

Along with the trend of financial deepening, loans to the household sector have also expanded. While the net financial asset position (i.e., a sum of cash, deposits, and financial security holdings minus gross debt) of the household sector as a whole remained stable and even increasing as a percentage of GDP, household borrowings have increased rather sharply since 2008, causing concerns about possible defaults and forced deleveraging by households. Over a longer term, however, the ratio of total household loans to total corporate loans has been roughly stable.

Structural changes since the 1997–1998 crisis

Prior to the 1997–1998 crisis, there has been a large increase in foreign capital inflows following financial liberalization and deregulations. Between 1994 and 1996, net foreign capital inflows amounted to USD 52.3 billion, more than three times the total net inflows for the 1990–1993 period. The interest differentials between the Republic of Korea and the rest of the world and between short-term and long-term borrowings, combined with partial and unbalanced deregulations and the lack of market principles, caused a surge in dollar-denominated short-term liabilities especially among non-bank institutions. Most of the increased credit was channeled to finance long-term investment by domestic corporations, generating severe currency and maturity mismatches.

After the 1997–1998 crisis, the government implemented various restructuring measures including financial sector reform plans. It continued the efforts to remove structural weaknesses in the financial sector and improve macroeconomic and financial policy frameworks (Lee and Rhee 2007). Financial sector reforms started with an injection of public capital and purchase of non-performing loans for financial institutions. When possible, the government sold troubled financial institutions to foreign investors. Once the economy recovered from the crisis and the financial sector stabilized, gradual privatization of banks and redemption of public funds were pursued. In the process of privatization, government shares of financial institutions were sold to the private sector including foreign investors.

One of the most notable changes in the financial system that took place through the structural reform was financial consolidation and conglomeration (Hahm 2008). During the drastic restructuring of the financial sector that required public funds of approximately 30% of the Republic of Korea's GDP in 2000, the government promoted purchases and assumptions and mergers and acquisitions among financial institutions to reduce the total number of financial institutions to 1,315 by the end of 2006, from 2,103 prior to the crisis. In particular, weaker banks with a capital adequacy ratio below the 8% threshold were acquired by healthier banks, and healthier banks were encouraged to form financial holding companies together with non-bank financial institutions.[2] As a result, the number of commercial banks dropped from 26 at the end of 1997 to 14 in 2005, and four major banks – Woori, KB Kookmin, Shinhan, and Hana – became a subsidiary of their respective holding companies by 2008.[3] Confirming the trend of market concentration, the Herfindahl-Hirshman index (He HI), calculated from deposit market shares of individual banks, increased from 772 in 1999 to 1,158 in 2014 (Suh 2016). The increased market concentration, however, may not necessarily imply that the banking industry became less competitive.[4]

Consolidation and conglomeration in the banking sector was followed by immediate improvement in profitability and financial soundness of banking institutions (Figure 7.2). However, the improvement may have been caused by short-term impacts of public fund injection and temporary cost cuts through rationalization of branches and employees, rather than by economies of scale and/or scope that the structural reform was aiming for. As will be discussed in the next section, the profitability of the Republic of Korea's banking sector still remains low by international standards. Also, as mentioned earlier, the share of the banking sector in corporate financing has been stagnant. Large corporations with high credit shifted to internal financing and capital markets, generating limited demand for bank loans. At the same time, banks, which have grown more risk averse since the 1998 crisis, have increased their collateralized loans to the household sector instead of providing unsecured loans to small and medium-sized enterprises (SMEs). This is consistent with the existing evidence on how banks shift their portfolios in response to capital constraints and enforcement of supervisory regulations (Peek and Rosengren 1995). It also suggests that the Republic of Korea's banking sector has yet to develop more effective credit risk evaluation skills and diversified business models.

In order to support SME lending, the government has been providing loan guarantees. As of 2014, the Republic of Korea's government-guaranteed loans for SMEs as a proportion of GDP was 4.1%, the third highest among 26 OECD member countries, next to Greece (9.2%) and Japan (5.7%) (OECD 2016). Also, the interest rate spread between SMEs and large firms dropped from 79 basis points in 2008 to 18 basis points in 2014 with almost automatic rollovers,

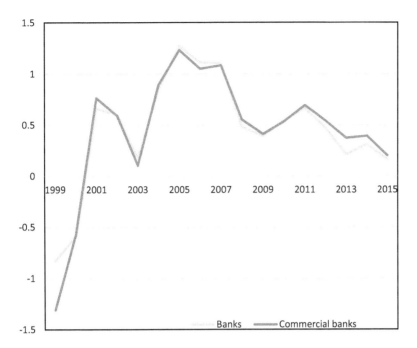

Figure 7.2   Return on asset (ROA) of the banking sector (in percentage)

Notes: Banks include both commercial banks and special banks. Special banks refer to state-run banks such as Industrial Bank of Korea, Korea Development Bank, National Federation of Fisheries Cooperatives, and NongHyup Bank.

Source: Financial Supervisory Service (http://fisis.fss.or.kr/fss/fsi).

probably "because of the government's advice" (OECD 2016). Despite these government policies, however, the share of SME lending in total bank loans gradually decreased from a peak of 91.4% in 2006 to 77.3% in 2015 (Bank of Korea, various years). This confirms the view that capital constraints and strengthened supervisory regulations that followed the crisis made banks prefer large firms and households over SMEs.

Another notable development in the Republic of Korea's financial sector after the 1998 crisis was the establishment of a newly integrated financial regulatory framework. In particular, four previously separate supervisory agencies were consolidated into the Financial Supervisory Service (FSS) in order to provide supervision of the whole financial sector in close cooperation with its decision-making body, the Financial Supervisory Commission (FSC). The Republic of Korea's supervisory authorities have implemented various microprudential regulation measures, including forward-looking criteria and the Basel capital adequacy ratio, and requirements on the deposit and/or loan ratio and the liquid asset and/or liquid debt ratio.

In many economies hit by the financial crisis, the lack of system-wide macroprudential oversight allowed systemic failures to occur in the financial system. Within the existing regulatory framework, which emphasizes microprudential supervision over individual institutions and specific financial instruments, the authorities were unable to identify the buildup of systematic risks and revealed its incompetence in introducing effective regulation for increasingly interdependent financial institutions and markets. Another major weakness in the regulatory and supervisory structure was its inability in tackling the innate procyclicality of financial systems.

Building up an adequate framework of macroprudential oversight can counter the procyclical effects of prudential regulations.

Even before the 2008 global financial crisis, the Republic of Korea had strong regulations on residential mortgage lending by introducing conservative loan-to-value (LTV) and debt-to-income (DTI) ratio requirements. The LTV ratio was introduced in 2002, responding to sharp increases in housing prices, and then complemented by the DTI ratio requirement in 2005. Since then, the authority repeatedly tightened and loosened the regulation depending on the economic circumstances.

Since the onset of the global financial crisis, authorities have introduced a number of macroprudential policies to mitigate procyclicality of the banking sector, to identify the buildup of systemic risks, and to monitor liquidity and foreign exchange vulnerabilities of the banking system. The policies include a series of measures such as a ceiling on the banks' loan-to-deposit ratio in 2009, a regulation on banks' foreign exchange derivatives positions in 2010, and a macroprudential stability levy (a levy on non-core foreign currency liabilities held by domestic and foreign banks) in 2011. These measures contributed to improving financial sector resilience and systemic stability (Bruno and Shin 2014; IMF 2014).

Macroprudential policies in the Republic of Korea have been conducted mainly at the discretion of the relevant financial authorities, while being coordinated through a range of inter-agency meetings. During the crisis, the agencies gathered in formal and informal inter-agency meetings to assess systemic risk and discuss policy measures at various levels. On July 2012, a Macroeconomic and Finance Meeting at the deputy level was set up by involving the five major agencies – the Ministry of Strategy and Finance (MOSF), Bank of Korea (BOK), Korea Deposit Insurance Corporation (KDIC), FSC, and FSS. The MOSF is in charge of developing and integrating economic and fiscal policies, and of making decisions in the other agencies as the financial regulator. In addition to its price stability mandate, the BOK is responsible to "pay attention to financial stability in carrying out its monetary and credit policies."[5] The KDIC contributes to the protection of depositors and the maintenance of the stability of the financial system. The five agencies have cross representation at key decision-making levels (IMF 2015a).

To further enhance financial stability, the government tried to set up the improved and effective crisis management and resolution mechanism. In accordance with the relevant laws and enforcement decrees, the five financial authorities together play a comprehensive role to identify, monitor, and tackle threats to financial stability in the event of a financial crisis (IMF 2015a). The FSC is in charge of financial sector and supervisory policies, including early intervention and resolution of troubled financial institutions. The FSS is an integrated supervisor for all supervised financial entities and operates under the guidance of the FSC. The FSC and KDIC are assigned to serve as the resolution authorities for distressed financial institutions, with the FSC acting as the lead authority. The BOK is responsible to support a financial safety net by its comprehensive liquidity facilities including emergency liquidity assistance. The KDIC provides a deposit insurance scheme that protects depositors in the banking and non-banking sectors, up to KRW 50 million per depositor in each covered financial institution.

Major challenges and issues

Coping with volatile capital flows

The Republic of Korea's financial sector has been closely linked to global financial markets, remaining highly exposed to volatile cross-border capital flows. It was in 1997 and 1998 when Korea was hit by the Asian financial crisis triggered by a huge, sudden reversal of short-term capital flows. The balance sheets of financial institutions in the Republic of Korea deteriorated. Banks suffered from double mismatch problems – currency and maturity mismatches.

The Republic of Korea showed a speedy recovery from the crisis with swift macroeconomic adjustment and structural reforms. Despite significant progress in strengthening financial resilience and soundness, however, the economy experienced another significant financial distress in the year of 2008 when the global financial crisis prompted a large outflow of foreign capital (Figure 7.3). The intensified global liquidity shortage disrupted the cross-border funding from global banks and international money markets. The sudden reversal of short-term foreign currency borrowings caused significant instability in the financial sector. As shown in Figure 7.4, during the fourth quarter of 2008 after the failure of Lehman Brothers, the short-term liabilities of the banking sector fell by over USD 50 billion.

Relatively high volatility of capital flows partially resulted from the activities of foreign bank branches in the Republic of Korea that accounted for about 40% of the banking sector's foreign debt in 2008, of which relatively little was balanced by foreign assets (Tsutsumi, Jones, and Cargill 2010). The gross liabilities of domestic branches of foreign banks fell sharply, reflecting financial and economic troubles in their home countries.

The authorities' timely and comprehensive responses helped the financial sector restore its stability quickly in early 2009 (Tsutsumi, Jones, and Cargill 2010; IMF 2014). The Bank of Korea, rapidly shifting its stance to expansionary monetary policy, cut the policy interest rate six times from 5.25% in October 2008 to 2% in February 2009 and provided KRW 28 trillion (2.7% of GDP) in order to alleviate the credit crunch. The government and public

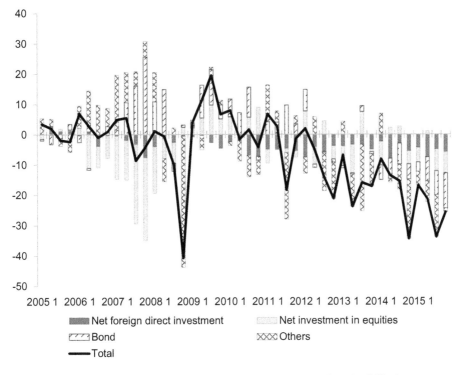

Figure 7.3 The Republic of Korea's capital account, 2005–2015 (quarterly, USD billion)

Source: Compiled from Bank of Korea.

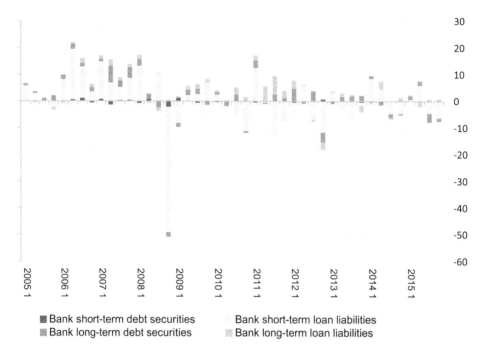

Figure 7.4 Capital flows to the banking sector, 2005–2015 (quarterly, USD billion)

Source: Compiled from Bank of Korea.

organizations together created a KRW 10 trillion Bond Market Stabilization Fund to pro-vide additional liquidity to the market. The government strengthened financial institutions by injecting capital into banks through a KRW 20 trillion Bank Recapitalization Fund. The government also established a KRW 40 trillion Corporate Restructuring Fund to address the bad asset problem in financial institutions.

The government promised USD 100 billion payment guarantee in banks' short-term liabili-ties in October 2008. The Bank of Korea actively sought for currency swap deals. It signed a USD 30 billion currency swap agreement with the US Federal Reserve in October 2008, and expanded the volume of the bilateral KRW-JPY swap arrangement with the Bank of Japan from the equivalent of USD 3 billion to USD 20 billion.

Thanks to the efforts made by the authorities as well as the global liquidity injection by central banks in major advanced economies, the financial markets showed a quick recovery in net capital inflows. However, volatile capital flows have frequently destabilized the Republic of Korea's financial markets (Figure 7.3). Amid the reversal of the Fed's monetary policy with the tapering of the long-term securities purchases and the increase in interest rate, the Republic of Korea's currency value and asset prices substantially dropped due to the capital outflows.

As a consequence of the government's continuous efforts to eliminate the economy's financial vulnerabilities, the financial system became more transparent and resilient, which would help maintain foreign confidence and better respond to external shocks. In fact, the financial sector has been less affected by financial turmoil than other emerging markets over the recent years (IMF 2015b). However, as an export-oriented economy with an open capital account and non-reserve currency, the country still remains vulnerable to broad contagion from global financial market turbulence. Volatile capital flows are one of the major challenges the economy continues to face.

How to improve profitability of banks?

The financial sector restructuring efforts led by the government after the 1997–1998 crisis caused remarkable improvement in capital adequacy and profitability of financial institutions and contributed to the economy's quick recovery from the crisis. With a debt guarantee by the government, the KAMCO (Korea Asset Management Corporation) and the KDIC were able to raise an adequate amount of public funds that was subsequently used for equity participation, non-performing loan purchases, and deposit payoffs. As a result, the Basel capital ratio of commercial banks increased from 8.2% in 1998 to 12% in 2005 and the return on assets (ROA) increased from −3.3% to 1.23% during the same period. However, while capital adequacy continued to improve subsequently, profitability of banks deteriorated after reaching a peak in 2005 (Figure 7.2). The ROA of banks was 0.38% in 2013, substantially lower than the world average of 1.28% (The Banker 2014).

The recent downward trend in bank profitability suggests that the improvement in ROA that immediately followed the financial restructuring was of temporary nature. As mentioned earlier, larger and fewer banks created through financial restructuring did exhibit an improvement in profitability, at least for the first few years. This is consistent with the common perception that market concentration and profitability are positively correlated (Gilbert 1984; Berger et al. 2004). Banks in a concentrated market may achieve high profitability for two reasons: first, the increased market power enables banks to extract non-competitive rents; second, only those banks with superior efficiency can increase their relative market shares, leading to higher market concentration and an improvement in overall market efficiency. However, the profit increase of banks did not last long. Under the new oligopolistic market structure, banks tried to maintain or increase their market share by competitively expanding their assets. The banks' race for size generated increased competition for deposits and a greater reliance on wholesale funding, which in turn implied higher funding costs. At the same time, interest rates remained low worldwide, reducing the net interest margin for banks from 2.81% in 2005 to 1.54% in 2015.

While the decreasing net interest margin was not confined to the Republic of Korea, it was particularly consequential for banks whose main revenue source had been interest income. The Republic of Korea's banks still generate about 90% of total revenue from retail banking and have very limited non-interest-income business. For US banks, the share of interest income in total revenue is about two-thirds. It appears that, despite the financial consolidation and conglomeration in the banking sector, economies of scope or financial synergies have not yet materialized. At the same time, financial deregulation and the development of new financial technology (fintech) are causing competition from non-bank institutions. In attempts to cope with these problems and improve profitability, banks are searching to develop more diversified business models and increase the share of non-interest income. The government also has been encouraging banks to further diversify the revenue sources and to explore global markets.

It is not clear how profitability of the Republic of Korea's banks will evolve in the future. According to exiting studies, the effect of market concentration on the profitability of banks is ambiguous, both theoretically and empirically. For example, the X-inefficiency hypothesis argues that high concentration may reduce incentives to minimize costs, thereby causing inefficiencies in production that may offset efficiency gains from economies of scale. Among empirical studies on the Republic of Korea's banking sector, Park (2011) finds that consolidation of banks resulted in an increase in X-inefficiency along with other measures of inefficiency but no clear benefits from economies of scale or economies of scope. Also, to the extent that the risk-return trade-off holds, the relationship between market concentration and the risk-taking behavior of banks may have important implications regarding profitability. Previous studies provide conflicting results on this as well (see, for example, Beck, Demirguc-Kunt, and Levine 2006; Boyd and De Nicolo 2005).

In the Republic of Korea, regardless of increased market concentration, bank loans to large corporations and households grew more rapidly than loans to SMEs, suggesting that banks have become more cautious after going through the two financial crises in 1998 and 2008. The increasing weight on low-risk loans has been another contributing factor to the low profitability.

To summarize, financial consolidation and conglomeration in the Republic of Korea has not yet resulted in a sustainable increase in bank profitability. In order to achieve an uptrend and stability in profit margins, banks will have to develop better risk evaluation methods, to diversify revenue sources, and to reduce dependence on the domestic market.

Household and corporate debt

Household debt has been increasing steadily in the Republic of Korea since the 2000s. The Republic of Korea's household debt to GDP ratio was about 85% in 2015, substantially higher than its 2002 value of 65% and the OECD average of 75%. The expansion of household debt caused growing concerns that it can potentially weaken financial sector stability and become a drag on domestic consumption. In fact, several survey results show that financial market participants regard the surge in household debt as one of the greatest systemic risks to the Republic of Korea's financial sector.

An increase in household debt may arise for two reasons: asset acquisition (or debt repayment) and consumption smoothing. For households, the primary reason for debt financing has been acquisition of assets such as houses and other real estates. According to the Survey of Household Finances and Living Conditions data for 2010 through 2015, people responded that about one-third of their debt holding was caused for asset acquisition purpose. Another one-third of household debt corresponded to homeowners' holding of rental deposit. Under the Republic of Korea's unique rental system called *Jeonse*, the tenant pays the landlord a large fixed-sum deposit, amounting to 50%–90% of the house purchase price, instead of monthly rent. Due to its large magnitude, Jeonse deposits account for a major portion of household debt.[6] Since Jeonse is essentially a housing repo contract where the landlord borrows from the tenant putting up the house as collateral, the homeowner's holding of Jeonse deposit can also be regarded as a mode of debt financing for asset acquisition (Kim and Shin 2013). Of the remaining portion of household debt, about 20% was for business financing and about 15% for consumption financing.

Various factors contributed to the high and increasing household borrowings for asset acquisition. First, the traditionally high housing price generated proportionately large demand for mortgage loans. Second, the record low interest rates combined with more risk-conscious lending practices by financial institutions expanded the market for collateralized loans. Third, as the accessibility of households to the formal financial sector increased, landlords switched from the direct financing through the Jeonse system to the indirect financing through financial intermediaries. Since the official aggregate measures of household debt does not include Jeonse deposits, the replacement of Jeonse deposits with bank loans contributed to an increase in the aggregate household debt measure.

Considering the composition of household debt in the Republic of Korea, the likelihood of mass bankruptcy in the household sector appears to be low. Most household debt has an offsetting asset, and the financial supervisory authority has been actively using prudence measures such as LTV and DTI regulations since 2006. As a result, the household debt delinquency rate has remained low since the 2000s and even decreased recently from 1.1% in 2005 to 0.5% in

2015, suggesting that financial soundness of households is still in place. Also, most stress tests on household debt report that, even under pessimistic scenarios, the overall debt delinquency ratio will increase only marginally and have limited impacts on the balance sheet of first-tier financial institutions. It is noted, however, that the subset of households who have borrowings from the second-tier financial market has higher DTI and LTV ratios and thus is more susceptible to negative shocks, such as an increase in the interest rate and a fall in the property price.

A similar statement can be made about corporate debt. Although the overall balance sheet of the corporate sector does not pose immediate systemic risks, there exist troubled firms in certain industries – including steel, shipbuilding, and shipping – that have been particularly susceptible to the global economic crisis and thus are in great need of restructuring.

Since the 1997–1998 Asian crisis, corporate leverage in the Republic of Korea has continued to decrease. The debt and/or equity ratio, which was 3.41 on average during 1999–2004, declined to 2.75 in 2008, and to 1.37 in 2014. The rapid deleveraging, initially imposed by the government for corporate restructuring, was further strengthened by changed attitudes of corporations and financial institutions toward risk. As investment decisions started to be made with a heightened appreciation of risk, the investment rate decreased and firms became less dependent on external debt financing. This, combined with accommodative interest rate policy, contributed to improving financial health of corporations as measured by the interest coverage ratio.

However, aggregate measures do not provide a full account of corporate debt issues. There are concerns that a relatively large portion of corporate debt is concentrated in firms with high leverage and low profitability. For example, IMF (2015b) points out that almost 20% of corporate debt is owed by firms with negative profits and 20% by firms with the interest rate coverage ratio below one. Also, as Figure 7.5 shows, the NPL ratio of domestic banks, measured by the proportion of "substandard-or-below" loans, has been gradually increasing since 2006.[7] The

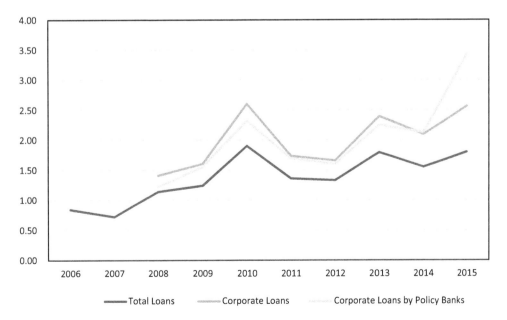

Figure 7.5   The proportion of non-performing (substandard-or-below) loans of domestic banks (in percentage)

Source: Financial Supervisory Service (http://fisis.fss.or.kr/fss/fsi).

increase in the NPL ratio was more pronounced for the specialized policy banks including the Korea Development Bank and Korea EXIM Bank.

These features suggest that the credit allocation practice of financial institutions in the Republic of Korea still needs improvement. In particular, inefficiencies inherent in state-run policy banks need to be adequately addressed.

Public pension funds and demographic changes

The Republic of Korea has the world's most rapidly aging population. The proportion of elderly people aged 65 or above is forecast to reach over 37% by 2050 (Korea Statistical Information Service 2012). The rapid trend of population aging will have fundamental structural impacts on all of the economy including the financial sector.

According to the life-cycle variation in consumption and saving, there will be massive accumulation of assets by the working-age population for the next few decades. A prominent example is the expansion of pension funds including the National Pension Fund. The Republic of Korea's National Pension Fund managing assets of KRW 533 trillion as of end-May 2016 or 34% of GDP, the third largest of its kind in the world, is expected to continue to expand for the next decade.[8] The widening of the gap between supply and demand for capital will cause a decreasing trend in the rate of return. These changes imply that there will be increasing demand for efficient asset management and supporting financial infrastructure.

The management of the National Pension Fund so far has been marked by low risk exposure and a high weight to domestic assets. As a result, the rate of return on the National Pension Fund has been relatively low compared to other major funds (KDI 2015). Also, because of the dominant size of the National Pension Fund market, various issues of market power and illiquidity may arise with respect to the Fund's transactions in the domestic market. In order to reduce these problems and to achieve more efficient asset management, pension funds will have to develop measures for enhanced global diversification and better governance structure.

Improving corporate governance of the financial sector

To develop a robust financial system and increase the competitiveness of the financial sector, the Republic of Korea should tackle poor governance of financial institutions. Since the Asian financial crisis in 1997–1998, the government introduced a series of reforms in the financial sector, notably the introduction of outside directors and audit committees. With the slow pace of progress, the financial sector has faced criticism for insufficient checks and balances of outside directors and disproportionately strong control of managers.

In the aftermath of the crisis, there were concerns that information asymmetries and misaligned incentives in the financial markets caused short-sightedness and excessive risk-taking behaviors of management and employees in the financial firms. At the same time, there were strong demands for reinforcing the internal risk management by reforming compensation schemes, for increasing the role of the board of directors in risk oversight, and for changing procedures to evaluate credit and trading decisions.

The weakness in the succession of the chief executive officer (CEO) was also pointed out as a problem. The Republic of Korea's financial holding companies and banks had higher uncertainties in the CEO turnover process, compared to global financial companies, which increased management instability and thereby reduced corporate value.

The FSC issued a model corporate governance code for financial companies in December 2014. The Law on Corporate Governance passed the National Assembly in 2015 and was enacted in August 2016. The new law is expected to enhance transparency and soundness in corporate governance rules and strengthen internal control and risk management (Lee, S 2015). It explicitly states the roles and authorities of the board of directors, increasing independence of outside directors. It improves independence of the chief risk officer and the chief compliance officer from the CEO, and changes compensation schemes to reduce excessive risk-taking. The law requires the board to establish an internal regulation on the CEO succession plan. Financial companies and institutions are required to disclose their internal rules and practices on corporate governance. Effective implementation of the law is expected to significantly enhance corporate governance of the financial sector.

Balancing between innovation and regulation

Financial innovation, like many other modern technologies, comes with benefits and risks. In theory, financial innovation improves allocative efficiency of financial resources, mitigates risks and hence ultimately enhances economic growth and welfare. However, the global financial crisis has highlighted the dangers of unrestrained financial innovation. Modern, sophisticated finance has become complex, obscure, and excessively leveraged. As such, in regard to financial innovation, the ways to improve transparency and to set up the right incentives system must be addressed. How to stimulate and effectively manage innovation without stifling it is one of the key challenges that the policy-makers need to deal with.

Recently financial technology, or "fintech," has been a buzzword not just in the Republic of Korea but worldwide. This unprecedented financial innovation including digital payment and money transfer services, crowdfunding, and automated wealth management, is considered to disrupt the traditional banking system. However, in the Republic of Korea, the development of the fintech sector has been slow. Only a few new fintech firms have been successful so far, while traditional financial companies continue to be the dominant providers in online financial services. The development of the fintech sector was slow mainly due to the government regulation on financial sectors such as separation of industrial and financial capital, pre-registering requirements, and compulsory authentication requirements in online purchases.

The government has recently embarked on a series of policies to nurture the fintech industry. However, it faces a challenge of creating a favorable environment with relaxed regulations for fintech start-ups, while at the same time reinforcing adequate standards on security and protection for consumers in the sector (Lee, Y 2015). The financial regulatory structure must continue to upgrade the institutional capacity and policies to keep in step with rapid financial innovation.

Notes

1 While the consolidated budget balance of the central government has recorded a surplus in most years, the operational balance (defined as the consolidated budget balance minus social security balance plus redemption of public funds and perceived as a better indicator of fiscal soundness) has been persistently negative.

2 By Fair Trade Act and Financial Holding Company Act, *chaebols* (Republic of Korea's non-financial conglomerates) are limited in owning shares of banks. In the non-banking sector, however, chaebols own an increasingly large number of financial companies.

3 Woori Financial Group, established in 2001 as the first financial holding company in Republic of Korea, was later merged into Woori Bank in 2014.

4 Suh (2016) finds that the Panzar and Rosse H-statistic, a measure of industry competition, has been strictly positive since 1999 with the average of 0.6 and even increased after the 2008 global financial crisis.

5 Article 1 of the Bank of Korea Act.

6 However, Jeonse deposit is not included in official aggregate measures of household debt.

7 According to the Financial Supervisory Service, the NPL ratio of Republic of Korea banks, 1.71% as of 2015, was higher than the comparable ratio of US (1.59%) and Japan (1.53%).

8 National Pension Service Investment Management (http://fund.nps.or.kr/jsppage/fund/fund_main_e.jsp).

References

Bank of Korea. Various Years. *Financial Market Trends*. Seoul: Bank of Korea.

Beck, T., A. Demirguc-Kunt, and R. Levine. 2006. Bank Supervision and Corruption in Lending. *Journal of Monetary Economics* 53: 2131–2163.

Berger, A., A. Demirguc-Kunt, R. Levine, and J. G. Haubrich. 2004. Bank Concentration and Competition: An Evolution in the Making. *Journal of Money, Credit and Banking* 36(3): 433–451.

Boyd, J. H., and G. De Nicoló. 2005. The Theory of Bank Risk-Taking and Competition Revisited. *Journal of Finance* 60(3): 1329–1343.

Bruno, V., and H. S. Shin. 2014. Assessing Macroprudential Policies: Case of South Korea. *The Scandinavian Journal of Economics* 116(1): 128–157.

Demirgüç-Kunt, A., E. Feyen, and R. Levine. 2013. The Evolving Importance of Banks and Securities Markets. *World Bank Economic Review* 27(3): 476–490.

Financial Supervisory Service. Various Years. *Securities Investment by Foreign Investors*. Seoul: Financial Supervisory Service.

Gilbert, R. 1984. Bank Market Structure and Competition: A Survey. *Journal of Money, Credit and Banking* 16(4): 617–644.

Hahm, J. 2008. Ten Years After the Crisis: Financial System Transition in Korea. In *Ten Years After the Korean Crisis: Crisis, Adjustment and Long-run Economic Growth*, edited by M. Karasulu and D. Yang. Seoul: Korea Institute for International Economic Policy.

International Monetary Fund. 2014. *Republic of Korea Financial System Stability Assessment*. Washington, DC: International Monetary Fund.

International Monetary Fund. 2015a. *Republic of Korea Financial Sector Assessment Program – Crisis Preparedness and Crisis Management Framework – Technical Note*. Washington, DC: International Monetary Fund.

International Monetary Fund. 2015b. Republic of Korea 2015 Article IV Consultation – Staff Report; Press Release; and Statement by the Executive Director for the Republic of Korea. IMF Country Report No. 15/130. Washington, DC: International Monetary Fund.

Investment Company Institute. 2016. *2016 Investment Company Factbook*. Washington, DC: Investment Company Institute.

Kim, S., and H. Shin. 2013. Financing Growth without Banks: Korean Housing Repo Contract. 2013 Meeting Paper No. 328, Society for Economic Dynamics.

Korea Development Institute (KDI). 2015. *KDI Focus*, 15 May. Seoul: Korea Development Institute.

Korea Statistical Information Service. 2012. Population Projections. http://kosis.kr/eng/statisticsList/statisticsList_01List.jsp?vwcd=MT_ETITLE&parentId=A#SubCont (accessed 12 August 2016).

Lee, S.-Y. 2015. Keys to Effective Implementation of the Law on Corporate Governance of Financial Companies in Korea. *KIF Weekly Financial Brief* 15(22): 2–3.

Lee, Y. 2015. Key Considerations for Fintech Innovation in Korea. *KIF Weekly Financial Brief* 15(10): 6–7.

Lee, J.-W., and C. Rhee. 2007. Crisis and Recovery: What We Have Learned from the South Korean Experience? *Asian Economic Policy Review* 2(1): 146–164.

Organization for Economic Cooperation and Development (OECD). 2016. *Financing SMEs and Entrepreneurs 2016*. Paris: OECD.

Park, K. 2011. What Happened to Efficiency and Competition After Bank Mergers and Consolidation in Korea? *KDI Journal of Economic Policy* 33(3): 33–55.

Peek, J., and E. Rosengren. 1995. The Capital Crunch: Neither a Borrower Nor a Lender Be. *Journal of Money, Credit and Banking* 27(3): 625–638.

Suh, J. 2016. *Market Competition in Korea's Banking Industry and the Implications*. Seoul: Korea Institute of Finance.

Swiss Re. 2015. *World Insurance in 2015: Steady Growth and Regional Disparities*. Zurich: Swiss Re.

The Banker. 2014. *Top 1000 World Banks 2014*. London: The Banker.

Tsutsumi, M., R. S. Jones, and T. F. Cargill. 2010. The Korean Financial System: Overcoming the Global Financial Crisis and Addressing Remaining Problems. OECD Economics Department Working Paper No. 796. Paris: OECD Publishing.

8

FINANCIAL SYSTEM IN MALAYSIA

Sukudhew Singh

Introduction

In the aftermath of the Asian financial crisis, it became apparent to policy-makers in Malaysia that the concentration of financing in the banking system and the fragmented nature of the financial system were a major source of vulnerability to the economy. With rising international economic and financial integration, that vulnerability was likely to get larger as the economy experienced more frequent external shocks. Policy-makers acted preemptively and initiated steps to undertake a consolidation and deepening of the financial system, even as they progressively undertook financial liberalization and increased the overall level of competition in the financial system. This chapter describes the results of those efforts. It looks at the overall structure of the financial system, the institutional and legal framework, the governance and oversight of financial stability, as well as some of the policy issues and dilemmas faced by policy-makers today.

Structure of the Malaysian financial system

The Malaysian financial sector has changed significantly over the past two decades. Malaysia today is home to a modern, sound, progressive, and inclusive financial system that is well connected regionally and globally. The financial sector caters for a full range of products and services delivered seamlessly through a dual financial system comprising both conventional and Islamic finance. As at end-2015, the size of the financial system stood at MYR 4.6 trillion (or 400% of GDP), from MYR 1.2 trillion (351% of GDP) in 2000.[1]

The recent evolution of Malaysia's financial sector is a result of holistic and planned reforms undertaken since the Asian financial crisis. A series of 10-year development master plans have reshaped the Malaysian financial landscape in terms of its institutions, markets, systems, infrastructure, and regulatory and supervisory frameworks (Figures 8.1 and 8.2).[2]

The role of financial institutions

The Malaysian financial sector is well developed and diversified, with a wide range of domestic and foreign financial institutions (Table 8.1). The banking system comprises commercial banks,

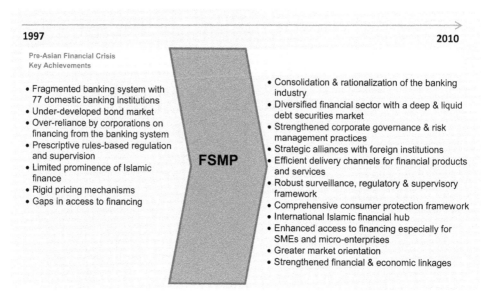

Figure 8.1 Evolution of the Malaysian financial sector under the financial sector masterplan 2001–2010 (FSMP)

Source: Compiled by author.

Islamic banks, and investment banks, and has total assets of approximately MYR 2.4 trillion or over 200% of GDP as at the end of 2015 (Figure 8.3a). Commercial banks are the most prominent providers of funds, performing a broad spectrum of banking activities including acceptance of deposits, giving loans, and providing payment and remittance services. Islamic banks conduct a similar range of banking activities based on Shariah principles.[3] Meanwhile, investment banks are primarily involved in capital market activities such as dealing in securities and corporate advisory services. Malaysia's banking system now consists of 27 commercial banks (8 domestic and 19 foreign), 16 Islamic banks, and 11 investment banks. Collectively, the banking system has a total of MYR 1.4 trillion in outstanding financing, equivalent to over 120% of GDP.

The role of the banking system is complemented by development financial institutions (DFIs) (Figure 8.3c). These are specialized financial institutions established by the government to serve the specific financial needs of targeted strategic sectors, which may involve projects that carry higher credit or market risk and have long gestation periods. The presence of DFIs have served to promote greater financial inclusion and the development of strategic sectors including agriculture, small and medium-sized enterprises (SMEs), infrastructure, maritime, and export-oriented sectors, as well as capital-intensive and high-technology industries.

The insurance sector offers a variety of life, nonlife, family *takaful* and general *takaful* products (Figure 8.3b).[4] Currently, there are 32 insurance companies (12 domestic and 20 foreign), 11 *takaful* operators, seven reinsurers, and four *retakaful* operators present in Malaysia, performing an important role in meeting the protection and savings needs of Malaysian businesses and households. While the insurance penetration rate has risen significantly over the past decade to 54.9% in 2015 (2004: 42.6%), certain protection gaps still remain, with reforms currently underway in the life insurance sectors aimed at achieving the national target of a 75% penetration rate.

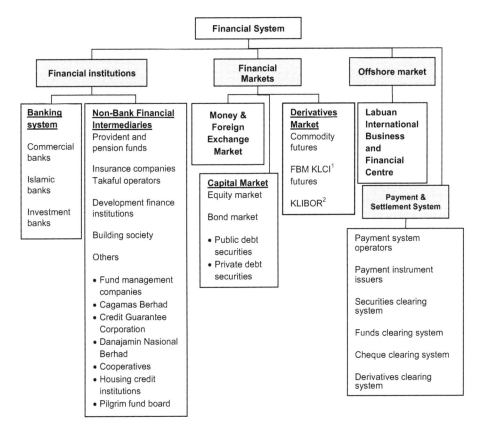

Figure 8.2 Components of the Malaysian financial system

Notes: [1]FTSE Bursa Malaysia Kuala Lumpur Composite Index, [2]Kuala Lumpur Interbank Offered Rate, [3]Malaysian Government Securities.

Source: Compiled by author.

Table 8.1 Structure of financial stability oversight in Malaysia

REGULATORY AUTHORITIES	*RESPONSIBILITIES*	
	SAFETY and SOUNDNESS • *Safety and soundness of financial institutions* • *Orderly functioning of financial markets* • *Stable and efficient financial market infrastructure*	*CONSUMER PROTECTION AND MARKET CONDUCT* • *Protection of rights and interests of financial consumers* • *Fair, responsible, and professional market conduct*

Bank Negara Malaysia	• Regulation and supervision of:
	  − Banking, insurance, and *takaful* sector
	  − Development financial institutions (DFIs)
	  − Money and foreign exchange markets
	  − Payment systems
	  − Money changing, remittances, wholesale currency business
	• Surveillance of systemic non-bank financial entities outside its regulatory reach
		• Promotion of:
		  − Fair and equitable market practices
		  − Financial capability of consumers
		• Supervision and enforcement of market conduct practices of financial service providers

(*Continued*)

Table 8.1 (Continued)

REGULATORY AUTHORITIES	RESPONSIBILITIES	
Securities Commission Malaysia (SC)	• Oversight of capital market intermediaries, e.g., fund management companies, broker-dealers • Regulation of all matters relating to securities and derivatives • Monitoring and mitigation of systemic risk in the capital market • Supervision and surveillance of exchange holding companies, exchanges, clearing houses, and central depositories	• Investor protection in the capital and derivatives markets • Promotion and maintenance of the integrity of all licensees in the securities and derivatives industries
Malaysian Deposit Insurance Corporation (PIDM)	• Resolution authority for member institutions, i.e., commercial and Islamic banks, insurers, and takaful operators	• Protection against loss of deposits or takaful/insurance benefits for which a member institution is liable • Administration of Deposit Insurance System (DIS) and Takaful and Insurance Benefits Protection System (TIPS)
Government ministries and other enforcement agencies	**Cooperatives Commission Malaysia** • Regulation of credit cooperatives **Ministry of Finance** • Oversight of public pension funds, Pilgrim Fund Board, other DFIs, social security organizations **Ministry of Housing and Local Government** • Licensing of moneylenders and pawnbrokers **Ministry of Domestic Trade, Cooperatives and Consumerism** • Oversight of hire purchase activities governed by the Hire Purchase Act 1967	**Malaysia Competition Commission (MyCC)** • Ensuring competition in the financial sector **Ministry of Education** • Integration of financial education into school curricula **Law enforcement agencies** • Combating financial scams, banking fraud, money laundering, and terrorism financing

Source: Compiled by author.

Bank Negara Malaysia (BNM) regulates and supervises all banking and insurance institutions (including Islamic banks and takaful operators) under the Central Bank of Malaysia Act 2009, the Financial Services Act 2013 and the Islamic Financial Services Act 2013. It also has regulatory and supervisory oversight over the DFIs under the Development Financial Institutions Act 2002, while investment banks are co-regulated with the Securities Commission Malaysia. Oversight of other capital market intermediaries such as fund management companies (Figure 8.3d) and brokerage houses are undertaken by the Securities Commission Malaysia. For governance of offshore financial activities in Labuan International Business and Financial Centre which are carried out in non-ringgit currencies, the Labuan Financial Services Authority supervises offshore banking, insurance, trusts, and fund management.[5]

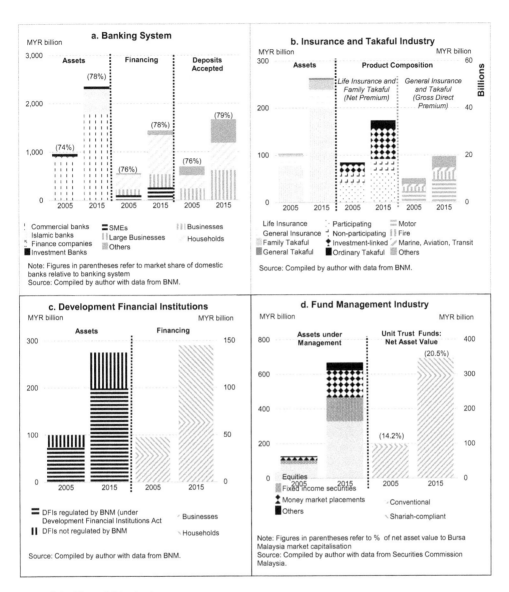

Figure 8.3 Financial institutions

The role of capital markets

Since the Asian financial crisis, Malaysia's capital markets have evolved to become an important source of financing to the Malaysian economy. The Malaysian debt securities market has grown in breadth and depth over the recent decade, enabling both the public and private sectors to raise funds efficiently, while also acting as a conduit for diversifying risks within the financial system. Total outstanding debt securities in the market amounted to MYR 1.13 trillion as at end-2015, or around 101.6% of GDP (Figure 8.4a). This development has not only led to the bond market functioning as an important alternative avenue for fund-raising, but has also paved the way for innovation and product development to support hedging and securitization activities.

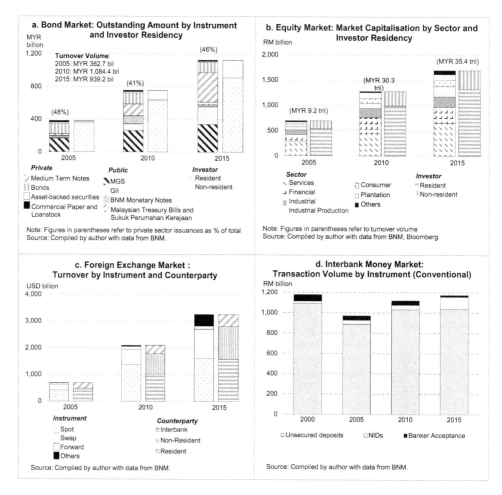

Figure 8.4 Financial markets

The vibrancy of the debt securities market in Malaysia is largely due to the presence of numerous active market players – interbank players and wholesale participants (corporates, institutional investors, insurance companies, and foreign investors). Various enhancements have also been made in developing the supporting infrastructure, which has served to facilitate fund-raising activities by corporates. These measures include improving the transmission of information and price discovery process through the Electronic Trading Platform under Bursa Malaysia, as well as enhancements to the Fully Automated System for Tendering (FAST) for tendering of both government and corporate bonds on the platform.

Supporting the country's government debt securities market is a system of principal dealers (for conventional and Islamic markets) and Islamic principal dealers (solely for Islamic market) that serve as primary bidders for Malaysian Government Securities, Government Investment Issues, Malaysian Treasury Bills, and other Real Time Electronics Transfer of Funds and Securities (RENTAS) securities specified by BNM.[6] Their role is crucial in supporting the market-making activities for these securities, as well as stimulating the development and growth of trading in the secondary market.

Another defining element of Malaysia's capital market is the *sukuk* market for Islamic securities.[7] Malaysia is host to the largest *sukuk* market globally, with total outstanding *sukuks* of MYR 644.4 billion as at end-2015, representing 54% of *sukuks* outstanding globally. In line with its growing prominence, the share of *sukuk* has also increased from 25% of the total debt securities market in 2001 to 54.8% as at end-2015. More importantly, the development of the debt securities and *sukuk* markets has enabled Malaysia to finance infrastructure projects critical to the long-term growth of the economy, such as the issuance of the MYR 30.6 billion *sukuk* by the highway operator PLUS in 2012 for the development of Malaysia's highways.

Malaysia's equity market is similarly well developed. Market capitalization expanded at a compounded annual rate of 9.3% from MYR 695 billion in 2005 to MYR 1.7 trillion in 2015, equivalent to around 147% of GDP (Figure 8.4b). The stock exchange, Bursa Malaysia, now has around 900 companies listed on its two boards – the Main Market and the ACE market, which caters for newer and smaller listings. As at end-2015, the net asset value of Malaysia's unit trust industry stood at MYR 347 billion, one of the largest in the ASEAN region. With the progressive deepening of the capital market, it is expected to provide an increasing share of the financing needs of the Malaysian economy.

Complementing debt and equity markets are the Malaysian foreign exchange, money and derivatives markets, which provide investors with important avenues for the exchange of currency and management of risks (Figures 8.4d, 8.4e, and 8.4f). The transition toward a flexible exchange rate regime in 2005 and subsequent efforts to liberalize the Malaysian markets have contributed toward the development of a wide variety of foreign exchange and derivative instruments, in turn improving the efficiency of the financial intermediation process. This has translated to greater ease of doing business in Malaysia as well as enhanced flexibility for foreign investors intending to invest in Malaysia. Turnover in the foreign exchange market was USD 3.25 trillion in 2015 (Figure 8.4c), while derivatives turnover amounted to USD 1.25 trillion.

Supporting financial system infrastructure

Supporting financial infrastructure has been an essential part of Malaysia's financial development efforts and today forms the bedrock of a modern and progressive financial sector. It has ensured that all viable economic participants continue to have access to financial services. Figure 8.5 depicts the infrastructure and institutions that have been established over the years with mandates to address gaps in financial intermediation activities and support the fund-raising capacity of the financial system.

Ensuring an adequate supply of trained financial professionals

Even after ensuring that the financial system has adequate depth and diversity, and that the financial institutions are financially sound, there is still an additional component in ensuring that the financial system is able to serve the needs of the Malaysian economy in a globalized environment. That critical ingredient is the talent pool within the financial system. While there is some reliance on international talent, the most reliable and sustainable source of talent is domestic, and it is in developing this source that policy-makers have devoted immense effort and resources.

The intervention of policy-makers was necessary because while individual financial institutions looked at their own talent needs, there was no one else looking at the overall talent needs of the industry. With a limited talent pool, staff pinching is likely to be as important a talent enhancement strategy as talent development. The intervention of policy-makers

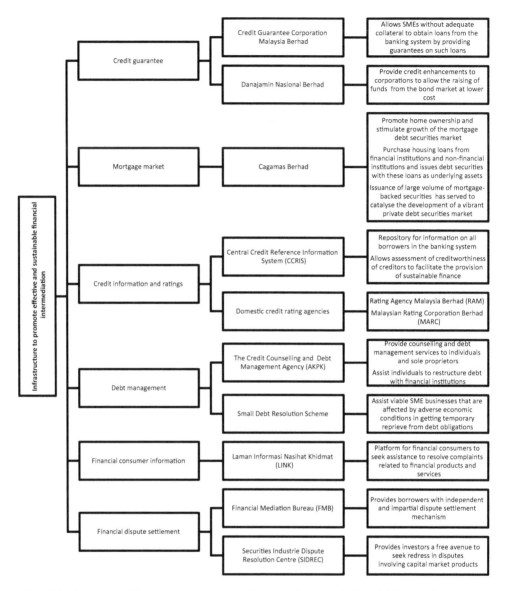

Figure 8.5   Supporting infrastructure to promote effective and sustainable financial intermediation

Source: Compiled by author with information from BNM sources.

is even more necessary in areas that require anticipation of the future talent needs of the industry. One such area is Islamic finance. Therefore, there were strong incentives for the regulators and policy-makers to take a leadership role in a collaborative industry-driven effort to develop talent and create the infrastructure to train finance professionals. The outcome of these efforts in terms of the components of the talent development and training infrastructure is depicted in Figure 8.6.

The comprehensive talent development infrastructure is intended to serve the distinct talent needs of financial services professionals at each of the stage of their career, ranging from entry

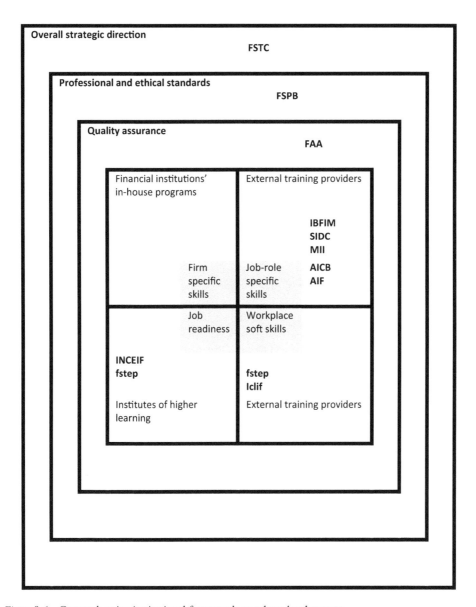

Figure 8.6 Comprehensive institutional framework on talent development

Note: FSTC (Financial Services Talent Council): recommends strategies to develop, attract, retain, and deploy domestic and international talent to meet the demand; FSPB (Financial Services Professional Board): develops and advocates voluntary professional and ethical standards for the financial sector; FAA (Finance Accreditation Agency): responsible for quality assurance of learning initiatives, including program, individual and institutional accreditation; AIF (Asian Institute of Finance): enhances human capital development and talent management in the financial sector; AICB (Asian Institute of Chartered Bankers): professional education body for the Malaysian banking and financial services industry; MII (The Malaysian Insurance Institute): professional body and education institution for the Malaysian insurance and takaful industry; SIDC (Securities Industry Development Corporation): provides capital markets education, training, and information for ASEAN; IBFIM: Islamic finance training and reference center for industry and academia; Iclif (The Iclif Leadership and Governance Centre): provides training for senior management in strategic management and leadership; fstep (Financial Sector Talent Enrichment Programme): provides training for top graduates to acquire a foundation in the financial services industry; INCEIF (International Centre for Education in Islamic Finance): builds Islamic finance talent and skills by offering both graduate and professional programs.

Source: Compiled with information from the BNM's Financial Stability and Payment Systems Report 2014.

positions to senior management and board levels (Figure 8.6). These include, among others, the Financial Sector Talent Enrichment Programme for entry-level graduates, the Asian Institute of Finance for professional training and skills development, the ICLIF Leadership and Governance Centre for senior management and board of directors and the International Centre for Education in Islamic Finance. These dedicated agencies are further complemented by higher-level bodies such as the Financial Services Professional Board, which develops voluntary professional standards, and the Financial Services Talent Council, which oversees the overall strategic direction of talent development within the financial sector.

Institutional and legal framework governing the financial system

The Malaysian financial system is governed by a number of important legislations to ensure that it is well regulated, safe, and stable. These are summarized in Table 8.2.

One of the key legislative changes was the enactment of the Central Bank of Malaysia Act 2009 (CBA), which replaced the previous Central Bank of Malaysia Act of 1958, and provides greater clarity to the Bank's mandates for promoting monetary stability and financial stability. With respect to the financial stability mandate, the CBA clearly sets out the Bank's primary functions, namely to (1) regulate and supervise financial institutions under the Bank's purview, (2) provide oversight over the money and foreign exchange markets, (3) exercise oversight over payment systems, and (4) develop a sound, progressive and inclusive financial system.

It is upon these primary functions codified in CBA that the regulatory laws administered by the Bank are founded. The Financial Services Act 2013 (FSA) and the Islamic Financial Services Act 2013 (IFSA) provide the Bank with the requisite powers to effectively perform its regulatory and supervisory roles. Integrating six now repealed statutes,[8] the FSA and IFSA provide a more cohesive and integrated legal framework that delivers a consistent and comprehensive treatment across similar risks regardless of origin, thus limiting prospects of regulatory gaps or arbitrage. Broadly, they reflect the Bank's increased emphasis on early intervention to address emerging risks in the financial system, and a more risk-focused and integrated approach to the regulation and supervision of financial institutions.

The Development Financial Institutions Act 2002 entrusts the regulation and supervision of six major development financial institutions (DFIs) to the Bank to ensure that their development mandates can be achieved in a financially sustainable manner, while contributing to the stability and development of the financial system.

Over the past two decades, global efforts to combat money laundering and terrorism financing have intensified in response to new political realities and increasingly sophisticated money laundering techniques. The Anti-Money Laundering, Anti-Terrorism Financing and Proceeds of Unlawful Activities Act 2001 (AMLATFPUAA) provides a comprehensive framework to counter money laundering, thus preserving the integrity of the financial system. The AMLATFPUAA also supports more effective collaboration between the Bank, financial institutions and law enforcement agencies in the areas of crime prevention and national security. Recognizing that certain sectors, such as money-changing and remittance services, can be particularly vulnerable to the flow of illicit funds, the Money Services Business Act 2011 and supporting regulatory and supervisory frameworks have been put in place to strengthen the Central Bank's oversight of these activities.

Taken together, the legislative framework for financial stability serve to promote greater resilience and efficiency of the financial sector, strengthen the regulatory and supervisory regime, provide greater protection for consumers, and preserve a high level of confidence in the financial system.

Table 8.2 Comprehensive laws for financial stability

| | Deterrence of financial crime | Fair, responsible and professional business conduct | Financial stability | | | | Shariah compliance |
			Prudential regulation and supervision	Tools for crisis management and prevention	Financial safety nets	Orderly financial markets and payment systems	
Central Bank of Malaysia Act 2009 (CBA)							
Islamic Financial Services Act 2013 (IFSA)							
Financial Services Act 2013 (FSA)							
Development Financial Institutions Act 2002 (DFIA)							
Anti-money Laundering and Ant-terrorism Financing Act 2001 (AMLATFA)							
Money Services Business Act 2011 (MSBA)							
Malaysia Deposit Insurance Corporation Act 2011 (MDICA)							

Source: Compiled by author drawing on BNM's Financial Stability and Payment Systems Report 2012.

Collaboration to better manage risks to financial stability

Although the central bank regulates financial institutions that collectively account for two-thirds of assets of the financial system, it is not the only regulator of the financial system. As Table 8.3 highlights, there are a number of other regulatory agency looking after different parts of the financial system.

When several agencies have a role in financial regulation, coordination becomes necessary to avoid regulatory arbitrage and to ensure that no risks and vulnerabilities are left undetected. Coordination is also necessary to ensure that policies achieve their intended outcomes and that risks do not migrate to different parts of the financial system.

The collaboration and coordination mechanisms among the three major financial regulators – that is, the bank, Securities Commission (SC), and PIDM – are codified by way of memorandums of understanding (MoUs). The MoU between the bank and SC sets out the roles and responsibilities of both parties and clarifies cooperation arrangements in various areas, including:

- Management of financial stability threats and systemic risk in the capital market;
- Development of and changes to legislation and policies;
- Access to and exchange of information; and
- Examination, regulation, and supervision of entities under joint regulatory purview.

Coordination between the bank and SC is further strengthened with the recent development of the BNM-SC Operational Framework for Financial Crisis Management and Resolution. The Framework sets out the operational guidance for inter-agency coordination in dealing with a financial crisis situation that has implications on the stability of the financial system and capital markets, with the aim of ensuring a high degree of preparedness in managing, containing and resolving a system-wide crisis in a cohesive, effective, and efficient manner.

Similarly, BNM and PIDM have entered into a Strategic Alliance Agreement since 2006 to enhance the ability of BNM and PIDM to carry out their respective mandates. Some of the core areas of collaboration include (1) information-sharing protocols for risk assessment and monitoring; and (2) coordination arrangements for supervisory intervention and failure resolution (e.g., early intervention triggers, non-viability triggers, and operational protocols).

For market conduct oversight activities, the Bank mainly coordinates with SC and the Malaysia Competition Commission (MyCC). The Technical Working Group on Financial Services, which comprises the Bank, MyCC and SC, was established in 2013 to support the respective authorities in dealing with competition issues in the financial sector and harmonizing current industry practices with competition principles. In combating financial scams and banking fraud, the bank works closely with numerous enforcement agencies and government ministries including, but not limited to, the Ministry of Domestic Trade, Cooperatives, and Consumerism, Companies Commission of Malaysia, the Inland Revenue Board, and the Royal Malaysian Police. With regards to financial education, the bank actively collaborates with the Ministry of Education to integrate financial education into school curricula.

On a global scale, regulators and supervisors are increasingly placing greater focus on developing and operationalizing effective cooperation and coordination arrangements across borders. The expansion in the cross-border activities of financial groups and capital mobility across borders adds an international dimension to the management of systemic risks. Effective cross-border cooperation among supervisors is therefore crucial to facilitate sound implementation of regulatory frameworks within borders as well as support the consolidated supervision of large

Table 8.3 Financial system: total assets and financing by type of institution

RM million		Banking Institutions	Insurers and Takaful Operators	Development Financial Institutions (DFIs)	Pension Funds	Fund Management Industry	Credit Cooperatives, and Building Societies	Cagamas (National Mortgage Corporation)	Others
Assets	2005	958,546	103,465	99,868	263,877	127,200	15,480	32,023	34,080
	2015	2,355,728	263,770	274,809	824,963	667,880	65,694	40,347	129,442
Financing	2005	558,071		47,496	55,650		2,987	21,178	17,924
	2015	1,445,139		144,868	89,362		40,728	30,345	18,815

Source: Compiled by author with data from BNM, Securities Commission Malaysia, Malaysia Cooperatives Societies Commission, financial statements and internal BNM estimates.

financial groups. In good times, ongoing communication among regulatory agencies will help identify and address regulatory inconsistencies across jurisdictions, deter potentially destabilizing risk-taking, and lay the groundwork for enhanced cooperation during crises. In stressed times, strong cross-border relationships help minimize cross-border disruptions and reduce the likelihood of inefficient, fragmented policy responses.

As the home supervisor to several banking groups with notable regional presence, the Bank regularly engages with host regulators on the development and performance of the banks abroad through established supervisory colleges and bilateral meetings. The Bank takes a two-tiered approach to membership in colleges, taking into consideration the materiality of the operations to the group and its systemic importance in the host countries. The continued strengthening of such home-host engagements and consolidated supervision enable the early identification of vulnerabilities at the entity and group level, and facilitate timely supervisory responses.

The intensification of trade and financial linkages in the Asia-Pacific region has also accentuated the need for collective efforts to safeguard monetary and financial stability. Cross-border cooperation with regards to regional surveillance and crisis management is supported by the Executives' Meeting of East Asia-Pacific Central Banks (EMEAP) through the Monetary and Financial Stability Committee, Working Group on Banking Supervision, Working Group on Financial Markets and Working Group on Payment Systems. Recognizing that member countries have a common interest and joint responsibility in managing the cross-border implications of different types of crises, the EMEAP Regional Crisis Management and Resolution Framework was put in place in 2014. This framework aims to facilitate integrated surveillance and support cohesive crisis responses among authorities to manage the cross-border effects of economic crises, financial market disruptions, and distressed systemic financial institutions. This framework complements existing cross-border cooperation arrangements to safeguard regional stability and support national crisis management frameworks and resolution regimes.

Policy interactions and policy governance within the central bank

Given its multiple mandates and its wide-ranging responsibilities for the stability of the financial system, it is very important for the central bank to ensure that it has a robust framework for considering policies and making decision. BNM has had a monetary policy committee since 2002. Considerations that favor decision-making by committee for monetary policy are increasingly also relevant to decision-making on financial stability. In particular, with a globally integrated financial system that has grown significantly in size, financial stability issues tend to be multifaceted and require broad-based expertise and perspectives to support sound judgments and decisions. Such committees provide an avenue for rigorous debate on macroprudential policies which often entail managing multidimensional interactions with other policies (monetary, fiscal, and regulatory) and finding the appropriate policy mix to mitigate systemic risks. Whether the committees are internal or external, the quality of the financial stability decisions would depend critically on the strength and robustness of the processes (including analytical frameworks and supporting structures) within the lead macroprudential authority that provides support to these committees.

Within the bank, the Financial Stability Committee (FSC) is the high-level decision-making committee responsible for safeguarding financial system stability (Figure 8.7). Chaired by the governor of the bank, its members comprise high-level executives from various policy sectors and departments within the bank, such as financial regulation, supervision and development, consumer and market conduct, payment systems, economics, monetary policy, and treasury operations. The FSC meets at least four times a year to discuss and deliberate on emerging issues

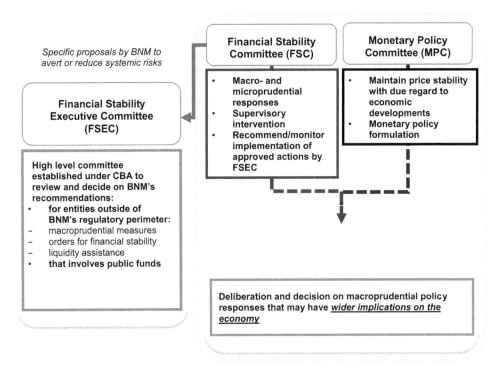

Figure 8.7 Key decision-making committees for financial stability policies in Bank Negara Malaysia
Source: Compiled by author.

and areas of vulnerability that may pose risks to financial stability. Synthesizing information from various functional areas across the Bank, the FSC deliberates and decides on the appropriate use of financial stability policy instruments, be they macro- or microprudential policies.

The dual objectives of monetary and financial stability typically raise concerns about the increased scope for policy conflicts. In general, central banks practice some degree of separation between members of the monetary policy and financial stability committees. This is intended, for example, to reduce potential conflicts that can arise when concerns over the viability of individual financial institutions may influence monetary policy decisions. While this remains a legitimate concern, it is also important to recognize that financial stability responses (both of a microprudential and macroprudential nature) and monetary policy can also play an important complementary role in preventing the build-up of systemic risks within the financial system.

Recognizing these challenges, the central bank established the Joint Policy Committee to deliberate and decide on macroprudential policies that have wider implications on the real economy. Comprising members from the FSC and Monetary Policy Committee, the JPC seeks to address the common concerns confronting both financial stability and monetary stability. Since its inception, the JPC has deliberated on a number of issues, including those related to the sustainability of household indebtedness and developments in the property sector. This has resulted in several targeted macroprudential and microprudential measures to ensure that household debt remains within prudent levels and that the property market is not affected by excessive speculation.

The enhanced oversight function and powers to address financial stability concerns in CBA are complemented by a strengthened framework for governance, transparency, and accountability. Under the circumstances where any of the financial stability powers are invoked on institutions that are beyond the regulatory reach of the Bank or where it involves public funds or impinge on personal rights, the Act provides that such decisions are taken by the FSEC. In essence, the FSEC decides on proposals relating to the (1) issuance of orders to entities which are not regulated by the Bank to undertake measures to avert and reduce risks to financial stability; (2) extension of liquidity assistance to entities that are not regulated by the Bank or to overseas subsidiaries or branches of Malaysian financial institutions; (3) provision of capital support; and (4) issuance of an order for compulsory transfers. The FSEC comprises the governor, one deputy governor, and three to five other members to be appointed by the minister on the recommendation of the Board of Directors, based on their professional expertise and experience:

- The secretary-general of Treasury to provide views on the implication of any proposal on the government's fiscal position;
- The chief executive officer of PIDM for the knowledge and experience in dealing with resolution of FIs and financial sector risks;
- The chairman of the Securities Commission of Malaysia for its role in identifying and addressing systemic risks in the capital markets;
- Private sector experts who are knowledgeable in financial industry issues, typically drawn from a mix of legal, accounting, and financial services or markets background and experience; and
- Heads of other relevant authorities, for situations when the FSEC deliberates on measures affecting persons/entities under their direct purview.

The composition of FSEC is designed to reinforce the element of independent external oversight and enhance the efficacy of decision-making. The clear majority of non-executives in the composition is intended to ensure the robustness of discussions and the independence of decision-making in extending financial support or imposing certain financial stability measures. Representation from the various agencies is intended to facilitate thorough policy consideration and effective inter-agency coordination, especially with regards to entities beyond the Bank's regulatory purview.

Policy issues and challenges

The development of the Malaysian financial system has also brought a number of policy issues and challenges to the forefront. Four of these issues are briefly highlighted here. These include the role of a deeper financial system in managing external volatility, promoting consumer protection in the face of increased complexity of financial products, making the financial system inclusive to ensure that it benefits all sectors of society, and balancing the availability of financing against the accumulation of excessive debt by society.

Greater openness and rising integration result in greater susceptibility to global financial cycles through shifts in capital flows

Rising financial integration has resulted in the increased presence of foreign investors in Malaysia's financial system. Greater liberalization of the financial system during the mid-2000s, coupled with strong economic growth, attracted sizeable cross-border capital inflows into the domestic financial system, in particular into the domestic capital markets, across the different asset classes (Figure 8.8).

However, the openness to foreign portfolio flows means that Malaysia is increasingly influenced by global financial cycles through shifts in cross-border flows. As noted recently by Cerutti, Claessens, and Puy (2015), apart from domestic pull factors, cross-border flows since 2009 largely reflect global push factors from years of low interest rates and abundant liquidity from advanced economies. For Malaysia, the bulk of inflows were channeled into the bond market, notably into Malaysian Government Securities (MGS) and BNM bills (Figure 8.9).

However, the heightened uncertainty in the global financial markets since September 2014 has led to significant capital outflows from EMEs, including Malaysia, which led to larger co-movements between global and domestic asset prices. This is reflected by a more positive relationship between the returns in global financial markets (proxied by daily returns in Dow Jones) and domestic equity market (daily returns in KLCI) over the past decade. This is consistent with Ananchotikul and Zhang (2014) which notes that as the degree of financial integration rises, domestic asset prices are likely to become more susceptible to global risk aversion shocks, leading to stronger spillovers, particularly to the domestic equity market.[9]

However, the volatility in the domestic financial markets has been partly mitigated by the presence of a diverse base of large institutional investors, which includes pension funds, banks, and insurance companies. These large institutional investors have played a stabilizing role in containing the excessive movements in asset prices, especially in bond markets during both periods of large inflows and outflows (Figure 8.10). In recent times, non-resident flows in the MGS market have mostly been facilitated by banks, rather than non-bank institutional investors such as pension funds. This is due to the fact that these non-bank domestic institutional investors have a long-term investment strategy to buy and hold such financial assets, which limits their ability to actively play an offsetting role in the MGS market.

One additional point is that while deeper financial markets may help to mitigate the impact of these flows on domestic financial markets, the larger inflows and outflows can cause large swings in the exchange rate. If this is uncomfortable for the economy, then the central bank

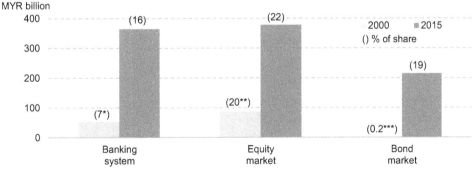

* % of total liabilities
** % of market capitalisation
*** % of total bond outstanding

Figure 8.8 Growing presence of foreign investors across asset classes

Source: Compiled by author with data from Bank Negara Malaysia and Bursa Malaysia.

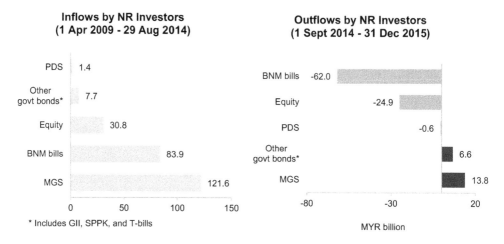

Figure 8.9 MGS received the largest inflows and the trend continued during the period of capital reversal while the outflows contained to BNM bills

Source: Compiled by author with data from BNM.

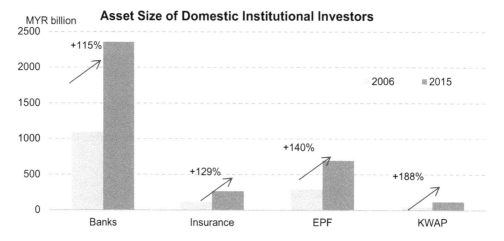

Figure 8.10 Rapid asset growth enables domestic institutional investors to play stabilizing role

Source: Compiled by author with data from BNM.

will have to have large foreign exchange reserves buffers to support its intervention operations – that, or adopt more aggressive measures to dissuade the flows from coming in. With globalized financial markets, the benefits of having deeper and more open financial markets can be less clear-cut when the rest of the economy matters, especially in small economies.

With greater liberalization, resident outflows have also increased. Notably, Malaysian banks and corporations have expanded their regional presence through establishing subsidiaries in neighboring countries. These flows were partly facilitated by a key liberalization measure in 2005 which allowed residents to freely invest abroad with their own foreign currency funds. Further liberalization of foreign exchange administration rules in 2009 coincided with the expanded investment mandates of Malaysia's domestic institutional investors that created

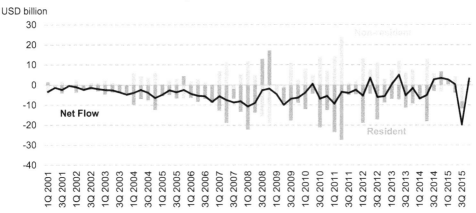

Figure 8.11   Overseas expansion by residents has led to greater two-way flows

Source: Compiled by author with data from the Balance of Payments Statistics, Department of Statistics Malaysia.

incentives to diversify assets across borders to increase potential returns. The role of resident external investment flows can be helpful or unhelpful depending on the situation, especially in terms of their role in mitigating non-resident flows. During times of large non-resident inflows, the resident outflows helped to reduce the pressure on the exchange rate and facilitated orderly market conditions (Figure 8.11). However, given that resident flows have generally been negative, they can be unhelpful when the country is facing non-resident outflows and lead to additional pressure on the exchange rate and foreign exchange reserves of the country.

Promoting financial consumer empowerment and protection

The increasing complexity in financial products and services underscores the importance of equipping financial consumers with the necessary knowledge and skills to make informed financial decisions. Financially competent consumers are not only able to protect themselves against unfair market practices, but would also promote greater competition and innovation in the financial system. Financial education also plays an important role in the prevention of over-indebtedness both by increasing an individual's ability to understand his contractual obligations and by helping raise awareness about the effects that consumption patterns and lifestyles have on individual finances.

To inculcate good financial management skills among young Malaysians, the Central Bank collaborates with the Ministry of Education to strengthen the knowledge and skills of teachers and lecturers to effectively deliver financial education to students of all ages. The focus for adult financial education is directed at educating young adults and low-income households given their propensity to borrow and their relatively lower financial buffers. The Bank has put in place the POWER! program, which covers debt management, building wealth, and preparing households for unexpected events to address specific concerns associated with these target groups.

Similarly, the Securities Commission investor education program seeks to strengthen the capabilities of investors by equipping them with the requisite skills, knowledge, and tools to exercise good judgment in making investment decisions. The SC launched *InvestSmart*, a comprehensive investment literacy initiative in 2014 to provide investors with investment information presented in an easily understood format, leveraging on new technology and multimedia platforms to supplement existing investor education channels. By leveraging on digital and social media, *InvestSmart* provides reliable and independent information and investment tools to the public.

Malaysia fosters an integrated and collaborative approach to financial education, which enable the Bank, the SC, the Malaysia Deposit Insurance Corporation, AKPK, and the Employees Provident Fund to coordinate strategies and action plans, including research initiatives and national outreach programs.

The Bank has undertaken considerable effort to put in place a coherent financial consumer protection framework to foster fair and responsible business conduct by financial institutions as well as to protect the rights and interests of consumers of financial services and products. This includes enforcing key business conduct requirements that focus on achieving fair treatment of consumers, which include requiring meaningful product disclosure, assessments on suitability of financial products and services, provision of proper advice, responsible lending practices, fair debt collection practices, equitable banking charges, and protection of customer information. The Securities Commission also has similar standards of conduct for intermediaries in the capital market to guard against practices such as market manipulation and insider trading that could undermine the integrity of the market.

Given the important role of financial services professionals in dealing with consumers, investors, financial markets and the greater economy, a strong culture of ethical conduct in the financial industry is central to its long-term sustainability. Based on a shared vision for high standards of ethics and professionalism within the financial services industry, the SC and the Bank have established the Financial Services Professional Board (FSPB). As an industry-led standard-setting body, the FSPB focuses on developing practical and applicable standards of professionalism and ethics for the industry and its workforce.

Promoting financial inclusion for sustainable growth

In looking at the role of the financial system in the economy, it was clear that a sophisticated financial system by itself would not necessarily serve the needs of all sectors of society. Consequently, the need to realign policy priorities toward ensuring that the Malaysian financial system is able to serve all segments of society by providing access to quality and affordable financial products. Figure 8.12 summarizes the key objectives and strategies of the financial inclusion framework. Various initiatives have been undertaken to increase access. In particular, the design of dedicated products such as the *Skim Pembiayaan Mikro* (Micro Financing Scheme), microinsurance/microtakaful and microsavings products, have been successful in extending the benefits of finance toward the targeted and unserved segments. The percentage of adults with deposit accounts in 2015 stood at over 90%, while 99% of Malaysians now enjoy convenient access to reliable financial services.

In view of the significant infrastructure cost in setting up bank branches in the more rural areas, a significant innovation in the Malaysian market has been the development of agent banking, which has had a profound impact on access to financial services. At its core, agent banking enables consumers to obtain formal banking services from financial institutions through third-party agents such as retail outlets and post offices. Since its introduction in 2012, agent banking has significantly increased the availability of financial access points in Malaysia, with 6,902 agent banks having been established nationwide by end-2015 (2012: 460 agent banks). This

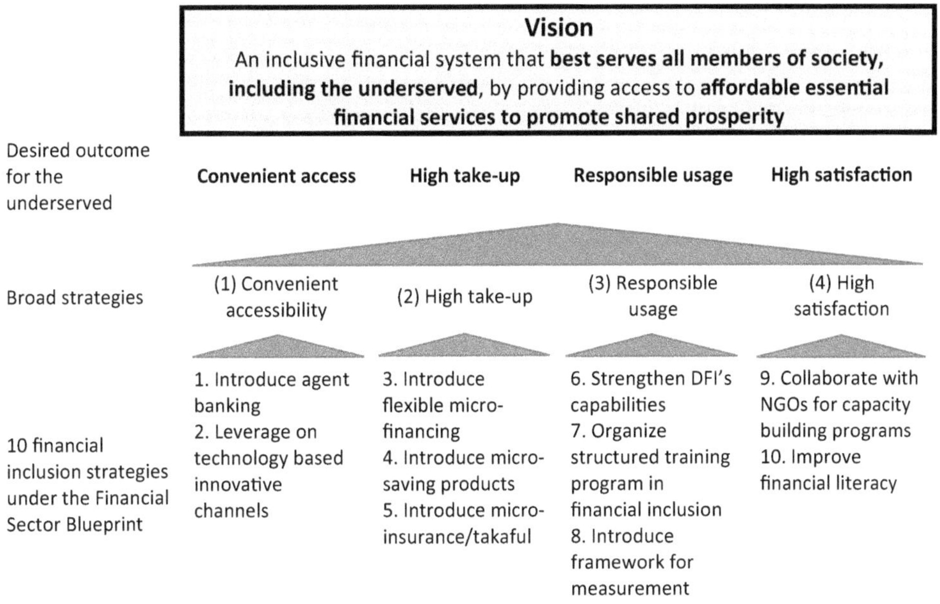

Vision
An inclusive financial system that **best serves all members of society, including the underserved,** by providing access to **affordable essential financial services to promote shared prosperity**

Desired outcome for the underserved	Convenient access	High take-up	Responsible usage	High satisfaction
Broad strategies	(1) Convenient accessibility	(2) High take-up	(3) Responsible usage	(4) High satisfaction
10 financial inclusion strategies under the Financial Sector Blueprint	1. Introduce agent banking 2. Leverage on technology based innovative channels	3. Introduce flexible micro-financing 4. Introduce micro-saving products 5. Introduce micro-insurance/takaful	6. Strengthen DFI's capabilities 7. Organize structured training program in financial inclusion 8. Introduce framework for measurement	9. Collaborate with NGOs for capacity building programs 10. Improve financial literacy

Figure 8.12 The financial inclusion framework

Source: Compiled by author.

has greatly facilitated access to financial services in rural areas. By end-2015, 97% of the 866 sub-districts in Malaysia with a population of more than 2,000 had access to financial services.

Despite the progress to date, financial inclusion continues to be a strong policy priority, with more efforts planned ahead to improve outreach toward the final 8% of the population that remains unbanked. This includes, among others, greater usage of electronic payments, digital technology and cost effective solutions that are better able to transcend the unique boundaries facing this last segment. With further progress, it is expected that the unbanked population will be further reduced to 5% by 2020.

Balancing access to financing against avoiding excessive leverage

One of the desired outcomes of the central bank's efforts to widen the reach of the formal banking system has been the availability of greater access to financing. As their large corporate clients increasingly turned to the capital market to meet their funding needs, the banks have found it necessary to focus their lending strategies more on households and small and medium-scale businesses. The emergence of a more diversified and competitive banking system has also reduced lending rates and increased competition for customers. The outcome of this easier access has been the growth of household indebtedness. The share of loans to the household sector increased from 35% of total loans in 1999 to 56.8% in 2015. These household borrowings have been primarily concentrated in financing for the purchase of residential properties (48.6% of loans to households), which have grown at an annual rate of 11.6% since 2010. The increased prominence of non-bank credit providers has also aided credit expansion. Although non-bank financial institutions (including DFIs regulated by the bank) account for only 20% of credit to the household sector, these institutions provide a significant share (59%) of the personal financing to individuals that has driven the rapid expansion in household indebtedness in recent years.

The bank has been closely monitoring developments in domestic credit growth, particularly in light of ample liquidity conditions, low borrowing costs and rising property prices. Based on past experience in other countries, a protracted and rapid pace of credit expansion can give rise to vulnerabilities that could lead to financial instability if left unattended. These vulnerabilities include (1) imprudent underwriting practices and risk mispricing; (2) inadequate financial buffers to absorb losses from shocks; (3) weak regulation and supervision of major credit providers; (4) high proportion of externally sourced foreign currency loans that are vulnerable to foreign exchange and rollover risks; (5) credit-fueled asset price distortions; and (6) high and unsustainable leverage positions of households and businesses which are not supported by commensurate balance sheet strength. In the case of Malaysia, while such fragilities were assessed to be low or well contained, the bank has taken a series of measures since 2010 to preemptively address potential vulnerabilities in the household and residential property sectors that could increase risks to financial stability over the longer term. These measures reflect a targeted and incremental approach which aims to avoid unintended consequences that could result in an over-adjustment in the economy, while allowing market participants, including households and businesses, to gradually adjust their expectations, behavior, and risk appetite, thereby ensuring that these risks continue to be well managed (Figure 8.13).

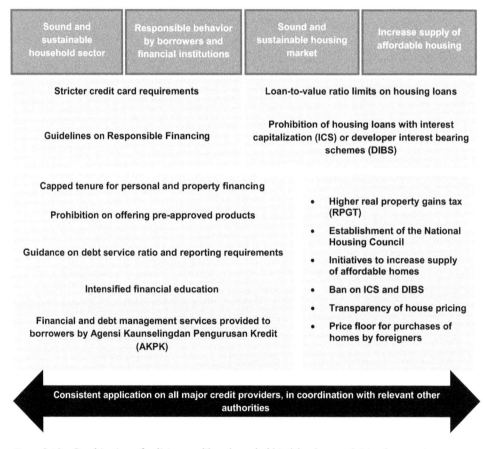

Figure 8.13 Combination of policies to address household indebtedness and rising house prices

Source: Compiled by author.

The design and implementation of macroprudential measures in Malaysia are broadly based on several key elements and considerations. First, the deployment of macroprudential policies is based on discretion, rather than being rule-based (i.e., no set fixed threshold levels or automatic triggers for implementation of such policies). The bank's macroprudential policies are often deployed preemptively with their effects closely monitored to prevent "overshooting." Second, the bank adopts a targeted approach, with policies aimed at specific segments. This allows for a more focused analysis of the efficacy and relevance of such measures over time. Designing overly complex policies aimed at a broader segment of the economy would give rise to implementation issues such as regulatory arbitrage, circumvention, and even confusion. Third, macroprudential measures introduced by the bank are designed to be flexible, which allow for them to be recalibrated in response to changing circumstances. Finally, the bank ensures that such measures are implemented within the context of a holistic policy approach which also includes microprudential, monetary, and fiscal measures.

Conclusion

The evolution of the Malaysian financial system has been as much an outcome of policy initiatives and market reforms as it has been of market forces. The outcome is a financial system that is not only able to handle the financing needs of the economy but one that has also proved to be resilient in the face of various shocks to the economy. However, as the financial system has increased in depth and breadth, it has given rise to new challenges for policy-makers, and some of these are mentioned in this chapter. There also remain other areas of the financial system that still need further development. These include the need to develop more market-based financing to support the innovation and creativity-driven industries that would be a key determinant of the Malaysian economy moving up the value chain. Overall, the financial system will continue to evolve in response to developments in the Malaysian economy and society, as well as global financial and technological trends. As part of this evolution, aside from guarding against the emergence of systemic risks, policy-makers would have an important role in ensuring that the development of the financial system is consistent with the developments in the real economy.

Notes

1 The size of the financial system is proxied by the sum of loans outstanding, stock market capitalization, and bonds outstanding.
2 The Financial Sector Masterplan 2001–2010 (FSMP) and Financial Sector Blueprint 2011–2020 (FSBP) issued by Bank Negara Malaysia (BNM 2001, BNM 2011) as well as the Capital Market Masterplan 1 and 2 by the Securities Commission Malaysia (SCM 2001, SCM 2011).
3 Islamic banking refers to a system of banking that complies with Islamic law also known as Shariah law. The underlying Shariah principles that govern Islamic banking are mutual risk and profit sharing between parties, the assurance of fairness for all, and that transactions are based on an underlying business activity or asset.
4 Takaful refers to an arrangement based on mutual assistance under which takaful participants agree to contribute to a common fund providing for mutual financial benefits payable to the takaful participants or their beneficiaries on the occurrence of pre-agreed events. Similar to life insurance, family takaful refers to an arrangement by which takaful benefits are payable to takaful participants on death or survival, including those takaful benefits payable in respect of personal accidents, disease or sickness. General takaful refers to all non-family takaful.
5 Labuan is a designated offshore financial center, which conducts financial activities such as banking, insurance, trust, and fund management.
6 As of January 2015, there are 12 principal dealers and seven Islamic principal dealers in the Malaysian financial system.

7 *Sukuk*, or Islamic bonds, are certificates that represent the holder's proportionate ownership in an undivided part of an underlying asset where the holder assumes all rights and obligations to such assets.
8 Namely the Banking and Financial Institutions Act 1989, Insurance Act 1996, Payment Systems Act (PSA), Exchange Control Act 1953 (ECA), Islamic Banking Act 1983, and Takaful Act 1984.
9 This trend, however, is not observed in the bond market as the sensitivity of bond yields is more closely related to domestic fundamentals and macroeconomic stability.

References

Ananchotikul, N., and L. Zhang. 2014. Portfolio Flows, Global Risk Aversion, and Asset Prices in Emerging Markets. International Monetary Fund Working Paper 12/156. Washington, DC: International Monetary Fund.

Bank Negara Malaysia (BNM). 2001. *Financial Sector Masterplan 2001–2010*. Kuala Lumpur: Bank Negara Malaysia.

BNM. 2011. *Financial Sector Blueprint 2011–2020*. Kuala Lumpur: Bank Negara Malaysia.

Cerutti, E., S. Claessens, and D. Puy. 2015. Push Factors and Capital Flows to Emerging Markets: Why Knowing Your Lender Matters More Than Fundamentals. International Monetary Fund Working Paper 15/127. Washington, DC: International Monetary Fund.

Securities Commission Malaysia (SCM). 2001. *Capital Market Masterplan 1*. Kuala Lumpur: Securities Commission Malaysia.

SCM. 2011. *Capital Market Masterplan 1* and *Capital Market Masterplan 2*. Kuala Lumpur: Securities Commission Malaysia.

9

THE PHILIPPINE FINANCIAL SYSTEM

Developments, challenges, and opportunities

Nestor Aldave Espenilla Jr.

Overview of the Philippine financial market

Macroeconomics and the Philippine financial market

Understanding the Philippine financial market requires an appreciation of its macroeconomic environment. While there are references to financial institutions operating in the country as early as the 18th century, one has to consider that they were doing so without the formal oversight by a financial regulator.[1] These regulators – the Insular Treasurer was designated as the Insurance Commissioner in 1914, the office of which was the precursor of the Insurance Commission (IC); the Securities and Exchange Commission (SEC) was established in October 1936; while the Central Bank of the Philippines (CBP) came into being in 1948 – were all in place in the first half of the 20th century, but coming out of the ruins of World War II, one can imagine that the focus was on reconstruction and recovery rather than development.

An inward view pervaded the 1950s and 1960s as the Philippines pursued an import-substitution policy and economic nationalism exemplified by the "Filipino First" program. Land reform was a major initiative but import and exchange controls were likewise put in place. The economic policy was to substitute against imports rather than promote exports:

> trade policies heavily penalized the primary and agricultural sectors and benefited the manufacturing sector. In addition, the overvaluation of the Philippine peso during several periods between the 1950s and the 1980s contributed to declines in the prices of exports in peso terms and diverted resources away from agriculture and toward import-substituting manufacturing.
>
> *(Gerson 1998)*

As a result of these polices, as late as 1990, "the poverty rate was dramatically higher in the Philippines than in its neighbors. . . . The distribution of assets has also shown little improvement over the last few decades. Between 1960 and 1990, for example, the Gini coefficient[2] on landholding worsened slightly" (Gerson 1998). All of these economic issues matter in the pattern of saving and the development of the financial market. Charting gross domestic saving over time will necessarily show a rising trend (Figure 9.1). However, what is equally noticeable is that the saving rate (i.e., gross domestic saving as a percentage of GDP) has an extended period where it is declining, specifically from the mid-1970s to at least 1998, and then maintains a relatively flat trend until 2012.

The economic shocks (oil rationing, high inflation, etc.) and the political dynamics in the post-war period appeared to have nurtured a heavy reliance on the banking sector that was operating on fixed rates (Figure 9.2). The fixed and low rates encouraged a short-term view

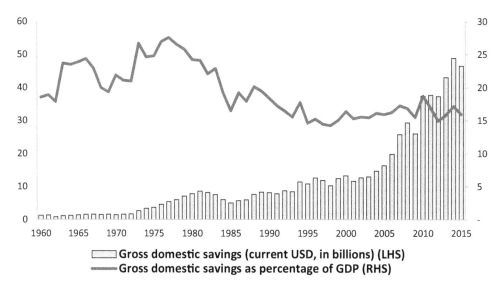

Figure 9.1 Philippine gross domestic savings (1960–2015)

GDP = gross domestic product.

Source: World Bank Development Indicators.

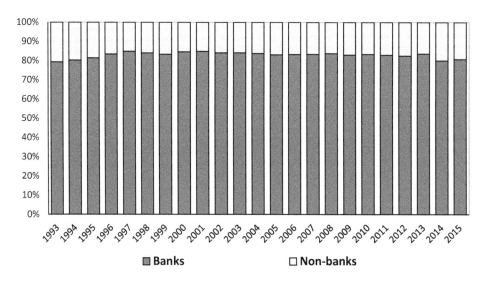

Figure 9.2 Share of banks' assets in total financial assets (1993–2015, in percentage) (PHP billion)

Source: Bangko Sentral ng Pilipinas.

on saving since the "penalty" for missing out on longer-term options was low. This meant that there was no market developing for outright long-term saving. Moreover, as noted by the International Monetary Fund and CBP (1972: 1),

> in the years 1950 to 1969, both the government and the private sector relied heavily on Central Bank credit: on the average 53.7% of increases in liquidity from domestic origin. Obviously, exclusive of the Central Bank, the financial system, with total resources of PHP27.03 billion, liabilities of PHP19.33 billion and net worth of PHP7.70 billion, may not be able to provide for the PHP32.24 billion financial requirements for the Four-Year Development Program (1972–1975) simultaneous with other exigencies of the economy.

Reforms were then pushed in various fronts, including the repeal of the anti-usury law, the liberalization of the foreign exchange market, the entry of foreign banks, and the strengthening of the prudential norms in the banking system. The Asian financial crisis exacerbated the need to accelerate these reforms, particularly in developing a capital market, instilling market conduct, and shifting toward risk-based analysis. The fact that the country stood firm during the global financial crisis reflects some degree of resilience, but clearly there is more that needs to be done.

Banking industry

Like in many Asian countries, the Philippine banking system until the early 1980s was primarily tasked with a developmental role (Gochoco-Bautista 1997). It was viewed as the conduit of credit to sectors deemed as high priority by the state. Controls on interest rates, subsidies, and directed lending were some of the ways this was carried out. Beginning in 1980, however, financial liberalization and reforms were undertaken including, among others, the lifting of interest rate ceilings, and the promotion of bank consolidation and mergers.

The 1990s saw fundamental changes in the banking industry. In 1994, foreign bank entry was allowed under Republic Act 7721. The foreign exchange market was also liberalized, taking away the exclusive right of banks to manage and trade foreign exchange. With the liberalization of the financial and capital markets, foreign capital inflows began to surge in the early 1990s, peaking at a little over 7% of GDP in 1996.

The hard lessons of the 1997 Asian financial crisis paved the way for the broad-based restructuring of the financial sector. Throughout the years, the Bangko Sentral ng Pilipinas (BSP) remains steadfast in pursuing meaningful reforms to promote continuing financial stability. Efforts toward this end are threefold: (1) broad-based and continuing financial sector restructuring to develop a dynamic, stable, and truly inclusive financial system; (2) cross-sectoral cooperative arrangements with financial regulators,[3] legislators, and the private sector to harmonize regulatory standards and align the same with international norms; and (3) reform-oriented and integrated advocacy on financial inclusion, consumer education, and protection.

As of end-December 2015, there was a notable streamlining in the banking landscape as the number of operating banks (measured by the number of head office) went down to 632 banks from 648 banks in 2014. This was 1.7 times lower than the peak of 996 banks in 1998 when the BSP started introducing its merger and consolidation policy. On the other hand, bank network (measured by branches, microbanking offices and other bank offices) expanded by 411 additional bank offices to 10,124 branches in 2015 (vs. 9,713 in 2014), and this was 1.9 times wider than the network of 6,650 bank offices recorded in 1998.

This streamlining in banking footprint occurred amid continued credit expansion with improving asset quality. Both the non-performing loan (NPL) and distressed asset ratios improved to 2.1% and 4% as of end-2015. Of the distressed assets, banks' holdings of real and other properties acquired with tenure of beyond 10 years have been declining, on average, at slower pace of 7.7%[4] for 2010 to 2014. Thus, interest-based earnings buoyed overall profitability of banks in 2015. Net interest income grew annually by PHP 30.4 billion to PHP 351.9 billion for the period ending 31 December 2015. Banks' risk-taking activities likewise had minimal impact on capital as capital adequacy ratio of universal and commercial banks stood at 14.9%, on a solo basis, as of end-December 2015 (Figure 9.3a–d).

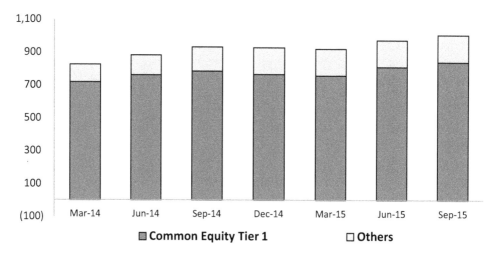

Figure 9.3a   Banking industry indicators (PHP billion)

Source: Bangko Sentral ng Pilipinas.

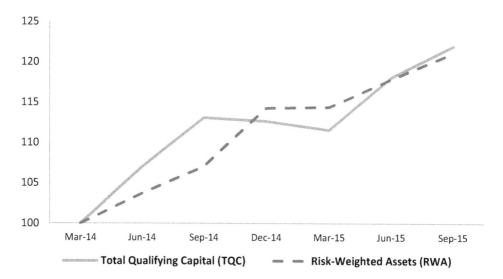

Figure 9.3b   Banking industry indicators (PHP billion)

Source: Bangko Sentral ng Pilipinas.

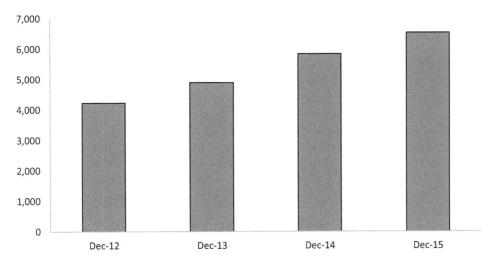

Figure 9.3c Banking industry indicators (PHP billion)

Source: Bangko Sentral ng Pilipinas

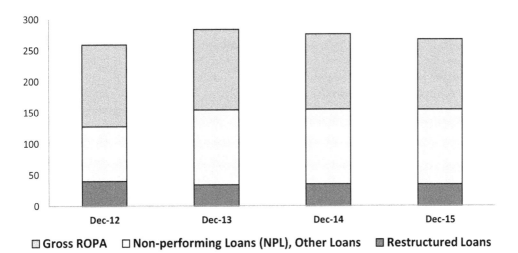

Figure 9.3d Banking industry indicators (PHP billion)

Source: Bangko Sentral ng Pilipinas.

Securities market

It is not clear when the first security was issued in the Philippines, but it is evident that the securities market is at least a century old since the Manila Stock Exchange (MSE) was established in 1917. Tasked with the oversight of this market and to safeguard public interest is the SEC, which was established on 26 October 1936.

The legal mandate of the SEC is embodied under Republic Act 8799 or the Securities Regulation Code (SRC). The SRC provided for the reorganization of the SEC to give greater focus on its role in developing the capital market, fostering good governance, and enhancing investor protection.[5] The Implementing Rules and Regulations of the SRC was revised in 2015 to liberalize the capital raising environment and to help market players meet the challenges posed by increasing market sophistication.

The operations of the equities market are managed through the Philippine Stock Exchange (PSE) which was established in 1992 out of the unification of the MSE and the Makati Stock Exchange. The SEC granted the PSE "self-regulatory organization" status in 1998, allowing the exchange to define and implement rules for the equities market and to establish governance guidelines for trading participants and listed companies. The Market Regulation Division of the PSE was largely tasked to oversee rules, compliance and governance. This was subsequently spun-off and re-established in 2011 as a separate juridical entity, the Capital Markets Integrity Corporation (CMIC). By 2012, the CMIC had taken the role of the self-regulatory organization for the equities market, effectively making the CMIC the primary regulator of the trading participants.

In terms of size, the local stock market has been growing. Market capitalization has been rising (Figure 9.4) and so has the Philippine Composite Index (PSEi). In recent periods, the PSE maintains one of the highest price-earnings ratios in the ASEAN (Figure 9.5), particularly if one adjusts for inflation over time (i.e., using a cyclically adjusted highest price-earnings ratio).

In 2008, the PSE started tracking investor accounts and profiling investors through the Stock Market Investor Profile. Data through 2012 show that the number of Filipino stock market investors continues to be limited, barely accounting for half a percentage point of the total population. Financial technology (fintech) is evident through the emergence of online trading platforms which make trading more convenient as well as to the greater awareness by the public in the nuances of stock market investment (Crisostomo, Padilla, and Visda 2013). Thus, the profile of the Filipino retail investor reflects the rise of online investors and the ongoing shift in the age composition of investors to a younger group.

An organized fixed income market has had a much shorter history. Despite the prevalence of government securities, its trading was done through bilateral over-the-counter arrangements.

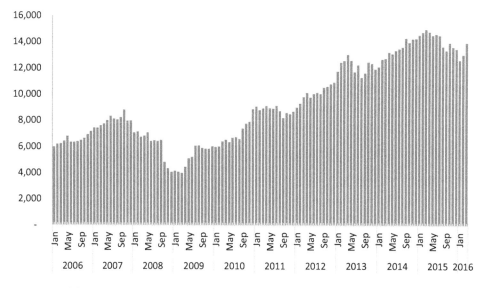

Figure 9.4   Philippine stock market capitalization (PHP billion)

Source: Bangko Sentral ng Pilipinas.

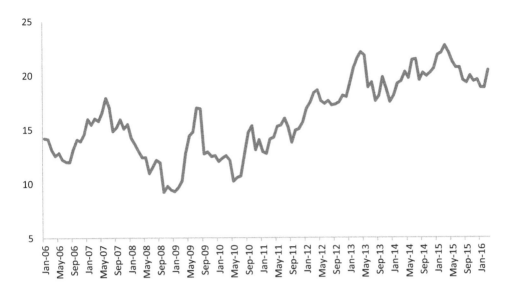

Figure 9.5 Philippine stock market P/E ratio

Source: Bangko Sentral ng Pilipinas.

Apart from a functionally opaque market of bilateral trading, there was no "price discovery" to speak of. Since the Deposit Secrecy Act (Republic Act 1405) prohibits disclosure of or inquiring into anyone's deposits with a bank, retail investors were effectively limited to buying securities from the inventory made available by the bank where the investor has a bank account. This arrangement nurtured an opaque environment of conflicted interests, since retail investors would not have a choice over the full array of securities outstanding and would not know if the price they were agreeing on was in fact inferior to prices trading bilaterally in the professional market.

Two major scandals involving debt securities as well as the 1997 Asian financial crisis significantly affected the market. In response, the Bankers Association of the Philippines[6] (BAP) spearheaded the creation of an exchange market for fixed income (i.e., debt) instruments (Figure 9.6). The Philippine Dealing and Exchange Corporation (PDEx) was incorporated in 2003 as the trading platform for debt securities but the BAP vision had evolved into an end-to-end (i.e., from trading to clearing and settlement to post-settlement facilities) solution by then. Apart from PDEx, the Philippine Depository and Trust Corp. (for Securities Services), the Philippine Securities Settlement Corp. (for Payment and Transfer Services), and the PDS Academy for Market Development Corp. (for Market Education and Development) were likewise created under the Philippine Dealing Systems Holdings Corp.

Formally launched in March 2005, PDEx provides an online inter-dealer trading platform for the secondary trading of government securities. Designated by the BAP as its calculating and posting agent, price discovery is provided to trading participants and reported to the public subsequently.[7] In addition to its role as market operator, the SEC granted PDEx an SRO status for the exchange and over-the-counter trading of fixed income securities.

The Philippine bond market has seen in recent years more corporate issuances,[8] but by and large, it remains dominated by national government issued bonds. As of December 2015, the value of the Philippine bond market was calculated at PHP 4.8 trillion, 83% of which are issuances of the government (Figure 9.7). ADB notes that, moving forward, the challenge lies with

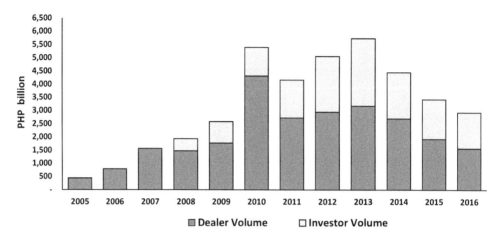

Figure 9.6 Annual fixed income trading volume (2005–2015)

Source: Philippine Dealing and Exchange Corporation.

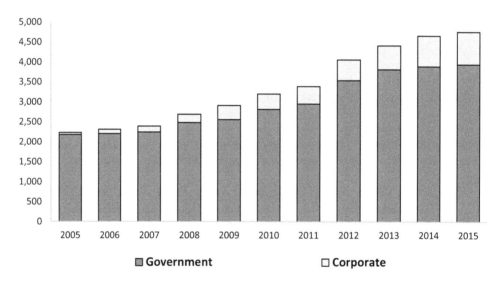

Figure 9.7 Outstanding amounts of LCY bonds (PHP billion)

LCY = local currency.

Source: Asian Bonds Online.

making the local bond market more robust through pricing, liquidity enhancements, increased private debt issues and development of hedging markets in line with regional integration.[9]

Insurance and contingent claims

Officially speaking, the insurance industry has a longer history in the Philippines than the securities market.[10] During the Spanish occupation, the concept of insurance was first introduced in the Philippines by Lloyd's of London by appointing Strachman, Murray and Co., Inc. as its representative in the country. The first life insurance company was established in 1898 with the entry of Sun Life Assurance of Canada, followed by Yek Tong Lin Insurance Company, the first domestic nonlife insurance company, in 1906. Shortly after, the Insular Life Assurance Co., Ltd., the first domestic life insurance company in the country, was established in 1910.

The Philippine insurance industry provides general and life insurance, which includes health, accident and disability insurance, to Filipino individuals, households, and businesses. It is regulated by the Insurance Commission (IC) under the Department of Finance (DOF). The IC is mandated to regulate and supervise the insurance industry in accordance with the provisions of the Insurance Code of the Philippines[11] in order to ensure that adequate insurance protection is available to the public at a fair and reasonable cost and to assure the financial stability of the insurance industry so that all legitimate claims of the insuring public are met promptly and equitably. Also, it issues licenses to pre-need companies, insurance agents and other agents involved in insurance activities such as general agents, resident agents, underwriters, brokers, adjusters, and actuaries.

Under the DOF Department Order No. 15-2012, minimum capitalization for domestic/foreign insurers (life or nonlife) and microinsurers were increased to PHP 1 billion and PHP 500 million,[12] respectively. The insurance industry adopted a risk-based capital (RBC) framework under Insurance Memorandum Circulars No. 6-2006 and 7-2006, wherein every insurance company is annually required to maintain a minimum RBC ratio of 100% and to successfully comply with the trend test. These regulations aim to boost the insurance industry to better compete globally and provide cushion against risks for the protection of the insured.

Latest performance indicators of the insurance industry are on an uptrend, with assets amounting to PHP 1.29 trillion as of June 2016. The combined premium generated by both life and nonlife insurance sectors declined by 9.11% to PHP 105.5 billion for the same period. However, latest data on insurance penetration rate is still low at 1.8% as of June 2015 (Table 9.1).

Industry players consist of 30 life insurance and 68 nonlife insurance companies in 2015. The significant number of players has resulted in competition and has affected premium pricing.[13] In addition, the life insurance sector also competes with other financial institutions such as mutual funds and banks.[14]

Figure 9.8 shows the net worth and premium income of the top five life and nonlife insurance companies in the Philippines as of 2014. The top five life insurance companies accounted for 74.2% share and 61.4% share of the sub-group's net worth and premium income, respectively, implying high concentration of the industry. On the other hand, the nonlife insurance

Table 9.1 Philippine stock market volume of transactions (in million shares)

Insurance Industry	In PHP billion		% Change
	June 2016	June 2015	
Total Assets	1,290.59	1,073.52	20.22
Total Liabilities	1,028.07	886.94	15.91
Total Net Worth	262.51	186.58	40.70
Total Paid-up Capital	42.55	40.8	4.27
Total Investments	1,125.44	929.87	21.03
Total Premiums	105.52	116.11	(9.11)
Total Benefit Payment/Losses Incurred	39.19	36.91	6.17
Total Net Income/(Loss)	19.17	10.86	76.56

Source: Compiled by author with information from the Insurance Commission website.

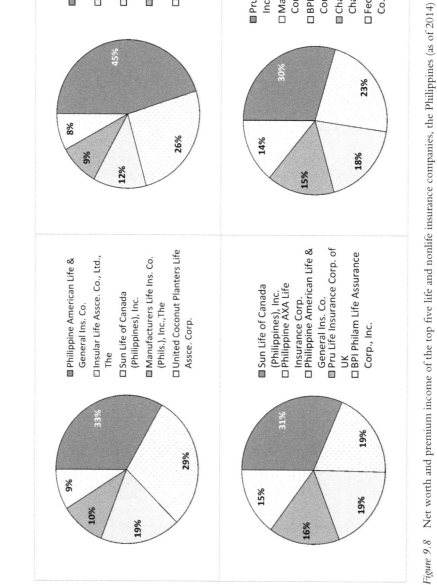

Figure 9.8 Net worth and premium income of the top five life and nonlife insurance companies, the Philippines (as of 2014)

Source: Insurance Commission.

industry is relatively dispersed as the top five nonlife insurance companies held a smaller 38.4% share and 37.7% share of the sub-group's net worth and premium earned, respectively.

Meanwhile, the challenges faced by the insurance industry are chiefly on the low penetration rate, growing natural catastrophe risks due to climate change and high reinsurance risk. The low penetration rate is mainly due to the lack of awareness and the generally conservative nature of majority of Filipinos when it comes to insurance. Meantime, the threat of climate change combined with the country's vulnerability to natural disasters is unavoidable and puts pressure on the income generation of the industry. Correspondingly, due to the high exposure of insurers to losses from the growing incidents of catastrophes, reinsurance risk has grown. In the Philippines, all nonlife companies are required to reinsure with the country's only Filipino-owned reinsurance firm, the National Reinsurance Corporation of the Philippines, although they are not prohibited from reinsuring with foreign reinsurance firms.

Critical contemporaneous issues

Notwithstanding significant progress as a result of systemic implementation of financial sector reforms, the Philippine financial sector does face some critical challenges. Two specific issues are being discussed in the following: (1) the need to collaborate across regulatory agencies and legal mandates arising from both microprudential oversight requirements and the macroprudential objective of financial stability; and (2) our continuing agenda on financial inclusion. These are prominent issues because they cut across traditional financial market segments. More importantly, the specific outcomes of these developments are likely to leave their footprint so as to strategically alter the regulatory landscape as the market moves forward.

Coordination and collaboration of microprudential and macroprudential responsibilities

Coordination and collaboration are certainly necessary when it comes to the supervision of financial institutions, but it is more so in cases such as that of the Philippines where the regulatory framework is based on the traditional demarcation between securities, insurance, and banking markets. In recent decades, these traditional demarcations have become much more opaque and much less binding, thus making the case for even stronger coordination and collaboration.

The Financial Sector Forum (FSF) was formally established on 5 July 2004 by the BSP, SEC, IC, and the Philippine Deposit Insurance Corporation (PDIC). This voluntary endeavor provided an institutionalized framework for coordinating common microprudential supervisory and regulatory issues. Formalizing this cooperative body through a Memorandum of Agreement (MoA) recognized the commitment of the four agencies while at the same time preserving the mandate of each agency under respective laws.

Currently, the focus of the FSF has been on the supervision of financial conglomerates, adherence to quality control standards in external audit, the protection of financial consumers and the streamlining of regulatory reports together with the sharing of information. From time to time, the FSF also has ad hoc work undertaken to assess immediate concerns such as the requirements of ASEAN integration, the enhancement of payment systems and, more recently, crowdfunding.

The prudential focus on conglomerates – particularly non-financial conglomerates with a financial group embedded within the conglomerate – is driven by the fact that the Philippine economy in general is dominated by such corporate structures. Although the size of these conglomerates has been cited as a possible cause for concentration risk,[15] the more compelling concern is their complexity and the degree of inter-connectedness that arise from intra- and inter-conglomerate dealings.

To improve financial conglomerate supervision, the FSF set up common governance expectations applicable to their respective supervised financial institutions, and strengthening coordination efforts to come up with a holistic assessment for the group. To implement this alternative, the FSF had drawn guidelines strengthening oversight and control standards for managing related party transactions (RPT) that will be implemented by each member agency. Further to this, FSF member agencies are reviewing their existing corporate governance standards to come up with common criteria applicable to all supervised institutions.

The BSP, for its part, issued such governance guidelines on RPTs through Circular No. 895 dated 14 December 2015. The guidelines highlight that while transactions between and among the entities within the same group create financial, commercial, and economic benefits, a higher standard should be applied to protect the interest of all stakeholders.[16]

Another key concern for the FSF is the important role of external auditors. Part of this is a concern over transparency, but the key underlying issue is the reliance of both the public and of regulators on the opinion rendered by external auditors in making subsequent decisions.

In line with the general objective of promoting the adherence of external auditors to quality control standards in auditing, the BSP, SEC, IC, and the Board of Accountancy forged an agreement on 12 August 2009 to formalize the framework and process for the synchronization of the accreditation requirements of external auditors. Following this, FSF member agencies adopted common standards on the expectations for an effective external audit function.

To further address the issues and challenges to improving the quality of external audit, the Forum has activated the Council for Accreditation and Quality Control of Practicing CPAs (Council). Under the MoA, the Council shall discuss policy issues on quality control standards of accredited external auditors, oversee the implementation of the MoA, and recommend improvements/enhancements of the synchronized accreditation/selection procedures and requirements. On 15 September 2015, the Council signed the Terms of References of the Council which ultimately aims to promote adherence to quality control standards in external audit.

The FSF has also recognized the critical facet of consumer protection as among the pillars of sustained macrofinancial health. The forum appreciates that the growth of the Philippine economy over the past decade and a half does not guarantee that the financial consumer is automatically better positioned to identify opportunities and improve their financial well-being. To the contrary, the expanding macrofinancial market gives rise to increased occasions where the financial consumer is compromised, either by unlawful and unethical business practices or by his own constraints on financial literacy.

In addition to the above, information sharing and providing a thriving database are necessary for the other initiatives. The existing multilateral MoA dated 19 April 2006 is being amended to capitalize on the use of information technology in facilitating a more efficient and fluid exchange of data and information relevant to the supervision and/or regulation of entities under the jurisdiction of the FSF agencies.

The other aspect of cooperation and collaboration arises from the pursuit of financial stability as the de facto prudential norm. Financial authorities are now tasked – whether explicitly under mandate of law or implicitly as part of general oversight – to consider the build-up and mitigation of systemic risks. While this is expected in the aftermath of the global financial crisis, it does pose specific challenges for authorities.

Knowing what to avoid (i.e., the ex post manifestations of instability) neither defines how to achieve what should be achieved nor identifies the accountable stakeholder who can lead this pursuit. Faced with these uncertainties while recognizing the importance of financial stability as the new normal for prudential policy and oversight, the BSP created a high-level Financial Stability Committee within the central bank and, in parallel, proposed to the legislature possible amendments to its charter to formally include financial stability as one of its mandates. The focus on financial stability has been extended with the creation of an inter-agency Financial Stability Coordination Council (FSCC).

The BSP Financial Stability Committee was created in September 2010. The Committee is chaired by the governor and has all three deputy governors as core members (Figure 9.9). A technical committee provides the link between the workstreams (i.e., working groups assigned to address a specific issue) and the high-level committee. The committee meets every two months to assess developments arising out of its continuing surveillance of the markets as well as to discuss the progress of the various workstreams.

The BSP recognized and appreciated early on that the pursuit of financial stability will necessarily be beyond the legal remit of the central bank and will therefore involve other stakeholders. On this premise, the FSF discussions led to an agreement to establish a parallel inter-agency body specifically focused on financial stability issues. This provided a natural complementation between the microprudential and sectoral risks that the FSF focuses on as against the macroprudential and systemic risks that this new body intends to manage.

This new body is the FSCC and its creation was formally agreed upon by the FSF members on 4 October 2011. Aside from the four FSF members, the FSCC also includes the DOF in the Executive Committee and the Bureau of the Treasury in the supporting subcommittees or work stream. The inclusion of the DOF puts the fiscal authority into the discussions on potentially systemic issues and having the Bureau of the Treasury in both the work stream and the Steering Committee ensures that capital market risks are likewise considered.

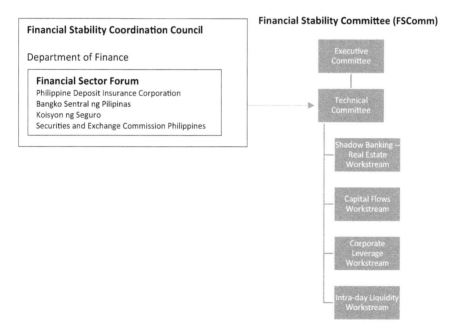

Figure 9.9   Financial stability coordination council membership

Source: Compiled by author with information from Bangko Sentral ng Pilipinas.

The FSCC is chaired by the governor of the BSP. It meets quarterly and the technical secretariat support is provided by a team from the BSP.

Financial inclusion

A second overarching strategic issue is that of financial inclusion. This is not just an initiative that is benefiting from a popular global focus but one that is fundamental to the sustainability of the Philippine financial market.[17] As an archipelago of 7,107 islands with a population of more than 100 million, 18 administrative regions, and 182 live languages, one can only imagine the socio-economic segmentation that prevails in the country. With Palma ratios of over three times,[18] one is not necessarily surprised with findings that only 31% of Filipino adults have a formal financial account and only 32.5% of the population has some form of insurance coverage.[19]

If the financial market is to maintain its value proposition as the venue for stakeholders to either mobilize economic saving through financial instruments or raise funding for entrepreneurial as well as consumption purposes, then it must necessarily be responsive to the needs of the economic consumer. The objective, as noted in the definition of financial inclusion, is to provide "effective access," and this is possible only if there is a broad menu of financial products and services which have been calibrated to the varied needs of differentiated consumers.

In the absence of such effective access and broad menu of calibrated financial products and services, the financial market will then simply cater to those that are "financially included." This perpetuates an economic imbalance by disenfranchising those who need the value proposition of financial markets the most at the margin.

Following a continuing commitment toward inclusion, data on access and usage of formal financial services in the Philippines suggest that the country's financial system has become more inclusive over the years. In terms of access, the number of bank branches from September 2014 to 2015 increased by 3.9%, from 10,160 to 10,560 offices, covering 64% of all cities and municipalities in the country, while the number of automated teller machines grew by 10.5% from 15,182 to 16,778 over the same period.[20] Non-bank financial service providers including credit cooperatives, non-stock savings and loan associations, microfinance non-government organizations, pawnshops, remittance agents, money changers, foreign exchange dealers and electronic money (e-money) agents remain important access points especially in those areas without physical banking presence. About 67% of cities and municipalities without banking offices are being served by these providers.

Usage of formal financial products is generally increasing, as gleaned from the 10% growth of the volume of bank deposits and 16% growth for loans between September 2014 and September 2015 while the total number of deposit accounts increased by 5% from 48 million to 50 million during the same period.

Microdeposits increased by 28% from PHP 3.8 million in September 2014 to PHP 4.8 million in September 2015. The number of microdeposit accounts likewise increased by 31% from 1.9 million accounts to 2.5 million during the same period. Meanwhile, microinsurance delivery and coverage also improved. Thirty-nine banks authorized to sell microinsurance products together with other licensed micro-insurance providers covered 29 million individuals in 2014 compared to 28 million in 2013.[21]

Under the e-money regulations of the BSP, there has been a notable growth of accounts, transactions, e-money issuers and agents. Thirty-one institutions, banks and non-banks alike, are now offering e-money products and services. These institutions employ 13,345 active agent outlets as distribution channels. This vast network enabled e-money issuers to reach almost 11 million account holders with outstanding balances of over PHP 9 billion.

All of these data are encouraging signs that ongoing efforts are indeed extending the frontiers of the financial market in a more inclusive manner. But they cannot be taken as measures of success as if the objective has finally been achieved. The more realistic view is that the initiative of making financial markets more inclusive will have to be a continuous cross-cutting task among many stakeholders and any gains along the way will fundamentally reshape the financial market, its product offerings and its relationship with the financial consumer.

The financial inclusion agenda has brought to fore the need for consumer protection because those previously "excluded" are not likely to have sufficient appreciation of the risks that they may be taking with specific products. By extension, they too may not yet be in a position to compare the nuances of financial risks across competing products. Either case is clearly a significant concern and should not be allowed to fester.

Aspiring for an inclusive financial system will mean that more financial transactions are expected. The sheer increase of transactions, let alone a potential increase in the take up of risk products as a result of more appetite over time for financial risks, should also translate to more occurrences of transactions that will be subject to disputes. Clearly, this could occur in the securities, insurance or banking markets, necessitating that a coordinated redress framework must already be in place to handle any disputes that arise.

The sheer volume of transactions is not the only premise for a redress framework (Figure 9.10). Financial sales agents are potentially conflicted if they singularly focus on making a sale without due consideration of the suitability of the client to the financial product. Having a redress mechanism provides a recourse to address either malpractices or temper the indiscriminate selling of sophisticated financial products and services to interested, albeit inexperienced, retail customers.

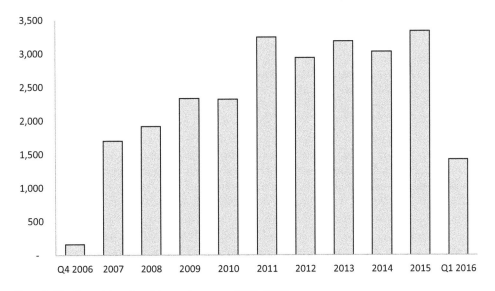

Figure 9.10 Complaints, inquiries, and requests (2006–2016)

Source: Bangko Sentral ng Pilipinas.

The BSP issued its Financial Consumer Protection Framework (Circular No. 857). Part of this framework focuses on five standards of market conduct that shall apply to financial service providers. The framework also lays down guiding principles to handle conflicts of interest:

1   Disclosure to the consumer prior to the execution of the transaction that the former or its staff has an interest in subject transaction;
2   Disclosure that the financial institution only recommends products issued by related companies, particularly when commissions or rebates are the primary basis for the recommendation;
3   Disclosure of the remuneration to be received from the transaction, at the pre-contractual stage; and
4   Institutionalization of adequate systems and controls to promptly identify issues and matters that may be detrimental to a customer's interest (e.g., cases in which advice may have been given merely to meet sales targets, or may be driven by financial or other incentives).

These guiding principles are geared toward giving the financial consumer full information about the gains that will accrue to the seller should the transaction be consummated.

Market direction: mitigating the risks of capital market underdevelopment

The preceding reflects the many moving parts of the Philippine financial market. While each facet has its own story to tell, the most interesting ones are those that cut across traditional markets. This is so because they will likely have the most impact in reshaping the market landscape and are also the obvious triggers for system-wide dislocations if they are not handled "appropriately."

As a policy objective, capital market development has been discussed for an extended period. The banking authority has a natural stake on this issue because a developed capital market reduces the reliance on bank credit with long-term exposures, provides a better environment within which banks operate as trading participants, and creates proper valuation between short-term and longer-term (credit, liquidity, time) risks.

The impression though is that progress has been much more modest when compared to desired outcomes. With global and regional markets volatile since the second semester of 2015, the risks arising from capital market *under*development has become rather elevated and, if not mitigated effectively, can easily escalate into a systemic risk.

Market stakeholders have long desired of a transparent, market determined, and binding yield curve which some have argued is not what is available today. They point out that the current reference rate is "too volatile" for purposes of being a benchmark (Figure 9.11).

The problem appears to be driven by the fact that the outstanding issues of government securities are not evenly distributed across benchmark tenors (Figure 9.12). Latest data show that only 7.22% of outstanding issues have a remaining term of less than one year (Figure 9.13). As a result, the rate tends to swing more erratically between done, bid, and interpolated rates.

There is a need to address the sources of volatility in the benchmark rates so that distortions do not arise. While it can factually be argued that the volatility may be reflecting the market's lack of uniform liquidity, it is also known that volatile benchmark rates mean that mark-to-market values of tradable securities will be just as volatile. There is further a consumer protection issue here since financial consumers may be acting upon (temporarily) favorable values when in fact these are volatile in nature.

Enhancing the benchmark-setting exercise is critical. It can mitigate systemic risks as well as consumer protection issues. But this will need a fiscal response since the underlying issue remains the distribution of outstanding government securities.

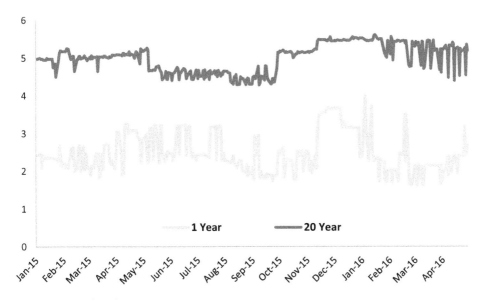

Figure 9.11 Benchmark rates

Source: Raw data sourced from the Philippine Dealing and Exchange Corp.

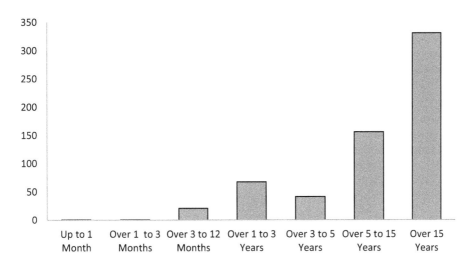

Figure 9.12 Residual maturity of HTM government securities (as of end-December 2015, PHP billion)

Source: Financial reports submitted by banks to the Bangko Sentral ng Pilipinas.

The discussion on capital market development naturally segues to the intent to integrate the Association of Southeast Asian Nations (ASEAN). Although it may sound ironic, one should expect that the desire to harmonize and converge will highlight in the process existing divergences. That said, the decision to integrate as a single market and production base was made two decades ago, and we find ourselves today at the point of executing this policy and political directive.

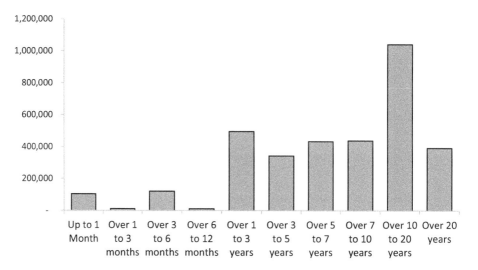

Figure 9.13 Outstanding amount of government securities by residual maturity (PHP million)

Source: Bureau of the Treasury.

For the rollout of the ASEAN Banking Integration Framework, preparations are needed for the banks and for the public. Quite frankly, to the extent that the qualified ASEAN banks will operate within the regulations of the host jurisdiction, the immediate challenge will be more about communicating to the banks and to the public what ASEAN integration is all about.

However, when these qualified ASEAN banks will be used as portals for intra-ASEAN investments, then there is a need to be more concerned with the readiness of the domestic capital market to integrate with the rest of ASEAN. The issue of having distortions from a volatile yield curve is just one issue. Integrating capital markets is about re-allocating saving through financial instruments and economic initiatives. It may mean that onshore saving may be diverted to offshore opportunities or that the local market may be immersed with foreign saving. Either case has its pros and cons, but for as long as integration is the policy directive, it will mean keeping the Philippine borders open to inflows and outflows. That becomes the issue because there will be times that it is inconvenient or untimely to keep the borders open.

To mitigate this selection bias problem, the onshore capital market must be an effective tool for attracting investment funds (both financial and real) and a linchpin for channeling funds offshore. Doing so means having in place needed infrastructure; a well-functioning pricing benchmark; strong banks which can properly identify, price and mitigate risks across borders; and a consumer protection framework that can nurture financial literacy and trigger redress mechanism, where necessary. In this context, the critical contemporaneous issues discussed earlier are significantly underpinned by the need to mitigate the risks from the underdevelopment of the local capital market.

Notes

1 The first credit institution in the Philippines, "The Obras Pias," was started by Father Juan Fernandez de Leon in 1754. The name literally means "works of piety" and was generally funded out of a directive of the Church to direct a portion of personal wealth to charitable foundations such as Obras Pias. The first Philippine Bank, on the other hand, was established in 1851 and named the "Banco Español-Filipino de Isabela II" as a tribute to the mother of then Spanish King Alfonso XII. This is the oldest bank in the Philippines and in Southeast Asia.

2 The Gini coefficient is a measure of inequality of a distribution.

3 Both domestic and international.

4 Compound annual growth rate.

5 Securities and Exchange Commission website (www.sec.gov.ph/aboutsec/history.html).

6 The Bankers Association of the Philippines (BAP), a non-stock and non-profit organization, was organized on 29 March 1949 with the distinct purpose and objectives of furthering the interest of banks. It was formally incorporated into a corporate organization duly registered with the Securities and Exchange Commission on 24 August 1964. The membership of the BAP covers the universal and commercial banks. These banks have a natural interest in the fixed income market because they are the largest players in this market.

7 Bangko Sentral ng Pilipinas website (www.bsp.gov.ph/financial/fixed.asp).

8 Asian Development Bank. *Asian Bonds Monitor March 2016*.

9 Asian Development Bank. *ASEAN+3 Bond Market Guide January 2012*.

10 Insurance Commission website (www.insurance.gov.ph/htm/_about_history.asp).

11 Amended by Republic Act No. 10607 in 15 August 2013, which aimed to strengthens and modernize the insurance industry. Some of the significant regulatory amendments introduced include (1) increased minimum capitalization requirements, (2) adoption of a financial reporting framework, (3) allows insurance companies to invest in more financial instruments, (4) institutionalizes bancassurance, microinsurance, and variable contracts, (5) modification of reserve valuation, and (6) additional powers and functions to the Insurance Commissioner.

12 Existing domestic and foreign insurers (life or nonlife) and microinsurers are allowed to comply with the minimum capitalization on a staggered basis until 2020. Meanwhile, new domestic and foreign insurers (life or nonlife) and microinsurers are required to comply upon operation.

13 Economic evidence shows that with fewer competitors, insurance premiums tend to be higher. Less competition among insurers produces higher prices for consumers (www.nytimes.com/2015/07/25/business/dealbook/anthem-cigna-health-insurance-deal.html?_r=2). Thus, higher number of industry players would generally lead to lower premiums for consumers and reduced profits to insurance companies.

14 Banks offer insurance products through bancassurance (i.e., partnership or relationship between a bank and an insurance company, or a single integrated organization, whereby the insurance company uses the bank sales channel in order to sell insurance products, an arrangement in which a bank and an insurance company form a partnership so that the insurance company can sell its products to the bank's client base), while some insurance companies sell investment type products like annuities and provide services such as tax and estate planning which compete directly with mutual funds (www.investopedia.com/features/industryhandbook/insurance.asp).

15 International Monetary Fund website (www.imf.org/external/pubs/ft/scr/2015/cr15246.pdf).

16 The BSP guidelines emphasized that RPTs are generally allowed on the condition that they be done on an arm's-length basis. This ensures that related parties are not favored – or equivalently, that non-related parties are effectively prejudiced – by the dealings of the covered institution. In the same guidelines, supervised financial institutions are required to create an RPT Committee. The said committee shall be responsible for the continuing identification and review of existing relations between and among businesses and counterparties, and for ensuring that RPTs are processed in the regular course of business, and are priced fairly.

17 We note that BSP's efforts in microfinance and financial inclusion has a 15-year track record, well ahead of the current focus in various forums. In 2000, the BSP declared that microfinance would be its flagship program for poverty alleviation. Defined as the "provision of a broad range of services (i.e., deposits, loans, payments/ money transfers, insurance) for the low-income entrepreneurial poor and their households," microfinance dovetails readily with the BSP's financial inclusion initiatives since financial inclusion is succinctly defined by the BSP as "a state wherein there is effective access to a wide range of financial services by all."

18 The Palma ratio (Cambridge University, January 2011) is a measure of inequality and is calculated as the top 10% of population's share of gross national income (GNI) divided by the poorest 40% of the population's share of GNI. Higher values for the ratio indicate greater inequality.

19 Figures taken from the National Strategy for Financial Inclusion. July 2015.

20 Unless otherwise stated, all data are from the BSP.

21 Insurance Commission.

References

Crisostomo, R. G., S. Padilla, and M. F. Visda. 2013. *Philippine Stock Market in Perspective*. Paper Presented at 12th National Convention on Statistics, Mandaluyong City, Philippines, 1–2 October.

Gerson, P. 1998. *Poverty and Economic Policy in the Philippines*. Finance and Development. Washington, DC: International Monetary Fund.

Gochoco-Bautista, M. S. 1997. The Past Performance of the Philippine Banking Sector and Challenges in the Postcrisis Period. In R*ising to the Challenge in Asia: A Study of Financial Markets*, Volume 10, Philippines. Manila: Asian Development Bank, pp. 29–78. https://aric.adb.org/pdf/aem/external/financial_market/Philippines/phil_bnk.pdf

International Monetary Fund (IMF) and Central Bank of the Philippines (CBP). 1972. *Recommendations of the Joint IMF-CBP Banking Survey Commission on the Philippine Banking System*. Manila: Central Bank Publishing Office.

10

FINANCIAL SECTOR IN SINGAPORE

Hwee Kwan Chow and Sai Fan Pei

Introduction

Over the past five decades, Singapore has established a sound and progressive financial center of international repute that serves both the local economy and the Asia-Pacific region. As an international financial center, it is home to a high concentration of over 1,200 financial institutions which offer myriad products and services across diverse asset classes. Financial markets in Singapore are well established, and the main financial services industries include banking (especially investment banking, wealth management and treasury activities), insurance, and capital market (securities, futures, and derivatives) services. The key descriptors of the financial center in Singapore are an efficient pro-business environment; an effective regulatory environment; excellent infrastructure; and the availability of a highly skilled and experienced pool of finance professionals.

Unlike other more laissez-faire major financial centers, however, financial development in Singapore since independence owes much to the government's proactive policies. The Singapore government has been actively undertaking financial liberalization and reforms since the 1960s. Financial liberalization was hastened in the aftermath of the Asian financial crisis in order to build a resilient and competitive financial sector in the advent of a more globalized environment. In particular, greater access was granted to foreign participants along with a wave of consolidation of domestic banks. Moreover, a different "risk-based" approach to regulation and supervision was adopted to facilitate financial development and innovation and at the same time guard against systemic risks of the financial sector.

This chapter reviews the financial development strategies adopted by the Singapore government as it navigates internal and external changes to build a vibrant center of finance in the Asia-Pacific region. The next two sections provide an overview of the structure of the financial system and the financial governance framework. This is followed by a discussion on the outward looking development strategy that underpinned the successful development of Singapore's financial sector. The penultimate section highlights the reforms undertaken in the aftermath of the Asian financial crisis that led to the building of a well-diversified and thriving international financial center. We conclude with the challenges Singapore faces in the new global financial landscape.

Overview of financial system

The banking sector in Singapore had a total asset size of around SGD 2 trillion in 2014, and there are currently more than 200 banks (including representative offices of banks) operating in Singapore. Of the 125 commercial banks, only five are local and 29 foreign banks are awarded full bank status.[1] The other foreign commercial banks are either wholesale banks or offshore banks, numbering 53 and 38, respectively. Foreign full banks include global players in the banking business such as HSBC, Citibank, and Standard Chartered among others. A growing number of foreign banks are choosing Singapore to be their regional headquarters or as a global platform for banking services.

The three dominant local banks are DBS Bank Ltd. (DBS), Overseas-Chinese Banking Corporation Ltd. (OCBC), and United Overseas Bank Ltd. (UOB), each ranking highly in Bloomberg's list of world's strongest banks. Table 10.1 records the key characteristics of the three banks in 2014. It is clear from the table that the individual banks have strong financial fundamentals in terms of being well capitalized and profitable. Moreover, each of these local banks has a low level of non-performing assets as well as healthy funding and liquidity profiles.

Apart from the traditional lending and deposit-taking functions, banks located in Singapore also provide sophisticated banking services like corporate and investment banking. In addition, Singapore has emerged as a leading wealth management and private banking hub as it capitalizes on the rising number of high net worth individuals in Asia, Europe, and other regions. In this respect, the deep and liquid capital markets in Singapore play an important role in facilitating greater financial intermediation, particularly within Asia.

Singapore's foreign exchange market is ranked third largest in the world by turnover, just after the UK (first) and the US (second), based on the 2016 Bank for International Settlements triennial central bank survey. The average daily volume of foreign exchange turnover and foreign exchange derivatives turnover amounted to USD 419.2 billion and USD 87.3 billion, respectively, in April 2016.[2] Singapore is also ranked the largest over-the-counter (OTC)

Table 10.1 Characteristics of Singapore's largest banks in 2014

	DBS	OCBC	UOB
(in million SGD)			
Total assets	440,667	401,226	306,736
Total loans	275,588	207,593	195,903
Total customer deposits	317,173	245,519	233,750
Shareholders' equity	37,783	34,185	29,772
Net interest income	6,398	4,842	4,606
Net fees and commissions	2,027	1,495	1,749
Profit (loss) before tax	4,906	4,763	3,825
Profit (loss) after tax	4,190	4,076	3,264
(in %)			
Tier 1 capital ratio	13.1	13.8	13.9
Non-performing assets to total assets ratio	0.3	0.3	0.8
Deposits to funding ratio	85.7	83.3	87.6
Loan loss reserves to non-performing assets ratio	141.9	173.7	132.9

Source: Compiled by authors with data from EIU Singapore Financial Services report, Banks (November 2015, www.eiu.com/industry/Financial%20services/asia/singapore/article/2013913385/banks); Bloomberg's list of World's Strongest Banks 2014 (www.bloomberg.com/visual-data/best-and-worst/world-s-strongest-banks).

interest rate derivatives center in Asia-Pacific by turnover. The large trading volume can partly be attributed to Singapore's time zone, which is well suited for trading the increasing important Asian currencies. Indeed, Singapore has positioned itself as a major global trading and treasury hub serving investment and risk management needs in the Asian time zone.

With over 40% of its listing originating from outside Singapore, the Singapore Exchange (SGX) is Asia's most internationalized exchange. The SGX has a listing of close to 800 companies and is the largest Real Estate Investment Trust (REIT) market in Asia ex-Japan. Its derivatives exchange is also one of Asia's largest and trades a wide range of international derivatives. These include interest rate futures, currency futures, bond and stock index futures, and commodity futures. Singapore's derivatives exchange has built a reputation of being a successful regional risk management center for global investors. In recognition of its continued innovation across the risk management portfolio, the SGX was awarded the Global Exchange of the Year, and Exchange of the Year for the region that includes Asia, Australasia and Middle East and Africa by Futures and Options World, in 2015.

Likewise, Singapore is a key international debt arranging hub in Asia. According to the annual survey of the Singapore corporate debt markets, total corporate debt capitalization reached a record high of SGD 200 billion with a record number of 149 issuers by the end of 2014 (MAS 2015a). In particular, yuan bonds shot up by 153% from 2013 exceeding RMB 35 billion in 2014. Besides corporates, there is also a steady flow of issuance from the Singapore government, statutory boards and supra-nationals.

Supported by well-developed capital markets, Singapore has become a premier asset management center in Asia. Assets under management by fund managers in Singapore reached a record high of SGD 2.6 trillion in 2015, with 80% of funds sourced from outside Singapore and 68% of funds invested in Asia-Pacific (MAS 2015b). The industry is essentially a pan-Asian asset management center that serves global investors in search of Asian growth. There were approximately 628 fund managers in 2015. The breadth and depth of players can be seen from global and locally owned asset managers in the traditional space, as well as alternative players including hedge funds, private equity and real estate managers. Diversification across asset classes is revealed in the following distribution in 2015: equities (43%), fixed income (23%), alternatives (20%), collective investment schemes such as mutual funds (10%), and cash/money markets (4%).

Singapore has also established itself as an insurance hub and is often used as a base to write risks from the region. Local as well as major international life and general insurers, reinsurers, captives, and intermediaries provide a range of services. Total insurance industry assets were SGD 197.4 billion in 2014. In particular, offshore insurance business has become a major driver of industry growth, accounting for more than half of the total general insurance business written.

The liberalization of the yuan by the government of the People's Republic of China (PRC) government has led to a new growth area for the Singapore financial services sector. According to the Society for Worldwide Interbank Financial Telecommunications (SWIFT), Singapore is the largest offshore yuan trading hub outside the PRC and Hong Kong, China by payment value. As of March 2015, yuan deposits were CNY 257 billion; outstanding yuan loans and trade financing exceeded CNY 300 billion; and the average daily turnover for yuan foreign exchange reached USD 60 billion (MAS 2015a). Direct trading for the yuan and the Singapore dollar has also commenced on the PRC Foreign Exchange Trade System. Other collaborative efforts include cross-border yuan flows arrangement whereby eligible companies in the Suzhou Industrial Park, Tianjin Eco-City, and Chongqing can borrow in yuan from the Singapore market.[3] An overnight yuan liquidity facility that caters to the short-term funding needs of financial institutions was also set up in Singapore in July 2014. In October 2014, Singapore Exchange also successfully launched the yuan currency futures, namely USD/CNY and CNY/USD futures.

Financial governance framework

The development of Singapore as a sound and reputable international financial center is under-pinned by the consistent high standards of financial regulation that allows well-managed risk-taking and innovation. The Monetary Authority of Singapore (MAS), established as a statutory board in 1971, is responsible for the supervision and development of the Singapore financial services sector. The MAS also functions as Singapore's central bank, formulating and implementing monetary policy.

Governed by the MAS Act, the MAS is conferred the powers to issue legal instruments for the regulation and supervision of financial institutions. As financial institutions develop mixed operation models with hybrid products and services cutting across different financial services industries, MAS takes an integrated supervisory approach by evaluating financial groups on a whole-of-group basis across their banking, insurance, and securities activities. The MAS also establishes supervisory frameworks, methods, and guidelines on topics which cut across various classes of financial institutions.

The supervisory objectives of the MAS include the promotion of (1) a stable financial system; (2) safe and sound intermediaries; (3) safe and efficient infrastructure; (4) fair, efficient, and transparent markets; (5) transparent and fair-dealing intermediaries and offerors; and (6) well-informed and empowered consumers (MAS 2004). To this end, the MAS performs the tasks of regulation, authorization, supervision, surveillance, enforcement, and resolution. A risk-focused approach is adopted. The MAS evaluates the risk profile of an institution, providing closer supervision for those that are systemically important and giving greater business latitude to well-managed institutions. At the same time, the MAS requires financial institutions to have a shared ownership of supervisory outcomes.

Additionally, the MAS collaborates with other authorities and principal regulators to facilitate corporate governance, market discipline, consumer education and consumer safety net. For instance, the MAS works with the Council of Corporate Disclosure, the Ministry of Finance, and the Accounting and Corporate Regulatory Authority to strengthen corporate governance and disclosure standards. For capital market enforcement, MAS collaborates with Singapore Exchange, Commercial Affairs Department of Singapore Police Force, and Attorney General's Chambers. While the MAS administers statutory laws regulating the capital markets and has oversight of SGX's regulatory function, the SGX has frontline responsibility of regulating market participants and ensuring compliance.

By benchmarking itself against international standards and best practices, such as capital rules by Basel Accords and recommendations by Financial Action Task Force (FATF) on combating money laundering, MAS' sound regulation and rigorous supervision have earned investor confidence in the Singapore financial system. This has resulted in financial stability, even amid external turmoil such as during the 1997–1998 Asian banking crisis and the 2007–2008 global financial crisis. Moreover, MAS has a long tradition of active consultation with the industry on proposed new rules and initiatives. Such a consultative approach to regulation has contributed to building a responsive and progressive financial system.

An outward-looking financial development strategy

At the outset, the Singapore government recognized the financial sector for its growth potential and regarded it as an important sector in its own right. Despite prevailing norms in Asia, an outward-looking financial development strategy was adopted in the 1960s. This was motivated by the desire to become a regional financial center. After all, the small size of the domestic market means a limited growth potential and posed the need to look outside to engender growth.

A two-tier banking system

The Singapore financial center has its beginnings in the financing of merchant trade in the region. Taking advantage of its status as a trading hub, Singapore started in the 1960s as an offshore trading center for foreign currencies.[4] It established the Asian dollar market (ADM) as an international money and capital market, channeling savings in foreign currencies mainly in USD from advanced and oil rich Middle Eastern countries to the growing economies in the region particularly during the 1970s and 1980s. The ADM also attracted multinational companies to set up regional treasury and financing operations in Singapore (Hew 2005)

A two-tier banking system was designed since 1968.[5] Banks were required to partition their offshore from local operations by using separate accounting units. The Asian Currency Unit (ACU) was a bookkeeping entity for non-Singapore dollar transactions while the Domestic Banking Units (DBUs) were for Singapore dollar transactions. This segregation of international vis-à-vis domestic banking activities ensures the flow of funds into the ADM did not disrupt monetary management in Singapore. It also protected domestic banks from larger and more sophisticated foreign financial institutions.

The MAS imposed liquidity requirements on the DBUs and subjected DBU activities to large exposure and equity investment limits in order to safeguard domestic financial stability. By contrast, ACU activities were minimally regulated and enjoyed withholding tax exemptions. Consequently, the ACUs grew spectacularly outpacing the expansion of DBUs. Starting with just USD 33.2 million in 1968, monies in ACU accounts grew quickly to cross the USD 1 billion mark only three years later and reached almost USD 2 trillion by the end of 2013.

Foreign exchange market

Singapore's favorable time zone, which bridges the gap between the close of US markets and the reopening of European markets, enabled its foreign exchange market to become part of the round-the-clock global market for foreign exchange trading. This, along with the success of the ADM, boosted the growth of the foreign exchange market. In 1984, the foreign exchange market was broadened with the establishment of Singapore International Monetary Exchange (SIMEX) which offers currency futures contracts. Singapore overtook Switzerland in 1992 and Tokyo in 2013 to become the third largest foreign exchange market in the world today, in terms of average daily forex turnover. This no doubt contributed to Singapore's rise in stature as a leading financial center.

The rise in foreign exchange trading and ADM activities, in turn, led to the robust growth in the banking sector. To protect the local banks from excessive competition, new types of banking licenses were issued. In 1973, the MAS established the offshore bank license category to attract foreign banks of good standing to operate mainly in the ADM and foreign exchange market and to conduct wholesale banking with nonresidents. Developmental incentives targeted at ACU activities were offered to encourage the growth of the offshore banking sector. By 1997, Singapore became a dominant offshore banking sector in Asia, as the ADM reached USD 557.2 billion and the financial center made up 12% of Singapore's GDP.

In spite of its notable achievements, the financial sector in Singapore faced an increasing competitive external environment with the advent of globalization. Advances in technology enabled financial institutions to introduce new products and distribution channels, as well as scale up their operations across geographical and industry barriers. The increasingly fierce competition across borders resulted in the growth of large financial conglomerates and the congregation of international financial activities in fewer centers. For instance, London as a financial hub partially replaced Zurich, Paris, and Frankfurt. Meanwhile, Euronext became the consolidated stock exchange between Paris, Amsterdam, and Brussels. To ensure Singapore stayed ahead of the competition, a major review of the financial sector was conducted in Singapore after the outbreak of the Asian financial crisis.

Review of the financial sector

A Financial Sector Review Group (FSRG) was formed in 1997 to conduct a comprehensive review of Singapore's financial sector. This was led by the then Deputy Prime Minister Mr. Lee Hsien Loong, who was the chairman of the MAS in 1998–2004. Inputs were sought from experts from the Bank of England and the US Federal Reserve, among others. Feedback was also obtained from private sector committees that worked on various aspects of reforming the financial sector. In addition, McKinsey and Arthur D. Little were commissioned to carry out strategy studies on the financial sector and financial sector information technology.

The review of the financial sector led to the development of the following three broad strategies: (1) promote a vibrant asset management industry; (2) develop deep and broad capital markets in debt, equity, and derivatives; and (3) build a strong and competitive banking industry. While the FSRG recommended bold measures to liberalize the financial sector, it urged the careful implementation of these measures in order to safeguard stability and confidence in Singapore's financial markets. Hence, the MAS decided to avoid a "big bang" liberalization approach, preferring instead to make a series of significant incremental changes. In particular, a careful balance was struck between supervision and development of the financial sector.

A dedicated financial promotion department

Inherent tension exists between taking risks to facilitate business innovation and enterprise for development versus the effective monitoring and mitigating of risks for safety. The FSGR believed this tension between promotion and supervisory roles is best managed within a single organization with a shared purpose instead of separate entities with conflicting goals. In 1998, the MAS Act was amended to include financial sector promotion as a principal objective so that the central bank can be more proactive in promotional efforts. Hence, a dedicated promotion department was set up in the MAS to work closely with the industry to bring in new products, technologies, and activities. Another function of the new Financial Sector Promotion Department was to champion industry's needs with various government agencies such as the Ministry of Finance and the Inland Revenue Authority of Singapore.

To encourage productive public-private sector collaboration and cross-pollination of ideas, the MAS set up two institutions. They are the Financial Sector Advisory Council, which facilitates regular feedback of ideas from market participants in Singapore, and the International Advisory Panel, which provides MAS with a global perspective from leading financial executives worldwide.

Asset management industry

A key strategic trust that emerged from the review was to develop Singapore into a premier asset management hub. MAS' vision was to attract more global fund managers to use Singapore

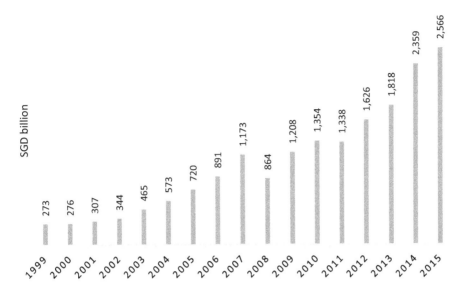

Figure 10.1 Total assets under management
Source: Compiled by authors with data from CEIC database (Monetary Authority of Singapore).

as a base to invest in Asia as well as for Asian investors to use Singapore as a base to diversify out of Asia. To realize this vision, capital markets needed to be deepened and widened to provide a greater variety of investment products that reached more market segments. Global investors could then have more instruments to gain Asian exposure across a wide range of asset classes.

Hence, the MAS streamlined regulations to make it easier for fund managers to enter domestic markets and distribute their products. The Government Investment Corporation (GIC)[6] and the MAS provided USD 35 billion and USD 10 million seed money, respectively, to fund managers with proven track record and who showed commitment to develop the local asset management industry. The rules of the Central Provident Fund (CPF) Investment Scheme were also relaxed to allow CPF members to engage professional asset managers to manage their investible funds.[7] Apart from the generous tax incentives, foreign fund managers were attracted by the opportunity to manage a substantial amount of funds from the national pension scheme.

Singapore became a major player in the management of offshore money for investors based overseas. We see from Figure 10.1 that assets under management by fund managers in Singapore shot up from SGD 273 billion in 1999 to SGD 2.6 trillion in 2015.

Capital markets

An important lesson drawn from the Asian financial crisis is that over-dependence on the banking system exacerbated problems for borrowers and national financial security. This prompted a greater push to develop broad and deep capital markets so as to diversify sources of funds. In particular, the development of a deep and liquid bond market would provide borrowers a good alternative source of long-term capital to match long-term expenditure needs, and a more diversified funding base for the national economy. Hence, the MAS issued Singapore Government Securities (SGS) despite persistent fiscal surpluses in order to create a benchmark Singapore dollar yield curve on which corporate debt issues can be priced. The inclusion of SGS in the JP Morgan Government Bond Global Broad Index in 2000 gave the debt market a further boost.[8] In addition, public sector agencies such as the Housing Development Board and the Land Transport Authority were encouraged to issue bonds in order to enlarge the pool of tradable Singapore dollar bonds.

The MAS also made it easier for foreigners to issue local currency bonds by gradually liberalizing the Singapore dollar non-internationalization policy. This policy, adopted in the early 1980s, restricted the international use of the domestic currency essentially to deter currency speculation so as to facilitate the effective conduct of Singapore's exchange-rate centered monetary policy (Ong 2003). The restrictions have been progressively removed over the years to facilitate the development of Singapore's capital markets. For instance, banks were allowed to lend any amount to nonresidents provided proceeds were for investment purposes in Singapore assets. At the same time, there was active promotion of Singapore as a regional hub for arranging and trading debt securities. Importantly, a strong talent pool with expertise and experience in debt origination, sales, and trading was built through the Approved Bond Intermediary tax incentive scheme.

With these changes, the bond market attracted a diverse range of local and foreign issuance. Figure 10.2 displays the rapid growth in corporate debt issuance from a total capitalization of SGD 19.5 billion in 1999 to SGD 174 billion in 2015, with less than 16% of issuance in Singapore dollars.

Turning to equities and derivatives, the Stock Exchange of Singapore and the Singapore International Monetary Exchange were merged and demutualized to form an integrated stock and derivatives exchange, the Singapore Exchange (SGX), a first in the Asia-Pacific in 1999. Synergies between the securities and derivative business were offered by the merger, which also increased the financial capability to undertake heavy capital investments and financial innovation. Besides improving its technological infrastructure, the SGX relaxed foreign listing requirements and pursued strategic alliances with other exchanges. The MAS liberalized brokerage commissions, opened access to foreign stockbroker participation and expanded product offerings by encouraging the creation and hedging of structured products, credit derivatives and the use of securitization. To maintain investor confidence, various measures were implemented

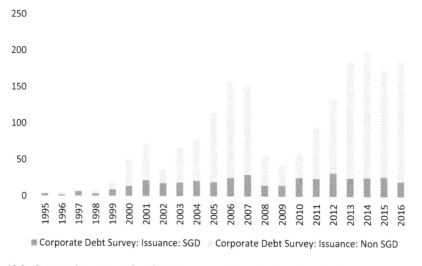

Figure 10.2 Issuance in corporate bond in Singapore dollar and other denominations

Source: Compiled by authors with data from CEIC database (Monetary Authority of Singapore).

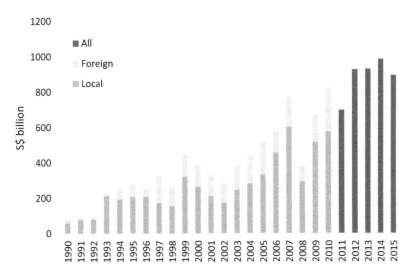

Figure 10.3 Market capitalization of SGX mainboard

Note: Data on the breakdown between foreign and local listings are available up to 2010 only.

Sources: Compiled by authors with data from CEIC Database (1990–2010), Monetary Authority of Singapore (2011–2015) (https://secure.mas.gov.sg/msb-xml/Report.aspx?tableSetID=III&tableID=III.7).

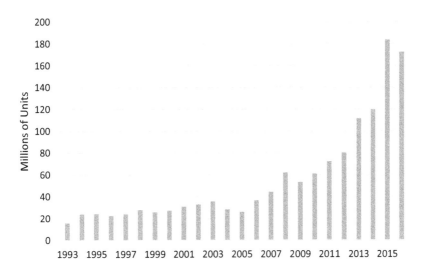

Figure 10.4 Annual turnover of SIMEX/SGX futures and options

Source: Compiled by authors with data from CEIC database (Monetary Authority of Singapore).

to improve corporate governance of listed companies, enhance disclosure and strengthen market discipline.

Consequently, the SGX became an access point for managing Asian capital and investment exposure. Total equity market capitalization of SGX grew from SGD 126 billion in 1999 to SGD 895 billion in 2015, with a significant proportion of the trades originating from outside Singapore (see Figure 10.3). As shown in Figure 10.4, financial derivatives trading volume in Singapore grew from 25.9 million contracts in 1999 to 172.3 million contracts in 2016.

Banking industry

Another strategic trust that emerged from the review was to build commercial banking as the bedrock of Singapore's financial sector. To this end, the domestic banking sector was liberalized and a five-year program to develop strong local banks through consolidation and competition was launched in 1999. Rather than opening the domestic retail market indiscriminately, the MAS granted access only to strong, well-managed foreign banks committed to growing in Singapore. It awarded a new license category – Qualifying Full Bank – and the Restricted Bank category was renamed Wholesale Bank with increased lending limits and lower restrictions on engaging in Singapore dollar swaps. These measures were successful in attracting foreign banks to base their operational headquarters in Singapore to service their regional activities.

Such an increase in foreign participation resulted in stiffer competition for the local banks. The government recognized that strong local banks with a significant home market share is vital for domestic banking system stability. The domestic banks were encouraged to consolidate, merge or form alliance to take on the more competitive environment.[9] A wave of consolidation took place such that by 2004, seven local banking groups had merged into three main local banking groups, namely DBS, OCBC, and UOB. As a result, the local banks' capabilities were strengthened with improved management teams, enhanced operational effectiveness, and expanded range of business activities and better risk management capabilities. The greater financial strength also enabled the local banks to embark on regional expansion through mergers and acquisitions.[10] According to Asian Banking and Finance (2012), overseas assets represented 37% of total assets of these three local banks in 2012.

In line with the FSGR recommendations, the MAS enhanced corporate governance and raised accounting standards in line with international best practices. Guidelines were issued to separate non-financial from financial activities of banking groups, as well as to limit cross-shareholding structures. All these boosted investor confidence in the domestic banking industry. At the same time, increased competition had the advantageous effect of spurring the development of innovative products, more competitive pricing and better services for the customers. Singapore's banking environment evolved to be one of the most liberal in Asia due to these liberalization measures and reforms.

Financial infrastructure

Apart from building capability in a broad range of clusters of activities, emphasis was also given to develop the financial infrastructure which includes rules and regulations, networks, and manpower capabilities. In 1999, the Financial Sector Development Fund was set up for the purpose of developing financial sector expertise, upgrading of infrastructure, and support of research and other projects to develop the financial sector. Cognizant that a successful financial sector depends much on the availability of a strong talent pool, the fund supports various training schemes to equip the Singapore financial sector workforce with relevant skills. At the same time, measures such as enhancing the living environment in Singapore were put in place to attract foreign talent with relevant expertise and experience. Steps were also taken to improve the infrastructure supporting financial sector development such as ensuring the availability of support services including telecommunications industry and networks; transport, legal and accounting services; and information technology.

Regulatory reforms

Prior to the Asian financial crisis, the MAS's regulatory approach was to take minimum risks to protect the financial system with extensive regulation. An often heard lament by the market participants then was that "in Hong Kong anything not expressly forbidden is permitted, whereas in Singapore anything not expressly permitted is forbidden."

To avoid over-regulation, the MAS moved from a one-size-fits-all approach to a risk-based supervision approach. An internal rating system for financial institutions was developed that takes into account the quality of an institution's internal risk management and internal control as well as the potential impact it poses to the entire financial system. Supervisory resources were allocated among financial institutions according to their level of systemic risks and risk management capability. While higher requirements or tighter restrictions were imposed on weaker institutions, more leeway was given to stronger and better managed ones so as to encourage financial innovation. Consequently, the financial institutions gained more agility in developing products in response to market conditions.

Furthermore, the MAS shifted away from a prescriptive, merit-based regulation whereby the suitability of a product is assessed by the regulator before it is allowed to be introduced in the marketplace. Instead, a disclosure-based approach was adopted where consumers make well-informed decisions when purchasing financial products and services based on material information being made available to them. By enforcing adequate disclosure and greater transparency for market scrutiny, and professional and ethical sale conduct, the competitive edge of financial institutions was sharpened as they faced pressure to operate more efficiently and professionally.

The implementation of reforms, opening of new markets, and enacting of sound regulations and fiscal incentives that attracted well-established foreign financial institutions to Singapore resulted in a globalized financial services sector. The outcome of such a concerted development strategy is the successful transformation of Singapore into an international financial center. Indeed, the recent Zen Global Financial Centers Index published in March 2016 listed London, New York, Singapore, and Hong Kong as the top four leading global financial centers (Yeandle 2016).

Challenges ahead

Successful though financial development has been, Singapore is currently facing various challenges posed by the new global financial landscape.

Digital revolution and fintech[11]

The digital revolution is transforming the way customers access financial products and services. Fintech has been accelerating the pace of financial innovation at a remarkable rate and is reshaping the financial services industry's status quo. MAS has to rise to the challenge once again in navigating this digital revolution.

In order to promote financial innovation in a comprehensive way, MAS is building the necessary ecosystem. This includes bringing a whole range of players, both global and local, together such as technology players, and finance players and start-ups. At the same time, MAS provides horizontal infrastructures which can spur innovation in banking and finance including smart regulation for fintech; grooming more tech-savvy professionals; developing efficient and secure storage of data in the cloud; and encouraging the use of common technological platforms and application program interfaces.

In smart regulation, MAS must remain adaptable and nimble, thinking out of the box when warranted. While regulation must not and cannot front-run innovation, regulators must run alongside innovation. It is interesting to note that MAS will introduce a "regulatory sandbox" approach that aims to give fintech more confidence in experimenting and launching their innovative products or services within controlled boundaries.[12] The idea is not to remove all risks, since failure is an inherent part of innovation. Rather, this will create an environment where if an experiment fails, it fails safely or without systemic adverse consequences.

In June 2015, MAS also announced a SGD 225 million Financial Sector Technology and Innovation Scheme to be spent over five years. The funding is targeted at helping financial firms set up innovation labs and building infrastructure to deliver financial technology services.

Combating money laundering

Like other international financial centers which thrive on openness and free capital movement, Singapore has always been a suitable venue for possible international money laundering activities. As Singapore's financial center grows in scale and sophistication, it has to be even more vigilant against the risk of its abuse for illicit financing activities, and MAS has to enhance the supervisory regime for tackling money laundering and illicit financing risks.

MAS' supervisory regime against money laundering comprises four key elements: strict regulations, rigorous supervision, effective enforcement, and good cross-border co-operation. MAS views financial institutions as the critical gatekeepers against the flow of illicit funds. It therefore requires financial institutions to comply with strict anti-money laundering regulations and expects financial institutions to put in place robust controls to detect and deter illicit activities. It has recently taken further measures to strengthen the supervisory regime which include (1) criminalizing the laundering of serious tax offenses; (2) enhancing regulations and guidelines to comply with evolving international standards; and (3) stepping up inspections of financial institutions.

A recent case in point is the decisive actions taken by MAS in 2016 to revoke the banking licenses of BSI Bank and Fulcon Bank for serious failures in anti-money laundering controls and improper conduct by management staff discovered during several inspections of these institutions. Furthermore, the referral of the banks' management staff to public prosecution for possible criminal offense also demonstrated MAS' resolve to fight against money laundering.

To enhance MAS' supervisory focus and effectiveness at a time of increasing sophistication of illegal money flows globally and to respond to the increasing use of financial technology in money laundering activities, MAS set up a dedicated Anti-Money Laundering department in August 2016. The responsibilities for regulatory policies relating to money laundering and other illicit financing risks are streamlined, with the department monitoring these risks and carrying out on-site supervision of how financial institutions manage these risks. These functions used to be carried out by different departments in MAS and the new structure will enhance supervisory focus. In addition, MAS has also set up a new enforcement department that will work closely with the Commercial Affairs Department to investigate money laundering and other financial market offenses, and will be responsible for enforcement actions arising from regulatory breaches of MAS' banking, insurance, and capital market regulations.

Developing talent

Another challenge that relates to financial innovation is the need to continuously develop a sustainable talent pipeline relevant to the changing and growing needs of the industry. This is particularly important due to an increasingly complex environment, as consumers become more sophisticated and discerning with the advent of digital age.

MAS has continually placed great emphasis on talent development in the financial services industry. It recently formed the Financial Sector Tripartite Committee which brings together the industry associations, government authorities and labor movement. The aim of the Financial Sector

Tripartite Committee is to foster a financial sector workforce that is versatile and well equipped to seize new opportunities and adapt to the changing needs of the industry. Singapore is also facing an aging population and the current political climate places restraints on a large inflow of foreign workers. Efforts to promote continuing professional development in order to reskill finance managers and professionals, such as the launch of SkillsFuture, is therefore timely and critical.[13]

Expanding financial linkages and forming partnerships

Unlike Hong Kong, China, which has a vast hinterland to provide its financial services to, Singapore has always been under pressure to find its niches and a customer base. One of the reasons for Singapore's success as an international financial center has been its ability to attract top-notch foreign international financial institutions to operate in Singapore. However, in recent times, due to tighter regulatory requirements from Basel III, a more hostile trading environment and increasing operating costs, several foreign international financial institutions have shrunk their operations in Singapore.

Singapore will thus need to explore new linkages and new partnerships to continue growing its financial markets. One such linkage will be with ASEAN, a market of 640 million people with a combined GDP of USD 2.4 trillion. The ASEAN Economic Community came into existence on 31 December 2015. Singapore should and can enhance its regional capital market access by tapping into the Community. Nevertheless, challenges remain in aligning the regulatory and governance standards of the financial markets among the ASEAN member countries. Some progress has been made, but more remains to be done. For instance, the ASEAN Collective Investment Schemes Framework established in 2014 allows fund managers based in Singapore, Malaysia, and Thailand to offer funds constituted and authorized in their home jurisdictions directly to retail investors in each other's countries.

Another important strategy in broadening the market is to develop more PRC capability by working closely with PRC authorities in enhancing various schemes such as the CNY Qualified Foreign Institutional Investors, the CNY Qualified Domestic Institutional Investors, and the Qualified Domestic Institutional Investors to allow greater two-way portfolio investment flows between the PRC and Singapore. It is equally important to build a thriving RMB financial ecosystem in Singapore by introducing or expanding CNY/USD futures, "Lion City" bonds, and cross-border CNY financing in Shanghai, Tianjin, and Chongqing.

As highlighted by Prime Minister Lee Hsien Loong in 2011,

> MAS must constantly review Singapore's value proposition and growth strategy. Competition from emerging financial centers in the region is intensifying, but the opportunities in Asia . . . are growing rapidly too. MAS needs to continue leveraging on Singapore's system-wide capabilities to strengthen our position as an international financial centre.[14]

In other words, Singapore needs to continue to plan, invest, and anticipate changes to stay ahead as a financial center in the evolving global financial landscape.

Notes

1 Please refer to the Financial Directory at MASNET (https://masnetsvc.mas.gov.sg/FID.html).
2 As recorded by the Singapore Foreign Exchange Market Committee Survey of Singapore Foreign Exchange Volume April 2016 (www.sfemc.org/statistics/SFEMCFXSurveyApr16.pdf).

3 Both the Suzhou Industrial Park and Tianjin Eco-City are bilateral, national-level projects between Singapore and the PRC.

4 Over the years, the ADM developed to include foreign exchange and derivatives, foreign securities, loan syndication and bond issuance activities, see MAS (2000).

5 MAS has recently rationalized the regulatory framework that distinguished domestic versus international banking operations, citing market developments and global regulatory changes over the last half decade. See Tharman (2015).

6 The GIC is a sovereign wealth fund that manages Singapore's foreign reserves.

7 The CPF is a government administered compulsory savings scheme that is used for funding the citizens' housing, healthcare, and retirement needs.

8 This includes fixed-rate issuances from high-income countries and the indices are tools for measuring performance and quantifying risk across international fixed income markets.

9 See speech by then Deputy Prime Minister and Chairman of MAS Lee Hsien Loong on *Consolidation and Liberalization: Building World-Class Banks* at the Association of Banks Annual Dinner on 29 June 2001 (Lee 2001).

10 For instance, DBS acquired DoaHeng Bank the fourth largest bank in Hong Kong in April 2001.

11 FinTech is an economic industry that integrates finance and technology.

12 See panel remarks made by MAS Managing Director Ravi Menon on *Fintech – Harnessing Its Power, Managing Its Risks* at the Singapore Economic Policy Forum held on 2 April 2016 (www.mas.gov. sg/News-and-Publications/Speeches-and-Monetary-Policy-Statements/Speeches/2016/FinTech-Harnessing-its-Power-Managing-its-Risks.aspx).

13 SkillsFuture is a national movement to enable all Singapore citizens to develop to their fullest potential throughout life by providing a variety of resources to attain mastery of skills. For details, refer to www. skillsfuture.sg/.

14 Lee (2011).

References

Hew, D. 2005. Singapore as a Regional Financial Center. In *Capital Markets in Asia: Changing Roles for Economic Development*, edited by D. Vandenbrink and D. Hew. Singapore: Institute of South East Asian Studies.

Lee, H.L. 2001. Consolidation and Liberalisation: Building World-Class Banks. Speech by Deputy Prime Minister Lee Hsien Loong, Chairman MAS, at the Association of Banks Annual Dinner, 29 June. www.mas.gov.sg/news-and-publications/speeches-and-monetary-policy-statements/speeches/2001/consolidation-and-liberalisation--building-world-class-banks--29-jun-2001.aspx

Lee, H.L. 2011. Speech by Prime Minister Lee Hsien Loong at MAS 40th Anniversary Dinner, 28 November. www.mas.gov.sg/News-and-Publications/Speeches-and-Monetary-Policy-Statements/Speeches/2011/Speech-by-PM-Lee-Hsien-Loong-at-the-MAS-40th-Anniversary-Dinner.aspx

Monetary Authority of Singapore (MAS). 2000. Monetary Authority of Singapore: 30 Years of Central Banking Excellence. Singapore: Monetary Authority of Singapore.

MAS. 2004. *Objectives and Principles of Financial Supervision in Singapore*. Singapore: Monetary Authority of Singapore.

MAS. 2015a. Singapore Corporate Debt Market Development 2015. Singapore: Monetary Authority of Singapore.

MAS. 2015b. *Monetary Authority of Singapore Annual Report 2014/15*. Singapore: Monetary Authority of Singapore.

Ong, C.T. 2003. Singapore's Policy of Non-Internationalisation of the Singapore Dollar and the Asian Dollar Market. In *China's Capital Account Liberalisation: International Perspective*, BIS Papers No. 15. Basel: Bank for Internaional Settlements, pp. 93–98.

Tharman, S. 2015. Keynote address by Deputy Prime Minister Tharman Shanmugaratnam at the Association of Banks in Singapore on 30 June 2015. http://twww.mas.gov.sg/news-and-publications/speeches-and-monetary-policy-statements/speeches/2015/keynote-address-by-dpm-at-abs-annual-dinner.aspx

Yeandle, M. 2016. *The Global Financial Centres 19*. Z/Yen Group Limited, March. www.longfinance.net/global-financial-centre-index-19/992-gfci-19.html

11

BANKING AND FINANCE IN THAILAND

Yothin Jinjarak and Ulrich Volz

Introduction

Since the 1960s, Thailand has made remarkable progress in its social and economic development. Over the past five decades, per capita income has progressed with only short stalling periods during 1997–2001 due to the Asian financial crisis and during 2008–2009 due to the global financial crisis. The per capita income has increased from below USD 600 in the early 1960s, to around USD 6,000 in 2016.[1] In 2011, Thailand became an upper-middle-income economy.

Thailand's financial system is relatively large, with total finance amounting to 237% of gross domestic product (GDP) in 2015 (Figure 11.1). According to a new composite index of financial development constructed by the International Monetary Fund (IMF), Thailand's financial sector has witnessed significant development since the early 1980s (Figure 11.2). The different measures that make up the financial development indicator seem to almost converge by 2014. Financial institutions depth and financial institutions access, two of the three measures used for the financial institutions development indicator, show a clear upward trend, whereas the third component measure, financial institutions efficiency, has actually declined somewhat between 1980 and 2014, indicating deteriorating profit margins in the banking sector. The same applies to the three component measures used to calculate financial market development: the measures for financial market depth and financial market access have improved, whereas the financial market efficiency measure has deteriorated slightly (from 0.72 in 1980 to 0.69 in 2014).

The financial sector has seen substantial change in recent decades with an increasing importance of bond and equity markets. While capital markets have grown considerably, the Thai financial system is still dominated by banking. As can be seen in Table 11.1, depository corporations hold almost 70% of total assets of financial institutions, of which the majority are held by commercial banks. In 2016, 1,496 depository corporations were registered, 1,419 of which were savings cooperatives.

Figure 11.3 shows the various types of funding in the Thai financial system. While the share of total loans (i.e., lending by commercial banks, specialized financial institutions [SFIs], savings cooperatives, finance companies, and other financial institutions) in total funding of the economy has fallen from 57% in 2011 to 52% in 2016, lending by deposit-taking corporations is still by far the most important source of funding. Bond markets accounted for 17% (16%) and equity markets for 31% (27%) of funding in 2016 (2011), respectively.

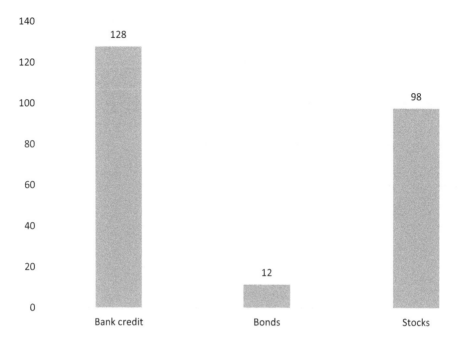

Figure 11.1 Total finance as a percent of gross domestic product, 2015

Source: Compiled by author with data from the World Bank Financial Development Index Database.

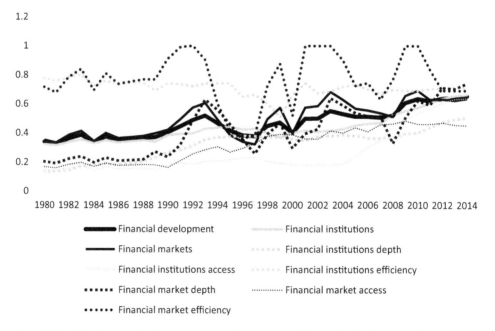

Figure 11.2 New international monetary fund measures of financial development for Thailand, 1980–2014

Source: Compiled by authors with data from Svirydzenka (2016).

Table 11.1 Financial institutions system: number and asset size of major financial institutions (third quarter of 2016)

Types of financial institutions	Number	% of total assets of financial institutions
Depository corporations		69.03
Commercial banks	31	46.70
Specialized financial institutions	6	15.32
Savings cooperatives[a]	1,419	6.28
Finance companies	2	0.04
Money market mutual funds	38	0.69
Other financial corporations		30.97
Mutual funds (excluding money market mutual funds)	1,394	11.02
Insurance companies	86	8.67
Leasing companies	796	1.91
Credit card, personal loan and nano-finance companies under regulation[c, d]	36	2.33
Provident funds	404	2.47
Government pension fund	1	1.98
Asset management companies	39	0.72
Securities companies	53	0.96
Agricultural cooperatives[b]	3,612	0.58
Pawnshops	616	0.19
Secondary Mortgage Corporation[e]	1	0.04
Thai Credit Guarantee Corporation[e]	1	0.10

Notes: P Preliminary data.
a Excluding credit unions.
b Agricultural cooperatives data are provided as of the fourth quarter of 2015.
c Only including financial institutions with licenses issued by the Bank of Thailand and operate in line with definitions of financial institutions according to Monetary and Financial Statistics Manual 2000.
d As of the third quarter of 2016, there were 22 nano-finance companies in total.
e The Secondary Mortgage Corporation and Thai Credit Guarantee Corporation are non-depository specialized financial institutions.

Source: Compiled by authors with data from Bank of Thailand (2017a).

Since the financial crisis of 1997–1998, the Thai government has set out to develop and strengthen the financial sector. The immediate concern was of course to stabilize the financial sector, stop the contraction of the economy, restore investor confidence, and address the vulnerabilities that became evident through the crisis. With the return of the banking sector to profitability in 2001, the Ministry of Finance (MoF) and the central bank, the Bank of Thailand (BOT), started to work on mapping out a longer term, comprehensive financial reform program. The Financial Sector Master Plan (FSMP) was developed over the period 2002–2003 and adopted in 2004.[2] The FSMP puts forward three goals or visions (BOT 2006: 11–12):

1 Vision 1: Provide financial services to all potential, economically viable, users whereby users should have access to basic financial products and services at the appropriate pricing.
2 Vision 2: Develop a competitive, efficient, stable, and balanced financial system, capable of servicing sophisticated and unsophisticated users; and
3 Vision 3: Ensure fairness and protection for customers whereby financial institutions must abide by good corporate governance standards, and consumers receive adequate information and advice from various financial institutions to make informed investment decisions.

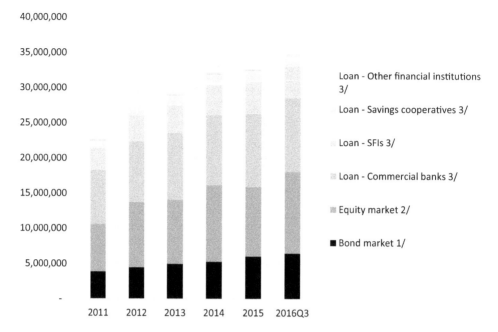

Figure 11.3 Thai financial system by type of funding

1 Par values of bonds issued in Thailand, excluding the issuance of financial sector and nonresidents.
2 Market values of listed equities in the Stock Exchange of Thailand and Market for Alternative Investment, excluding the issuance of financial sector.
3 Loans to households, non-financial corporations and the government.

Note: Loans from finance companies are so marginal they don't appear in this figure.

Source: Compiled by authors with data from the Bank of Thailand (2017a).

The FSMP put forward four supporting reform measures to achieve these visions: (1) improving the basic infrastructure of the financial system, (2) improving competitiveness of individual financial institutions, (3) removing regulatory impediments to financial sector development, and (4) improving systemic efficiency by strengthening market-based mechanisms (BOT 2006: 15). The implementation of the FSMP was set out in three phases, starting in 2004. The first phase was completed in 2009, and helped, according to the IMF, to "successfully consolidate [. . .] the banking sector, producing larger institutions, with high capital adequacy ratios, good profitability, and strong risk management systems" (IMF 2010: 6).

The second phase, from 2010 to 2015, focused on "increas[ing] efficiency and competitiveness of the financial institutions system as well as promot[ing] financial access and enhanc[ing] financial infrastructure, especially financial institutions' risk management" (BOT 2016: 1).

FSMP phase III, which is scheduled from 2016 to 2020, aims to create a more "competitive, inclusive, connected and sustainable" (BOT 2016: 1) financial system. FSMP III comprises four major initiatives for (1) promoting electronic financial and payment services and enhancing efficiency of the financial system; (2) facilitating regional trade and investment connectivity as part of the Association of Southeast Asian Nations' (ASEAN) plans to promote regional economic and financial integration under the ASEAN Economic Community; (3) promoting greater financial access of households and businesses; and (4) further developing the country's financial infrastructure, including through improved financial professional development, financial literacy and consumer protection, the legal infrastructure to enhance risk management and the operation of financial institutions, and strengthening regulations and supervision in line with international standards.

The following sections will in turn provide an overview of Thailand's banking sector, capital markets, the insurance sector, and asset management. The subsequent section reviews financial regulation in Thailand. The final section concludes.

Banking sector

Banking is dominated by commercial banks, which provided 54% of all loans to the economy in the third quarter of 2016 (Figure 11.3), with more than 70% of all corporate and around 40% of consumer loans coming from commercial banks (Table 11.2). There are 31 commercial banks, 15 of which are domestic commercial banks, 12 are registered foreign bank branches, and four are foreign bank subsidiaries. In September 2017, there were 6,841 branches of all commercial banks in Thailand, with 2,074 in Bangkok. The commercial banking sector is characterized by a high concentration of banking assets in the four largest banks: Bangkok Bank, Krungthai Bank, Siam Commercial Bank, Kasikorn Bank, and Bank of Ayudhya. Together, these five largest banks hold 69% of all commercial bank assets (Figure 11.4). Concentration in the banking sector increased significantly in the wake of the currency and banking crisis of 1997–1998. To stabilize the financial system, the government took drastic emergency measures, bringing about a consolidation of the sector. More than 50 banks and finance companies were

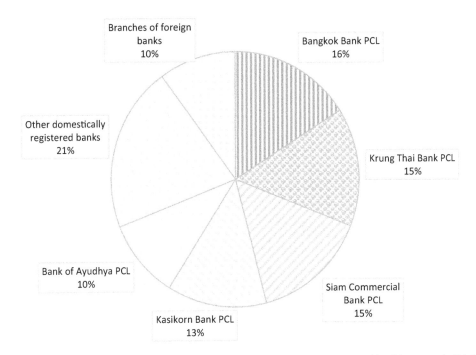

Figure 11.4 Shares of commercial bank by asset size (structure of the commercial banking system) (third quarter of 2016)

Note: Other domestically registered banks include CIMB Thai Bank PCL, Industrial and Commercial Bank of China (Thai) PCL, Kiatnakin Bank PCL, Land and Houses PCL, Standard Chartered Bank (Thai) PCL, Thancart PCL, Tisco Bank PCL, TMB Bank PCL, Unlimited Overseas Bank (Thai) PCL.

Source: Compiled by authors with data from the Bank of Thailand (2017a).

deemed nonviable and were wound down, while weak financial institutions were recapitalized and merged with stronger ones. All other domestically registered banks hold only 21% of commercial bank assets, and foreign bank branches hold only 10%.

The participation of foreign banks remains at a relatively low level. The assets held by foreign banks as share of total banking assets increased in the 2000s and stands now at 10% (Figure 11.5). As of October 2017, Thailand had four registered foreign commercial banks' subsidiaries and 12 registered foreign commercial bank branches. Foreign bank subsidiaries are defined as public limited companies licensed to undertake commercial banking business and are owned by at least 95% by a foreign commercial bank.[3] Foreign commercial banks' subsidiaries can undertake commercial banking business and are allowed to operate 20 branches and 20 off-premise ATMs (BOT 2017b). Branches of foreign commercial banks licensed to undertake commercial banking business in Thailand are allowed to open up to three branches including its head office.[4] The number of expatriate management is limited to six staff at full branches. Branches of foreign commercial banks must maintain minimum capital funds of THB 125 million invested in government or state enterprise securities, or directly deposited in the BOT.

The ratio of liquid assets to deposits and short-term funding was between 5% and 10% for most of the 2000s, then, following the global financial crisis, rising to its peak of 24% in 2011, before leveling out (Figure 11.6). The size of non-performing loans (NPLs) to gross loans has been steadily declining from around 40% after the financial crisis in the late 1990s to below 5% by the early 2010s.

The bank lending deposit spread (i.e., the difference between the rate charged by banks on loans to the private sector and the rate offered by commercial banks on three-month deposits)

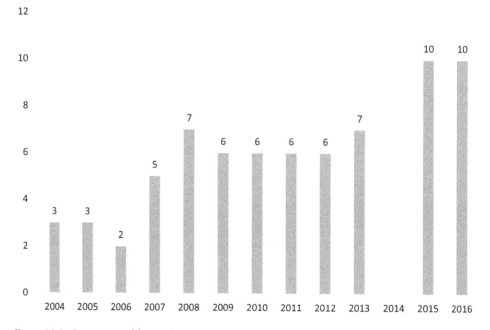

Figure 11.5 Percentage of foreign bank assets among total bank assets

Note: Data for 2014 could not be found.

Source: Compiled by authors with data from the World Bank's Global Financial Development Database and Bank of Thailand.

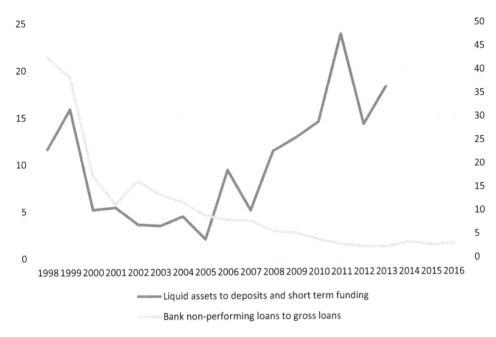

Figure 11.6 Liquid assets to deposits and short-term funding (in %, left scale) and bank non-performing loans to gross loans (in %, right scale)

Source: Compiled by authors with data from the World Bank's Global Financial Development database.

has been around 4%–5% since the mid-1990s (Figure 11.7). The late 1980s, early 1990s, and 2005–2006, when the spread was around 2%–3%, are exceptions. The net interest margin (i.e., the accounting value of banks' net interest revenue as a share of their average interest bearing assets) has been between 2% and 3% over the last two decades (Figure 11.7).

The share of financial sector assets held by SFIs has grown from 18% in 2008 to 25% in 2016, reflecting their proactive lending activity in response to the global financial crisis when commercial banks tightened their lending standards (IMF 2012; BOT 2017a). SFIs provided 15% of all corporate loans and 25% of all consumer loans in 2016 (Table 11.2). SFIs, which are all publicly owned, assume an important role in the Thai banking system by providing financial services to parts of the economy not sufficiently served by commercial banks, especially small and medium-sized enterprises (SMEs) and agricultural and rural enterprises (ADB 2011, BOT 2017a). SFIs contribute to the government's social and development policies, including by act-ing as distributor for welfare payments, providing financial support for target groups, and by supporting business development (BOT 2017a). Thailand has nine SFIs with 2,500 branches across the country, especially in rural areas: the Bank for Agriculture and Agricultural Coop-eratives, the Export-Import Bank of Thailand, the Islamic Bank of Thailand, the Secondary Mortgage Corporation, the Small and Medium Enterprise Development Bank of Thailand, the Thai Credit Guarantee Corporation (TCG),[5] the Small Business Credit Guarantee Corpora-tion, the Government Housing Bank, and the Government Savings Bank (GSB). Except for the Secondary Mortgage Corporation and TCG, all SFIs are deposit-taking institutions. The three most important SFIs together accounted for 95% of all assets held by SFIs in 2016, with 46% held by the GSB, 29% by the Bank for Agriculture and Agricultural Cooperatives and 20% by the Government Housing Bank (BOT 2017a: 52).

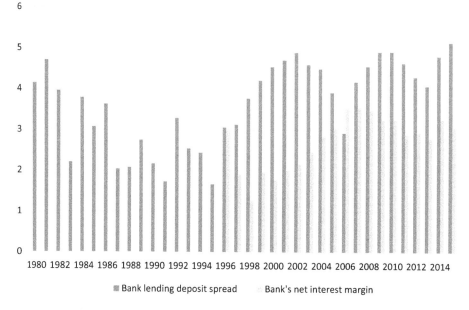

Figure 11.7 Bank lending deposit spread and net interest margin

Source: Compiled by authors with data from the World Bank's Global Financial Development database.

Table 11.2 Shares of consumer and corporate loans classified by type of financial institutions (third quarter of 2016)

Shares of consumer loans classified by type of financial institutions (third quarter of 2016)	41	25	19	15
Shares of corporate loans classified by type of financial institutions (third quarter of 2016)	73	15		12

Source: Compiled by authors with data from the Bank of Thailand (2017a).

The portfolio of SFIs has grown considerably over recent years, as the government has used SFIs to implement developmental policies or finance flood relief and reconstruction help after disasters. According to the IMF (2017), SFIs "appear sound, although many have lower profitability and higher NPLs than commercial banks, reflecting their policy bank mandate" (10–11).

A third of all loans extended by the banking sector are consumer loans, 19% of loans go to the manufacturing sector, 16% into commerce, 8% to financial business, 8% to public utilities, 7% to services, 5% to real estate, and 2% to construction (Figure 11.8).

The level of commercial banks' outstanding loans to households as percentage of GDP has increased from below 25% in 2005 to almost 40% in 2014 (Figure 11.9). For SMEs, the level of outstanding loans from commercial banks declined from 30% of GDP in 2005 to 23% in 2010, then reverted to a rising trend to the level almost 30% by 2016.

Still, despite their importance for the Thai economy, SMEs face significant challenges in accessing finance through the formal financial sector (Amornkitvikai and Harvie 2016). Table 11.3 shows significant differences in access to finance between small, medium, and large firms. Government-owned SFIs play an important role in the external financing of SMEs. The Thai government has developed various schemes aimed at improving SME's access to finance. For instance, a Portfolio Guarantee Schemes (PGS) for SMEs was launched in 2009 as part of

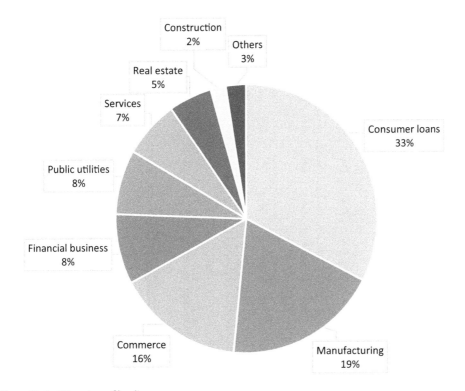

Figure 11.8 Direction of lending

Source: Compiled by authors with data from the Bank of Thailand (2017c).

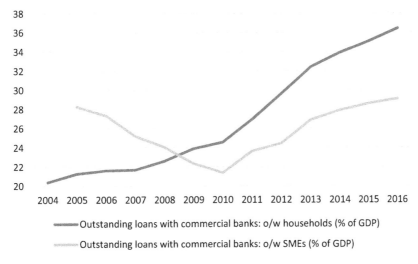

Outstanding loans with commercial banks: o/w households (% of GDP)

Outstanding loans with commercial banks: o/w SMEs (% of GDP)

Figure 11.9 Outstanding loans from commercial banks to households and small and medium-sized enterprises (percentage of GDP)

GDP = gross domestic product.

Source: Compiled by authors with data from the International Monetary Fund's Financial Access Survey.

Table 11.3 Access to finance by firm size (2016)

Firm size	Percent of firms with a bank loan/ line of credit	Proportion of loans requiring collateral (%)	Value of collateral needed for a loan (% of the loan amount)	Percent of firms whose recent loan application was rejected	Percent of firms using banks to finance investments	Proportion of investments financed internally (%)	Proportion of investments financed by banks (%)	Percent of firms using banks to finance working capital	Percent of firms using supplier/ customer credit to finance working capital	Proportion of working capital financed by banks (%)
Small	11.2	90.1	153.1	44.8	15.8	86.0	6.8	26.0	18.9	13.3
Medium	21.9	96.6	436.7	0.6	13.0	88.9	9.8	31.4	15.8	17.5
Large	35.0	93.9	139.7	0.0	27.1	72.7	14.9	43.7	18.2	25.2

Note: Small: 5–19 workers, Medium: 20–99 workers, Large: 100+ workers.

Source: Compiled by authors with data from the World Bank's Enterprise Surveys (www.enterprisesurveys.org).

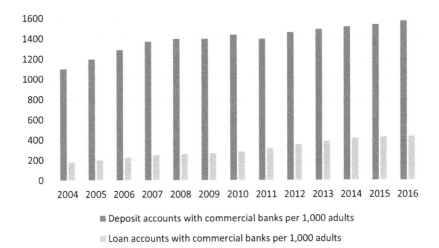

Figure 11.10 Household deposit accounts and loan accounts with commercial banks per 1,000 adults

Source: Compiled by authors with data from the International Monetary Fund's Financial Access Survey.

the Thai economic stimulus measures taken in response to the global financial crisis. The PGS was introduced through TCG – an SFI – to stimulate commercial bank loans to SMEs (Panyanukul, Promboon, and Vorranikulkij 2014). The government has since established further new SME support schemes, including the Business Security Act of April 2015, which aims to improve access to funding by accepting existing assets as collateral, and by providing financial assistance, mostly in the form of soft loans (Oxford Business Group 2016). In January 2016, the GSB (another SFI) and the Stock Exchange of Thailand announced the establishment of an SME Private Equity Trust Fund to provide working capital for SMEs (Ekvitthayavechnukul 2016a). This was followed by an announcement by Krungthai Bank in July 2017 to launch an SME Private Equity Trust Fund together with the Stock Exchange of Thailand and the National Science and Technology Development Agency (Ekvitthayavechnukul 2016b).

Accessibility of banking services has improved over the years for households. The number of household deposit accounts with commercial banks per 1,000 adults has increased from around 1,000 in the mid-2000s to almost 1,500 by 2014, while the number of loan accounts with commercial banks per 1,000 adults has reached 250 in the early 2010s (Figure 11.10).

Bond markets

Underlined by relatively stable fiscal and monetary environment of recent years, the bond markets continue to grow. As of the first quarter of 2017, the size of total debt securities issued by Thai residents and sectors amounted to USD 345 billion (Table 11.4). Of this outstanding amount, USD 138 billion is from financial corporations, USD 82 billion from non-financial corporations, and USD 124 billion from the general government. The majority is domestic debt securities, USD 331 billion, while international debt securities total USD 11 billion.

As a result of the Asian financial crisis, the level of public debt increased significantly in the five years after 1997 due to the government rescue and bailout of domestic financial institutions (Figure 11.11). The total amount of domestic public debt securities issued in domestic markets (including long-term bonds and notes, treasury bills, commercial paper, and other short-term notes) relative to GDP increased from 0.4% in 1997 to 10.4% in 1998 and further to 22.7 in

Table 11.4 Summary of debt securities outstanding by residence and sector of issuer, amounts outstanding in billions of US dollars (first quarter of 2017)

Total debt securities

Total	Financial corporations		Non-financial corporations	General government
345	138		82	124

Domestic debt securities

Total	Financial corporations		Non-financial corporations	General government
331	133		74	124

International debt securities

Total	Financial corporations		Non-financial corporations	General government
	Total	Banks		
11	3	1	7	0

Source: Compiled by authors with data from Bank of International Settlement, Summary of Debt Outstanding, Table C1 (www.bis.org/statistics/c1.pdf).

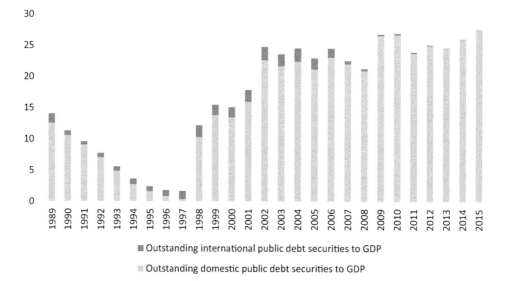

■ Outstanding international public debt securities to GDP

▨ Outstanding domestic public debt securities to GDP

Figure 11.11   Outstanding domestic public debt securities and international public debt securities to gross domestic product (in %), 1989–2015

Source: Compiled by authors with data from the World Bank's Global Financial Development database.

2003. The amount of outstanding public international debt securities (including long-term bonds and notes and money market instruments placed on international markets) relative to GDP increased from 1.3% in 1997 to 1.9% in 1998 and 2.1% in 2003. The size of public debt has stabilized at around 25% of GDP (27.5% in 2015), all of it being domestic.

While historically virtually all domestic bond issuances were denominated in US dollars (a phenomenon often referred to as "original sin"), Thailand and other countries that were badly hurt by the Asian financial crisis started to promote the development of local currency (LCY) bond markets to overcome the dependency on dollar funding as a lesson of the crisis. During the crisis, the practice of Thai banks to borrow in US dollars and lend in Thai baht became a major problem as the resulting currency mismatches became untenable when the baht was devalued against the dollar in July 1997. As shown in Figures 11.12 and 11.13, LCY bond markets started

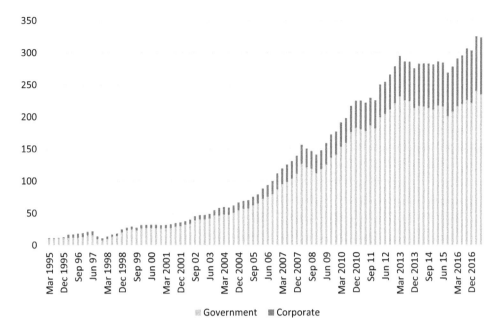

Figure 11.12   Size of local currency bond market (bonds outstanding in USD billion)

Source: Compiled by authors with data from AsianBondsOnline.

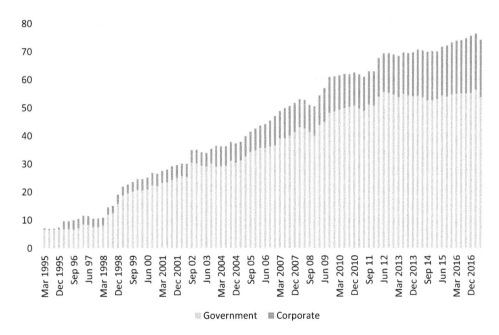

Figure 11.13   Size of local currency bond market as a percent of gross domestic product

Source: Compiled by authors with data from AsianBondsOnline.

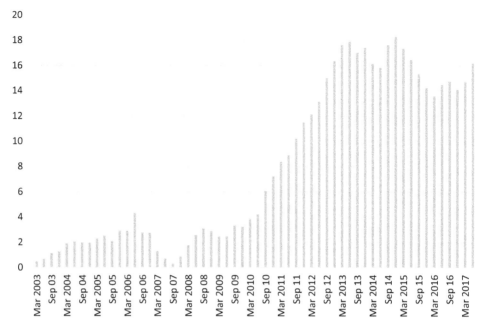

Figure 11.14 Foreign holdings in local currency government bonds as percentage of total

Source: Compiled by authors with data from AsianBondsOnline.

to grow quite rapidly since the early 2000s. As of June 2017, the value of outstanding government bonds was USD 235 billion and the value of outstanding corporate bonds was USD 89 billion. The share of foreign ownership in LCY government bonds has also grown rapidly since the early 2000s. In June 2017, 16% of LCY government bonds were held by foreigners (Figure 11.14).

Equity markets

Stock trading in Thailand dates back to the early 1960s. In 1962, the first Thai stock exchange was established as a private limited partnership. A year later, it became a limited company and was renamed into Bangkok Stock Exchange Company Limited (BSE). However, BSE failed to gain traction and ceased in the early 1970s. The government then made new efforts at developing a stock market with the support of the World Bank. In 1974, legislation establishing the Securities Exchange of Thailand was enacted and in 1975 the Securities Exchange of Thailand officially started trading. In 1991 it was renamed into Stock Exchange of Thailand (SET). In 2016, SET was the 13th largest Asian stock exchange with a total market capitalization of USD 0.4 trillion. It was also the fifth fastest growing stock exchange by market capitalization in the world, with a change of 25% compared to 2015.

The size and activity of stock market have undergone ups and downs over the past decades (Figure 11.15). Stock market capitalization as a percentage of GDP increased from around 30% at the beginning of the 2000s, to a pre-crisis peak of 88% in 1994, only to fall back to 23% in 1998. After the crisis it rebounded to 69% in 2004 and stayed at similar levels until 2007. The global crisis had its impact also on the Thai stock market, with stock market capitalization falling to 49% in 2009. Since then, the market has rebound and stock market capitalization reached almost 100% in 2015. Stock market total value traded, as measured by total value of all traded

Figure 11.15 Stock market capitalization to gross domestic product and stock market total value traded to gross domestic product

Source: Compiled by authors with data from the World Bank's Global Financial Development database.

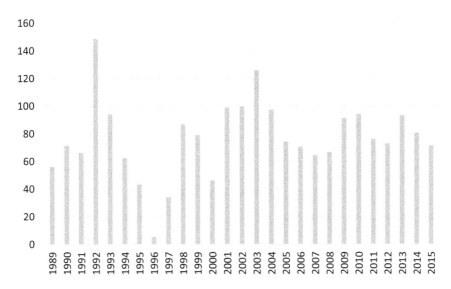

Figure 11.16 Stock market turnover ratio (value traded/capitalization) (in percentage)

Source: Compiled by authors with data from the World Bank's Global Financial Development database.

shares in a stock market exchange as a percentage of GDP, has followed closely the pattern of stock market capitalization.

Stock market turnover ratio, as measured by total value of shares traded during the period divided by the average market capitalization for the period, has been quite volatile (Figure 11.16). Since 2001, turnover was with the exception of 2003 somewhere between 60% and 80%.

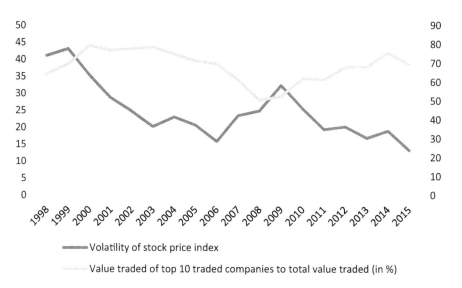

━━━Volatility of stock price index

┄┄┄ Value traded of top 10 traded companies to total value traded (in %)

Figure 11.17   Volatility of stock price index and value traded of top 10 traded companies to total value traded (right scale, in %)

Note: Volatility of stock price index is the 360-day standard deviation of the return on the national stock market index. Value of all traded shares of the top 10 traded companies as a share of total value of all traded shares in a stock market exchange.

Source: Compiled by authors with data from the World Bank's Global Financial Development database.

Stock market volatility fell after the Asian financial crisis, reaching the bottom in 2006 (Figure 11.17). The volatility of stock price index, as measured by the 360-day standard deviation of the return on the national stock market index, rose during 2007–2009, influenced by the global financial crisis, but dropped back to the low pre-crisis level by 2011. There seems to be a positive association, albeit with lag, of the stock market volatility and market activity notably the value of all traded shares of the top 10 traded companies as a share of total value of all traded shares in a stock market exchange.

Insurance sector

The size of insurance sector increased steadily over the past decade. The ratio of insurance company assets over GDP rose from 10% in the early 2000s to 22% by 2011, after which it decreased again somewhat (Figure 11.18). Life insurance accounts for more than two-thirds of the Thai insurance sector (Table 11.5). Thailand's life insurance sector has been ranked 30th globally and 10th in Asia in terms of premium income over recent years (Thai Re Group 2017). In 2016, 23 life insurers were active, with the four largest insurers (AIA, Muang Thai Life, Thai Life Insurance, and Krungthai AXA Life) having a market share of over 60%. The nonlife insurance market is relatively immature with insurance density – the ratio of total insurance premiums to whole population – of slightly more than USD 100 per capita (Thai Re Group 2017).

The total premium volume, as measured by the insurer's direct premiums earned (if property/casualty) or received (if life/health) during the previous calendar year, has increased from less than 2% of GDP in the 1990s to 5% by 2014 (Figure 11.19). The

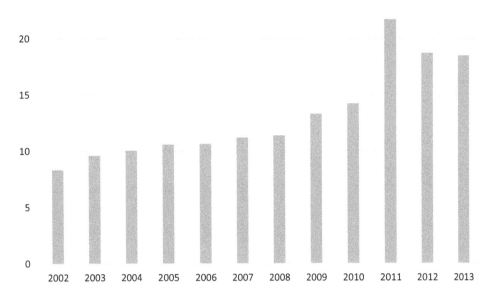

Figure 11.18 Insurance company assets as share of gross domestic product (in percentage)

Source: Compiled by authors with data from the World Bank's Global Financial Development database.

Table 11.5 Development of the insurance market, 2014–2016

	2016		2015		2014	
	USD billion	*Growth (%)*	*USD billion*	*Growth (%)*	*USD billion*	*Growth (%)*
Life sector	**16.1**	**5.7**	**15.6**	**6.8**	**15.4**	**13.2**
Ordinary	14.0	6.5	13.5	7.7	13.2	15.6
Industrial	0.2	−6.4	0.2	−6.1	0.2	−2.5
Group	1.7	2.5	1.7	2.0	1.7	0.4
Personal accident	0.2	−5.5	0.2	−2.2	0.2	3.9
Nonlife sector	**6.0**	**1.2**	**6.1**	**2.0**	**6.3**	**1.1**
Fire	0.3	−2.4	0.3	−5.2	0.3	−6.4
Marine and transportation	0.2	−1.4	0.2	0.9	0.2	−0.1
Motor	3.5	1.5	3.5	2.1	3.6	−0.4
Miscellaneous	2.1	1.5	2.1	2.9	2.2	5.2
TOTAL	**22.0**	**4.5**	**21.7**	**5.4**	**21.7**	**9.4**

Source: Compiled by authors with data from the Office of Insurance Commission.

relative size of life insurance and nonlife insurance subsectors has changed over the years, with the former becoming noticeably larger. In 1990, life insurance premium volume was about 0.9% of GDP, while nonlife insurance premium volume was 0.8% of GDP. In 2015, life insurance premium volume/GDP was 3.9%, while nonlife insurance premium volume/GDP was just 1.3%.

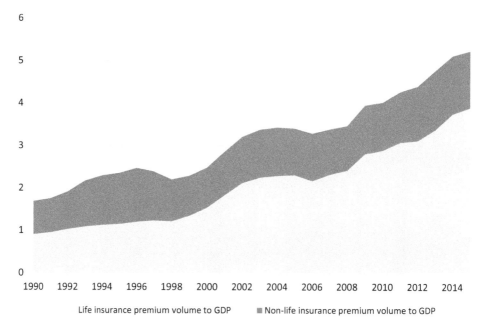

Figure 11.19   Life insurance and nonlife insurance premium volume to gross domestic product (in percentage)

GDP = gross domestic product, SFI = specialized financial institution.

Source: Compiled by authors with data from the World Bank's Global Financial Development database.

Asset management

The growth of assets under management in non-bank financial institutions has kept pace with the growth in deposit money banks. Across subsectors, mutual funds account for more than half of the assets in non-bank financial institutions, followed by pension funds, and insurance companies.

Total assets under management of mutual funds, pension funds, and insurance companies together rose from 21% of GDP in 2002 to 44% of GDP in 2013, a significant increase within a decade (Figure 11.20). Growth was driven primarily by mutual funds and pension funds.

Financial supervision

The BOT, which was established in 1942, is the regulator and supervisor of commercial banks, finance companies and credit foncier companies. It is also in charge of managing the country's foreign exchange. SFIs, which in practice operate alongside commercial banks and at times in competition to them, are under a specific regulatory and supervisory regime and benefit from special privileges. While the MoF has delegated operational supervision over SFIs to the BOT, the latter has no enforcement powers as the MoF continues to be the legal supervisor and regulator.

Capital markets are supervised by the Securities and Exchange Commission, which was established in May 1992 as an independent public agency. It controls and supervises securities

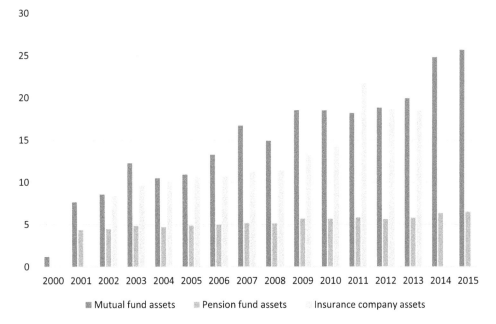

Figure 11.20 Mutual fund assets, pension fund assets, and insurance company assets as share of gross domestic product (in percentage)

Note: A mutual fund is a type of managed collective investment scheme that pools money from many investors to purchase securities. A pension fund is any plan, fund, or scheme that provides retirement income. Ratio of assets of pension funds to gross domestic product. A pension fund is any plan, fund, or scheme that provides retirement income.

Source: Compiled by authors with data from the World Bank's Global Financial Development database.

companies and the issuance and public offering of securities. The insurance sector is regulated by the Office of the Insurance Commission (OIC), which was established in 2007 to replace the Department of Insurance in the Ministry of Commerce. At the same time, responsibility for insurance was transferred from the Ministry of Commerce to the MoF. The OIC is the regulator for all aspects of both life and nonlife insurance.

Measures on regulatory oversight have been stepped up over the years. In the banking sector, the bank regulatory capital to risk-weighted assets has increased from 10.9% in 1998 to 17.1% in 2015 (Figure 11.21). The ratio of bank capital to total assets has followed similar pattern, increasing from 5.9% in 1999 to 10.0% in 2015. Between the financial crisis of 1997–1998 and 2008 the provision to NPLs has increased from just 29% to 98%, only to drop to 45% in 2009.

In 2016, the BOT established a financial stability unit responsible for monitoring financial risk and developing macroprudential policy tools to deal with systemic financial risk. The financial stability unit is also responsible for coordinating with other regulatory bodies. As shown in Table 11.6, the BOT has been developing macroprudential measures since the early 2000s.

The BOT is also in charge of capital account management. Both inflow and outflow restrictions were tightened in the late 1990s and up to 2005 (Figure 11.22). Faced with substantial capital outflows in 2008, inflow restrictions were lessened between 2008 and 2010. Inflow restrictions were reinstated again in 2012 in the face of large-scale capital inflows related to quantitative easing policies in the US and other advanced economies.

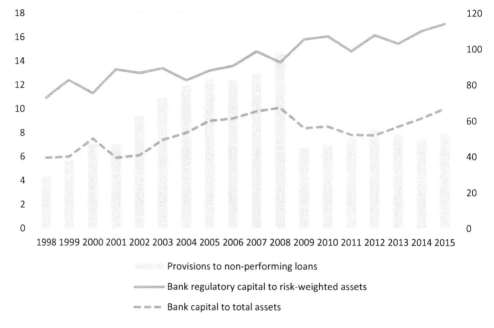

Figure 11.21 Bank regulatory capital to risk-weighted assets (left axis, in percentage), bank capital to total assets (left axis, in percentage), and provisions to non-performing loans (right axis, in percentage)

Source: Compiled by authors with data from the World Bank's Global Financial Development database.

Table 11.6 Thailand's macroprudential policies

Policy Measure	Purpose	Details
Setting a maximum loan to value ratio (LTV)	Preemptive measure to prevent speculation in the real estate market and to reduce overheating of mortgage loan growth	**2003**: set a mortgage ceiling for commercial banks to no more than 70% of collateral (LTV < 70%) for houses valued over THB 10 million. **2009**: canceled the LTV ceiling of 70% set in 2003, changed to a flexible LTV that better reflects credit risks. This is done by specifying risk-weighted capital requirement and allowing risk weight to adjust with LTV for houses valued over THB 10 million. o If LTV > 80%, risk weight is 75% o If LTV ≤ 80%, risk weight is 35% **2011**: issued a LTV measure for mortgage of high-rise housing valued less than THB 10 million. o If LTV > 90%, risk weight is 75% o If LTV ≤ 90%, risk weight is 35% **2013**: issued a LTV measure for mortgage of ground-level housing valued less than THB 10 million. o If LTV > 95%, risk weight is 75% o If LTV ≤ 95%, risk weight is 35%
Counter-cycle provisioning	Provisioning for possible impaired loans	**2012**: the BOT mandated commercial banks to set aside provisions to buffer against risks of NPLs in case of an economic slowdown.

Policy Measure	Purpose	Details
Setting a monthly credit limit and minimum payment for credit card loans	A measure to slowdown household indebtedness and instill financial discipline	Monthly credit limit should not exceed five times of monthly income for personal consumption and credit card loan. Setting a minimum monthly income for credit card loans from commercial banks at THB 15,000 and raising a minimum monthly payment from 5% to 10% of total amount owed.

Source: Compiled by authors with information from Bank of Thailand (2017: 41).

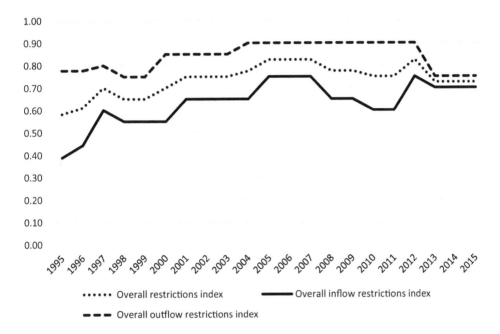

Figure 11.22 Capital control measures, 1995–2015

Note: A higher value indicates more restrictions. A value of 0 indicates a completely liberalized capital account.

Source: Compiled by authors with data from Fernández et al. (2016) (dataset updated 2017) (www.columbia. edu/~mu2166/fkrsu/).

Conclusion

For the last two decades, the banking and finance sector in Thailand has seen rapid growth and development. Against the backdrop of the Asian financial crisis in 1997–1998, hard lessons have been learned by both market participants and regulators alike, but concluding that the banking and finance sector in Thailand is resilient to adverse shocks and mishaps from top to bottom would be jumping the gun. With constantly evolving financial innovations and their ramifications, evidently after the global financial crisis of 2007–2009, the Thai economy is becoming ever more exposed to the influence of global markets and their development.

Several important challenges remain for the financial sector in Thailand. With the FSMP, which is now in its third phase, the BOT is seeking to address four key challenges, namely

(1) promoting the digitization of financial services; (2) facilitating regionalization of trade and investment under the ASEAN Economic Community; (3) increasing access to finance by households and SMEs; and (4) further developing the financial infrastructure, including the regulatory framework.

Notes

1 GDP per capita (constant 2010 US dollars). Source: World Bank's World Development Indicators.
2 For details on the development of the FSMP, see BOT (2006).
3 These are the ANZ Bank (Thai) PCL, Bank of China (Thai) PCL, Mega International Commercial Bank PCL, and Sumimoto Mitsui Trust Bank (Thai) PCL. See www.bot.or.th/English/FinancialInsti tutions/WebsiteFI/Pages/InstList.aspx?pie1=3.
4 These are the Bank of America, BNP Paribas, Citibank, Deutsche Bank, Indian Oversea Bank, JP Morgan Chase Bank, Mizuho Bank, Over Sea-Chinese Banking Corporation, RHB Bank Berhad, Sumimoto Mitsui Banking Corporation, and HSDB. See www.bot.or.th/English/FinancialInstitu tions/WebsiteFI/Pages/InstList.aspx?pie1=4.
5 TCG was established under the Small Industry Credit Guarantee Corporation Act in 1991.

References

Amornkitvikai, Y., and C. Harvie. 2016. The Impact of Finance on the Performance of Thai Manufacturing Small and Medium-Sized Enterprises. ADBI Working Paper No. 576. Tokyo: Asian Development Bank Institute.

Asian Development Bank (ADB). 2011. Thailand: Restructuring of Specialized Financial Institutions. Performance Evaluation Report, Independent Evaluation Office. Manila: Asian Development Bank.

Bank of Thailand (BOT). 2006. *Thailand's Financial Sector Master Plan Handbook*. Bangkok: BOT.

BOT. 2016. *Financial Sector Master Plan Phase III (2016-2020)*. Bangkok: BOT.

BOT. 2017a. *Financial Stability Report 2016*. Bangkok: BOT.

BOT. 2017b. Financial Business under the Bank of Thailand's Supervision and Examination. www.bot. or.th/English/FinancialInstitutions/Scope/Documents/ScopeOfSupervision.pdf.

BOT. 2017c. Performance of the Thai Banking System in the First Quarter of 2017. BOT Press Release 22/2017. www.bot.or.th/English/FinancialInstitutions/Publications/FIProformance_Press/n2260e.pdf.

Ekvitthayavechnukul, C. 2016a. Thailand's Government Saving Bank to Launch First PE Fund for SMEs. *Deal Street Asia*, 14 January. www.dealstreetasia.com/stories/thailands-government-saving-bank-launch-first-pe-fund-smes-27016/

Ekvitthayavechnukul, C. 2016b. Thailand: Krungthai Bank Launches SME Private Equity Trust Fund. *Deal Street Asia*, 25 July. www.dealstreetasia.com/stories/48435-48435/

Fernández, A., M. Klein, A. Rebucci, A. Schindler, and A. Uribe. 2016. Capital Control Measures: A New Dataset. *IMF Economic Review* 64(3): 548–574.

International Monetary Fund (IMF). 2010. Thailand: 2010 Article IV Consultation. IMF Country Report No. 10/344, www.imf.org/en/Publications/CR/Issues/2016/12/31/Thailand-2010-Article-IV-Consultation-Staff-Report-Public-Information-Notice-on-the-24394

IMF. 2012. Thailand Article IV Consultation. IMF Country Report No. 12/124. www.imf.org/external/pubs/ft/scr/2012/cr12124.pdf

IMF. 2017. Thailand: 2017 Article IV Consultation. IMF Country Report No. 17/136. www.imf.org/~/media/Files/Publications/CR/2017/cr17136.ashx

Oxford Business Group. 2016. Programmes to Stabilise Lending to SMEs in Thailand. www.oxfordbusi nessgroup.com/analysis/supportive-measures-new-programmes-aim-stabilising-lending-smes

Panyanukul, S., W. Promboon, and W. Vorranikulkij. 2014. Role of Government in Improving SME Access to Financing: Credit Guarantee Schemes and the Way Forward. Paper Presented at the BOT Symposium 2014. www.bot.or.th/Thai/MonetaryPolicy/ArticleAndResearch/SymposiumDocument/Paper3_SME2557.pdf

Svirydzenka, K. 2016. Introducing a New Broad-Based Index of Financial Development. IMF Working Paper No. 16/5. Washington, DC: International Monetary Fund.

Thai Re Group. 2017. The State of Insurance Market in Thailand 2016–2017. www.thaire.co.th/thaire_backend/upload/ourservices/publice_20170331141039.pdf.

12

THE FINANCIAL ECONOMY OF VIET NAM IN AN AGE OF REFORM, 1986–2016

Quan-Hoang Vuong

Introduction

Before the *Doi Moi* reforms in 1986, Viet Nam's economy was devastated by 30 years of warfare with two major military powers, France and the US, ending in 1975. In the subsequent 10 years, Viet Nam suffered from failing economic experiments, including agricultural cooperatization, "industry-commerce rehabilitation," price-wage-currency reform, among others, under the centrally planned mechanism (Wood 1989), as well as the international isolation and a US trade embargo when its troops entered Cambodia to overthrow the Khmer Rouge (Riedel and Turley 1999). Its per-capita gross domestic product (GDP) declined to USD 97 in 1989 whereas the ratio of external debt to GDP reached 330%.[1] The economy languished and became one of the poorest in the world (VGP 2016).

Things have since changed. With a population of 92 million, its GDP was USD 204 billion in 2015, after 30 years of socio-economic transitions. *Doi Moi* has enabled the marketization and internationalization of the economy, bringing about the fruits of the market (Dutta 1995; Riedel and Turley 1999), with the financial system facilitating the transformation (Siregar 1997). The banking system then had total assets of USD 307 billion, about 150% of GDP.

Economic foundations and governance framework

Economic foundations

With 2015 per-capita GDP of approximately USD 2,300, Viet Nam has become a lower-middle-income country. Households have more money to spend and invest as the gross domestic savings ratio remains high, at around 30% of GDP (Figure 12.1). Improved savings ratio in turn helps to counter future economic shocks (Sepehri and Akram-Lodhi 2005).

Foreign direct investment (FDI) facilitated transformations with financial resources, technologies, markets, and new business methods. The stock of FDI-capital realizations by 2015 totaled USD 139 billion, while 2,013 new FDI projects were licensed in 2015 with the new capital registration worth USD 22.76 billion (Figure 12.2). Figure 12.2 shows an evolution of changing FDI projects licensed (vertical axis) and new capital registration (radius of data point) since 1990.

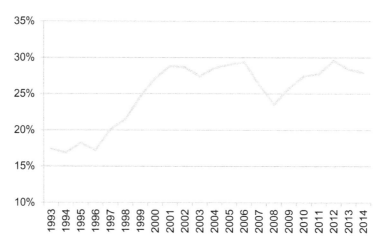

Figure 12.1 Gross domestic savings ratio, 1993–2014 (percentage of GDP)

GDP = gross domestic product.

Source: General Statistics Office.

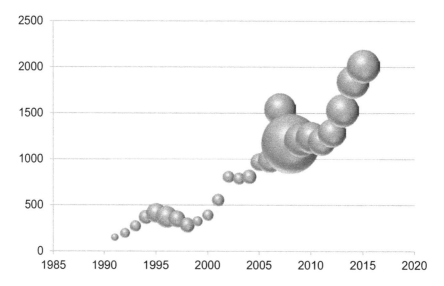

Figure 12.2 FDI projects and registered capital in Viet Nam, 1991–2015

FDI = foreign direct investment.

Source: General Statistics Office.

Financial markets had been virtually non-existent before 1990, although money, bank deposits, and loan transactions did exist. With financial reforms this component economy has grown fast (Román 1995). Over time, the State Bank of Viet Nam (SBV) has also built up national foreign reserves that are regarded as *coussin-de-sécurité* against economic shocks that tend to occur frequently in an open emerging economy (Figure 12.3).

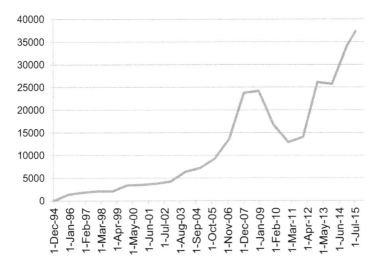

Figure 12.3   National foreign reserves (foreign exchange and gold, USD million)

Source: WB-WDI/SBV/Author's estimate.

Governance framework

Along with the process of reforms, new regulations constitute the governance framework required for achieving strategic goals. The transition period has made lawmaking and enforcement particularly challenging. There are different promulgators in Viet Nam: the Politburo; the National Assembly; the president, the government/prime minister, ministries, and ministerial-level agencies; and the SBV. Legal documents consist of resolutions, laws, circulars/decisions/directives, and decrees. The regulatory framework that governs the financial economy has been built up over the past 10 years (Table 12.1), of which the SBV has issued a relatively large number of regulations. These are important for regulating a large spectrum of financial activities.

Table 12.1 Legal documents governing financial system of Viet Nam

Issuer	2007	2008	2009	2010	2011
Govt/PM	46	36	16	6	11
SBV	94	106	103	35	57
NA	1	1	0	6	3
Ministries	3	34	3	9	4
	2012	2013	2014	2015	2016
Govt/PM	16	3	6	2	0
SBV	50	49	87	55	23
NA	4	0	0	0	0
Ministries	16	0	1	3	0

Source: SBV (www.sbv.gov.vn/portal/faces/vi/pages/vbqppl).

The contemporary history

With *Doi Moi* and a two-tiered banking system, the financial system was to fight late-1980s inflation. The battle was continuing well into the early 1990s. In 2010s, once again inflation plagued the economy. Important events of Viet Nam's financial system are summarized in Table 12.2. Correlated with the pace of inflation and economic expansion, the process of monetizing Viet Nam's economy started in the early 1990s, and accelerated in the mid-2000s, when the equity market boomed, leading broad money supply (M2) to surge (Figure 12.4), standing at USD 267 billion at 2015 year-end.

In 1986, total credit supply jumped to 1,897% of the 1976 level. The surge continued, and credit supply in 1990 was 4,361% of the 1986 amount. Without proper measures, this monetizing

Table 12.2 Milestones of the financial system since *Doi-Moi*

Year	Events	Remarks
1986–1987	Launching *Doi Moi* at the Sixth National Congress of the Communist Party of Viet Nam.	Recognizing/legalizing different economic ownerships in Viet Nam's economy; Passing Law on Foreign Investment
1986–1992	• Hyperinflation. • Banking reforms started with the birth of a two-tiered banking system, introducing a central bank and a system of four state-owned commercial banks (SOCB) into the economy. Ordinances on the SBV and commercial banking issued. • Chain collapse of credit cooperatives. • Amended Constitution 1992. • Birth of joint-stock commercial banks (JSCB) and foreign-owned commercial banks (FOCB) following Law on Credit Institutions 1990	• 3-digit inflation: 748% (1986), 223% (1987) and 394% (1988). • 26/3/1988: Decree 53/HDBT to "transform the banking system." SBV was consolidated to manage the monetary/credit and credit institutions. State Treasury was spun off from the SBV. Four SOCBs focused on commercial specializations (Decision 403-CT). Positive real interest rate policy implemented. • Thanh Huong credit scandal broke out in March 1990 as a consequence of mass borrowings by Nguyen Van Muoi Hai, via a large system of 900 money-receiving outlets, offering 12%–15% interest rate/month during 1987–1989. A chain collapse occurred, causing an irrecoverable loss of VND 37 billion (0.235% of 1989 GDP).
1992–1993	• Financing arrangement by France and Japan. US government allowed American firms to do business in Viet Nam. • IMF restored Viet Nam's borrowing eligibility after an eight-year suspension. • WB granted loans of USD 320 million through IDA. • ADB granted USD 76 million.	• USD 55 million grant and USD 85 million loans arranged for Viet Nam to pay its USD 142 million arrears to IMF since 1985. • IMF approved a USD 233 million loan. • Paid off USD 13.5 million arrears to ADB.
1992–1993	Historic visit of François Mitterrand. French ODA flowed in.	French ODA: USD 33 million (1992), USD 65 million (1993), followed by Republic of Korea: USD 50 million; Australia: AUD 100 million.

Year	Events	Remarks
1994–1995	Lifting of the US trade embargo and normalizing diplomatic relations with the US; Becoming member of ASEAN.	Reintegrating into the world economy. IMF, WB, and ADB opened offices. Donors community became active.
1997–1998	Collapse of the Minh Phung-Epco group of 50 companies; Asian currency/financial crisis.	Irrecoverable loss of VND 3,000 billion during 1993–1996. Viet Nam issued Brady Bonds for settling USD 553 million distressed loans in 1998.
2000–2001	Inauguration of the first stock market: HSTC (now Ho Chi Minh City Stock Exchange/ HOSE).	Started with four privatized SOEs. Ultra-thin trading. Primitive products. First collapse in May 2001.
2005	Opening HaSTC (today's Hanoi Stock Exchange/HNX). The 2nd Vietnamese government bond offering internationally since *Doi Moi*.	USD 750 million bond issue; rate of 7.125%.
2006	Stock prices surged, leading to overoptimistic sentiment and high P/Es.	HSBC and ML "bullish reports" about VSM prospects released, triggering stock market fever.

Post-WTO

Year	Events	Remarks
2007	Viet Nam joining WTO. HOSE reached the historic height.	USD 10.2 billion of foreign portfolio investment (FPI) flooded during 2006–2007 without proper sterilization. HOSE VNIndex peaked at 1,171 on 12/3/2007.
2007–2008	2-digit inflation recurred.	12.6% (2007); 19.9% (2008).
2008–2009	Stock market in turmoil. USD 6 billion stimulus package during 2008Q4–2009Q1.	Decision 131/QD-TTg subsidizing borrowings costs by 4% max.
2010	Vinashin's default on its financial obligations to international lenders.	Its collapse causing an irrecoverable loss estimated at USD 4.4 billion.
2011	Arrest of banker Huynh Thi Huyen Nhu.	Largest financial fraud, causing estimated loss of USD 200 million; four banks, nine companies involved during 2007–2011.
2011–2012	Struggled to control credit growth below 20%, and M2 growth below 16%; two-digit inflation recurred.	Inflation: 11.75% (2011); 18.13% (2012). Policy rate jumped from 9% to 11% (17/2/2011), then 12% (1/5/2011).
2012	Arrest of mogul Nguyen Duc Kien (ACBBank). Arrest of Vinalines former CEO and Chair arrested.	6/2012: SBV removed interest rate cap, liberalized interest rates. Vinalines on the verge of bankruptcy.
2013	VAMC created.	Dealing with bad debt problems in the banking system. Back to restrictive monetary policy.
2014	External debt: USD 72 billion.	38.6% GDP.
2015	State budget showed signs of stress.	MPI Minister stated needs of renewed reforms.
2016	AEC officially came into existence.	ASEAN regional economy: 660 million population; USD 2,500 billion GDP.

Source: Compiled by the author from numerous government, WB, IMF, ADB, and media sources.

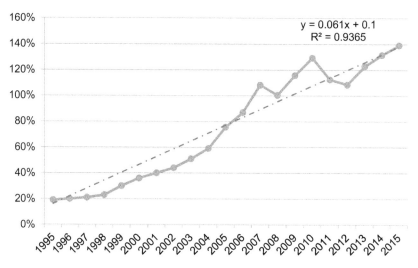

Figure 12.4 M2/GDP (1995–2015)

GDP = gross domestic product.

Sources: SBV, GSO, ADB, and author's estimates using ADB ARIC (https://aric.adb.org/macroindicators/userde fined); WDI (http://data.worldbank.org/indicator/DT.DOD.DECT.CD) (accessed 20 August 2016).

process led to a high inflation period of two and three digits. Most counter-inflation measures employed then were ad hoc reactions, not without negative consequences. Early adoption of so-called monetary policy measures only started in 1991, having learned the market-based economic mechanism the hard way: slower money velocity could help weather hyperinflation, given certain economic conditions. A significant slowdown in credit growth then followed.

In 1990s, this critically important task has been performed through a two-tiered banking system, with the SBV in the command, and the state-owned commercial banks (SOCBs) and/ or joint-stock commercial banks (JSCBs) playing the role of market performers. Credit growth went down to 70% in 1992, and 27.5% in 1999, helping reduce inflation from about 400% in 1988, down to 67.5% (1991), then 17.5% (1992), and then 0.1% (1999).

Institutions; markets; instruments

Institutions

The most important types of financial institutions are presented in Figure 12.5 and Table 12.3.

The financial system in Viet Nam has been bank-based, with 80% of financial intermediation conducted by a handful of powerful banks. But banks resources had been limited until mid-2000s with size of the banking sector being modest, with M2/GDP standing below 80% (Figure 12.4), while Thailand and Malaysia had M2/GDP over 100% in 2000 (ADB 2014). In 2015, the banking sector accounted for 92.25% of total financial assets.

People's Credit Funds (PCF) resemble credit cooperatives in terms of social traits, but with market principles and joint-stock ownership. They are particularly suitable for delivering rural microfinance. At present, the system of PCFs collectively has total equity of USD 140 million, and total assets USD 3,545 million. Non-bank financial institutions, PCFs included, accounted for 8.5% of total assets in 2016.

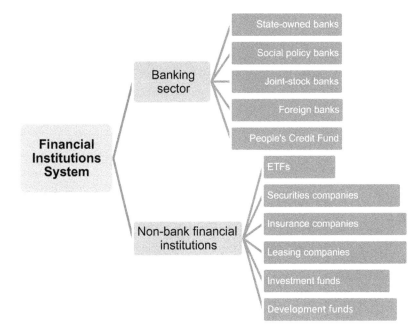

Figure 12.5 Viet Nam's financial system structure

ETFs = exchange-traded funds.

Sources: Author and Vuong and Associates.

Table 12.3 Financial institutions in Viet Nam

	2001	*2006*	*2008*	*2011*	*2016*
SOCB	5	5	5	4	4
SPB	1	2	2	2	3
JSCB	39	34	39	37	31
FOCBs – Branches	26	31	44	48	55
FOCBs – 100%	NA	NA	2	5	6
FOCBs – Joint Ventures	4	5	6	6	7
People's Credit Funds (PCFs)	959	–	–	906	–
NBFI – Financial Cos.	7	8	22	18	17
NBFI – Financial Leasing Cos.	8	8	12	12	11
Securities Companies	8	15	87	105	81
Insurance Companies	18	29	38	38	61

SOCB = state-owned commercial bank, JSCB = joint-stock commercial bank, FOCB = foreign-owned commercial bank, JV = joint-venture, NBFI = non-bank financial institution, SPB = social policy bank.

Note: NA: not applicable; – : not available.

Sources: SBV, MoF.

Markets and instruments

Credit markets and products

The banking industry has been dominated by four SOCBs: Vietcombank, BIDV, VietinBank, and Agribank. They are largest in terms of equity and assets (Figures 12.6 and 12.7). The second "family" consists of 31 JSCBs. Tier-1 JSCBs were founded during 1992–1993 with such names as ACB, Eximbank, Sacombank, VPBank, and Techcombank.

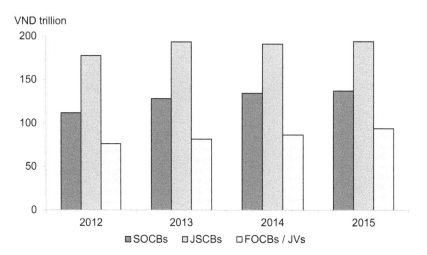

Figure 12.6   Banks' capital aggregates by ownership

Source: SBV.

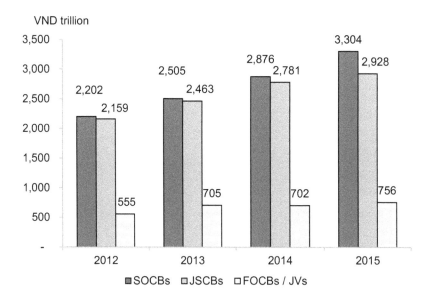

Figure 12.7   Bank assets by ownership

Source: SBV.

During 1990–1996, the SBV issued licenses for 20 rural areas commercial banks. Following SBV Decision 1557/QD-NHNN (9/8/ 2006), rural banks, if satisfying financial and operational conditions, may be "converted" to normal JSCBs and allowed to conduct business in urban areas. Most of them formed the tier-2, although some moved up the value chain and have become stronger and sizeable (e.g., HDBank).

After the US-Viet Nam bilateral trade agreement in 2001, and 2007 WTO membership, Viet Nam's banking market has opened to FDI and FPI, leading to a surge in foreign banks' operation in the domestic market.

Since 2005, the SBV has required banks to maintain a minimum 8% capital-asset ratio, defined by total equity/total risky assets. Banks then rushed to issue shares to shore up their capital base. By the end of 2006, most banks had equity three times of the 2004 level.

Figures 12.7 and 12.8 show although total assets of SOCBs have still been the largest in the system, JSCBs collectively have become larger, and on par with SOCBs.

There are also special entities, established to serve the development and poverty reduction programs, namely Viet Nam Bank for Social Policy, Viet Nam Development Bank, and Cooperative Bank of Viet Nam.

Domestic commercial banks have been able to increase their equity base thanks to public offerings on the Viet Nam Stock Market (VSM). Since 2005, banks have collectively raised the additional equity amount of USD 13 billion. In 2015 the capital adequacy ratios were 9.4% for SOCBs, 12.7% for JSCBs, and 33.8% for foreign-owned commercial banks (FOCBs).

Banks' profitability and investment efficiency have generally been considered modest, and showed some sign of decline in recent years, with ROEs in 2014 standing at 6.92% for SOCBs, 4.64% for JSCBs, and 3.79% for FOCBs. ROA was 0.53% for SOCBs, 0.40% for JSCBs, and 0.61% for FOCBs.

The development of the banking sector is correlated to the expansion of credit supply to the economy. Credit-to-GDP ratio was 71% in 2006 and 116% in 2010. On average, annual credit growth was 33% during 2006–2010. In this period, FDI and foreign portfolio investment (FPI) inflows surged abruptly, adding a lot of liquidity the economy. In 2007 alone, USD 17.7 billion flowed in,

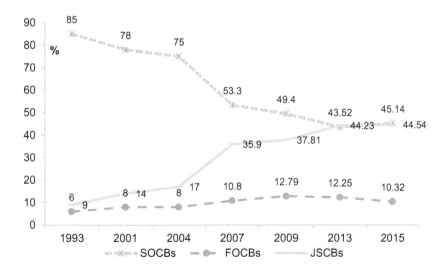

Figure 12.8 Shares of bank assets by ownership

Source: Author's compilation/Vuong and Associates.

leading to SBV net forex purchase of USD 10.2 billion. Without being sterilized properly, M2 surged by 46% in the year, creating a tremendous inflation pressure. For fighting inflation, the rate dropped to 11% in 2011, and 9% the next year, choking off the credit flows and causing tens of thousands of firms to collapse each following year. After years of restrictive monetary-policy measures, credit growth rate was 18% in 2015 when M2 and deposits expanded by about 14% (Figure 12.9).

Banks also earn their incomes from forex operations, thanks to fluctuations in forex rates (Figure 12.10) and increasing transaction volumes. Vietnamese individuals are allowed to keep foreign currency deposits, mostly US dollars, at banks. A high foreign currency deposits/M2 ratio reflects the "dollarization" issue, which varied from 5% during 1992–1996, to 19% (2000–2001), 15% (2008–2009), 20% (2010), and 15% (2011–2015).

In addition, banks have expanded retail banking to reach out to individuals with more bank cards, ATMs, and POS. Domestic debit cards and ATMs appeared first in 1993, and

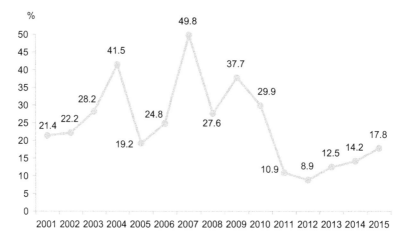

Figure 12.9 Credit growth (percentage/year)

Source: SBV.

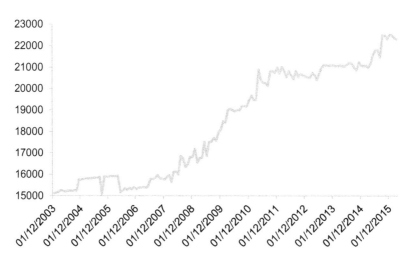

Figure 12.10 USD-VND exchange rate, 2003–2016

Source: OTC-Interbank.

international credit cards in 1996. But ATM/POS became popular only in 2003, when the number of cards nationwide reached 234,000. Electronic banking activities have since flourished, with 31.7 million cards in 2010 and 88.21 million in 2015.

Viet Nam Stock Market

The Viet Nam Stock Market (VSM) consists of two stock exchanges: Ho Chi Minh Stock Exchange (HOSE), established in July 2000; and Hanoi Stock Exchange (HNX), established in July 2005. Figure 12.11 shows the evolution of two widely cited market indexes during 2005–2015 (VNIndex/HNXIndex), where average price/earning for HOSE peaked at 50–70(X) during 2007–2008, and plunged to 8(X) in 2011. As of 2015 year-end, this ratio stood at 9 and 11(X) for HNX and HOSE, respectively.

In mid-2016, VSM had 312 joint-stock companies listed on HOSE and 388 on HNX. Both size and liquidity have grown over time. In 2005, the average daily trade volume was less than 700,000 shares, and the figure increased to 2.6 million in 2006, and 18 million in 2008. In 2014, the VSM saw the largest yearly trade volume of 47.4 billion shares, worth USD 35 billion (Table 12.4). In 2016Q1, the average value was approximately USD 100 million/day.

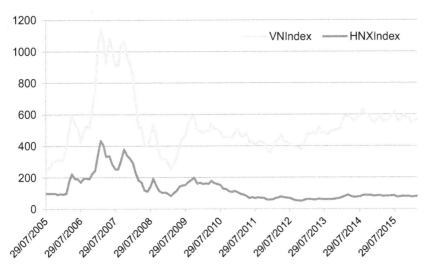

Figure 12.11 VNIndex (HOSE) and HNXIndex

Source: Compiled by author with data from Ho Chi Minh City Stock Exchange.

Table 12.4 Liquidity on VSM, 2011–2015

Year	Trade volume (billion shares)		Trade values (VND billion)	
	HOSE	*HNX*	*HOSE*	*HNX*
2011	18.88	7.94	–	–
2012	–	12.14	216,881	–
2013	16	10.57	260,985	82,081
2014	30.45	16.98	533,052	199,527
2015	28.13	11.54	482,046	135,035

Source: HNX data.

The VSM's market size grew quickly during 2006–2015, with 2015 year-end market capitalization standing at 33% of GDP (Figure 12.12). The VSM performs better now than in the pre-World Trade Organization (WTO) period in terms of both IPOs and seasoned offerings. Firms have issued shares worth about USD 100 billion in VSM's first 17 years. During 2010–2015, USD 53 billion was raised, of which the total value of funds raised reached USD 13.2 billion in 2015, about 28% of Viet Nam's total capital expenditures. In addition, the VSM helped to attract about USD 15 billion of FPI.

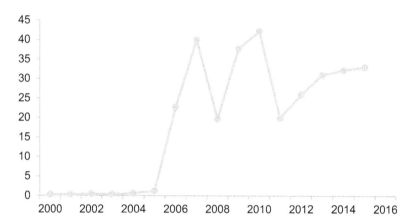

Figure 12.12   VSM market capitalization (percentage of GDP)

Source: Author's compilation from SSC/HOSE/HNX reports.

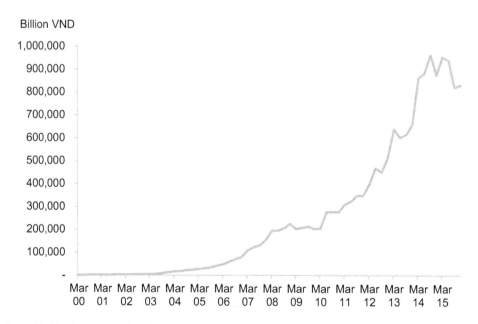

Figure 12.13   Government bonds (outstanding)

Source: ADB/AsianBondOnline (23 March 2016).

Bond markets

From 2005, the VSM has also served as a major distribution system of government bonds, with the HNX being authorized to organize public auctions. The government borrowed from public bonds investors approximately USD 48 billion in 2010–2015, mostly with tenures of three and five years. In 2011, the bond market was worth 15% of GDP, with over 90% being government bonds. Total value of outstanding government bonds is now estimated 22% of GDP, making them a major source for financing state budget deficit. While the government bond market has been picking up since 2005, the corporate bond market remains quite modest, about VND 42.8 trillion (USD 1.92 billion) in 2015, according to the HNX. In fact, the corporate bond is the game where few large corporations – banks included – dominate and seek to tap public sources of debt finance.

Securities broker firms

The number of securities companies grew with VSM's size. Dozens of securities broker firms have made their fortune on VSM, especially those with strong equity and dominating market shares. The 10 most active broker firms in HNX occupied more than 62% of market share, while they also took 67% of HOSE brokerage fees in 2015. About 800,000 stock trading accounts were registered with the Viet Nam Securities Depository Center (VSD) in 2009, a substantial increase from 530,000 in 2008. But in March 2016, the VSD already counted 1.48 million trading accounts.

High inflation and restrictive monetary policy caused brokerage firms to make a substantial loss in 2011. In 2014, surviving firms were able to improve their performance, and their collective profits jumped to USD 150 million. The sector's ROA and ROE were 5.15% and 8.58%, respectively in 2014, twice of those of 2010.

By the end of 2015, only 81 firms survived the fierce competition who collectively held total assets of USD 3,395.5 million, and total equity of USD 1,891 million. Among them, the 20 largest made total revenues of USD 345.5 million, and profits of USD 131.8 million.

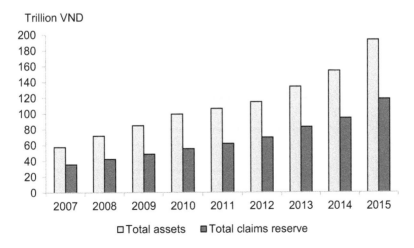

Figure 12.14   Financial aggregates of the insurance industry
Source: DIMA.

Insurers/insurance markets

Before *Doi Moi*, the insurance business had been monopolized by Bao Viet Insurance, an SOE established on 17 December 1964 offering two dozen basic insurance needs. Changes came with Decree 100/CP (18/12/1993), which allowed private and foreign firms to participate. The scope of activities also expanded. The market boomed in 1995 when dozens of new insurance firms, including joint ventures, were licensed. Additionally, 40 foreign insurers' representative offices and about 70,000 insurance agents were approved. Nowadays, 61 insurance and related service firms are fully operational in Viet Nam, offering 800 different products meeting almost every consumer's need.

It is also noteworthy that six life insurance businesses have been offering pension products – namely Manulife, AIA, Daiichi, PVI Sun Life, Bao Viet Life, and Prudential. Conventional nonlife insurance needs are mainly served by domestic firms with PetroVietnam Insurance occupying the largest share due to the surge of risky oil exploring/mining activities during 1995–2015.

In 2015, total insurance revenues reached USD 3.13 billion, representing an annual growth of 21.43%, of which nonlife took USD 1.46 billion, and life USD 1.67 billion. Revenue growth for life insurance was at 29.5%, outpacing nonlife, 14%. Insurers also honored total financial obligations worth USD 955 million.

Total assets of the insurance sector stood at USD 8.78 billion in 2015, a 12.68% annual growth during 2011–2015, of which, nonlife subsector accounted for 31.8%, and life 68.2%. Total revenues of 12 insurance broker firms also reached USD 26.8 million in 2015, representing a 14.3% annual growth.

Insurers also reinvest into the economy, with total 2015 stock worth USD 6,383 million, 79.2% of which came from life insurers. They are the main buyers of government bonds, with total purchases reaching USD 283 million in 2015.

With over 200,000 registered agents, life insurers increased new policies sold during 2013–2015: 1,178,390; 1,252,157; 1,298,776. Industry experts expect the life insurance market to annually expand by 25%, and nonlife by 18%.

Financial companies

The first financial companies were licensed in 1997 to provide consumer finance and serve domestic trades. Their collective balance sheets showed an increase of shareholders' equity from USD 520.8 million in 2012 to USD 815.6 million in 2015; and assets decreased from USD 7.49 billion to USD 4.04 billion.

As non-deposit-taking firms, they are focused on non-bank services, especially riskier consumer goods financing. In the 2014–2016 period, they financed 20% of consumer goods purchases, with interest rates typically running from 25% to 30% per annum, twice the normal bank rates.

Leasing

Six financial lessors appeared in mid-1990s, providing small-scaled term-finance alternatives to private small and medium-sized enterprises (SMEs), who then suffered from discriminatory lending by SOCBs. Banks also established their wholly owned financial leasing subsidiaries, as lessors could be more flexible in terms of decision-making. From 2000, the government raised the bar for new entrants, requiring USD 5 million equity minimum. Lessors then entered a race in equity. Their equity base increased to USD 70.5 million in 2005, and then USD 136.4 million in 2007.

In the post-WTO period, lessors performed poorly, with profit margins declining over time. The industry average ROE was only 3.5% in 2007. Flexible contract terms became dangerous as executives manipulated regulations and made financing decisions for personal profiteering, especially at SOCB-founded lessors such as the case of Vu Quoc Hao – former CEO of Agribank Leasing Co. 2 – who was sentenced to death in an embezzlement trial in 2014.

By 2016Q1, only Vietinbank Leasing, Vietcombank Leasing, BIDV Leasing, ACB Leasing, and Sacombank Leasing remain active while the rest struggle with bad debts and losses.

Merger and acquisitions market

Merger and acquisition (M&A) activities started in Viet Nam in the mid-1990s. The risk spillover during the 1997 Asian financial turmoil triggered early transactions such as the merger between Phuong Nam JSCB and Dong Thap Rural JSCB in 1997. The first noteworthy cross-border M&A deal was Colgate Palmolive's acquisition of Da Lan Toothpaste – then occupying 30% market share – for USD 3 million. But the real surge in M&A activities started in 2006, speculating on Viet Nam's continuous prosperity post-WTO, with 47 deals completed, worth total USD 0.6 billion.

Larger M&A deals appeared in 2013 with Warburg Pincus's acquiring 20% of Vincom Retail and KKR's USD 400 million purchase of Masan's equity. The market peaked in 2012 and 2015, with total value each year standing at USD 4.2 billion, counting 367 and 525 deals, respectively (Figure 12.15). M&A among domestic firms also increased during 2008–2012, from 22% to 45% of market. Acquiring firms from Japan, Singapore, the Republic of Korea, and the US dominate the market.

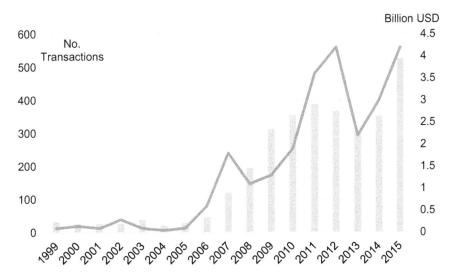

Figure 12.15   M&A transactions in Viet Nam

Source: Institute for Mergers, Acquisitions and Alliances (IMAA) and Vuong, Napier, and Samson (2014).

The relation of banking, finance, and economic growth

Monetary policy and financial sector reform

Implementing more modern monetary policy has helped Viet Nam fight inflation and supported growth (Roman 1995; Riedel and Turley 1999; Camen 2006). But over time, the goals, tools, and implementation processes have shown weaknesses and limitations. For example, management of forex fluctuations has been a burden on SBV/SOCBs, limiting the ability to pursue an independent monetary policy (Pham and Riedel 2012; ADB 2014; World Bank 2014). Also, Pham and Riedel (2012) argue that the conduct of monetary policy in Viet Nam during the higher inflation period was generally "clumsy." To this end, financial sector liberalization helped not only promote growth but also maintain macroeconomic stability, thanks to more predictable commercial lending rates in the marketplace (Figure 12.16).

Viet Nam's leadership now considers steps for further liberalizing the financial system, giving more freedom to market players. Although interventions are still unavoidable at times, they are now used more cautiously, and policy-making tends to be increasingly evidence-based.

Viet Nam's integration into the world economy increases its domestic capital market's dependence on world markets, which also bring contagion risks. There is evidence that the VSM has been influenced by American, PRC, and Japanese stock markets (Wang and Lai 2014).

Inclusive financing: microfinance, venture capital, crowdfunding

Microfinance

Jobs creation has been a major economic achievement. From mid-1990s, most jobs have been created by private SMEs. The problem with the SMEs subsector has been a constant lack of access to financing and unequal playing field where they are subjected to higher costs of fund and operations (O'Toole and Newman 2012; Yoshino and Taghizadeh-Hesary 2014).

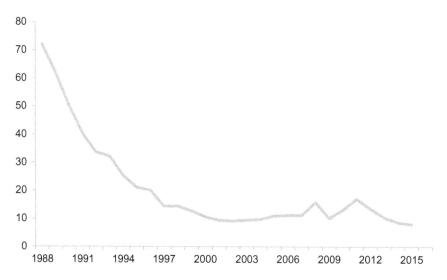

Figure 12.16   Average lending rate (in percentage)

Source: SBV and GSO (2014–2016).

Kalra (2015) reports only 8% of Vietnamese saved money and 16% had a loan with a financial institution in 2011.

In this context, microfinance has been an important solution and a sign of financial market liberalization, although evidence on its positive effects has been mixed (IFC 2014).

According to the IFC (2014), only 16.5% of the adults in rural areas and 29.8% of adults in urban areas have an account at a formal financial institution as of 2011, whereas the averages for the East Asia and Pacific developing region are 50.1% and 68.7%, respectively.

Although still limited in scale, improvements of MFI activities can be seen with more recent statistics. The three major domestic systems that are partly responsible for microfinance activities, namely Bank for Social Policy, Agribank, and PCFs collectively served 9.6 million clients by the end of 2013, providing a total amount of credit worth USD 8,034 million. By the end of 2012, genuine MFIs (exclusive of VBSP/VBARD/PCFs) provided USD 108 million micro-credit to 480,000 clients (IFC 2014). This cause of sustainable development – supported by multilateral organizations – also leads to microfinance initiatives such as the Asian Development Bank-managed USD 40 million Asian Development Fund program in conjunction with Japan Fund for Poverty Reduction's technical assistance.[2]

Venture capital financing

Due to the predominantly credit-based financing agenda by the Vietnamese government, venture-capital activities had a slow start in 1990s, and Viet Nam's entrepreneurial financing initiatives have significantly diverged from international venture-capital policy patterns (Klingler-Vidra 2014). Today's best-known venture-capital funds (VCF) include IDG Ventures, Kamm Investment, CyberAgent, DFJ/VinaCapital, IndochinaCapital, MekongCapital, and Viet Nam Partners.

IDG is the pioneer with its presence in Viet Nam dating back to 1992, with IDG financing PCWorldVietnam – its first computer publication. Formally established in 2004, it now holds a USD 100 million portfolio consisting of 42 tech, ICT/media, and consumer-sector companies, including successful projects as VNG, Apollo, VC-Corp, and VietnamWorks.

In 2015, the government explored the opportunity of setting up a VCF to support a new-born ecosystem for tech-related entrepreneurs, with assistance from state-financed sci-tech supports agencies such as NAFOSTED/NATIF/NATEC, Viet Nam Startup Fund, and Viet Nam Silicon Valley Project. The government and its research institutes believe a national VCF will be a prime solution, helping nurture this critically important component of the entrepreneurship ecosystem with seed funding.

Crowdfunding

Crowdfunding has become a buzzword in recent years when entrepreneurs seek to find alternative finances for their creative, yet risky, ideas. It was heard of for the first time in Viet Nam in 2012, but the legal framework for governing crowdfunding operations has not been in place leading to higher perceived risks. Viet Nam finally got the first ever crowdfunding platform IG9 in mid-2013.

Most crowdfunding activities center around a handful of internet-based platforms: including ig9.vn, fundstart.vn, 500.co, inspireventures.com, and cyberagentventures.com. Despite its novelty, local entrepreneurs are receptive to crowdfunding, and on steep learning curves.

The crowdfunding industry has still been nascent, but with a fast growing and dynamic entrepreneurship community, Viet Nam would likely become the second country in ASEAN – after Malaysia – that institutionalizes a crowdfunding framework with a development roadmap.

Inherent risks and challenges

The bank-based nature induces inherent risks of structural problems as at present, total banking assets amount to 180% of GDP, and 92% of total financial assets. During 2005–2010, state institutions increased holdings in SOCBs/JSCBs from USD 70 million to USD 700 million without facing regulatory restrictions (Pincus 2015), although inefficiencies of state-owned non-core investments had been well informed. Meanwhile the inflation problem remains, making the system even more vulnerable to economic shocks (Nguyen, Cavoli, and Wilson 2012; Kalra 2015; Vuong 2016).

Use of credit in Viet Nam has generally been regarded as inefficient. The real estate market consumed 80% of credit supply in 2013, crowding out other productive sectors. More recently, the government's stimulus package in 2008 induced risk-taking and arbitrage-seeking (e.g., turning to speculative assets), causing irrational bubbles in these connected assets markets (Dinh et al. 2013). The risk of misallocation of financing to three to six times the formal banking rates (Thanh et al. 2011). This is a serious issue for the economy in general (O'Toole and Newman 2012; Vuong 2016). Selfish interests tend to entice banks – currently under interest controls – to protect their margins by transferring operational costs to customers, for instance by imposing fees on numerous lending transactions (Pham 2015).

Another persistent challenge is habitual practices of using a large portion of short-term funds to provide long-term credit, causing mismatch risk and adversely affecting asset-liability management equations. The ratio changed for SOCBs over time from 21.5% (2012) to 25% (2014) and 34% (2016); and for JSCBs: 18%, 21%, and 37%, respectively. The issue appears to worsen even though the size of the banking system has increased significantly, thus a structural issue remains structural!

In reality, the aforementioned risks are reflected through the problem of non-performing loans. Official bad debt ratio (Figure 12.17) is usually regarded by experts as well below international standards, triggering disagreements even among concerned authorities.

The creation of Viet Nam Assets Management Company in June 2013 and its questionable credibility show how serious the problem of bad debts is. The government had planned this for

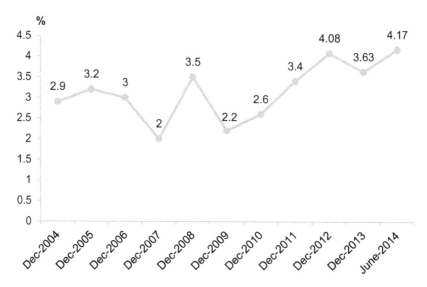

Figure 12.17 Bad debt ratio

Source: SBV reports.

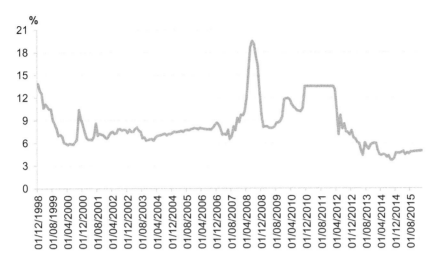

Figure 12.18   Three-month interbank rate

Source: SBV.

about three years, and it finally took three major sub-law regulatory documents to establish it: Decree 53/2013/ND-CP by the government; Decision 843/QD-TTg by the prime minister; and Decision 1459/QD-NHNN by the SBV governor.

Facing these issues, recent positive signs of the banking system such as a lower lending-to-deposit ratio, about 80% during 2014–2016, and positive growth rate of deposits at banks may reduce stress in the financial system for some time, with short-term lending rates going below 10% per annum during 2013–2015 (Figure 12.18). However, there have also been signs of a lower capacity to consume finance within the productive sector. In addition, the increasing society's liquidity preference becomes phenomenal, representing some doubt over the financial system's long-run stability.

Reform needs

It is generally agreed that financial reforms have to a large extent supported the transformation of Viet Nam's economy (Kovsted, Rand, and Tarp 2005; Bayraktar and Wang 2006; ADB 2014; World Bank 2014). However, persistent problems are now putting pressure on renewed reforms (Leung 2009; Pham and Riedel 2012). The following three issues need to be urgently addressed by policy-makers.

The skewness of financial assets by sector and ownership will need to be addressed adequately, as with fast growing assets – now already 200% of Viet Nam's GDP – all the risks pertaining to the system as discussed will be amplified, making the economy increasingly vulnerable to economic shocks (ADB 2014, 2015). Viet Nam's financial deepening is high compared to the majority of lower-middle-income countries. Although openness improves the access to financial services and the efficiency of financial intermediaries, its functions of reducing the cost of funds and stimulating capital accumulation/economic growth face serious limitations (Bayraktar and Wang 2006; Vuong and Napier 2014). The opening of the sector alone does not suffice to address the risks (Leung 2009; Pham and Riedel 2012). Renewed reforms of the governance system based on rules of law and arm's-length-transaction principles will have to be institutionalized (Malesky and Taussig 2009; Bhattacharya 2014; Pincus 2015). That means a departure from the existing system – primarily based on personal relationships, cronyism, and unchecked commercial interests – with cross-holdings of banks' equity as a manifestation (Sarath and Pham 2015).

The flaws in making and implementing monetary policy, such as sudden changes of policy rates or putting the brakes on credit flows, are related to the complexity, and most probably the impossibility of its multi-objective macro decision-making framework (Pham and Riedel 2012), thus a reform need is well beyond just fixing the "clumsy policy behavior" (Nguyen and Nguyen 2009; Nguyen, Cavoli, and Wilson 2012; Kalra 2015). The two bouts of two-digit inflation during 2008–2012 remind policy-makers of the problem posed by the so-called impossible trinity (Das 2006; Grenville 2011).

The weaknesses that prevent the economy from attaining its optimal balance between growth and sustainability include an inadequate speed of institutional reforms, macro institutions, and the entrepreneurial ecosystem; as well as a lack of an independent central bank with effective policy-making and efficient set of policy implementation tools, which has the skills, rules, resources and capabilities of balancing between stability-oriented interventions and profitable risk-taking (Camen 2006; Kraay and Nehru 2006; Leung 2009; Volz 2013; Volz 2016).

The SBV's relative independence will become critical, as compromising on quality of policy-making will ultimately lead to uncontrollable risks and failures to plan even in the short run. As the monetary and capital markets have already been strongly connected and very sensitive even to a vague sign of failures (Bellocq and Silve 2008), monetary policy quality will have far-reaching effects – positive or negative – on the whole economy and its future. Toward such a reform, the value of increasing central bank's autonomy should ultimately be for public interests and national sustainable prosperity (Stiglitz 2016).

Acknowledgments

The author thanks the staff of Vuong and Associates – Dam Thu Ha, Nghiem Phu Kien Cuong, Vuong Thu Trang – for their assistance; and the following experts for their views: Nancy K. Napier (Boise State University), André Farber (Université Libre de Bruxelles), James Riedel (Johns Hopkins University), Joseph Stiglitz (Columbia University) and Pham Muoi (*Wall Street Journal*). Thanks also go on to Tran Van Dzung (HOSE) and Vu Thuy Nga (HNX) for helps on stocks and bonds data.

Notes

1 Financials reported in USD are for comparison while national accounts and market transactions are required by laws to report in Vietnamese Dong (VND).
2 ADB/NewsBrief (5/7/2012) (www.adb.org/news/briefs/viet-nam-microfinance-development-program).

References

Asian Development Bank (ADB). 2014. *Viet Nam: Financial Sector Assessment, Strategy, and Roadmap.* Manila: Asian Development Bank.
ADB. 2015. *Key Indicators for Asia and the Pacific 2015.* Manila: Asian Development Bank.
Bayraktar, N., and Y. Wang. 2006. Banking Sector Openness and Economic Growth. World Bank Policy Research Paper No. 4019. Washington, DC: World Bank.
Bellocq, F.-X., and A. Silve. 2008. The Banking System of Vietnam After the Accession to WTO: Transition and Its Challenges. AFD Working Paper No. 77. Paris: Agence Française de Développement.

Bhattacharya, R. 2014. Inflation Dynamics and Monetary Policy Transmission in Vietnam and Emerging Asia. *Journal of Asian Economics* 34: 16–26.

Camen, U. 2006. Monetary Policy in Vietnam: The Case of a Transition Country. *BIS Papers* 31: 232–252.

Das, D. K. (2006). Globalization in the World of Finance. *Global Economy Journal* 6(1): 1–22.

Dinh, T. M., E. Malesky, T. T. To, and D. T. Nguyen. 2013. Effect of Interest Rate Subsidies on Firm Performance and Investment Behavior During Economic Recession: Evidence from Vietnam. *Asian Economic Journal* 27(2): 185–207.

Dutta, M. 1995. Vietnam: Marketization and Internationalization of Its Economy. *Journal of Asian Economics* 6(3): 311–326.

Grenville, S. 2011. The Impossible Trinity and Capital Flows in East Asia. ADBI Working Paper No. 318. Tokyo: Asian Development Bank Institute.

IFC. 2014. *Responsible Finance in Vietnam*. Washington, DC: International Finance Corporation.

Kalra, S. 2015. Vietnam: The Global Economy and Macroeconomic Outlook. *Journal of Southeast Asian Economies* 32(1): 11–25.

Klingler-Vidra, R. 2014. Building a Venture Capital Market in Vietnam. *Asian Studies Review* 38(4): 582–600.

Kovsted, J., J. Rand, and F. Tarp. 2005. *From Monobank to Commercial Banking: Financial Sector Reforms in Vietnam*. Singapore: ISEAS.

Kraay, A., and V. Nehru. 2006. When Is External Debt Sustainable? *World Bank Economic Review* 20(3): 341–365.

Leung, S. 2009. Banking and Financial Sector Reforms in Vietnam. *ASEAN Economic Bulletin* 26(1): 44–57.

Malesky, E. J., and M. Taussig. 2009. Where Is Credit Due? Legal Institutions, Connections, and the Efficiency of Bank Lending in Vietnam. *Journal of Law, Economics, and Organization* 25(2): 535–578.

Nguyen, H. M., T. Cavoli, and J. K. Wilson. 2012. The Determinants of Inflation in Vietnam, 2001–09. *ASEAN Economic Bulletin* 29(1): 1–14.

Nguyen, T. P., and D. T. Nguyen. 2009. Exchange Rate Policy in Vietnam, 1985–2008. *ASEAN Economic Bulletin* 26(2): 137–163.

O'Toole, C. M., and C. Newman. 2012. Investment Financing and Financial Development: Firm Level Evidence from Vietnam. IIIS Discussion Paper No. 409. Dublin: Institute for International Integration Studies, Trinity College Dublin.

Pham, H. 2015. Bank Efficiency, Ownership Structure and Regulations in Vietnam. Doctoral dissertation, Limoges.

Pham, T. T. T., and J. Riedel. 2012. On the Conduct of Monetary Policy in Vietnam. *Asian-Pacific Economic Literature* 26(1): 34–45.

Pincus, J. 2015. Why Doesn't Vietnam Grow Faster? *Journal of Southeast Asian Economies* 32(1): 26–51.

Riedel, J., and W. S. Turley. 1999. The Politics and Economics of Transition to an Open Market Economy in Vietnam. Technical Paper No. 152. Paris: OECD Development Centre.

Román, L. 1995. Institutions in Transition: A Study of Vietnamese Banking. Doctoral dissertation, Stockholm School of Economics.

Sarath, D., and D. V. Pham. 2015. The Determinants of Vietnamese Banks' Lending Behavior: A Theoretical Model and Empirical Evidence. *Journal of Economic Studies* 42(5): 861–877.

Sepehri, A., and A. H. Akram-Lodhi. 2005. Transition, Savings and Growth in Vietnam. *Journal of International Development* 17(4): 553–574.

Siregar, R. 1997. Management of Macroeconomic Policies Vietnam. In *Rising to the Challenge in Asia: A Study of Financial Markets*. Manila: Asian Development Bank.

Stiglitz, J. E. 2016. *Rewriting the Rules of the American Economy*. New York: W. W. Norton.

Thanh, V. T., T. T. Cuong, B. Dung, and T. D. Chieu. 2011. Small and Medium Enterprises Access to Finance in Vietnam. In *Small and Medium Enterprises Access to Finance in Selected East Asian Economies*, edited by C. Harvie, S. Oum, and D. Narjoko. Jakarta: ERIA, pp. 151–192.

VGP. 2016. Vietnamese Government Portal (23/5/2016). http://chinhphu.vn/portal/page/portal/chinhphu/tinhhinhthuchien

Volz, U. 2013. ASEAN Financial Integration in the Light of Recent European Experiences. *Journal of Southeast Asian Economies* 30(2): 124–141.

Volz, U. 2016. Regional Financial Integration in East Asia against the Backdrop of Recent European Experiences. *International Economic Journal* 30(2): 272–293.

Vuong, Q. H. 2016. Determinants of Firm Performance in a Less Innovative Transition System: Exploring Vietnamese Longitudinal Data. *International Journal of Transitions and Innovation Systems* 5(1): 20–45.

Vuong, Q. H., and N. K. Napier. 2014. Resource Curse or Destructive Creation in Transition: Evidence from Vietnam's Corporate Sector. *Management Research Review* 37(7): 642–657.

Vuong, Q. H., N. K. Napier, and D. E. Samson. 2014. Relationship Between Innovations, Capital Expenditures and Post-M&A Performance: Evidence from Vietnam, 2005–2012. *IUP Journal of Business Strategy* 11(1): 1–8.

Wang, K. M., and H. C. Lai. 2014. Which Global Stock Indices Trigger Stronger Contagion Risk in the Vietnamese Stock Market? *Panoeconomicus* 60(4): 473–497.

Wood, A. 1989. Deceleration of Inflation with Acceleration of Price Reform: Vietnam's Remarkable Recent Experience. *Cambridge Journal of Economics* 13(4): 563–571.

World Bank. 2014. Vietnam's Financial Sector Assessment. WB/FSAP. Washington, DC: World Bank.

Yoshino, N., and F. Taghizadeh-Hesary. 2014. Analytical Framework on Credit Risks for Financing Small and Medium-sized Enterprises in Asia. *Asia-Pacific Development Journal* 21(2): 1–21.

PART II

Thematic chapters

13

COMMERCIAL BANKING IN ASIA

Ilhyock Shim

Introduction

Asia's financial system is bank-centric. The bulk of financial intermediation in almost all major Asian economies has been done in the form of bank financing. Figure 13.1 shows that the share of domestic bank credit to total domestic debt financing, which include both bank loans and bond issuances, is around 60%–80% in many Asian economies as of the end of 2014. Therefore, it is crucial to understand the activity of banks in the region and potential risks they may pose.

The Asian financial crisis of 1997–1998 was an important wake-up call for both commercial banks and financial authorities in Asia. After such experience, financial authorities in Asia have strengthened capital requirements and other regulations to require banks to hold sufficient amounts of capital against negative shocks, improved their system of managing capital flows, and increased the flexibility their exchange rate regimes.

In addition to strengthening microprudential regulation, Asian financial authorities also strengthened their macroprudential orientation. Even before the crisis, a few jurisdictions in Asia used macroprudential policies on housing markets to slow down rapid growth in housing loans or housing prices. After the 1997–1998 crisis, many Asian economies actively introduced various forms of macroprudential policies to mitigate housing and credit booms.

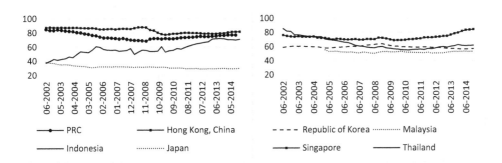

Figure 13.1 Share of domestic bank credit to total domestic debt financing (in per cent)

Sources: Compiled by author with BIS debt securities statistics and IMF *International Financial Statistics*.

Such conservative approaches helped most of the Asian banking systems withstand the turmoil of the global financial crisis of 2007–2009 well. Overall, Asian banks remained profitable and resilient over the past 10 years. The Asian financial authorities have also adopted Basel III and other international financial reforms in line with the internationally agreed timeline or even earlier than other advanced economies.

However, the prolonged low interest rate environment generated by major advanced economies after the global financial crisis and the European sovereign debt crisis have put pressure on the profitability of commercial banks in Asia due to lowering short-term rates in many Asian economies, flattening yield curves and greater capital market financing by Asian corporates. More recently, weakening growth in emerging Asia combined with a turn in the domestic credit cycle in many Asian economies added to pressure on the profitability of Asian banks through greater likelihood of loan losses.

After the European banks retreated from the Asian region in the aftermath of the global financial crisis, many Asian banks have filled the gap and started to increase their cross-border lending to other economies in the region in search for greater profits and diversification of income sources. Asian banks have also increased their presence in other economies in the region by setting up branches and subsidiaries.

Such an increase in the intra-regional cross-border banking activity brings benefits of greater intra-regional financial integration and of using regional savings for the region's economic growth. However, it can also increase systemic risks through a few channels such as the common and concentrated lenders within the region, liquidity risk in foreign currency funding, and the shortening maturity of foreign currency loans.

This chapter provides an overview of commercial banking in Asia from the perspective of both domestic and cross-border banking, focusing on the developments after 2007. The first section will focus on the profitability and soundness of commercial banks in Asia in the context of macroeconomic challenges such as low interest rates, turning of credit cycles, and slowing growth. The second section will in turn look at the cross-border activity of Asian banks, focusing on their intra-regional activity, their intra-regional presence in the form of branches and subsidiaries, and potential risks in expanding their cross-border business.

Domestic commercial banking in Asia

In this section, we first look at the business models of Asian commercial banks focusing on their overall profitability and the main profit sources. Then, we consider if their capital and liquidity buffers are at adequate levels. Next, we examine the relationship between bank credit cycle and non-performing loan cycle in Asia. Finally, this section provides a brief overview on the progress in implementing Basel III in major Asian jurisdictions in Box 13.1.

Business models and profitability of Asian banks

The first step to understand Asian banks is to look at their business models. Roengpitya, Tarashev, and Tsatsaronis (2014) classify banks into three groups by their business model: a retail-funded commercial bank, a wholesale-funded commercial bank and a capital-markets-oriented bank. The first two models differ mainly in terms of banks' funding mix, while the third category stands out primarily because of banks' greater engagement in trading activities. Following the method of Roengpitya, Tarashev, and Tsatsaronis (2014), which considers 222 banks headquartered in 34 economies, most banks domiciled in Asia are classified as retail-funded commercial banks.

Most Asian banks heavily rely on net interest margin (NIM) as their main source of income. Table 13.1 shows that the ratio of interest margin to gross income is greater than 50% for most Asian banks, except those in Hong Kong, China, between 2011 and 2015. Therefore, the share of non-interest income is relatively small.

In many Asian economies, the current low interest rate environment has compressed NIM. One factor is the flattening of the yield curve driven by the market expectation of future rate cuts or a prolonged period of low short-term interest rates, as well as by strong demand for long-term Asian bonds by both domestic and foreign investors. When the yield curve is steeper, banks can increase earnings from maturity transformation. By contrast, when the yield curve is flat or negatively sloped, banks' lending rates tend to become subject to downward pressure. Another factor is the very low policy rates in a number of economies in the Asia-Pacific region. When the policy rate approaches zero or becomes negative, banks have little room to lower their deposit rates in line with the policy rate, while the lending rate remains subject to downward pressure. Even when both short-term and long-term interest rates fall at the same time, the short-term loan rate adjusts relatively quickly, while the long-term deposit rate changes more slowly. Therefore, banks with a large share of short-term loans and long-term deposits could face a narrowing in NIM.

The upper panels of Figure 13.2 show that since 2009 the NIM of banks has indeed narrowed in the economies (Hong Kong, China; Japan; and Singapore) where the policy rate has remained close to zero. The lower panels of Figure 13.2 illustrate that for a few other countries (Republic of Korea, Malaysia, and Thailand), a tightening in term spreads has generally coincided with a fall in NIM.

However, the return on assets (ROA) of these banking systems remained relatively stable between 2009 and 2015 except the Republic of Korea (Figure 13.2). In some cases, the ROA and the policy rate moved in opposite directions, mainly driven by increases in banks' non-interest income, which has more than compensated for the declines in traditional interest income. The increases in non-interest income partly reflect increases in trading profits, which may not be sustainable. In addition, when bond yields fell, banks holding a large amount of bonds were able to enjoy valuation gains – but these could quickly reverse when long-term interest rates increase.

Finally, over the past two decades, the volume of bank lending in Asia has grown substantially relative to gross domestic product (GDP), mainly driven by household loans, especially housing loans. Schularick and Shim (2016) decompose the change in the ratio of total bank lending to

Table 13.1 Interest margin to gross income (in per cent)

	2011	*2012*	*2013*	*2014*	*2015*
People's Republic of China	80.7	80.2	78.9	78.5	76.3
Hong Kong, China	45.3	48.0	46.7	51.2	46.5
India	71.8	70.3	69.4	67.7	68.7
Indonesia	59.8	65.0	68.8	69.0	70.3
Japan	–	–	62.6	63.8	62.6
Republic of Korea	73.6	78.3	82.2	72.5	–
Malaysia	–	–	52.9	60.7	62.0
Philippines	–	–	50.4	67.8	68.9
Singapore	65.1	55.6	61.6	64.9	62.9

Notes: For Japan, the value for each year is the average of the previous year's Q4 and the current year's Q1 to Q3. For Korea, the value for 2014 is the average of data for Q1 and Q2 2014.

Source: IMF *Financial Soundness Indicators*, author's calculation.

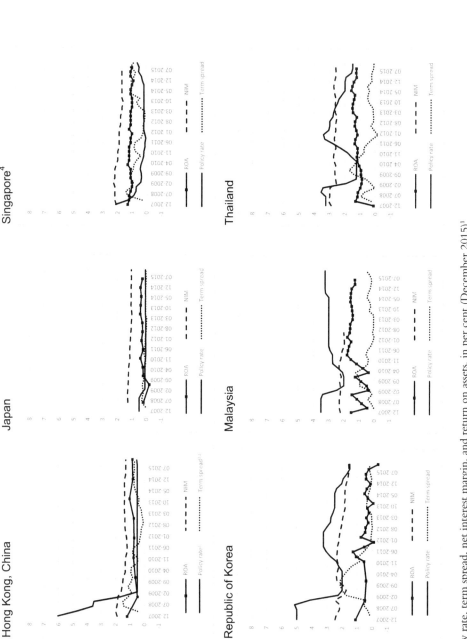

Figure 13.2 Policy rate, term spread, net interest margin, and return on assets, in per cent (December 2015)[1]

ROA = return on assets; NIM = net interest margin.

Notes: [1]For Hong Kong, China, all authorised institutions, Hong Kong, China offices; for Japan, all banks; for Singapore, local banks; for the Republic of Korea, domestic banks; for Malaysia, banking system; and for Thailand, commercial banks. [2]Quarterly average. [3]Three-year government bond yield minus three-month government bill yield; For Singapore; five-year government bond yield minus three-month government bill yield. [4]For policy rate, one-month overnight interest swap rate.

Sources: IMF, *Financial Soundness Indicators*; Bloomberg; national data.

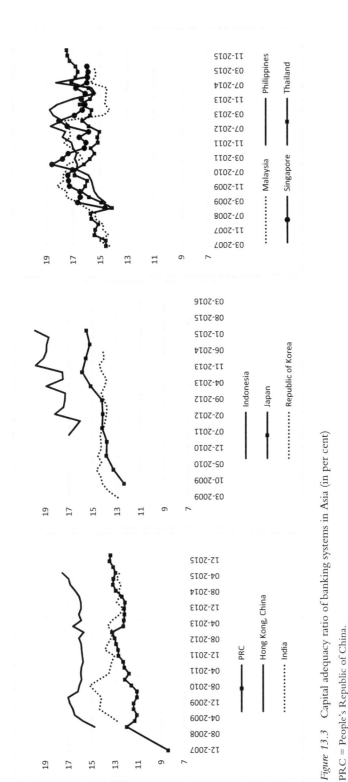

Figure 13.3 Capital adequacy ratio of banking systems in Asia (in per cent)

PRC = People's Republic of China.

Note: Total regulatory capital to risk-weighted assets.

Sources: IMF, *Financial Soundness Indicators*; Bloomberg; CEIC; national data.

the private non-financial sector to GDP into the change in the ratio of household lending to GDP and the change in the ratio of corporate lending to GDP. They show that increases in household lending explain about 70% of increases in total bank lending over 1994–2014, and that increases in housing lending account for 78% of such increases in household lending.

Adequacy of capital and liquidity of Asian banks

During the global financial crisis of 2007–2009 and stresses in the euro area sovereign debt market after 2010, most Asian banks maintained sizeable capital buffers above the level required by the regulators in their jurisdictions (Figure 13.3). Asian banking systems generally held regulatory capital well above 10% of their risk-weighted assets as of end-2015. Because banks in the region are generally well capitalized and follow business models less affected by the tighter capital requirements, concerns over the impact of new capital requirements are less pronounced in the region than elsewhere.

Box 13.1   Recent developments in banking regulation in Asian economies

After the global financial crisis, the Basel Committee on Banking Supervision (BCBS) revamped the bank capital and liquidity requirements, called "Basel III." It is a wide range of reform measures, developed by the BCBS, to strengthen the regulation, supervision, and risk management of the banking sector. It includes both bank-level, or microprudential, regulation, which will help raise the resilience of individual banking institutions to periods of stress, and macroprudential regulation to mitigate system-wide risks that can build up across the banking sector as well as the procyclical amplification of these risks over time.[1]

As of 2016, the regulatory authorities of almost all major economies in the region (including both BCBS member jurisdictions and non-BCBS member jurisdictions) had implemented the main components of Basel III capital requirements either in line with the BCBS agreed date of implementation or earlier. In terms of liquidity requirements, most jurisdictions in Asia also implemented the liquidity coverage ratio rules according to the BCBS agreed timeline, and on track to introduce the net stable funding ratio rules in line with the BCBS target date. Most jurisdictions in Asia have also introduced rules on domestically systemically importance banks. Finally, many jurisdictions in Asia are in the process of introducing the leverage ratio rules, with some of them having introduced the rule much earlier than the deadline of January 2018 agreed by the BCBS members.

Box Table: Basel III Implementation in Major Asian Economies

		BCBS agreed date of implementation	People's Rep. of China	Hong Kong, China	India	Indonesia	Japan	Rep. of Korea	Malaysia	Singapore	Thailand
Risk-based capital	Definition of capital	Jan 13	Jan 13	Jan 13	Apr 13	Jan 14	Mar 13	Dec 13	Jan 13	Jan 13	2013
	Capital conservation buffer	Jan 16	Jan 13	Jan 15	Mar 16	Jan 16	Mar 16	Dec 13	–[13]	Jan 16	2016[19]

		BCBS agreed date of implementation	People's Rep. of China	Hong Kong, China	India	Indonesia	Japan	Rep. of Korea	Malaysia	Singapore	Thailand
	Counter-cyclical buffer	Jan 16	Jan 13[1]	Jan 15	Feb 16	Jan 16	Mar 16	Jan 16	–[13]	Jan 16	–[19]
Liquidity standards	Liquidity coverage ratio (LCR)	Jan 15	Mar 15	Jan 15	Jan 15	Jan 16	Mar 15	Jan 15	Jun 15	Jan 15	–[20]
	Net stable funding ratio (NSFR)	Jan 18	–[2]	–[3]	–[4]	–[7]	–	–[10]	–	–[16]	–
Leverage ratio		Jan 18	Jan 15	Mar 15	Apr 15[5]	–[8]	–	Mar 15[11]	–[14]	–[17]	–[21]
Globally systemically important bank (G-SIB) requirements		Jan 16	Jan 13	Jan 15	–[6]	–[9]	Mar 14	–[12]	–	–[18]	–
Domestically systemically important bank (D-SIB) requirements		Jan 16	Jan 13	Jan 15	Apr 16	Jan 16	Mar 16	Jan 16	–[15]	Apr 15	–[21]

1 High-level principles were published in June 2012 and are in force from January 2013; and detailed policy framework is under development as of end-March 2016.

2 The NSFR policy framework is under development as of end-March 2016.

3 A draft rule is expected to be published in 2017.

4 A draft rule was published in May 2015.

5 Revised guidelines on the leverage ratio framework, incorporating amendments based on the BCBS leverage ratio framework of January 2014, are in force from April 2015. A rule migrating to Pillar 1 treatment will be issued as and when decided by the BCBS.

6 There are no Indian banks on the list of G-SIBs as of end-March 2016. For one Indian bank included in the sample of global banks for identification of G-SIBs, instructions to make disclosures were issued starting from the financial year ending in March 2014.

7 A consultation paper is being drafted as of end-March 2016.

8 A consultative paper on Leverage Ratio regulation was issued in October 2014. Selected banks have been required to calculate the leverage ratio using December 2014 data. The final regulation on the leverage ratio and its disclosure will be issued before 2018.

9 Indonesia is not home to any G-SIBs.

10 A draft rule is expected to be published in 2017.

11 The final rule is in force from March 2015. A rule migrating to Pillar 1 treatment is expected to be published in 2017, in line with the BCBS timeline.

12 Rules requiring public disclosure of 12 indicators for assessing G-SIBs published and in force from December 2013.

13 The headline capital conservation and counter-cyclical buffer requirements was published in 2013. Details on the buffer requirements were provided in 2015. The buffer requirements will come into force in 2016.

14 A final decision to formally adopt the leverage ratio as a binding measure will be made closer to the targeted 2018 deadline.

15 The regulator is currently assessing the need to adopt the D-SIB rules.

16 Consultation is expected to be issued in 2016.

17 A draft rule is expected to be issued in 2017.

18 The public disclosure and submission requirements for assessing G-SIBs are implemented with effect from January 2014.
19 The rules regarding the capital conservation buffer and counter-cyclical buffer were published in 2012. As of early 2015, the former will not take effect until 2016 and the latter will take effect only if the circumstances warrant it.
20 In 2014, the regulator conducted the Quantitative Impact Studies and analyzed data.
21 Under consideration as of early 2015.

Notes: The dates in the cells are the first month the relevant rules were enforced.

Sources: Basel Committee on Banking Supervision *Tenth Progress report on adoption of the Basel regulatory framework,* April 2016; Financial Stability Institute *Survey on Basel II, 2.5 and III implementation,* July 2015.

On the liquidity side, most Asian banks have retail deposits as the main source of funding. Even though strong loan growth has exceeded deposit growth in some Asian economies over the past several years, the loan-to-deposit ratios for banks in most countries remain well below 100%.

Table 13.2 compares Asian banks with non-Asian banks in Group of 20 (G20) economies in terms of capital adequacy, asset quality, profitability, and liquidity adequacy at the end of 2015. In particular, the total risk-weighted capital ratio, Tier 1 risk-weighted capital ratio and (risk-unadjusted) leverage ratio of Asian banks are on average higher than those of non-Asian G20 economy banks, respectively. In addition, the Asia banks' average non-performing loan ratio is lower than the ratio for non-Asian G20 economy banks. Moreover, in terms of the two key profitability measures, Asian banks' average ROA and return on equity are higher than those of non-Asian G20 economy banks, respectively. Finally, Asian banks have more liquidity buffers and a better liquidity profile than non-Asian G20 economy banks in terms of both the liquid asset ratio and the loan-to-deposit ratio.

Bank credit cycle and NPL cycle in Asia

Another major determinant of the medium- and longer-term profitability of banks is the state of the credit cycle. Credit expansion has slowed in some jurisdictions in Asia and turned negative in other jurisdictions. By the end of 2015, prolonged booms in bank credit in most emerging Asian economies had ended (Figure 13.4). Several macroeconomic factors such as weak external demand, falling commodities prices and deleveraging pressures on the corporate and household sectors are likely to reduce the scope for credit expansions in Asian economies, and hence profits from the traditional banking business.

In addition, adverse macroeconomic developments may increase the ratio of non-performing loans (NPLs) to total loans. In the backdrop of the rapid credit expansion in Asia in the last decade and the turn of the credit cycle in some economies, this is of particular relevance. Indeed, based on available data from selected economies, it appears that the NPL cycle tends to follow the credit cycle with a lag (Figure 13.5). The historical experience suggests that strong credit booms combined with severely negative macroeconomic developments could soon be followed by a surge in NPLs. It should be noted that one difference between the surge in credit in the run-up to the Asian financial crisis in 1997–1998 and the recent surge in credit after 2009

Table 13.2 Comparison of Asian and non-Asian banks (in percentage, as of end-2015[10])

	10 Asian economies[1]	Non-Asian G20 economies[2]
Regulatory capital to risk-weighted assets	16.12	15.31
Regulatory Tier 1 capital to risk-weighted assets	13.53	13.05
Capital to assets	9.21	8.51
Non-performing loans to total gross loans	2.00	3.81[3]
Return on assets	1.95	1.41[4]
Return on equity	17.23	14.27[4]
Interest margin to gross income	65.51[5]	56.24[6]
Liquid assets to total assets (liquid asset ratio)	28.47	24.00[7]
Total (non-interbank) loans to customer deposits	85.67[8]	100.72[9]

Notes: [1]Ten Asian economies include People's Republic of China; Hong Kong, China; India; Indonesia; Japan; Republic of Korea; Malaysia; the Philippines; Singapore; and Thailand. [2]G20 economies excluding Asia include Argentina, Australia, Brazil, Canada, France, Germany, Italy, Mexico, Russian Federation, Saudi Arabia, South Africa, Turkey, the UK, and the US. [3]Excluding Germany. [4]Excluding Australia and Germany. [5]Excluding Thailand. [6]Excluding Australia, France, and Germany. [7]Excluding France. [8]Excluding People's Republic of China, Malaysia, and Thailand. [9]Excluding Australia and France. [10]For Italy, as of 2015Q2; for Japan, as of 2015Q3; for Republic of Korea, as of 2014Q2; for Mexico, as of February 2016; for South Africa, as of January 2016; for the UK, as of 2015Q2.

Source: IMF *Financial Soundness Indicators*; author's calculation.

shown in Figure 13.5 is that the former was mainly due to corporate credit booms, while the latter was driven by both household and corporate credit booms.

Indeed, the signs of deteriorating credit quality have surfaced already. Export-sensitive sectors such as steel, shipbuilding, and shipping have been especially hard hit by prolonged deceleration of global growth in recent years. With property markets turning weak in some economies, some construction companies and developers as well as mortgage borrowers are also having difficulty in paying back their loans. As in the cases of Hong Kong, China and Taipei,China in the late 1990s, however, it may take some time until this is fully reflected in the actual NPL ratios.

NPL recognition may also be slower in tough times. When banks are generating robust growth in income either due to strong economic growth or fast loan growth, banks can handle rising NPLs by actively disposing of them and incurring losses through loan sales or loan charge-offs from defaulted loans. In a downturn, however, sagging bank income may limit the capacity of banks to absorb the losses that result from NPL recognition. Under these circumstances, banks may be tempted to provision inadequately for potential losses or to "evergreen" potentially problematic loans by rolling over existing loans or lending more to existing borrowers. Thus, low current NPL ratios may not fully reflect the true credit risk or credit quality of bank assets.

Cross-border banking in Asia

Commercial banks also engage in international activities. In general, banks expand abroad to take advantage of growth opportunities in other markets and also to widen and diversify their income sources and funding base. Additional motives for cross-border expansion include strong competition in domestic banking markets and the resulting low margins; limited lending

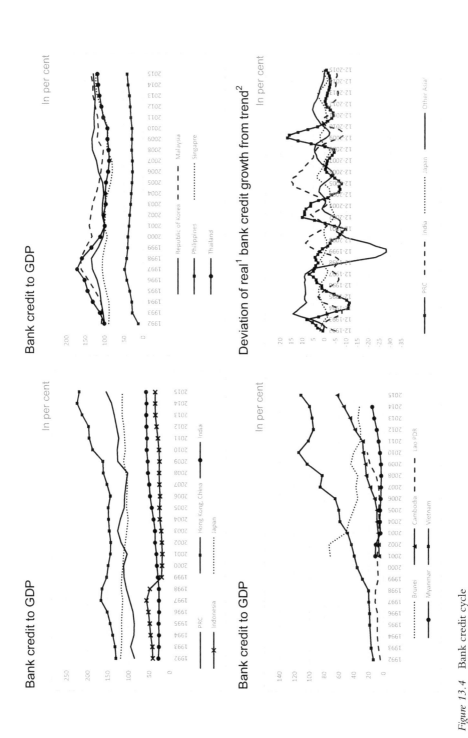

Figure 13.4 Bank credit cycle

GDP = gross domestic product, Lao PDR = Lao People's Democratic Republic, PRC = People's Republic of China.

Notes: [1] Deflated by CPI inflation. [2] Actual growth minus its linear time trend calculated over the period of Q1 1992 to Q4 2015 for each series; four-quarter moving average. [3] Weighted averages of Hong Kong, China; Indonesia; the Republic of Korea; Malaysia; the Philippines; Singapore; and Thailand. Based on 2005 GDP and PPP exchange rates.

Sources: IMF, *International Financial Statistics*; CEIC; national data; BIS.

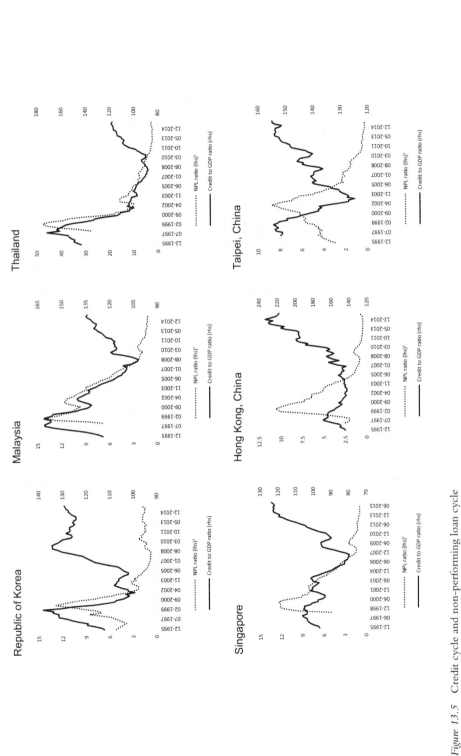

Figure 13.5   Credit cycle and non-performing loan cycle

NPL = non-performing loan.

Notes: LHS: as a percentage of total loans; RHS: as a percentage of annualized GDP.

[1] For Republic of Korea, substandard loan ratio of commercial banks; for Malaysia, net of interest in suspense and specific provision in both non-performing loans and total loans; for Thailand, gross non-performing loans; for Singapore, classified loans to non-banks; for Hong Kong, China, gross classified loans; for Taipei,China, past-due loan ratio.

Sources: Compiled by author with data from Bloomberg, CEIC, IMF, national sources, and BIS.

opportunities in domestic markets combined with ample deposit funding; or tight domestic banking regulations that could encourage banks to look for business opportunities in less tightly regulated jurisdictions.[2]

When it comes to the choice of legal entity, banks expanding abroad can start with a representative office focusing on offshore businesses, set up an onshore branch to serve mainly existing home-country customers, or establish a full subsidiary serving local customers with a limited or a full range of services. Alternatively, banks can purchase part or all of an existing branch network or particular business units from an established bank.

Several major banks in Asia are also global systemically important banks (G-SIBs) designated by the Basel Committee on Banking Supervision. As of November 2016, four PRC banks and three Japanese banks are in the list of 30 G-SIBs. In addition to the seven G-SIBs, many banks headquartered in Asian economies are actively engaged in cross-border banking within the region.

In this section, we consider various aspects of cross-border banking in Asia. In particular, we first provide some evidence of the increasing regionalization of cross-border banking in Asia, and an overview of the intra-regional presence of Asian banks in terms of branches and subsidiaries. Next, we consider two specific aspects of the regional banks' cross-border banking business model: funding models of foreign banking activity and the maturity of foreign currency lending. Finally, the section provides a brief discussion on potential financial stability concerns stemming from the increasing trend of regionalization of cross-border banking in Asia.

Growing importance of regional banks in cross-border lending to Asia

Cross-border banking in the Asian region exhibited a strong growth over the last 15 years. Between 2002 and 2007, international bank lending in foreign currency by banks' headquarters or by local branches and subsidiaries (henceforth, international claims) to the emerging Asia-Pacific region almost quadrupled, reaching USD 844 billion in 2007 (Figure 13.6). At the end of 2007, euro area banks accounted for about a third of these claims, Asian banks for a similar share, and Swiss, UK, and US banks for roughly the other third. Over the same period, international claims on Latin America and the Caribbean grew more slowly than those on Asia by 52%, while those on emerging market economies (EMEs) in Europe almost quintupled (that is, grew by 388%), albeit from a smaller base.

During the peak of the global financial crisis period, international banking activity collapsed, and the Asia-Pacific region was no exception. Between 2007 and 2008, international lending in the emerging Asia-Pacific region fell by USD 120 billion. But this halt was only temporary. The growth in international lending in the region resumed strongly in 2009. International claims on the region more than doubled over 2009–2014 (Figure 13.6). Banks headquartered in Japan and outside area banks, defined as banks located in the Bank for International Settlements (BIS) reporting area but not headquartered in one of the countries reporting to BIS consolidated statistics (assuming that they are headquartered in Asia), have rapidly increased their lending to the emerging Asia-Pacific region (Figure 13.7). Hong Kong, China and Singapore also played an important role as regional banking centers, by intermediating a large amount of cross-border funds compared to their respective GDP. The strong growth in international claims on emerging Asia between 2009 and 2014 stands in contrast to what happened elsewhere. During the same period, international claims on Latin America and the Caribbean grew by 48%, while those on EMEs in Europe shrank by 11%.

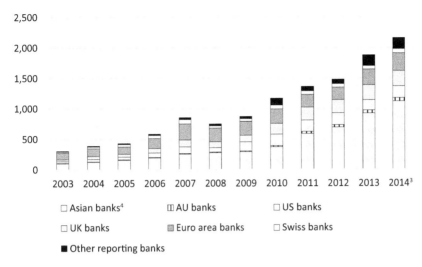

Figure 13.6 International claims[1] on emerging Asia-Pacific economies[2] (USD billion)

Notes: [1]Sum of all cross-border claims and locally extended claims in foreign currency on an immediate borrower basis. [2]All economies in the Asia-Pacific region excluding Australia; Hong Kong, China; Japan; New Zealand; and Singapore. [3]As of the end of 2014Q3. [4]The sum of international claims on emerging Asia by Japanese banks, regional banks, Asian offshore banks and outside area banks (assuming these are headquartered in Asia).

Source: Compiled by author with BIS consolidated banking statistics (immediate borrower basis).

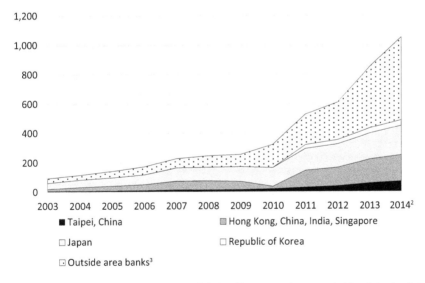

Figure 13.7 International claims on emerging Asia-Pacific economies extended by Asian banks[1] (USD billion)

Notes: [1]Amount outstanding. Exclude "inside area offices" since data on country breakdown for claims extended by inside area offices are unavailable. [2]As of 2014Q3. [3]It is assumed that these are headquartered in Asia. From 2003Q4 to 2011Q3, they do not include banks headquartered in Australia; Taipei,China; Hong Kong, China; India; Japan; and Singapore. From 2011Q4 to 2014Q3, they also exclude banks headquartered in the Republic of Korea. Therefore, they are possibly banks headquartered in countries such as the People's Republic of China, Indonesia, Malaysia, the Philippines, and Thailand.

Source: BIS consolidated banking statistics (immediate borrower basis).

With the resurgence of cross-border lending, the set of leading players changed. In the wake of the crisis and amid sovereign debt problems in Europe, euro area banks' cross-border activity fell off. As a result, euro area banks failed to keep up with the Asian region's growing demand for dollar funding. By 2015, the share of euro area banks in international claims on emerging Asia-Pacific was down to 13%, less than half its 2007 share, although the absolute level of their claims was largely unchanged. The banks that stepped in were largely from Asia.

When we examine cross-border lending data based on the location of the creditor bank ("residence basis" rather than "consolidated basis"), cross-border banking in Asia excluding Japan looks much more intraregional than that in EMEs in Europe and Latin America. This is largely because of the special intermediary role played by two banking centers: Hong Kong, China and Singapore.

Asian economies excluding Japan get a larger share of their financing from other economies within the region than do EMEs in Europe and Latin America. The larger share could partly be due to funds that originate elsewhere, but are channeled to borrowers in Asia excluding Japan through domestic and foreign banks located in Hong Kong, China and Singapore. This is also the case for portfolio investment, but it is more pronounced for bank lending.

One important aspect of foreign bank activity is the choice of currency in lending. Over the past decade, foreign banks have lent more to emerging Asian economies in their local currencies (Figure 13.8). However, the locally extended claims on emerging Asia in local currency

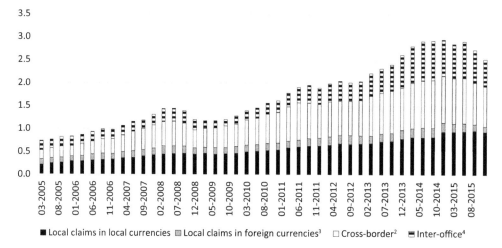

■ Local claims in local currencies ▨ Local claims in foreign currencies[3] ☐ Cross-border[2] ▤ Inter-office[4]

Figure 13.8 Foreign claims on emerging Asia[1] (USD trillion)

Notes: Emerging Asia = People's Republic of China; Taipei,China; India; Indonesia; Republic of Korea; Malaysia; the Philippines; and Thailand.

[1]BIS reporting banks' total outstanding foreign claims (immediate borrower (IB) basis) on residents of the region expressed at constant end-2015 exchange rates. [2]Cross-border claims (ultimate risk (UR) basis) excluding interoffice positions, adjusted for exchange rate movements using the currency breakdown available for cross-border claims (including interoffice positions) from the locational banking statistics. [3]Local claims in foreign currency, estimated as the difference in international claims (IB basis) and cross-border claims (UR basis). This estimate will be increasingly biased the greater the net risk transfers (i.e., the gap between the red and dashed black lines). [4]Interoffice claims on subsidiaries in the borrower country/region; estimated as the difference between cross-border claims from the consolidated statistics (UR basis) and cross-border claims from the locational statistics, and adjusted for currency movements using the currency breakdown available for total cross-border positions in the locational banking statistics.

Sources: BIS consolidated banking statistics (ultimate risk and immediate borrower basis); BIS locational banking statistics by residency.

extended by all foreign bank branches and subsidiaries take up less than 35% of foreign claims, which are the sum of cross-border claims, locally extended claims in all currencies and interoffice claims. This implies that the majority of foreign bank lending to emerging Asia is denominated in foreign currency.

Foreign branches and subsidiaries of regional banks

Regional cross-border banking is done either by banks in one country lending directly to borrowers in another or by lending through local branches or subsidiaries. To the extent that intra-regional cross-border banking activity in Asia and the Pacific continues to intensify, the regional expansion of Asia-Pacific banks in the form of branches and subsidiaries will become more important. It will matter for financial stability how these branches and subsidiaries fund themselves.

Over the past several years, 10 member countries in the Association of Southeast Asian Nations (ASEAN) have taken steps to accelerate banking integration under the initiative of the ASEAN Economic Community. In particular, the member countries agreed on the ASEAN Banking Integration Framework and introduced a scheme called Qualified ASEAN Banks. Under this scheme, a bank qualified in one jurisdiction receives equal treatment in the other jurisdictions within ASEAN. To recognize the different levels of readiness among the member countries, the five larger ASEAN countries plan to implement the Qualified ASEAN Banks scheme first, and later include the other five countries.

All BIS member economies in Asia have banks with foreign branches or subsidiaries elsewhere in the Asian region (Table 13.3, reading each row). As of the end of 2014, the banks headquartered in the People's Republic of China, India, Japan, the Republic of Korea, and Singapore, respectively, had 20 or more foreign branches and subsidiaries in the region. From the viewpoint of host countries, the People's Republic of China; Hong Kong, China; Japan; and Singapore each had 20 or more foreign branches and subsidiaries of banks headquartered elsewhere in the region. This home-host pattern is mainly explained by the cross-border activities of the domestic customers of Asian banks, ready access to US dollar borrowing from international markets, the role of regional financial centers and growth opportunities abroad.

In establishing a presence elsewhere in the region, Asian banks tend to use branches rather than subsidiaries. In particular, their branches outnumber subsidiaries by a ratio of almost three to one (Table 13.3, the cell where the Asia row and the Asia column intersect). Nonetheless, this preference for branches is more moderate than that of foreign banks from outside the region, which have branches that outnumber their subsidiaries by a ratio of more than five to one. Banks from ASEAN countries represent an exception to this general pattern. As shown by the figures inside the box in Table 13.3, ASEAN banks generally have more subsidiaries than branches within the ASEAN region. As a host country, Indonesia in particular shows a striking preference for subsidiaries over branches: the country hosts more than twice as many subsidiaries as branches (Table 13.3, the cell where the bottom row and the Indonesia column intersect).

Funding models of regional banks' foreign banking activity

Banks operating outside their home markets make use of a range of different funding sources to support their lending business. To fund assets acquired in the course of cross-border expansion, banks can look to home-country deposits swapped into the host currency, borrow in wholesale markets in the host currency, or tap into local host country retail deposits. Banks in

Table 13.3 Foreign bank branches and subsidiaries in Asia

Host Home	CN[1]	HK	IN	JP	KR	ID	MY[2]	PH	SG	TH	Asia
CN		9/11	–/1	–/5	–/5	1/1	2/–	–/1	2/6	2/–	16/30
HK	3/2		–/–	–/–	–/–	–/–	–/1	–/–	1/–	–/–	4/3
IN	–/4	–/12		–/2	–/1	2/–	1/–	–/–	6/1	–/1	9/21
JP	3/3	1/10	–/3		–/4	3/1	3/4	–/2	3/3	–/3	13/37
KR	6/3	2/5	–/2	1/8		3/–	–/–	–/1	–/5	–/–	12/24
ID	–/3	–/2	–/1	–/1	–/–		–/–	–/–	1/1	–/–	1/8
MY	–/3	1/3	–/–	–/1	–/–	3/–		1/–	4/–	1/1	10/8
PH	2/–	1/2	–/–	–/2	–/–	–/–	–/–		–/1	–/–	3/5
SG	4/–	2/4	–/2	–/3	–/3	3/–	2/3	–/–		1/1	12/16
TH	2/2	–/4	–/1	–/1	–/–	1/1	1/–	–/–	1/2		5/11
Asia	20/20	16/53	–/10	1/23	–/13	16/3	9/8	1/4	18/19	4/6	85/236
Others	18/45	12/92	–/35	1/48	2/26	6/7	18/16	1/9	10/74	2/7	70/359
Total	38/65	28/145	–/45	2/71	2/39	22/10	27/24	2/13	28/93	6/13	155/595

AU = Australia; CN = People's Republic of China; HK = Hong Kong, China; ID = Indonesia; IN = India; JP = Japan; KR = Republic of Korea; MY = Malaysia; NZ = New Zealand; PH = the Philippines; SG = Singapore; TH = Thailand.

Notes: The first figure in each cell represents the number of foreign bank subsidiaries located in a host country owned by ultimate parent banks headquartered in a home country, while the second represents the number of foreign banks that have branches in a host country. The outlined box represents foreign bank branches and subsidiaries among the ASEAN-5 home-host countries. [1]Based on the 2013 Annual Report of the China Banking Regulatory Commission. [2]Includes foreign banks and branches in Labuan.

Sources: National sources (retrieved from the websites of central banks and financial regulators in early January 2015); author's calculations.

mature banking markets with ample deposits and limited lending opportunities are more likely than others to rely on home-country deposits for their foreign expansion, although they still run a rollover risk in terms of hedging currency exposure. By contrast, banks in high-growth economies with strong loan demand are more likely to rely on wholesale markets. Except in the case of an outright bank acquisition, host country retail deposits take time to accumulate.

Retail funding tends to be viewed as more "sticky" than wholesale or market funding. During the global financial crisis, foreign banks' local affiliates that had strong local retail funding base such as those in many Latin American countries weathered funding market stresses better than those relying mainly on wholesale funding.[3]

When we look at the degree of reliance on wholesale and retail funding regardless of currency, Asian banks' foreign subsidiaries located in Asia show relatively strong core funding ratios, defined here as the ratio of customer deposits to funding from all sources. Table 2 in Remolona and Shim (2015) provides more details.

Another key aspect of business models is the funding currency. For foreign bank subsidiaries, local currency funding is generally more stable than funding in other currencies such as US dollars. This is partly because local currency deposits mainly consist of relatively stable customer deposits for domestic use, while foreign currency deposits are made mainly by corporations or financial institutions that are sensitive to exchange rate and other developments. Lending by international banks' foreign affiliates that are funded in local currency is considerably less volatile than cross-border lending (see Ehlers and Wooldridge (2015) and references therein).

In aggregate, banks headquartered in selected Asian economies tend to rely on local currency funding for their lending to the region to almost the same degree as those headquartered elsewhere (see table 3 in Remolona and Shim (2015) for details). However, in many host countries in Asia, banks headquartered in Asia have a lower share of local currency liabilities than those headquartered elsewhere. In particular, Asian banks in the People's Republic of China; Taipei,China; Hong Kong, China; India; the Republic of Korea; the Philippines; and Singapore have a lower share of local currency liabilities than non-Asian banks in the respective economies. By contrast, Asian banks that lend to Indonesia, Japan, Malaysia, and Thailand maintain higher levels of local currency funding than those headquartered in Americas and Europe.

Another way to look at the funding model is in terms of the local currency funding gap. This gap is defined as the difference between local currency assets and local currency liabilities. Banks would fill this gap by borrowing foreign currency and converting it into local currency. Banks choose to either keep open currency positions and expose themselves to exchange rate risks or hedge their positions by entering into derivatives contracts, such as currency swaps, at a cost. The gap is the maximum amount since it does not include local currency funding via the swap market.

In aggregate, the funding gaps of banks headquartered in selected Asian economies and that lend to the region are about the same size as those of banks headquartered elsewhere. Local currency liabilities are 66% of local currency assets in the region for Asia-Pacific banks, compared with 64% for those based in Americas and Europe (see table 3 in Remolona and Shim (2015) for details). As regards individual host economies, Asian banks' lending to Taipei,China: India; the Republic of Korea; and the Philippines tends to have relatively large funding gaps with the ratio of their local currency liabilities to local currency assets smaller than 50%, while their lending to Japan has a relatively small gap, with a ratio of 95%.

Maturity of foreign currency lending

Mismatches between the maturity structures of foreign currency borrowing and lending can be an important source of risk, as experience during the 1997–1998 Asian financial crisis shows. These days, Asian banks typically borrow in US dollars and other international currencies, mostly from US and European banks, and lend in the same currencies to banks and non-banks in the region. Given their funding, do Asian banks lend more in short-term maturities than do banks of other nationalities?

We can look at the issue of loan maturity from the perspectives of both creditors and borrowers. From the creditor perspective, before 1997 it was Swiss, UK, and US banks that tended to make the most use of short-term loans in providing financing to the emerging Asia-Pacific region (Figure 13.9, left-hand panel). In 1998, in the wake of the Asian financial crisis, banks from all regions cut back their short-term foreign currency loans to the region, although they eventually started lending short term again.[4] In the wake of the global financial crisis, Asian banks increased their share of short-term loans, reaching a share of about 70% in 2014. This contrasts with the declining share of US banks and the slightly rising share of euro area banks during the same period.

Turning to the borrower perspective, there is some heterogeneity among Asian economies in terms of their reliance on short-term foreign currency liabilities (Figure 13.9, right-hand panel). Before the Asian financial crisis, international borrowing by Hong Kong, China and Singapore was almost entirely short term, while that by the People's Republic of China was largely long term. Short-term borrowing fell sharply across all countries in the region immediately after the

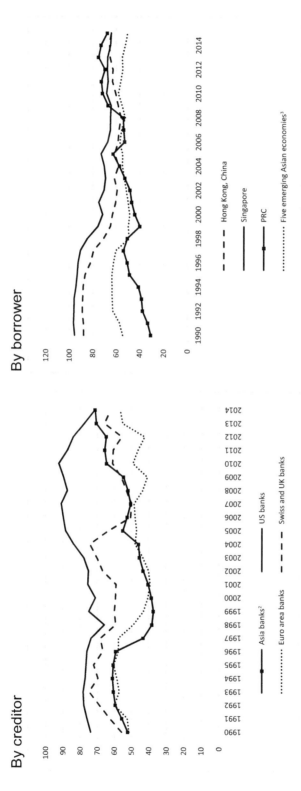

Figure 13.9 Share of Asian banks' short-term claims[1] in all international claims on emerging Asia–Pacific economies (in per cent)

PRC = People's Republic of China, US = United States, UK = United Kingdom.

[1]Maturity equal to or less than one year. [2]Includes outside area banks, that is, those that do not report to BIS consolidated banking statistics at a given point in time, on the assumption that outside area banks lending to emerging Asia–Pacific economies are headquartered in Asia. Also includes Japanese banks (from Q2 1990); Taipei,China and Singapore banks (from Q4 2000); India banks (from Q4 2001); Hong Kong, China banks (from Q2 2005); Republic of Korea banks (from Q4 2011). [3]Indonesia, the Republic of Korea, Malaysia, the Philippines, and Thailand.

Source: BIS consolidated banking statistics (immediate borrower basis).

Asian financial crisis. During the period between the Asian financial crisis and the great financial crisis, the share of short-term international borrowing by the People's Republic of China increased steadily from 30% to 60%, while that of five emerging Asian economies (Indonesia, the Republic of Korea, Malaysia, the Philippines, and Thailand) increased only slightly. Since 2009, the People's Republic of China's share has grown sharply, approaching 70% by 2015. During the same period, the share of short-term borrowing of Hong Kong, China grew somewhat more modestly, while that of the five emerging Asian economies was broadly stable.

The increasing share of short-term foreign currency borrowing can be explained by the following two factors: (1) the increasing share of interbank borrowing in total borrowing by all entities; and (2) the increasing share of short-term non-bank borrowing in all non-bank borrowing. Over the past two decades, the share of interbank borrowing has shown a similar trend to the share of short-term borrowing, with their correlation ranging around 0.5–0.6. Since we can expect banks to borrow from each other in short maturities in the normal course of business, the increasing share of interbank borrowing is likely to have contributed to the increasing share of short-term borrowing by the Asian economies.

A more important question is whether the share of short-term borrowing by non-banks has also increased. BIS data, however, do not provide a maturity breakdown separately for non-banks. Nonetheless, we can assume that all interbank foreign currency loans are short-term and subtract these loans from the amount of all short-term loans to each economy. This gives us a conservative estimate of the amount of short-term loans to non-banks in a country. We then find that between Q1 2009 and Q1 2015, the share of short-term loans to non-banks in all non-bank loans increased by 21 percentage points for Hong Kong, China, 20 percentage points for Singapore, 12 percentage points for the People's Republic of China, and 4 percentage points for the five emerging Asian economies. Such large increases in the share of short-term borrowing by non-banks are a cause for concern.

Potential financial stability concerns

Whether at the global or regional level, banking integration involves benefits and risks. Benefits include greater competition and enhanced efficiency, availability of a wider range of banking services and greater risk-sharing. The trends discussed in the previous sections suggest three potential sources of risks. The first is the growing systemic importance of foreign banks in host jurisdictions, both as common and concentrated lenders within the region, and through foreign branches and subsidiaries. The second is liquidity risk in foreign currency funding associated with the funding models of Asia-Pacific banks, and the third is shortening maturity of foreign currency loans.

The financial regulators and supervisors in Asia would need to seek a good balance between the benefits and costs of the rising intra-regional banking. It is also necessary for them to make efforts to identify systemic risks stemming from the integration of cross-border banking within the region and discuss potential ways to deal with such risks.

Acknowledgments

The views expressed in this chapter are my own, and not necessarily those of the Bank for International Settlements. I thank Peter Morgan, Ulrich Volz, and Naoyuki Yoshino for comments and helpful suggestions, and Jimmy Shek for excellent research assistance. All remaining errors are mine.

Notes

1 In December 2010, the BCBS released Basel III, which set higher levels for risk-adjusted capital requirements and introduced a new global liquidity framework. BCBS members agreed to implement Basel III from January 2013, subject to transitional and phase-in arrangements. In terms of Basel III leverage ratio, the BCBS plan to make final adjustments to the definition and calibration of the leverage ratio by 2017, with a view to migrating to a Pillar 1 (minimum capital requirements) treatment in January 2018. For liquidity requirements, the BCBS issued the revised liquidity coverage ratio (LCR) rule in January 2013, which came into effect in January 2015 subject to a transitional arrangement before reaching full implementation in January 2019. In October 2014, the BCBS also issued the final standard for the net stable funding ratio (NSFR), which will become a minimum standard by 1 January 2018. Finally, in July 2013 the BCBS published an updated framework for the assessment methodology and higher loss absorbency requirements for globally systemically important banks (G-SIBs). The requirements came into effect on 1 January 2016 and will become fully effective on 1 January 2019. Finally, in October 2012, the BCBS issued a set of principles on the assessment methodology and the higher loss absorbency requirement for domestic systemically important banks (D-SIBs).

2 Broadly speaking, banks can take on one of the following two expansion models when they decide to go abroad. First, they can "follow their customers," tailoring their expansion to existing customer needs. In this model, banks support their customers by providing cross-border trade-related banking services and helping them raise capital abroad, for example. Second, banks can expand via cross-border acquisitions and partnerships. In this model, banks take on or co-manage foreign franchises with distinct client bases in sectors such as consumer finance, project finance and wealth management.

3 The legal form of subsidiaries is often associated with a more stable retail funding base than that of branches. However, this is not always the case. The experience in central and eastern Europe testifies to this point. For example, in Hungary during the euro area debt crisis, the subsidiaries of western European banks that relied on wholesale funding from their parent banks were the ones vulnerable to deleveraging by the parents.

4 The share of short-term loans in all foreign currency loans decreased sharply for a few years after the Asian financial crisis partly because the stock of short-term loans adjusted much more than that of long-term loans, and also partly because trade activity requiring short-term credit fell significantly during the period.

References

Basel Committee on Banking Supervision. 2016. *Tenth Progress Report on Adoption of the Basel Regulatory Framework*, April. Basel: Basel Committee on Banking Supervision.

Ehlers, T., and P. D. Wooldridge. 2015. Channels and Determinants of Foreign Bank Lending. BIS Paper No. 82. Basel: Bank for International Settlements.

Financial Stability Institute. 2015. *Survey on Basel II, 2.5 and III Implementation*, July. Basel: Bank for International Settlements.

Remolona, E., and I. Shim. 2015. The Rise of Regional Banking in Asia and the Pacific. *BIS Quarterly Review*, September, 119–134.

Roengpitya, R., N. Tarashev, and K. Tsatsaronis. 2014. Bank Business Models. *BIS Quarterly Review*, December, 55–66.

Schularick, M., and I. Shim. 2016. Household Credit in Asia and the Pacific. Paper Presented at the BNM-BIS Conference on "Financial Systems and the Real Economy," 18 October 2016, Kuala Lumpur, Malaysia.

14

DEVELOPMENT BANKS IN ASIA

Magic bullets that invariably disappoint

Vikram Nehru

Introduction

National development banks (NDBs) are normally defined as state-owned financial institutions with a mandate to provide credit to borrowers that would otherwise be underserved by private lenders. NDBs operate in virtually every country in developing Asia and often constitute the main source of long-term credit.[1] Asia is also served by bilateral development finance institutions (BDFIs), such as the Japan Bank for International Cooperation (JBIC) and China Development Bank (CDB), and international multilateral development banks (MDBs), such as the World Bank and the Asian Development Bank (ADB), and more recently the Asian Infrastructure Investment Bank (AIIB) and the New Development Bank (NeDB).[2] This chapter covers all three types of development banks in Asia – national, bilateral, and multilateral – and examines the rationale for their establishment, what services they render, how well they perform, and what challenges they face. The chapter concludes that while the rationale for establishing NDBs may have been laudable, their record has been mixed for political economy and other reasons. Nevertheless, even though NDBs have been criticized for their poor performance, they retain a significant presence in every developing Asian economy – in numbers and in their relative share of the banking system's assets and lending. MDBs, on the other hand, have been generally seen as helpful in supporting Asia's development, yet their presence appears to be shrinking in overall financial inflows and they now face intense competitive pressure from new competitors that will test their resilience and their business model in coming years.

In 1998, developing Asia had 121 NDBs (Bruck 1998).[3] A more recent survey in 2012 reported that this had declined to 72 (Musacchio and Lazzarini 2012).[4] An examination of developing Asia's national central bank websites for this study found 63 NDBs in developing Asia.[5] In addition, there are about 18 important BDFIs, most of which are European and many of which have operations in Asia, although the largest is the People's Republic of China (PRC)-based (the China Development Bank).[6] As for international MDBs, the World Bank and ADB have played an important role in Asia over the last half century, while the Islamic Development Bank (which counts Afghanistan, Bangladesh, Indonesia, Malaysia, and Pakistan as among its members) and the European Investment Bank (owned by the 28 European member states) have been less important, and AIIB and NeDB are the most recent entrants.

Rationale for national development banks

As in other parts of the world, governments in developing Asia established NDBs to overcome market failures, real or perceived. The belief was that market failures led private banks to under-deliver long-term finance to sectors (such as agriculture, industry, housing, infrastructure, and small and medium-sized enterprises) considered crucial for sustained, inclusive development. The big push on NDBs occurred from the late 1940s to the 1970s when they were in vogue worldwide and supported by international MDBs such as the World Bank and the Asian Development Bank. In Asia, this was a period that saw the establishment of BAPINDO (Indonesian Development Bank) in 1946, Industrial Finance Corporation of India (1948), Indonesia's Bank Industri Negara (1951), Korean Development Bank (1954), Nepal's National Industrial Development Corporation (1959), Pakistan's Industrial Development Bank (1961), and Bank Pembangunan Malaysia (1973), to name a few. The argument went that correcting for market failures – such as myopic savings behavior, information asymmetries, and the large gap between shadow and market prices – through appropriate policies and institutions would take too long. State intervention was therefore necessary to jump-start development by financing projects directly in these sectors which (as a result of market failures) usually exhibit low financial, but high economic and social rates of return.[7] Without such long-term financial instruments, households and firms in these key sectors would be constantly exposed to high interest rates and high rollover risk, leading to suboptimal investment decisions, fewer positive externalities, and consequently lower, sustained growth in welfare.

Over time, in the 1980s and 1990s, NDBs extended their operations from beyond their core business of supplying long-term investment finance for socially profitable projects and development programs, and diversified into other areas such as working capital financing, project preparation and appraisal, technical assistance, leasing, credit guarantee and insurance, restructuring, and investment banking. MDBs also went through significant changes during this period, shifting the sectoral composition of their lending and introducing new financial instruments to meet new development challenges in their client countries.

The 1980s and 1990s were also a time when the limitations and challenges of development banking became more apparent. Despite operating for half a century or more in Asia, there is no conclusive evidence that NDBs have been able to successfully direct long-term finance to specific sectors with sustained results. In many instances, the political economy of state ownership, state capture, and poor corporate governance in NDBs have undermined national development. In some instances, NDBs have increased directed lending to priority sectors, but even in such cases it is difficult to show conclusively that this hasn't come at the expense of crowding out the private sector (Caprio et al. 2004).

Increasingly, globalization, technological advancements, economic crises, and other economic reforms have encouraged Asian developing countries to liberalize and strengthen their financial sectors. These liberalization efforts have occasionally involved the privatization of NDBs,[8] but NDBs nevertheless continue to occupy a prominent place in developing Asia. Indeed, NDBs continue to operate even in Republic of Korea and Japan – both high-income economies with well developed, market-oriented financial sectors (Amyx and Toyoda 2006; de Aghion 1999).[9] There are arguably three reasons that account for this: first, during economic downturns, as in the Asian financial crisis in 1997–1998 and the global financial crisis in 2009–2010, NDBs proved valuable for macroeconomic management because they played a counter-cyclical role by extending additional credit when private sector banks were cutting back on loan exposure or stopped lending altogether; second, there appears to be a widespread belief among policy-makers that market failures in banking and finance tend to be stubborn and resist withering away with economic and financial sector development, and consequently still require corrective measures through direct or indirect state intervention; third, NDBs and other forms of state-driven directed lending are a convenient means for governments to demonstrate that they are responding actively to politically important segments of the population who would otherwise find it difficult to access finance from private banks; and fourth, sheer policy inertia and the political power of vested interests can extend the lives of these institutions well beyond their usefulness.

Size, orientation, and performance of national development banks

An analysis of data taken from a World Bank survey published in 2012 reveals that NDBs in developing Asia vary more in size than in other developing regions (sub-Saharan Africa, Latin America, and Eastern Europe), whether measured by assets, equity, or loan portfolio (Figure 14.1a–c).[10] In part, this reflects the fact that developing Asian economies vary so much in size themselves, from the PRC, India, and Indonesia at one extreme to Afghanistan, Nepal, and Lao People's Democratic Republic (Lao PDR) on the other.

One reason for this large variation in size is that developing Asia also has by far the largest NDB in the world – CDB – which is ranked the 16th largest bank in the world with assets almost five times those of the World Bank,[11] and is set to become larger. Established in 1994 with the Ministry of Finance and Central Huijin Investment (a state-owned investment company) as its two largest shareholders, CDB grew rapidly initially by lending to state enterprises and special financing vehicles set up by local governments to fund infrastructure projects. In 2011, such loans accounted for half of CDB's loan book and accounted for a third of all loans to local government special financing vehicles (for CDB's international operations, see below; Sanderson and Forsythe 2013). At the other extreme, among the smallest development banks in Asia is the Myanmar Agricultural Development Bank (MADB). MADB is run by the Myanmar

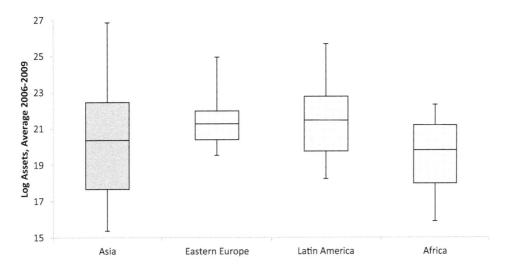

Figure 14.1a Variation in size of NDBs, by asset size, by region

Note: End points depict largest and smallest NDBs by absolute size (measured in USD); horizontal lines depict 25th, 50th, and 75th percentile in size distribution.

Source: Luna-Martínez and Vicente (2012).

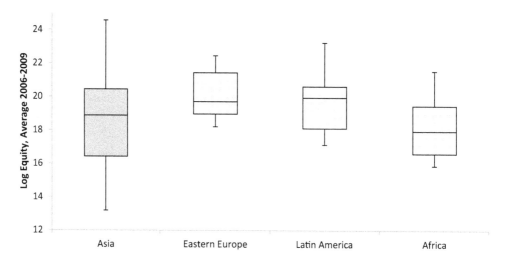

Figure 14.1b   Variation in size of NDBs, by equity, by region

Note: End points depict largest and smallest NDBs by absolute size (measured in USD); horizontal lines depict 25th, 50th, and 75th percentile in size distribution.

Source: de Luna-Martínez and Vicente (2012).

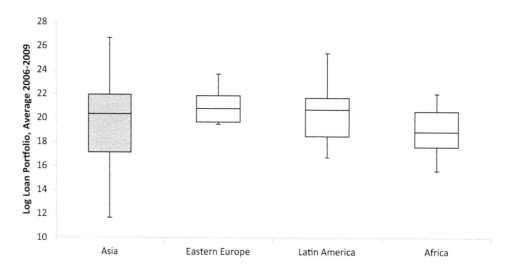

Figure 14.1c   Variation in size of loan portfolios of NDBs, by region

Note: End points depict largest and smallest NDBs by absolute size (measured in USD); horizontal lines depict 25th, 50th, and 75th percentile in size distribution

Source: de Luna-Martínez and Vicente (2012).

Ministry of Agriculture and provides institutional credit to groups of small-scale farmers for short-term cultivation needs. Loan size is usually small in relation to farmers' needs, in part because of the limitations imposed by collateral requirements, but also because of MADB's somewhat parlous financial condition.

The two extremes exemplified by the CDB and the MADB reflect the wide variety of functions, history, and settings that characterize development banks across developing Asia.

Of the 63 Asian NDBs examined for the purposes of this chapter, about 35% could be considered multisectoral, while 22% are mandated to support agricultural and rural development, 10% small and medium-sized enterprises (SMEs), 10% industrial development, 11% export and import activities, 8% housing, and 3% infrastructure. Such sectoral classifications, however, break down in practice: agricultural development could be supported through construction of warehouses or rural roads, industry could be supported through export or import financing, SMEs could be in manufacturing, agriculture, or services, and so on. Just as important, the number of development banks in each sector gives little idea of the credit and asset breakdown of banks by sector which would require detailed research beyond the scope of this chapter.

Data on 24 NDBs in developing Asia collected by the World Bank yield some interesting insights on the range of activities these financial institutions cover (de Luna-Martínez and Vicente 2012). For example, the vast bulk (96%) count SMEs among their clients, 57% lend to large private corporations, 43% provide services to individuals and households, and 57% cover state-owned enterprises.[12] Around nine out of every 10 NDBs lend directly to borrowers; the remainder act as wholesale financial institutions, lending to other (retail) financial institutions. Retail NDBs in developing Asia include such organizations as the Bank Pembangunan Malaysia Berhad, Bhutan Development Finance Corporation, the Nepal Industrial Development Corporation, and the SME Development Bank of Thailand. Wholesale DFIs tend to be very few, although they are large. Examples include the Industrial Development Bank of India, which refinances other financial institutions that provide medium- and long-term loans to industry; the Indonesia Infrastructure Guarantee Fund which provides government guarantees for infrastructure public-private partnership projects in Indonesia; and the National Bank of Agriculture and Rural Development in India, which refinances financial institutions that invest in India's rural development.

A key role of NDBs is to extend long-term finance, so it is notable that over half (53%) extend loans with a maturity in excess of 10 years, while only 26% offer a maximum maturity of five years or less. Half offer subsidized interest rates and as many as 64% offer loans with repayments guaranteed by the government to offset default losses (Rothschild and Stiglitz 1976).[13] Of course, in many if not all instances, governments extend NDBs an implicit guarantee which helps them raise capital from capital markets more cheaply than private financial institutions. Occasionally, however, when non-performing loans exceed prudent levels and threaten financial solvency or pose a systemic risk, governments often find it expedient to bailout NDBs, restructure their capital, and inject fresh equity, whether the guarantee is explicit or implicit.[14] In the PRC, for example, the Central Huijin Investment Corporation (a state-owned investment company), has often been called upon to recapitalize PRC state-owned banks, including NDBs. Research suggests that such bailouts, unless accompanied by structural and credible actions forbidding future bailouts, only tend to encourage moral hazard (Berger et al. 2010; Duchin and Sosyura 2011; Farhi and Tirole 2012; Gropp, Hakenes, and Schnabel 2011).

Some cross-country studies suggest that NDBs are less efficient than private banks because they are less profitable and argue that state ownership is largely to blame. While this may be true to some extent,[15] assessing the profitability of NDBs on the basis of published financial accounts alone can be misleading (Micco, Panizza, and Yañez 2007; Altunbas, Evans, and Molyneux 2001). NDBs are not profit-maximizing institutions and the social mandate imposed by governments tends to distort their true financial condition. Moreover, data on development bank profitability should be treated with caution, because accounting standards are not uniform within and between countries. Moreover, subsidies may distort net income (as would operations of development banks in protected markets), and treatment of non-performing loans in the financial accounts may vary and thereby affect net income. Finally, cross-country studies show that the impact of privatization on efficiency and profitability tends to be small or insignificant, in sharp comparison to privatization of non-financial corporations (Clarke, Cull, and Shirley 2003). Of course, if NDBs (and state-owned banks more generally) crowd out private financial institutions, then this would be a strong argument in favor of privatization; there is no clear-cut evidence on this either.[16]

With these important caveats, data collected for this study on the rate of return on assets and equity for 63 Asian NDBs suggest that, for the most part, they appear profitable (Figure 14.2a–b). Data for the five years in the period 2010–2014 show that for many banks in many years, the return on assets is between 1% and 2%, with only a few making outright losses in some years.

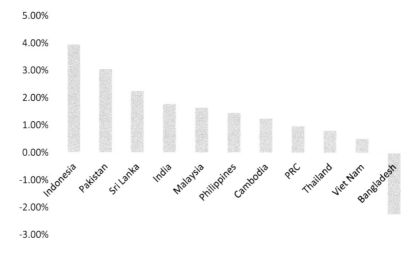

Figure 14.2a   Variation in average return on assets of NDBs, by country (2010–2014)

PRC = People's Republic of China.

Source: Data collected from central bank websites.

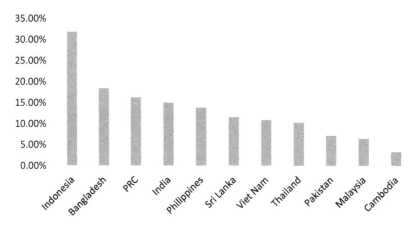

Figure 14.2b   Variation in average return on equity of NDBs, by country (2010–2014)

PRC = People's Republic of China.

Source: Data collected from central bank websites.

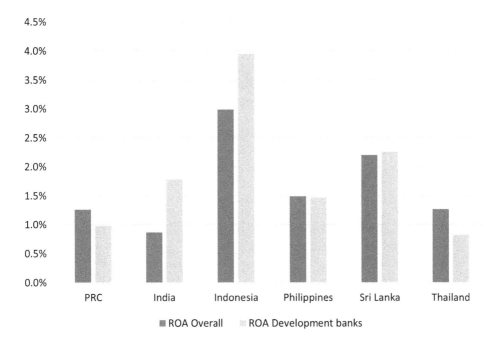

Figure 14.3 Comparisons of return on assets between NDBs and the overall banking system, selected countries

Obviously, the rate of return on equity varies considerably more, in large part because equity as a share of total liabilities differs widely across banks.

Average profitability of NDBs in some Asian countries can be skewed on account of one or two large NDBs.[17] Thus, Indonesia's high average returns on equity largely reflect the operations of Bank Rakyat Indonesia, which has a low ratio of equity to total liabilities, but also has efficient microfinance operations in rural areas which accounts for its relatively high rate of return on assets. Similarly, Bangladesh's NDBs make losses in aggregate, but this is largely due to the Bangladesh Krishi Bank (which also has significant negative equity); Bangladesh's other large NDB – the Bangladesh Development Bank – has relatively strong profitability, with a return to assets of around 3% and return to equity of 6%–8%.

In the case of five countries, our estimates for the return on assets for NDBs can be compared to those of the entire banking sector (Figure 14.3). In the case of the PRC and Thailand, the NDBs have a lower return on asset than the rest of the banking system. In the case of India and Indonesia, it is higher. And in the case of the Philippines, the two are broadly comparable. These results suggest no overall pattern, indicating that the return on asset for NDBs can be higher or lower than those of other banks depending on the specific circumstances of individual institutions and individual countries.

Challenges confronting NDBs

NDBs in developing Asia operate in financial sector and national policy settings that differ widely, but most face challenges across a broad range of dimensions. For example, the World Bank survey revealed a third (33.3%) of the NDBs in developing Asia had operations which were not sustainable without financial support from government. Almost a fifth (19%) considered themselves under-supervised with standards of reporting to the central bank that fell below the standards applicable to private financial institutions. Over a quarter (27%) said they did not disclose their capital (as required by regulation) as part of their reporting requirement and slightly under a quarter (23%) reported non-performing loan ratios of 30%, an order of magnitude above those normally reported by commercial banks. The corporate governance standards of NDBs also appear to be well below those required by their commercial brethren: nearly a quarter (23%) do not require directors to demonstrate their own solvency track record, slightly under a fifth (19%) reported that directors were not required to possess minimum requirements in technical skills, and a few (10%) did not even have independent board members.

Since they are state-owned, NDBs in poorly regulated financial systems tend to face soft budget constraints (much like other state-owned financial and non-financial institutions), which means few incentives to promote efficiency and financial viability.[18] Moreover, large rents from interest and subsidy distortions and discretionary power of banking officials tend to promote corruption and political bias. In Pakistan, for example, a study found that state-owned banks allocated credit on political considerations, even though such loans led to higher default rates (Khawaja and Mian 2005; Sapienza 2004). Similarly, prior to 1998, Indonesian NDBs (Bank Pembangunan Indonesia being a good example) were politically pressured to lend to conglomerates with strong ties to the political elite, and the fragility of their portfolio was exposed by the 1998 financial crisis.

Finally, during the global financial crisis in 2010, Asian NDBs played a counter-cyclical role that won them several proponents. Despite their well-recognized deficiencies, these banks were able to maintain a credit supply when private sector sources of finance all but dried up. More broadly, lending by state-owned banks tends to be less procyclical than private banks, and this effect is stronger the larger the downturn in lending by private banks (Micco, Panizza and Yañez 2007). Nevertheless, policy-makers need to be aware that counter-cyclical lending comes with risks, and that contingent liabilities associated with rising NPLs during such episodes must be carefully considered. Perhaps the most striking example of such risks was the quasi-fiscal counter-cyclical lending of PRC banks during the global financial crisis, the after-effects of which are now complicating the PRC's macroeconomic management half a decade later.

In summary, it is hard to conclude categorically whether NDBs have helped or hurt financial sector development specifically, or economic growth more generally. Cross-country studies that include NDBs in developing Asia show no definitive evidence either way. One can, however, be more certain that NDBs tend to play a valuable counter-cyclical role, although this may weaken loan portfolios if not done appropriately.

Nevertheless, one broad conclusion emerging from the preceding discussion is that NDBs are certainly not the magic bullets they were expected to be, and that they are just as likely to become victims to the same market failures they are expected to overcome. Moreover, given weaknesses in the regulatory and institutional environment in most developing Asian countries, NDBs can become prey to powerful political forces that can undermine their effectiveness. When addressing market failures in the financial sector, governments are best advised to work indirectly through regulatory, policy, and institutional design rather than directly through state-owned banks with mandatory sectoral lending requirements. For example, housing finance is best supported not by establishing a housing finance institution, but by developing the market, legal, regulatory, liquidity, guarantee, risk management, and tax frameworks that would support a stable, sustainable, and affordable supply of long-term housing finance.

More specific policy recommendations, however, need to be firmly embedded in the specific political, institutional, and policy circumstances of each country. In some cases, it may make sense to close down an NDB or merge it with another bank, as was done with BAP-INDO (Indonesian Development Bank) in 1999 after the financial crisis (Saro 2005).[19] In other instances, it may make sense to expand an NDB's operations, as was the case with India's National Housing Bank, which refinances loans by primary lending institutions to low-income households (World Bank 2013). A third category would be those that would be allowed to continue lending, but under stricter controls and supervision to avoid an accumulation of non-performing loans, as was the case with the Lao Development Bank (World Bank 2009).

Bilateral development finance institutions (BDFIs)

Although 15 of the 18 important BDFIs in the world are European, the three in Asia are among the largest: China Development Bank (CDB), Japan Bank for International Cooperation (JBIC), and China EXIM Bank (Downs 2011).[20]

With a loan portfolio of USD 1.2 trillion and total assets of USD 1.6 trillion, CDB is among the world's largest development banks (the only other BDFI of comparable size is JBIC; see below). Even though CDB's focus is primarily domestic (see above), its international lending between 2005 and 2015 increased 17-fold to reach USD 276 billion.[21] It started financing international investments in 2008, primarily to secure access to natural resources, especially energy (Kroeber 2015). CDB accelerated its cross-border energy acquisitions following the global financial crisis, when energy assets were available at bargain-basement prices and the PRC's energy demands had grown following its own fiscal stimulus. Since 2013, however, upon government instructions to be less adventurous abroad, CDB's international lending has declined and its emphasis has shifted back to its domestic operations. Nevertheless, CDB is, and will continue to be, a major lender supporting the PRC's Belt and Road Initiative, which it finances directly through loans for international infrastructure projects as well as indirectly through the PRC's Silk Road Fund and the China-Africa Development Fund.

JBIC began life in 1950 as the Export-Import Bank of Japan and, after a series of reorganizations and name changes, emerged in its current form in 2012. Owned by the Japanese government and with total financial assets of around USD 1.5 trillion, its objective is to develop and secure natural resources overseas for Japan, support the international competitiveness of Japanese industries, prevent disruptions to the international financial order, and promote the global environment.[22] The rapid growth of lending by PRC BDFIs and new PRC-supported MDBs (such as AIIB and NeDB; see below) has stimulated JBIC to relax its lending requirements and accelerate its investment lending, especially in Asia. This is part of a recent Japanese government effort under the rubric of Japan's Quality Infrastructure Initiative to increase overseas infrastructure lending by Japanese development institutions, including JBIC, and compete more effectively with the PRC's expanded development finance operations in the region.

The PRC's EXIM Bank, with total assets of around USD 500 billion, may not be as large as CDB, but its stock of overseas lending has overtaken CDB's.[23] Its operations increasingly resemble those of a traditional development bank (for example, it is an official conduit for government concessional assistance to support other developing countries), and its investment lending abroad now exceeds its trade financing.[24]

A paucity of good data makes it difficult to assess the operational efficiency and development effectiveness of these large Asian BDFIs. While JBIC has an excellent reputation for high-quality projects, concerns have been raised about the quality of lending by the two PRC BDFIs, especially lately under the BRI. Nevertheless, an examination of their activities suggests that they are probably neither profligate investors nor are they paragons of development virtue. On balance, their development impact is probably positive and they earn positive returns, but as with all development finance institutions, they also tend to have their fair share of poorly performing loans (Brautigam 2015; Dollar 2016; Myers and Gallagher 2017).

The World Bank and Asian Development Bank: an introduction

The two large MDBs operating in developing Asia – ADB and the World Bank – operate across the entire developing Asia region under policies laid down by boards representing their international membership. Both were created to assist developing countries access international finance for development purposes and function at the core of a broad, evolving, and increasingly complicated global aid and development architecture.

Created in 1944, the World Bank now includes 188 member countries and five separate organizations.[25] The two agencies that lend to sovereign borrowers, the International Bank for Reconstruction and Development (IBRD) and International Development Association, form the core of the World Bank Group and provide development finance and technical assistance to low- and middle-income countries through a variety of loan and grant instruments. The International Finance Corporation focuses exclusively on encouraging private sector development and provides loan and equity investments to private sector borrowers in developing countries. The World Bank Group's lending, guarantee, and insurance operations cover the entire range of development challenges facing poor countries, such as health, education, infrastructure, agriculture, public administration, macroeconomic management, institutional development, governance, financial and private sector development, environmental protection, and natural resource management.[26]

ADB has much the same mandate as the World Bank, except that its development lending is restricted to developing Asia.[27] Established in 1966, two decades after the World Bank, ADB is now owned by 67 members, 48 of which are from within the Asia and the Pacific region (including Japan, Australia, and New Zealand) and 19 are from outside the region (including Canada, the US, and 17 European countries).[28] Its initial emphasis was on food and rural development projects, but it subsequently diversified into education, health, and infrastructure development. In the late 1990s, ADB joined the International Monetary Fund and the World Bank in responding to the Asian financial crisis, supporting financial sector development and strengthening social safety nets.

The international community has periodically called for greater coordination and a clearer division of labor in Asia between the World Bank and ADB as part of broader efforts to revamp the global development architecture (G20 Information Center 2009).[29] The World Bank justifies its engagement in Asia on the grounds that its value rests on its global membership and involvement in all developing regions. It leverages its global reach by disseminating development experience across regions and setting global standards in areas such as sanctions, safeguards, transparency, research, and procurement. ADB, on the other hand, focuses on regional interests, including regional economic integration and regional public goods (World Bank 2010).

Comparing ADB and the World Bank

Over the last two decades, the World Bank, together with regional multilateral banks and multilateral financial institutions, have jointly occupied a shrinking role in global financial flows.[30] The rapid growth of cross-border private investment, portfolio, and other financial flows, including the rise of philanthropic organizations,[31] as well as the emergence of non-traditional bilateral creditors (such as the PRC) has meant that official multilateral creditors now account for only a small proportion of financial flows to developing countries. This is particularly true in the case of Asia, which has attracted a significant share of private financial flows to developing regions worldwide.

With its authorized capital of USD 147 billion, ADB is by far the largest of the world's regional MDBs and some indicators of its financial size, such as commitments and disbursements, are approaching those of the World Bank's operations in Asia (Table 14.1). Although it is focused on only one developing region, ADB's authorized capital is almost 60% of the World Bank's, and it still has significant room for expanding its lending. As of end-2015, it had used up only 40% of its maximum lending ceiling of USD 159 billion. whereas the IBRD had exhausted 82% of its headroom for ADB see ADB 2016; for World Bank see World Bank 2015).

A recent analysis of 3,821 World Bank-financed projects in Asia and 1,342 ADB-financed projects in the region reveal several interesting insights (Bulman, Kokma, and Kraay 2015).[32] There is little to choose between them when comparing sectoral shares by total numbers or value (Figures 14.4a and 14.4b).

Both institutions show a very high proportion of their projects were rated as successful (usually between 70% and 80%), but the variation over time was higher for ADB than the World Bank (Figure 14.5).

In general, a higher proportion of World Bank projects were considered successful compared to ADB (Figure 14.6). Furthermore, while the variation in success rates *across* countries is significant (for both institutions), country characteristics (such as GDP growth and the policy environment) still only account for 10%–25% of project success.[33] Civil liberties and political freedom appear negatively correlated against project outcomes (probably owing to high success rates in the PRC, Lao PDR, and Viet Nam; Cevdet, Kaufmann, and Kraay 2013). The larger variation in success rates *within* countries points to the importance of project-specific factors, including the time taken to implement projects, the quality of the project officer or team leader in the MDB, and the willingness to close non-performing projects early.[34]

External assessments of the two agencies also give the two institutions high marks. Four studies that rank the quality of aid agencies place the World Bank among the top five; ADB appears in that select group in two of those studies (Knack, Rogers, and Eubank 2010;

Table 14.1 ADB and the World Bank: selected financial indicators, 2015[a]

	ADB	World Bank[c]
Loan commitments to Asia[b]	10.8	13.8[d]
Disbursements to Asia[b]	8.2	11.4[d]
Outstanding loans to Asia[b]	57.4	128.6[d]
Authorized capital	147.1	252.8
Outstanding debt	66.1	158.8
Total assets	117.7	343.2
Net income	0.6	−0.8

a For ADB, end-December 2015; for World Bank, end-June 2015.
b To sovereign borrowers only.
c Includes IBRD and IDA, but excludes IFC.
d For end-2014.

Note: The regions and countries for the World Bank corresponding to the ADB's borrowing member countries include East Asia and the Pacific, South Asia, Armenia, Azerbaijan, Georgia, Kazakhstan, Kyrgyz Republic, Tajikistan, Turkmenistan, and Uzbekistan.

Sources: ADB financial information statement, April 2016. www.adb.org/documents/series/financial-information-statements; World Bank Financial Statement, 30 June 2015.

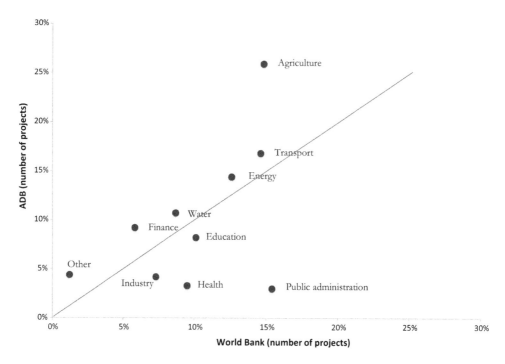

Figure 14.4a Sectoral composition in developing Asia for the World Bank and ADB portfolios, by number of projects

Source: Compiled by author with data provided by Bulman, Kokma, and Kraay (2015).

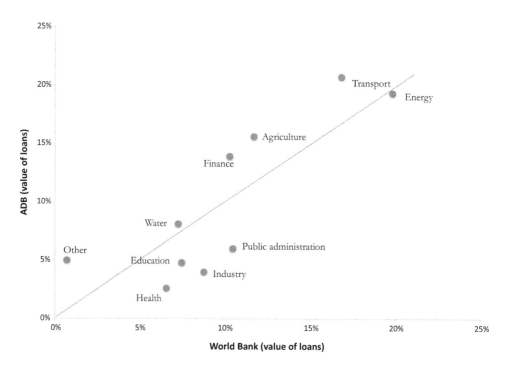

Figure 14.4b Sectoral composition in developing Asia for World Bank and ADB portfolios, by value of loans

Source: Compiled by author with data provided by Bulman, Kokma, and Kraay (2015).

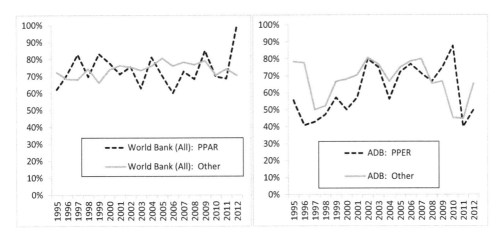

Figure 14.5 World Bank and ADB portfolio comparisons: trends in average project performance by evaluation type

Notes: These charts show average project success ratings by evaluation year. For the World Bank, PPAR refers to "Project Performance Audit Reports," the more detailed project evaluations conducted by its Independent Evaluation Group. ADB, PPER refers to detailed "Project Performance Evaluation Reports."

Source: Compiled by author with data provided by Bulman, Kokma, and Kraay (2015).

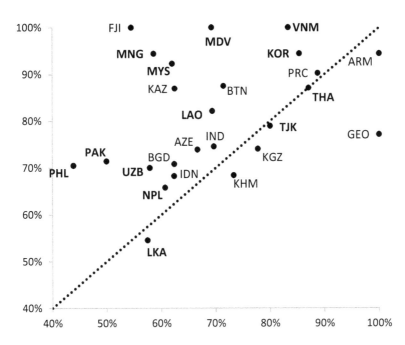

Figure 14.6 Distribution of average success rates of World Bank and ADB projects in developing Asia, by country

Source: Compiled by author with data provided by Bulman, Kokma, and Kraay (2015).

Table 14.2 Comparison of the publication records of the World Bank and ADB

	Articles		
	mentioning a developing country	in the top development economics journals	in 27 specialized development journals
World Bank	1,757	1,343	1,702
ADB	69		56

Source: Compiled with data from Ravallion and Wagstaff (2010).

Easterly and Pfutze 2008; Roodman 2006; Birdsall and Kharas 2010). IDA was the only multi-lateral agency that ranked in the top 10 in all four indicators of the quality of aid – maximizing efficiency, fostering institutions, reducing burdens, and transparency and learning – while ADB appeared in the top 10 for two indicators. In a fifth study, IDA and the Asian Development Fund (ADF) were rated "very good," with IDA better at focusing on poor countries, and ADF better at partnerships, strategic management, and operations in fragile contexts (DFID 2011). Similarly, in separate studies that used a common performance assessment methodology, both institutions scored highly in the strategic, operational, relationship, and knowledge management areas (MOPAN 2009, 2010).

Arguably the World Bank and ADB make their most important contribution through knowledge transfer to their developing country clients. Unfortunately, no studies measure how well they do this. A possible proxy – the publications record of the research of the two institutions (Table 14.2) – ranks the World Bank second only to Harvard University on the volume of journal articles it publishes each year on development economics (Ravallion and Wagstaff 2010), whereas ADB's publication record is considerably less stellar (Ravallion and Wagstaff 2010).

Challenges confronting MDBs

Going forward, there are three challenges that confront the World Bank and ADB in Asia.

The first is the very fundamental issue of relevance. Given the declining role of official development assistance in overall capital flows to developing countries, and the diminishing role of multilateral development banks within that space, the World Bank and ADB need to constantly re-evaluate the value they bring to developing countries through their operations. They face competition from two directions. The first is the growing importance of non-traditional donors, some of whom provide resources without the strings that normally come attached to World Bank and ADB lending. On the other hand, a Gallup poll conducted in East Asia found that the World Bank's knowledge, research, and data outputs were given higher ratings compared to international universities and private consulting firms in all the countries surveyed (Figure 14.7).

But this raises the second challenge – that the development knowledge space has become highly contestable. Although the World Bank and ADB enjoy unique access to policy-makers in many Asian developing countries, their comparative advantage is diminishing rapidly, especially in middle-income Asia which has less need for MDB financing. True, ADB and the World Bank can act as conveners, matching demand for knowledge with those who have the best expertise available on the subject. But other agencies – private and public – are increasingly providing these services, sometimes more efficiently than the World Bank or ADB.

The third challenge confronting both institutions is governance. This is perhaps more keenly felt in the World Bank, where there has been considerable concern that the voting structure

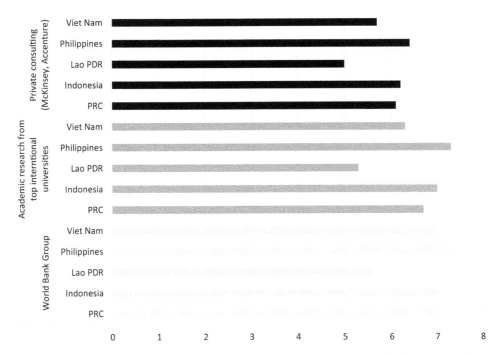

Figure 14.7 How much impact does the knowledge, research, data produced by the following organizations have (mean score)?

Source: Compiled by author with data from a World Bank Group global poll conducted by Gallup Consulting in 2008.

does not represent the increasing influence of developing countries. Recent increases in the shares of developing countries, particularly the PRC's, has raised the share of developing countries from 42.6% to 44.1% to 47%, still short of parity with the developed (Part I) countries.

The Asian Infrastructure Investment Bank and the New Development Bank

Notwithstanding developing Asia's rapid economic progress, its growing access to capital markets, and its own rapidly evolving development capabilities, the reality is that the region could benefit from additional MDB financing. For developing Asia, MDBs will continue to be an important source of long-term finance, implementation know-how, and development knowledge based on global experience. The bulk of the financing need is for infrastructure. Asia's growth potential of 5%–7% a year has meant that transport and energy infrastructure has become a growth bottleneck in most developing countries in the region. Increased infrastructure is not only expected to unleash growth, it will also be expected to help promote inclusive, sustainable, and resilient development. The total infrastructure investment financing need in developing Asia is estimated at USD 1.34 trillion a year, or around 7.9% of GDP through 2030 (ADB 2017), leaving considerable room available for incremental sources of long-term finance. These large unmet infrastructure financing needs in Asia provide the backdrop for two recent entrants into Asia's MDB space: AIIB and NeDB, both the result of PRC initiatives that have acquired multilateral support and participation.

PRC President Xi Jinping announced the creation of AIIB in October 2013 and the new organization's articles of agreement entered into force on 25 December 2015 with 57 founding member countries and USD 100 billion in subscribed capital. A further 24 countries have indicated an interest in joining, the latest being Canada (the US and Japan are perhaps the two most prominent countries that have refused to join so far). By end-2017, its membership is expected to exceed that of the ADB (which has only 67 members). The PRC is AIIB's largest shareholder, accounting for almost 30% of total equity, which gives it effective veto over key board decisions that require a three-quarters super majority vote. AIIB's first PRC president has taken special pains to allay international concerns about the new institution's commitment to meet globally recognized social and environmental safeguards. By end-June 2016 – with just 38 staff on its payroll – the newly formed AIIB had already committed over USD 500 million in financing for four projects (in Bangladesh, Indonesia, Pakistan, and Tajikistan), three of which were co-financed with the World Bank, ADB, and the European Bank for Reconstruction and Development, respectively. AIIB's intent is to commit USD 1.2 billion in 2016 and double that in 2017.

NeDB – sometimes called the BRICS Development Bank – was first proposed in the Fourth BRICS Summit at New Delhi in March 2012. It was formally launched at its Shanghai headquarters in July 2015 with an authorized capital of USD 100 billion to meet the development funding requirements of its five founding member countries: Brazil, Russia, India, the PRC, and South Africa (BRICS), although the intention is to expand membership later to include other developing countries. Of the USD 50 billion in subscribed capital, USD 10 billion is paid-in capital and each founding member country has agreed to pay USD 2 billion in installments over a seven-year period. The remaining USD 40 billion constitutes callable capital. NeDB has already allocated a total of USD 911 million in new loans, comprising one loan each to its five founding members.

The creation of AIIB and NeDB has meant that PRC development financing far exceeds that of all Western-led multilateral development institutions combined. On the other hand, the creation of these two new MDBs poses little threat to western-led MDFIs, especially in Asia. After all, the demand for long-term development finance in the region far exceeds supply, so there is more than enough business for all four MDBs. Moreover, the World Bank and ADB are already competing against the China Development Bank, the operations of which are actually much larger than AIIB is ever likely to be. At another level, however, these new entrants will increase contestability for Asia's relatively few high-quality, well-prepared infrastructure projects which constitutes the real binding constraint to infrastructure development in the region. The PRC's contribution of USD 50 million toward an AIIB project preparation special fund reflects the importance attached to investing in designing quality projects suitable for MDB financing. At the same time, AIIB's intention to be "lean, clean, and green" will force its MDB competitors in Asia to improve operational efficiency if they are to retain the confidence of their important clients.

Acknowledgments

The author acknowledges excellent research assistance by Patrick Farrell, Junior Fellow, Carnegie Endowment for International Peace.

Notes

1 For the purposes of this chapter, developing Asia includes the developing countries (as defined by the World Bank) in East, Southeast, and South Asia. For data limitation reasons, it does *not* include Central Asia and the Pacific Islands.

2 This chapter neither covers development banks in high-income Asian economies (Japan, Republic of Korea, Singapore, and Taipei, China), nor does it cover privately owned development banks in developing Asia. But it does cover export-import banks in developing Asia, which are usually mandated to ease barriers to trade finance and thereby support the development of export-oriented firms.

3 Bruck (1998) includes the Pacific, but it is not clear if he includes Central Asia or development banks with a subnational focus.

4 The number includes NDBs in developing Asia as defined in this chapter; see note 2.

5 For lack of data, we exclude development banks covering subnational regions as well as NDBs in Central Asia.

6 One each in the PRC, Japan, and the US, and 15 in Europe.

7 Financial rates of return are calculated on the basis of market prices; economic rates of return are calculated on the basis of shadow prices; and social rates of return are calculated on the basis of economic costs and benefits at shadow prices appropriately weighted by their incidence on different segments of the income distribution.

8 State-owned commercial banks have also been candidates for privatization.

9 Even the US has large loan and loan-guarantee programs, such as Fannie Mae, Freddie Mac, student loan programs, the Federal Housing Administration, and over 100 other smaller programs.

10 The author is extremely grateful to Jose De Luna Martinez and Carlos Leonardo Vicente of the World Bank for making this data available. The results of the global survey can be found in de Luna-Martínez, J. and C.L. Vicente (2012). The survey includes data for 2006–2009 and covers 12 developing countries in Asia, 12 in Latin America, seven in Eastern Europe (including Turkey), and 11 in sub-Saharan Africa. The global survey also includes data for advanced economies, but these were excluded for the purposes of this chapter. The World Bank's global survey data for developing Asia were compared to data collected for this chapter from 63 NDBs in 16 developing Asian countries and were found to be broadly comparable.

11 CDB's assets of USD 1,664 billion in 2014 were almost five times larger than the World Bank's USD 343 billion in 2015.

12 The shares add to well above 100% because many NDBs serve multiple types of clients.

13 Subsidized interest rates (or government guarantees) tend to encourage borrowing because: (1) the demand for loans by existing borrowers increases when the costs of borrowing falls; and (2) those unable to borrow at any rate from private lenders are able to access loans. The second channel can sometimes be the more important of the two.

14 Debts can be restructured without being forgiven by extending maturities, lowering interest rates, or postponing interest and/or amortization payments. All these methods effectively imply a debt write-off in net present value terms.

15 When compared to private banks, state-owned banks in developing countries tend to have lower profitability, higher non-performing loans, and higher overhead costs; these differences tend to be insignificant in state-owned and private banks in industrial countries.

16 While there are no Asia-focused studies on this issue, broader cross-country studies suggest no significant negative correlation between state ownership of banks (of which NDBs form a significant part) and lending to the private sector. See Yeyati et al. (2007).

17 In fact, our analysis shows that the average equity-asset ratio across developing Asia can vary from less than 5% to over 40%, and there is a significant inverse relationship between the return on equity and the equity assets ratio.

18 State ownership of banks may be associated with higher NPL ratios, but this is more a symptom of poor regulation than state ownership, per se (Barth, Caprio, and Levine 2001).

19 BAPINDO was merged with three other state banks to form Bank Mandiri, which continues to operate today as Indonesia's largest state-owned commercial bank. (Saro 2005).

20 The Overseas Private Investment Corporation (OPIC), a US government agency, is another non-European BDFI, but with total assets of USD 8.5 billion, its operations are relatively small. (OPIC 2017).

21 See the International Cooperation section of the China Development Bank website (www.cdb.com. cn/English/ywgl/xdyw/gjhzyw/).

22 Assets as of end-March 2016. See JBIC (2016).

23 The stock of overseas lending at end-2016 was USD 329 billion for CDB and USD 346 billion for EXIM (Dollar 2017).

24 See China EXIM Bank's website, especially http://english.eximbank.gov.cn/tm/en-TCN/index_640. html (also see Kroeber 2015: 34).

25 IBRD has 188 members, while IDA has 172 members. The World Bank Group's five organizations are the International Bank for Reconstruction and Development (IBRD), the International Development Association (IDA), the International Finance Corporation (IFC), the Multilateral Investment Guarantee Agency (MIGA), and the International Center for the Settlement of Investment Disputes (ICSID).

26 Based on various issues of World Bank and ADB annual reports.

27 Developing Asia comprises Central Asia and the South Caucasus, South Asia, and East Asia and the Pacific.

28 Based on various issues of ADB annual reports.

29 It should be noted that the Pittsburgh communiqué raises concerns about overlaps between the World Bank and all regional development banks, and doesn't specifically mention ADB by name.

30 Besides ADB, the world's regional MDBs include the Corporacion Andina de Fomento; Caribbean Development Bank; Central American Bank for Economic Integration; East African Development Bank; and West African Development Bank. Multilateral financial institutions include the Asian Infrastructure Investment Bank, European Bank for Reconstruction and Development, European Investment Bank, International Fund for Agricultural Development, the Islamic Development Bank, the Nordic Development Fund, the New Development Bank, the Nordic Investment Bank, and the OPEC Fund for International Development.

31 The largest and best-known among these would be the Gates Foundation.

32 Note that the study includes Republic of Korea (which used to borrow from the World Bank until 1998) and defines Asia as including Central Asia and the Pacific Islands.

33 This is consistent with previous studies (Cevdet, Kaufmann, and Kraay 2013).

34 Bulman, Kokma, and Kraay (2015) estimated within country variation by using a regression of project outcomes with country dummy variables on the right-hand side.

References

Altunbas, Y., L. Evans, and P. Molyneux. 2001. Bank Ownership and Efficiency. *Journal of Money, Credit, and Banking* 33(4): 926–954.

Amyx, J., and A. Maria Toyoda. 2006. The Evolving Role of National Development Banks in East Asia. The International Centre for the Study of East Asian Development Working Paper No. 2006–26, Kitakyushu: The International Centre for the Study of East Asian Development.

Asian Development Bank (ADB). 2016. Financial Information Statement, April. www.adb.org/documents/series/financial-information-statements

ADB. 2017. *Meeting Asia's Infrastructure Needs*. Manila: Asian Development Bank.

Barth, J., G. Caprio, and R. Levine. 2001. The Regulation and Supervision of Banks Around the World. In *Integrating Emerging Market Countries into the Global Financial System*, edited by R. E. Litan and R. Herring. Brookings-Wharton Papers on Financial Services. Washington, DC: Brookings Institution Press.

Berger, A. N., C. H. S. Bouwman, T. Kick, and K. Schaeck. 2010. Bank Liquidity Creation and Risk Taking During Distress. Discussion Paper 2, No. 05/2010. Frankfurt: Deutsche Bundesbank.

Birdsall, N., and H. Kharas. 2010. Quality of Official Development Assistance. Washington, DC: Brookings Institution and the Center for Global Development.

Brautigam, D. 2015. 5 Myths About Chinese Investment in Africa. *Foreign Policy*, 4 December. http://foreignpolicy.com/2015/12/04/5-myths-about-chinese-investment-in-africa/

Bruck, N. 1998. Role of Development Banks in the Twenty-First Century. *Journal of Emerging Markets* 3: 39–68.

Bulman, D., W. Kokma, and A. Kraay. 2015. Good Countries or Good Projects: The Macro and Micro Correlates of World Bank and Asian Development Bank Performance. World Bank, Policy Research Working Paper No. 7245. Washington, DC: World Bank.

Caprio, G., J. Fiechter, R. E. Litan, and M. Pomerleano. 2004. The Future of State-Owned Financial Institutions. Brookings Institution, Conference Report #18, September 2004.

Cevdet, D., D. Kaufmann, and A. Kraay. 2013. Good Countries or Good Projects? Macro and Micro Correlates of World Bank Project Outcomes. *Journal of Development Economics* 105: 288–302.

Clarke, G., R. Cull, and M. Shirley. 2003. Empirical Studies of Bank Privatization: An Overview. Paper Prepared for the Conference on Bank Privatization in Low- and Middle-Income Countries, 23 November. Washington, DC: World Bank.

de Aghion, B. A. 1999. Development Banking. *Journal of Development Economics* 58: 83–100.

de Luna-Martínez, J., and C. L. Vicente. 2012. Global Survey of Development Banks. World Bank Policy Research Working Paper No. 5969. Washington, DC: World Bank.

Department of International Development of the United Kingdom (DFID). 2011. Multilateral Aid Review. London: Department of International Development of the United Kingdom. www.dfid.gov. uk/Documents/publications1/mar/multilateral_aid_review.pdf

Dollar, D. 2016. *China's Engagement in Africa: From Natural Resources to Human Resources.* The John L. China Center at Brookings. Washington, DC: Brookings Institution Press.

Dollar, D. 2017. *Yes, China Is Investing Globally, But Not so Much in Its Belt and Road Initiative.* Washington, DC: Brookings Institution, 8 May 2017. www.brookings.edu/blog/order-from-chaos/2017/05/08/yes-china-is-investing-globally-but-not-so-much-in-its-belt-and-road-initiative/

Downs, E. 2011. *Inside China, Inc.: China Development Bank's Cross-Border Energy Deals.* John L. Thornton China Center Monograph Series 3. Washington, DC: John L. Thornton China Center at Brookings.

Duchin, R., and D. Sosyura. 2011. Safer Ratios, Riskier Portfolios: Banks' Response to Government Aid. Ross School of Business Paper No. 1165. Ann Arbor: University of Michigan.

Easterly, W., and T. Pfutze. 2008. Where Does the Money Go? Best and Worst Practices in Foreign Aid. *Journal of Economic Perspectives* 22(2): 29–52.

Farhi, E., and J. Tirole. 2012. Collective Moral Hazard, Maturity Mismatch and Systemic Bailouts. *American Economic Review* 102(1): 63–90.

G20 Information Center. 2009. G20 Leaders Statement: The Pittsburgh Summit, 24–25 September 2009, Pittsburgh. www.g20.utoronto.ca/2009/2009communique0925.html

Gropp, R., H. Hakenes, and I. Schnabel. 2011. Competition, Risk-Shifting, and Public Bail-Out Policies. *Review of Financial Studies* 24(6): 2084–2120.

Japan Bank for International Cooperation (JBIC). 2016. JBIC Annual Report 2016. Tokyo: Japan Bank for International Cooperation. www.jbic.go.jp/wp-content/uploads/page/2016/12/53051/2016E_01. pdf

Khawaja, A., and A. Mian. 2005. Do Lenders Favor Politically Connected Firms? Rent Provision in an Emerging Financial Market. *Quarterly Journal of Economics* 120(4): 1371–1411.

Knack. S., H. Rogers, and N. Eubank. 2010. Aid Quality and Donor Rankings. World Bank Policy Research Working Paper 5290. Washington, DC: World Bank.

Kroeber, A. 2015. Financing China's Global Dreams. *China Economic Quarterly*, November. https://chinaeconomybookdotcom.files.wordpress.com/2016/02/ceq_2015q34_kroeber_financingglobaldreams.pdf

Micco, A., U. Panizza, and M. Yañez. 2007. Bank Ownership and Performance: Does Politics Matter? *Journal of Banking and Finance* 31(1): 219–241.

MOPAN. 2009. MOPAN Common Approach – World Bank 2009. www.mopanonline.org/upload/documents/World_Bank_Final_February_19_issued.pdf

MOPAN. 2010. MOPAN Common Approach – Asian Development Bank 2010. www.mopanonline. org/upload/documents/ADB_Final-Vol-I_January_17_Issued1.pdf

Musacchio, A., and S. G. Lazzarini. 2012. Leviathan in Business: Varieties of State Capitalism and Their Implications for Economic Performance. Harvard Business School Working Paper No. 12-108. Cambridge, MA: Harvard University.

Myers, M., and K. Gallagher. 2017. Chinese Financing to LAC in 2016. *The Dialogue*, February. www. thedialogue.org/wp-content/uploads/2017/02/Chinese-Finance-to-LAC-in-2016-Web-and-email-res.pdf

OPIC. 2017. Annual Management Report of the Overseas Private Investment Corporation for Fiscal Years 2016 and 2015. www.opic.gov/sites/default/files/files/2016_Annual_Management_Report.pdf

Ravallion, M., and A. Wagstaff. 2010. The World Bank's Publication Record. World Bank Policy Research Working Paper No. 5374. Washington, DC: World Bank.

Roodman, D. 2006. An Index of Donor Performance. Center for Global Development Working Paper No. 67. Washington, DC: Center for Global Development.

Rothschild, M., and J. Stiglitz. 1976. Equilibrium in Competitive Insurance Markets: An Essay on the Economics of Imperfect Information. *Quarterly Journal of Economics* 90(4): 629–649.

Sanderson, H., and M. Forsythe. 2013. *China's Superbank: Debt, Oil and Influence – How China Development Bank Is Rewriting the Rules of Finance*. Singapore: Wiley.

Sapienza, P. 2004. The Effects of Government Ownership on Bank Lending. *Journal of Financial Economics* 72(2): 357–384.

Saro, Y. 2005. Bank Restructuring and Financial Institution Reform in Indonesia. *The Developing Economies*, XLIII-1(March 2005): 91–120.

World Bank. 2009. Implementation Completion and Results Report for a Series of Three Poverty Reduction Support Operations, Report No. ICR0000592, p.28. Washington, DC: World Bank.

World Bank. 2010. New World, New World Bank Group: Post-Crisis Directions. Paper Prepared for the Development Committee of the World Bank, 20 April. Washington, DC: World Bank.

World Bank. 2013. Low Income Housing Finance Project. World Bank Project Appraisal Report, Report No. 76829-IN, 18 April. Washington, DC: World Bank.

World Bank. 2015. Management's Discussion and Analysis and Condensed Quarterly Financial Statements, 31 December. http://treasury.worldbank.org/cmd/pdf/IBRD_MDA_and_Financial_Statements_December_2015.pdf

Yeyati, E. L., A. Micco, U. Panizza, E. Detragiache, and A. Repetto. 2007. A Reappraisal of State-Owned Banks. *Economía* 7(2): 209–259.

15

DEVELOPING LOCAL CURRENCY BOND MARKETS IN ASIA

Cyn-Young Park

Introduction

Following the 1997–1998 Asian financial crisis, the development of local currency bond markets has become a policy priority for many Asian economies. The Association of Southeast Asian Nations plus the People's Republic of China (PRC), Japan, and the Republic of Korea (ASEAN+3) Finance Ministers introduced the Asian Bond Markets Initiative (ABMI) to develop efficient and liquid local currency bond markets in member countries. National policy efforts coupled with regional initiatives focused on developing local currency bond markets to balance their highly bank-dominated financial systems, reduce heavy reliance on foreign debts,[1] and mobilize the region's excess savings more effectively for development finance.

Many emerging Asian economies have seen local currency bond markets grow dramatically in the past two decades. The total outstanding local currency bonds in emerging Asia, including India, stands about USD 10,228 billion as of December 2015, up from USD 2,568 billion in 2005.

Asian local currency bonds now also emerge as a new asset class as many traditional assets have lost their shines in the wake of the global financial crisis. At the height of the global financial crisis in the last quarter of 2008, Asian local currency bond markets experienced high volatility and low liquidity associated with large capital outflows from emerging markets. However, Asian local currency bonds quickly regained investor confidence on the back of relatively strong growth performance in the region and subsequent monetary easing and fiscal stimuli around the world. Fueled by favorable global liquidity conditions and regional initiatives, the total bond issuance almost doubled since 2008.

While the progress made in Asian local currency markets has been remarkable, it isn't universal across the region. Especially, the growth in local currency bond markets has been largely concentrated in government bonds, leaving room for substantial improvement for emerging Asia's corporate borrowers. There are also remaining hurdles in market infrastructure and institutions, inconsistent policies and regulations, and more broadly corporate governance to further development of local currency corporate bonds.

This chapter reviews the progress made in developing local currency bond markets in emerging Asia. The following sections look at the development and current situation of local currency bond markets and examine key regional initiatives to foster local currency bond markets.

The last section discusses the remaining obstacles to further development and suggests policy responses.

Asia's local currency bond markets: then and now

Size and depth of local currency bond markets

The size of local currency bond markets rose to USD 10,228 billion in emerging Asia as of December 2015, with 14.8% compounded annual growth rate between 2005 and 2015 (Table 15.1). The PRC was the largest (local currency) LCY bond market in emerging Asia with outstanding bonds worth USD 6,150 billion, or 60% of the region's total bonds outstanding. The Republic of Korea is the second largest at USD 1,720 billion, with a share of about 17%. The third largest bond market in the region was India at USD 1,121 billion with an 11% share. Excluding the PRC, the Republic of Korea, and India, growth in outstanding bonds was at 10.6% compounded annual growth rate between 2005 and 2015 (on LCY basis).

The LCY bond markets have deepened as well. The total outstanding as a share of gross domestic product (GDP) increased to 62.9% at end-2015 from 50.2% at end-2005 (Table 15.2).

Table 15.1 Bonds outstanding in local currency bond markets (USD billion)

Economy	as of Dec 2015			as of Dec 2005			as of Dec 1995[1]		
	GOV	COR	Total	GOV	COR	Total	GOV	COR	Total
US	18,901.7	21,019.4	39,921.1	9,801.2	16,629.1	26,430.3	5,499.4	6,102.9	11,602.3
JPN	8,274.0	656.0	8,930.0	6,301.6	743.7	7,045.3	2,763.5	1,093.6	3,857.1
Emerging Asia	**6,431.5**	**3,796.5**	**10,228.0**	**1,886.4**	**681.9**	**2,568.3**	**244.2**	**36.5**	**280.6**
PRC	4,067.0	2,083.0	6,150.0	835.2	64.5	899.6	57.7	0.0	57.7
HKG	120.0	90.0	210.0	16.3	69.2	85.6	7.6	18.2	25.8
IND	832.5	288.2	1,120.7	376.7	84.7	461.4	87.1	6.8	94.0
INO	109.0	18.0	127.0	48.3	5.9	54.2	0.0	2.8	2.8
KOR	700.0	1,020.0	1,720.0	392.9	360.8	753.7	67.0	0.0	67.0
MAL	142.0	118.0	260.0	61.3	45.6	107.0	–	–	–
PHI	84.0	17.0	101.0	41.1	1.0	42.1	–	–	–
SIN	129.0	91.0	220.0	46.9	36.2	83.1	13.1	7.8	20.9
THA	208.0	70.0	278.0	64.9	14.1	79.0	11.5	0.9	12.4
VIE	40.0	1.3	41.3	2.7	0.0	2.7	–	–	–

– = unavailable; GOV = Government bonds; COR = Corporate bonds; US = United States; JPN = Japan; PRC = People's Republic of China; HKG = Hong Kong, China; IND = India; INO = Indonesia; KOR = Republic of Korea; MAL = Malaysia; PHI = Philippines; SIN = Singapore; THA = Thailand; VIE = Viet Nam.

1 As of December 1998 for Japan, and as of December 1997 for the People's Republic of China.

Note: For the US, government bonds include municipal, treasury, and federal agency securities; while corporate includes corporate debt, asset-backed securities, mortgage-related securities, and money market securities. For the rest of the economies, government bonds include obligations of the central government, local governments, and the central bank. Corporates comprise both public and private companies, including financial institutions. Financial institutions comprise both private and public sector banks, and other financial institutions. Bonds are defined as long-term bonds and notes, treasury bills, commercial paper, and other short-term notes.

Source: Compiled by author with data from *AsianBondsOnline* and Securities Industry and Financial Markets Association for US data.

Table 15.2 Depth of the local currency bond market (outstanding bonds as percentage of GDP)

Economy	as of Dec 2015			as of Dec 2005			as of Dec 1995[1]		
	Government	*Corporate*	*Total*	*Government*	*Corporate*	*Total*	*Government*	*Corporate*	*Total*
US	105.3	117.1	222.4	74.9	127.0	201.9	71.8	79.6	151.4
JPN	199.4	15.8	215.2	147.3	17.4	164.6	61.3	24.2	85.5
Emerging	**39.6**	**23.3**	**62.9**	**36.9**	**13.3**	**50.2**	**10.6**	**1.6**	**12.2**
Asia									
PRC	39.0	20.0	59.0	36.3	2.8	39.1	6.0	0.0	6.0
HKG	39.2	29.4	68.6	9.0	38.0	47.0	5.3	12.6	17.8
IND	42.2	14.6	56.8	46.0	10.3	56.3	22.7	1.8	24.5
INO	13.0	2.2	15.2	17.1	2.1	19.2	0.0	2.4	2.4
KOR	52.7	76.9	129.6	43.2	39.6	82.8	12.6	0.0	12.6
MAL	52.9	43.9	96.7	42.7	31.7	74.4	–	–	–
PHI	29.7	6.1	35.8	38.5	0.9	39.4	–	–	–
SIN	45.5	32.2	77.7	36.8	28.4	65.2	14.9	8.8	23.7
THA	55.4	18.6	74.0	35.0	7.6	42.6	6.9	0.5	7.4
VIE	21.5	0.7	22.2	5.1	0.0	5.1	–	–	–

– = unavailable; US = United States; JPN = Japan; PRC = People's Republic of China; HKG = Hong Kong, China; IND = India; INO = Indonesia; KOR = Republic of Korea; MAL = Malaysia; PHI = Philippines; SIN = Singapore; THA = Thailand; VIE = Viet Nam.

1 As of December 1998 for Japan, and as of December 1997 for the People's Republic of China.

Note: For the US, government bonds include municipal, treasury, and federal agency securities; while corporate includes corporate debt, asset-backed securities, mortgage-related securities, and money market securities. For the rest of the economies, government bonds include obligations of the central government, local governments, and the central bank. Corporates comprise both public and private companies, including financial institutions. Financial institutions comprise both private and public sector banks, and other financial institutions. Bonds are defined as long-term bonds and notes, treasury bills, commercial paper, and other short-term notes.

Source: Compiled by author with data from *AsianBondsOnline* and Securities Industry and Financial Markets Association for US data.

The Republic of Korea posted the highest bonds-to-GDP share at 129.6%, followed by Malaysia (96.7%), Singapore (77.7%), and Thailand (74%). However, the corporate sectors show generally shallow market depth compared with the government sectors. The average depth of emerging Asia's corporate bond markets is 23.3% of GDP. The Republic of Korea has the deepest market at 76.9% of GDP and it alone has the depth above 50%. The shallowest three corporate bond markets are Indonesia (2.2%), the Philippines (6.1%), and Viet Nam (0.7%).

Government bonds continue to dominate most emerging Asian markets except in the Republic of Korea (Figure 15.1). Government bonds in the region account for about 60% of the total LCY bond outstanding. The Republic of Korea is the only market where the size of the corporate bond market is larger than that of the government bond market.

The Asian financial crisis of 1997–1998 played a catalytic role in creating active LCY bond markets. Since then, the LCY bond markets have emerged as an important funding source for both government and corporate issuers. Especially, in the aftermath of the global financial crisis of 2008–2009, monetary easing and fiscal expansion fueled growth in the region's LCY bond markets. The region's governments turned to the LCY bond markets to finance their fiscal stimulus packages in the post-crisis economic slowdown. The corporate issuers also resorted to the use of LCY bonds as banks became reluctant to lend while liquidity evaporated in global markets, particularly after the collapse of Lehman Brothers in 2008.

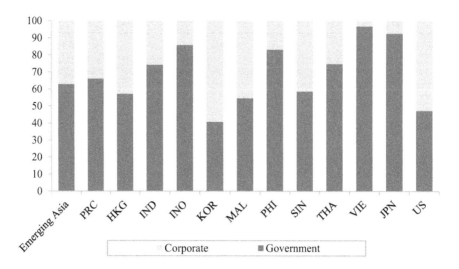

Figure 15.1 Outstanding local currency bonds by sector (percentage of total, as of end-December 2015)

PRC = People's Republic of China; HKG = Hong Kong, China; IND = India; INO = Indonesia; KOR = Republic of Korea; MAL = Malaysia; PHI = Philippines; SIN = Singapore; THA = Thailand; VIE = Viet Nam; JPN = Japan; US = United States.

Note: For the US, government bonds include municipal, treasury, and federal agency securities; while corporate includes corporate debt, asset-backed securities, mortgage-related securities, and money market securities. For the rest of the economies, government bonds include obligations of the central government, local governments, and the central bank. Corporates comprise both public and private companies, including financial institutions. Financial institutions comprise both private and public sector banks, and other financial institutions. Bonds are defined as long-term bonds and notes, treasury bills, commercial paper, and other short-term notes.

Source: Compiled by author with data from *AsianBondsOnline* and Securities Industry and Financial Markets Association for US data.

The corporate bond market plays an increasingly important role in corporate financing (Table 15.3). While bank lending continues to play a dominant role in corporate financing in many emerging Asian economies, equity and bond financing has gained prominence. Stock market capitalization increased from 77.7% of GDP in 1995 to 91.6% in 2015; and corporate bonds outstanding rose from 1.6% of GDP to 23.3%. The share of bank lending in corporate financing is the highest at 50% in 2015, down somewhat from 53% in 2005. The equity market's share declined from 46% to 41%; while the corporate bond market's share jumped from less than 1% to 10%.

The total volume of LCY bond issuance in emerging Asia excluding India rose substantially to USD 1,046.0 billion in 2015 from USD 346.5 billion in 2005 (Figure 15.2).[2] There was a drop in the issuance at the height of the global financial crisis in 2008, but the issuance volume recovered quickly in 2009 driven largely by the PRC and the Republic of Korea. Other regional economies such as Hong Kong, China; Singapore; and Thailand have also shown strong issuance activities since 2009.

With the exception of the PRC, the lion's share of government bond issuance is from the central bank and the central government. A majority of corporate bond issuance is originated from government-owned corporations, banks, and other non-bank financial institutions. Energy, transport, and other utility companies are the largest issuers.

Table 15.3 Corporate financing as percentage of GDP

Economies	2015			2005			1995		
	Corporate Bonds	Stock Market	Bank Credit	Corporate Bonds	Stock Market[1]	Bank Credit	Corporate Bonds[2]	Stock Market[3]	Bank Credit
US	117.1	139.5	48.1	127.0	129.8	41.9	79.6	90.7	33.7
JPN	15.8	118.9	93.6	17.4	100.0	74.0	24.2	66.5	87.4
Emerging Asia	**23.3**	**91.6**	**116.0**	**13.3**	**66.8**	**84.2**	**1.6**	**77.7**	**78.2**
PRC	20.0	71.9	131.8	2.8	17.7	105.3	0.0	70.1	94.1
HKG	29.4	1034.8	313.7	38.0	581.0	164.2	12.6	210.0	334.3
IND	14.6	69.5	73.8	10.3	66.3	59.0	1.8	76.1	39.7
INO	2.2	40.5	32.9	2.1	26.2	22.8	2.4	27.3	20.4
KOR	76.9	88.4	83.4	39.6	79.9	67.6	0.0	32.7	35.4
MAL	43.9	122.2	111.5	31.7	121.8	93.6	–	224.1	79.5
PHI	6.1	79.8	37.3	0.9	38.6	26.1	–	98.2	35.1
SIN	32.2	217.7	132.1	28.4	202.0	83.8	8.8	168.4	82.1
THA	18.6	93.4	91.4	7.6	65.4	74.6	0.5	82.9	133.2
VIE	0.7	26.1	111.6	0.0	16.4	60.2	–	–	18.5

– = unavailable; US = United States; JPN = Japan; PRC = People's Republic of China; HKG = Hong Kong, China; IND = India; INO = Indonesia; KOR = Republic of Korea; MAL = Malaysia; PHI = Philippines; SIN = Singapore; THA = Thailand; VIE = Viet Nam.
1 As of 2008 for Viet Nam.
2 As of December 1998 for Japan, and as of December 1997 for the People's Republic of China.
3 As of 1998 for the Philippines and as of 2003 for the People's Republic of China and India.

Note:
(1) On corporate bonds: For the US, government bonds include municipal, Treasury, and Federal agency securities; while corporate includes corporate debt, asset-backed securities, mortgage-related securities, and money market securities. For the rest of the economies, government bonds include obligations of the central government, local governments, and the central bank. Corporates comprise both public and private companies, including financial institutions. Financial institutions comprise both private and public sector banks, and other financial institutions. Bonds are defined as long-term bonds and notes, treasury bills, commercial paper, and other short-term notes.
(2) Bank credit refers to the following: Commercial Bank Credit: Loans and Lease (US); Loans and Discount: Outstanding: Domestically Licensed Banks (Japan); Financial Institution Loans (PRC); Authorized Institutions: Loans and Advances to Customers (Hong Kong, China); Commercial Bank: Domestic Credit (India); Commercial Banks: Loans to Deposit Ratio: Total Credit to Third Party (Indonesia); Loans of Commercial and Specialized Banks (Rep. of Korea); Commercial Banks: Loans and Advances (Malaysia); Loans : Universal Commercial Bank (Net of Reverse Repurchase Agreement) (Philippines); Domestic Banking Unit: Loans and Advances (Singapore) ; Commercial Bank: Loans (Assets) (Thailand); Banking Institutions: Claims on Private Sector (Viet Nam).

Source: Compiled by author with data from *AsianBondsOnline*, ADB; Securities Industry and Financial Markets Association; World Development Indicators, World Bank; International Monetary Fund; and national sources.

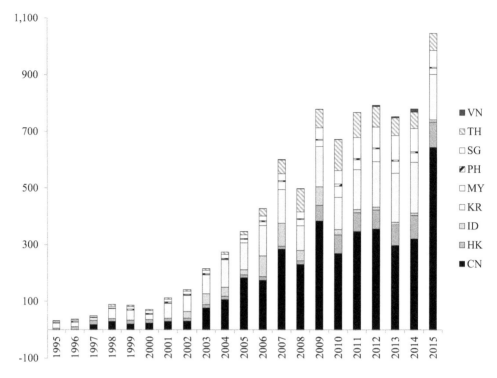

Figure 15.2   Issuance volume of local currency bonds in emerging Asia excluding India (USD billion)

VN = Viet Nam; TH = Thailand; SG = Singapore; PH = Philippines; MY = Malaysia; KR = Republic of Korea; ID = Indonesia; HK = Hong Kong, China; CN = People's Republic of China.

Source: Compiled by author with data from *AsianBondsOnline*, ADB (https://asianbondsonline.adb.org/regional/data.php).

Maturity profile of local currency bond markets

LCY bonds can be issued for the short term (less than 5 years), medium term (between 5 and 10 years) and long term (more than 10 years).The term refers to the length of time from issuance until maturity, when the final payment of a debt security (the principal and all remaining interest) is due to be made. The term structure of a market has implications for (1) the rollover or refinancing risk from an issuer perspective and (2) the sensitivity of bond prices to changes in interest rates and more broadly economic conditions from an investor perspective. In general, longer-term bonds tend to offer higher yields to compensate investors for greater risk exposures to economic factors.

Figures 15.3 and 15.4 show the maturity profiles of LCY government and corporate bonds outstanding respectively. Maturities in the government bond sector have been generally extended over time, but they are still relatively concentrated at the short-end in Hong Kong, China (74.6% of total government bond outstanding less than five years); and Viet Nam (79.9%). Together with these markets, the PRC, the Republic of Korea, and Malaysia have more than 50% of their government bonds outstanding with maturities of less than five years. Indonesia and the Philippines have structured their debt since early 2000s to extend the maturities and their government bonds of more than 10 years are the largest segment of their markets.

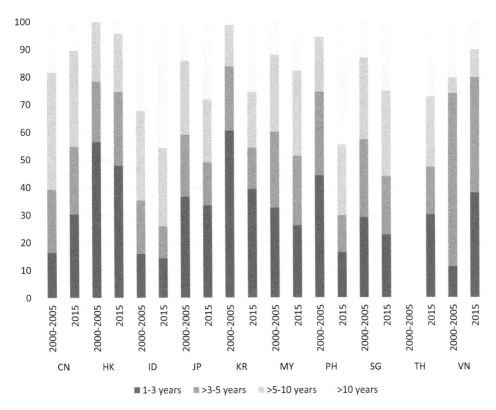

Figure 15.3 Maturity profiles of government bonds outstanding (percentage of total)

VN = Viet Nam; TH = Thailand; SG = Singapore; PH = Philippines; MY = Malaysia; KR = Republic of Korea; ID = Indonesia; HK = Hong Kong, China; CN = People's Republic of China.

Source: Compiled by author with data from AsianBondsOnline, ADB (https://asianbondsonline.adb.org/regional/data.php).

The maturity profiles of the corporate bond sectors present generally greater concentration on shorter end than those of the government sectors. The Indonesian and Vietnamese corporate sectors have issued proportionately large share of short-term debts; corporate bonds less than five years account for 83.5% and 88.1% of their total corporate bonds outstanding respectively. The maturity structure of most emerging Asian corporate debt markets has improved, but is still generally positioned toward short term under five years. With the exception of Malaysia (29.3%), the Philippines (46.1%), and Singapore (49.6%), all other emerging Asian economies have more than 60% of their corporate bonds in short term less than five years.

Interestingly, the corporate bond sectors of Hong Kong, China and Malaysia have proportionately less short-term and more long-term debts than their respective government bond sectors do. This may be related to the fact that many of the corporate issuers in these economies are in the property development, energy companies, and infrastructure industries, which require longer-term financing.

Extending the maturity profile of corporate bonds has been one of major long-term goals for many emerging Asian markets. Over the past decade or so, the medium- to long-term issuance of emerging Asian corporate bonds has increased. This trend continued true even with the onset of the global financial crisis and the subsequent low interest rate environment,

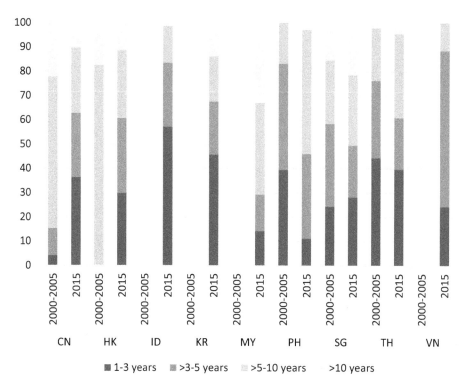

Figure 15.4 Maturity profiles of corporate bonds outstanding (percentage of total)

VN = Viet Nam; TH = Thailand; SG = Singapore; PH = Philippines; MY = Malaysia; KR = Republic of Korea; ID = Indonesia; HK = Hong Kong, China; CN = People's Republic of China.

Source: Compiled by author with data from *AsianBondsOnline*, ADB (https://asianbondsonline.adb.org/regional/data.php).

contributing to the extension of the maturity profile. In the next few years, a large amount of emerging Asian corporate bonds would be due to mature. As interest rates are expected to rise, however, the corporate sector may find it difficult to refinance their retiring debts and hence challenging the ongoing maturity extension.

Issuers and investors of local currency bond markets

A diverse and good-quality issuer base is an essential element of well-developed corporate bond markets. A sizeable pool of quality companies is critical for the potential market size. Major infrastructure companies and financial institutions are often the largest issuers in the early stage of bond market development, but the challenge is to increase the pool of quality issuers over time by encouraging successful companies in a variety of sectors to tap the bond market. This activity will support private sector growth and help enhance financial resilience of the corporate sector from various economic shocks.

Emerging markets have seen growth in both financial and non-financial issuances over the past decade, even with the effect of the crisis in 2008 (Tendulkar and Hancock 2014). In 2000, corporate bond issuances by the financial sector accounted for just 20% of total emerging market issuances, increasing to 43% in 2007 (Figure 15.5). Between 2007 and 2013, financial

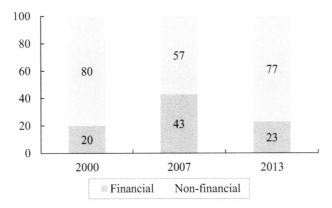

Figure 15.5 Corporate bond issuances by sector in emerging markets (percentage of total)

Source: Compiled by author with data from Tendulkar and Hancock (2014).

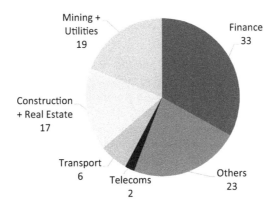

Figure 15.6 Corporate bond issuances by sector in emerging Asia (percentage of total)

Note: Emerging Asia includes the People's Republic of China; Hong Kong, China; India; Indonesia; the Republic of Korea; Malaysia; the Philippines; Singapore; Taipei,China; and Thailand.

Source: Compiled by author with data from Levinger and Li (2014).

issuance more than doubled reaching USD 241 billion in 2013. However, non-financial issuances grew faster by more than four times to reach USD 692 billion in 2013. As a result, the share of financial issuances declined to 23% in 2013.In Emerging Asia, corporate bond issuances are also concentrated in the non-financial sector, mostly from construction, mining, and utilities sectors (Figure 15.6). Finance comprised around one-third of total corporate bond issuances in 2009–2013.

The risk-return profile of both government and corporate issuers in emerging Asia is also an important factor in promoting active participation in local currency bond markets. Credit ratings represent the creditworthiness of the borrower where a poor rating indicates high probability of default. With their sovereign credit ratings steadily improving over time, emerging Asian issuers offer relatively stable ratings and attractive yields compared to other developing region counterparts (Table 15.4).

Table 15.4 Standard & Poor's sovereign credit rating (local currency, long-term)

Economy	as of Dec 2015	as of Dec 2000
Japan	A + u	AAA
United States	AA + u	AAA
Emerging Asia		
China, People's Rep. of	AA−	BBB
Hong Kong, China	AAA	A+
India	BBB − u	BBB
Indonesia	BB+	B
Korea, Rep. of	AA−	A
Malaysia	A	A
Philippines	BBB	BBB+
Singapore	AAAu	AAA
Thailand	A−	A−
Viet Nam	BB−	BB

Note: For Viet Nam, earliest rating is as of December 2002. "u" indicates that the rating was unsolicited without involvement of the borrower.

Source: Compiled by author with data from Bloomberg.

Similarly, the credit default swap (CDS) spreads for sovereign emerging Asian issuers have narrowed over time (Figure 15.7). The CDS spreads indicate market sentiment on the riskiness of bond issues. The buyer (bondholders) pay a premium to the seller of the swap agreement for protection in the event of default, thus acting as a guarantor of the creditworthiness of the bond issue. This premium is called the CDS spread. The premium is quoted in basis points per year of the contract's notional amount and the payment is made quarterly. Higher CDS spreads represent higher default risks. The relatively stable and narrow CDS spreads for emerging Asian issuers suggest favorable market sentiment for their risk conditions.

The investor base for emerging Asian local currency bonds has broadened over time. Prior to the global financial crisis, a majority of the government bonds were held by domestic banks. The growth of local institutional investors, such as pension funds and insurance companies, contributed significantly to the diversity of the investor base. The share of contractual savings' and other investors' (including foreign) holdings combined increased to 65.9% of total government bonds in Indonesia, 63.7% in the Republic of Korea, 68.5% in Malaysia, and 81.0% in Thailand at the end of 2015, even compared to their 2010 figures at 63.4%, 51.5%, 64.9%, and 72.7%.

Emerging Asian local currency bonds have attracted foreign investors for their relatively good risk-return profiles. While improved credit ratings represent relatively low risks, emerging Asian bonds offer attractive yields, on the back of the region's robust economic performance following the crisis and gains from ongoing and anticipated currency appreciation. The share of foreign holding now reaches nearly 40% of government bonds in Indonesia, more than 30% in Malaysia, around 14% in Thailand, and over 10% in the Republic of Korea (Figure 15.8). With growing foreign investors' participation, regulatory authorities need to be more mindful of its implication for market stability and carefully monitor the types of investors and their risks behaviors in local currency bond markets.

There is a growing interest from emerging market bond funds and global institutional investors like pension and insurance agencies in emerging Asian local currency bond markets. As foreign investors have become increasingly comfortable with the credit profiles of emerging

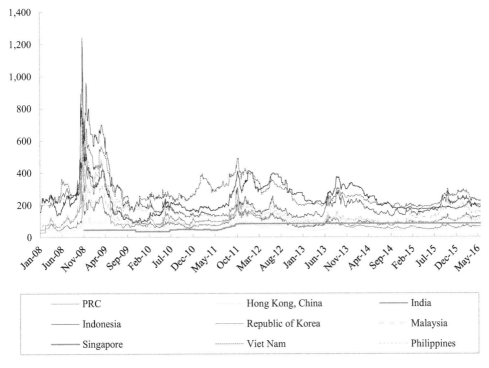

Figure 15.7   Credit default swap spreads (senior five-year, mid-spread in basis points)

PRC = People's Republic of China.

Note: Data as of 20 May 2016.

Source: Compiled by author with data from AsianBondsOnline, ADB (https://asianbondsonline.adb.org/regional/ data.php).

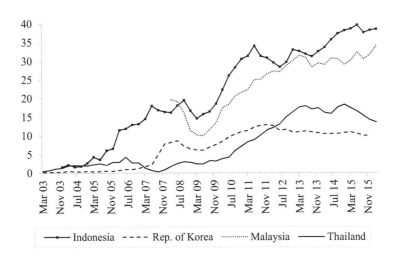

Figure 15.8   Foreign holdings in local currency government bonds (percentage of total)

Source: Compiled by author with data from *AsianBondsOnline*, ADB (https://asianbondsonline.adb.org/regional/ data.php).

Asian issuers, global bond flows will likely channel more global savings into the region's local currency bond markets.

Secondary market liquidity and trading

The growth in the size of the local currency bond markets has not translated automatically to a significant improvement in market liquidity. Although secondary market liquidity and trading have been improving in several emerging Asian markets, the level of liquidity varies significantly across the region's local currency bond markets depending on their overall size, turnover, issuance, and investor base.

Liquidity is a multi-dimensional concept and can be measured in terms of market tightness, depth, and resilience. Tightness, often measured by the bid-ask spreads, refers to "how far transaction prices (bid or ask prices) diverge from the mid-market price" (Bank for International Settlements 1999: 5). Depth, shown as the average turnover ratio or bond yield volatility, refers to "either the volume of trades possible without affecting prevailing market prices, or the amount of orders on the order books of market-makers at a given time" (Bank of International Settlements 1999: 5). Resilience can be defined as either "the speed with which price fluctuations resulting from trades are dissipated, or the speed with which imbalances of order flows are adjusted" (Bank for International Settlements 1999: 5).

However, data on secondary market liquidity and trading is scarce. For example, bid-ask spreads for particular corporate bonds are not readily available or publicly accessible. Similarly, data on turnover ratios and dealer inventories of corporate bonds is very limited. Where data is available, liquidity appears to be improving in selected emerging Asian markets. The government bond markets are also relatively more liquid than corporate bond markets.

Emerging Asian government bond market liquidity can be characterized as moderately improving as bid-ask spreads have narrowed and yield volatility declined (Figures 15.9 and 15.10).

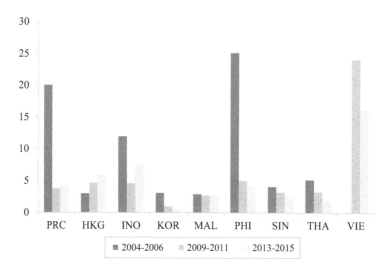

Figure 15.9 Government bond market bid-ask price (average over the period specified, basis points)

PRC = People's Republic of China; HKG = Hong Kong, China; INO = Indonesia; KOR = Republic of Korea; MAL = Malaysia; PHI = Philippines; SIN = Singapore; THA = Thailand; VIE = Viet Nam.

Source: Compiled by author with data from AsianBondsOnline, ADB (https://asianbondsonline.adb.org/regional/data.php).

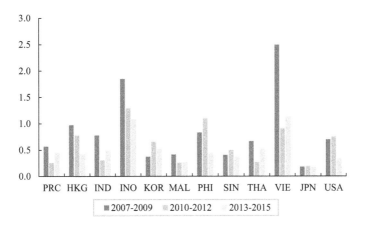

Figure 15.10 10-year bond yield volatility (standard deviation)

PRC = People's Republic of China; HKG = Hong Kong, China; INO = Indonesia; KOR = Republic of Korea; MAL = Malaysia; PHI = Philippines; SIN = Singapore; THA = Thailand; VIE = Viet Nam; JPN = Japan; USA = United States.

Source: Compiled by author with data from Bloomberg.

Table 15.5 Local currency bond market volatility indicators

Economy	Trade Volume (USD billion)				Turnover Ratio			
	2015		*2005*		*2015*		*2005*	
	Government	*Corporate*	*Government*	*Corporate*	*Government*	*Corporate*	*Government*	*Corporate*
PRC	2,476.69	447.12	214.19	40.11	0.63	0.29	0.27	0.73
HKG	71.14	13.75	246.31	2.29	0.61	0.16	15.15	0.03
INO	53.72	2.96	6.21	0.42	0.52	0.16	0.15	0.07
JPN	10,395.57	36.98	7,402.82	130.00	1.24	0.06	1.19	0.18
KOR	413.05	97.80	270.02	57.14	0.59	0.10	0.69	0.16
MAL	38.38	5.60	19.51	7.42	0.27	0.05	0.32	0.17
PHI	39.07	–	12.19	–	0.49	–	0.30	–
SIN	34.61	–	29.84	–	0.47	–	0.62	–
THA	126.50	5.47	22.10	0.56	0.62	0.08	0.35	0.04

– = unavailable; PRC = People's Republic of China; HKG = Hong Kong, China; INO = Indonesia; JPN = Japan: KOR = Republic of Korea; MAL = Malaysia; PHI = Philippines; SIN = Singapore; THA = Thailand.
Source: Compiled by author with data from *AsianBondsOnline*, ADB. https://asianbondsonline.adb.org/regional/data.php

Liquidity in the corporate bond markets is relatively poor with the corporate bond turnover ratios are much lower than those of government bonds and even deteriorated since 2005 (Table 15.5).

Regional initiatives to develop local currency bond markets

The experience of the 1997–1998 Asian financial crisis gave rise to the establishment of regional institutions to safeguard financial stability and build economic and financial resilience. One of the key policy thrusts in this context was to develop local currency bond markets.

Table 15.6 Timeline of bond market development

Year	Initiatives
2003	Asian Bond Markets Initiative (ABMI), launched under ASEAN+3, to develop a liquid and well-functioning bond market
2003	Asian Bond Fund 1: launched by central banks of Executives' Meeting of East Asia and the Pacific (EMEAP) countries to invest pooled savings in the region's (sovereign and quasi-sovereign) bond markets.
2004	ABMI launched the AsianBondsOnline as a one-stop data and information portal for institutional investors, policy-makers and researchers participating in local currency debt markets
2005	Asian Bond Fund 2, follow-up to ABF1, with investment channeled into local currency bonds. Primary goal is to reduce market barriers for investors and improve liquidity in sovereign bond markets.
2008	New ABMI Roadmap was signed to set up task forces to address specific issues in local bond market development.
2010	ASEAN+3 established the Asian Bond Market Forum (ABMF) as a platform to foster standardization of market practices and harmonization of regulations relating to cross-border bond transactions in the region
2010	Launch of the Credit Guarantee and Investment Facility (CGIF) as a trust fund within the ADB to provide guarantees for local currency denominated bonds issued by companies in the region
2013	ASEAN+3 established the Cross-Border Settlement Infrastructure Forum (CSIF) to discuss the preparation of a roadmap and an implementation plan for the improvement of regional cross-border settlement infrastructure
2015	ABMF released implementation guidelines for the ASEAN+3 Multi-Currency Bond Issuance Framework (AMBIF), which helps facilitate intraregional transactions through standardized bond and note issuance and investment processes

Source: Compiled by author with information from Levinger and Li (2014) and ADB (2008, 2012, 2015a).

Table 15.6 summarizes key regional initiatives to help develop local currency bond markets. Especially, the ABMI aims to "develop efficient and liquid bond markets in Asia, which would enable better utilization of Asian savings for Asian investments. The initiative would also contribute to the mitigation of currency and maturity mismatches in financing" (AMRO 2013: 1). The ABMI activities have been further supported by the introduction of the Credit Guarantee and Investment Facility (CGIF) and the Asian Bond Market Forum (ABMF).

Separately, the Asian Bond Funds (ABF) was established to facilitate the investment of the region's international reserves in the region's financial assets. Initially, the ABF was invested in a basket of liquid US dollar bonds of major Asian economies, but subsequent ABFs were invested in the local currency bonds issued by the region's sovereign issuers.

Asian Bond Markets Initiative

ASEAN+3 Finance Ministers launched the ABMI in August 2003 to develop a liquid and well-functioning bond market. ABMI activities focus on increasing issuance and circulation of local currency bonds in the member countries by encouraging market participation of a broader investor base and by building and strengthening market infrastructure.

A new ABMI roadmap was signed in May 2008 to take forward the initiative and four task forces were created to (1) promote issuance of local currency denominated bonds co-chaired by the PRC and Thailand, (2) facilitate the demand of local currency denominated bonds by Japan and Singapore, (3) improve regulatory framework by Japan and Malaysia, and (4) improve related infrastructure for the bond markets with view to encouraging domestic issuance and increasing secondary market liquidity by the Republic of Korea and the Philippines, respectively (ADB 2008). The new roadmap also aims to encourage member economies to take further voluntary actions to develop the LCY bond market and the national efforts are expected to lead to the creation of a more accessible regional bond market.

A Steering Group was established to ensure effective and efficient work under the new ABMI framework. The Steering Group was to (1) review and revise the ABMI Roadmap; (2) oversee and provide guidance to the ABMI activities; (3) formulate strategies to promote public awareness on the ABMI; (4) monitor the progress of studies by the Task Forces; (5) assign a task to an appropriate Task Force or create, if necessary, a Working Team; and (6) promote information exchanges among member countries on the developments of local currency-denominated and regional bond markets through a self-assessment process. The Steering Group will report to the ASEAN+3 Finance Deputies' Meeting (AFDM+3), which then reports to the ASEAN+3 Finance Ministers' Meeting (AFMM+3).

Other efforts included the establishment of a group of public and private sector experts from the region to look at the possibility of creating a regional settlement intermediary in ASEAN+3 to enhance cross-border settlement infrastructure, introducing measures to harmonize cross-border regulations and strengthen domestic credit rating mechanisms, and creating a credit guarantee mechanism for local-currency bonds.

Credit Guarantee and Investment Facility

The Credit Guarantee and Investment Facility (CGIF), a key component of Task Force 1 under ABMI, was established in November 2010 by ASEAN+3 and ADB. ASEAN+3 finance ministers endorsed the creation of a credit guarantee and investment mechanism as a trust fund of the Asian Development Bank at their annual meeting in May 2009 in Bali. Subsequently, ADB's Board of Directors approved in April 2010 the establishment of the CGIF trust fund with an initial capital of USD 700 million.[3] As of May 2016, CGIF has issued 13 guarantees to bonds issued in five ASEAN currencies by 10 companies in six countries, amounting to USD 888 million.

The CGIF aims to promote the development of Asian bond markets by providing credit guarantees for local currency denominated bonds issued by investment grade companies in ASEAN+3 countries. Such guarantees would make it easier for firms to issue local currency bonds with longer maturities. It is also expected to encourage the harmonization of standards and practices for bond issuance and help tap into the region's savings to finance long-term investment, notably in infrastructure and other public utilities. CGIF also aims to guarantee securitization of SME credits.

Asian Bond Market Forum (ABMF)

The ABMF is a working group of experts under Task Force 3 of ABMI, developing a strategy to harmonize regulations across the ASEAN+3 economies. The ABMF has expanded steadily as more market participants sign up.

ASEAN+3 Bond Market Guide (ADB 2012) was published in Phase 1, which provided a comparative analysis on market infrastructures and detailed information on bond transaction flows. In Phase 2, ABMF created two sub-forums: (1) Sub-Forum 1 (SF1) to close the information gap in regulations, market practices, and other areas in the region's bond markets, and (2) Sub-Forum 2 to enhance regional straight-through-processing through the harmonization of transaction procedures and standardization of messages. Two reports were produced, summarizing the activities of SF1 and SF2 respectively: (1) Proposal on ASEAN+3 Multi-Currency Bond Issuance Framework (AMBIF) (ADB 2014a) and (2) ASEAN+3: Information on Transaction Flows and Settlement Infrastructures (ADB 2014b). In Phase 3, ABMF continued to work on the proposal in the Phase 2 reports by SF1 and SF2 in order to set up procedures on how to implement AMBIF in the region (ADB 2015a, 2015b).

One of the major goals under AMBIF is to achieve a common understanding and mutual recognition among regulatory agencies and financial authorities in the region. Existing differences in the current market rules and procedures are substantial across the member economies and hence it would be quite challenging to achieve mutual recognition of the procedures and requirements on public offering for general public participants. Therefore, AMBIF has been also focusing on licensed or exempt markets, including the private placement market, where full disclosure requirements for ordinary public offering would be waived for professional investors or Qualified Institutional Buyers.

Asian Bond Fund (ABF) initiative

The Executives' Meeting of East Asia Pacific Central Banks (EMEAP) is a forum of central banks and monetary authorities in the East Asia-Pacific region to enhance financial cooperation among its members (Hyun and Jang 2009). It launched the first Asian Bond Fund (ABF1) in June 2003 which pooled USD 1 billion of international reserves from EMEAP central banks and invested in USD-denominated sovereign and quasi-sovereign debt issued in eight economies (the PRC; Hong Kong, China; Indonesia; the Republic of Korea; Malaysia; the Philippines; Singapore; and Thailand).

The EMEAP launched the second Asian Bond Fund (ABF2) in 2005, which extended the concept of ABF1 to an investment of additional USD 2 billion in local-currency-denominated sovereign and quasi-sovereign issues in the same eight EMEAP markets. USD 1 billion was allocated to the eight national index funds and a further USD 1 billion was to the Pan-Asian Bond Index Fund, a single index fund, which invests in local-currency sovereign and quasi-sovereign bonds issued in the EMEAP markets. These funds are index funds tracking the benchmarks provided by the International Index Company (IIC). The iBoxx ABF index family, which includes sovereign and quasi-sovereign LCY debt, serves as benchmark for the ABF2 funds (Table 15.7).

Table 15.7 Asian Bond Fund 2 net asset value

Funds	Inception date	Net Asset Value (USD per unit)	Net Asset Value (USD million)
China Bond Index Fund	27 May 2011	0.17	451.50
Hong Kong Bond Index Fund	17 Jun 2005	12.97	429.37
Korea Bond Index Fund	21 Apr 2010	152.10	17.19
Malaysia Bond Index Fund	18 Jul 2005	0.28	368.81
Philippines Bond Index Fund	27 Apr 2005	4.74	295.47
Singapore Bond Index Fund	31 Aug 2005	0.86	437.34
Thailand Bond Index Fund	24 Feb 2006	34.95	201.24
Pan-Asia Bond Index Fund	07 Jul 2005	119.38	2,998.00

Note: Based on local currency values for all except Korea Bond Index Fund and Pan-Asia Bond Index Fund; converted to US dollars using the latest official exchange rate from International Monetary Fund as of 5 June 2016.

Source: Compiled by author with data from Bloomberg (accessed 5 June 2016) and ABF Pan-Asia Bond Index Fund Factsheet.

The ABF initiative acted as a catalyst for regulatory reforms and improvements in market practices and infrastructure in the region. Although it is difficult to evaluate the gains exclusively attached to this initiative, foreign exchange restrictions and capital controls have been gradually liberalized. Restrictions on the convertibility of local currencies have been removed and foreign exchange administration rules have been relaxed over time. Currency hedging has been made possible by the development of FX swap or derivatives markets. It also made significant contributions to reducing market impediments in the areas of financial regulation and taxation. Together with the ABMI, the ABFs[4] have also prompted domestic regulatory reforms, improvements in leading to improvements in market practices and infrastructure in the region.

Challenges ahead

Emerging Asia has come a long way in building local currency bond markets, but significant variations exist in the level of development across the region's local currency bond markets. While the bond markets of Hong Kong, China; the Republic of Korea; and Singapore are relatively well developed and liquid, markets in the PRC, India, Indonesia, Malaysia, and Thailand are still at an early stage of development. Although the PRC and India have the largest local currency bond markets, in terms of market depth and liquidity, the level of development remains low. Bond issuance data also shows variations in sectoral diversity, issuing volume and consistency. The bond markets in the PRC and India also remain relatively less open to foreign investors despite their large sizes compared to those of Indonesia, the Republic of Korea, Malaysia, and Thailand.

More needs to be done to enable the private sector to seek funding from a broader range of sources without increasing vulnerability to shocks. The region's demographic changes and substantial needs for infrastructure and urban development also suggest increasingly large long-term funding needs. Asia's investment needs for infrastructure are indeed substantial – as much as USD 8 trillion in the 10 years to 2020 (ADB and ADBI 2009). Fiscal spending alone would not be able to address the funding gap. Robust local capital markets are essential to diversify the sources of funding necessary to support longer-term investments and sustain emerging Asia's high growth levels.

However, there remain structural impediments to growth in corporate bond markets. To manage the transition to a more resilient corporate bond market, key areas of reform focus are improving market efficiency, broadening the investor base, deepening secondary markets, and integrating regional markets. These reform efforts will also help the region to more efficiently absorb large capital flows and channel these into long-term productive investments.

Size and liquidity in secondary markets

Despite fast growth in primary issuance, secondary market trading volumes and liquidity remain limited in many emerging Asian markets. A deep and liquid secondary market can reduce liquidity risks and allows investors to exit from long-term bonds before their maturity, contributing to greater demand for long-term bonds. However, various measures of market liquidity indicate room for improvement in the region's corporate bond markets. Bid-ask spreads for corporate bonds are typically wider than those for sovereign bonds. Corporate bond turnover ratios, which measure the value traded in the secondary market relative to the size of bonds outstanding, are also low. New issues are often traded only for a short period of time. Lack of risk management products hampers secondary market trading and liquidity.

The introduction of bond buybacks and exchanges and building active cash management capacity can have a positive impact on secondary market liquidity, along with the development of a broader range of more sophisticated market instruments and segments. Encouraging foreign investors' participation in local currency bond markets can also help boost liquidity. One means to this end is to remove or reduce withholding taxes and other restrictions on local currency convertibility. The legal infrastructure also needs to be improved to develop a repo and derivative market.

The key reforms in this area typically include (1) enhancing primary and secondary market architecture to provide the appropriate level of market transparency; (2) promoting market-making activities (including a primary dealers system, where it is appropriate) to increase liquidity; (3) introducing prudential norms and risk management practices of market participants; (4) increasing the size of benchmark bonds and extending the yield curve; (5) moving toward a more market-based implementation of monetary policy and more emphasis on the interbank repo market; and (6) fostering institutional investor and encouraging foreign participation.

Supporting market infrastructure

The region also needs to improve supporting market infrastructure such as standardized credit rating systems, risk management products and a functioning trading and settlement system, and strengthen the legal and regulatory frameworks to encompass various auxiliary markets such as interest futures, accounting, and tax issues with international best practices. The establishment of a reliable benchmark yield curve also helps enhance market efficiency and transparency in the pricing of corporate bonds. It is also important to broaden the investor base and develop appropriate risk management instruments along with the extension of the yield curve. In emerging Asian markets, where banks are the predominant investors, efforts to extend the yield curve could simply transfer the interest rate and liquidity risks from the government to the banking sector.

The region's credit rating system is not sufficiently developed. Locally based credit rating agencies may know more about the companies they rate and be familiar with the local business environment. However, these local credit rating agencies should meet the standards of qualification to gain the trust of investors. Unless they are fully qualified, they may become a cause of systemic risks. While local credit rating agencies can play an important role in developing a corporate bond market, it is important to ensure that these local credit rating agencies are credible, commercially viable, and independent.

The development of active money markets and efficient derivatives markets can be instrumental for local currency bond market development. An active money market, especially the repo market, allows market makers to fund their inventories of bonds flexibly and cost-efficiently, while providing tools for better risk management. The ability of primary dealers and/or other market makers to hold inventory and to hedge temporary accumulations of long positions by taking short positions in issues with similar maturities, is a fundamental building block for market-making activities. Developing a liquid foreign exchange derivatives market can also help encourage foreign investors' participation in local currency bond markets.

While reform efforts should continue to refine and upgrade supporting market infrastructure and other legal and institutional framework to be brought in line with those of more advanced markets, more targeted efforts would be needed to address cross-border barriers to regional integration. The launch of a pilot platform for cross-border clearing and settlement of debt securities in Hong Kong, China and Malaysia is a good example, aimed at strengthening post-trading infrastructure and promoting standardization and dissemination of corporate announcements across emerging Asian markets.

Broad investor base

Banks are often the largest group of investors in emerging Asia's corporate bond markets, but tighter capital requirements facing these banks may contribute to lack of liquidity in secondary markets. Lack of investor diversity can also lead to high volatility and expose the market to some sector specific risks and conditions. In the PRC, a majority of outstanding corporate bonds are held by state-owned commercial banks, which are in turn heavily exposed to state-owned enterprises.

Fostering institutional investors, such as pension funds and insurance companies, can help contribute to the development of long-term bond markets. Although the size of domestic institutional investors' assets in most emerging Asian markets remains small relative to that of advanced markets, these investors tend to play an increasingly important role in corporate bond markets. In the Republic of Korea, the combined holdings of pension funds and insurance companies reached nearly a half of the market.

Foreign investors may have different investment horizons and preferences from domestic investors, which can result in improved demand structure and secondary market liquidity. Foreign investors could be allowed to operate in local markets with fewer restrictions, especially though eliminating withholding taxes and undue restrictions on the convertibility of local currency. Foreign financial institutions may also assume new roles in the domestic market, such as intermediaries or asset managers.

Regional integration of bond markets

Emerging Asian bond markets are growing at a healthy clip. It is important that this expansion is accompanied by strengthening market infrastructure within the context of regional cooperation. Integration has lagged behind the level of inter-connectedness seen in other markets, for example, equities. Deutsche Bank Research (2013) finds that Asian local currency bond markets are not effectively integrated, although the degree of integration varies across the region. Some markets (Malaysia, Taipei,China, and Thailand) are relatively better integrated then others (the PRC, Indonesia, and the Philippines).

Various regional initiatives and policies have focused on promoting regional integration of emerging Asian bond markets. The latest example is the launch of a bond pricing portal among five banks across ASEAN economies in 2013, which is meant to pave the way for an electronic trading platform, mirroring a similar project to integrate trading of equities. Five banks from Indonesia, Malaysia, the Philippines, Singapore, and Thailand quote the prices for local bonds and distribute them through Bloomberg. The initiative is part of the efforts to create a more integrated capital market in the ASEAN economies by facilitating access to cross-border bond price information. A roadmap for capital market integration has been also agreed on as part of the ASEAN Economic Community (AEC) by 2015. This should pave the way for greater, and more resilient, use of the corporate bond market in the future.

While greater market integration bring about many benefits in theory, such as more efficient resource allocation and better enforcement of market disciplines, it can increase the risk of financial contagion and spillovers. It is therefore critical to enable regional regulatory authorities to develop and implement appropriate regulatory frameworks to facilitate market development and integration, while safeguarding financial stability during transition, where increased competition and financial innovation could lead to increased risk-taking and risk financial stability.

Acknowledgments

The author gratefully acknowledges the research support by the following consultants of the Regional Cooperation and Integration Division of the ADB's Economic Research and Regional Cooperation Department: Pilar Dayag, Grendell Vie Magoncia, Ana Kristel Molina, and Mara Claire Tayag. All remaining errors are the author's.

Notes

1 The crisis exposed the risk of a double mismatch of currency and maturity on the private sector balance sheets. On the back of the relatively stable exchange rates prior to the crisis, firms borrowed short-term in foreign currency for long-term investment whose returns are tied to domestic currency. Such transactions were also often coursed through domestic banking systems, leading to massive bank failures during the crisis.
2 Data on total issuance (government and corporate) are not available for India.
3 CGIF has received capital contribution of USD 700 million from ADB, ASEAN, the PRC, Japan, and the Republic of Korea and is operating with 2.5 leverage ratio, thus having a guarantee capacity up to USD 1.75 billion.
4 The launch of the ABFs may have inspired multilateral agencies to introduce similar funds in other emerging markets. For example, the World Bank launched the Global Emerging Markets Local Currency Bond Fund as part of its strategy to develop bond markets in developing countries by opening them up to foreign investors, thereby providing an additional source of local financing.

References

ASEAN+3 Macroeconomic Research Office (AMRO). 2013. Chairman's Press Release on the Asian Bond Market Initiative, 1 August. http://asean.org/chairman-s-press-release-on-the-asian-bond-markets-initiative-3/

Asian Development Bank (ADB). 2008. *ASEAN+3 New ABMI Roadmap*. Manila: Asian Development Bank.

ADB. 2012. *ASEAN+3 Bond Market Guide*. Manila: Asian Development Bank.

ADB. 2014a. *Proposal on ASEAN+3 Multicurrency Bond Issuance Framework*. Manila: Asian Development Bank.

ADB. 2014b. *ASEAN+3: Information on Transaction Flows and Settlement Infrastructures*. Manila: Asian Development Bank.

ADB. 2015a. *Implementation of the ASEAN+3 Multi-Currency Bond Issuance Framework: ASEAN+3 Bond Market Forum Sub-Forum 1 Phase 3 Report*. Manila: Asian Development Bank.

ADB. 2015b. *Harmonization and Standardization of Bond Market Infrastructures in ASEAN+3: ASEAN+3 Bond Market Forum Sub-Forum 2 Phase 3 Report*. Manila: Asian Development Bank.

ADB and ADB Institute. 2009. *Infrastructure for a Seamless Asia*. Tokyo: Asian Development Bank Institute.

Bank for International Settlements. 1999. Market Liquidity: Research Findings and Selected Policy Implications. www.bis.org/publ/cgfs11.htm

Credit Guarantee and Investment Facility (CGIF). 2016. CGIF Guarantees PT MitraPinasthikaMustika Finance's Debut Indonesian Rupiah Bonds; Press Release, 11 March. https://support.cgif-abmi.org/wp-content/uploads/2016/04/MPMF_TA_CGIF_Closing-Announcement_EN_20160311_F.pdf

Deutsche Bank Research. 2013. Asian Bond Market or Markets? Global Economic Perspectives. Frankfurt: Deutsche Bank Research.

Jang, H.B., and S. Hyun. 2009. A Way Forward for Asian Bond Market Development. Working Paper No. 383. Seoul: Institute for Monetary and Economic Research, Bank of Korea.

Levinger, H., and C. Li. 2014. What's Behind Recent Trends in Asian Corporate Bond Markets? In *Current Issues: Emerging Markets,* 31 January. Frankfurt: Deutsche Bank.

Tendulkar, R., and G. Hancock. 2014. Corporate Bond Markets: A Global Perspective. Staff Working Paper of the IOSCO Research Department. Madrid: International Organization of Securities Commissions.

16

ASIAN STOCK MARKETS

Jonathan A. Batten, Igor Lončarski, and Péter G. Szilágyi

Introduction

Asian stock markets have undergone enormous transformation in both scale and scope over the last decade. Led by privatization and initial public offerings (IPOs), Asia-Pacific stock markets in aggregate increased in US dollar terms by nearly 150% in the period 2005–2015. Collectively, their combined value exceeded USD 23.2 trillion by the end of 2015. By comparison, over the same period, stock markets worldwide increased 64.1% to USD 68.1 trillion, while in the US and Europe increases were only 47.5% and 31.2%, with market capitalization now at levels of USD 25.1 trillion and USD 15.9 trillion, respectively.

This increase is even more impressive given the effects of the global financial crisis and the more recent contagion within the region from slowing growth in the People's Republic of China (PRC). These two critical events represent milestones of regulatory developments in the region over the past decade. In addition, the impacts of these events reflect the highly integrated nature of the Asia-Pacific stock markets compared to other regions worldwide. This has been due to the effects of ongoing capital market deregulation and greater economic integration through trade and policy initiatives such as various free trade agreements.[1] In this respect, the efforts of ASEAN are especially noteworthy and include the decision in 2003 to create the ASEAN economic community.[2]

The global financial crisis in 2008 saw stock market values fall worldwide with falls of nearly 50% in many Asia-Pacific markets, with the largest falls in stock prices occurring in September and October 2008 due to the bankruptcy of Lehman Brothers on 15 September 2008. A detailed account and timeline of these events is provided by Guillen (2012), while Filardo et al. (2010) provide information on the subsequent policy response by government, which included quite specific measures to boost the value of the stock market. For example, on 22 October 2008, the Malaysian government injected MYR 5 billion into a special-purpose vehicle, Value Cap Sdn Bhd, for investment in undervalued companies.

This chapter takes an overall perspective on the scale and scope of stock market development in the Asia-Pacific region, broadly defined, with the aim of providing insights into the manner of its structure and extraordinary development in recent years. First, a perspective on the level of development of the Asia-Pacific markets is provided with comments made on the impact of recent changes in the regulatory framework where relevant. To some extent this section updates the earlier work by Purfield et al. (2006) and Lipinsky and Ong (2014), who also investigate at the growth and opportunities that exist in the Asian stock markets. Then, the key issues confronting stock market development is considered along with discussion of factors that affect the levels of investor demand and supply, along with discussion of any relevant infrastructure impediments. The final section allows for concluding remarks.

Level of stock market development

In 2005 the Japanese stocks markets based in Osaka and Tokyo comprised nearly 80.0% of the market capitalization of the Asia-Pacific region. Ten years later they comprise just 21.0% and have fallen in value from USD 7.4 trillion to USD 4.9 trillion. On the other hand, the two PRC stock markets based in Shanghai and Shenzen have increased in value as a result of privatization and new listings to have a market capitalization of USD 8.2 trillion, which represents 21.1% of a much larger regional capitalization of USD 23.7 trillion in December 2015.

The economic rise of the PRC and decline of Japan over the past decade, as evidenced by their relative levels of stock market development, are themes that have implications, not just for the Asia-Pacific region, but worldwide. Many of these themes are also considered in this volume. For example, capital flows as direct and portfolio investment into and out of the PRC have contributed to debates on the effectiveness of capital controls and the presence of asset bubbles, not just in asset markets in the PRC but also to others in the Asia-Pacific region that have been the beneficiary of PRC investment.

The internationalization of the PRC's currency, the yuan (CNY), as part of a wider program of capital account liberalization and internationalization of the PRC's state-owned enterprises, are all factors that reflect a realignment of the PRC's economic as well as political influence worldwide. Xiao and Kimball (2005) show that a decade ago the PRC successfully used its capital controls to favor foreign direct investment over portfolio and bank asset and liability flows. This had not changed by 2015, with Hatzvi, Meredith, and Nixon (2015) writing that PRC private capital flows remain dominated by foreign direct investment and banking-related flows (average of 3.5% of GDP from 2001 to 2015), with portfolio flows remaining relatively small by comparison.

Data available from the World Federation of Exchanges provides detailed information on domestic stock market capitalization, based in US dollar terms, for the period from 2005 to 2015. In December 2015, the US dollar value of the American stock markets was USD 28.0 trillion, with the largest exchange being the New York Stock Exchange and the NASDAQ with USD 17.8 and USD 7.3 trillion, respectively. At this time, these two American markets comprised 37.4% of world stock market capitalization of USD 67.1 trillion. The remaining American markets, excluding the US markets, are tiny by comparison and comprise just 4.32%, while Europe, Africa, and the Middle East comprise 23.7%. It is the Asian markets with the balancing 34.6% (USD 23.2 trillion) that now almost match the US markets in terms of size. Whether these financial markets collectively will dominate world stock markets in terms of scope – and the implication of such ascendency – remains a key policy question and one where further analysis of market structure is required. Figure 16.1 shows the evolution of the regional shares of global stock markets (in USD terms) in the period from December 2005 to December 2015.

In terms of the absolute size of the stock exchanges in Asia, there have been significant developments over the past 10 years. As shown in Table 16.1, at the end of 2005 by far the largest markets/exchanges were those in Japan (Tokyo and Osaka) with the combined market capitalization exceeding USD 7.5 trillion. Significantly lagging behind at the time was the Hong Kong Exchanges and Clearing with more than USD 1 trillion in market capitalization,

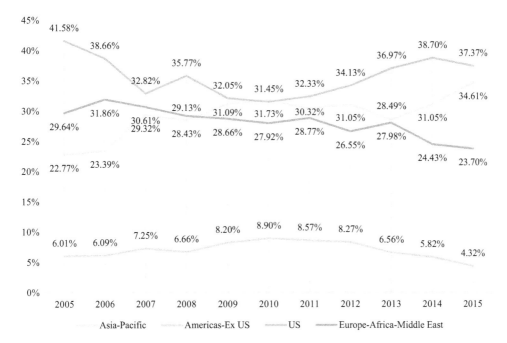

Figure 16.1 Share of global stock markets by region

The figure shows the share of global stock market (based on the market capitalization in US dollar terms) per selected World regions as a percent of the total number of listed companies as reported by the World Federation of Exchanges. The data is based on the statistics provided by the World Federation of Exchanges.

Source: World Federation of Exchanges and own calculations.

Table 16.1 The largest exchanges in Asia by market capitalization, 2005 and 2015

2005			2015		
Exchange	USD million	% largest	Exchange	USD million	% largest
Japan Exchange Group–Tokyo	4 572 901.0	100.0%	Japan Exchange Group★	4 894 919.1	100.0%
Japan Exchange Group–Osaka	2 964 297.7	64.8%	Shanghai Stock Exchange	4 549 288.0	92.9%
Hong Kong Exchanges and Clearing	1 054 999.3	23.1%	Shenzhen Stock Exchange	3 638 731.3	74.3%
Korea Exchange	718 010.7	15.7%	Hong Kong Exchanges and Clearing	3 184 874.2	65.1%
BSE India Limited	553 073.7	12.1%	BSE India Limited	1 516 216.7	31.0%
National Stock Exchange of India	515 972.5	11.3%	National Stock Exchange of India	1 485 088.6	30.3%
Taipei,China Stock Exchange Corp.	476 018.0	10.4%	Korea Exchange	1 231 199.8	25.2%
Shanghai Stock Exchange	286 190.3	6.3%	Taipei,China Stock Exchange Corp.	744 999.7	15.2%

(*Continued*)

Table 16.1 (Continued)

2005			2015		
Singapore Exchange	257 339.8	5.6%	Singapore Exchange	639 955.9	13.1%
Bursa Malaysia	180 517.5	3.9%	Bursa Malaysia	382 976.7	7.8%
Stock Exchange of Thailand	123 885.0	2.7%	Indonesia Stock Exchange	353 271.0	7.2%
Shenzhen Stock Exchange	115 661.9	2.5%	Stock Exchange of Thailand	348 798.0	7.1%
Indonesia Stock Exchange	81 428.1	1.8%	Philippine Stock Exchange	238 819.9	4.9%

★ On 1 January 2013, Tokyo and Osaka merged into JPX.
Source: The World Federation of Exchanges.

while the Shanghai and Shenzhen exchanges were, by comparison, relatively small in size. Ten years later the Japan Exchange Group (Osaka) remained the single largest exchange (almost USD 4.9 trillion in market capitalization), while the most important PRC exchanges (Shanghai, Shenzhen, and Hong Kong) represented the largest markets with a combined market capitalization of over USD 11.3 trillion. Other exchanges in the region have more or less kept their relative rankings and growth, while the Indian exchanges overtook the Korea Exchange. These developments highlight the growing importance of the emerging economies of the PRC and India, not just in Asia, but also worldwide.

An additional perspective is provided by considering the role these markets play in terms of the broader economy. The benchmark US stock markets in December 2015 had stock market capitalization relative to GDP of 139.68%. This statistic may be compared with the same number for selected economies in the Asia-Pacific region and provided in Table 16.2. For example, the PRC's stock markets by 2015 accounted for about 75.35% of GDP (and an average of 102.65% for the region), up significantly from a year earlier – 58% at the end of 2014; a number which is more comparable with the European and central Asian stock markets with 64.3%. Not surprising is the fact that the two major regional financial centers of Hong Kong, China and Singapore have relatively more significant stock markets in terms of size relative to GDP (about 1,028% and 219% of GDP, respectively). This table highlights the enormous diversity between the developed financial centers of Asia and, for example, the frontier and emerging markets of Viet Nam and Indonesia. The level of underdevelopment in some markets (e.g., Viet Nam) carries through to underdevelopment in other financial segments (e.g., banking and derivatives), while there are also significant differences between some developed countries such as Malaysia and the financial products available. For example, according to stock market value relative to GDP (around 130% at the end of 2015) one could argue Malaysia has a relatively developed stock market. However, the stock market traded value and turnover (see Tables 16.3 and 16.4) are among the lowest in the region.

Another statistic that facilitates regional and worldwide comparisons of the degree of financial market development is the traded value of stocks as a percentage of GDP. Trading volume is also consistent with liquidity – the more liquid a market, the more likely it is to approach theoretical levels of efficiency in terms of price discovery and trading. US stock markets in 2015 had traded value of 230.7% of GDP. The statistics for selected Asia-Pacific countries are provided in Table 16.3. The Asia-Pacific markets, by comparison with the US markets, had substantially less trading, with the notable exception being Hong Kong, China with a value in

Table 16.2 Stock market capitalization to GDP

Country, Region/Year	2000	2005	2008	2010	2012	2014	2015
United States	146.89	129.84	78.75	115.50	115.56	151.78	139.68
South Asia	**NA**	**58.54**	**44.98**	**84.13**	**67.62**	**74.53**	**71.30**
East Asia and Pacific	**72.33**	**88.30**	**61.91**	**97.07**	**77.36**	**91.79**	**102.65**
PRC	NA	17.71	39.02	66.69	43.70	58.01	75.35
Hong Kong, China	363.14	581.04	605.97	1185.86	1078.30	1110.13	1027.61
India	NA	66.30	52.87	95.51	69.23	76.30	73.12
Indonesia	16.25	28.48	19.36	47.73	46.65	47.40	40.99
Japan	66.73	100.02	64.25	69.61	58.40	95.25	118.71
Korea, Rep.	30.49	79.94	46.98	99.76	96.45	85.93	89.36
Malaysia	120.65	125.77	81.99	160.26	148.39	135.76	129.29
Pakistan	8.96	41.38	13.73	21.42	NA	NA	NA
Philippines	32.06	38.61	29.87	78.82	91.69	91.95	81.80
Singapore	159.47	201.97	137.85	273.76	264.49	245.75	218.61
Thailand	23.12	65.44	35.39	81.46	98.10	106.46	88.24
Viet Nam	NA	NA	9.56	25.98	NA	24.74	26.80

GDP = gross domestic product, NA = not available, PRC = People's Republic of China.

Source: World Bank: World Development Indicators.

Table 16.3 Stock market traded value to GDP

Country, Region/Year	2000	2005	2008	2010	2012	2014	2015
United States	289.57	196.98	320.99	240.74	200.24	224.67	230.67
South Asia	**8.71**	**58.27**	**63.55**	**53.58**	**28.03**	**28.91**	**32.91**
East Asia and Pacific	**67.67**	**79.48**	**110.12**	**113.24**	**66.24**	**103.01**	**242.37**
PRC	62.44	17.30	85.67	136.73	59.41	115.54	361.90
Hong Kong, China	217.28	231.97	715.17	650.63	409.98	498.21	667.47
India	4.61	55.60	75.60	63.28	33.76	35.78	37.23
Indonesia	7.82	9.75	14.87	13.83	10.02	10.19	8.71
Japan	52.44	94.88	128.04	77.66	56.17	105.41	135.12
Korea, Rep.	88.20	133.58	118.46	148.90	129.59	90.96	133.81
Malaysia	55.99	31.10	35.67	45.01	39.33	42.19	37.64
Pakistan	41.92	127.34	24.86	6.57	5.33	0.22	N/A
Philippines	9.10	5.19	7.10	11.15	14.27	14.82	13.16
Singapore	99.29	91.53	131.63	129.34	90.14	65.48	67.65
Thailand	15.29	47.44	36.40	65.24	60.12	76.83	68.64
Viet Nam	NA	NA	7.12	16.51	NA	11.71	9.64

GDP = gross domestic product, NA = not available, PRC = People's Republic of China.

Source: World Bank: World Development Indicators.

2015 of 667.5%. Regional averages for East Asia and the Pacific were around 100% in 2014 and spiked to above 240% in 2015, predominantly at the account of the huge increase in the PRC (from 115.5% in 2014 to 361.9% in 2015). Most of other markets in the East Asia and Pacific region experienced an increase in the traded value relative to GDP as well in 2015, but nowhere near the numbers that the PRC saw. The average for South Asian markets stood much lower at around 33%, predominantly reflecting the situation in India (37.2%).

Key regional developing economies, such as the Philippines, Viet Nam, and India have low stock market turnover and traded value ratios that suggest lower levels of liquidity than other regional markets. The lower level of liquidity may impose potential costs – as well as asymmetric information – on foreign investors when investing in these markets. For example, Batten and Vinh (2015) show that foreign investors need to adopt a long-term investment horizon and employ a buy and hold strategy to exploit potential growth prospects given the high market entry costs. These investors avoid firms with riskier financial management practices and where information asymmetries provide advantages to domestic investors. Overall, their findings support the importance of linking deregulation with financial market openness and transparency to enhance and encourage international portfolio investment.

A related statistic is the stock market turnover ratio, which is the value of domestic shares traded divided by their market capitalization, instead of GDP. This statistic measures the frequency that shares change hands and is typically annualized by multiplying the monthly average by 12. The US in December 2015 had a turnover ratio of 165.0. The values for selected Asia-Pacific countries are reported in Table 16.4. Interestingly, while most of the listed countries in the Asia-Pacific region have turnover ratios less than 100 – an expected result for undeveloped markets such as the Philippines and Viet Nam that have ratios of 16 and 36, respectively, in 2015 – East Asian developing nations overall had a higher value of 192.9. The PRC also had a ratio greater than the US (239.3 in 2014).[3]

In 2001, an article in the *Economist* (2001)[4] highlighted the fact that the trading frequency in certain developing markets – notably Pakistan, the Republic of Korea; Taipei,China; and India – had ratios higher than in the US. These higher ratios are due to differences in regulations concerning free-float, liquidity restrictions, transaction costs as well as culture. For example, Beracha, Fedenia, and Skiba (2014) examine the effects of cross-cultural differences on institutional investors' trading frequency. These authors show that as cultural distance between

Table 16.4 Stock market turnover ratio

Country, Region/Year	2000	2005	2008	2010	2012	2014	2015
United States	197.13	151.71	407.63	208.44	173.29	148.03	165.15
South Asia	**327.90**	**102.83**	**142.78**	**63.95**	**48.15**	**46.33**	**50.31**
East Asia and Pacific	**97.63**	**89.06**	**178.83**	**118.81**	**86.85**	**107.86**	**221.98**
PRC	NA	97.64	219.54	205.02	135.97	199.16	480.29
Hong Kong, China	59.83	39.92	118.02	54.87	38.02	44.88	64.95
India	NA	83.87	142.99	66.25	48.77	46.89	50.92
Indonesia	48.12	34.21	76.80	28.98	21.47	21.49	21.24
Japan	78.58	94.86	199.27	111.56	96.19	110.66	113.82
Korea, Rep.	289.24	167.09	252.17	149.26	134.36	105.85	149.75
Malaysia	46.41	24.73	43.50	28.09	26.50	31.08	29.11
Pakistan	467.95	307.69	181.04	30.66	NA	NA	NA
Philippines	28.38	13.45	23.77	14.14	15.56	16.12	16.09
Singapore	62.26	45.32	95.49	47.25	34.08	26.65	30.94
Thailand	66.16	72.50	102.84	80.09	61.28	72.17	77.79
Viet Nam	NA	NA	74.44	63.57	NA	47.33	35.98

NA = not available, PRC = People's Republic of China.

Source: World Bank: World Development Indicators.

the investors and their stock holdings increases, institutions trade with lower frequency. They also show that traders from different cultural backgrounds behave differently when faced with information asymmetry that cultural differences generate.[5]

It is also worth pointing out that turnover ratios are time-varying and the important role this plays in driving market liquidity. According to data available from the St. Louis Federal Reserve, the stock market turnover ratio (value traded/capitalization) for the US,[6] prior to the global financial crisis in 2005 was 153.4. This ratio peaked at 292.6 in 2008 and was 153.0 in December 2014. The St. Louis Federal Reserve also reports this statistic for a number of other countries, including the PRC. For example, in 2009 the statistic was 291.0, and later fell to 139.6 in 2012 as a result of trading restrictions imposed by the Peoples Bank of China. The later relaxation of these same rules increased trading. For example, in 2015 the China Securities Regulatory Commission banned the margin-trading businesses of brokerages from using so-called umbrella trusts and allowed fund managers to lend shares to short sellers. Later they relaxed rules on margin trading after measures including an interest-rate cut failed to stop equities falling.[7]

Analysis of data showing the number of listed companies in any given stock market highlights an important trend in the Asia-Pacific region: the increase in market capitalization of regional stock markets is primarily driven by an increase in the number of listed companies, with many of these new listings being the result of privatization of state-owned enterprises. Worldwide listings of the number of firms are presented in Figures 16.1 (numbers of firms) and Figure 16.2 (percentages of listed firms) for the period from 2005 to 2015.

Figure 16.2 shows that worldwide the number of listed firms, as reported by the World Federation of Exchanges, has increased from around 41,829 in 2005 to above 51,403 in 2016. There was minimal growth in listed firms in the Americas and Europe and declining listings in the US: the latter attributed to the withdrawal of many non-US based multinationals from US exchanges due to the high cost of regulatory compliance. Thus, the increase in firm numbers worldwide is largely driven by new listings in Asia and the Pacific. Figure 16.3 shows this more clearly when the number of listed firms is expressed as a percentage of the total. In this case the Asia-Pacific region accounted for 43.8% of listed firms in 2005, while this region in 2015 now accounts for 51.3%. Given that US stock markets have greater capitalization this highlights the fact that on average the market capitalization of firms in the Asia-Pacific region is less than that for the other regions.

Figure 16.4, provides further detail on the number of listed firms in the Asia-Pacific region by comparing the number of firms in the PRC, India, and Japan. This figure clearly shows that the increase in the number of listed firms in the region is being driven by new listings in the PRC (total now 2,828 in 2014) and India (5,860 in 2014). In fact, in Japan, the numbers of listed firms have fallen from 4,361 in 2005 to 3,509 in 2014. Interestingly, many of these new firms are genuine start-ups often based in technology and financial services.

Zhang's (2004) analysis of the privatization process in the PRC provides relevant insights into the process of privatization within the region. Privatization invariably brings about a change in the corporate governance in many of these institutions, along with an increase in industry concentration, with many failing to significantly improve financial performance. The paper by Greacen and Greacen (2004) analyzing reforms in the Thai electricity sector also highlight externalities associated with the privatization process unless there is due regulatory oversight. In the Thai case, Greacen and Greacen (2004) conclude that electric utilities have been able to successfully reject certain aspects of neo-liberal reform (competition, regulatory oversight) while embracing others (stock market capitalization).

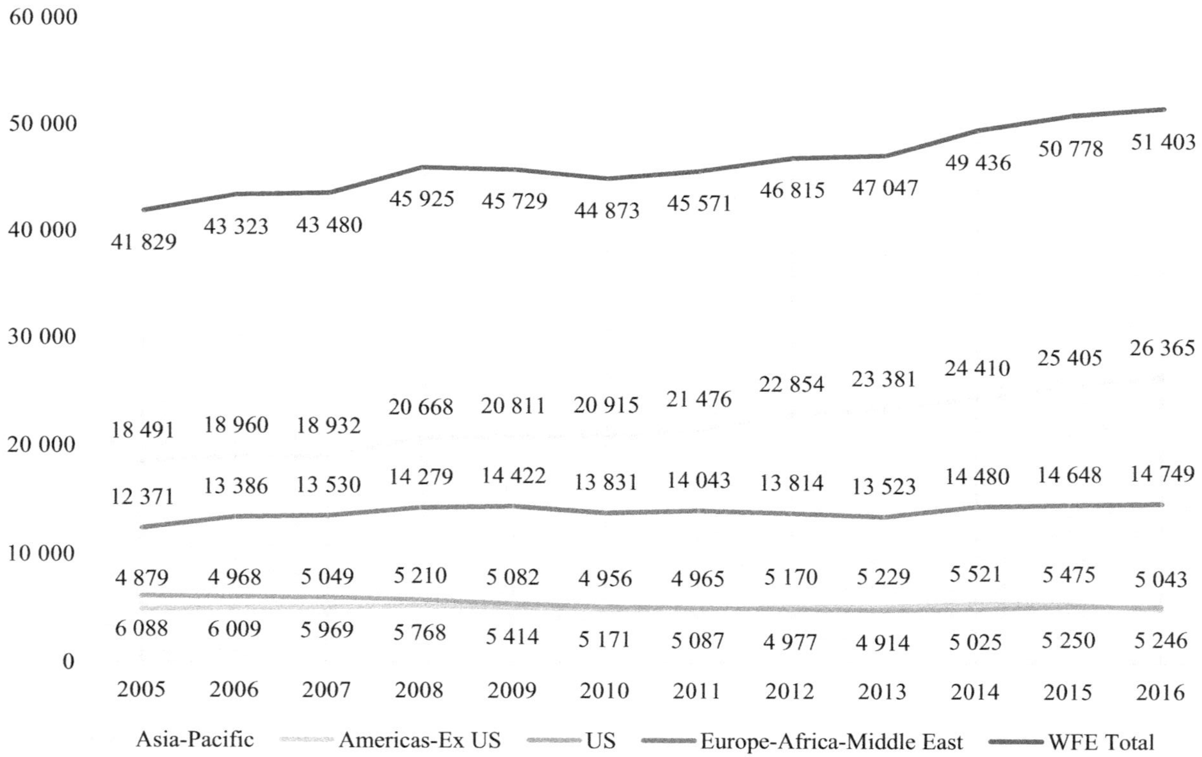

Figure 16.2 Number of listed companies worldwide

The figure shows the number of listed companies per selected World regions. The data is based on the statistics provided by the World Federation of Exchanges. In order to make the time-series data comparable, we assumed that prior to becoming members of WFE exchanges had the same number of listed companies as reported in the year of joining the WFE and that after discontinuing its membership (while the stock exchange remained independently operational) the number of listed companies remained the same.

Source: World Federation of Exchanges and own calculations.

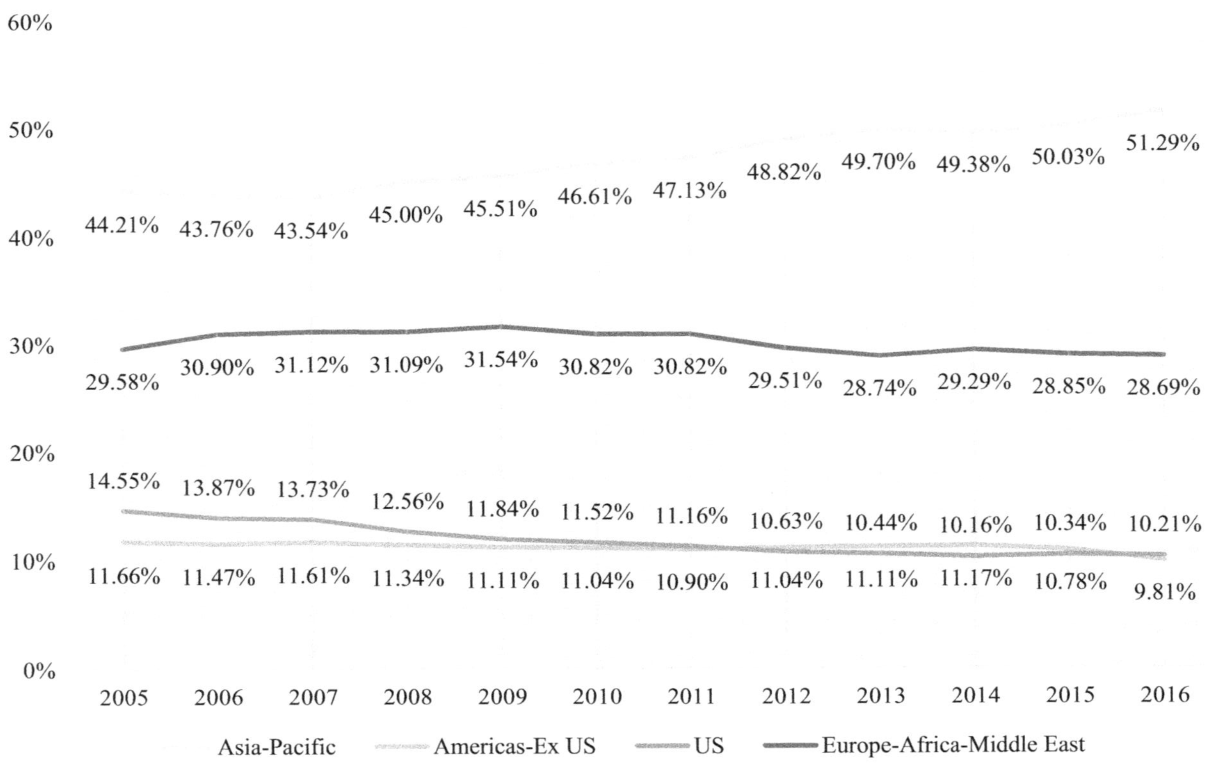

	2005	2006	2007	2008	2009	2010	2011	2012	2013	2014	2015	2016
Europe-Africa-Middle East	44.21%	43.76%	43.54%	45.00%	45.51%	46.61%	47.13%	48.82%	49.70%	49.38%	50.03%	51.29%
Asia-Pacific	29.58%	30.90%	31.12%	31.09%	31.54%	30.82%	30.82%	29.51%	28.74%	29.29%	28.85%	28.69%
Americas-Ex US	14.55%	13.87%	13.73%	12.56%	11.84%	11.16%	11.52%	10.63%	10.44%	10.16%	10.34%	10.21%
US	11.66%	11.47%	11.61%	11.34%	11.11%	11.04%	10.90%	11.04%	11.11%	11.17%	10.78%	9.81%

Figure 16.3 Share of listed companies worldwide

The figure shows the share of listed companies per selected World regions as a percent of the total number of listed companies as reported by the World Federation of Exchanges. The data is based on the statistics provided by the World Federation of Exchanges. In order to make the time–series data comparable, we assumed that prior to becoming members of WFE exchanges had the same number of listed companies as reported in the year of joining the WFE, and that after discontinuing its membership (while the stock exchange remained independently operational) the number of listed companies remained the same.

Source: World Federation of Exchanges and own calculations.

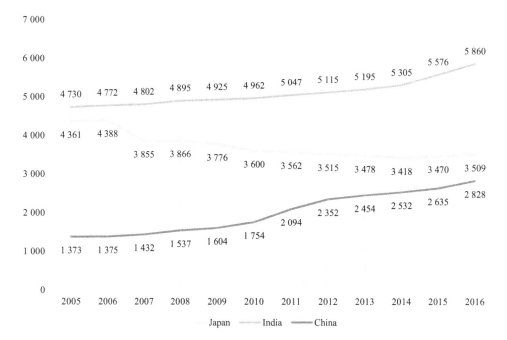

Figure 16.4 Number of listed companies in the major Asian stock markets

The figure shows the number of listed companies in Japan, India, and the PRC. The data is based on the statistics provided by the World Federation of Exchanges. In order to make the time-series data comparable, we assumed that prior to becoming members of WFE exchanges had the same number of listed companies as reported in the year of joining the WFE and that after discontinuing its membership (while the stock exchange remained independently operational) the number of listed companies remained the same.

Source: World Federation of Exchanges and own calculations.

Table 16.5 Distributional statistics of CAPE for the selected Asian markets

Market	Current	Max	Median	Min	25th pct.	75th pct.	Start Date
Japan	22.3	92	37	15	23	58	1969
PRC	11.4	49	17	10	15	25	1995
India	17.1	49	20	16	18	27	1994
Indonesia	17.8	69	23	10	19	28	1992
Malaysia	15.8	35	21	16	20	24	1992
Korea, Rep	11.9	29	15	11	13	20	1995
Taipei,China	18.5	29	19	11	17	22	1995
Thailand	16.9	148	20	12	18	51	1992

Data as of 16 November 2016.

Source: Research Affiliates LLC.

Valuations in the Asian markets

Many characteristics and special features of the Asian stock markets are also reflected in their valuations and relative performance measures. As shown in Table 16.5, using data provided by Research Affiliates,[8] the most recent valuations (November 2016), as proxied by the so-called Shiller's CAPE measure (also termed a cyclically adjusted P/E ratio), for the largest markets in the Asian region are below the historical 25th percentile of CAPE distribution. This implies that Asian markets are currently undervalued from both ahistorical and global perspective. These valuations may be compared to those where central banks have engaged in recent years in massive unconventional monetary policies in recent years to facilitate economic recovery post global financial crisis. For example, according to the same data, the comparable CAPE ratio for the large cap US stocks is 26.9 (well above 75th percentile of the CAPE distribution for US), while on the other hand, stock markets in Germany, France, or the UK fare similarly to their Asian counterparts, with CAPE values around historical 25th percentile.

Capital raising in primary markets

According to recent market reports by EY, Asian markets have taken a global lead when raising capital in primary equity markets.[9] Of particular concern has been the pricing of initial public offerings (IPOs). Asian markets accounted for 54% of the value of all deals in 2016, and 60% of all deals by number. In terms of deal volume, the PRC has ranked first for the past five years or so, with Hong Kong, China exchanges raising almost twice as many funds in December 2016 (USD 25.2 billion) as the NYSE (USD 13.6 billion). Shanghai came in second in 2016 with USD 14.2 billion raised, while the TSE came in fourth (USD 9.3 billion). The EY report also provides a very positive outlook for the IPO deals in Asian markets in the near future, as many small and medium-sized companies in the PRC, are in the pipeline, with up to 55% to be listed on the Shenzhen Stock Exchange). Even though the main focus and growth potential lies within the PRC market, primary markets in Japan and the Republic of Korea were also very active and maintain good prospects for the near future as well. In the rest of ASEAN, markets investors seem to be more cautious and primary markets there are modest.

Seven countries in the region have specialized capital markets that specifically cater to SMEs (ADB 2015).[10] The oldest one has been established in the Republic of Korea (KOSDAQ) back in 1987 within the Korea Exchange, while the newest initiatives emerged in India in 2012 (within Bombay Stock Exchange and National Stock Exchange). By far the largest in market capitalization are the specialized SME exchanges in the PRC (within Shenzhen Stock Exchange), with a combined market capitalization of around USD 1.2 trillion at the end of 2014 which translates into an average market capitalization of around USD 1 billion per company. The second largest exchange according to the same measure is KOSDAQ with the market capitalization of USD 130 billion (company average of around USD 122 million). The smallest such exchange is EMERGE in India with the market capitalization of USD 68 million and the average company capitalization of around USD 11 million. All other specialized SME exchanges in the region have market capitalizations of below USD 12 billion. This huge heterogeneity raises issues related to the definition of SMEs in various countries in the region and the capital market potentials for start-ups and SMEs.

Issues confronting stock market development

There is a rich literature that argues that countries are motivated to improve the structure of their financial systems, including stock markets, due to the positive effect that stock market development has on economic growth. Yartey (2008) provides an excellent summary of the relevant literature, which may be expressed in terms of the following impacts: (1) stock markets provide a mechanism for growing companies to raise capital; (2) they provide an alternative to bank financing; (3) and this financing – in the form of equity – is long term, thereby facilitating the difficult process of mobilizing savings to long term financing of industry. Nonetheless, there is the possibility of perverse incentives arising from having more developed markets. This is evident in the creative forms of financial engineering that many benefit the few, rather than the many, and the fact that greater stock market liquidity may negatively influence corporate governance and enhance investor myopia, to name two well-known criticisms.

Despite these criticisms, as noted by Yartey (2008), the empirical evidence shows that the development of local stock markets has been a key regulatory feature of the domestic financial liberalization programs of most emerging markets and a major channel for foreign capital flows. In conclusion, Yartey (2008) finds that income level, domestic investment, banking sector development, private capital flows, and stock market liquidity are important determinants of stock market development in emerging markets, and once established, at the later stages of financial market development, stock markets provide competition to banks.

In the Asian region, a market long dominated by its banking sector and with a relatively undeveloped bond market, this competition may improve pricing and ensure a better range of financing products and services are available. Yartey's findings support earlier work by Caporale et al. (2004) that show that a well-developed stock market can foster long-run economic growth with a well-functioning stock market facilitating the process of capital accumulation, and better resource allocation. More recently, Levine, Lin and Xie (2016), along with a number of other authors, highlight the importance of the rule of law in promoting development and ensuring sustainable growth. Their analysis shows that the adverse consequences of banking crises on equity issuances, firm profitability, employment, and investment efficiency are smaller in countries with stronger shareholder protection laws.

This finding adds to the debate on the relative merit of having bank-based versus market-based financial systems. Thus, while an earlier work by Levine (2002) showed that financial development was linked with economic growth, with no support for either the bank-based or the market-based view, more recent efforts by La Porta et al. (2006) further qualified the role of the rule of law by finding little evidence that public enforcement benefits stock markets, but strong evidence that laws mandating disclosure and facilitating private enforcement through liability rules benefit stock markets.

While there may have been limited region wide take up of some of key G20 regulatory priorities (e.g., cross-border, post-trade, automated trading and high frequency trading [HFT], operational resilience and cybercrime, and capital issues), there has been considerable attention paid to local issues include greater electronification of exchanges and trading, increasing participation in financial markets (especially foreign participation), and ensuring that there is availability of new technologies to transform the way markets operate. Collectively these initiatives have been directed at improving market efficiency and openness. Interestingly, as noted by a OECD-UNCTAD (2016) report on investment measures "the majority of the investment policy changes introduced by G20 members since September 2015 enhanced openness for international investment, such that more than 80% of newly taken measures specific to foreign direct investment were liberalizing in nature. This confirms the long-term trend since monitoring of G20 policy measures began in 2009." Some of the recent measures identified included:

The PRC simplified the capital registration system for companies in the PRC; India liberalized rules on inward FDI in a variety of sectors.

Indonesia adopted a new "negative list" for foreign investment, with the new list increasing the allowed ceiling for foreign investment in a number of sectors

The Republic of Korea adopted amendments to the Foreign Investment Promotion Act in order to simplify FDI registration procedures (OECD-UNCTAD 2016: 2).

Despite these liberalizing initiatives, many challenges remain. The most recent Bank for International Settlements (BIS 2016) survey once again revealed the extent that foreign exchange and derivative trading remain concentrated in the existing financial centers of London and New York. Many local markets remain undeveloped in terms of the scale and scope of these markets, which are necessary for risk management. In addition, high transactions costs may impede or set limits to arbitrage, thereby inhibiting price convergence between related financial products.

Other key impediments

It is well known that when a stock market is segmented, a local investor can benefit in terms of maximizing return and minimizing risk through international investment. What may impede these potential investments are impediments, both structural and regulatory, such as capital controls, high transactions costs and asymmetric and costly information. However, even if these costs are low, or absent entirely, when markets are highly integrated there are few benefits arising from international investment. Collectively, such factors may encourage investor behavioral responses such as home bias; the favoring of local investment despite benefits from cross-border investment.

A number of international studies, including the recent paper by Batten, Morgan, and Szilágyi (2015) demonstrate limited diversification benefits to Asian stock market investors for engaging in cross-border regional portfolio investment due to the high degree of integration of countries in the Asia-Pacific region. However, the degree of integration varies over time and so provides benefits over different investment horizons for investors. For example, short-term investors, with an investment horizon of one year, receive some benefits, whereas longer-term investors receive few diversification benefits due to the well-documented increasing integration of domestic, regional, and world markets caused by enhanced communications, better trading and information technology, and market deregulation.

Another impediment to stock market development is the absence of liquidity in some markets. The market turnover statistics discussed earlier reveal the highly segmented nature of stock market liquidity with the financial centers of Singapore and Hong Kong, China being the most liquid. Charoenwong, Ding, and Yang's (2013) analysis of Asian stock market liquidity reveals a sharp decline in stock liquidity during both the Asian and the more recent global financial crisis. Stock liquidity and trading activity are both found to decrease after large market declines, although there is cross-sectional variation: the Republic of Korea and Taipei,China are more sensitive than Singapore. Their findings confirm earlier results by Wong and Fung (2001) on the impact of crisis on the liquidity in the Hong Kong, China stock market.

Conclusion

Asian stock markets now play a vital role worldwide. From a regional perspective, they also provide an important avenue for mobilizing domestic savings for both lower risk infrastructure investment, and higher risk technology and other innovative start-ups. In many cases, private sector, or possibly private-public sector partnerships, represent a departure from historic government financing of infrastructure. From an international investor viewpoint, however, opportunities for portfolio diversification may arise due to the time-varying nature of stock market integration. That said, the failure to build adequate derivatives and other securities market infrastructure may impede risk management and thereby limit potential foreign and domestic investment despite the best intensions of government to promote an investment agenda. Longer term, domestic or home bias limits – as in most developed markets – the appetite for regional investment despite its attractiveness from an investment viewpoint. Encouraging the development of stock and other financial markets, by limiting information asymmetries, relaxing capital controls and encouraging technological innovation, provide broader benefits in terms of market scale and scope that in turn should facilitate the attainment of broader economic objectives and goals.

Notes

1 For example, see Armstrong (2015).
2 See http://asean.org/asean-economic-community/.
3 Also, see Cruz, Gao, and Song (2014: 22) for other international comparisons with the PRC's stock markets.
4 www.economist.com/node/731687.
5 www.uwyo.edu/hskiba/web/papers/skiba_culture_turnover.pdf.
6 https://fred.stlouisfed.org/series/DDEM01USA156NWDB.
7 See SCRC Announcements, Decrees and Policy Interpretation: www.csrc.gov.cn/pub/csrc_en/laws/overRule/PolicyInterpretation/.
8 www.researchaffiliates.com/en_us/asset-allocation/equities.html.
9 www.ey.com/ipo.
10 PRC, India, Malaysia, Philippines, Republic of Korea, Thailand, and Viet Nam.

References

Armstrong, S. 2015. The Economic Impact of the Australia-United States Free Trade Agreement. AJRC Working Paper No. 01/2015. Canberra: Australia-Japan Research Centre.

Asian Development Bank (ADB). 2015. Asia SME Finance Monitor 2014. Manila: Asian Development Bank.

Batten, J.A., P. Morgan, and P.G. Szilágyi. 2015. Time-Varying Stock Market Integration: Asian Perspectives. *Singapore Economic Review* 60(1).

Batten, J.A., and V.V. Xuan. 2015. Foreign Ownership in Emerging Stock Markets. *Journal of Multinational Financial Management* 32–33(1): 15–24.

Bank for International Settlements (BIS). 2016. Triennial Central Bank Survey of Foreign Exchange and OTC Derivatives Markets in 2016. Basel: Bank for International Settlements.

Beracha, E., M. Fedenia, and H. Skiba. 2014. Culture's Impact on Institutional Investors' Trading Frequency. *International Review of Financial Analysis* 31(C): 34–47.

Caporale, G.M., P.G.A. Howells, and A.M. Soliman. 2004. Stock Market Development and Economic Growth: The Casual Linkage. *Journal of Economic Development* 29(1): 33–50.

Charoenwong, C., D.K. Ding, and Y.C. Yang. 2013. Liquidity and Crises in Asian Equity Markets. In *Market Microstructure in Emerging and Developed Markets*. Research Collection Lee Kong Chian School of Business, Singapore: Singapore Management University, pp. 407–424.

Cruz, P.C., Y. Gao, and L.L. Song. 2014. The People's Republic of China's Financial Markets: Are They Deep and Liquid Enough for Renminbi Internationalization? ADBI Working Paper No. 477. Tokyo: Asian Development Bank Institute.

Filardo, A., J. George, M. Loretan, G. Ma, A. Munro, I. Shim, P. Wooldridge, J. Yetman, and H. Zhu. 2010. The International Financial Crisis: Timeline, Impact and Policy Responses in Asia and the Pacific. BIS Papers 52, July: 21–82.

Greacen, C.S., and C. Greacen. 2004. Thailand's Electricity Reforms: Privatization of Benefits and Socialization of Costs and Risks. *Pacific Affairs* 77(3): 517–541.

Guillen, M. 2012. The Global Economic and Financial Crisis: A Timeline. Philadelphia, PA: The Lauder Institute, Wharton School, University of Pennsylvania.

Hatzvi, E., J. Meredith, and W. Nixon. 2015. Chinese Capital Flows and Capital Account Liberalisation. Reserve Bank of Australia Bulletin December Quarter: 39–48.

La Porta, R., F. Lopez-De-Silanes, and A. Shleifer. 2006. What Works in Securities Laws? *Journal of Finance* 61(1): 1–32.

Levine, R. 2002. Bank-Based or Market-Based Financial Systems: Which Is Better? *Journal of Financial Intermediation* 11(4): 398–428.

Levine, R., C. Lin, and W. Xie. 2016. Spare Tire? Stock Markets, Banking Crises, and Economic Recoveries. *Journal of Financial Economics* 120(1): 81–101.

Lipinsky, F., and L.L. Ong. 2014. Asia's Stock Markets: Are There Crouching Tigers and Hidden Dragons? Monetary and Capital Markets Department, International Monetary Fund. IMF Working Paper No. 14/37. Washington, DC: International Monetary Fund.

OECD-UNCTAD. 2016. Fifteenth Report on G20 Investment Measures, 21 June. www.oecd.org/daf/inv/investment-policy/15th-Investment-Report-on-G20-Investment-Measures.pdf

Purfield, C., H. Oura, C. Kramer, and A. Jobs. 2006. Asian Equity Markets: Growth, Opportunities, and Challenges. IMF Working Paper No. 06/266. Washington, DC: International Monetary Fund.

Wong, J., and L. Fung. 2001. Liquidity of the Hong Kong Stock Market since the Asian Financial Crisis. Basel: Bank for International Settlements. www.bis.org/cgfs/conf/mar02n.pdf

Xiao, F., and D. Kimball. 2005. Effectiveness and Effects of China's Capital Controls. *China & World Economy* 13(4): 58–69.

Yartey, C.A. 2008. The Determinants of Stock Market Development in Emerging Economies: Is South Africa Different? IMF Working Paper No. 08/32. Washington, DC: International Monetary Fund.

Zhang, L.-Y. 2004. The Roles of Corporatization and Stock Market Listing in Reforming China's State Industry. *World Development* 32(12): 2031–2047.

17

INSTITUTIONAL INVESTORS AND SOVEREIGN WEALTH FUNDS IN ASIA

Choong Lyol Lee

Introduction

Institutional investors are defined as non-bank institutions or organizations that trade securities or other financial assets in large share quantities or amounts. They usually pool together large amounts of funds on behalf of others, and invest them in a variety of different financial instruments and asset classes. Major examples are sovereign wealth funds, insurance companies, pension funds, and investment funds.

The number and size of assets of institutional investors has increased globally but also in Asia for the past decade. Several new sovereign wealth funds have been established and the asset sizes of investment fund have grown substantially.

Despite their rapid expansion in Asian and global financial markets, relatively little is known about institutional investors. Although some case studies on the activities of institutional investors on economic development and their influence on financial market have been made recently, including Genberg (2015), Inderst and Stewart (2014), and Park and Estrada (2009), a comprehensive study of these investors has not been provided yet, especially in Asia.

Several reasons explain it. First, institutional investors are so diverse in terms of its purpose of establishment that it is not easy to analyze. Second, it is very difficult to collect and consolidate the data and its information. Their financial statements and data are not consolidated in different financial supervisory agencies of different countries and sometimes in different forms.

This chapter examines the activities of institutional investors in Asia. The focus is mostly on institutional investors in the People's Republic of China (PRC); Hong Kong, China; Japan; India; the Republic of Korea; Malaysia; and Singapore. It investigates both the time series and cross-sectional data. It focuses on the investment activity of institutional investors such as recent asset trends or its portfolios or, if possible, financial performances.

The remainder of this chapter is structured as follows. The next section describes different types of institutional investors in Asia. It provides definitions of major institutional investors, including sovereign wealth funds, pension funds, insurance companies and investment funds, and then describes their asset sizes, types and characteristics. The following section provides details of two of major institutional investors for each type of institutional investor. The final section concludes.

Institutional investors in Asia

Sovereign wealth funds

Sovereign wealth funds (SWFs) are public investment agencies which manage part of the mostly foreign assets of national state. They are usually state-owned and have no or only very limited explicit liabilities. SWFs are typically created when governments have budgetary surpluses or extra financial sources. They utilize a sovereign wealth fund as a way to funnel it into investments rather than simply keeping it in the central bank or channeling it back into the economy.

SWFs are classified either by the purpose of establishment or by the source of the fund. Major sources of SWFs are a fiscal surplus, a balance of payment surplus, or extra foreign exchange reserve. It can be made by the commodity export revenue such as oil and gas exports or a tight government policy.

Several reasons can be given to the government to establish SWFs. First, it is a stabilization fund. It may reduce the volatility of government revenues or to counter the boom-bust cycles' adverse effect on government spending and the national economy. Second, it can be a saving fund to transfer current resources to future generations. When a country has a large amount of natural resource or financial one today, it may worry about the future depletion of those resources. Then the SWFs can be good way to transfer it to the future generation because government fund is usually made of long-term financial assets. Third, it can be a development fund to help a specific projects or industrial policies. Finally, it can be made by some political or strategic reasons such as war chests for uncertain times.

In reality, many SWFs tend to serve the several purposes at the same time. For example, several SWFs in the Middle East were made not only to protect the national economy from the volatility of oil price but also to transfer the wealth to the future generation.

While few SWFs reveal their full portfolios, *it is known that SWFs* use a variety of investment strategies. Some funds invest exclusively in publicly listed financial assets such as government bonds, equities but others invest in all of the major asset classes *including* foreign direct investment. *They purchase almost* all types of companies and assets, including start-ups like Xiaomi or renewable energy companies like Bloom Energy.

The size of SWFs in the world has substantially increased for the past decade. While it was only USD 3,417 billion in September 2007 but it reached about USD 7,400 billion at the end of 2015.

Table 17.1 shows some characteristics of major SWFs in Asia. First, currently, 10 SWFs exist in Asia and their assets amount 28.0% of the total assets of global SWFs. SWFs in Asia are mainly sourced by foreign reserve and the share of resource related funds is very small.

Second, almost half of SWFs in Asia are established since 2005. China Investment Corporation, the largest SWF in Asia and Korea Investment Corporation were established in 2005 and Timor-Leste Petroleum Fund of East Timor, State Capital Investment Fund of Viet Nam, Government of Investment Unit of Indonesia were done in 2006.

Third, the PRC dominates the SWF market in Asia. About 64.7% of SWFs in Asia are originated from the PRC. It is because the PRC, which maintained a large amount of trade surplus since 2000 began to exploit SWF as a tool to manage its extra foreign exchange reserve.

Fourth, there is no sovereign wealth fund in South Asia. It is because most countries of South Asia such as India and Pakistan did not have current account or budget surplus for a long time or did not have any large amount of specific natural resource to export to the rest of the world.

Table 17.1 Major sovereign wealth funds in Asia

	Name	Country	Total Assets (USD billion)	Founded Year	Purpose	Source
1	China Investment Corporation	PRC	847.6	2007	Reserve Investment Fund	Foreign Reserves
2	SAFE Investment Company	PRC	474.0	1997	Reserve Investment Fund	Foreign Reserves
3	Government of Singapore Investment Corporation	Singapore	344.0	1981	Reserve Investment Fund	Foreign Reserves
4	Tamasek Holdings	Singapore	193.6	1974	Development Fund	Legacy State Ownership
5	Korea Investment Corporation	Republic of Korea	91.8	2005	Reserve Investment Fund	Foreign Reserves
6	Brunei Investment Agency	Brunei Darussalam	40	1983	Stabilization Fund	Commodity – Oil and Gas
7	Khazanah Nasional	Malaysia	34.9	1993	Development Fund	Legacy State Ownership
8	Timor-Leste Petroleum Fund	Timor-Leste	16.9	2005	Stabilization Fund	Commodity – Oil and Gas
9	State Capital Investment Fund	Viet Nam	0.5	2006	Development Fund	Legacy State Ownership
10	Government of Investment Unit	Indonesia	0.3	2006	Development Fund	Legacy State Ownership
	Asia Total		2043.6			

PRC = People's Republic of China.

Source: Sovereign Wealth Funds Institute (www.swfinstitute.org/sovereign-wealth-fund-rankings/).

Several kinds of SWFs exist in Asia. First, the stabilization and saving funds was established by the countries with oil and gas exporting country such as Brunei and Timor-Leste or the countries with manufacturing products such as the PRC and the Republic of Korea. Second, development funds such as Singapore's Temasek and Malaysia's Khazanah Nasional was also made. They started to invest internationally and be operated more like a commercial investment company with the expansion of its fund asset size. While these institutions operate on a commercial basis today, they are established as a tool to pursue national economic development policies. In that sense, it is fully consistent that they allocated a large volume of funds to the home market.

The China Investment Corporation may be seen as a hybrid between a reserve fund like the GIC or KIC and that of a private equity fund. Its size is so large that it is better to take care of wider objectives.

Pension funds

Pension funds are funds providing retirement income for the employees or contributors. Usually, it is contributed by both the employer and employees. The liability and asset of pension fund are with very long-term maturity. Its amount of asset is very large and in many nations it is the largest institutional investor. Many large-scale pension funds are public, although they are commonly run by independent financial intermediaries. In some cases, large funds operate their pension funds in-house.

Pension funds are categorized in several ways. First, they are classified as open vs. closed pension funds. Open pension funds support at least one pension plan with no restriction on membership while closed pension funds support only pension plans that are limited to certain employees. Second, pension funds can be distinguished into public pension fund and private pension funds.

The size of pension funds in the world has rapidly increased for the past decade. The asset size of pension funds of major 16 economies have increased from USD 20,507 billion in 2002 to USD 36,023 billion in 2014.[1] It annual average growth rate recorded 7.0%. Another study by Towers Watson (2015) shows that the asset size of the world's top 300 pension funds increased from USD 5,528 billion in 2002 to USD 15,361 billion in 2014. It annual average growth rate recorded 9.3% for this period.

According to the statistics on 300 world largest pension funds as in Tables 17.2 and 17.3, several characteristics of pension funds in Asia can be observed. First, only 28 funds from 10

Table 17.2 Pension funds in Asia of 300 world largest pension funds in 2015

	Economy	Asset Value (USD billion)	Ratio (%)	Number of Funds
1	Japan	1,788,531	56.6	15
2	Republic of Korea	459,101	14.5	3
3	PRC	247,361	7.8	1
4	Malaysia	215,450	6.8	2
5	Singapore	207,872	6.6	1
6	Taipei,China	102,043	3.2	3
7	India	80,741	2.6	1
8	Thailand	21,489	0.7	1
9	Philippines	20,313	0.6	1
10	Viet Nam	17,283	0.5	1
	Total	3,160,184	100.00	28

PRC = People's Republic of China.

Source: Towers Watson (2015a). P&I/TW 300 Analysis. September 2015.

Table 17.3 Major pension funds in Asia

Rank in Asia	Name	Economy	Asset (USD billion)	World Rank
1	Government Pension Investment Fund	Japan	1,143.8	1
2	National Pension Service of ROK	Republic of Korea	429.8	3
3	National Social Security	PRC	247.4	7
4	Central Provident Fund	Singapore	207.9	10
5	Local Government Officials	Japan	194.7	11
6	Employees Provident Fund	Malaysia	184.7	13

(Continued)

Table 17.3 (Continued)

Rank in Asia	Name	Economy	Asset (USD billion)	World Rank
7	Pension Fund Association	Japan	98.1	25
8	Employees' Provident	India	80.7	34
9	National Public Service	Japan	67.5	46
10	Labor Pension Fund	Taipei,China	64.8	53
11	Public School Employee	Japan	48.8	69
12	Organization for Workers	Japan	46.3	78
13	Private School Employee	Japan	34.7	111

PRC = People's Republic of China.

Source: Towers Watson (2015b).

Asian countries are among the 300 largest pension funds in the world, with assets amounting to 20.6% of the total assets of the 300 world largest pension funds.

Second, Japan dominates the Asian pension fund markets. Assets of Japanese pension funds hold up to 58% of total asset of Asian pension funds and especially, asset of the Government Pension Investment of Japan amounts to 37.2% of total Asian pension fund asset.

Third, the pension funds of relatively high-income countries in Asia such as the Republic of Korea (14.9%), PRC (8.0%), Malaysia (7.0%), and Singapore (6.8%) take high portion. Those of low-income countries such as India, Thailand, Philippines, and Viet Nam only count less than 5% of total assets of Asian pension funds.

In the asset allocation, it was shown that pension funds of the Asian countries put more assets in the bonds and less assets on equities. It is either because Asian equity market is less developed or more volatile or because pension fund managers of the Asia and Pacific region are more conservative in terms of asset allocation.

Insurance

Insurance is a contract in which an individual or entity receives financial protection or reimbursement against losses from an insurance company. Insurance companies are made of life insurance companies, nonlife or property/casualty insurance one and composite one.

Generally, assets and liabilities of life insurance company are with longer-term maturity that that of nonlife insurance company because policies of nonlife insurance including automobile and homeowner policies provide payments depending on the loss from a particular financial event.

While there are many important indicators to represent the recent trend of insurance market, we rather focus on those of asset management of insurance company because this chapter only focus on the role and activities of institutional investors on the financial market. According to the Organisation for Economic Co-operation and Development (OECD) Insurance Statistics database and other national data sources on insurance, the assets of insurance industry in Asia amounted USD 6.4 trillion in 2014, taking 26.6% of the world insurance market.[2] Its annual growth rate for the past five years of 2009 to 2014 recorded 4.8%, higher than that of OECD countries of 1.6% of the same period. As a result, the share of insurance industry of Asia has increased from 24.0% in 2009 to 26.6% in 2014. The assets of insurance industries of the PRC, India, and the Republic of Korea increased substantially while those of Japan decreased for this time. Especially, the asset of insurance industry of Japan fell by 17.7% in 2013 and by 8.9% in

2014, respectively. On the contrary, that of the PRC and India have increased by 22.6% and 12.2% on average respectively from 2009 to 2015.

Despite this rapid expansion of the PRC's and India's insurance industry in Asia, still the insurance market of Asia is dominated by Japan. In 2014, the assets of the Japanese insurance industry amounted to 51.8% of the total assets of Asia while that of the PRC was 24.2%. The sum of those of these two countries amounted to almost 75% of the total assets of the insurance industry of Asia.

The composition rates of life insurance, nonlife insurance and composite insurance of Asian insurance industry are different from those of world. As seen in Figure 17.1a–c, the life insurance dominates the insurance market while those of composite insurance company make a very limited operation in Asia.

The portfolios of Asian insurance industry are not much different from those of rest of the world. Bond takes 55% to 60% of total assets and stock and loan and deposit do 10 to 15% in Asia.

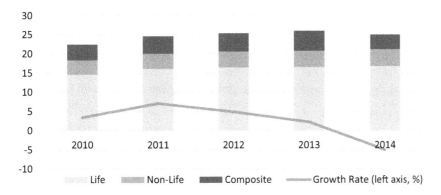

Figure 17.1a   Insurance industry in Asia by type: asset trend and growth rate in the world (USD trillion)

Sources: OECD. http://stats.oecd.org/; National Bureau of Statistics of China, *China Statistical Yearbook*, 2015; Insurance Regulatory and Development Authority of India, *Handbook on Indian Insurance Statistics* 2015–2016.

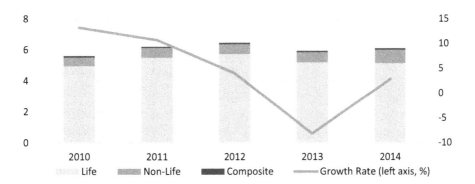

Figure 17.1b   Insurance industry in Asia by type: asset trend and growth rate of Asia (USD trillion)

Sources: OECD. http://stats.oecd.org/; National Bureau of Statistics of China, *China Statistical Yearbook*, 2015; Insurance Regulatory and Development Authority of India, *Handbook on Indian Insurance Statistics* 2015–2016.

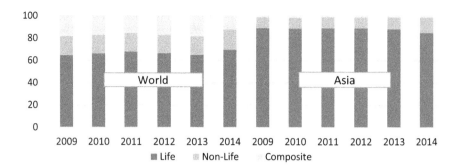

Figure 17.1c   Insurance industry in Asia by type: types of insurance company (in percentage)

Sources: OECD. http://stats.oecd.org/; National Bureau of Statistics of China, *China Statistical Yearbook*, 2015; Insurance Regulatory and Development Authority of India, *Handbook on Indian Insurance Statistics* 2015–2016.

Investment funds

Investment funds are institutional units, excluding pension funds and insurance companies, that consolidate investor's funds for the purpose of acquiring financial assets. Mutual funds including money market funds, investment trusts, unit trusts, and other collective investment units are included in this category.

According to the fund asset statistics from International Investment Fund Association (2016), the asset values of the world's investment funds have increased from USD 21.8 trillion in 2006 to USD 37.2 trillion in 2015. Investment funds in Asia held a total of USD 3.0 trillion assets in 2015, 8.5% of the world investment market. The ratio is relatively low when compared with those of other institutional investors such as SWFs (28.0%) or pension funds (20.0%) in Asia. It is because investment funds are relatively new financial instruments and Asian financial markets are relatively less developed than those in North America or Europe.

Despite their low stage of development, Asian investment funds have rapidly expanded very recently (Figure 17.2a). While the growth rate of assets of world investment funds was 4.4% and 18.5% in 2014 and 2015, respectively, the growth rate of Asian investment funds was 42.3% and 31.5%, respectively.

Investment funds in Asia have developed particularly in Japan, the PRC, and the Republic of Korea, whose shares amount to 92.5% of the region (Figure 17.2b). Especially, Japan and the PRC took 41.9% and 39.8%, respectively in 2015. It is quite noticeable that PRC investment funds rapidly expanded for the past several years. It is because the investment funds are introduced into the PRC as a new way of investment in addition to traditional bank deposits.

Asset portfolios of investment funds differ across Asian countries (Figure 17.2c). For example, the PRC's investment funds put 54.2% into the money market, compared to only 1.0% for Japanese investment funds at the end of 2015. The share for the Republic of Korea's and Taipei,China's investment funds is 23.3% and 48.6%, respectively. In general, the ratio of relatively long-term financial assets such as bond or equity are low while that of short-term ones such as money market is high. It is surprising that investment funds which seek high returns allocate such large amounts to a short liquidity market. It is because still the money market return rate in Asia is relatively high with low risk. It is shown that in Asia, equity (45.7%) is the most important financial asset, with money market investments coming second (26.9%).

Major institutional investors in Asia

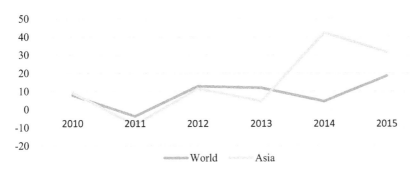

Figure 17.2a Assets of investment funds: growth rate (in percentage)

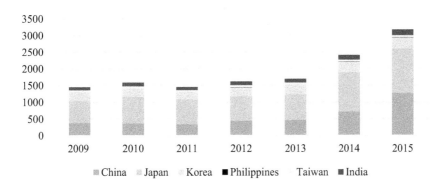

Figure 17.2b Assets of investment funds: asset of investment fund by countries (USD billion)

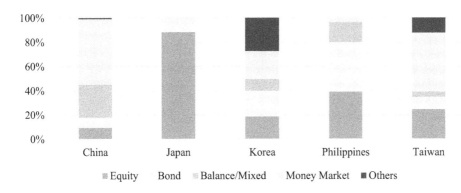

Figure 17.2c Assets of investment funds: asset composition of investment fund by type (in percentage)

Source: International Investment Fund Association. *Worldwide Regulated Open-End Fund Assets and Flows* (www.iifa. ca/industry_statistics/index.html).

Sovereign Wealth Funds

In this section, we provide a detailed overview of activities of two major Asian SWFs, namely the Government of Singapore Investment Corporation (GIC) and China Investment Corporation (CIC). The GIC is one of the oldest SWFs which has become a model for other SWFs in terms of management style and performance. The CIC is chosen because it was the largest SWF in Asia amounting to 40% of Total SWFs assets in Asia.

Government of Singapore Investment Corporation

The Government of Singapore Investment Corporation (GIC) was founded in 1981 to manage Singapore's foreign exchange reserves. Its major mission is to preserve and to enhance the international purchasing power of the foreign exchange reserves. GIC's mandate is to achieve good long-term returns over the investment time horizon of 20 years.

The governance structure of the GIC is unique. The GIC fund is owned by the government and as a result, the Ministry of Finance of Singapore sets the investment objective, risk parameters and investment horizon for the asset portfolio. It also ensures that a competent board of directors is in place. The GIC Board assumes responsibility for asset allocation and the overall performance of the portfolio while GIC's Management is responsible for formulating and executing investment strategies and for individual investments.

At the end of 2014, the GIC invested more than USD 100 billion into a variety of international financial assets. Equity and bond are the most investment asset of GIC. Equity takes 54% of total assets and bonds and cash take 34%. More detail, developed market equity and emerging market equity take 26% and 19% of total asset and private equity, 9%. With a network of nine offices in key financial capitals around the world, the GIC plays as a global investor in diverse assets.

From 2001 up 2015, annualized rolling 20-year real rate of return of the GIC portfolio recorded 4.0% above global inflation rate (Figure 17.3). In nominal USD terms, the portfolio generated an annualized return of 5.7% over the 20 years.

China Investment Corporation

The China Investment Corporation (CIC) was founded by the government of China in 2007 to take care of its surplus foreign exchange reserves. Its initial asset of USD 207.9 billion increased to USD 847.6 billion at the end of 2015 (CIC 2016). Currently, it is the largest SWF in Asia amounting to 41.5% of total SWF assets in Asia.

The CIC was established as a vehicle to diversify the PRC's foreign exchange holdings and to seek high returns for its shareholder within acceptable risk tolerance. The CIC has three subsidiaries: CIC International Co., Ltd. (CIC International), CIC Capital Corporation (CIC Capital), and Central Huijin Investment Ltd. (Central Huijin). These three subsidiaries of CIC have different roles. CIC International is mainly responsible for investing and managing

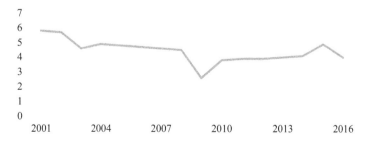

Figure 17.3 Annualized rolling 20-year real rate of return of the GIC portfolio since 2001 (in percentage)

Source: Government of Singapore Investment Corporation of Singapore (2016). *Report on the Management of the Government's Portfolio for the Year 2015/16.*

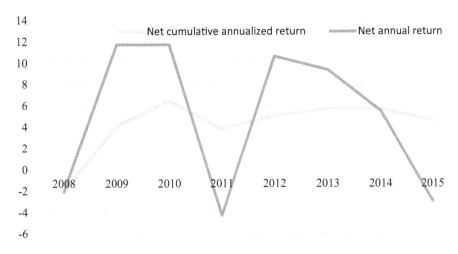

Figure 17.4   Investment performance of the CIC

Source: CIC website (www.china-inv.cn/wps/portal).

overseas assets while CIC Capital is specialized in direct investments. Central Huijin focuses on equity investments in key state-owned financial institutions in the PRC. The CIC observes several principles for its investment activities as below. First, the CIC invests on a commercial basis. Its objective is to seek maximum returns for its shareholder within acceptable risk tolerance. In addition, CIC takes the role of a financial investor and does not seek control of the companies in its portfolio. It also emphasizes the role of a responsible investor, abiding by the laws and regulations of China and recipient countries and conscientiously fulfilling its corporate social responsibilities and to ensure a prudent and disciplined decision-making process.

The CIC invests 67% of its investment through external financial institution while its in-house investment only amounts 33%. The CIC invests its asset mainly into public equity and relatively safe investment. Almost half (47.5%) of its investment are allocated into public equity while about a quarter (22.2%) of its investment are into a long-term investment. Fixed income and absolute income amount 14.4% and 12.7%, respectively.

The rate of return of the CIC changed very much since its establishment of 2007. As seen in Figure 17.4, its return rate fell into −4.3% in 2011 and rose to 10.6% in 2012 although its net cumulative annualized return reached 4.58% from 2008 to 2015.

Pension Funds

This section introduces two major government pension funds: the Government Pension Investment Fund of Japan and the Employees Provident Fund of Malaysia. The Government Pension Investment Fund of Japan is currently the largest pension fund in the world and the Employees Provident Fund of Malaysia established in 1951 is one of the oldest and very active working pension funds in Asia.

Government Pension Investment Fund in Japan

The Government Pension Investment Fund of Japan (GPIF) is an incorporated administrative agency taking care of pension funds for Japanese public sector employees. It is the largest pension fund in the world, whose asset value reached up to USD 1,143.8 billion in 2014. The assets of the GPIF have continuously increased for the past 15 years, except a few years around 2010.

The objective of the GPIF is to achieve the investment returns required for the public pension system to be sustainable. Its investment strategies are summarized as the following four principles: (1) to obtain the investment returns required for the public pension system with minimal risks, solely for the benefit of pension recipients from a long-term perspective diversification by asset class, region, and timeframe, (2) to achieve investment returns in a more stable and efficient manner by taking advantage of its long-term investment horizon; (3) to formulate the policy asset mix and manage and control risks at the levels of the overall asset portfolio, each asset class, and each investment manager; and (4) to fulfill the stewardship responsibilities and maximizing medium to long-term equity investment returns for the benefit of pension recipients.

A large amount of the GPIF's assets are invested by external money managers, who are selected and monitored by GPIF managers. Only a small portion of the assets in the domestic bond category are invested by in-house investment managers.

About 60% of investment is allocated in domestic assets while 40% is in foreign assets. Domestic bonds take 37.6%, while domestic equity 23%. International bonds amount to 13.2%, while international equity amounts to 21.9%. So, in the domestic market, more assets are allocated into bonds but in the international market, more assets are in stocks.

The return rate of the GPIF has been volatile for past years despite strict guidance on investments (Figure 17.5). It was on 3.11% on average for the past 14 years and 3.68% for the past nine years. It fell into the negative for 2007, 2008, and 2010 but afterwards, it turned positive.

Employees Provident Fund in Malaysia

The Employees Provident Fund of Malaysia (EPF) is a provider of retirement savings for all private and non-pensionable employees in Malaysia. It manages a mandatory savings scheme through which both employees and employers contribute a fixed percentage of the employees' monthly salary into the employee's account. A contribution constitutes the amount of money credited to members' individual accounts in the EPF. The amount is calculated based on the monthly wages of an employee.

Since its establishment in 1951, the total asset of EPF has continuously increased into RM 684.5 billion (USD 184.7 billion) in 2015 (EPF 2016; Figure 17.6 a,b). Its average annual

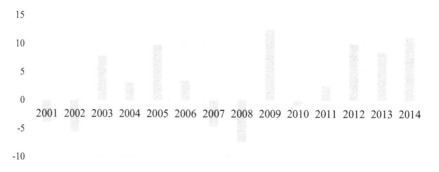

Figure 17.5 Real investment return rate of the GPIF

Source: Government Pension Investment Fund. 2016. *Periodic Review of Policy Asset Mix*, June.

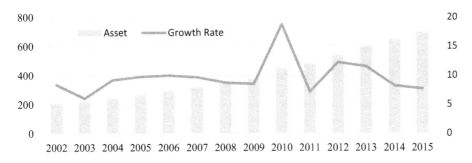

Figure 17.6a Employees Provident Fund of Malaysia: size of asset

Sources: Employees Provident Fund of Malaysia. *Annual Report*, various issues.

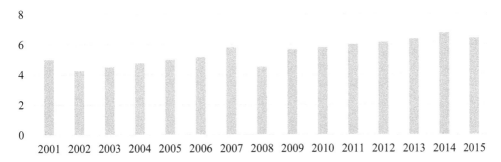

Figure 17.6b Employees Provident Fund of Malaysia: return rate of investment (%)

Sources: Employees Provident Fund of Malaysia. *Annual Report*, various issues.

growth for the past 15 years records 9.7%. The number of members reached 14.55 million and that of active and contributing members is 6.79 million.

The major investment assets are equity. The ratio of equity investment is as high as 44% and Malaysian government and loans and bonds amount 26% and 25%, respectively. An average rate of return was 5.47% from 2001 to 2015. Despite the global financial crisis of 2007–2008 and the European crisis, of 2010–2011, it has managed 4%–6% of return rates for the past 15 years.

Insurance companies

The China Life Insurance (CLI) is the biggest public life insurance company in terms of market capitalization in the world and Samsung Life Insurance is one of the fastest growing insurance companies for the past several decades in the world.

China Life Insurance

China Life Insurance is the largest state-owned insurance and financial services company in the PRC (Figure 17.7). It is also a key player in the PRC capital market as an institutional investor. It originated as the People's Insurance Company of China (PICC) formed in 1949 and has seven subsidiaries: (1) China Life Insurance Company Limited, (2) China Life Asset Management Company Limited, (3) China Life Property and Casualty Insurance Company Limited,

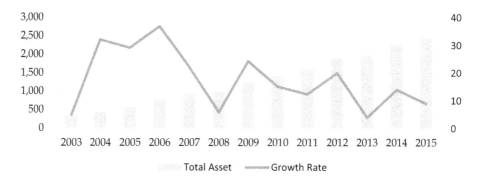

Figure 17.7 Total asset and its growth rate

Source: China Life Insurance. 2016. *Annual Report 2015*. April.

(4) China Life Pension Company Limited, (5) China Life Insurance (Overseas) Company Limited, (6) China Life Investment Holding Company Limited, and (7) Insurance Professional College.

CLI is also the biggest public life insurance company in terms of market capitalization in the world. It possesses the most extensive distribution and service network among all insurers in China. It has about 216 million long-term in-force insurance policies offering individual and group life, annuities, and health insurance protections in 2015.

The objective of CLI is to be a world-class financial and insurance group trying to a comprehensive insurance service provider with property and casualty insurance, and the pension business. It also plans to gradually integrate banking, funds, securities, and the trust business into its core business through various channels.

CLI has played an active role in utilizing the insurance capital to serve the development of the national economy. It has effectively invested in a series of major projects and participated in some large-scale capital operations, thus making great contributions to national economic development, financial institutional reform and IPOs of state-owned enterprises.

In 2015, 73% of its investment were on fixed-maturity investments made up of term deposits, bonds, insurance asset management products, and other fixed-maturity investments. Equity related investment only takes 17%.

Samsung Life Insurance

Samsung Life Insurance (SLI) is the largest insurance company Korea belonged to the Samsung Group. It was a private company founded in 1957 whose principal products are life, health insurance and annuities. When it went public in May 2010, it recorded the largest IPO in the Republic of Korea's history and made SLI one of the country's most valuable companies measured by market capitalization.

The asset size of SLI has rapidly increased over the past 15 years. Its annual average asset growth rate recorded 9.5% from 2002 to 2015 as seen in Figure 17.8 due to the popularity of insurance in the Republic of Korea. Of its assets, 58.2% are financial assets available for sale and 16% are loans, advances, and financing. The ratio of held to maturity investment assets only amounts of 0.2%. Of the available for sale financial assets, the bond takes 77.7% while that of equity does 13.0%. Foreign security takes only 7.5%.

Recently, it tried to diversify and expand its asset management business into oversea markets. For example, it built an office building in Beijing's key commercial district in 2014 and

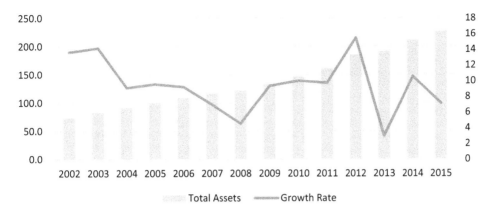

Figure 17.8 Asset and their growth rate

Sources: Samsung Life Insurance. *Consolidated Financial Statements*, various issues.

extended its business into financing infrastructure construction by the build-transfer operate and build-transfer-lease schemes.

Investment fund industry

Investment fund industry in Japan

The fund market of Japan has increased quickly in the past 15 years. As seen in Table 17.4, its asset value and the number of funds increased by 10.5% and 7.7% from 2002 to 2015, respectively. Considering the low growth rate of GDP and inflation in Japan, it was a very high number.

Types of investment funds have changed a lot since 2001. In 2002, the fund held in publicly offered amounted almost 90% while that of private placement investment fell to 12%. The real-estate investment trusts only take 1%. However, in 2015, the publicly offered fund only takes 58.2% while that of private placement investment fund amounts to 36.9%. Still the real estate investment takes less than 5%.

The type of invested asset of fund has also changed much for the same years. In early 2000, the most favored fund was a bond related fund amounting 46.2% of total assets while stock related fund took 38.8%. The money market related fund amounted 12%. Since then, stocks became more attention and in 2015, its ratio reaches 88% while that of bond related one takes only 10.7%. It is because interest rate in Japan has been so low for this year.

The investment on overseas funds amounts to 32.3% of the total fund. Interestingly, the 73.7%of overseas funds are bond related, while those of stock related, are only 21.6%. It is different from those of domestic investment which more focused the investment on stock market.

Investment fund industry of Korea

The investment trust business came to be carried out after Korea Investment Trust, the country's first specialized investment trust company, was launched in September 1974. Afterward, several new investment trust companies have been established and laws and regulations has been changed several times. During the Asian financial crisis of 1997–1998, it has undergone the restructuring process like most other financial institutions in the Republic of Korea.

Table 17.4 Assets of investment funds in Japan

Year	Total Funds				Number of Funds	Average Fund (JPY trillion)
	Amount (JPY trillion)	Growth Rate (%)	Held in Publicly Offered	Private Placement Investment		
2001	51,624		45,280.0	6,106.0	3529	14.6
2002	43,839.0	−15.1	36,016.0	7,381.0	3809	11.5
2003	48,586.0	10.8	37,435.0	10,384.0	3933	12.4
2004	57,839.0	19.0	40,996.0	15,596.0	4,155	13.9
2005	83,041.0	43.6	55,347.0	25,643.0	4,549	18.3
2006	105,068.0	26.5	68,927.0	32,987.0	4,985	21.1
2007	119,478.0	13.7	79,760.0	36,030.0	5,516	21.7
2008	81,670.0	−31.6	52,146.0	25,555.0	5,978	13.7
2009	95,143.0	16.5	61,455.0	29,667.0	6,337	15.0
2010	98,255.0	3.3	63,720.0	30,626.0	6,629	14.8
2011	89,979.0	−8.4	57,327.0	28,542.0	6,928	13.0
2012	100,461.0	11.6	64,063.0	31,818.0	7,174	14.0
2013	128,014.0	27.4	81,523.0	40,413.0	7,857	16.3
2014	147,512.0	15.2	93,504.0	46,870.0	8,817	16.7
2015	167996.4	13.9	97756.2	61973.8	9856.0	17.0

Source: Japan Securities Dealers Association, *Fact BOOK 2015* (2015).

Table 17.5 Assets of investment funds of the Republic of Korea

Year	Total Fund				Number of Funds	Average Size of Funds
	Amount	Growth Rate	Unit Trusts	Mutual Funds		
2001	157.9	−	−	−	6740	23.4
2002	173.0	9.6	−	−	5616	30.8
2003	148.3	−14.3	−	−	8771	16.9
2004	190.1	28.2	183.3	6.8	6,492	29.3
2005	216.8	14.0	204.2	12.6	7,319	29.6
2006	242.4	11.8	229.9	12.6	8,137	29.8
2007	318.4	31.3	304.0	14.4	8,907	35.7
2008	288.5	−9.4	277.3	11.2	9,678	29.8
2009	318.5	10.4	306.3	12.2	9,005	35.4
2010	318.8	0.1	306.9	12.0	9,159	34.8
2011	277.3	−13.0	266.5	10.8	9,735	28.5
2012	307.6	10.9	296.6	11.0	9,864	31.2
2013	328.4	6.8	317.7	10.8	10,807	30.4
2014	376.1	14.5	365.4	10.7	11,997	31.3

Source: Korea Financial Investment Association. *2015 Capital Market in Korea*. August 2015.

The asset of investment fund in the Republic of Korea increased from KRW 157.8 trillion in 2001 to KRW 376.1 trillion in 2014 (Table 17.5) and its annual average growth rate recorded 7.8%. Almost 95% of investment funds are unit trust fund and less than 5% is a mutual fund. In 2014, 47.3% was a privately placed funds while 53.7% was a public offering funds. The number of funds increased from 6,740 in 2001 to 11,997 in 2014 and the average size of the fund also did from KRW 23.4 billion to KRW 30.4 billion, over the same time.

The asset portfolio in investment funds in the Republic of Korea show a substantial change for these years. First, the ratio of bond and hybrid bond types of asset continuously decreased for the past decades while the importance of derivative and others representing real estate, commodities, and special assets continuously increased. The ratios of derivative and other funds increased from 2.5% and 1.9% in 2004 to 8.8% and 20.4% in 2014.

Second, the ratio of equity and hybrid equity fund changes very much for the past years. In 2004, their ratio was only 9%–10%, but it has increased to 46.7% in 2007. In 2014, it records 22.3%.

Third, oversea investment has been getting more attention throughout the years. In 2004, the overseas fund only amounted the 3.0% of the total fund, but it increased continuously up to 16.1% in 2014.

Concluding remarks

The preceding analysis gives rise to three observations. First, institutional investors in Asia have gained in importance since 2000. With high income and accumulation of current account surplus, governments of this region launched several institutional investment funds and its related agencies. In addition, the development of financial industry also contributed into its expansion.

Second, the total value of four major institutional investors in Asia amounts USD 14.7 trillion and when examining the size of four major institutional investors in Asia, insurance sector is the largest (43.7%) and the investment fund (21.5%) and the pension fund sectors (20.9%) are the next in terms of the size of the assets. That of SWFs is the least. The investment fund records the highest growing rate of 15.1% on average for the past six years while those of assets of insurance and pension fund did only about 4%.

Third, the business activities of institutional investors including formulating asset portfolio are quite different from each other and it is very difficult to formulate them. Some institutional investors put their financial resource into domestic market while others did not. Some investors emphasize investment on equity and equity related one while others do not. It is mainly because the object of institutional investors in Asia are very different with each other and because the development stage of financial market and system of each Asian country is different with each other. For example, the insurance and pension funds are more conservative in composing asset component while investment fund are more aggressive. In addition, their portfolio also changed very substantially in some cases.

Notes

1 The 16 economies are Australia, Brazil, Canada, France, Germany, Hong Kong, China, Ireland, Japan, Malaysia, Mexico, Netherlands, South Africa, Republic of Korea, Switzerland, the United Kingdom, and the United States (Towers Watson 2015b).
2 The assets of insurance industry in Asia include those of major Asian countries of such as the People's Republic of China, India, Indonesia, Japan, the Republic of Korea, Malaysia, Singapore, and Thailand. The assets of insurance companies of Indonesia, Japan, the Republic of Korea, Malaysia, Singapore, and Thailand are provided in the OECD Insurance Statistics database (http://www.oecd.org/finance/insurance/oecdinsurancestatistics.htm). Those of the People's Republic of China and India are given in *China Statistical Yearbook 2015 and Handbook on Indian Insurance Statistics 2015–2016*.

References

China Investment Corporation (CIC). 2016. Annual Report 2015. Beijing: China Investment Corporation.
China Life Insurance. 2016. Annual Report 2015. Beijing: China Life Insurance.

Employees Provident Fund of Malaysia (EPF). Annual Report 2015. Kuala Lampur: Employees Provident Fund of Malaysia.

Government Pension Investment Fund. 2016. *Periodic Review of Policy Asset Mix*, June. www.gpif.go.jp/en/

Government of Singapore Investment Corporation of Singapore. 2016. Report on the Management of the Government's Portfolio for the Year 2015/16. Singapore: Government of Singapore Investment Corporation of Singapore.

Genberg, H. 2015. Capital Market Development and Emergence of Institutional Investors in the Asia-Pacific Region. UN ESCAP Working Paper No. 15/03. Bangkok: UN Economic and Social Commission for Asia and the Pacific.

Inderst, G., and F. Stewart. 2014. Institutional Investment in Infrastructure in Emerging Markets and Developing Economies. Washington, DC: World Bank.

Insurance Regulatory and Development Authority of India. 2015–2016. *Handbook on Indian Insurance Statistics*. Hyderabad: Insurance Regulatory and Development Authority of India.

International Investment Fund Association. 2016. Worldwide Regulated Open-End Fund Assets and Flows. www.iifa.ca/industry_statistics/index.html

Japan Post Insurance. 2016. Annual Report, April 2016. Tokyo: Japan Post Insurance.

Japan Securities Dealers Association. 2015. *Fact Book 2015*. Tokyo: Japan Securities Dealers Association.

Korea Financial Investment Association. 2015. 2015 Capital Market in Korea, August. Seoul: Korea Financial Investment Association.

National Bureau of Statistics of China. 2015. *China Statistical Yearbook, 2015*. Beijing: National Bureau of Statistics of China.

Park, D., and G. B. Estrada. 2009. Developing Asia's Sovereign Wealth Funds and Outward Foreign Direct Investment. ADB Economics Working Paper No. 169. Manila: Asian Development Bank.

Towers Watson. 2015a. *The World 300 Largest Pension Fund*. London: Towers Watson.

Towers Watson. 2015b. *Global Pension Assets Study 2015*. London: Towers Watson.

World Bank. 2008. *Sovereign Wealth Funds in East Asia*. Washington, DC: World Bank.

18

INSURANCE MARKETS IN ASIA

W. Jean J. Kwon

Introduction

We have been relatively successful when it comes to reducing uncertainty. This innate risk-reduction drive motivates the formations of groups, societies, and economies. Nonetheless, risks continue to emerge and expand. Our income-dependent lifestyles make us vulnerable to economic changes over which we have little control. Natural calamities and other environmental changes result in devastating monetary losses and casualties in developing and developed economies in Asia and other regions. Man-made catastrophes are also on the rise.

Increasingly, we employ structured risk management techniques not only to mitigate adverse consequences of old and new risks effectively but also to enable us to use our limited economic resources efficiently. Risk control and financing are two broad classes of the techniques, where the former focuses on pre-loss activities and the latter on post-loss matters. Risk financing can be classified into structured retention programs (e.g., self-insurance) and transfer programs (particularly, insurance). The private sector plays a leading role in supplying insurance coverages, especially in the countries where the government moves away from functioning as a de facto supplier of public policy-based social insurance to the provider of last resort when the loss outcome of catastrophic risk – natural and man-made alike – is beyond the capacity of the private insurance sector alone.

The insurance industry, in Asia and elsewhere, offers both short- and long-term risk control and financing services to policyholders. While financial capital underpins all operations, insurance companies rely heavily on human capital for product design and pricing, distribution, underwriting, claims management and investment management. The success of the industry depends on the insurer's ability to meet its contractual obligations *timely* and in full, and the government is obliged to preserve this security. For this purpose, most governments have established the insurance regulatory authority, which may belong to a government ministry or may operate autonomously. Some countries have a dual authority system in which, for example, the central bank functions also as the prudential supervisory authority.

Governments use various approaches for insurance regulation. There are ex ante standards and rules that new and incumbent insurance market players must abide by (e.g., market entry control, ownership structure, capital requirements, approval of premium rates and products, and solvency requirements). There are ex post approaches mainly for correction of distortions in the insurance market and insurer operations, including review (as opposed to approval) of premium rates and examination of insurers' financial statements. Additionally, self-regulation (e.g., corporate governance and enterprise risk management) and monitoring of member activities by insurance associations are observed in many countries. Most governments use a combination of these approaches with an increasing preference to ex post and self-regulation.

Numerous insurance markets, which were nationalized or were under a controlled economy, have been privatized and liberalized.[1] In selected cases, these actions are in response to the standards set by intergovernmental organizations (e.g., as a condition to become a World Trade Organization member). As a result, private insurance companies are in competition with state-administered insurers and overseas insurance companies increase their direct investment in the supply of insurance and reinsurance in liberalized markets.

Not all such markets are *comparatively* privatized or liberalized from the viewpoint of developed economies. As also alluded to above, few governments have, or are likely to build, a completely deregulated market. Some governments strongly believe that the government, which is deemed to have an unlimited supply of financial capital and is bankruptcy free, should provide certain social insurance protections. In other countries, certain risks are too large (e.g., nuclear radiation risk) or carry too big a problem of adverse selection (e.g., flood risk) for private companies to underwrite, thus requiring the government to be the underwriter.

Merely shifting the weight to ex post approaches for insurance regulation and supervision or simply adopting a policy of deregulation, privatization or liberalization of the local insurance market does not guarantee that the market will be competitive and mature. A mature market calls for regulation and supervision of international standards, the presence of financially and technically sound insurance and other financial services institutions and well developed social and economic infrastructure. With these requisites in place, policyholders' interests can be best protected and a further growth of the insurance industry is expected. In this chapter, we examine the current status as well as recent development in insurance regulation and supervision of insurance markets in Asia.

Asian insurance markets

Asia exhibits diversity in history, culture, religion, government structure and economic development.[2] The influence of such diversity is observed in Asian insurance markets as well. Taipei,China, Japan, the Republic of Korea, and Singapore are known to have developed insurance markets, revenues of which contribute significantly to the nation's GDP. There are World Bank-classified least developed economies, the destitute in which insurance protection would be viewed not at a necessity but as a luxury. Religion (e.g., Buddhism and Islam) and demographic change also affect insurance consumption.

Swiss Re (2016b) reports that Asia (excluding Middle Eastern and Central Asian countries) generated insurance premiums amounting to about USD 1,300 billion in 2015 or 28.49% of global insurance premiums.[3] By country and as presented in Table 18.1, Japan, the People's Republic of China (PRC), the Republic of Korea, and Taipei,China ranked 2nd, 3rd, 8th and 10th in the world in terms of total premium revenues in US dollar in 2015. Their aggregate share of the global premium was 23.84% during the year. In contrast, the premium shares in the world market were 0.03% by Bangladesh, 0.05% by Pakistan, 0.02% by Sri Lanka and less for several developing and underdeveloped economies in Asia. The premium share of all 10 ASEAN members in the global insurance market was only 1.52% as compared to Group of Seven) G7's 63.27%. The size of respective insurance markets as share of the Asian market is shown in Figure 18.1.

Table 18.1 Premium shares by economy and region in Asia: total (1981–2015)

TOTAL (USD million)	1981		1991		2001		2011		2015	
	Premium (USD)	World Share	Premium (USD)	World Share	Premium (USD)	World Share	Premium (USD)	World Share	Premium (USD)	World Share
Japan	79,488	16.63%	386,963	25.54%	444,601	18.10%	636,904	13.97%	449,707	9.88%
Bangladesh			81	0.01%	237	0.01%	1,107	0.02%	1,473	0.03%
People's Republic of China			3,999	0.26%	25,484	1.04%	221,903	4.87%	386,500	8.49%
Hong Kong, China			2,481	0.16%	9,265	0.38%	28,864	0.63%	45,748	1.00%
India	1,911	0.40%	4,220	0.28%	13,173	0.54%	72,346	1.59%	71,776	1.58%
Indonesia	472	0.10%	1,054	0.07%	1,898	0.08%	14,620	0.32%	14,930	0.33%
Malaysia	595	0.12%	1,670	0.11%	5,433	0.22%	14,349	0.31%	14,351	0.32%
Pakistan	218	0.05%	374	0.02%	344	0.01%	1,436	0.03%	2,182	0.05%
Philippines	560	0.12%	524	0.03%	971	0.04%	2,888	0.06%	5,550	0.12%
Singapore	426	0.09%	1,896	0.13%	10,109	0.41%	21,304	0.47%	28,004	0.61%
Korea, Rep. of	716	0.15%	31,059	2.05%	48,641	1.98%	123,656	2.71%	153,620	3.37%
Sri Lanka					189	0.01%	710	0.02%	892	0.02%
Taipei,China	800	0.17%	7,923	0.52%	24,243	0.99%	78,427	1.72%	95,979	2.11%
Thailand	331	0.07%	1,733	0.11%	3,362	0.14%	15,337	0.34%	21,682	0.48%
Viet Nam				0.00%	336	0.01%	1,770	0.04%	2,997	0.07%
Asia	88,016	18.42%	450,153	29.71%	602,104	24.51%	1,276,659	28.00%	1,350,974	29.67%
ASEAN	2,383	0.50%	6,900	0.46%	22,201	0.90%	70,574	1.55%	87,921	1.93%
G7	404,305	84.59%	1,267,735	83.68%	1,954,306	79.57%	2,981,487	65.39%	2,809,967	61.71%
World	477,932	100.00%	1,515,045	100.00%	2,456,148	100.00%	4,559,244	100.00%	4,553,785	100.00%

ASEAN = Association of Southeast Asian Nations, G7 = Group of Seven.

Source: Swiss Re (2016b).

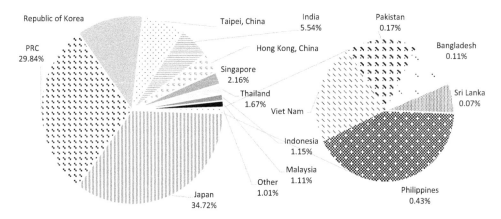

Figure 18.1 Insurance market size and share in Asia (direct premiums in USD million, 2015)

PRC = People's Republic of China.

The total includes other Asian countries and thus deviates slightly from the sum of the countries in the table.

Source: Swiss Re (2016b).

Asian life insurance markets show a similar pattern. As summarized in Table 18.2, Asia generated 35.18% of global life insurance premiums and five countries (Japan, the PRC, the Republic of Korea, Taipei,China, and India) were ranked within the global top 10 in terms of premium revenues in US dollar in 2015. At the same time, each of several countries (including Bangladesh, Pakistan, Sri Lanka, and Viet Nam) claimed less than 0.1% of the global life insurance market share. The premium share of all ASEAN members in the global life insurance market was 2.26% as compared to G7's 60.46%. As shown in Table 18.3, Asian nonlife markets account for a relatively smaller global market share – that is, 22.10% – than life markets. Besides, the PRC became the 2nd largest nonlife insurance market in the world, followed by Japan (4th), and the Republic of Korea (9th).

Evaluation of Asian insurance markets becomes more complete, although not complete, with an analysis of the insurance markets' contribution to the local economy and per capita consumption of insurance. We summarize the findings for 2015 in Table 18.4 where the density is the per capita consumption of insurance (nation's premium revenue divided by the population) and the insurance penetration ratio is a proxy of the importance of the insurance industry (nation's premium revenue divided by GDP). With respect to the total market and also to the life market, the density distribution for 2015 clearly separates developed economies (e.g., Hong Kong, China; Taipei,China; Singapore; Japan; and the Republic of Korea) from other economies. Commonly, the higher the per capita GDP of a country, the higher the share of savings-oriented, investment-linked life and annuity products in the country's life insurance market. Income tax policies of the government also affect life insurance consumption. In nonlife insurance, we often find a positive relationship with the economic development and infrastructure of the country. In fact, those countries that are export-oriented (e.g., the Republic of Korea; Singapore; Japan; Taipei,China; Hong Kong, China; Malaysia; and the PRC) – especially when they are economically developed – tend to exhibit a relatively high nonlife insurance consumption rate.

A number of Asian countries are vulnerable to natural catastrophes. Tropical storms (e.g., Typhoon Haiyan in the Philippines in 2013), earthquakes and tsunamis (e.g., earthquakes and

Table 18.2 Premium shares by economy and region in Asia: life (1981–2015)

TOTAL (USD million)	1981 Premium (USD)	1981 World Share	1991 Premium (USD)	1991 World Share	2001 Premium (USD)	2001 World Share	2011 Premium (USD)	2011 World Share	2015 Premium (USD)	2015 World Share
Japan	59,107	29.32%	299,777	37.08%	357,388	24.30%	505,597	19.29%	343,816	13.57%
Bangladesh		0.00%	25	0.00%	150	0.01%	847	0.03%	1,082	0.04%
People's Republic of China		0.00%	1,555	0.19%	15,556	1.06%	134,566	5.14%	210,763	8.32%
Hong Kong, China		0.00%	1,385	0.17%	7,290	0.50%	25,555	0.98%	41,255	1.63%
India	1,214	0.60%	2,803	0.35%	10,504	0.71%	59,870	2.28%	56,675	2.24%
Indonesia	116	0.06%	288	0.04%	886	0.06%	10,883	0.42%	11,013	0.43%
Malaysia	211	0.10%	789	0.10%	3,678	0.25%	9,385	0.36%	9,588	0.38%
Pakistan	88	0.04%	182	0.02%	131	0.01%	811	0.03%	1,451	0.06%
Philippines	217	0.11%	218	0.03%	572	0.04%	1,913	0.07%	4,010	0.16%
Singapore	94	0.05%	768	0.09%	7,803	0.53%	12,060	0.46%	16,258	0.64%
Korea, Rep. of	0	0.00%	24,706	3.06%	34,511	2.35%	77,083	2.94%	98,218	3.88%
Sri Lanka		0.00%		0.00%	84	0.01%	318	0.01%	383	0.02%
Taipei,China	417	0.21%	5,526	0.68%	16,947	1.15%	64,142	2.45%	79,627	3.14%
Thailand	157	0.08%	889	0.11%	2,000	0.14%	10,142	0.39%	14,619	0.58%
Viet Nam		0.00%		0.00%	189	0.01%	775	0.03%	1,583	0.06%
Asia	61,920	30.72%	340,528	42.12%	462,030	31.41%	924,215	35.27%	904,569	35.70%
ASEAN	795	0.39%	2,953	0.37%	15,166	1.03%	45,239	1.73%	57,172	2.26%
G7	175,128	86.88%	681,764	84.32%	1,168,468	79.44%	1,712,941	65.37%	1,531,861	60.46%
World	201,573	100.00%	808,513	100.00%	1,470,953	100.00%	2,620,360	100.00%	2,533,818	100.00%

ASEAN = Association of Southeast Asian Nations, G7 = Group of Seven.

Source: Swiss Re (2016b).

Table 18.3 Premium shares by economy and region in Asia: nonlife (1981–2015)

TOTAL (USD million)	1981		1991		2001		2011		2015	
	Premium (USD)	World Share	Premium (USD)	World Share	Premium (USD)	World Share	Premium (USD)	World Share	Premium (USD)	World Share
Japan	20,381	7.37%	87,186	12.34%	87,213	8.85%	131,307	6.77%	105,891	5.24%
Bangladesh		0.00%	56	0.01%	87	0.01%	260	0.01%	390	0.02%
People's Republic of China	311	0.11%	2,444	0.35%	9,928	1.01%	87,337	4.50%	175,737	8.70%
Hong Kong, China		0.00%	1,095	0.16%	1,975	0.20%	3,308	0.17%	4,494	0.22%
India	697	0.25%	1,418	0.20%	2,668	0.27%	12,476	0.64%	15,101	0.75%
Indonesia	355	0.13%	766	0.11%	1,013	0.10%	3,738	0.19%	3,916	0.19%
Malaysia	384	0.14%	881	0.12%	1,755	0.18%	4,964	0.26%	4,762	0.24%
Pakistan	130	0.05%	192	0.03%	213	0.02%	625	0.03%	731	0.04%
Philippines	343	0.12%	305	0.04%	399	0.04%	974	0.05%	1,539	0.08%
Singapore	332	0.12%	1,128	0.16%	2,306	0.23%	9,245	0.48%	11,746	0.58%
Korea, Rep. of	716	0.26%	6,353	0.90%	14,130	1.43%	46,572	2.40%	55,402	2.74%
Sri Lanka		0.00%	60	0.01%	105	0.01%	392	0.02%	508	0.03%
Taipei;China	383	0.14%	2,397	0.34%	7,296	0.74%	14,284	0.74%	16,352	0.81%
Thailand	174	0.06%	844	0.12%	1,362	0.14%	5,195	0.27%	7,063	0.35%
Viet Nam		0.00%	24	0.00%	147	0.01%	995	0.05%	1,414	0.07%
Asia	26,097	9.44%	109,625	15.52%	140,074	14.22%	352,444	18.18%	446,405	22.10%
ASEAN	1,588	0.57%	3,947	0.56%	7,035	0.71%	25,334	1.31%	30,749	1.52%
G7	229,177	82.93%	585,971	82.94%	785,838	79.76%	1,268,546	65.43%	1,278,105	63.27%
World	276,359	100.00%	706,532	100.00%	985,195	100.00%	1,938,884	100.00%	2,019,967	100.00%

G7 = Group of Seven.

Source: Swiss Re (2016b).

Table 18.4 Insurance density and penetration ratios by economy and region in Asia: nonlife (2001 and 2015)

| | Insurance Density (USD) (Per Capita Premium) | | | | | | Insurance Penetration (Insurance Premium ÷ GDP) | | | | | |
| | 2001 | | | 2015 | | | 2001 | | | 2015 | | |
	Total	Life	Nonlife	Total	Life	Nonlife	Total	Life	Nonlife	Total	Life	Nonlife
Japan	3,528.1	2,836.0	692.1	3,553.8	2,717.0	836.8	11.08%	8.91%	2.17%	10.82%	8.27%	2.55%
Bangladesh	1.8	1.1	0.7	9.1	6.7	2.4	0.42%	0.27%	0.15%	0.67%	0.50%	0.18%
People's Republic of China	19.9	12.2	7.8	280.7	153.1	127.6	1.91%	1.17%	0.75%	3.57%	1.95%	1.63%
Hong Kong, China	1,355.8	1,066.8	289.0	6,271.2	5,655.2	616.0	5.47%	4.30%	1.17%	14.76%	13.31%	1.45%
India	12.3	9.8	2.5	54.7	43.2	11.5	2.68%	2.14%	0.54%	3.44%	2.72%	0.72%
Indonesia	8.8	4.1	4.7	57.9	42.7	15.2	1.09%	0.51%	0.69%	1.73%	1.28%	0.45%
Malaysia	226.6	153.4	73.2	472.3	315.6	156.7	5.42%	3.67%	1.75%	5.05%	3.37%	1.68%
Pakistan	2.4	0.9	1.5	11.5	7.7	3.9	0.47%	0.18%	0.29%	0.82%	0.54%	0.27%
Philippines	12.2	7.2	5.0	55.0	39.8	15.3	1.27%	0.75%	0.52%	1.90%	1.37%	0.53%
Singapore	2,164.5	1,885.7	278.8	3,825.1	2,931.5	893.7	10.03%	8.74%	1.29%	7.25%	5.55%	1.69%
Republic of Korea	1,027.1	728.7	298.4	3,034.2	1,939.9	1,094.3	8.98%	6.37%	2.61%	11.42%	7.30%	4.12%
Sri Lanka	10.0	4.4	5.5	43.1	18.5	24.5	1.20%	0.53%	0.67%	1.15%	0.49%	0.66%
Taipei,China	1,084.3	758.0	326.3	4,094.1	3,396.6	697.5	8.10%	5.67%	2.44%	18.97%	15.74%	3.23%
Thailand	53.0	31.5	21.5	318.9	215.1	103.9	2.79%	1.66%	1.13%	5.49%	3.70%	1.79%
Viet Nam	4.1	2.3	1.8	32.1	16.9	15.1	0.94%	0.53%	0.41%	1.57%	0.83%	0.74%
Asia	162.5	125.0	37.6	311.7	209.8	102.0	6.92%	5.32%	1.60%	5.34%	3.59%	1.74%
ASEAN	108.5	28.4	11.0	128.2	90.3	37.9	3.42%	2.46%	0.96%	3.35%	2.36%	0.99%
G7	2,756.0	1,668.4	1,088	3,637.1	2,014.5	1,622.6	9.01%	5.46%	3.56%	8.05%	4.46%	3.59%
World	390.3	236.0	154.2	602.8	337.1	265.7	7.26%	4.39%	2.87%	6.05%	3.38%	2.67%

ASEAN = Association of Southeast Asian Nations, G7 = Group of Seven.

Source: Swiss Re (2016b).

Table 18.5 Average annual losses and exceedance probability of catastrophic exposures (2015)

Region	Average Annual Losses (US Billion)			Aggregate Exceedance Probability Losses (US Billion)					
				1-in-100-year Loss Event			1-in-250-year Loss Event		
	Insured	Insurable	Insured Percentage	Insured	Insurable	Insured Percent	Insured	Insurable	Insured Percent
Asia	10.4	36.3	28.7%	52.8	355.5	14.9%	74.7	688.7	14.9%
Europe	10.7	13.7	78.1%	61.4	80.2	76.6%	85.3	110.6	76.6%
Latin America	4.5	7.5	60.0%	37.7	65.6	57.5%	56.4	89.9	57.5%
North America	47.1	76.7	61.4%	196.2	303.1	64.7%	267.9	399.0	64.7%
Oceania	1.6	1.7	94.1%	21.7	21.2	102.4%	37.1	40.4	102.4%
All Exposed Areas	**74.4**	**135.9**	**54.7%**	**232.8**	**518.7**	**44.9%**	**304.8**	**847.0**	**44.9%**

Notes: Exceedance probability quantifies the risk profile for whole portfolios or individual risks. Aggregate exceedance probability areas are not additive in this table.

Latin America comprises the Caribbean, Central America and South America, and North America comprises Canada, the US, Mexico, and Bermuda.

The insured percentage is insured losses divided by insurable losses.

Source: AIR Worldwide (2015).

tsunamis in the Indian Ocean in 2004 and in Japan in 2011 and earthquakes in Nepal in 2015), floods (e.g., Thailand floods in 2011 and North India floods in 2013), and other natural catastrophes have caused casualties and property damages – and even economic slowdowns. Asian governments have built up stronger and expansive infrastructure and programs to minimize pre-loss damages and casualties. Many of them also offer financial subsidies to people and small businesses for the purchase of insurance against natural calamities. Owing to lack of education, the general dependency of people on government and lack of income, the consumption rate of such insurance remains relatively low throughout Asia. As presented in Table 18.5, the consumption ratios – which do not include data for Africa – in all three categories are the lowest in Asia. The 2015 data for Asia indicates only 28.7% of the insurable properties were actually insured (not necessarily with a proper coverage amount), but the percentage drops for the loss probabilities of once per 100 years or 250 years. Swiss Re (2016a) also reports that Asia's share of victims of worldwide catastrophes in 2015 was 71.8%, which support the premises that casualty rates tend to be higher in developing and underdeveloped economies than in developed economies. With respect to property damages, Asia sustained 41% of the economic losses resulting from catastrophes, but its share of insured losses was merely 19.0%.

Insurance markets in a number of Asian countries continue to grow at a fast rate, despite the prevailing low-interest environment which tends to affect significantly life insurance businesses and long-tail nonlife businesses. Swiss Re (2016b) reports that in 2015, the real growth rate of direct premiums (thus less reinsurance premiums) was 3.8% globally, 2.7% among G7 countries, 3.5% in North America and 1.4% in Western Europe. The growth rate for the same year was 8.2% in Asia and 8.1% in ASEAN. In fact, Asia surpassed the world growth rate in most years during the recent decades. The rates in 2015 were relatively high in the PRC (18.3%), Viet Nam (16.9%), the Philippines (16.0%), Singapore (16.0%), Pakistan (11%), and Indonesia (9.7%) for the total market. As expected, emerging economies had a relatively fast growing life insurance market (e.g.: Viet Nam [21.2%], the PRC [19.7%], the Philippines [17.1%], and Pakistan [11.0%]). A similar pattern is observed for the nonlife market, with double digit growth rates in the PRC, (16.6%), Singapore (13.2%), the Philippines (13.0%), and Viet Nam (12.4%). Only Japan and Malaysia are known to have a growth rate below the world average in both life and nonlife markets in 2015.

South Asian markets

A number of insurance markets in Asia have a relatively long history, especially those in South and Southeast Asia. The markets in South Asian countries – Bangladesh, India, Pakistan, and Sri Lanka – were created in the early 20th century. In India, for example, the history dates back to the pre-independence era, then mainly to serve foreign companies operating in the region.[4] By 1956, there were 245 life insurance companies operating in India. The then government claimed that insurance was essentially a social device and insurance should be available to all people. This resulted in the introduction of the Life Insurance Corporation Act of 1956 and a subsequent merger of all life insurance businesses into a single state-run corporation. The government also nationalized nonlife businesses in 1972. The Indian insurance market was closed until the government created the Insurance Regulatory and Development Authority in 1999 and initiated re-invitation of foreign insurance companies in the form of joint venture. As part of India's preparation to be a WTO member, the government increased the maximum limit of foreign insurer partner's share to 49% in 2015 and is expected to permit operations by foreign reinsurers (branches) in 2016.

Bangladesh, Pakistan, and Sri Lanka have followed a similar path. Bangladesh introduced the Insurance Corporation Act of 1972 to nationalize the insurance industry and established two state-owned monopoly insurers. The market remained nationalized until the government initiated privatization, albeit not fully, in the mid-1980s and deregulation, again to a certain degree, in the 1990s. The Bangladeshi government introduced the Insurance Act of 2010 (effective in 2011) and established the Insurance Development and Regulatory Authority in 2011. The private sector led insurance operations in Sri Lanka until the government initiated nationalization of the market with the introduction of a series of laws and regulations, notably the Insurance Corporation Act of 1961 and the Control of Insurance Act of 1962. The World Bank (2016), jointly with other intergovernmental agencies, currently runs the Health Sector Development Program to help the Bangladesh government alleviate problems of public health issues and insurance. The program includes investment up to USD 100 million for improvement in regulation and supervision of the insurance industry in Bangladesh.

The Sri Lankan insurance market was re-open to the private sector with the introduction of the Control of Insurance (Amendment) Act of 1986. Pakistan repealed the Insurance Act of 1938 and enacted the Insurance Ordinance of 2000. The Insurance Board of Sri Lanka issued the final risk-based capital (RBC) framework in October 2013 for implementation in 2016, following a period of consultation and testing. This framework became effective in 2016 and replaced the previous solvency margin requirements. With effect from the first quarter of 2014, all insurers have been required to submit two sets of financial returns (in accordance with both the current and RBC regimes).

The former state-owned insurance corporations in South Asian countries remain competitive – some as national reinsurers – in today's South Asian markets. As discussed later, the presence of compulsory cession of (mainly nonlife) business to the national reinsurer remains as a deadlock for the development of private insurance operations in Bangladesh and Pakistan.

Like several other governments in the region, Pakistan promotes insurance business. As a result, the life insurance market grows steadily which is led by State Life Insurance Corporation along with a small number of private companies. It promotes microinsurance, which is viewed more or less as a long-term project. It also promotes health insurance, especially for the poor. Finally, the government could manage the separation of Islamic principle-based *takaful* operations[5] from conventional insurance operations, thus making it possible to run *takaful* operations with a minimum PKR 50 million (about USD 500,000).

Nepal is in need of an insurance market with a stronger financial and human capital basis, let alone its need to build a resilient economic and social infrastructure to fight again natural catastrophes, especially earthquakes. This would require a further deregulation of the insurance business, the presence of more domestic and foreign insurers, political stability and consumer education about the value of insurance. At the time of writing, the Insurance Board of Nepal plans to increase the minimum paid-up capital for insurance business and has created Nepal Re as an outcome of the government's initiative to transform the national terrorism pool into a reinsurance company.

ASEAN markets

Foreign insurers (and intermediaries) were also the first to develop the insurance markets, particularly those in the countries under control of colonial powers, in Southeast Asian countries. Independence of the nation and nationalization of the insurance industry was also a pattern that many Southeastern countries passed through until modernization of the political system and economic development has transformed them to the more privatized, deregulation, and liberal insurance markets today. There are a few commonalities we find in selected Southeastern countries. One is the influence of Islam. The Quran, Shariah principle, and other Islamic guidelines did not approve the concept of insurance at all until the scholars proposed *takaful insurance* (close to the mutual, cooperative form of conventional insurance but in compliance with Islamic principle) in the mid-1980s. As a result, *takaful* insurance is observed not only in Muslim populous countries (that is, Brunei Darussalam, Indonesia, and Malaysia) but also in Singapore. As further discussed later, the combining effect of poverty and a natural catastrophe has resulted in a number of deadly events, some evening causing a derailing the growth of the country's economy. Finally, it is ASEAN's move toward freer trade in goods and services across the member countries in the region. The ASEAN Insurance Council is responsible for the regionalization of insurance businesses. As presented in Tables 18.1–18.3, the consumption of life insurance within ASEAN is below the global average – in fact, much below when Singapore is excluded but that of nonlife insurance above the average owing to the export-oriented nature of the economy in a number of member countries. The Council is also working on loss control measures and modeling of natural catastrophes.

The insurance market environment in Myanmar is reshaping. On the one hand, the changes are rather unusual. The government restricted foreign insurer presence in the Special Economic Zones except for three Japanese insurance companies in 2015 and requires them (as well as any newly licensed companies in 2016 and thereafter) to abide by the premium rates set by the Insurance Business Regulatory Board. On the other hand, the government permits all insurance companies to offer health insurance.

The Lao PDR government introduced the Law on Insurance in 2012, effective in 2012, as an attempt to develop life and health insurance as well as microinsurance for life and nonlife businesses. The government has also initiated a partnership with foreign companies for the provision of insurance. Nonetheless, the market is still at its infancy, needs a wider and stronger basis for human capital development and waits for a stronger, private sector-led capital market environment.

The history of insurance, especially of private insurance, in Cambodia is relatively short. Cambodian National Insurance Company (Caminco) was established in 1990 as the first insurance company in Cambodia. The Royal Government of Cambodia privatized 75% of Caminco in 2009. Today there are several private life insurance companies as well as microinsurance companies.

Brunei Darussalam is a rich country with comprehensive government-led economic and social welfare programs. As a result, insurance penetration, especially in life insurance, remains relatively low in the country. Muslim dominance in the country is another factor that affects the low consumption of life insurance, whether it being offered by conventional or *takaful* insurance companies.

Indonesia, large in population size, has a great potential for further growth in insurance business. It is Muslim populous and the government is actively promoting *takaful* insurance and microinsurance, along with conventional insurance. The population is relatively young and thus is a large market for various types of life and nonlife insurance products. There has been a constant influx of foreign insurer capital, especially to the microinsurance market, in addition to the long-term presence of foreign companies in the conventional insurance market.

The insurance markets in the Philippines shows signs of improvement. The government has adopted policies to remove a large number of licensed but non-performing companies and to improve the capital position of incumbent companies via higher initial paid-up capital and solvency capital requirements. The Insurance Code of 2013 has brought into new measures of insurer solvency and is likely to encourage mergers and acquisitions to result in a smaller number of financially and operationally stronger insurance companies. This trend is expected to continue during the next few years, as the government is expected to gradually increase insurer capital requirements. The market is served by both private domestic and foreign insurance companies.

Singapore leads the ASEAN markets. Insurance density and penetration remain considerably high, and the market is served by both a large number of domestic and foreign insurance and reinsurance companies. A number of foreign entities claim Singapore home to their captive operations. Singapore generates a substantial amount of offshore premium revenues, thus helping the country remain a regional hub for insurance operations in Asia. Laws and regulations governing the insurance market in Singapore are known for transparency and high standards, including the RBC 2, the Insurance (Amendment) Act 2015, and the Financial Advisers (Amendment) Act 2015. Several local insurance companies, particularly those affiliated with domestic banks, are expanding their operations to other ASEAN countries.

The market environment in Thailand has been significantly improved in recent decades. As a stepping stone for insurance operations under the ASEAN Economic Community, the government has separated the insurance authority from the government and revised existing laws and regulations and introduced new ones of a high standard. Besides, Thai insurance companies are actively promoting the development of insurance markets in neighboring countries via direct investment. Viet Nam is also in preparation for the single ASEAN insurance market.

Northeast Asian markets

Insurance is fast developing in the PRC. The country continues to break the record in terms of premium growth and market size. The life insurance market in the PRC accounts for about 8.3% of the global premium, as compared to 0.01% in 1984. The nonlife market claims 8.7% of the global market share, as compared to 0.2% in 1984 (Swiss Re 2016b). The life and nonlife markets are 4th and 2nd largest markets globally, respectively. In contrast, the PRC is ranked at

53rd in terms of insurance density and 40th in terms of penetration. These findings altogether indicate a relatively strong growth potential in the PRC. Hong Kong, China – a former colony of the UK and today a special administrative region of the PRC – maintains a relatively liberal insurance market and is a regional hub for insurance transactions.

There are two key developments worth elaboration. One is the introduction of the China Risk Oriented Solvency System or C-ROSS, to be fully effective in 2017. The C-ROSS has three pillars. The capital adequacy pillar covers quantitative regulatory requirements including: balance sheet evaluation, actual capital standards, minimum capital standards, capital adequacy standards and other regulatory measures. The risk management pillar is primarily associated with qualitative regulatory solvency requirements including company-wide risk management requirements, regulatory capital measurement and risk management supervision and inspection. The information disclosure pillar is mainly related to the transparency of the regulatory and solvency requirements including: regulatory reporting requirements and public disclosure of information (Kwon 2014). The other is the expansion, a movement supported by the PRC government, of insurer's operations in foreign soils. The expansion is not limited to insurance operations as large insurance groups acquire real properties and other non-insurance businesses.

Taipei,China continues to focus on savings and investment-linked life insurance and leads the world in terms of the life insurance penetration ratio, being the 2nd highest in 2015. The government maintains a high standard in insurance regulation and supervision. In 2014, the Executive Yuan approved the Insurance Act (Amendment) that allows the insurance authority to take over insurers with a RBC ratio below the minimum threshold if it fails to improve the capital position within a stipulated period. Besides, life insurers have been permitted since 2014 to sell policies denominated in renminbi – not yet popular in the country.

Japan and the Republic of Korea have large and developed insurance markets, especially in life insurance. In nonlife insurance, the Republic of Korea claims the greater density of the two in part because of depreciation of the Japanese yen in recent years (whereas the density is often measured in US dollar or euro) and in part because of the Republic of Korea's government's permission of annuities with a limited tem by nonlife insurance companies.

The future of the Japanese life insurance market is not necessarily bright. The country has suffered from low economic growth since the early 1990s, coupled with an extremely low-interest environment, as well as from a negative spread between guaranteed returns in old policies (especially those issued around the Asian economic crisis in the late 1990s) and lower-than-expected investment performance of life insurance companies. Consumers have also shifted their preference from high premium, savings, and investment-oriented policies to low cost, death protection policies. Population aging is also demanding a transformation of annuity products and target customers (Life Insurance Association of Japan 2015). Nonlife insurance companies have also been affected by the prevailing economic condition in Japan. After a series of mergers and acquisitions, nonlife insurance companies became bigger in size and stronger in capital position. A number of them are active in expanding their overseas operations in Asia, Americas, Europe, and the Middle East, for example (General Insurance Association of Japan 2015). The Financial Services Agency of Japan uses Japan's own Economic Capital Solvency approach for financial regulation of licensed insurance companies. Japan favors a Solvency II equivalence status, a requisite for Japanese insurance companies to operate throughout the EU.

The environments surrounding the Korean insurance market share some similarities to those in Japan. Both life and nonlife insurance companies are *Chaebol* affiliated, whose financial and operational positions are stronger, if not much, than smaller companies. The market deals with the low-interest environment, although the situation is not as worse as in Japan. Population aging has already become a critical issue in the Republic of Korea. The Financial Supervisory

Services uses a Korean version of Risk-based Capital regulation for insurer solvency monitoring. The Republic of Korea is active in drafting its own version of the IFRS 4 Phase 2 – a new international accounting standard – as a means to make the domestic accounting and valuation methodologies more comparable with international standards (Financial Supervisory Service 2015). The nonlife insurance market in the Republic of Korea carries a unique structure in that companies can sell long-term pension funds and annuities (subject to 10 years for the maximum coverage period). The share of these businesses as well as long-term accident and health insurance continues to rise, consequently making the nonlife market more comparable in size with the life market. The Republic of Korea is also known for an advanced data sharing at the government and association level to detect fraud and fraudulent claims.

We observe some diversity in regulatory approaches in Asian insurance markets. One is the variation of the market share of the five largest insurance companies. Table 18.6 shows the

Table 18.6 Key market and regulation status by economy in Asia: nonlife

Economy	Top Five Company Market Share (Premium)[a]	Initial Capital Requirement Range (USD Million) (Nonlife and Composite) (Effective Year)	Solvency Regulation Methodology (Current to Planned)
Japan	82.38%	8.2	Economic Value Solvency
Bangladesh	54.41%	1.92–5.13	Solvency Margin
Brunei	94.45%	6.5	Solvency Margin
Cambodia	78.30%[b]	7.1	Solvency Margin
PRC	74.30%	32–80	C-ROSS
Hong Kong, China	29.87%	1.8–2.56	RBC[d] (to Solvency II?)
India	59.84%	16.32	Solvency Margin (to RBC)
Indonesia	51.91%	8	RBC
Malaysia	45.34%	25	RBC
Myanmar	Not Applicable	40	Solvency Margin
Nepal	47.86%	1–2.5	Solvency Margin
Pakistan	66.28%	6.9 (2017)	Solvency Margin
Philippines	47.82%	22 (2022)	Solvency Margin
Lao PDR	78.20%[c]	1.85	Solvency Margin
Singapore	48.04%	4.8	RBC 2
Korea, Rep. of	76.48%	4.5–30	RBC/Solvency Margin II[e]
Sri Lanka	70.76%	60	Solvency Margin
Taipei,China	60.16%	60	RBC
Thailand	44.95%	7	RBC
Viet Nam	67.46%	14	Solvency Margin

a The information may not include reinsurance and *takaful* operation data.
b This share represents only three companies.
c This share represents only two companies.
d Risk-based capital (RBC).
e Currently under review for revision.

Source: AXCO Reports (February 2016) and author's compilation.

shares in selected nonlife insurance markets in Asia in 2013 (Axco 2016). Hong Kong, China; Malaysia; Nepal; Singapore; the Philippines; and Thailand show a share below 50% while the findings for other countries (including the PRC, Taipei,China; Japan; and the Republic of Korea) signals possible dominance of the largest companies. In contrast, the majority of insurance markets in the Western Hemisphere are serviced by a large number of companies, each unlikely being the market leader. Second, there is a diversity in the initial capital requirement that a new company applying for an insurance license in the respective jurisdiction must meet along with other requirements. Table 18.6 shows the minimum initial paid-up capital that an insurance license applicant is required to raise. The countries highlighted in light green require capital in excess of USD 25 million. There are more developing economies than developed economies in this group. In contrast, several developed economies in Asia require a relatively smaller initial capital (e.g., USD 4.8 million in Singapore as compared to USD 8 million in Indonesia or USD 32–80 million in the PRC). The higher the initial capital requirement, the more stringent the access to the market becomes. However, a higher capital requirement does not necessarily indicate that the local insurance market is developed. There is risk that such a requirement may simply work as an entry barrier to the market. Finally, Table 18.6 presents the distribution of the current (or planned) solvency regulation tools in Asia. The countries in light green have, or are expected to have, risk-based, sophisticated statistical models for the measurement of the *minimum* capital each incumbent insurance company must maintain not only to meet its insurance obligations but also to absorb the tail-end shocks in in investment operations. The countries in orange still have non-statistical solvency margin regulations.

Investment environments

Insurance policies can be described as a type of contingent claim contracts that rely on pricing inversion, meaning that the product is priced before final costs are known. Therefore, insurers add a margin for unfavorable pricing deviations (e.g., risk charges). Insurance companies must manage this portfolio of internal risks through stringent corporate governance, expertise in all functional areas and utilization of reinsurance, among others. They must manage assets, which include their liabilities to policyholders, efficiently and maintain solvency. Financial capital provides insurance companies with a cushion against the possibility that actual losses, expenses or investment results deviate negatively from assumptions implicit in coverage pricing. A poorly diversified or low-quality investment management may, and can, lead to financial difficulties and even insolvency.[6]

Insurers, especially life insurers, manage significant investment portfolios. They are key institutional investors in capital markets worldwide. Generally, insurance companies manage their investment in line with the duration and embedded interest in their policies and invest in high-quality products in capital markets. Besides, regulatory authorities are concerned about the financial soundness of the insurance market and companies, thus paying close attention to the composition and management of invested assets of the regulated companies. They commonly encourage, sometimes force, insurance companies to invest in high-quality areas (e.g., blue chips government bonds and rated corporate bonds), all other things being equal.

The developmental status of investment markets in Asia is in sync with the status of insurance markets. The markets, for example, in Taipei,China; Hong Kong, China; Japan; the Republic of Korea; Malaysia; and Singapore are of international standards, whereas the infrastructure of the markets in a number of emerging or landlocked economies tends to be relatively weak.

In Singapore, which adopted a RBC regime in 2004, we find a diversity in insurers' asset portfolios, which signals that insurance companies can develop a wide array of insurance policies based on the asset-liability matching principle both in return and duration. (Of course, they are still exposed to external systemic risk.) Singapore has a highly developed and transparent financial services sector in which a large number of domestic and foreign institutions compete. Freedom of capital movement in and out of the country also helps Singapore to maintain its status as a regional hub for financial services, certainly including insurance. Hong Kong, China is considered another regional hub for financial services with a complete an open capital market system. This free capital market allows insurance companies to maintain diversified investment portfolios, thus being able to offer a wide variety of short and long-term protection products. Insurance companies from the PRC have also found Hong Kong, China home to their expansion of business beyond the PRC. Today, Hong Kong, China's economic policies are closely linked with those of mainland China.

Japan has a well-developed investment market, which helps the insurance industry maintain stability and growth. Nevertheless, the country continues to live with a low interest rate environment. In April 2015, the Financial Services Agency announced a new basis for the calculation of standard interest rates which affect life, annuity, pension and other long-term insurance policies. All these other major policies affect insurance operations within Japan. Insurers seem to find solutions in part by re-engineering their policies that reflect the prevailing conditions in investment (thus reducing their exposure to asset and liability valuation risk and other investment-related risks) and in part by finding business opportunities outside Japan. These movements seem to be acceptable as the insurance industry as a whole maintains a significantly higher Solvency Margin Ratio than the required minimum.

The prevailing global economic condition affects the Republic of Korea's investment market. The interbank and commercial interest rates continue to fall and capital market performance stagnates. This condition, on the one hand, affects the performance of the insurance industry. The industry experienced insolvencies in the recent past and small companies generally seem to face challenges in strengthening their capital positions. On the other hand, large insurance companies commonly maintain their solvency status, especially when measured by the government-implemented solvency methodology. What remains relatively unknown is the impact of IFRS 4 Phase 2. Scheduled to be implemented in 2018–2019, this new accounting standard may require local insurance companies, especially life companies, to increase their solvency capital because their liabilities will be valued on a realistic basis as opposed to the current net premium valuation basis.

Taipei,China continues to add stimuli to the local economy via several new measures. In 2014, the Financial Supervisory Commission relaxed the regulations on real estate investment (especially those affecting investment in real property in the country, mainland China and abroad) (Financial Supervisory Commission 2014) as well as on the use of derivatives by insurance companies. In 2015, the Financial Supervisory Commission amended regulations related investment and insurance transactions in foreign currency. Nevertheless, the insurance industry is still waiting for the development of a long-term investment market, durations of the products in commensuration with those of long-term insurance coverages. It seems Taipei,China does not have a long-term investment market that adequately covers all the needs of the life insurance market.

Malaysia has a relatively developed investment market. It is also known as the first country that has introduced a Shariah-compliant exchange. This has not only helped *takaful* companies in Malaysia to strengthen their investment portfolios but also attracted investment by overseas companies in need of Islamic principle-based investment choices. Malaysian takaful companies are also in partnership with foreign takaful companies for cross-border operations between Malaysia and the Middle East and North African countries.

In Thailand, insurance companies tend to hold government bonds, corporate bonds and other fixed interest investment products. In Brunei Darussalam, it seems the investment decisions for local companies are made by their corporate offices in home countries, for example, Singapore. Indonesia has the Jakarta Stock Exchange (privatized in 1992) and the Jakarta Futures Exchange (for derivative trading). Takaful companies in Brunei Darussalam and Indonesia are expected to manage investment in compliance with Islamic principle.

In the PRC, insurance companies did not have much choice for the management of investment portfolios in part due to the stringent investment guidelines set by the China Insurance Regulatory Commission and in part due to the limited choices in the local stock exchanges. This was, and still is to a certain degree, a problem for policyholders who own savings or investment-linked life insurance policies. The aforementioned C-ROSS and amendment of related laws and regulations, on the one hand, are likely to offer more investment choices for insurance companies in the PRC: for example, investment in infrastructure finance, real property, unlisted shares and unsecured corporate bonds. On the other hand, the risk charges based on specific types of invested assets, insurance businesses and policyholder liabilities will force the companies to be more careful and effective in managing their capital in the country.

India, an emerging market in Asia, seems to maintain a stringent policy on investment choices for insurance companies. The government prefers investment within India and would require approval by the State Bank for investment in foreign soils.

The capital markets in many other Asian economies are not strong and in need of development. Alternatively, insurance companies (most of them with a limited capital) seem to be conservative in investment and do not deviate much from principle guaranteed investment choices. Bangladesh, for example, offers a limited investment choice to insurance companies. The regulatory authority adds an additional layer of restriction on investment by the companies (e.g., a minimum holding of invested assets on government securities). Investment in foreign stock is not permitted. In Cambodia, the Cambodia Securities Exchange began its operation only March 2012. Viet Nam also maintains stringency when it comes to investment portfolio management by insurance companies.

Reinsurance

Reinsurance is vital to portfolio diversification functioning of insurance risks internationally, with virtually every insurance company relying on it. Due to the large size of some loss exposures, insurance companies find it necessary to share their exposures with reinsurance companies that may even distribute the risk regionally and internationally. It is not thus uncommon that an insurance company maintains multiple reinsurance programs, each with a sharing of risk portfolios by a number of reinsurance companies. Reinsurance is very well developed in the Western Hemisphere, especially in the EU and North America. Large international professional companies – and foreign to most Asian countries – dominate reinsurance markets globally.

Reinsurance is critical to building the domestic insurance market. Domestic companies in a number of developing economies in Asia, due mainly to low capitalization, have low risk underwriting and retention capacity and a correspondingly high demand for reinsurance. Historically, large global reinsurers have provided their client companies – sometimes state-administered companies – with risk management and underwriting services. The value of these services plus low capitalization of the majority of insurers in developing economies have led to dependence on reinsurance supplied by foreign reinsurers. Some governments, certainly including those in Asia, view reinsurance positively, while others mistakenly treat reinsurance transactions merely as an outflow of capital from their home countries.

Reinsurance business is strong in Hong Kong, China and Singapore, the two regional hubs for financial services. Hong Kong, China has about 20 companies registered for reinsurance business (including eight for life reinsurance) but a few of them are not actively underwriting reinsurance risks at the time of writing. Singapore has dozens of reinsurance companies, including branches of foreign companies. Both Hong Kong, China and Singapore promote offshore reinsurance, meaning that locally licensed insurance companies assume risks from other countries. Both countries share a commonality that foreign reinsurers (mainly from Europe and the US) lead the business.

Japan, the Republic of Korea, and Taipei,China maintain liberal reinsurance market environments in which both domestic and foreign reinsurance companies compete fairly. Natural catastrophe risks, such as earthquakes in Japan and typhoons in both Japan and Korea, are often the subject matters for reinsurance. The Japanese government maintains a national earthquake reinsurance scheme jointly with private sector insurance companies and Japan Earthquake Reinsurance (Ministry of Finance Japan 2016). The consumption of catastrophe insurance went up recently, albeit not substantially, especially after the 2011 Tohoku earthquake and tsunami. Toa Re is known as the only local life reinsurance company. Several reinsurance companies, including a former monopoly Korean Re, operate in the Republic of Korea. Taipei,China has one domestic company (Central Reinsurance Corporation) plus several foreign reinsurance companies (branches). It is the first Asian economy – other than Japan – that completed insurance-linked securitization (catastrophe notes) of natural catastrophe risk (specifically, earthquake as part of the economy's earthquake pool of about USD 1.5 billion capacity).

The PRC hosts several domestic reinsurance companies. Some of them were domestic and the other foreign. Several other foreign reinsurance companies are in preparation to enter the PRC market in part reflecting the potential growth possibility in the PRC and in part reflecting the substantial rise in risk charges (thus requiring more capital) for reinsurance ceded abroad when the C-ROSS regulation is fully imposed.

The reinsurance markets in other Asian countries are different in structure. In India, the government has been planning to introduce another local reinsurance company but is still keeping state-owned General Insurance Corporation (GIC Re) as the sole reinsurance company. All nonlife insurance businesses are subject to a mandatory cession to GIC Re, which is scheduled to phase out soon in the future. Thailand has Thai Re Life as the only life reinsurance company. Thai Re Life is a wholly owned subsidiary of Thai Re. Insurance companies in Thailand were subject to a 5% compulsory cession but are free today to place risks with qualified reinsurance companies of their preference. Indonesia had four local reinsurance companies, of which three are state-owned. The government strongly advises local life and nonlife companies to seek reinsurance locally (Otoritas Jasa Keuangan 2014). The government took a step farther to merge all four reinsurers to PT Reasuransi Indonesia Utama (also known as Indonesia Re) in 2015. Nonetheless, reinsurance with large global international reinsurance companies continues. The Philippines also has one professional reinsurance company, National Reinsurance Corporation of the Philippines, which was state-owned. Both life and nonlife insurance companies are subject to the mandatory reinsurance cession requirement (e.g., a minimum of 10 of the life business to be placed in the reinsurance market).

In Pakistan, Pakistan Reinsurance Company is the only professional reinsurance company. It is a state-run company under the Ministry of Commerce, to which all licensed insurance companies in the country are required to check if the national reinsurer is willing to accept 35 percent of their nonlife business (and health insurance business by nonlife companies) for treaty reinsurance. The national reinsurance company may decline the cession. Facultative placement of reinsurance risks must also be offered to the national reinsurance company. In

Bangladesh, state-owned Sadharan Bima Corporation is the only nonlife reinsurance company and all licensed companies are subject to the 50% mandatory cession to the reinsurance company. In contrast, the government does not impose a compulsory cession for life risks. Compulsory session of life risks is also observed in Cambodia which has Cambodia Re as the sole reinsurance company.

The mechanism by which reinsurance is placed in the international market often is specified by local laws. In a few countries, all reinsurance (especially in nonlife business) must be placed through national reinsurance companies, although the trend is to abandon such practices. With such compulsory cession policies, the governments believe – incorrectly – that they could enhance the domestic insurance market by merging part of the pools of risks from individual companies to the national reinsurance company. They may also believe – again incorrectly – that would limit reinsurance premiums to foreign companies, thus reducing foreign currency outflows. Such belief is incorrect because insurance and reinsurance work better when risks are not concentrated in a certain territory and because they ignore reinsurance claims benefits. Compulsory cessions usually harm insurance markets. Regulators and insurers now know that the resultant concentration of insured exposures usually fails to diversify risks and exposes the industry to catastrophic loss potential.

Government's role in insurance

The insurance industry plays an important role in the economy. The industry is a vital source of capital for economic development, especially in developing economies. It provides society with effective and cost-efficient means on which their members – individuals and businesses alike – can safely rely for preservation and enhancement of wealth. Consumption of insurance coverages are treated, and should be treated, as (quasi-)necessities for any societal member, for example: protection against, loss of health, disability, unemployment, and pension. Certain other coverages protect the rights to which the social member is entitled, for example: financial compensation for victims of accidents, workplace injuries and sometimes victims of natural and man-made disasters. Guaranteeing the provision of these necessities and rights is so important that no governments treat insurance simply as a private sector matter. They are actual underwriters of certain risks (e.g., longevity risk under public pension), require the purchase of insurance compulsory (e.g., third-party motor liability and workers' compensation) and regulate the insurance market and all players in the market stringently.

There are two key objectives – in fact, two sides of the same coin – which governments wish to achieve in the insurance market. One is protecting policyholders' rights by ensuring that the market is serviced by financially sound and operationally healthy insurance companies only. The other is making the insurance market sustainable and attractive by making it free of undue regulation and other forms of government control. A deregulated (and liberalized) market environment forces companies to increase their efficiency and be more competitive. Companies in a competitive insurance market will focus their *modus operandi* on developing expertise and enhancing capital and underwriting capacity, thus being able to offer consumers a wide array of insurance products. When the market is also liberalized, not necessarily fully, foreign capitals and expertise will flow into the domestic market and all the participants in the market can receive the benefits from the resulting scale- and scope-economy effects. Inefficient or uncompetitive insurers cannot survive long in the market.

In selected cases, however, policy-makers do not correctly understand the functioning of insurance and prefer retaining protectionism or upholding non-market-based regulatory policies and measures. Policy-makers should impose only the rules and regulations that promote fair competition within the market, and must not attempt to use the insurance industry merely as a source of capital for economic development. Insurers in the countries should be financially sound, technically competent in insurance matters, and must remain prudent in management and operation. The people as well as public and private entities in each of those countries must enhance their understandings about the benefits of insurance, and demand for and consume insurance products that meet their insurance needs.

Notes

1 Other reasons for strong control of the insurance market exist. The government in a developing or underdeveloped economy may treat insurance premiums as an important source of capital for economic development and try to minimize, if not prohibit, the flow of premiums out of the country. Some governments believe that the industry is of national interest and must be protected until the local insurers possess sufficient financial and human capital to compete with foreign insurers. Generally, policies based on this non-economic reasoning are more prevalent in the reinsurance market than in the insurance market.
2 The discussion in this section is in part based on the broad references to the following: Kwon (2007), Axco (2016), Insurance Information Institute (2015), A. M. Best (2013) and information publicly available from government and insurance authority websites (unless otherwise noted).
3 The premium and its share of global premium by the Middle East and Central Asia were approximately USD 53.7 million and 1.18%, respectively, in 2015.
4 The first known life insurers in India were Oriental Life Insurance Company established in 1818 in Calcutta, and Bombay Life Assurance Company founded in 1823.
5 See the next section.
6 A related but different concern arises with cross-border insurance transactions. Unlike the situation with a locally established subsidiary of a foreign insurance company whose assets typically must be kept locally, the assets backing cross-border insurance liabilities (e.g., reinsurance sold by offshore companies) are not usually maintained in the host country. If an offshore insurance company fails to meet its obligations, the policyholders in the host country would be at risk, as compared with the policyholders with a locally established company. Hence, governments tend to control, even prohibit in extreme cases, cross-border trade in insurance and reinsurance.

References

A. M. Best. 2013. *Asia-Pacific Review*. Oldwick: A. M. Best Company.
AIR Worldwide. 2015. *2015 Global Modeled Catastrophe Losses*. Boston: AIR Worldwide.
Axco. 2016. *Insurance Market Information and Statistics (Online)*. London: Axco.
Financial Supervisory Commission. 2014. *Regulations Governing Permission of Insurance Business Transactions and Investment Between the Taiwan Area and the Mainland Area (Amended)*. Taipei: Financial Supervisory Commission of Taiwan. http://law.tii.org.tw/Eng/FLAWDAT0201.asp?No=1A0020003&lsid=FL006778&hasChar=True&btnType=0&rlType=
Financial Supervisory Service. 2015. *FSS Handbook*. Seoul: Financial Supervisory Service of Korea.
General Insurance Association of Japan. 2015. *Fact Book 2014–2015*. Tokyo: The General Insurance Association of Japan.
Insurance Information Institute. 2015. *World Insurance Fact Book 2015*. New York: Insurance Information Institute.
Kwon, W. J. 2007. *Risk Management and Insurance Perspectives in a Global Economy*. New York: Wiley/Blackwell.
Kwon, W. J. 2014. *The C-ROSS and Insurer Operations in China and Abroad*. Zurich: Swiss Re.
Life Insurance Association of Japan. 2015. *Life Insurance Business in Japan 2014–2015*. Tokyo: The Life Insurance Association of Japan.
Ministry of Finance Japan. 2016. *Japan's Earthquake Insurance System*. Ministry of Finance. www.mof.go.jp/english/financial_system/earthquake_insurance/index.html

Otoritas Jasa Keuangan. 2014. *Letter on Optimization of Local Capacity (No S-77D.05/2014)*. Jakarta: Otoritas Jasa Keuangan.

Swiss Re. 2016a. *Natural Catastrophes and Man-Made Disasters in 2015*. Zurich: Swiss Re.

Swiss Re. 2016b. *World Insurance 2015*. Zurich: Swiss Re.

World Bank. 2016a. *Combined Project Information Documents/Integrated Sateguards Data*. Washington, DC: The World Bank. http://www-wds.worldbank.org/external/default/WDSContentServer/WDSP/SAR/2016/04/06/090224b08426994f/1_0/Rendered/INDEX/Concept0Projec0nt0Project000P156823.txt

World Bank. 2016b. *List of Economies*. Washington, DC: The World Bank. http://siteresources.worldbank.org/DATASTATISTICS/Resources/CLASS.XLS

19

INFRASTRUCTURE FINANCE OF ASIA

Shubhomoy Ray

Introduction

Against the backdrop of the financial crisis that affected Europe and the US over the later part of the last decade, Asian economies have been trying to shed their over-reliance on the financial resources of the West and find financing solutions in their local and regional financial markets. At the same time, the global growth engine was largely driven by Asia during this period, fueled by expanding regional production networks, integration into the global economy, foreign direct investment (FDI), falling trade and investment barriers, a commodity boom, and heightened demand from a rising Asian middle class.

As a result, the region launched its own initiatives of institutional development and integration, seeking to deviate from traditional US dollar-denominated financing and creating its own financing backbone through regional cooperation and bilateral support mechanisms. This, since the beginning of the current decade, led to formation of institutions like the Asian Infrastructure Investment Bank (AIIB); creation of risk-mitigated down-sell models like take-out financing; long-term, cross-border, project finance loans denominated in People's Republic of China (PRC) yuan and Japanese yen; and larger bilateral involvement in project financing of publicly conceived projects through softer government-to-government loans.

This chapter analyzes the current financing trends and assesses the depth and capabilities of the region's local credit and equity markets for financing infrastructure projects, while also trying to identify supplementary sources of capital that could augment both the quantum and tenor of the local financial resources. The chapter also delves into financial market and policy-related issues that need to be addressed to free up the flow of local and foreign capital into infrastructure projects, and proposes capacity building solutions for increasing sustainability of local level equity and credit market financing.

Important characteristics of infrastructure projects

The Cambridge Dictionary defines infrastructure as the basic systems and services, such as transport and power supplies, that a country or organization uses in order to work effectively. A more technical definition given by the Asian Development Bank (ADB) says that infrastructure consists of hard and soft components (ADB 2012). The hard components of infrastructure include all those activities that facilitate the movement of goods and people, and provide services for households and businesses. This includes roads, railways, airports, water transport, utilities (electricity, gas, water, and sanitation), and telecommunications. Soft components of infrastructure include the rules and regulations governing the use and functioning of the physical infrastructure. It helps in providing an environment which is conducive in the development and functioning of infrastructure service. An ideal policy environment must be (1) clear, consistent, and fairly applied; (2) reflect international best practices; and (3) encourage economically viable trade and travel. The hard components must be accompanied and supported by the soft components. In other words, a right mix of the two is very important to ensure that the infrastructure system performs well.

Infrastructure projects are typically characterized by four points:

1 *Long gestation period.* Infrastructure projects generally take a long time to get completed, particularly in larger, complex project situations involving multiple stakeholders. Typically, the development period of these projects alone can range from three to eight years with another four to seven years in construction, which means that for most projects cash flows do not materialize for 7 to 15 years of first investment. With such long gestation period, there is an inherent risk of changes in the regulatory environment or delays leading to an increase in the project cost or making the original project concept and design redundant.

2 *Large initial capital outlay and maintenance costs.* Infrastructure projects require a large amount of funds to meet the initial investments; also, there is a need to make provisions throughout the project life to meet the ongoing capital expenditure needs.

3 *High sunk cost.* Even before the infrastructure project starts operating a large proportion of the cost is incurred upfront in the form of "sunk costs." These costs may act as a barrier to investment in such projects by the private sector, as such expenditures cannot be recovered.

4 *Stable yield and cash flows.* Infrastructure projects are generally long duration projects providing a stable yield and relatively stable cash flow over the life of the project. However, they can be subject to considerable uncertainty from a variety of sources, including political and regulatory changes, which makes their returns potentially risky.

Infrastructure demand projections

Regional and sub-regional financing needs for infrastructure projects

According to Bhattacharyay (2010), Asia (East Asia, South Asia, and Southeast Asia) will need at least USD 7.84 trillion in this decade in infrastructure investment (Table 19.1).

According to ADB (2009), in value terms, only 1%–5% of the intra-regional trade between South Asia and Southeast Asia was conducted with neighboring countries, compared with a global average of 25%, mostly because of infrastructure shortfalls.

The reasons for the bottlenecks were largely due to the immaturity of regional financial markets and their inability to provide sufficient infrastructure financing. This implies a strong need to develop regional financing capabilities which would help foster infrastructure investment and insulate regional infrastructure growth from shocks from developed markets. Countries in the region need to enhance their own financing and risk management abilities in order to prevent and resolve any future financial crises. Strengthening of regional financial cooperation, together

Table 19.1 National infrastructure investment needs in Asia, 2010–2020: per subregion and per sector (2008 USD billion)

Sector/Subsector	East and Southeast Asia	South Asia
Electricity	3,182.46	653.67
Transportation	1,593.87	1,196.12
Airports	57.73	5.070
Ports	215.20	36.08
Rails	16.14	12.78
Roads	1,304.80	1,142.20
Telecommunications	524.75	435.62
Telephones	142.91	6.46
Mobiles	339.05	415.87
Broadband	42.78	13.29
Water and Sanitation	171.25	85.09
Water	58.37	46.12
Sanitation	112.88	38.97
Total	**5,472.33**	**2,370.50**

Source: Bhattacharyay (2010).

with support from international financial organizations, including the International Monetary Fund (IMF) and from developed countries, would be critical to attain this objective.

One Belt One Road initiative

In 2013, the PRC's president, Xi Jinping, proposed establishing a modern equivalent of the ancient trade routes linking the PRC with the rest of Eurasia, by creating a network of railways, roads, pipelines, and utility grids. The initiative, One Belt One Road (OBOR), comprises the Silk Road Economic Belt (SREB), and the 21st Century Maritime Silk Road (MSR).

In its largest definition, OBOR would include 65 countries, 4.4 billion people, and about 40% of global GDP (Hofman 2015). To backup this initiative, the PRC has set up a new Silk Road Fund of USD 40 billion. The New Silk Road Fund is sponsored by the PRC's foreign exchange reserves, as well as government investment and lending arms.

The AIIB is also expected to support the OBOR initiative with a considerable share of its USD 100 billion in lending while the China Development Bank said that it would invest around USD 900 billion in more than 900 projects involving 60 countries. The *Economist* magazine has reported that USD 1 trillion would be spent in "government money" on this initiative (The Economist 2015).

Status of traditional finance supply and shortfalls

Asian financial markets have been characterized by the predominance of banks. Furthermore, Asian financial systems are generally loan-centric, with underdeveloped bond markets forcing a majority of credit onto banks and other credit intermediaries. The development of debt capital markets in the region has been slow owing to lack of market depth, legal, and regulatory hurdles. With global developments in financial markets, stricter risk allocation and compliance norms and overall credit shortage in the West, investment in infrastructure projects in the Asian region has been impacted by a reduction in commercial bank participation in project financing, which has significantly increased the role of multilateral financial institutions and export credit agencies. Traditionally, only commercial banks have been able to provide consistent funding toward project financing requirements of infrastructure projects globally. They have historic organizational expertise (together with their technical and legal advisers) to structure project risks so that their organizations can bear them. They also have the experience needed to supervise projects in construction, monitoring borrowers, considering waivers and consents on a case-by-case basis, restructuring projects when necessary.

However, the long-term global need for infrastructure has simply outgrown the capital available from commercial banks. Simultaneously, and particularly after implementation of the Basel III norms, banks' ability to provide debt has declined as the global need for investment has increased. As it has become clear that banks' balance sheets will not be able to support the need to finance infrastructure, attention has increasingly turned to institutional investors. The sums held by institutional investors, principally insurers, pension funds and sovereign wealth funds, approach the funding gap in scale. The OECD (2011) has estimated the total global infrastructure funding required from 2010 to 2030 to be USD 50 trillion. The same report estimated the total sums held by pension funds, insurance companies and mutual funds to be in excess of USD 65 trillion. The pricing, ticket sizes, and tenor that institutional investors can offer to borrowers can also make them more attractive than traditional bank financing.

The financing model thus needs to change to more sustainable local market and local currency financing by harnessing domestic savings in local financial institutions. Across the region, the growth of total credit has exceeded nominal GDP growth rates for many years. Equivalently, total credit and loans as a percentage of GDP have risen, so that many Asian countries are now well leveraged (Figure 19.1).

Investment finance methods; assessment of options

Traditional, non-recourse project financing in the Asian region has been largely impacted by the lack of a mature and liquid debt capital market, the traditional collateral-based banking model, and the generally high rate of inflation in the region which has left interest rates high.[1]

Historically, traditional infrastructure financing models have been heavily reliant on a leveraged structure. The monopolistic revenue model of such projects is largely sponsored by

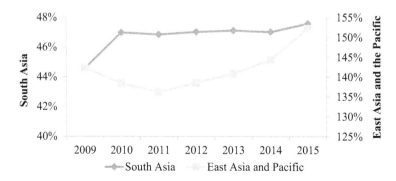

Figure 19.1 Domestic credit to private sector as a percentage of GDP, 2009–2015

GDP = gross domestic product.

Source: Compiled by author with data from the World Bank's Global Development Data.

Table 19.2 Infrastructure financing options

Type	Domestic Sources	External Sources
Equity	Domestic investors	Foreign investors
	Public utilities	Equipment suppliers (in collaboration with domestic and international developers)
	Dedicated government funds	Dedicated infrastructure funds
	Institutional investors	Other international equity investors
	Domestic commercial banks	International commercial Banks
Debt	Domestic term lending Institutions	Export credit agencies
	Domestic bond markets	International bond markets
	Specialized infrastructure financing options such as infrastructure debt funds	Multilateral agencies (financing with development perspectives and in long tenors)

Source: Finnacle Capital Research (2013).

state-owned developers and executed by competitively selected private sector counterparties. Subsequently, with the entry of private sector in project development, there was a conscious effort to break monopolies, leading to revenues being largely determined by market forces and the least cost bidding model, and for projects which were operating as regional monopolies, the financing and execution risk was largely transferred to private sector players whose own abilities to raise financing was limited. Thus, a substantial part of project-specific financing requirements was raised from the banking system.

Various options for financing infrastructure exist, both from domestic and external sources, as explained in Table 19.2.

Developments to expand public finance

The high asset value of infrastructure, long gestation periods, lumpiness of capital flows and high financing costs have deterred, and will continue to deter, private sector investment in development-stage projects.

The commercial and non-commercial components of a public infrastructure project make it unattractive for the private sector to invest and thus the non-commercial components are required to be unbundled for government funding through budgetary allocations, supported, and supplemented by financing from development finance institutions (DFIs) and under government-to-government programs.

In the Asian region, the Reserve Bank of India and the People's Bank of China are the only central banks which have been active in creating an environment conducive for the financing of infrastructure projects, while other central banks have continued investing large portions of their foreign exchange reserves in safe, but low-yielding securities like US Treasury bills and gold, among others.

For many countries in the region, foreign exchange reserves have come to exceed the amounts needed to provide for short-term import financing and maintaining exchange rate stability and hence part of these reserves have been channeled into sovereign wealth funds (SWFs), which can play an important role in funding projects spanning multiple countries. SWFs in the region have increased in both size and number over the past decade. These funds have become large and active participants in global financial markets and they frequently make high-profile foreign investments.

Table 19.3 Global ECA league table, Q1 2017 (USD million)

Company	USD million	Number of Deals
China EXIM Bank	3,581	5
JBIC	2,263	11
Export-Import Bank of India	956	4
Korea Exim Bank	608	4
Hungarian Export-Import Bank	270	1
UK Export Finance	124	1
Eksportkreditt Norge	107	2
KfW	88	2
Bladex	75	1
Export Development Canada	65	2

Source: Trade Finance League Table Analysis, Q1 2017.

The role of export credit agencies (ECAs) in infrastructure is expected to increase in the coming years with Asian ECAs taking the lead. PRC institutions are particularly active and are increasingly willing to work with other international finance providers. The Export-Import Bank of China (China EXIM Bank) and Japan Bank for International Cooperation (JBIC) have closed the largest number of deals globally in Q1 2017 (Table 19.3).

Multilateral development banks

Multilateral development banks (MDBs) can play an important role in a project's financial lifecycle, starting as a provider of development support to the host country parastatal. As the project progresses, this role evolves in that of a policy influencer, technical advisor, and honest broker. Subsequently, at financial closure, the MDBs will be expected to commit capital and debt to the project and leverage their network among other MDBs to take the project to financial closure. Simultaneously with this exercise, the MDBs are also needed to play an active role in influencing capital market reforms, promoting policy initiatives and introducing effective risk management tools.

MDBs support their member countries in achieving their development goals through financial support and technical assistance. In addition, MDBs help countries generate, attract, and manage additional flows to support sustainable development. MDBs provide in-depth and global expertise on infrastructure policy and design, as well as bring in practitioners engaged in the business of structuring, financing, and implementing of infrastructure projects. The MDBs are aiming to build a more harmonized approach for project preparation, procurement supervision, monitoring, and reporting.

The recently established Global Infrastructure Forum (GIF), which was jointly organized by various MDBs, aims at enhancing the level of coordination among different multilaterals and their development partners. The GIF is a platform to provide sustainable, accessible, resilient, and quality infrastructure for developing countries. The objective is to try and attract more resources for infrastructure, through government and their working partners.

AIIB

The landscape of MDBs has changed in January 2016 with the launch of AIIB, which was established to address the vast infrastructure financing needs in the region. AIIB's focus areas include development of infrastructure and other productive sectors in Asia, including energy and power, transportation and telecommunications, rural infrastructure and agriculture development, water supply and sanitation, environmental protection, urban development and logistics, and so forth. With 57 member countries, AIIB has invested over USD 1.7 billion in nine projects till January 2017, of which the two largest are the Trans-Anatolian natural gas pipeline project in Azerbaijan (USD 600 million) and the Tarbela 5 hydro power extension project in Pakistan (USD 300 million). AIIB is cooperating with the existing MDBs to jointly address Asia's infrastructure needs. AIIB has signed non-binding memoranda of understanding with ADB, the European Bank for Reconstruction and Development (EBRD), and the European Investment Bank (EIB).

ADB

As a multilateral development finance institution, ADB provides loans, technical assistance and grants to its members. In addition, ADB provides direct assistance to private enterprises of developing member countries, both, in the form of equity and debt. The aim of ADB is to support the three complementary agendas of inclusive economic growth, environmentally sustainable growth, and regional integration.

World Bank

The World Bank provides low-interest loans, zero- to low-interest credits, and grants to support a wide array of investments in such areas as education, health, public administration, infrastructure, financial and private sector development, agriculture, and environmental and natural resource management. It has also co-financed projects with governments, other multilateral institutions, commercial banks, export credit agencies, and private sector investors.

Shifting focus of MDBs and DFIs

Over the years, there has been a strong shift in global project financing away from projects, which relate to mining, processing, transportation, and consumption of fossil fuels. While the MDBs have traditionally been most vocal against such projects with adverse environmental impact, large global commercial banks and financial institutions too have weaned away in the last few years from financing fossil fuel projects, driven largely by shareholder and financier concerns.

While the MDBs and DFIs, including several bilateral and directed financing institutions, are well justified in their views against projects based on fossil fuel, a large number of countries in South Asia and Southeast Asia continue to largely remain engaged in such projects to sustain their long-term economic growth rates. Such consideration takes further credence because not only the energy output in this region is low with one of the lowest per capita energy consumption in Asia, but also because of their natural access to fossil fuel, the marginal cost of mining, and its lower use in energy production.

This situation makes it imperative for developers of such projects to procure most of their financing from local markets or ECAs who have not adopted such stringent policies against fossil fuel based projects like the DFIs and MDBs have.

Reducing the impact of currency shocks

A large number of DFIs, particularly the IFC and ADB, have taken several steps to augment availability of local currency financing to projects in Asia in order to mitigate the risk of depreciation of local currencies against hard currencies. Traditionally, they have done it through credit enhancement route, by providing guarantees to local financial institutions, replacing their direct lending with guarantee products. As DFIs increasingly shift their focus from direct lending and financing to providing guarantee products, commercial banks will need to be informed and actively encouraged to take part in projects that previously they would not have financed. The guarantees, thus provided, will ensure that the projects' residual risk profile (in terms of project, currency, and political risk) is acceptable to commercial financiers.

In direct financing, DFIs are increasingly seeking to finance projects through local currency denominated bonds placed by them in the local market. Through issuance of such local currency bonds, DFIs also contribute to building the financial and regulatory environment that is necessary for a well-functioning, robust local capital market. Further, issuance of local currency bond help extends the range of investable local financial instruments, which is key for increasing the participation of market players, as local investors need to have a sufficient variety of securities to be able to make efficient asset allocation decisions matching their risk-return profiles and time horizon. Given the shallow status of most capital markets in the region, a DFI involvement through bond issuance can largely help in harnessing their capacity and international expertise needed for widening the capital market environment that allows other international or domestic issuers to raise capital in local currency. Increased market participation results in better liquidity, which, in turn, makes it easier for domestic developers to raise money from the non-bank financing system in the local market, providing them with an opportunity to borrow directly from capital markets, particularly if their size made it previously impossible for them to access international capital markets.

ECAs

ECAs are public agencies and entities that provide government-backed loans, guarantees, and insurance to corporations from their home country seeking to do business overseas in countries that are considered too risky (commercially or politically) for conventional corporate financing. ECAs are part of a broader government policy context of industrial policy, trade, and investment promotion.

One of the main impacts of the global financial crisis has been the retrenchment of commercial bank lending which has led to the increasing share of the DFIs and ECAs in the project finance space. The presence of ECAs also helps deepen the bank funding market by lowering the risk and cost of funding. Asian governments are most active in the ECA space, promoting the industrial base of their home economies.

The long tenor required in infrastructure financing matches the long-term goals of ECAs like export promotion. Due to government backing, ECAs enjoy a lower cost of borrowing, capital reserves, and return expectations, and such cost savings are often passed on to the borrowers. ECAs help mitigate political risks which helps the project avail of traditional bank funding as well. They can also offer the benefit of relationships with multilateral agencies such as ADB and IFC.

While commercial banks are seen reluctant to adapt to market changes, the ECAs and their mandates have constantly evolved to adapt to such changes, new opportunities, competitions, and political situations. Helping small and medium-sized enterprises (SMEs) is now a key focus of most ECAs. For instance, Korea EXIM Bank has earmarked USD 24.5 billion for such purposes in 2015. A number of ECAs now also support energy investments with natural resources as a key policy aim.

With the continued prominence of the Asian region in the global economy and huge infrastructure gap in the region, Asian economies attract an ever-increasing share of ECA transactions globally. With an ever-increasing demand for energy, Indonesia has been a key focus for ECAs. China EXIM Bank was involved in the financing of Indonesia's Fast Track 1 procurement process for 10,000 MW of power in 2008–2009.

Even though ECAs are not as active as other MDBs in the area of renewable energy, they are increasingly responding to the growing funding needs of the region. Korea EXIM Bank, for instance, has taken the lead by included green financing as one of its priority sectors.

Developments to expand private finance

As mentioned earlier, Bhattacharyay (2010) estimated the need for infrastructure investment in the region, for the period 2010–2020, at USD 7.84 trillion. According to World Bank data, Asians had gross domestic savings of USD 8.37 trillion in 2014 alone. The household savings rate has been traditionally high in the region as compared to more developed nations. However, most of the savings are invested in real estate, precious metals listed securities, and liquid investments in US treasuries. To channel these savings into "bankable" infrastructure investments and attract private investment, there is a need to develop the domestic financial markets.

The insurance and pension funds are affected by statutory constraints restricting these funds from investing in infrastructure assets, being allowed to invest only in instruments having an investment grade rating which is impossible for a project financing asset class to achieve.

The regional commercial banks prefer to stay away or have an ultra-conservative perspective toward the non-recourse project finance proposals. The concern arises from risk concentration, peaking exposure norms, low asset yield, high moratorium and high payback periods of these loans, in a volatile interest and exchange rate regime.

Developing local and regional capital markets is an essential step in reducing reliance on foreign financiers while creating enabling conditions for growth. Most countries in the region have enough domestic savings to finance the infrastructure financing gap with only the access to and immaturity of the capital markets preventing savings being channelized toward funding this gap.

Efforts have been taken by many countries in the region to deepen financial markets by introducing new instruments and reforming the stock market. With liberalization and deregulation of financial activities allowing market participants to assume greater risks, prudential regulations and supervision need to be strengthened.

Foreign direct investment

Fueled by expanding regional production networks, integration with the global economy, falling trade and investment barriers, Asian economies have attracted significant amounts of FDI, especially from western countries driven by low demand in their native countries for creation of new infrastructure and high rate of return in Asian economies. In the Asian region, most FDI went to East Asia (World Investment Report 2016); total inflows to the region increased by 25% to USD 322 billion (Figure 19.2). In East Asia, Hong Kong, China was the largest recipient with USD 175 billion in 2015, making it the second largest recipient in the world after the US. The PRC saw an inflow of USD 136 billion. Singapore was the leading recipient country in Southeast Asia with FDI inflows of USD 65 billion, followed by Indonesia (USD 16 billion). India was the largest recipient country in South Asia with total inflows of USD 44 billion, making it the fourth largest recipient in the Asia region.

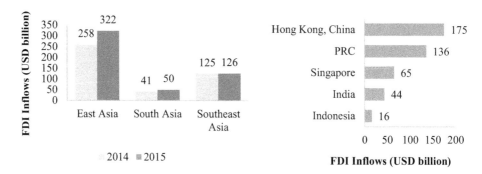

Figure 19.2   FDI inflows by subregion, 2014 and 2015, and top five economies by FDI inflows in the
region, 2015

FDI = foreign direct investment, PRC = People's Republic of China.

Source: Compiled by author with data from the United Nations Conference on Trade and Development, World
Investment Report 2016.

In the light of turbulent financial markets, it is crucial for countries to take a more liberal
view in creating an enabling FDI environment and open their doors to FDI from all credible
and sanitized sources.

However, FDI in the region is constrained by political risk, change in laws, sub-investment
grade procurers of finance, local currency exposure, and illiquid exit options.

Private participation in infrastructure

Over the last few decades, public-private partnership (PPP) has emerged as an often-preferred
tool in to complement sovereign efforts in developing infrastructure and providing related
services.

The infrastructure financing needs in the region exceed public sector resources, making the
role of the private sector engagement vital. The overall participation of the private sector has
a potential to improve dramatically. Momentum in the private sector can accentuate the efficiency and competitiveness of the region drastically.

In 2015, in the Asian region in terms of investment projects reaching financial closure, the
largest destination for PPI was the East Asia and Pacific region, attracting USD 13.5 billion
in 79 projects, followed by the South Asian region which attracted a combined total of USD
3 billion in 43 projects. In East Asia and Pacific region, the PRC accounted for a majority
of the projects, with a total investment of USD 3 billion in 49 projects out of the total 79
(Table 19.4), the Philippines, on the other hand, witnessed a commitment of USD 5.9 billion
across 13 projects. In the South Asian region, there were 43 deals for a combined value of
USD 5.6 billion, representing 5% of the total investment – a decline of 82% from the five-year
average of USD 30.5 billion, with India accounting for a majority of the projects (36 out of
43 projects).

Financing needs for energy in the region are expected to be supplemented by needs for
projects in the transportation and urbanization sectors, leading to enhanced connectivity. The
number of PPI projects in East Asia and the Pacific region[2] as well as the South Asia region has
seen a downward trend (Figure 19.3) along with the total investments made in the region over
the recent years (2012–2016).

Table 19.4 Number of projects (PPI) reaching financial closure

Country	2015	2014
Bangladesh	1	5
PRC	49	57
India	36	35
Indonesia	1	2
Lao PDR	1	2
Malaysia	1	1
Pakistan	4	0
Thailand	14	5

PRC = People's Republic of China.

Source: World Bank. Global PPI Update Report (2014–2015) (http://ppi.worldbank.org/).

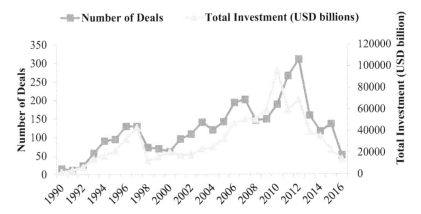

Figure 19.3   Number of PPI projects and total investment in the East Asia and the Pacific region and the South Asia region, 1990–2016

Source: Compiled by author with data from the World Bank's Private Participation in Infrastructure Database.

Barriers to public–private partnerships

PPPs in South Asia and Asia and the Pacific region have had a mixed track record of success and disappointment, with large amount of project delays and financing incapability often arising out of inadequate pre-investment work, insufficient project planning, absence of proper feasibility studies, flawed project evaluations, absence of competitive tendering, poor contract design, complexities in land acquisition, and inaccurate estimation of demand. Poorer compliance with the "environmental-social-governance" framework and lack of transparent governance mechanisms also lead to complicating project situations, creating perceptions of conflicts of interest and leading to arbitrary and populist government interference, lack of judicial independence, and lack of strong legal framework defining the rights and obligations of private investors.

In recent times, following the financial crisis of 2008, commercial banks have largely stayed away from infrastructure finance, which, together with the lack of liquidity and depth in the underdeveloped regional bond markets, has created an over-reliance on ECA and MDB financing. Given the stringent procurement requirements of DFIs, the PPP development model is

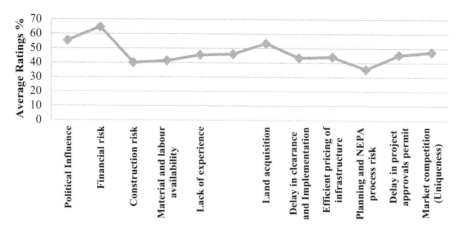

Figure 19.4 Risk factors versus viability

Source: Compiled with data from Hake et al. (2016).

increasingly focusing on reducing development lead time and minimizing execution risks, seeking better structured, readily financeable, and ready-to-construct project propositions. Apart from financial risk, the mitigation of political and land acquisition risks is the most pertinent. Figure 19.4 depicts the most significant risk factors affecting PPPs.[3]

Infrastructure projects have lifecycles which are much longer than the political tenors mandated through electoral system. Hence, there is an inherent political risk involved in financing of such projects, particularly if a newly elected government seeks to review projects allocated in the previous regime. One of the most important issues driven by political shifts relates to land acquisition which has caused several projects to be either stalled or delayed. The reason for this is resistance from local communities, often influenced by political considerations. It has also been observed that there is a huge difference between the registered value offered and the actual market value, resulting in disputes and litigation. Another issue is the delay in obtaining regulatory and environmental clearances, the reason for this is that the procedure for clearances is cumbersome and complex, and often is subject to ad hoc and arbitrary changes.

Regulatory and political hurdles aside, at the developers end, land acquisition issues also arise due to lack of an inclusive community engagement. This can be mitigated to an extent with ongoing community involvement during design, construction, and operation phases of a project.

At the regulatory end, there is a need for robust infrastructure regulation and contracts with possible government role in land acquisition prior to project allocation. Countries with successful PPP models in infrastructure are characterized by general stability of laws and regulation ensuring non-partisan alignment on infrastructure vision and strategic decisions. A reliable and efficient administration with clear agency setup, and efficient procurement and permit processes, reliable, and fair dispute-resolution mechanisms, and strict implementation of anti-corruption and transparency standards is a must.

Barriers to infrastructure finance and way forward

Project-level constraints

While in earlier days it used to be only quantitative parameters like debt service coverage ratio, interest coverage ratio, debt equity ratio, project internal rate of return, length of cash cycle and project payback, that determined the bankability of a project, today, in the complex world of environmental fragility and human rehabilitation, several qualitative parameters and capability to assess these have become equally crucial. These include environmental clearances, afforestation plan, relocation, and rehabilitation plan, wild life and marine life safeguard plan, along with the cumulative impact assessment of the project.

Regulatory and systemic constraints impeding access to financing and possible mitigants

The regulatory environment of the region is vastly divergent having different incentive structures. Several regulatory and institutional problems constrain the participation of financial institutions and reluctance of the sovereign system in rationalizing user charges and creating a market-making environment, along with a substantial disconnect between policy and implementation which act as a deterrent, especially for the private sector.

Key areas of regulatory concern are:

1   Commercial banks are impaired by possibilities of asset-liability mismatch, exposure caps and stringent provisioning norms, restricting expansion of bank lending for infrastructure projects.
2   Long-term savings in insurance and pension funds are difficult to route to infrastructure financing as those are subject to stringent guidelines in respect of the credit rating of the facility they invest in.
3   FDI limitations in some countries and the inability of the developer to exit in fully developed projects in favor of more conservative but a deep-pocket, utility scale private investor, constrain project capitalization for construction financing.
4   Pricing of user charges by a regulator is often conflicted and governed by political compulsions.
5   In the typical high-risk, low-return infrastructure investment model, the host country regulations need to permit combinations of fiscal subsidy by way of exemption from taxes and duties, revenue subsidy to supplement user charges, and bankable credit enhancement for lowering risk pricing.

Institutional constraints

Public insurance and pension fund companies are inherently highly risk averse. The safest way for these institutions to participate in creation of new infrastructure capacity could be through "take-out financing."[4]

The low level of stand-alone ratings (tells about accountability of future cash flows and risk) achieved by infrastructure projects further restricts the flow of foreign non-bank financing in the debt of these entities. In Asian economies, the slow pace of reforms and evolution of the commercial debt capital markets has also been an impediment.

After the global financial crisis, the liquidity for debt has become further constrained with introduction of more stringent compliance, capital adequacy and provisioning norms for commercial banks. Together with reforms in the insurance and pension sector asset allocation and in the credit rating framework, there is also an urgent need to add depth and liquidity to the debt capital markets that can go a long way to attract retail and household savings.

One way to facilitate debt capital market investment by the retail and household sectors is to offer fiscal incentives in the form of tax rebate or tax credit. This also brings out the issue of designing structured products for the market, which is an investment banking role. With Asian banks being mostly focused on fund-based businesses, investment banking is conflicted in their attempt to sell their own credit products, with very little effort at exploring possibilities to create market friendly credit solutions for project finance.

Another area that requires strong institutional intervention is creating hedging solutions against interest and currency related risks. Foreign exchange hedging is not available for long tenures. Likewise, the inherent asset-liability mismatch of banks creates interest rate risk for projects borrowing on floating rates.

An effective way of backstopping the currency risk could be through an effective central bank intervention enabling foreign banks and ECAs to lend in local currency from their overseas resources.

PPP agreements are often poorly structured and drafted due to a lack of skills or experience in government departments. Additionally, investors need to guard against the possibility of continuing political, legal, and regulatory uncertainty with respect to foreign ownership restrictions, capital controls, and partnership terms.

High risk in several Asian countries in contract enforcement is an established concern among all investors. In the World Bank's (Ease of) Doing Business report for 2014, several Asian countries rank in the bottom fifth percentile in respect of contract enforcement risk, which points toward the need for rapid judicial reforms, bringing in transparency in litigation processes, fast track resolution of conflicts and firm enforcement of contracts under local laws.

Finally, an area of institutional reform that requires direct sovereign level support relate to provisioning of credit enhancement. It is extremely important for project developers to have recourse under sovereign guarantee to terminate a project and exit by recovering a termination payment if such changes become untenable for project ownership, construction and/or operation.

Policy proposals to ease constraints

The broad policy initiatives which are crucial for facilitating infrastructure financing in the region are summarized below:

1   Create policy enablers for insurance and pension funds to lend in debt refinancing of post-construction infrastructure projects;
2   Liberate FDI limits in non-strategic infrastructure businesses to create a larger investment pool;
3   Facilitate policy environment for bank financing of promoter buyout of financial investors in profitable operational projects;
4   Undertake sector reforms to levy market determined user charges, indexation, and pass through provisions without being conflicted and governed by political compulsions;
5   Permit well-directed fiscal and revenue subsidies to reduce project payback and attract investment;
6   Procure measures for debt market reforms by incentivizing market making in debt securities;
7   Create policy interventions to provide sovereign level support for mitigating currency and interest rate risks;
8   Encourage rating institutions for creating an infrastructure rating framework, enabling well-structured projects with bankable contracts to access funds in debt capital markets;
9   Promote an environment of transparent documentation, project allocation and contract enforcement to instill confidence in private participants;

10 Support regional cooperation mechanisms for cross-border projects by identifying the roles, responsibilities, obligations, and liabilities of each host nation;

11 Promote transparent policies for cross-border and international trade in capital equipment and services by lowering non-tariff barriers;

12 Implement judicial reforms for better contract enforcement and faster disposal of legal disputes;

13 Develop a mature regulatory framework for PPP projects, clearly identifying the roles, responsibilities and overall accountability of the government counterpart; and

14 Consider project specific sovereign support toward credit enhancement, including provisions of termination payment on account of default by a state entity.

It is critical to align regional connectivity initiatives with national projects to facilitate resource mobilization. Governments should be encouraged to work together and supply the needed cross-border infrastructure. The MDBs need to play a crucial role here.

Developing regional and national-level infrastructure is a long-term process that requires strong coordination mechanism. Therefore, countries need to create bankable project development, documentation, and transparent legal and institutional frameworks that can improve the acceptability of such projects among private sector counterparties, as well as promote competition and improve regulatory frameworks that protect public interests.

Development of national and regional capital markets and institutional financing mechanisms for improving access to finance

The capital markets in the Asian region are highly diverse. Developing approaches to narrow the infrastructure financing gap has been among the key issues in every regional forum. A well-developed regional capital market can enhance resilience and capacity to cope with global financial shocks, especially those originating in the western hemisphere.

The vulnerability of the region to sudden reversal of short-term capital inflows, which are particularly risky for long-term investments, came to light first in the 1997–1998 Asian financial crisis, prompting most central banks in the region to create poison pills for such capital flight through fiscal and monetary policies, while at the same time emphasizing on the creation of a more resilient financial system. In the years that followed, the ASEAN+3 (ASEAN, PRC, Japan, and Republic of Korea) countries (Addressing Infrastructure Financing in Asia) have been working together to strengthen the resilience of the financial system in the region by developing local currency bond markets to mitigate capital flight and mobilize domestic savings for long-term investment. The development of local currency bond markets reduces foreign currency risk for borrowers and helps to minimize currency and maturity mismatches, which is crucial for infrastructure investments.

MDBs can play a crucial role in deepening regional capital markets by playing the role of an honest broker and coordinator in regional forums. Additionally, at the country-specific level, MDB support can take the form of augmenting or supplementing national budgets through sovereign lending, leveraging private sector participation through guarantees covering political and credit risks, financing feasibility studies through technical assistance and providing project-structuring support, and improving business and governance practices. To increase local level retail participation in capital markets, there is a need to de-risk projects from currency and political risks. Guarantees and credit enhancement by MDBs can play an important role in this regard with mechanisms to transfer specific risks from investors and lenders to guarantee providers.

There is also a strong need to deepen derivatives markets to provide local currency hedging instruments. Exchange rate fluctuations can significantly affect the bankability of any infrastructure project that relies on foreign financing. Currency hedging instruments such as foreign exchange forwards and swaps play a substantial role in facilitating international transactions. In many of the markets in the Asian region, basic currency hedging instruments are not available. Also, the markets lack depth making hedging uneconomical. Governments and MDBs need to play an active role as market makers, providing pricing and sufficient liquidity in the currency market. Development of local capital markets needs to be supported by widespread regulatory, fiscal, and legal changes.

Notes

1 Non-recourse financing refers to the financing in which the lender is only entitled to repayment from the profits of the project for which the loan is given and not from other assets of the borrower.
2 In World Bank Reports and Database, East Asia and the Pacific region includes East Asia and Southeast Asia.
3 Hake et al. (2016) consider 20 risk factors, which are then put in a tabulated format with rating from 0 to 10 so that the most viable factors can be rated toward higher side and less viable factors rated toward lower side (i.e., 0 for most irrelevant factor and 10 for highly relevant factor).
4 Take-out financing refers to a structured refinancing of an existing debt through pre-committed loan buyout by another lender upon attainment of certain pre-agreed milestones.

References

Asian Development Bank (ADB). 2009. *Intraregional Trade and Investment in South Asia*. Manila: Asian Development Bank.
ADB. 2012. *Infrastructure for Supporting Inclusive Growth and Poverty Reduction in Asia*. Manila: Asian Development Bank.
Bhattacharyay, B. 2010. Estimating Demand for Infrastructure in Energy, Transport, Telecommunications, Water and Sanitation in Asia and the Pacific: 2010–2020. ADBI Working Paper No. 248. Tokyo: Asian Development Bank Institute.
Cambridge Dictionary. Definition of Infrastructure. http://dictionary.cambridge.org/dictionary/english/infrastructure
Economist Special Report. 2015. Business in China: Foreign Investment, The New Silk Road, 10 September. www.economist.com/news/special-report/21663326-chinas-latest-wave-globalisers-will-enrich-their-countryand-world-new-silk-road
Hake, S., T. Mohite, V. More, S. Salunke, and R. Shekade. 2016. Analysis of Risk Factors in PPP Projects. *IRJET* 3(4), April 2016. www.irjet.net/archives/V3/i4/IRJET-V3I4617.pdf
Hofman, B. 2015. China's One Belt One Road Initiative: What We Know Thus Far. http://blogs.world bank.org/eastasiapacific/china-one-belt-one-road-initiative-what-we-know-thus-far
OECD. 2011. *Pension Funds Investment in Infrastructure – A Survey*. Paris: Organization for Economic Co-operation and Development.
The Economist. 2015. Special Report on Business in China: Foreign Investment, September. https://www.economist.com/special-report/2015/09/12/back-to-business
Trade Finance League Table Analysis, Q1. 2017. https://tradefinanceanalytics.com/uploads/TFA_League-Tables_Q1%202017.pdf
UNCTAD. 2016. *World Investment Report*. Geneva: United Nations Conference on Trade and Development. http://unctad.org/en/PublicationsLibrary/wir2016_en.pdf

20

FINANCIAL INCLUSION IN ASIA

Peter J. Morgan

Introduction

Financial inclusion (i.e., access to finance) is receiving increasing attention as having the potential to contribute to economic and financial development while at the same time fostering more inclusive growth and greater income equality. Leaders of the G20 countries have approved the Financial Inclusion Action Plan and established the Global Partnership for Financial Inclusion[1] to promote the financial access agenda. The Asia-Pacific Economic Cooperation Finance Ministers' process has a dedicated forum looking at financial inclusion issues.[2] The implementation of the Association of Southeast Asian Nations (ASEAN) Framework on Equitable Economic Development has made the promotion of financial inclusion a key objective (ASEAN 2014). The Asian Development Bank has approved 121 projects (amounting to USD 2.59 billion as of 2012) to support microfinance in countries in Asia and the Pacific region (ADB 2012). Many individual Asian economies have adopted strategies on financial inclusion as an important part of their overall strategies to achieve inclusive growth.

However, there is still much to achieve. One key indicator of household access to finance is the percentage of adults who have an individual or joint account at a formal financial institution such as a bank, credit union, cooperative, post office, or microfinance institution, or with a mobile money provider. According to the most recent Global Findex database for 2014, the total number of adults without accounts is about two billion. East Asia and the Pacific region and South Asia combined account for 55% of the world's unbanked adults, mainly in India and the People's Republic of China (PRC) (Demirgüç-Kunt et al. 2015).

This chapter surveys the policies and experience of Asian economies in the areas of financial inclusion, financial regulation, financial literacy and financial education programs. The next sections provide definitions of financial inclusion and the rationale for expanded access. Then the current situation of financial inclusion in Asia is described, as well as barriers to financial inclusion. The following sections summarize strategies to expand financial inclusion, describe regulatory issues, and summarize the situation of financial literacy and education in Asia.

Definitions of financial inclusion

Financial inclusion broadly refers to the degree of access of households and firms, especially poorer households and small and medium-sized firms, to financial services. Here "access" doesn't mean just any kind of access, but implies convenient access at reasonable cost, and with accompanying safeguards such as adequate regulation of firms supplying financial services and laws and institutions for protecting consumers against inappropriate products, deceptive practices, aggressive collection practices, and so forth. Two examples of definitions are:

> ready access for households and firms to reasonably priced financial services.
>
> *(ADB 2015: 71)*

> the process of promoting affordable, timely and adequate access to a wide range of regulated financial products and services and broadening their use by all segments of society through the implementation of tailored existing and innovative approaches including financial awareness and education with a view to promote financial well-being as well as economic and social inclusion.
>
> *(Atkinson and Messy 2013: 11)*

Of course, it is difficult to define "reasonable cost" in cases where amounts involved are small, access costs in rural areas are high, there are information asymmetries, and so forth. This perspective also highlights the need for adequate financial education and consumer protection, as consumers cannot take proper advantage of access to financial services if they do not understand them properly or trust them.

Access to financial services has a multitude of dimensions, reflecting the range of possible financial services, from payments and savings accounts to credit, insurance, pensions, and securities markets. The relevant services vary for individuals and for firms. Another important dimension is actual usage of such products and services. For example, campaigns to increase the number of bank accounts fail if those accounts end up being rarely or never used.

Rationale for financial inclusion

There are various arguments in favor of greater financial inclusion. Poor households are often severely cash-constrained, so innovations that increase the efficiency of their cash management and allow them to smooth consumption can have significant impacts on welfare. Relying on cash-based transactions imposes many costs and risks. Also, many studies find that the marginal return to capital in small and medium-sized enterprises (SMEs) is large when capital is scarce, which suggests that they could reap sizeable returns from greater financial access (Demirgüç-Kunt and Klapper 2013). Greater financial inclusion can also contribute to reducing income inequality by raising the incomes of the poorest income quintile disproportionately (Beck, Demirgüç-Kunt, and Levine 2007). Financial inclusion may also contribute to financial stability by increasing the diversity of (thereby decreasing the risk of) bank assets and by increasing the stable funding base of bank deposits (Khan 2011; Morgan and Pontines 2014; Morgan and Zhang 2015).

A growing body of evidence suggests that access to financial services can reduce poverty, raise income, and promote economic growth. Some of the key earlier studies in this area finding benefits from financial inclusion were Honohan (2004), Beck, Demirgüç-Kunt, and Levine (2007), and World Bank (2008). There has also been a large volume of research on the impacts of microfinance, including McKernan (2003), Pitt et al. (2003), and Kaboski and Townsend (2005), but the reliability of the results of many of the studies suffered from possible selection bias (Karlan and Morduch 2009). More reliable studies with randomized control trials or natural experiments are still relatively rare. Some recent ones include Burgess and Pande (2005) and Bruhn and Love (2013), who found evidence that increases in bank branches reduced poverty and raised income and employment levels.

Status of financial inclusion in Asia

Households

One of the main measures of financial inclusion is the percentage of adults with accounts at a formal financial institution.[3] Account holdings tend to rise with per capita GDP, as would be expected, but there is still huge variation across countries (Figure 20.1). The large variation implies that other factors besides income play important roles, including overall financial development, financial system structure, regulatory, institutional, social, and geographic factors. The majority of Asian economies (for which data are available) have penetration shares of less than 55%: Afghanistan, Azerbaijan, Bangladesh, Cambodia, Georgia, India, Indonesia, Kazakhstan, Kyrgyz Republic, Lao PDR, Nepal, Pakistan, Philippines, Tajikistan, Uzbekistan, and Viet Nam. Penetration is even less than 20% in Afghanistan, Cambodia, Pakistan, and Tajikistan.

In contrast, Figure 20.2 shows that the relationship between per capita GDP and the share of adults obtaining loans from a formal financial institution is actually negatively sloped. For emerging economies, the relative positions are somewhat similar to those in Figure 20.1. However, high-income countries such as Japan, Republic of Korea, Malaysia, and Singapore have relatively low ratios. This presumably reflects access to other forms of credit in those countries, such as credit cards.

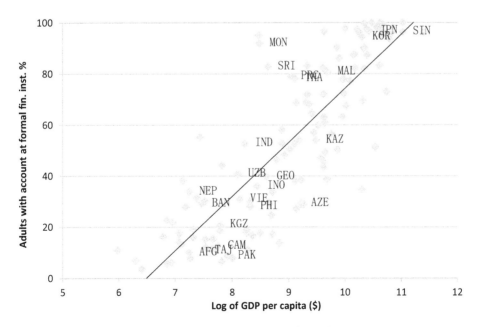

Figure 20.1   Relation of per capita GDP to deposit penetration for adults, 2014

Source: Compiled with data from the World Bank's Global Findex database, http://www.worldbank.org/en/programs/globalfindex.

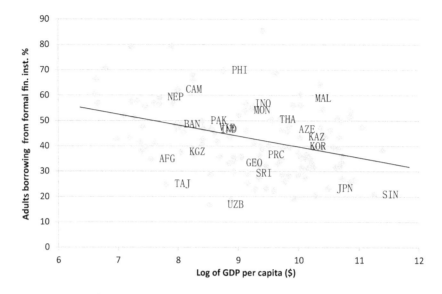

Figure 20.2 Relation of per capita GDP to loan penetration for adults, 2014

Source: Compiled with data from the World Bank's Global Findex database, http://www.worldbank.org/en/programs/globalfindex.

Data on individual access to insurance policies in the Global Findex Survey are relatively scarce, and also vary widely. High-income and high-middle-income economies such as Japan, Republic of Korea, and Malaysia have at least one life insurance policy for every adult. The penetration ratio in Thailand is 39%. On the other hand, penetration of life insurance policies is quite low in Bangladesh (14%), Georgia (11%), Kyrgyz Republic (6%), Myanmar (8%), and Tajikistan (5%). Information on penetration of nonlife insurance policies is even more scarce.

Firms

Figure 20.3 shows a fairly strong relationship between per capita GDP and the share of small firms with a line of credit overall, but, again, the pattern among emerging Asian economies shows a high degree of variation. Data are available for considerably fewer countries than in the case of household financial access. Central and West Asian economies, Indonesia, Lao PDR, and the Philippines stand out as having relatively low financing for SMEs.

Barriers to financial inclusion

Barriers to financial inclusion can be classified as either supply side or demand side. Supply side barriers reflect limitations on the capacity or willingness of the financial sector to extend financial services to poorer households or SMEs. These can be further subdivided into three categories: market-driven factors, regulatory factors, and infrastructure limitations.

Market-driven factors include aspects such as relatively high maintenance costs associated with small-size deposits or loans, high costs associated with providing financial services in small towns in rural areas, lack of credit data or usable collateral, and lack of convenient access points. Lack of credit data and reliable financial records worsens the problem of information asymmetry that discourages banks from lending to poorer households and SMEs.

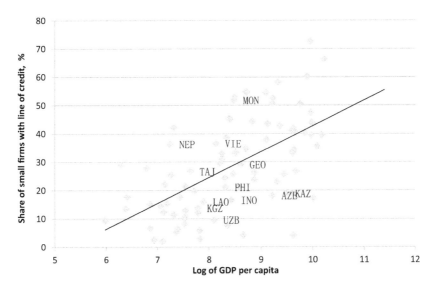

Figure 20.3 Share of small firms with line of credit, 2011

Source: Compiled with data from the World Bank's Global Findex database, http://www.worldbank.org/en/programs/globalfindex.

Regulatory factors include capital adequacy and supervisory rules that may limit the attractiveness of small-size deposits, loans or other financial products to financial institutions. Strict requirements regarding opening of branches or ATMs may also restrict the attractiveness of doing so in remote areas. Identification (ID) and other documentation requirements are important both with respect to "know your customer" (KYC) requirements and monitoring of possible money laundering and terrorist financing activities, but these can pose problems for poor households in countries which do not have universal individual identification systems (and few do). Regulatory requirements can also restrict the entry of microfinance institutions, such as restrictions on foreign ownership, inspection requirements, and so forth.

Infrastructure-related barriers include lack of access to secure and reliable payments and settlement systems, the availability of either fixed or mobile telephone communications, and the availability of convenient transport to bank branches or ATMs. These can pose particular problems in archipelagic countries such as Indonesia and the Philippines. Numerous studies have identified lack of convenient transport as an important barrier to financial access (e.g., Tambunlertchai 2015).

Demand-side factors include a lack of funds, lack of knowledge of financial products (i.e., financial literacy), and lack of trust. Lack of trust can be a significant problem when countries do not have well-functioning supervision and regulation of financial institutions and programs of consumer protection that require, among others, adequate disclosure, regulation of collection procedures, and systems of dispute resolution.

Strategies to promote financial inclusion

Asian economies are putting increasing emphasis on promoting financial inclusion, including financial education. Strategies for doing so can be implemented at the national level, as well as by central banks, financial regulatory agencies, private institutions, and non-governmental organizations (NGOs). Indonesia, the Philippines, and Thailand are relatively advanced in having developed broad national strategies for financial inclusion. Efforts to promote SMEs in Thailand are well advanced and are organized through the SME Promotion Master Plan. South Asian countries such as Bangladesh, India, and Sri Lanka are lagging at the national strategy level, but their central banks have been active in this area.

Strategies for promoting financial inclusion encompass five broad areas: (1) promotion of inclusion-oriented financial institutions; (2) subsidized funding; (3) development of innovative products and services; (4) development of innovative delivery technologies; and (5) development of innovative systems to enhance access to credit. These elements are shown in Table 20.1 for a number of emerging Asian economies.

Inclusion-oriented financial institutions

Inclusion-oriented financial institutions include microfinance institutions (MFIs), state-owned banks, post offices offering financial services, credit cooperatives and community organizations. India has operated mainly through state-owned agricultural banks and local banks. Thailand established a number of specialized financial institutions (SFIs) which operate as banks and cater to lower-income households and smaller firms. The PRC and Indonesia also have numerous specialized lending institutions. MFIs are active in most emerging Asian economies, although there are significant differences in their status and regulation across countries, as will be discussed below.

Innovative products and services

Innovative products and services include various "micro" products such as no-frills bank deposits, microcredits and microinsurance, the development of agent banking, and establishment of "micro" branches. India has seen an impressive rollout of 150 million no-frills accounts by April 2015. However, 85 million of them contain no funds, and even many of those with funds are basically dormant (The Economist 2015). Indonesia has introduced Grameen Bank-style credit products, and also offers three types of Islamic microfinance products, including a profit- and loss-sharing approach for credit and savings, Grameen-model Islamic microfinance, and Islamic style microinsurance (Tambunan 2015). In the Philippines, regular insurance companies and mutual benefit associations have begun to provide microinsurance and similar products by to help the low-income sectors to deal with vulnerability risks and catastrophic events (Llanto 2015). Use of agents or correspondents can help to overcome problems of distance and shortages of branches.

Innovative delivery technologies

Innovative delivery technologies such as mobile phones, electronic money (e-money), and internet banking can also help to bridge distances and save time. Telephone banking has great potential as a result of the rapid diffusion of mobile phone ownership in many developing and emerging economies. Telephone banking has enjoyed substantial success in the Philippines (UNESCAP 2014). On the other hand, use of mobile phones to pay bills in India is still quite limited, reaching only about 2% of the population, and a much lower rate for the rural poor (Barua, Kathuria, and Malik 2015). In Sri Lanka, bank representatives visit rural homes, use a point-of-sale electronic device to connect to a mobile phone network, and then take a deposit and provide an instant electronic confirmation to the depositor (Kelegama and

Table 20.1 Elements of financial inclusion strategies

Country	Inclusive financial institutions	Subsidized funding	Innovative financial products and services	Innovative delivery technologies	Innovative systems to enhance credit access
Bangladesh	Cooperative societies, postal savings bank, Grameen Bank, licensed NGO-MFIs	Palli Karma Sahayak Foundation for MFIs; refinancing of bank loans to SMEs	Microdeposits, microloans, "Taka Ten" bank accounts for farmers, school banking program	Mobile phone banking	
PRC	Agricultural Bank of China, rural credit cooperatives, Postal Savings Bank of China, village and township banks, poverty alleviation microfinance, microcredit companies, P2P		Microloans, farmers benefit credit card, mutual guarantee loans for SMEs	Branchless and mini-branch banking services, P2P lending platforms, third-party payment services, mobile banking	SME Board and ChiNext of Shenzhen Stock Exchange, SME collective notes (bonds), Credit Reference Center
India	Regional rural banks, united community banks, Local Area Banks, NBFC-MFIs	MUDRA Bank	No-frills bank accounts (with additional services to be added), business correspondents	Telephone bill-paying	Stock exchange platforms for SMEs, credit bureaus
Indonesia	Bank Perkreditan Rakyat, Bank Pembangunan Daerah, Bank Rakyat Indonesia		Grameen Bank-style microcredit products, Islamic microfinance products	Telephone banking, e-money	Loan guarantee programs
Philippines	Rural banks, cooperatives, credit cooperatives, and credit NGOs		Microdeposits, microloans, and microinsurance products, agents for insurance, e-money and payments	Telephone banking, e-money	
Sri Lanka	Cooperatives, NGO-MFIs, CBOs, Samurdhi, rotating savings, and credit associations			Telephone banking via POS terminal, e-remittance services	
Thailand	State financial institutions, cooperatives, and occupational groups, savings groups for production, and village funds			Telephone banking, e-money	Loan guarantee program, credit database (in development)

PRC = People's Republic of China, CBO = community-based organization, MFI = microfinance institution, NBFC = non-bank finance company, NGO-MFI = non-government organization microfinance institution, P2P = peer-to-peer lending, POS = point of sale, SME = small and medium-sized enterprise.

Sources: ADBI (2014), BUCFLP (2017), Barua, Kathuria, and Malik (2015), Kelegama and Tilakaratna (2014), Khalily (2015), Llanto (2015), Peng, Zhao, and Wang (2014), Tambunan (2015), and Tambunlertchai (2015).

Tilakaratna 2014). Peer-to-peer lending has become an important source of finance for SMEs in the PRC.

The development of e-money can make a substantial contribution to reducing the cost and inconvenience of making payments. Llanto (2015) notes that e-money accounts and e-money transactions have grown significantly in the past few years in the Philippines. For example, registered e-money accounts increased by 34% to 26.7 million accounts in 2013 from 2010. Also, there are 10,620 active e-money agents performing cash-in/cash-out transactions. However, there are issues with regard to identification and monitoring of money laundering and possible terrorism-related transactions, which are discussed below.

Innovative systems to enhance credit access

It is well known that informational asymmetries such as the lack of credit data, bankable collateral and basic accounting information discourage financial institutions from lending to SMEs. Some Asian economies have been active in the area of expanding and consolidating credit databases on households and SMEs, but such efforts in most cases are still at an early stage, while in others such efforts have not yet started. In Thailand, Tambunlertchai (2015) notes that the existing credit database of the Thai National Credit Bureau provides little credit information on low-income individuals and micro-enterprises. There is no formal credit bureau in Indonesia, which could be used to monitor risks of over-indebtedness in areas of strong credit growth (Tambunan 2015). Llanto (2015) also cites the problem of the slow implementation of a credit information system in the Philippines. In Sri Lanka, membership of the Credit Information Bureau (CRIB) of Sri Lanka is mandatory only for the formal financial institutions, while most MFIs are not integrated into the CRIB (Kelegama and Tilakaratna 2014).

Credit guarantees can also ease access to finance for SMEs, although they confront a number of problems, mainly issues of moral hazard and high costs due to non-performing loans. In Thailand, the Thai Credit Guarantee Corporation offers credit guarantee products that assist SMEs in obtaining commercial bank loans (Tambunlertchai 2015). In Indonesia, loans to micro, small, and, medium-sized enterprises (MSMEs) under the program for people/community business credit (KUR) are guaranteed (70%) by two insurance companies (PT. Asuransi Kredit Indonesia and Perusahaan Umum Jaminan Kredit Indonesia) and by other companies which have voluntarily joined the program (Tambunan 2015). Some governments have introduced measures in this area. India set up dedicated platforms for SMEs by both the National and Bombay Stock Exchanges, and Thailand has similar programs.

Strategies for financial inclusion

Strategies for financial inclusion are needed to set priorities and coordinate overall approaches. Table 20.2 summarizes the major strategies adopted by the countries in this study. National-level strategies would be most desirable, followed by strategies of the central bank and major ministries and/or financial regulatory bodies. Table 20.2 shows a range of approaches in the subject countries. In Asia, the Philippines and Thailand have the most well-articulated financial inclusion strategies, which are incorporated in their national economic planning strategies. Bangladesh, India, Indonesia, and Sri Lanka have long-standing policies to promote financial inclusion through devices such as loan quotas for priority sectors, but no national strategy. Indonesia has a detailed "National Strategy for Financial Inclusion" maintained jointly by Bank Indonesia and the Ministry of Finance. At the regulatory level, Thailand's Master Plan for SME

Table 20.2 Strategies for financial inclusion

Country	National	Central bank	Ministries, regulators
Bangladesh	No national strategy; legal basis for Grameen Bank; establishment of Microcredit Regulatory Authority	Taka Ten Account for farmers, expansion of rural bank branches, refinancing, mobile banking, SME financing, and school banking	
PRC	Reform measures endorsed by State Council	Promotion of increased bank branches and services in rural areas	China Banking Regulatory Commission: Introduction of new kinds of rural financial institutions; guidelines for microcredit business; China Securities Regulatory Commission: guidance for SME stock exchanges
India	Priority Sector Lending targets; "PMJDY" bank account strategy; biometric ID program	Rural branch opening rules; establishment of innovative bank types; promotion of no-frills bank accounts; business correspondents; financial education	
Indonesia	Subsidized credit and bank lending targets for MSMEs and farmers; establishment of Grameen-type banks and other microfinance institutions	National Strategy for Financial Inclusion (with MoF): payment system infrastructure; financial education; credit-related information; supporting regulation; campaigns; and consumer protection	MoF (see central bank)
Philippines	Included in Philippine Development Plan 2011–2016: Increase confidence in financial system; expand offerings of financial products; financial education	Lead government institution to formulate specific financial inclusion strategies: numerous circulars	Department of Finance–National Credit Council: Credit Policy Improvement Project
Sri Lanka	10% bank loan target for agriculture; creation of Samurdhi banking societies	Branch opening regulations	
Thailand	Aspects included in 11th National Economic and Social Development Plan: focus on SME finance, financial education		MoF: National Strategy for Financial Inclusion; Master Plan of SME Promotion

PRC = People's Republic of China, MoF = Ministry of Finance, MSME = micro, small, and, medium-sized enterprises, SME = small and medium-sized enterprises.

Sources: Barua, Kathuria, and Malik (2015), Kelegama and Tilakaratna (2014), Khalily (2015), Llanto (2015), Peng, Zhao, and Wang (2014), Tambunan (2015), and Tambun-lertchai (2015).

Promotion stands out, along with the Credit Policy Improvement Project of the Philippines and various programs of the China Banking Regulatory Commission in the PRC.

Regulatory issues for financial inclusion

Efforts to promote financial inclusion raise many challenges for financial regulators, and creative responses to these challenges could contribute substantially to promoting financial inclusion. Traditionally, regulators have been skeptical of schemes to promote financial inclusion, due to the higher credit risks and lack of documentation associated with small borrowers. However, a more recent strand of literature focuses on the positive implications of financial inclusion for financial stability. Khan (2011) suggests three main ways in which greater financial inclusion can contribute positively to financial stability. First, greater diversification of bank assets as a result of increased lending to smaller firms could reduce the overall riskiness of a bank's loan portfolio. Second, increasing the number of small savers would increase both the size and stability of the deposit base, reducing banks' dependence on wholesale funding, which tends to be more volatile during a crisis. Third, greater financial inclusion could also contribute to a better transmission of monetary policy, also contributing to greater financial stability.

Therefore, regulators need to strike a balance between the need to provide a fertile environment for providers of financially inclusive services, while at the same time guaranteeing the stability of the financial system and protecting consumers. Table 20.3 summarizes the major features of regulations related to financial inclusion in the subject countries, including regulatory agencies, ID-related measures, regulation of MFIs, regulations of lending (mainly interest rate caps) and consumer protection.

Two broad conclusions have emerged from the various country experiences. First, programs to promote financial inclusion must be aligned with financial incentives. Otherwise, they will face great difficulties in achieving their targets. Second, regulation of microfinance needs to be "proportionate" to the risks to financial stability involved.

Need for financial inclusion strategies to be aligned with economic returns

The performance of state-owned banks and government finance programs has been mixed, and there has been a gradual learning process that has shifted the emphasis away from specialized state-owned lenders, often operating with subsidies, to more market-based solutions. In Indonesia, Tambunan (2015) argues that the supply led subsidized microcredit programs initiated by the government do not provide a conducive environment where sustainable microfinance providers can operate, and that it should shift resources from subsidized program credits to capacity building of existing microfinance institutions for expanded outreach and their sustainability. In the Philippines, Llanto (2015) notes that the government recognized the failure of subsidized or directed credit programs to reach the intended targets – mostly small farmers and other small-scale clients – in a sustainable manner, and reforms pursued by the government and regulators in collaboration with private sector stakeholders led to a greater private sector role, chiefly by MFIs.

Regulatory measures to promote access

Governments have relied on a number of different measures to promote financial access, but with varying degrees of success. India sets minimum lending quotas for banks in so-called

Table 20.3 Financial inclusion regulatory measures

Country	Regulatory agencies	ID-related measures	Regulation of MFIs	Lending regulation	Consumer protection
Bangladesh	Bank of Bangladesh, Microcredit Regulatory Authority, Insurance Development and Regulatory Authority		Licensing of MFIs over certain size, can take deposits	Interest rate cap, deposit rate rate floor	
PRC	China Banking Regulatory Commission		Credit cooperatives can take deposits; microcredit companies cannot; also limits on funding		National Consumer Protection Agency; Consumer Dispute Settlement Board, Credit Information Bureau
India	Reserve Bank of India, MUDRA Bank	"Aadhaar" biometric ID program, linked to access to micro-accounts	Not licensed, self-regulated, but rules on disclosure; can convert to Small Bank	Lending rate caps for banks, NBMFIs	RBI: Grievance redress mechanism in banks; banking ombudsman system
Indonesia	Bank Indonesia, OJK, multiple others		Multiple regulatory entities	Interest rate caps: KUR (22%), 5%–7% for agriculture/energy programs	
Philippines	Bangko Sentral ng Pilipinas (BSP), Insurance Commission	Easier ID requirements in cases where documentation lacking	BSP regulates most entities; only rural banks and credit cooperatives can accept deposits	Only disclosure rules	BSP: Consumer Affairs Group; Securities and Exchange Commission; National Anti-Poverty Council; National Credit Council; Microfinance Consumer Protection Guidebook
Sri Lanka	Central Bank of Sri Lanka		NGO-MFIs can register under various acts; not licensed; only cooperative societies and Samurdhi Banking Societies can take deposits		Consumer Affairs Authority; Voluntary Financial Ombudsman system; Consumer Affairs Council; Credit Information Bureau of Sri Lanka
Thailand	Bank of Thailand, Ministry of Finance, multiple others		Various agencies depending on type of MFI, some not regulated at all	Interest rate cap of 28% for SFIs, 15% for non-formal lenders	Bank of Thailand: Financial Consumer Protection Center

FCA = Financial Conduct Authority, KUR = non-collateralized credit scheme for MSMEs, MFI = microfinance institution, MSME = micro, small, and medium-sized enterprise, NGO-MFI = non-government organization microfinance institution, OJK = Financial Supervisory Agency, PRC = People's Republic of China, RBI = Reserve Bank of India, SFI = Specialized Financial Institution.

Sources: Barua, Kathuria, and Malik (2015), Kelegama and Tilakaratna (2014), Khalily (2015), Llanto (2015), Peng, Zhao, and Wang (2014), Tambunan (2015), and Tambunan lertchai (2015).

priority sector loans such as agriculture and SMEs. Also, the Prime Minister's Task Force on MSMEs stipulated a target of 20% credit growth to micro and small enterprises on a year-on-year basis (Barua, Kathuria, and Malik 2015). The Reserve Bank of India (RBI) also established guidelines for "convenient access," which stipulate that the number and distribution of electronic payment access points be such that every single resident would be within a 15-minute walking distance from such a point anywhere in the country by January 2016. It also set a target of opening 80,000 new rural bank branches in 2013–2016 (Barua, Kathuria, and Malik 2015). However, these targets seem very difficult to achieve.

In the Philippines, banks are required to allocate at least 8% of their loan portfolio for micro and small enterprises, and at least 2% for medium-sized enterprises (Llanto 2015). In Sri Lanka, the banking sector is required to allocate 10% of credit to agriculture, and the central bank required banks to open two branches in rural areas for every branch opened in metropolitan areas (Kelegama and Tilakaratna 2014). However, without adequate incentives, banks will not achieve the targets, and have a tendency to cherry-pick customers within the target groups, and leave the poorer segments unserved.

In Thailand, banks receive various incentives to increase lending to lower-income groups. These efforts are undertaken as part of broader reforms of the financial sector, and are outlined in the various Financial Sector Master Plans (the latest from 2012 through 2016). These include the upward revision of the interest rate cap to 28% per year (interest and fees) for unsecured personal and microfinance loans, and the issuing of further guidelines to facilitate microfinance loan approvals by commercial banks (Tambunlertchai 2015).

Interest rate caps

Table 20.3 shows that many countries impose caps on loan interest rates. However, costs of making small loans to poor households and firms are inherently high, due to lack of economies of scale and information, and costs of access in remote areas. Therefore, such limits can be counterproductive if they mainly act to limit supply. In this regard, CGAP (2004) examined the experience of 30 countries and found that interest rate ceilings impeded the penetration of microcredit. India's RBI took a major step in April 2014 by removing the price cap of 26% on loans advanced by non-bank finance company MFIs, the only lenders eligible to lend through the microfinance channel (Barua, Kathuria, and Malik 2015).

Proportionate regulation

The observation that loans to poorer households and SMEs have less systemic risk than do loans to large firms provides the basis for the concept of "proportionate regulation" (i.e., that financial institutions should be regulated in a way commensurate with their potential benefits and financial systemic risks). The Philippines has perhaps implemented this concept most thoroughly in the region. The General Banking Act of 2000 and the National Strategy for Microfinance provided the regulatory framework for proportionate regulation and risk-based supervision adopted by the Bangko Sentral ng Pilipinas (BSP) for microfinance (Llanto 2015).

Proportionate regulation means taking into account the features of microlending methodology used by MFIs and adjusting prudential norms accordingly, including: reduced capital and documentation requirements; loan appraisal based on personal contact rather than scoring; more emphasis on overall risk management practices than collateral; and development of appropriate micro products such as microdeposits, micro-enterprise loans, micro-agriculture loans, housing microfinance, and microinsurance (CGAP 2011). It also means being open to new delivery technologies and other systems to enhance access to credit. For example, microbanking offices have become important access points of financial services in areas where regular branch banking is not available.[4] Finally, proportionate regulation also paved the way for adoption of innovative delivery technologies, such as telephone banking (Llanto 2015).

Regulatory coordination and regulation of MFIs

A consistent financial inclusion policy requires a coordinated regulatory approach. Microfinance organizations typically have greater restrictions imposed on them in terms of their activities compared with banks. Therefore, they tend to be regulated separately from the system for banks, which are typically supervised by the central bank or financial regulator, and they are typically regulated more lightly than banks. However, having a variety of lenders can spawn a multitude of regulatory frameworks which can lead to inconsistencies and gaps. Table 20.3 suggests that this is particularly the case for Indonesia, Sri Lanka, and Thailand.

Table 20.3 shows that a number of countries do not allow many MFIs to take deposits, including India, Indonesia, and Sri Lanka. In the Philippines, only rural banks and credit cooperatives are allowed to accept deposits (Llanto 2015). Bangladesh does allow MFIs of a certain size to be licensed and take deposits. Khalily (2015) finds that this development has improved both the efficiency of MFIs and their attractiveness to customers. The proposed Microfinance Act in Sri Lanka provides for establishing a Microfinance Regulatory and Supervisory Authority that will be responsible for licensing, regulating, and supervising all the NGO-MFIs and cooperatives engaged in microfinance. Importantly, under the Act licensed and registered MFIs will be allowed to accept deposits from their members. This is expected to have significant positive effects for development of Sri Lanka's microfinance sector (Kelegama and Tilakaratna 2014). It seems that more countries should consider an explicit licensing regime for MFIs to promote efficiency in the sector.

ID requirements

Banking transactions are normally subject to strict requirements regarding identification, both in view of "know your client" prudential norms and the need to monitor possible cases of money laundering or terrorist financing. However, proof of identification is often difficult in poorer rural areas. There are two main approaches: (1) relaxing ID requirements and (2) establishing a national identification system. As shown in Table 20.3, the Philippines has moved in the direction of the former when such evidence is difficult to provide. On the other hand, India has an ambitious program of rolling out the biometric Unique Identity Card (UID) or "Aadhaar" as the sole KYC document for both account opening and access to other microfinance products. These UIDs have already been created for 850 million individuals (The Economist 2015).

Development of regulatory frameworks for mobile phones, e-money

New delivery technologies such as mobile phones and e-money hold great promise for promoting financial inclusion, but need appropriate regulatory frameworks to achieve their potential while being consistent with financial stability and other regulatory requirements. In many cases, service providers are not banks, which makes a consistent approach more difficult. In India, currently 27 private pre-paid instrument providers (PPIs) are allowed to offer digital wallets up to a maximum of INR 50,000.

In the Philippines, the BSP played an enabling role in developing the regulatory framework of e-money schemes for both bank and non-bank companies. It regulated e-money as a service independently of the legal character of the e-money issuer, while still imposing conditions to mitigate risks presented by non-bank e-money issuers. The regulations effectively created a level playing field between banks and non-banks, ultimately enabling entry of a greater number of firms and products with the potential to promote financial inclusion (Ehrbeck, Pickens, and Tarazi 2012). Peer-to-peer lending platforms in the PRC are not regulated.

Consumer protection

Consumer protection programs are at various stages of development in Asia. In Thailand, the Bank of Thailand has the power to monitor consumer protection. In 2013, it opened its Financial Consumer Protection Center to inform consumers about their rights and responsibilities as consumers of financial services, to reduce consumers falling prey to fraudulent practices, and to facilitate informed decision-making by consumers. However, consumer protection programs seem less well developed in India, Indonesia, and the Philippines.

Financial literacy and education[5]

There are many channels by which financial literacy can plausibly contribute to economic and financial development. Benefits from financial education come principally from better financial allocation decisions of households, both regarding savings and borrowing, and these benefits affect not only large companies, but also SMEs. Second, a more financially literate population is likely to increase domestic savings rates and provide longer-term sources of financing, thereby reducing reliance on foreign capital, and helping to foster faster economic growth. Financial education can contribute to better retirement planning, which is important since many Asian economies have aging populations. Better financial education of households and SME entrepreneurs can reduce financial stability risks such as the probability of household or SME loan defaults.

Current situation of financial literacy in Asia

Mapping the current status of financial literacy (or financial capability) in Asia presents challenges to researchers and policy-makers alike. The coverage of available surveys is relatively spotty, and methodologies and results are not consistent. Only a limited number of Asian economies and target groups within them have been surveyed so far and their results vary widely. There is some relation of financial literacy with per capita income but rankings differ significantly across different studies. Table 20.4 shows one compilation of financial literacy surveys. The first column is the overall ranking based on the responses to three questions: the understanding of compound interest, understanding of the impact of inflation, and understanding of risk diversification. Germany ranked highest overall, while Japan and Indonesia ranked highly among Asian economies. However, since the results come from different surveys, they should not necessarily be regarded as being comparable.

Table 20.4 Selected financial literacy survey results from around the world

Country (Year of Survey)	Overall Ranking★	Q1. Compound Interest	Q2: Inflation	Q3: Risk Diversification	Survey Sample (Number)
High Income					
United States (2009)	60	65	64	52	1,488
Italy (2006)	48	40	60	45	3,992
Germany (2009)	74	82	78	62	1,059
Sweden (2010)	64	35	60	68	1,302
Japan (2010)	57	71	59	40	5,268
New Zealand (2009)	65	86	81	27	850
Netherlands (2010)	71	85	77	52	1,324
Upper Middle Income					
Russia (2009)	33	36	51	13	1,366
Romania (2010)	34	24	43	–	2,048
Azerbaijan (2009)	46	46	46	–	1,207
Chile (2006)	25	2	26	46	13,054
Lower Middle Income					
Indonesia (2007)	56	78	61	28	3,360
India (2006)	38	59	25	31	1,496
West Bank and Gaza (2011)	58	51	64	–	2,022

Note: Percentage of correct answers.
★Calculated as average of questions 1, 2, and 3.
Source: Xu and Zia (2012) and authors' estimates.

Current policies and gaps in financial education in Asia

There are still many policy gaps in Asia in the areas of financial literacy and financial education (Table 20.5). So far only India, Indonesia, and Japan have established and implemented such national strategies, while the Philippines is in the process of finalizing its national policy in this area. Central banks active in this area include the Reserve Bank of India (RBI), Bank Indonesia (BI), BSP, and Bank of Thailand. Financial regulators active in this area include the Financial Services Authority of Indonesia (OJK). In Sri Lanka, however, measures to enhance financial literacy have been rather ad hoc in nature and there is no national policy on financial education.

Indonesia's financial education program is particularly well developed, as it includes cooperative efforts by the Ministry of Finance (MoF), BI, and the OJK. In the Philippines, the BSP has been active in developing strategies for financial education. However, most financial education programs in Asia tend to be small scale and targeted at individual groups rather than the broad population. Only Japan actually includes financial education in its school curriculum, but even that program faces many problems, including a lack of experienced teachers, lack of time, and lack of motivation of students. Few programs address the needs of seniors or SMEs, either. In many countries, financial education programs are conducted independently from one to another. Japan has been consolidating financial education programs and a coordinated system has been created, where duplication can be eliminated.

Table 20.5 Policies and programs for financial education in Asia

Country	National-level	Central bank	Other regulators/ministries	Private bank, MFI, NGOs	Coverage	Channels
Bangladesh	None	None	None	None	None	None
PRC	None	None	China Banking and Regulatory Commission, programs: Website for public financial education; requested financial institutions to provide clients and public with basic financial knowledge	None	None	None
India	Financial Stability and Development Council launched National Strategy on Financial Education in 2012	Financial literacy project to enhance financial literacy among target groups; Standardized literacy material (2013)	None	Bank literacy centers that work with MFIs	School children, senior citizens and military personnel	Schools
Indonesia	Financial education one pillar of Indonesia National Strategy for Financial Inclusion organized by BI and MoF; "My Saving" program (2010)	Financial education, e.g., "Let's go to the bank" (2008)	OJK program: National Financial Literacy Strategy	None	Students, children, and youth, migrant works, fishermen, communities in remote areas, factory workers	Schools, media
Japan	None	Oversight of Central Council for Financial Services Information and national network of local councils	Japan Financial Services Agency: Established targets for financial literacy	Programs of banks and insurance companies	Financial education part of high school curriculum	Schools, media
Philippines	Included in Philippine Development Plan 2011–2016	Economic and Financial Learning Program to promote public awareness of economic and financial issues	None	None	N/A	None
Sri Lanka	None	Some activities	Some activities	Some activities	None	None
Thailand	None	Programs on financial education	Government "Debt Doctor" program	Civil society groups and non-profit organizations financial education programs for low-income groups; Bank of Agriculture and Agricultural Cooperatives teaches budgeting to rural clients	Private programs generally small-scale	None

BI = Bank Indonesia, MoF = Ministry of Finance, PRC = People's Republic of China.

Sources: ADBI (2014), BUCFLP (2017), Barua, Kathuria and Malik (2015), Kelegama and Tilakaratna (2014), Khalily (2015), Llanto (2015), Peng, Zhao, and Wang (2014), Tambunan (2015), and Tambunlertchai (2015).

Conclusion

There are numerous barriers to financial inclusion both on the supply and demand sides. On the supply side, the high costs of handling small deposits and loans in physically remote areas, together with information asymmetries, lack of documentation and collateral, deter financial institutions from extending financial services to lower-income households and SMEs. Regulatory restrictions on capital adequacy, identification requirements, branch openings, and so forth, as well as inadequate infrastructure for transportation and payments systems, work in the same direction. On the demand side, the chief barriers are lack of cash, ignorance of financial products and services, and lack of trust.

As a result, financial inclusion in many emerging Asian economies is still relatively low. For the most widely used measure of financial inclusion, the share of adults with an account at a formal financial institution, the following economies had shares of less than 55% as of 2014: Afghanistan, Azerbaijan, Bangladesh, Cambodia, Georgia, India, Indonesia, Kazakhstan, Kyrgyz Republic, Lao PDR, Nepal, Pakistan, Philippines, Tajikistan, Uzbekistan, and Viet Nam. Levels of financial literacy are also generally low, which contributes to the demand-side barriers to financial inclusion. Asia's experience in the area of financial education is still limited, but there are significant potential gains from more concerted policy efforts in this area.

Notes

1 Global Partnership for Financial Inclusion (www.gpfi.org/).
2 The annual forum was held most recently in the Philippines in March 2015 (http://apec2015. ph/2015/03/03/philippines-opens-2015-asia-pacific-forum-on-financial-inclusion/).
3 Microfinance institutions (MFIs) are normally included in the definition of formal financial institutions.
4 Microbanking offices are scaled down branches that perform limited banking activities (e.g., accepting microdeposits and releasing microloans to microfinance clients).
5 This section is based on Yoshino, Morgan, and Wignaraja (2015).

References

Asian Development Bank (ADB). 2012. *Technical Assistance Report. Improving Financial Inclusion in Asia and the Pacific*. Manila: Asian Development Bank.

ADB. 2015. Financing Asia's Future Growth. In *Asian Development Outlook 2015*. Manila: Asian Development Bank.

Asian Development Bank Institute (ADBI). 2014. *Financial Inclusion in Asia: Country Surveys*. Tokyo: Asian Development Bank Institute.

Association of Southeast Asian Nations (ASEAN). 2014. *The ASEAN Framework for Equitable Economic Development*. Jakarta, Indonesia: ASEAN Secretariat. www.asean.org/news/item/the-asean-framework-for-equitable-economic-development

Atkinson, A., and F. Messy. 2013. Promoting Financial Inclusion Through Financial Education: OECD/INFE Evidence, Policies and Practice, OECD Working Papers on Finance, Insurance and Private Pensions No. 34. Paris: Organisation for Economic Cooperation and Development.

Barua, A., R. Kathuria, and N. Malik. 2015. The Status of Financial Inclusion, Regulation, and Education in India. ADBI Working Paper No. 568. Tokyo: Asian Development Bank Institute.

Beck, T., A. Demirgüç-Kunt, and R. Levine. 2007. Finance, Inequality, and Poverty: Cross-Country Evidence. *Journal of Economic Growth* 12(1): 27–49.

Boston University Center for Finance, Law and Policy (BUCFLP). 2017. *Financial Inclusion Guide*. Boston: Boston University. http://www.bu.edu/bucflp-fig/financial-inclusion-guide/

Bruhn, M., and I. Love. 2013. The Economic Impact of Expanding Access to Finance in Mexico. In *Banking the World: Empirical Foundations of Financial Inclusion*, edited by R. Cull, A. Demirgüç-Kunt, and J. Morduch. Cambridge, MA: Massachusetts Institute of Technology Press, pp. 137–156.

Burgess, R., and R. Pande. 2005. Do Rural Banks Matter? Evidence from the Indian Social Banking Experiment. *American Economic Review* 95(3): 80–795.

Chakraborty, K.C. 2011. Financial Inclusion: A Road India Needs to Travel. Speeches. Mumbai, India: Reserve Bank of India. https://rbi.org.in/scripts/BS_SpeechesView.aspx?Id=607

Consultative Group to Assist the Poor (CGAP). 2004. Interest Rate Ceilings and Microfinance, The Story So Far. Occasional Paper No. 9. Washington, DC: CGAP.

CGAP. 2011. *Global Standard-Setting Bodies and Financial Inclusion for the Poor: Toward Proportionate Standards and Guidance. A White Paper on behalf of the Global Partnership for Financial Inclusion (GPFI).* Washington, DC: CGAP.

Demirgüç-Kunt, A., and L. Klapper. 2013. Measuring Financial Inclusion: Explaining Variation Across and within Countries. Brookings Papers on Economic Activity (Spring): 279–321.

Demirgüç-Kunt, A., L. Klapper, D. Singer, and P. Oudheusden. 2015. The Global Findex Database 2014: Measuring Financial Inclusion around the World. Policy Research Working Paper No. 7255. Washington, DC: World Bank.

Ehrbeck, T., M. Pickens, and M. Tarazi. 2012. *Financially Inclusive Ecosystems: The Roles of Government Today.* Focus Note 76, February. Washington, DC: CGAP.

Honohan, P. 2004. Financial Development, Growth and Poverty: How Close Are the Links? World Bank Policy Research Working Paper No. 3203. Washington, DC: World Bank.

Kaboski, J., and R. Townsend. 2005. Policies and Impact: An Analysis of Village-Level Microfinance Institutions. *Journal of the European Economic Association* 3(1): 1–50.

Karlan, D., and J. Morduch. 2009. In *Handbook of Development Economics*, Vol. 5, edited by D. Rodrik and M. Rosenzweig. Amsterdam: Elsevier, pp. 4703–4784.

Kelegama, S., and G. Tilakaratna. 2014. Financial Inclusion, Regulation, and Education in Sri Lanka. ADBI Working Paper No. 504. Tokyo: Asian Development Bank Institute. www.adbi.org/working-paper/2014/11/18/6506.financial.inclusion.education.sri.lanka/

Khalily, B. 2015. Financial Inclusion, Regulation, and Education in Bangladesh. ADBI Working Paper No. 504. Tokyo: Asian Development Bank Institute.

Khan, H.R. 2011. Financial Inclusion and Financial Stability: Are They Two Sides of the Same Coin? Address by Shri H.R. Khan, Deputy Governor of the Reserve Bank of India, at BANCON 2011, Organized by the Indian Bankers Association and Indian Overseas Bank, Chennai, India, 4 November.

Llanto, G. 2015. Financial Inclusion, Education and Regulation in the Philippines. ADBI Working Paper No. 541. Tokyo: Asian Development Bank Institute.

McKernan, S. 2003. The Impact of Microcredit Programs on Self-Employment Profits: Do Noncredit Program Aspects Matter? *Review of Economics and Statistics* 84(1): 93–115.

Morgan, P.J., and V. Pontines. 2014. Financial Stability and Financial Inclusion. ADBI Working Paper No. 488. Tokyo: Asian Development Bank Institute.

Morgan, P.J., and Y. Zhang. 2015. Mortgage Lending and Financial Stability in Asia. ADBI Working Paper No. 543. Tokyo: Asian Development Bank Institute. www.adb.org/publications/mortgage-lending-financial-stability-asia/

Peng, R., M. Zhao, and L. Wang. 2014. Financial Inclusion in the People's Republic of China: Achievements and Challenges. In *Financial Inclusion in Asia: Country Surveys.* Tokyo: Asian Development Bank Institute.

Pitt, M., S. Khandker, O. Chowdhury, and D. Millimet. 2003. Credit Programs for the Poor and the Health Status of Children in Rural Bangladesh. *International Economic Review* 44(1): 8–118.

Prasad, E. 2010. Financial Sector Regulation and Reforms in Emerging Markets: An Overview. NBER Working Paper 16428. Cambridge, MA: National Bureau of Economic Research.

Tambunan, T. 2015. Financial Inclusion, Financial Education, and Financial Regulation: A Story from Indonesia. ADBI Working Paper No. 535. Tokyo: Asian Development Bank Institute.

Tambunlertchai, K. 2015. Financial Inclusion, Financial Education, and Financial Regulation in Thailand. ADBI Working Paper No. 537. Tokyo: Asian Development Bank Institute.

The Economist. 2015. *Modi's Many Tasks*, pp. 3–16, May 23.

UNESCAP. 2014. Sustainable Development Financing: Perspectives from Asia and the Pacific: Background Paper. Paper Prepared for the Regional Outreach of the Intergovernmental Committee of Experts on Sustainable Development Financing for the Asia-Pacific Region, Asia-Pacific Outreach Meeting on Sustainable Development Financing, Jakarta, 10–11 June.

World Bank. 2008. *Finance for All? Policies and Pitfalls in Expanding Access.* Washington, DC: World Bank.

Xu, L., and B. Zia. 2012. Financial Literacy Around the World: An Overview of the Evidence with Practical Suggestions for the Way Forward. World Bank Policy Research Working Paper No. 6107. Washington, DC: World Bank.

Yoshino, N., P. Morgan, and G. Wignaraja. 2015. Financial Education in Asia: Assessment and Recommendations. ADBI Working Paper No. 534. Tokyo: Asian Development Bank Institute.

21

REMEDIES FOR MITIGATING ASIAN SMEs' ACCESS-TO-FINANCE DIFFICULTIES

Naoyuki Yoshino and Farhad Taghizadeh-Hesary

Introduction

Asia has been continuously growing, and this growth has alleviated poverty and increased the number of middle-income countries in the region. However, the recent regional and global economic slowdown caused by several reasons, including limited access of small and medium-sized enterprises (SMEs) to bank credit. It requires new and sustainable models to ease the access of SMEs to finance and boost the economic growth and job creation in the region.

A survey conducted by the Asian Development Bank (ADB) on 20 countries from five ADB regions in 2014, the Asia SME Finance Monitor (ASM),[1] shows that SMEs accounted for an average of 96% of all enterprises and 62% of the national labor forces across the ASM countries. These countries cover Central Asia, East Asia, South Asia, Southeast Asia, and the Pacific region. Meanwhile, the latest data reveal that SMEs contributed an average of 42% of the gross domestic product (GDP) or manufacturing value added in ASM countries (ADB 2015).

SMEs have a big role in trade. The latest data show that SMEs in the People's Republic of China (PRC) and India accounted for more than 40% of total export values, followed by 26% in Thailand, 19% in the Republic of Korea, and 16% in Indonesia (ADB 2015).

Definitions of SMEs differ between countries, not only for a common indicator, such as employment, but also in the type of indicators used. Along with employment, the other common criteria are assets or capital, and revenue, which may be defined as sales or turnover. Many economies set two criteria: one is employment and the other is assets, capital or revenue. For example, manufacturing firms in Malaysia are considered SMEs if they have fewer than 200 workers or revenues of less than MYR 50 million (about USD 12 million). There also may be different criteria for different sectors. The PRC has 15 sector definitions, Japan has four, and Singapore has one. To make matters even more complicated, government agencies within the same country may use different definitions. A ministry uses one definition while the national statistics office uses another, and a priority lending policy may adopt yet another (Vandenberg, Chantapacdepong, and Yoshino 2016).

Four indicators are commonly used to gauge the importance of SMEs. They specify the SME share of the total for (1) the number of enterprises, (2) employment, (3) domestic output, and (4) exports. Not all economies compile data on all four indicators, with the first two being the most common. Tables 21.1 and 21.2 present recent available data on 14 Asian economies,

Table 21.1 SME share of enterprises, exports, and output, selected Asian economies

	Share of all Enterprises	Share of Exports	Share of Output	Indicators for Output	Data Year★
	%	%	%		
High income					
Japan	99.7	. . .	43.7	Sales	2012
Rep. of Korea	99.9	18.8	47.6	MVA	2012
Singapore	99.4	. . .	45.0	GDP	2012
Upper middle-income					
PRC	97.3	41.5	60.0	GDP	2013, 2011, 2013
Kazakhstan	97.5	. . .	26.0	GDP	2014, 2013
Malaysia	97.3	. . .	35.9	GDP	2014
Philippines	99.6	. . .	35.7	GVA	2013, 2006
Thailand	99.7	26.3	39.6	GDP	2014
Lower middle-income					
Bangladesh	99.0	. . .	25.0	GDP	2013, 2014
India	. . .	42.4	37.5	MVA	2013
Indonesia	99.9	15.7	60.3	GDP	2013
Sri Lanka	99.5	20.0	30.0	GDP	2013
Viet Nam	97.7	. . .	. . .		2012
Low-Income					
Cambodia	99.8	. . .	. . .		2014

GDP = gross domestic product, GVA = gross value added, MVA = manufacturing value added, PRC = People's Republic of China, SME = small and medium-sized enterprise.

Note: For the PRC, the definition of SME used for the share of enterprises is those with fewer than 1,000 workers, and the share of exports refers to the share of industrial exports.

★ When more than one year is indicated, the first year refers to share of the enterprises, the second refers to exports, and the third to output.

Source: Vandenberg, Chantapacdepong, and Yoshino (2016).

including the region's three largest: the PRC, Japan, and India. The share of the total number of enterprises is the most consistently used indicator across countries, both in Asia and around the globe. The share for our Asian group is in the narrow range between 97% and over 99%. Both Bangladesh, which until recently was a low-income country, and the Republic of Korea, a high-income one, have shares of 99% or more (Vandenberg, Chantapacdepong, and Yoshino 2016).

The ASM results show that limited access to bank credit is a structural problem across developing Asia. Bank loans to SMEs made up averages of 11.6% of GDP and 18.7% of total bank lending in the region, with a decreasing trend of the latter since the 2008–2009 global financial crisis. Comparing SME access to bank credit relative to the income level of the countries in which they operate, bank credit reaches out to a larger number of SMEs (with a relatively low ratio of non-performing loans) as the country's economy becomes more advanced (ADB 2015).

Recently, there are some concerns about the impact of Basel III (an international regulatory framework for banks) on SME lending. There may be a negative effect on banks' lending

Table 21.2 SME employment share, selected Asian economies

	SME Employment as a Share of:	SME Share (%)	Year
Bangladesh	non-agricultural employment	75.0	2014
Cambodia	enterprise employment	71.8	2014
PRC	industry employment	64.7	2011
Japan	enterprise employment	69.7	2012
Kazakhstan	total employment	32.1	2014
Rep. of Korea	enterprise employment	87.7	2012
Malaysia	total employment	65.0	2014
Philippines	enterprise employment	63.7	2013
Singapore	total employment	68.0	2012
Sri Lanka	total employment	35.0	2013
Thailand	enterprise employment	80.3	2014
Viet Nam	total employment	46.8	2012

PRC = People's Republic of China, SME = small and medium-sized enterprise.

Note: For Bangladesh, the figure is 70%–80%; we have taken the average.

Source: Vandenberg, Chantapacdepong, and Yoshino (2016)

attitudes toward SMEs in countries that have decided to introduce Basel III. These countries include the PRC, India, Indonesia, and the Republic of Korea (ADB 2015).[2]

If SMEs, which are the backbone of Asian economies, find it difficult to get access to finance, this might endanger the economic growth and employment in Asia, especially in developing Asian countries which are more vulnerable. This suggests that further policy support for SME finance is needed in low-income and lower-middle-income Asian economies. In particular, a set of financial infrastructure, such as credit risk database, credit guarantee corporation, needs to be developed. In addition, the establishment and development of banks specialized on SME lending, and the introduction of the community-based financing schemes such as hometown investment trust funds are other required policies. These are the remedies that will be highlighted and defined in this chapter by providing operational examples from development and developing Asian economies in order to provide policy recommendation for the developing Asian economies, especially for the lower-income countries.

SMEs' difficulties in accessing finance

Almost 70% of the financial systems in India, 80% of those in the PRC, and 90% of those in Malaysia are banks (Yoshino and Taghizadeh-Hesary 2015). Asian economies are often characterized as having bank-dominated financial markets and their capital markets, in particular venture capital, are not well developed. This means banks are the main source of financing. Although the soundness of the banking system has improved significantly since the Asian crisis, banks have been cautious about lending to SMEs even though such enterprises account for a large share of economic activity. Start-up companies, in particular, are finding it increasingly difficult to borrow money from banks because of strict Basel capital requirements. Riskier SMEs also face difficulty in borrowing money from banks. SMEs are difficult to be evaluated by banks since they often do not have solid accounting systems. Many SMEs in Asia borrow money by paying high rates of interest or offering costly collateral. Many banks prefer to lend to large enterprises rather than SMEs. The reason is that for large enterprises the financial statements are clearer and audited.

Figure 21.1, prepared based on data from the G20 Financial Inclusion Indicators databank of the World Bank, shows 10 Asian countries in different income levels (GDP per capita PPP) based on two indicators in order to show the lending attitude of financial institutions to SMEs in differ- ent- income-level Asian economies. These two indicators are (1) SMEs with an outstanding loan or line of credit (%) that denotes the percentage of SMEs (5–99 employees) with an outstanding loan or line of credit from a bank or other formal financial institution, and (2) SMEs with a pro- portion of loans requiring collateral (%) that denotes the percentage of SMEs (5–99 employees) required to provide collateral on their last bank loan (reflects the tightness of credit conditions).

Figure 21.1 shows that in countries with low-income levels (GDP per capita PPP) that mainly have less developed financial systems, SMEs have more difficulties in accessing finance. Accord- ing to the latest available data, in Afghanistan less than 4.5%, and in Vanuatu less than 3.8% of SMEs have an outstanding loan or line of credit. However, for Viet Nam and Mongolia, which are among the middle-income (GDP per capita PPP) Asian countries, and have more developed financial systems, this ratio is 39.4 and 49.3%, respectively. This means that existence of a rela- tively sound and well-established financial system is a *necessity* to improve SMEs' access to finance. However, this is not enough, and a sound credit guarantee scheme is necessary as well.

Lack of information infrastructure for SMEs

There is an asymmetric information problem between suppliers and demanders of funds in general. Information infrastructures are necessary to remedy this problem. Many big enterprises list their shares on stock markets and issue securities in bond markets. Therefore, institutional

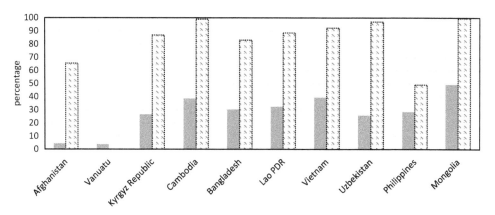

Figure 21.1 Lending attitude of financial institutions to SMEs in different Asian countries

Lao PDR = Lao People's Democratic Republic, SMEs = small and medium-sized enterprises.

Note: In making this figure, the latest available data were used. Year of data for each country is: Afghanistan (2014), Vanuatu (2015), Kyrgyz Republic (2014), Cambodia (2013), Bangladesh (2013), Lao PDR (2012), Viet Nam (2015), Uzbekistan (2013), Philippines (2015). and Mongolia (2013). Data of SMEs with a proportion of loans requiring collateral (%) for Vanuatu was not available.

Source: Compiled by authors with data from the World Bank's G20 Financial Inclusion Indicators database.

information sharing schemes of capital markets can facilitate access to a wide range of information necessary to estimate the creditworthiness of big enterprises.

However, most SMEs have no connection with capital markets. Financial institutions can closely and continuously observe borrowers, but it is costly to do so for borrowers of small loans.

The lack of information infrastructure for SMEs exacerbates the information asymmetry problem.

In collateral-based lending, the provision of collateral is the simplest way for SMEs and financial institutions to reduce the risk premium in loan formulations. However, by introduction of the Basel capital accord, many governments expanded policy-based finance for SMEs for mitigating the constraints on SME finance as an urgent countermeasure. Under such a situation, efficient and lower-cost credit risk evaluation tools were necessary for SME financing, especially for transaction-based lending. To address the serious credit constraints on SMEs after conforming to Basel requirements on risk management, a comprehensive information infrastructure is needed. This soft infrastructure will be explained later in this chapter.

Remedies for tackling the SMEs' difficulties for accessing finance

The previous section defined challenges that Asian SMEs face for raising money. Here in this section we provide some efficient remedies and the required soft infrastructures required for easing the SMEs' access to finance. These solutions were workable in some Asian countries and it is necessary to expand it to the rest of Asia.

Development of credit guarantee schemes by governments

Owing to the significance of SMEs to Asian economies, it is important to find ways to provide them with stable finance. In order to fulfill the under-supply of credit to SMEs, various government and donor initiatives have emerged in developed as well as developing and emerging economies, and created the so-called Credit Guarantee Scheme (CGS). The public credit guarantee scheme is a tool to reduce the supply demand gap in SME finance.

CGSs have been used over decades in many countries and in various forms as a way to increase the flow of funds into targeted sectors and groups. The purpose for the creation of such a scheme is to contribute to the flow of funds into sectors that have difficulties to raise funds including the SME sector. A CGS is making lending more attractive by absorbing or sharing the risks associated with lending to the targeted sector. Such schemes can also increase the amount of loan funds available to an enterprise beyond its own collateral limits, because the guarantee is a form of loan collateral. The guarantee manager can assume the additional role of loan assessor and monitor, which can improve the quality of the loans made (Zander, Miller, and Mhlanga 2013). However, guarantee funds have a cost, which is paid through the fees charged and/or subsidized by the government or by third-party institutions.

Many countries like Japan used to have full credit guarantee schemes which covered 100% of the default cost incurred by borrowers in Japan (Uesugi, Sakai, and Yamashiro 2006). Recently the Japanese government revised the credit guarantee policy and implemented a partial credit guarantee as the full guarantee had a moral hazard. If the government covers 100% of the SMEs' default costs and absorbs the full risk, then lending institutions would not monitor and analyze the healthiness of the borrowers, because their risk is covered by the government. Thus, it will raise the non-performing loans in the banking sector and will reduce the productivity of the public reserves. Hence, a partial credit-guarantee scheme can be an optimal case.

A CGS consists of at least three parties: a borrower, lender, and guarantor. The borrower is often a SME or a micro-enterprise, seeking debt capital. This borrower typically approaches private financial institutions (banks) for a business loan. For reasons of asymmetry of information, the loan request will frequently be turned down by the private lender. This is where the guarantor comes into the picture. The guarantor (Credit Guarantee Corporation), usually a government or trade association, seeks to facilitate access to debt capital by providing lenders with the comfort of a guarantee for a substantial portion of the debt (Riding and Haines 2001).

As it is clear in Figure 21.2, which is the Japanese example, CGCs' money is coming from the National Government (from Ministry of Finance to Ministry of Economy, Trade and Industry) and also from the local governments. National government is providing direct subsidies to CGCs, provides subsidies for compensation assets to Japan Federation of Credit Guarantee Corporation (JFG), and JFG provides it with compensation in case of losses to CGCs. Also, the national government provides funds for credit insurance to Japan Finance Corporation (JFC) and JFC uses this budget to insure the contracts. On the other hand, local governments are also supporters of CGCs that provide contributions and loans to them. In Japan, in fiscal year (FY) 2014, almost 3.852 million SMEs were operating, among which 36.6% means 1.412 million were guaranteed by the CGSs. There are 51 CGCs in Japan, one for each prefecture and one

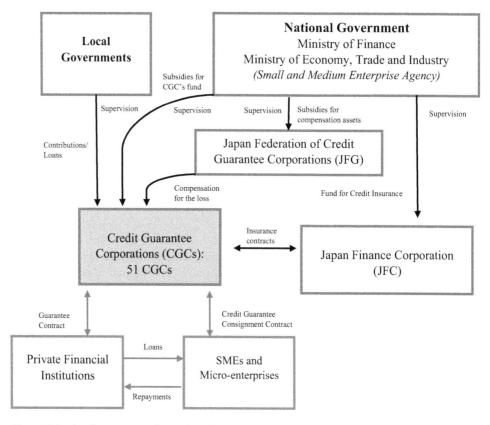

Figure 21.2 Credit guarantee scheme (Japan)

Source: Compiled by authors based on information from Japan Federation of Credit Guarantee Corporations (2014).

in each of the cities of Nagoya, Yokohama, Kawasaki, and Gifu. At the end of FY2014, their total liabilities stood at approximately JPY27.7 trillion (JFG 2015).

In Asia, credit guarantee schemes have been relatively widely established. India launched the Credit Guarantee Fund Scheme for Micro and Small Enterprises in 2000 as a partial guarantee scheme; it covers 75% of the credit applied force (statistics and information in this paragraph from ADB 2015). Indonesia started a public credit guarantee scheme for MSMEs – People's Business Credit, in 2007; it guarantees 70%–80% of the credit applied. Kazakhstan has a partial credit guarantee scheme for SMEs (up to 70%) under the Damu Entrepreneurship Development Fund. The Republic of Korea provides credit guarantees for SMEs mainly through two credit guarantee institutions: The Korea Credit Guarantee Fund and the Korea Technology Finance Corporation. In Malaysia, the Credit Guarantee Corporation provides guarantees for SMEs. In Papua New Guinea, a regional bank (Bank of South Pacific) provides partial credit guarantees for SMEs (50% of the credit applied). The Philippines has two credit guarantee programs for MSMEs: the partial guarantee scheme provided by the Small Business Corporation (70% of the credit applied), and the Credit Surety Fund Program under the central bank. In Solomon Islands, the central bank provides a credit guarantee scheme for SMEs, called the Small Business Finance Scheme, covering 90% of the credit applied. The central bank in Sri Lanka also provides credit guarantee schemes for SMEs as well as several credit lines. Thailand developed the portfolio guarantee scheme for SMEs in 2009 as part of the Thai economic stimulus measures against the global financial crisis. Viet Nam has two channels of credit guarantees, although they do not directly target SMEs: the credit guarantee fund operated by the Viet Nam Development Bank (85% partial guarantees), and the local credit guarantee funds operated by provincial authorities under the supervision of the Ministry of Finance.

Specialized banks for SME financing (SME bank)

In Japan, there is a good example of specialized private banks for SME financing, called *Shinkin* banks. *Shinkin* banks are deposit-taking cooperative banks that specialize in financing SMEs within a region. Just like city banks and regional banks, *Shinkin* banks are protected by deposit insurance and subject to the capital adequacy requirements and other banking regulations and supervisions.

Unlike city banks or regional banks, however, *Shinkin* banks make loans mainly to member SMEs who capitalize the *Shinkin* banks. They can make loans to non-member SMEs, but they have to restrict the share of the loans to non-member SMEs to 20%. On the other hand, they can accept deposits from anyone.

Shinkin banks are regional financial institutions in the sense that they can make loans only to SMEs that operate within the same region as the *Shinkin* banks. *Shinkin* banks are generally smaller than city banks and tier-1 and tier-2 regional banks and larger than credit cooperatives (*shinyokumiai*). *Shinkin* banks played a significant role in development of SMEs in different regions and in achieving the comprehensive growth throughout Japan (Hosono, Sakai, and Tsuru 2006).

In Republic of Korea, the Industrial Bank of Korea (IBK) was established in 1961 as the specialized policy banks for lending to SMEs; IBK has constantly expanded the corporate lending bases specially to SMEs and the number of clients reached 1.2 million corporates as of 14 December 2015. IBK retained the leadership role in financing competitive SMEs in financial distress over the past year. In 2015 alone, IBK extended new loans worth KRW 10.3 trillion, claiming 20% of the annual KRW 52.8 trillion net increase in SME loans extended by all Republic of Korea banks. IBK's SME loan balance stood at KRW 126.1 trillion in 2015 and accounted for 77.3% of the Bank's KRW 163.2 trillion total loan balance by the end of the year. Claiming 22.34% of the SME loan balance market share, this makes IBK the sole Republic of Korea financial institution with a market share of 20% or greater to SMEs.[3]

In Thailand, in 1964, the Council of Ministers approved a financing strategy to promote and develop small industries, as proposed by the National Economic and Social Development Board. A loan processing office for small industries was established under the Department of Industrial Promotion, Ministry of Industry's supervision to provide financial support to small manufacturing businesses. That office later became the Small Industry Finance Office (SIFO). However, SIFO's operations and growth were hampered by limited funds, which were dependent on state budget allocations, and cumbersome and inflexible government procedures and regulations. In 1991, the Thai government promulgated the Small Industry Finance Corporation Act and SIFO became the Small Industry Finance Corporation (SIFC) with registered capital of THB 300 million. On 20 December 2002, the Small and Medium Enterprise Development Bank of Thailand Act was enacted, re-establishing the SIFC as the Small and Medium Enterprise Development Bank of Thailand, or SME Bank. The Bank's mandate was "to conduct business with the aim of developing, promoting, and assisting small and medium enterprises to start-up expand or improve their businesses by providing loans, guarantees, venture capital, counseling, and other necessary services as prescribed by the Act."[4]

In Malaysia, the SME Bank was established in 2005 to function as a development financial institution to nurture and meet the unique needs of SMEs through the provision of financial and non-financial services to SMEs. While SME Bank's role is to complement the products and services provided by other development and commercial banking institutions, the Bank was also established to strengthen the national implementation infrastructure through enhanced SME capacity.[5] SME Bank governed by Shariah Governance Framework for Islamic Financial Institutions issued by Bank Negara Malaysia as a distinct feature in the organizational structure of the Bank, which includes establishment of the Shariah Committee in line with the requirement of Section 30(1) of the Islamic Financial Services Act. As of 31 December 2016, SME Bank had MYR 10.57 billion of total assets (SMEB 2017).

Development of hometown investment trust funds for risky SMEs

Given that Asian financial systems are dominated by banks, the creation of community-based funds (or hometown investment trust funds)[6] to promote lending to start-up companies and riskier borrowers, such as SMEs would help to maintain the soundness of the banking sector, as banks would not be exposed to the risks that lending to such companies inevitably poses. Selling those community trust funds through branch offices of regional banks, post offices, credit associations, and large banks would increase funding sources for start-up companies and riskier borrowers (Figure 21.3).

Such trust funds would not be guaranteed by a deposit insurance corporation and the associated risks would be borne by investors. The terms of a trust fund would have to be fully explained to investors, such as where their funds would be invested and what the risks associated with the investment would be in order to strengthen potential investors' confidence and help expand the trust fund market (Yoshino 2013).

Although government does not guarantee these funds, without government supervision and regulations there might be several cases of fraud. Japan's Financial Services Agency (FSA), the supervisor and the regulator of the financial system, regulates and supervises the internet companies that provide micro-investment platform for introduction and investment matchmaking of hometown investment trust (HIT) funds. Project owners can access these internet

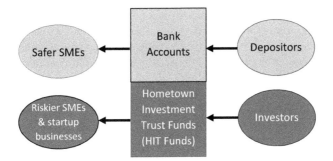

Figure 21.3 Utilizing HIT funds for investing in riskier SMEs and start-ups

HIT fund: hometown investment trust funds, SMEs = small and medium-sized enterprises.

Source: Compiled by authors drawing from Yoshino and Taghizadeh-Hesary (2014a).

companies, the internet companies will do some sort of due diligence, about the background of project owner, the quality of products, expected return and will do the project assessment. Then once it is approved, it will introduce the project and the amount of required investment, bid amount and the recruitment period on their website. FSA is monitoring and supervising the activities of these micro-investment internet companies; presently, there are seven companies in Japan and these companies are in direct relationship with project owners. These companies have significant roles for making the transparency in these HIT funds scheme.

There are examples of both successful and failed funds. Project assessors play a key role in evaluating each project to limit the number of non-performing investments and losses by investors. Some of the funds set up in Japan are regarded as charities, with some investors viewing them as a way to invest in their region to support new business ventures.

Such new ventures pose a problem for banks, as although some will have high expected rates of return, the high risks involved make it difficult for banks to finance them. However, if the projects are financed by hometown investment trust funds rather than by deposits transformed into bank loans, they will not create non-performing loans for banks. Banks can still benefit and compete with each other by selling the trust funds through their branch offices, although it has to be made clear that an investment in those funds is not guaranteed. If a bank sells successful HIT funds, it will be able to attract more investors; on the other hand, if it sells loss-making funds, it will lose investors in the future. Competition will improve the quality of projects and enhance the risk-adjusted returns for investors.

An HIT fund has three main advantages. First, it contributes to financial market stability by lowering information asymmetry. Individual households and firms have direct access to information about the borrowing firms, mainly SMEs that they lend to. Second, it is a stable source of risk capital. The fund is project-driven. Firms and households decide to invest by getting to know the borrowers and their projects. In this way, the fund distributes risk, but not so that it renders risk intractable, which has been the problem with the "originate and distribute" model. Third, it contributes to economic recovery by connecting firms and households with SMEs that are worthy of their support. It also creates employment opportunities at the SMEs as well as for the pool of retirees from financial institutions who can help assess the projects (Yoshino 2013; Yoshino and Taghizadeh-Hesary 2014b).

The main differences between HIT funds and conventional crowdfunding or venture capital is a "warm feeling" which is behind the HITs, because investors are sympathizing with the company/project owners and their efforts and not solely seeking the profit. However, in crowdfunding and venture capital, the investors are seeking solely for financial profit.

Examples of such funds in Japan include wind power generators and musicians' funds. In the first example, to construct 20 wind power generators, private-public partnerships were launched and local residents invested USD 1,000–5,000 in a fund. They received dividends every year through the sales of electricity by each wind power generator that they had invested in. Musicians' funds gather many small investors buying units for USD 150–500. If the musicians become successful and their DVDs sell well, the sales will generate a high rate of return for the fund.

During the recent years, there are several successful cases of HIT funds in Japan. For example, The Fukushima Daiichi nuclear disaster, an energy accident initiated primarily by the tsunami following the Tohoku earthquake on 11 March 2011, resulted in nuclear power plant shutdown in Japan due to government disapproval because of lack of safeness. After this disaster happened, in the suffering region and also in other parts of Japan, people who were opposing nuclear power supported use of renewable energy, especially wind power and solar power. However, renewable energy projects are costly and require private sector investments, and banks are reluctant to finance many of these projects as these projects are considered as risky projects from the point of view of most banks. Hence local communities created local funds and collected money in each region in order to collect sufficient capital for the establishment of wind power generators and solar power panels on roof of houses, and several projects could be started by this framework in Nagano prefecture, Hokkaido prefecture, and so on which are examples of HITs. Several solar and wind power projects started to generate electricity, hometown residents used the electricity and the spillover of it sold to the power companies in order to make profit and pay dividends to the investors.

There are many cases that shows the aforementioned "warm feeling," that is, for constructing a wind power generator in Japan, almost USD 2 million was required, 249 people of a hometown or those who were sympathizing with that region or with this specific project from all over Japan donated or invested in this fund, and the users of the electricity of this wind power generator accepted to purchase the generated electricity in 5% higher fees, in order to help that this project be a feasible project. Music Securities company,[7] which is an internet company that provides micro-investment platform for absorbing investments for projects through HIT and is one of the seven companies that FSA of Japan issued license of operation for them, through about 40 HIT funds, raised JPY 1.08 billion for earthquake reconstruction efforts and replacing renewable energy.

The second difference between HIT funds and conventional crowdfunding and venture capital is that the investors are eager to receive the products or services that the project generates (electricity, agricultural products, fish, etc.). However, in other two cases, the return is only in the form of liquid profit.

The third and last difference is the "transparency" which is existing in HIT funds, actually the base and nature of HIT funds is transparency. The internet micro-investment companies make the projects information, background of the project owner, results of project assessment and other further information concerning the projects completely transparent for the investors.

Development of SME credit risk databases, credit bureaus, and SME credit rating

Considering the importance of SMEs to many dimensions of Asian economic activity, further efforts are needed to offer them access to finance. Their financial and non-financial accounts are often difficult to assess, but the Credit Risk Database (CRD) in Japan shows how SMEs can be rated based on financial and non-financial data. The CRD includes a huge amount of data that can be used to rate SMEs through statistical analysis.

Credit risk database (CRD) (Japanese experience)

The CRD Association was established in 2001 as an initiative of the Japanese Ministry of Economy, Trade and Industry and the Small and Medium Enterprise Agency. Its aim was to facilitate fund-raising for SMEs and to improve their operational efficiency. The association's membership increased from 73 institutions at the end of March 2002 to 180 by 1 April 2016 (Kuwahara et al. 2016).

The CRD covers SMEs exclusively (Figure 21.4). As of 31 March 2016, it included 2,299,000 incorporated SMEs and 1,131,000 sole-proprietor SMEs, and it is by far the largest SME database in Japan. The database for enterprises in default covered 518,000 incorporated and sole-proprietor SMEs (Kuwahara et al. 2016). The CRD Association receives active support from both the private and public sectors, which has contributed to its success. For example, the Small and Medium Enterprise Agency nominates representatives of the CRD Association to government councils, which gives the association an opportunity to promote its activities and increase its membership. Credit guarantee corporations and private financial institutions use the CRD when they create a joint guarantee scheme.[8] Before the CRD was formally established, the government invested JPY1.3 billion from the supplementary budgets for fiscal years 1999 and 2000 to finance the setting up of the CRD's computer system and other operational costs. The association provides sample data and statistical information, and scoring services.

Member financial institutions use scoring models to evaluate creditworthiness, check the validity of internal rating systems, and align loan pricing with credit risk. In addition, the CRD Association provides consulting services to support the management of SMEs on the

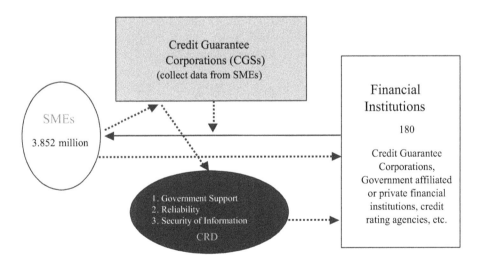

Figure 21.4 Credit risk database of small and medium-sized enterprises

CRD = credit risk database; SME = small and medium-sized enterprise.

Note: Numbers of financial Institutions are as of 1 April 2016. Number of SMEs show all SMEs in Japan at the end of FY2014.

Source: Authors, CRD website.[9] Source of number of SMEs: JFG (2015).

assumption that if SMEs are better managed, this will reduce the credit risk for member financial institutions and strengthen SME business operations. Consulting services have also been offered to member financial institutions to help them promote implementation of Basel III.

If such systems could be established in other parts of Asia to accumulate and analyze credit risk data, and to measure each SME's credit risk accurately, SMEs would not only be able to raise funds from the banking sector, they could also gain access to the debt market by securitizing their claims.

National Credit Bureau (Thai experience)

The National Credit Bureau (NCB) is well known among debtors, businessmen, and SMEs in Thailand as the organization that collects and processes the credit information of the clients of financial institutions. However, not many people know the exact responsibilities and duties of the NCB. Some people believe that the credit bureau can place people on a blacklist, or that it sells credit information to telesales businesses, and most people believe that the credit bureau is responsible for credit rejections.

The NCB was established in 1998 under a policy by the Thai government. The government realized that a significant cause of the economic crisis in Thailand was that the country's financial sector did not have an organization to collect credit information thoroughly and systematically. Financial institutions then performed an inaccurate analysis of credit because they did not know the overall obligations or payment histories of borrowers.

First, the government supported the establishment of two credit bureaus for collecting and assembling credit information and payment history of financial institutions' clients as well as serving credit inquiries to financial institutions under clients' consent. Later, in 2005, the two credit bureaus merged and became the National Credit Bureau running under the Credit Information Business Act B.E. 2545.

The NCB is a private credit bureau company that operates under a good governance policy and does not seek profit maximization. The shareholders are customers or members and the board of directors consists of experts and executives from the Ministry of Finance, financial institutions, and insurance companies. Credit information is treated impeccably to meet the international standards of credit bureaus in other countries (Yoshino et al. 2016).

SME credit rating

Credit ratings are opinions expressed in terms of ordinal measures, reflecting the current financial creditworthiness of issuers such as governments, firms, and financial institutions. These ratings are conferred by rating agencies – such as Fitch ratings, Moody's, and S&P – and may be regarded as a comprehensive evaluation of an issuer's ability to meet their financial obligations in full and on time. Hence, they play a crucial role by providing participants in financial markets with useful information for financial planning. To conduct rating assessments of large corporates, agencies resort to a broad range of financial and non-financial pieces of information, including domain experts' expectations. Rating agencies usually provide general guidelines on their rating decision-making process, but detailed descriptions of the rating criteria and the determinants of banks' ratings are generally not provided (Orsenigo and Vercellis 2013). In search of more objective assessments of the creditworthiness of large corporate and financial institutions, there has been a growing body of research into the development of reliable quantitative methods for automatic classification according to their financial strength.

In the short run, it is possible to implement various methods for performing credit risk analysis and credit rating of SMEs by lending institutions, credit guarantee corporations or by an independent local rating agencies, using data on SMEs. A comprehensive credit rating method developed by Yoshino and Taghizadeh-Hesary (2014c) employed statistical analysis techniques on various financial variables of a group of 1,363 SME customers of an Iranian bank by utilizing two statistical techniques (principle component analysis and cluster analysis) on various financial ratios of the sample of SMEs. These financial ratios are covering all characteristics of SMEs, including activity, profitability, coverage, leverage, and liquidity. The analysis classified SMEs into several groups: financially healthy SMEs, medium-risk SMEs, and financially risky SMEs. The detailed analytical framework is explained in Yoshino and Taghizadeh-Hesary (2014c).

For SMEs in the financially healthy group, banks can lend them more money by charging low rates of interest with no required collateral, or credit guarantee corporations can charge them a lower premium when guaranteeing the allocating credit. On the other hand, for SMEs in the high-risk group, banks can charge higher rates of interest with greater collateral requirements. If an SME's performance improves and it moves into a lower risk group, banks can change their interest rates from high to low, accordingly.

Similar SME data analysis is done by using NCB data for Thai SMEs (Yoshino et al. 2016). Yoshino et al. (2016) show how a credit rating scheme for SMEs can be developed, when access to other financial and non-financial ratios is not possible, by using data on lending by banks to SMEs. They employ statistical techniques on five variables from a sample of Thai SMEs from NCB database and classify them into subgroups based on their financial health.

By employing these techniques in Asian economies, banks could reduce information asymmetry and consequently set interest rates and lending ceilings for SMEs. This would ease financing to healthy SMEs and reduce the amount of non-performing loans to this important sector.

Conclusion

SMEs play a significant role in Asian economies as they are responsible for very high shares of employment and output in all Asian countries. However, SMEs have difficulty accessing cheap finance.

Asian financial systems are dominated by banks. Banks are cautious about lending to SMEs even though such enterprises account for a large share of economic activity. Start-up companies in particular are finding it increasingly difficult to borrow money from banks and the strict Basel III capital requirements made the situation tougher. Riskier SMEs also face difficulty in borrowing money from banks. SMEs are difficult to be evaluated by banks since they often do not have solid accounting systems and their credit risk is not obvious for lending institutions. Many SMEs in Asia borrow money by paying high rates of interest or offering costly collateral which hinder their growth.

Many banks prefer to allocate their resources to large enterprises rather than SMEs. The reason is that for large enterprises the financial statements are clearer. SMEs are mainly riskier from the point of view of lenders as they do not have clear accounting information.

This chapter highlighted the SMEs difficulties in access to finance and for easing the SME financing, provides three methods for diversifying channels of finance. These three methods are developing sustainable credit guarantee schemes by the governments, specialized banks for SMEs (SME Bank), and community-based financing schemes (i.e., HIT funds for financing risky SMEs and start-up businesses).

One of the major requirements for making the SMEs' credit risk transparent for lending institutions and for credit guarantee corporations is to have a nationwide credit risk database. In this chapter, a unique example of such a database from Japan is mentioned. The CRD Association was established in 2001 as an initiative of the Japanese Ministry of Economy,

Trade and Industry and the Small and Medium Enterprise Agency, aimed to facilitate fundraising for SMEs and to improve their operational efficiency. The CRD is providing credit risk analysis and credit scoring services and examining the probability of default of SMEs for banks and credit guarantee corporations which are members of CRD (presently 180 members).

If such systems could be established in other parts of Asia to accumulate and analyze credit risk data, and to measure each SME's credit risk accurately, SMEs would not only be able to raise funds from the banking sector, they could also gain access to the debt market by securitizing their claims. Establishment of CRD could be a medium-term infrastructure target in Asian economies.

In the short run, it is possible to implement various methods for measuring the credit risk and do credit rating of SMEs. These methods could be used by lending institutions, credit guarantee corporations, or by independent local rating agencies, using data of SMEs. A comprehensive SME credit rating method developed by Yoshino and Taghizadeh-Hesary (2014c, 2015) could be used by financial institutions and credit guarantee corporations in Asian companies who want to lend or guarantee SME finance.

Finally, it is important for Asian economies (especially for lower-income ones) that SMEs are the major parts of their economies to diversify channels of financing of SMEs. Try to accumulate the SME data in a nationwide database for categorizing SMEs based on their creditworthiness. Those who rank higher get higher credit guarantees from government with lower costs, so that they could succeed. They will have significant role in job creation and in production. In addition, for those which are risky we should avoid bank lending, because if they use bank loans it will cause non-performing loans. For promoting the start-ups and the riskier SMEs, community-based lending as explained in this chapter, such as HIT funds, are a suitable solution.

Notes

1 The countries and regions are as follows: (1) Kazakhstan, the Kyrgyz Republic, and Tajikistan in Central Asia; (2) the PRC, the Republic of Korea, and Mongolia in East Asia; (3) Bangladesh, India, and Sri Lanka in South Asia; (4) Cambodia, Indonesia, Lao People's Democratic Republic, Malaysia, Myanmar, the Philippines, Thailand, and Viet Nam in Southeast Asia; and (5) Papua New Guinea, Fiji, and Solomon Islands in the Pacific.
2 Even SMEs in Japan have suffered from implementation of Basel capital accord that limited their access to bank loans (Yoshino and Hirano 2011; Yoshino and Taghizadeh-Hesary 2016).
3 http://eng.ibk.co.kr/lang/en/au/corporateBanking.jsp (accessed 9 July 2017).
4 www.smebank.co.th/En/About (accessed 14 August 2017).
5 www.smebank.com.my/history/ (accessed 15 August 2017).
6 Hometown investment trust funds emerged in Japan during the current decade and were initiated by Yoshino (2013) and now have been adopted as a national strategy in Japan (Yoshino and Taghizadeh-Hesary, 2014b).
7 Music Securities micro-investment platform that allows users to invest in local regions or industries through HITs.
8 A credit guarantee system would make it easier for banks to lend money to SMEs. For example, in the case of an SME default, a percentage of the losses would be met by the credit guarantee corporation, which is a governmental organization. For example, assuming a credit guarantee corporation sets 80% as the guarantee ratio; if an SME went into bankruptcy, a bank could recover 80% of its loan. If there were no credit guarantee system in place and an SME went into bankruptcy, the bank would lose its entire loan. Arráiz, Meléndez, and Stucchi (2014) have provided a framework for a partial credit guarantee system.
9 www.crd-office.net/CRD/en/index.html.

References

Arráiz, I., M. Meléndez, and R. Stucchi. 2014. Partial Credit Guarantees and Firm Performance: Evidence from Colombia. *Small Business Economics* 43(3): 711–724.

Asian Development Bank (ADB). 2015. *Asia SME Finance Monitor 2014*. Manila: Asian Development Bank.

Hosono, K., K. Sakai, and K. Tsuru. 2006. Consolidation of Cooperative Banks (Shinkin) in Japan: Motives and Consequences. RIETI Discussion Paper No. 06-E-034. Tokyo: The Research Institute of Economy, Trade and Industry.

Japan Federation of Credit Guarantee Corporations (JFG). 2015. *Credit Guarantee System in Japan*. Tokyo: Japan Federation of Credit Guarantee Corporations.

Kuwahara, S., N. Yoshino, M. Sagara, and F. Taghizadeh-Hesary. 2016. Role of the Credit Risk Database in Developing SMEs. In *SMEs in Developing Asia New Approaches to Overcoming Market Failures*, edited by P. Vandenberg, P. Chantapacdepong, and N. Yoshino. Tokyo: Asian Development Bank Institute.

Orsenigo, C., and C. Vercellis. 2013. Linear versus Nonlinear Dimensionality Reduction for Banks' Credit Rating Prediction. *Knowledge-Based Systems* 47: 14–22.

Riding, A.L., and G. Haines, Jr. 2001. Loan Guarantees: Costs of Default and Benefits to Small Firms. *Journal of Business Venturing* 16(6): 595–612.

SMEB. 2017. *Leading SMEs towards Greater Achievements: Corporate Governance and Financial Report 2016*. Kuala Lumpur: Small and Medium Enterprise Development Bank Malaysia Berhad.

Uesugi, I., K. Sakai, and G.M. Yamashiro. 2006. Effectiveness of Credit Guarantees in the Japanese Loan Market. RIETI Discussion Paper Series 06-E-004. Tokyo: The Research Institute of Economy, Trade and Industry.

Vandenberg, P., P. Chantapacdepong, and N. Yoshino. 2016. Small Firms, Market Failures, and Government Policy. In *SMEs in Developing Asia New Approaches to Overcoming Market Failures*, edited by P. Vandenberg, P. Chantapacdepong, and N. Yoshino. Tokyo: Asian Development Bank Institute.

Yoshino, N. 2013. The Background of Hometown Investment Trust Funds. In *Hometown Investment Trust Funds: A Stable Way to Supply Risk Capital*, edited by N. Yoshino and S. Kaji. Tokyo: Springer.

Yoshino, N., and T. Hirano. 2011. Pro-Cyclicality of the Basel Capital Requirement Ratio and Its Impact on Banks. *Asian Economic Papers* 10(2): 22–36.

Yoshino, N., and F. Taghizadeh-Hesary. 2014a. An Analysis of Challenges Faced by Japan's Economy and Abenomics. *The Japanese Political Economy* 40(3–4): 37–62. https://doi.org/10.1080/2329194X.2014.998591

Yoshino, N., and F. Taghizadeh-Hesary. 2014b. Hometown Investment Trust Funds: An Analysis of Credit Risk. ADBI Working Paper No. 505. Tokyo: Asian Development Bank Institute.

Yoshino, N., and F. Taghizadeh-Hesary. 2014c. Analytical Framework on Credit Risks for Financing SMEs in Asia. *Asia-Pacific Development Journal* 21(2): 1–21.

Yoshino, N., and F. Taghizadeh-Hesary. 2015. Analysis of Credit Ratings for Small and Medium-Sized Enterprises: Evidence from Asia. *Asian Development Review* 32(2): 18–37.

Yoshino, N., and F. Taghizadeh-Hesary. 2016. Causes and Remedies of the Japan's Long-lasting Recession: Lessons for China. *China and World Economy* 24: 23–47.

Yoshino, N., F. Taghizadeh-Hesary, P. Charoensivakorn, and B. Niraula. 2016. Small and Medium-Sized Enterprise (SME) Credit Risk Analysis Using Bank Lending Data: An Analysis of Thai SMEs. *Journal of Comparative Asian Development* 15(3): 383–406.

Zander, R., C. Miller, and N. Mhlanga. 2013. *Credit Guarantee Systems for Agriculture and Rural Enterprise Development*. Rome: Food and Agriculture Organization of the United Nations.

22

MONETARY POLICY AND CENTRAL BANKING IN ASIA

Takatoshi Ito

Introduction

This chapter is an overview of monetary policy and central banking in Asia. Asian countries, in which northeast, southeast, and south Asian countries are included, are very diverse in monetary and currency arrangements as well as in the economic development stage. Also, they have gradually changed from countries with a closed capital account to those with an open capital market account in the last three decades. Historically, the Asian financial crisis of 1997–1998 was a turning point in policy thinking and implementation for many southeast and northeast Asian countries.[1]

The People's Republic of China (PRC), Republic of Korea, and Southeast Asian countries had adopted (de facto) fixed exchange rate regimes before the Asian financial crisis. Governments and central banks put a high priority on exchange rate stability, if not the highest priority. Domestic price stability was secondary in those countries. Due to their high growth, the PRC, Republic of Korea, and Southeast Asian countries experienced a strong pressure and realization for capital inflows, which made it possible to sustain large current account deficits without losing international reserves. When Thailand experienced capital outflows in 1996 and early 1997, the government and the central bank found it very difficult to maintain a stable exchange rate. This was a textbook case of the "impossible trinity," or the trilemma of international finance. The impossible trinity says that it is impossible to have a fixed exchange rate, free capital mobility, and autonomous domestic monetary policy pursuing domestic purposes.

The dollar peg of Thailand was abandoned on 2 July 1997, and the exchange rate started to depreciate. The capital outflows and resulting depreciation spread to other countries in Southeast Asia and to Republic of Korea. This was the beginning of the Asian financial crisis. The International Monetary Fund (IMF) programs for Thailand, Indonesia, and Republic of Korea did not stop depreciation, and some of the IMF prescriptions were counterproductive. These economies went into severe recessions due to large depreciations and resulting banking crises.

The Asian financial crisis left several important lessons to Asian countries. A country has three options to escape from the impossible trinity: flexible exchange rate, capital controls, or giving up autonomous monetary policy. Asian countries started to accumulate large foreign reserves in order to deter a speculative attack, and to fight the speculative capital outflows. Strengthening financial supervision was another lesson. Banks had vulnerable balance sheets before the crisis. They tended to borrow in the US dollar with short-term instruments, while they lent in local currencies with long-term loans. The problem was known as double mismatch.

After the Asian financial crisis, several countries, including Republic of Korea, Thailand, Indonesia, and the Philippines, moved to a managed floating regime with inflation targeting. Hong Kong, China maintained the fixed exchange rate (or currency board to be precise), pegging its currency to the US dollar. By pegging to the key currency in the global financial markets, while giving up on the autonomy of the monetary policy, the Hong Kong, China dollar gains credibility. Others were in between. The PRC maintained the peg to the US dollar through the Asian financial crisis and after until 2005, when it moved to a crawling peg allowing a gradual appreciation. This was partly a response to the US criticism of a large current account surpluses of the PRC. The PRC went back to the US dollar peg from mid-2008 to mid-2010, when it resumed orderly appreciation. During the slow appreciation, the PRC accumulated the international reserves to the level of USD 4 trillion, suggesting that the currency was undervalued and interventions were necessary to limit the degree of appreciation. Then since 2015, the yuan started to depreciate. In the following two years, the international reserves declined by USD 1 trillion.

The Monetary Authority of Singapore has been managing the Singaporean dollar against a basket of currencies of Singapore's major trading partners (i.e., the Monetary Authority of Singapore) is targeting the real effective exchange rate being relatively stable. The economy is highly dependent on exports and imports, so that stabilizing the real effective exchange rate is indirectly stabilizing the domestic inflation. Brunei Darussalam pegged its currency to Singapore. Brunei Darussalam's fiscal and trade surpluses come from its huge oil reserves, and pegging to the Singaporean dollar is to make import low and stable inflation.

After the Asian financial crisis, the government and the central bank of northeast and southeast Asian countries started to pay more attention to financial stability and foreign reserves. Many northeast and southeast Asian countries increased the international reserves.

South Asia, in particular India, Bangladesh, and Pakistan, has suffered from high fiscal deficits and high inflation, dissimilar to northeastern and southeastern Asia. Monetary policy has not been strong enough contain the inflation rate until very recently. India adopted inflation targeting in 2016.

The rest of this chapter is organized as follows. The next section reviews how Asian countries are avoiding the impossible trinity, or trilemma by learning lessons from the Asian financial crisis of 1997–1998. Then the relationship between monetary and exchange rate policy is examined, and inflation targeting in Asia is reviewed. Finally, financial stability is discussed before concluding the chapter.

Taxonomy: the exchange rate and monetary policy regimes

As many Asian economies learned the peril of the impossible trinity, they have implemented regime changes in the exchange rate policy, the monetary policy framework and the speed of capital account liberalization. Many economies shifted to floating or managed exchange rates, trying to maintain monetary policy autonomy in the face of (partially) liberalized capital accounts. Some even went one step further to make the inflation target explicit so that the monetary policy is explicitly assigned for controlling the inflation rate rather than the exchange rate which becomes more flexible to maintain the external balance. Foreign exchange interventions and moderate capital controls were added to manage capital flows. A combination of inflation targeting and managed floats was adopted by the Republic of Korea, Thailand, Indonesia, and the Philippines in the 2000s; by Japan in 2013; and by India in 2016.

Two economies have maintained a fixed exchange rate with free capital flows: Hong Kong, China and Brunei Darussalam. Hong Kong, China fixed the exchange rate to the US dollar and Brunei Darussalam to the Singaporean dollar. Since both economies operate the central bank as a currency board, there is little room for maneuver but to follow the monetary policy of the US and Singapore, respectively.

The PRC has shifted between a fixed exchange rate (until July 2005 and between July 2008 and June 2010) and a managed exchange rate arrangement. The managed exchange rate between July 2005 and June 2008 can be best described as a crawling peg, while the managed exchange rate regime after July 2010 shows limited flexibility depending on the market conditions, but still with an allowable band of daily fluctuation. When the PRC monetary authority resisted appreciation during the period of the crawling peg, not to mention the fixed exchange rate periods, the accompanying foreign exchange interventions led to a rapid growth of foreign reserves. Moreover, monetary policy was most likely maintained to be looser than a position that would have pursued with purely domestic purposes. The resulting ample liquidity in the domestic financial markets at times contributed to booms in real estate prices. Consumer price inflation rate, however, was kept reasonably low on average.

The four low-income countries in ASEAN – Cambodia, Lao People's Democratic Republic (Lao PDR), Myanmar, and Viet Nam – belong to a camp of a near-fixed exchange rate (to the US dollar). However, some parts of their economies are "dollarized" and the degree of freedom for monetary policy is severely limited.

Taipei,China has not adopted an inflation targeting framework, although its exchange rate has been relatively flexible and the monetary policy seems to have discretionary room. Capital flows are relatively restricted in Taipei,China.

Malaysia has been limiting the exchange rate volatility with capital controls. The Malaysian ringgit has been closely correlated with the PRC yuan.[2]

South Asian countries, in particular India, Pakistan, Bangladesh, and Sri Lanka, have experienced higher inflation rates. India adopted an inflation targeting framework in 2016, but it is too early to make assessment of the policy framework. Sri Lanka is classified by the IMF as a "crawling like" exchange rate arrangement since late 2015. Bangladesh is classified by the IMF as a basket currency country with a large weight on the US dollar. However, exchange rate movement suggests that Bangladesh, Pakistan, and Sri Lanka have either followed fixed or crawling peg regimes in the past 10 years. All these four countries have experienced large depreciations whenever the domestic inflation rate rose suddenly.

Asian countries vary in their openness to capital flows, from very rigid to very open like Japan. It is difficult to summarize the degree of openness, but Fernandez (2015, table 22.2), following Klein (2012), categorized economies into three: Wall, Gate, and Open. Japan, the Republic of Korea, Hong Kong, China, Singapore, and Brunei Darussalam qualify for "Open" capital markets. Indonesia, Thailand, Myanmar, and Viet Nam qualify for a "Gate" status, which are more liberalized than "Wall," to which the PRC, Malaysia, and the Philippines belong. Taipei,China is judged to be a "Gate" economy by the author of the present chapter, after interpreting the description on capital flows.[3] Another popular index is the Chinn-Ito openness index, as proposed by Chinn and Ito (2006, 2008). The index has been updated to 2014 (Chinn and Ito 2016).

Table 22.1 provides an overview of the monetary policy framework, the exchange rate regime, and the openness of the capital account of Asian economies. The table implies that there are a number of ways that the country can escape from the trilemma. Four observations emerge from the table: first, northeast and southeast Asian countries have very diverse exchange rate regimes and monetary policy frameworks. Second, the degree of openness in the capital accounts varies across northeast and southeast Asian countries. The diversity poses a challenge for regional financial integration and cooperation, as it makes it difficult for the region to respond to external shocks, such as the global financial crisis. For example, Hong Kong, China

Table 22.1 Trilemma table

	Economy	Income Group[1]	Exchange Rate Regime[2]	Monetary Policy Target[3] with inflation target being for 2016	Capital Controls[4]	Chinn-Ito Openness Index for 2014[5]
Northeast	Japan	High	Free Floating	Inflation Targeting 2%	Open	1.000
	PRC	Upper Middle	Crawling Peg (USD), 2005–2008 Fixed, 2008–2010	No explicit framework	Wall	0.165
	Rep. of Korea	High	Floating	Inflation Targeting 2%	Open	0.716
	Taipei,China	Upper Middle	Floating	M2 growth 2.5%–6.5%	Open	NA
	Hong Kong, China	High	Currency Board (USD)	Currency Board (USD)	Open	1.000
ASEAN	Indonesia	Lower Middle	Floating	Inflation Targeting 4% ± 1%	Gate	0.413
	Thailand	Upper Middle	Floating	Inflation Targeting 2.5% ± 1.5%	Gate	0.165
	Malaysia	Upper Middle	Managed (CNY)		Wall	0.413
	Singapore	High	Basket Currency (REER)	(exchange rate targeting)	Open	1.000
	Philippines	Lower Middle	Floating	Inflation targeting 3% ± 1%	Wall	0.449
	Brunei Darussalam	High	Currency Board (SGD)	Currency Board (SGD)	Open	NA
	Cambodia	Low	Managed (USD)	(dollarization)	Open	0.716
	Lao PDR	Low	Crawling Peg (USD)	(dollarization)	Wall	0.165
	Myanmar	Low	Managed (USD)	(dollarization)	Gate	0.000
	Viet Nam	Lower Middle	Basket Currency (High USD)	No explicit framework	Gate	0.413
South Asia	India	Lower Middle	Floating	Inflation targeting, 4% (2016)	Wall	0.165
	Pakistan	Lower Middle	Floating	No explicit framework	Wall	0.165
	Sri Lanka	Lower Middle	Crawling-like	Monetary Aggregate target	Wall	0.165
	Bangladesh	Lower Middle	Basket Currency (High USD)	Monetary Aggregate target	Gate	0.165

Lao PDR = Lao People's Democratic Republic, PRC = People's Republic of China, REER = real effective exchange rate.

Notes:
[1] As classified by the IMF, with Taipei,China; Cambodia, and the Lao PDR being judged by the author.
[2] IMF (2016: table 2) with additional information by the author.
[3] See text, as judged by the author.
[4] Capital Controls are as classified by IMF (2016), with Taipei,China; Cambodia, and Lao PDR being judged by the author. Following Klein (2012), "Open" ("Wall") countries have, on average, capital controls on less than 10% (more than 70%) of their transactions subcategories over the sample period and do not have any years in which controls are on more than 20% (less than 60%) of their transaction subcategories. "Gate" countries are neither Walls nor Open.
[5] Chinn and Ito (2006), and updated in the homepage, Chinn and Ito (2016) for data up to 2014. Chinn-Ito index for Malaysia and the Philippines rose to 0.4489 in 2014 from 0.1648 in 2013.

Source: Author.

Table 22.2 Trilemma summary

Fixed Exchange Rate	Autonomous Monetary Policy	Free Capital Mobility	Consequences	Economies
Yes	Yes	Yes (Open)	Impossible Trinity	
No	Yes with FIT	Yes (Open)	Floaters FIT	Japan, Republic of Korea, Indonesia, Thailand, Philippines
No	Yes without FIT	Yes (Open)	Floaters no-FIT, open	Taipei,China; Singapore; Cambodia
No	Yes without FIT	Yes (Gate)	Floaters no-FIT, no-open	Myanmar, Viet Nam, India
Yes	No	Yes	Currency Board	Hong Kong, China; Brunei Darussalam
Yes less flexibility	Yes without FIT	No (Wall)	Capital Controllers no-FIT	PRC, Malaysia, Sri Lanka, Bangladesh, Pakistan

PRC = People's Republic of China.

Source: Prepared by author.

maintains its dollar peg at any cost; Republic of Korea experiences capital outflows depreciating its currency with respect to the US dollar; and Japan experiences capital inflows as a safe haven country. As a consequence, the intra-regional cross rates become volatile. Thus, it makes it difficult to develop monetary cooperation in the whole Asian region. Third, south Asian countries have not had explicit frameworks for monetary policy, until India adopting the inflation targeting framework in 2016, and they have heavy capital controls. Fourth, middle-income emerging market economies maintain managed exchange rate regimes and moderate capital controls. The combination allows them to conduct flexible monetary policy pursuing price stability.

It should be noted that determination of capital account openness is not so clear cut, as many control items have to be measured and aggregated. The Chinn-Ito index disagrees with the IMF three groups – Open, Gate, and Wall in four countries, if we categorize those countries with the Chinn-Ito index of 0.7–1.0 as "Open"; 0.4–0.7 as "Gate" and "0.0–4.0" Wall. According to the Chinn-Ito index, Thailand should be "Wall" rather than "Gate"; Malaysia and the Philippines should be "Gate" rather than "Wall" and Myanmar should be "Wall" rather than "Gate." Hence, the IMF categorization, or any other attempt, would be arbitrary.

From Table 22.1, it is possible to re-categorize the countries into the group that shows how they avoid the impossible trinity, or trilemma. Table 22.2 shows such categories. A country has to deny one of the three institutions: fixed exchange rate; autonomous monetary policy; or free capital mobility. Each category in the table shows which institutions the country denies. Most countries now adopt the managed exchange rate regime.

Interaction between monetary and exchange rate policy

Trade-off or complement? Long-term analysis

Both floating and managed floating regimes, which allow wide fluctuations around some sort of a desired (equilibrium) exchange rate, allow the central bank to put a higher priority on domestic price stability (i.e., low and stable inflation rate). The more flexibility of the exchange rate the central bank allows, the more policy space the central bank gains. In this sense, there is a trade-off between exchange rate stability and price stability.

There can be an opposite view. If the central bank fails to contain inflation, the exchange rate is likely to depreciate as the inflation rate soars. Conversely, if the exchange rate, for external reasons, depreciates, the inflation rate will be raised as prices of imports soar. In fact, the Monetary Authority of Singapore argues that they pursue the stability of effective exchange rate in order to achieve price stability. The link between the two is explicitly recognized. Hence, whether price stability and exchange rate stability are trade-off or complement is an interesting empirical question.

Inflation among northeast Asian countries have been contained almost always below 5% since 2000 (Figure 22.1a). Inflation among southeast Asian countries has been mostly under 10%, with dramatic exceptions of Cambodia and Viet Nam reaching 25% in 2008. In other countries, there was also a spike in 2008, reflecting the commodity price booms in 2007 and 2008, and a big dip in 2009, reflecting a deep recession following the Lehman Brothers failure. Viet Nam, Lao PDR, and Indonesia had more than 10% inflation for a few years. More recently, all southeast Asian countries have contained inflation below 5% (Figure 22.1b). The inflation rates in the southeast region have been converging to the range between 0% and 5%. South Asian countries, as shown in Figure 22.1c, have had more volatile inflation. Sri Lanka had very high inflation from 2000 to 2008, and then a dramatic shift to moderate inflation after 2009. Bangladesh, India, and Pakistan had increasing inflation rates until 2009–2010, and then decreasing inflation rates in the 2010s. In general, the inflation rates were highest in southern Asia, followed by southeastern Asia, and then northeastern Asia the least. But, in all three subregions, the inflation rate seems to have converged to less than 5% by 2016. This is consistent with a global trend, where the Asian region is no exception, in which the central bank has

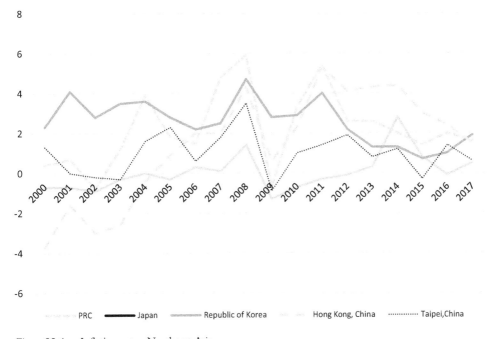

Figure 22.1a Inflation rates: Northeast Asia

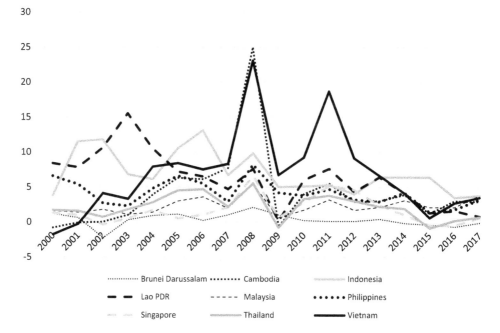

Figure 22.1b Inflation rates: Southeast Asia

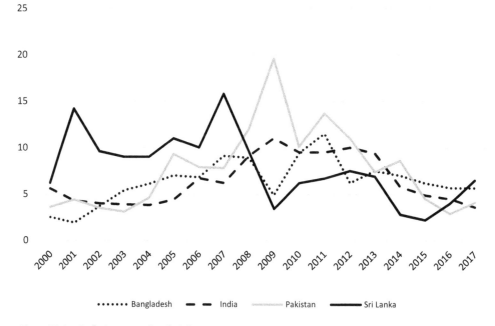

Figure 22.1c Inflation rates: South Asia

Source: Compiled by author with data from the IMF's World Economic Outlook database.

become increasingly independent from the government, and has become capable to achieve low and stable inflation rate.

The exchange rate is another key variable for macroeconomic stability. Figure 22.2a shows the annual change of the exchange rate (with respect to the US dollar, average of the year) of the northeastern economies. Hong Kong, China maintained a fixed exchange rate to the US dollar. While the PRC and Taipei,China have relatively stable currencies, the Republic of Korea and Japan saw wide fluctuations, with negative correlation since 2004. The Republic of Korea had large depreciation in 2008–2009, while Japan experienced large appreciation. The trend reversed in 2013–2014. These opposite movements of the Korean won and the Japanese yen is the difference of the two countries in the structure of the economy and capital markets. When there is a global shock originating in the US or Europe, the Japanese yen is regarded as a safe haven currency, while the Korean won is regarded as an emerging market currency that should be sold in the "risk-off" phase on global investment. Japan, Indonesia, and Malaysia have experienced large depreciation in 2013–2015. Figure 22.2b shows the exchange rate movements for southeastern countries. They move broadly in sync. There are a few countries that depreciated more or appreciated more, but a general trend is the same. This is indicative of financial integration in the region and similar economic development stages. Figure 22.2c shows the exchange rate movements of south Asian countries. The four currencies show large depreciations in 2009 and 2012.

In Figure 22.3, the pair of average inflation rate and the average change in the exchange rate over the period of 2001–2015 is plotted for each of the countries that were shown in Figures 22.1 and 22.2. It is expected that they are positively correlated. Higher inflation, as a domestic shock, tends to cause a nominal depreciation of the exchange rate; and the exchange rate depreciation due to external reasons would cause imported inflation. Assuming the first channel being dominant the following regression result is obtained.

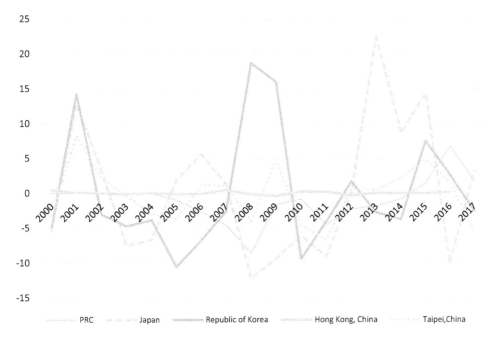

Figure 22.2a Annual change, exchange rates: Northeast Asia

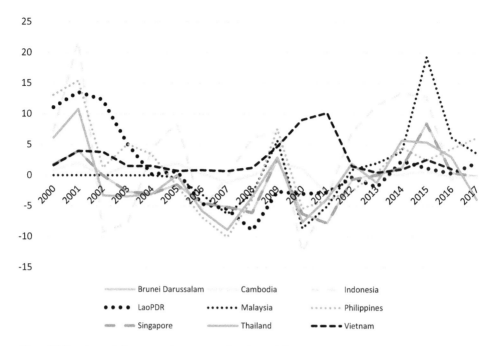

Figure 22.2b   Annual change, exchange rates: Southeast Asia

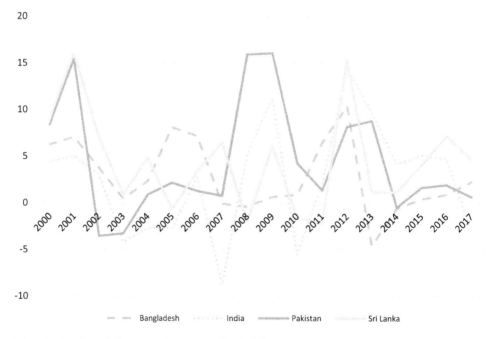

Figure 22.2c   Annual change, exchange rates: South Asia

Note: National currency per US dollar, period average.

Source: Compiled by author with data from the IMF's International Financial Statistics database and the Central Bank of Taipei,China.

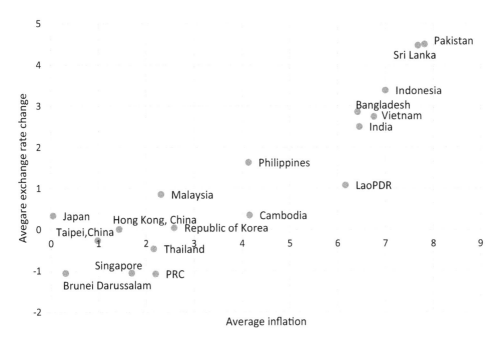

Figure 22.3   Average inflation rate and the exchange rate change

Source: Compiled by author based on own calculations

Samples: 18 countries (k = 1, . . ., 18), Variables are annual average of 2001–2016

$$\Delta ExR_k = -1.40 + 0.67\ \pi_k \qquad \text{Adjusted R2} = 0.68$$
$$(-2.54)\ \ (6.11)$$

where the t-statistic is shown in the brackets. The slope coefficient is statistically significant at 1%. The result implies that the 1% increase in the inflation rate tends to be associated with depreciation by 0.67 percentage point.

Whether the central banks in the region experienced a trade-off between price stability and exchange rate stability can be tested in a different way. The trade-off should be a relationship between the volatility in inflation rates and the volatility in the exchange rate changes. Without building a reliable model of the monetary policy reaction function, such a crude relationship should be viewed only as a casual observation. With this proviso, the pair of standard deviation of the monthly inflation rate and standard deviation of the monthly exchange rate changes is plotted. Figure 22.4 shows such pairs for the northeast, southeast, and south Asian countries of our interest. There is weak negative correlation between the standard deviation of inflation and exchange rate changes. The negative correlation implies the trade-off between the price stability and the exchange rate stability. The central banks that put a high priority to the price stability, such as inflation targeters, tolerate volatility in the exchange rate; the central banks that put a high priority to the exchange rate stability, such as with the crawling peg, would tolerate price volatility.

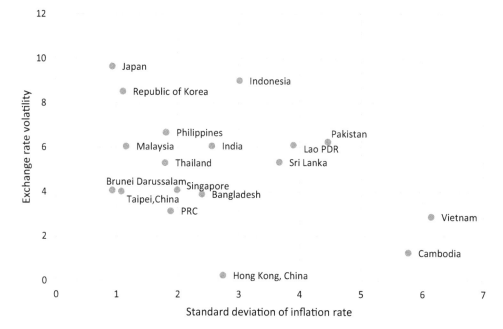

Figure 22.4 Average standard deviation of inflation rate and exchange rate volatility

Source: Compiled by author based on own calculations.

Formally, the slope of the trade-off can be estimated as follows:

Samples: 18 countries (k = 1, . . ., 18), Variables are annual average of 2001–2016

$$\text{STDDEV}(\Delta\text{ExR}_k) = 6.71 - 0.52 \text{ STDDEV}(\pi_k) \qquad\qquad \text{Adjusted R2} = 0.06$$
$$(5.79)\quad(-1.43)$$

Since the coefficient on standard deviation of inflation is not statistically significant, we do not have a conclusive evidence of the trade-off. That is the conclusion of a linear regression.

Yet another possibility is to estimate a hyperbola relationship between the two variables. By imposing the hyperbola formula, we will be estimating the following relationship:

$$\text{STDDEV}(\Delta\text{ExR}_k) \times \text{STDDEV}(\pi_k) = c$$

Where c is a constant. The higher k means the hyperbola is farther from the origin. In order to estimate k, natural log is applied to the both sides.

$$\ln\{\text{STDDEV}(\Delta\text{ExR}_k)\} + \ln\{STDDEV(\pi_k)\} = \ln c$$

By estimating this relationship, one obtains the following estimate:

$$\ln c = 2.28$$
$$(10.39)$$

Where the number in the bracket () shows the t-value. The value of c is now calculated as follows: c = 9.788.

Therefore, a hyperbolic relationship fits better than the linear relationship. Figures 22.3 and 22.4 use the averages of inflation and exchange rate changes over 16 years. However, some of the Asian countries have gone through the regime changes in the exchange rate policy or the monetary policy, which is not well depicted in these kinds of figures based on annual averages.

Trade-off or complement? With regime changes

Monthly price stability can be defined in several ways. The month-to-month variations in the exchange rate may be one way. The deviation from the medium target, especially for the inflation targeters, is another criterion. Or a deviation from the trend may be yet another one when the target is not publicly or explicitly stated. Here, we define price volatility (P-volatility) as the absolute value of the difference between the inflation rate and the 12-month moving average of the past inflation rate, where the inflation rate, $\varpi(t)$, is the rate of change in the CPI (headline) from the same month of a year earlier (i.e., year on year).

$$P\text{-volatility} = \text{period average of } \left| \pi(t) - MA(\pi(t)) \right|$$

$$\text{Where } MA(\pi(t)) = \text{Average of } \{\pi(k), k=t\text{-}12 \text{ to } t\text{-}1\}$$

$$\text{and } \pi(t) = 100\star\{CPI(t)\text{-}CPI(t\text{-}12)\}/CPI(t\text{-}12)$$

Exchange rate volatility (E-volatility) is defined as in the absolute value of monthly percent change of the exchange rate (with respect to the US dollar).

$$E\text{-volatility} = \text{period average of } \left| er(t) - er(t\text{-}1) \right|$$

Where er(t) is the exchange rate of average of month t.

Over the past 16 years of our sample, some countries have gone through regime changes in their exchange rate policies and monetary policy framework. The most important was the changes in the PRC exchange rate policies. It has been shown that the weight of the PRC currency, the yuan, is increasing in Asian currencies' explicit or implicit basket. This is natural that an economic integration of Asian countries with the PRC is proceeding steadily. Therefore, the changes in PRC exchange rate policies, summarized in the next paragraph, give a good sub-period definition.

The yuan exchange rate was fixed against the US dollar until July 2005. Then a very gradual (almost constant percentage) appreciation took place after the exchange rate reform in July 2005. During the global financial crisis, July 2008–June 2010, the PRC central bank reverted to a fixed exchange rate. Then a gradual appreciation resumed from July 2010, but this time with higher degree of flexibility. From the late 2015 to 2016, the yuan depreciated significantly. The following four sub-periods are identified.

I   2001/01–2005/06
II   2005/07–2008/06
III   2008/07–2010/06
IV   2010/07–2016/12

A pair of E-volatility and P-volatility is calculated for each country in each sub-period. The total of 72 dots (18 countries multiplied by four sub-periods) are shown in Figure 22.5. Three observations are obtained from the Figure. First, there seems a negative correlation between E-volatility and P-volatility. Second, the relationship may be non-linear, since there seem to be more dots along the two axes, rather than along a positive slope line. Third, there seems to be a mixture of several different kinds of countries reflecting various exchange rate and monetary regimes. If a central bank emphasizes and succeeds in achieving price stability, there may be more dots along a vertical line at the targeted inflation rate. Instead, if a central bank keeps the fixed or near fixed exchange rate regime, then dots should distribute horizontally near E-volatility zero line. Indeed, Hong Kong, China and the PRC in the first and third periods are very close to, if not on, the horizontal axis.

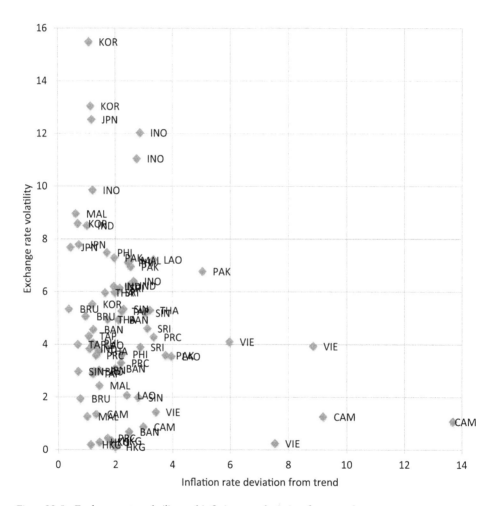

Figure 22.5 Exchange rate volatility and inflation rate deviation from trend

Note: BAN: Bangladesh, BRU: Brunei Darussalam, CAM: Cambodia, HKG: Hong Kong, China, IND: India, INO: Indonesia, JPN: Japan, LAO: Lao PDR, MAL: Malaysia, PAK: Pakistan, PHI: Philippines, PRC: People's Republic of China, KOR: Republic of Korea, SIN: Singapore, SRI: Sri Lanka, TAP: Taipei,China, THA: Thailand, VIE: Viet Nam.

Source: Compiled by author based on own calculations.

Given the three observations, the following specification for regressions will be examined.

$$\ln(E - \text{volatility}(j,k)) = \alpha + \beta \ln(P - \text{volatility}(j,k)) + \{\text{Controls}\}$$

where j = country; and k = I, II, III, IV. Controls may include dummy variables for different periods, k, and the Openness Index (Chinn and Ito 2016). Controls include period (I, II, III, IV) dummy variables; and openness index for each period.[4] This specification cannot accommodate the currency peg countries, as the E-volatility is at or close to zero. We eliminate samples with zero or near zero E-volatility.[5]

The above specifications can be transformed once the estimates are obtained as follows:

$$\left\{ E - \text{volatility}(j,k) \star \left(P - \text{volatility}(j,k) \right)^{\beta} \right\} = \exp\{\alpha + \{\text{controls}\}\}$$

In a special case of $\beta = 1$, the relationship between the two volatility measures will be a hyperbolic line, with a distance from the origin be determined by the value inside the value in the exp brackets. The higher the value, the farther away from the origin, suggesting more volatilities.

Regression results are shown in Table 22.3. There is a trade-off between exchange rate volatility and price stability with β coefficient being negative. Controlling for the period effect, which stems from global shocks, such as energy prices, global financial crisis, and PRC

Table 22.3 Regression results

		Log	*Period Dummy*	*Openness*
A	Coefficient	−0.037	−0.124	−0.335
constant	Std. Error	0.086	0.142	0.181
	t-Statistic	−0.427	−0.871	−1.851
	Prob.	0.671	0.387	0.069★
B	Coefficient	−0.250	−0.487	−0.419
pvolatility	Std. Error	0.104	0.111	0.115
	t-Statistic	−2.402	−4.393	−3.649
	Prob.	0.019★★	0.000★★★	0.001★★★
Dum2	Coefficient		0.093	0.059
	Std. Error		0.195	0.192
	t-Statistic		0.478	0.307
	Prob.		0.634	0.760
Dum3	Coefficient		0.762	0.685
	Std. Error		0.223	0.223
	t-Statistic		3.411	3.069
	Prob.		0.001★★★	0.003★★★
Dum4	Coefficient		−0.083	−0.081
	Std. Error		0.194	0.190
	t-Statistic		−0.426	−0.427
	Prob.		0.672	0.671
Openness	Coefficient			0.452
	Std. Error			0.247
	t-Statistic			1.831
	Prob.			0.072★
Adj. R2		0.070	0.238	0.267

exchange rate regime changes, the estimate of βbecomes higher suggesting the trade-off. Openness has a positive coefficient suggesting that when the country opens the capital market, capital inflows and outflows make the exchange rate and/or inflation rate more volatile.

When only high-income countries are considered, inflation volatility is very low, and the variation is mostly in the exchange rate. It is obvious from the data that high-income countries place a higher priority on domestic price stability. This is expected from having the independent central bank and the exchange rates are either freely floating or only managed occasionally. For upper middle-income countries, there seems to be a trade-off between the price and exchange rate stability, as a trend line would be downward sloping. These countries are transitioning to a model of more independent central banks with an inflation targeting.

Inflation targeting in Asia

Inflation targeting framework

The inflation targeting framework has become popular among central banks in emerging market economies as well as advanced countries since 1990 when New Zealand first adopted the framework. Inflation targeting central banks make explicit a numerical target for price stability to guide their monetary policy. However, inflation targeting as a monetary framework goes beyond just declaring the numerical target. The central bank has to be transparent and accountable to communicate monetary policy in relation to the targeted inflation rate so that the public would expect that the inflation rate should converge to the targeted level.

Since it is to place a higher priority on domestic price stability, a country to adopt inflation targeting has to be floating relatively freely. A country with a fixed exchange rate regime is not advised to adopt inflation targeting. As almost all Asian emerging and developing countries had adopted de facto dollar pegs prior to the Asian currency crisis of 1997–1998, it was natural that none of them had adopted an inflation targeting regime.

Many experts who studied the Asian currency crisis identified the fixed exchange rate regimes, coupled with partial opening of capital accounts, as a source of financial vulnerability that either led to the crisis or made the crisis much worse than just a one-time exchange rate adjustment. Huge capital inflows that created vulnerability to high-performance Asian emerging market economies were attracted to the high interest rates and relatively stable exchange rates. Thus double (maturity and currency) mismatch developed.

After the Asian currency crisis, several emerging market economies moved to floating exchange rate regimes, in order not to repeat the same mistake in the future. When a country moves from the fixed exchange rate regime to the floating exchange rate regime, the country has to face a trade-off between price stability and exchange rate stability. Previous sections of the chapter described how different Asian countries have chosen along the trade-off relationship. In this section, we focus on the four early adopters of inflation targeting in Asia – Republic of Korea, Thailand, the Philippines, and Indonesia – to assess their monetary policy. Republic of Korea adopted the framework in 1998, followed by Thailand in 2000, and the Philippines in 2002. Indonesia also adopted inflation targeting in 2000 (implemented in 2001), but substantially strengthened it in 2005.[6]

Among the advanced countries, Japan adopted inflation targeting in 2013, joining the list of advanced country inflation targeters relatively late.[7] Newly appointed Governor Haruhiko Kuroda announced in April 2013 that the Bank would aim at achieving 2% in two years, by raising the inflation rate, which had been in negative territory for most of the preceding 15 years. As of mid-2017, the inflation rate in Japan is stubbornly at near 0%, although now in the positive territory.

The latest adopter of inflation targeting in Asia is India. In August 2016, the inflation targeting framework was agreed between the finance minister and then Reserve Bank governor, Raghuram Rajan. The target was set at 4% with a tolerance band of ±2% in the next five years. It is too early to assess their performance.

Republic of Korea

Republic of Korea adopted inflation targeting in the midst of it currency crisis. In parallel to its negotiation with the IMF for its emergency loans, Republic of Korea introduced an inflation targeting framework. As the won was depreciating quickly, resulting high inflation was a concern. Inflation targeting was expected to keep down the inflation rate.[8] The revised Bank of Korea Act (December 1997) provided the Bank with policy independence and established an inflation targeting framework. The Bank of Korea formally started to implement inflation targeting in 1998. In the case of Republic of Korea, the currency crisis provided an additional incentive and urgency for adoption of inflation targeting.

The history of Republic of Korea inflation targets is summarized in Table 22.4. In 1998, when the sharp depreciation of the won in late 1997 was expected to produce a relatively high

Table 22.4 Republic of Korea

As of May 2017					Annual Inflation Rate		
Year	Target Ranges	Based On	Period(s)	Mid-term Inflation Target		Headline	Core
1998	9% ± 1%	Headline CPI inflation	annual		1998	7.5	5.9
1999	3% ± 1%	Headline	annual		1999	0.8	0.3
2000	2.5% ± 1%	Core CPI Inflation	annual	a level of 2.5%	2000	2.3	1.9
2001	3% ± 1%	Core	annual	2.5%	2001	4.1	3.6
2002	3% ± 1%	Core	annual inflation target	2.5%	2002	2.8	3.0
2003	3% ± 1%	Core	annual inflation target	2.5%	2003	3.5	3.1
2004	2.5%–3.5%	Core	2004–2006 (medium term)		2004	3.6	2.9
2005	2.5%–3.5%	Core			2005	2.8	2.4
2006	2.5%–3.5%	Core			2006	2.2	1.8
2007	3% ± 0.5%	Headline	2007–2009 (medium term)		2007	2.5	2.3
2008	3% ± 0.5%	Headline			2008	4.7	4.3
2009	3% ± 0.5%	Headline			2009	2.8	3.6
2010	3% ± 1%	Headline	2010–2012 (medium term)		2010	2.9	1.8
2011	3% ± 1%	Headline			2011	4.0	3.2
2012	3% ± 1%	Headline			2012	2.2	1.7
2013	2.5%–3.5%	Headline	2013–2015 (medium term)		2013	1.3	1.6
2014	2.5%–3.5%	Headline			2014	1.3	2.0
2015	2.5%–3.5%	Headline			2015	0.7	
2016	2%	Headline	2016–2019 (medium term)		2016	1.0	
2017	2%						
2018	2%						

inflation, the target was set at 9% ± 1%. (Note that the inflation rate is measured as the change in period average; percent per annum.) However, the inflation was controlled in 1998, as the exchange rate rebounded. The inflation rate fell significantly in late 1998.

Republic of Korea first adopted the headline CPI as a definition of the inflation rate. This was suggestion from the IMF as it was easy to communicate with the public.[9] However, in 2000, the benchmark CPI was switched to core inflation rate and the range was set at 2.5% ± 1%. Since 2000, the target central point has been either at 2.5% or 3%, only slightly higher than other Organisation of Economic Co-operation and Development countries. Republic of Korea moved to a medium-term target in 2004, to announce a three-year target. This is good from the viewpoint that the inflation targeting is the medium-term concept.

What is interesting about the Republic of Korea inflation targeting regime is the following characteristics. First, the benchmark CPI was switched back to headline in 2007. Second, the expression of target has switched back and forth between the range (such as 2.5%–3.5% in 2004–2006 and 2013–2015) and the central point with allowable deviation band around it (such as 3.0% ± 0.5% in 2007–2009 and 3.0% ± 1% in 2013–2015). Finally, it settled with the single point target (2%) for the medium-term target of 2016–2019.

Thailand

Thailand introduced inflation targeting in May 2000. By then, the foreign exchange and financial markets had recovered from the volatility of the Asian currency crisis of 1997–1998, which originated in Thailand. The Bank of Thailand considered a way to solidify stability and adopted the inflation targeting framework.

The original target was between 0.0 and 3.5 in the core inflation rate (Table 22.5). The range was much wider than other inflation targeters' ranges and the core inflation rate is less volatile than headline. The choice of a relatively easy target was deliberate. The Bank wanted to establish credibility first before raising the bar.

The record of successfully hitting the target range was excellent. More than 90% of time, the core inflation rate stayed in the target range between May 2000 and September 2009. The range was narrowed by trimming 0.5% on both the floor and the ceiling. The new range between 0.5 and 3.0 was introduced in September 2009 in the aftermath of the global financial crisis. The inflation rate undershot the floor in 2009, but got back into a new range by mid-2010.

Grenville and Ito (2010) assessed the 10-year history of the Thai inflation targeting as a commissioned work at the Bank of Thailand. Generally, they gave high marks on the Bank's performance: Controlling the inflation rate in the range with a high percentage, adopting an effective communication strategy and balancing the inflation targeting with other secondary objectives. They recommended to adopt a point target rather than a range target, as the point target, with or without an explicit allowable deviation band around it, is more effective in anchoring the expectation. They also suggested to change the benchmark CPI from core to headline. These suggestions were adopted five years later. In January 2015, the benchmark was changed from core to headline and the target became 2.5% ± 1.5%. The target and actual inflation rates are shown in Table 22.5.

In retrospect, the timing of switching from core to headline was not good, as the headline inflation rate became much lower in 2014–2015 due to declining energy prices. The actual inflation rate has been lower than the floor of the target since January 2015. It is a global phenomenon from advanced countries like the US, Japan, and the eurozone countries to emerging market economies that the inflation rate has stayed below the target.

Table 22.5 Thailand

	Period Average		Target	
	Headline	Core		
2000	1.6	0.8	Core	[0.0, 3.5]
2001	1.6	1.2	Core	[0.0, 3.5]
2002	0.7	0.5	Core	[0.0, 3.5]
2003	1.8	0.1	Core	[0.0, 3.5]
2004	2.8	0.4	Core	[0.0, 3.5]
2005	4.5	1.6	Core	[0.0, 3.5]
2006	4.7	2.3	Core	[0.0, 3.5]
2007	2.2	1.1	Core	[0.0, 3.5]
2008	5.5	2.4	Core	[0.0, 3.5]
2009	−0.8	0.3	Core	[0.5, 3.0]
2010	3.3	0.9	Core	[0.5, 3.0]
2011	3.8	2.4	Core	[0.5, 3.0]
2012	3.0	2.1	Core	[0.5, 3.0]
2013	2.2	1.0	Core	[0.5, 3.0]
2014	1.9	1.6	Core	[0.5, 3.0]
2015	−0.9	1.1	Headline	2.5 ± 1.5
2016	0.2	0.7	Headline	2.5 ± 1.5

Source: Author

There were two changes made to the target:

May 2000: Core inflation [0.0, 3.5]

September 2009: Core inflation [0.5, 3.0]

January 2015: Headline inflation 2.5% ± 1.5%

Indonesia

Bank Indonesia has been announcing the inflation target numbers since 2001 as shown in Table 22.6. However, inflation targeting as a monetary policy framework was not established until 2005. Bank Indonesia states: "[This] framework was formally adopted in July 2005, and replaces the previous monetary policy using base money as the monetary policy target." (Bank Indonesia, "Monetary Policy Framework," on its website).[10]

Between 2001 and 2009, the target was annually revised, but the actual inflation rate was constantly missing the target rate which had ±1% allowable deviation band. Frequent changes of the target were not contributing to anchoring expectation and missing the target made things worse. In addition, targeting a headline inflation has an additional challenge, many goods are under administered prices (price control by the government). When a good reform of removing subsidies is implemented, it results in a sudden inflation. This explains a surge in 2006 and 2008. It was a tall order to hit the target range with a narrow band with the benchmark of headline inflation that included a large number of administered prices. Moreover, the frequent changes of the target ranges did not contribute to anchoring inflation expectation.

A situation dramatically changed after 2010. The target became a three-year rolling plan and stable. The central point of the target range was 5% in 2010–2011 and has been 4.5% since 2012. The actual inflation rate is still missing the target. Indonesia is the only country among

Table 22.6 Indonesia

Year	Inflation Target	Inflation Actual (%, year-on-year)
2001	4%–6%	12.55
2002	9%–10%	10.03
2003	9% + 1%	5.06
2004	5.5% + 1%	6.4
2005	6% + 1%	17.11
2006	8% + 1%	6.6
2007	6% + 1%	6.59
2008	5% + 1%	11.06
2009	4.5% + 1%	2.78
2010	5% + 1%	6.96
2011	5% + 1%	3.79
2012	4.5% + 1%	4.3
2013	4.5% + 1%	8.38
2014	4.5% + 1%	8.36
2015	4% + 1%	3.35
2016	4% ± 1%	3.02
2017★	4% ± 1%	
2018★	3.5% ± 1%	

Source: Author.

many that it is overshooting the target in 2014 and 2015. For Indonesia, using the core inflation may be better to keep the inflation rate in the target range, so that credibility can be established first. See Table 22.6 for the inflation target and actual inflation rate.

The Philippines

The Central Bank of the Philippines adopted its inflation targeting framework in 2002. The history of inflation targeting and actual inflation rate is shown in Table 22.7. It started with the range target (4.5–5.5) in 2002–2003. The range target with the 1% width continued until 2007. The actual inflation rate overshot in 2005 and 2006. Oil price increases and VAT rate increases are blamed for the deviation. The inflation target was reformed to have a central point with a 1% allowable deviation band in 2008. The central point has been adjusted downward gradually from 4.5% in 2010 to 3.0% in 2015. The actual inflation rate has been in the allowable deviation band since 2010, except 2015, where the actual inflation rate undershot the floor. The framework seems to be working very well since 2010.

Japan

Japan adopted the inflation targeting with the target inflation rate being 2% in January 2013. This was a substantial development in the history of the Bank of Japan, as Japan had been suffering from deflation for 15 years. As the Bank of Japan was granted de jure independence with the revision of the Bank of Japan law in 1998, the inflation rate turned negative. The Bank of Japan was hesitant to take bold actions or aim a specific numerical target from the early years of independence.[11]

Mr. Shinzo Abe became prime minister, for the second time, in December 2012. He identified the 15-year deflation had had significant adverse effects on the Japanese economy. Getting

Table 22.7 The Philippines

Inflation Targeting History of the Philippines		
Year	Actual Inflation	Inflation Target
2002	2.9	4.5–5.5
2003	3	4.5–5.5
2004	5.5	4.0–5.0
2005	7.6	5.0–6.0
2006	6.2	4.0–5.0
2007	2.9	4.0–5.0
2008	8.3	4.0 ± 1.0
2009	4.2	3.5 ± 1.0
2010	3.8	4.5 ± 1.0
2011	4.6	4.0 ± 1.0
2012	3.2	4.0 ± 1.0
2013	3	4.0 ± 1.0
2014	4.1	4.0 ± 1.0
2015	1.4	3.0 ± 1.0
2016	1.8	3.0 ± 1.0

Source: Author.

out of deflation became his first priority. The Bank of Japan and the government signed a joint document that specified the responsibility of the Bank of Japan to target the 2% inflation rate in January 2013. At the expiration of the term of governor and deputy governors in March 2013, a new team that was more sympathetic to the inflation targeting framework was brought in.

Governor Kuroda introduced quantitative and qualitative easing (QQE) to significantly increase the balance sheet by purchasing a large amount of long-term government bonds. The government also expanded fiscal expenditures. The inflation rate rose from −0.9% in March 2013 to 1.6% by March–May 2014. The rise in the inflation rate, or an escape from deflation, was made possible by a sharp yen depreciation and a stock price surge.

However, the inflation rate (headline) started to decline since then and became at around 0% by the end of 2015. Much of the decline is blamed on the decline in oil and commodity prices. The Bank of Japan has never achieved its target of 2% since the introduction of the framework. Inflation expectation is also falling short of the target. It may take a few years before the Japanese inflation targeting framework becomes credible.

Summary of five inflation targeters

In summary, the experiences of the four Asian Emerging Market inflation targeters plus Japan are described and compared. The comparison shows that they are converging to the best practice of flexible inflation targeting with the following features:

1   The inflation targeting is treated as a medium-term objective, as opposed to annual revision. Initially, Indonesia, the Republic of Korea, and the Philippines had annual targets, but they were revised to be three-year intermediate targets by 2010. Stable target is better for anchoring the inflation expectation.

2   A point target (e.g., 2%) with or without an explicit allowable deviation band is adopted as opposed to a range (e.g., 1%–3%); Japan and Republic of Korea has a single point 2%. All others have point target with an allowable deviation band. Again showing the point is important to influence the inflation expectation.

3   The target point is reasonably low (consistent with the exchange rate stability);

4   Headline is used as opposed to core. However, this poses some problem in the environment of declining oil and other commodity prices. Only Indonesia is overshooting and all others are undershooting.

Financial stability

Central banks usually have two important wings (departments) in its organization in charge of monetary policy and financial stability. All central banks have a power of lender of last resort. However, in some countries, a main banking regulatory and supervisory function exists outside of the central bank.[12]

In the last 30 years in the global financial markets, bank regulation, supervision, and examination have become a key element for financial stability and development after a series of banking crises, which sometimes precede or follow a currency crisis. Crises often trigger institutional reform. After the banking crisis of Japan in 1997, the Financial Supervisory Agency (later, renamed as Financial Services Agency, FSA) was created. In the Republic of Korea, a similar reform took place that created the Financial Supervisory Services (FSS). In the PRC, the Banking Regulatory Commission is in charge of bank supervision. Indonesia created the Financial Services Authority (OJK) in 2011, and formally took over the function of regulation and supervision of banks from Bank Indonesia (the central bank) in 2014. The central bank remains the main bank supervisor in Cambodia, the Lao PDR, Malaysia, Myanmar, the Philippines, Singapore, Thailand, and Viet Nam; Table 22.8 summarizes the difference in institutional set-up of financial regulatory and supervisory authorities.

Table 22.8 Financial supervisor

	Central Bank, Stability Wing	*Other Financial Supervisory Authorities*

Japan	Bank of Japan
	Financial System and Bank
	    Examination Department
		★ Financial Services Agency
		Securities and Exchange Surveillance
		    Commission

Rep. of Korea	Bank of Korea Financial Stability Department	★ Financial Supervisory Service Financial Services Commission
People's Republic of China	People's Bank of China Financial Stability Bureau	★ China Banking Regulatory Commission China Securities Regulatory Commission China Insurance Regulatory Commission
Indonesia	Bank Indonesia Financial System Stability	★ Financial Services Authority
Thailand	★ Bank of Thailand Financial Institutions Stability	Office of the Securities and Exchange Commission
Singapore	★ Monetary Authority of Singapore Financial supervision	(NA)

	Central Bank, Stability Wing	Other Financial Supervisory Authorities
Malaysia	★ Bank Negara Malaysia Financial Surveillance	Securities Commission Malaysia Labuan Offshore Financial Services Authority
Philippines	★ Bangko Sentral ng Pilipinas Supervision and Examination Sector	Philippines Securities and Exchange Commission
Brunei Darussalam	★ Monetary Authority of Brunei Darussalam	Brunei International Financial Center of the Ministry of Finance
Viet Nam	★ State Bank of Viet Nam Banking Supervision Agency	State Securities Commission
Cambodia	★ National Bank of Cambodia Banking Supervision	(NA)
Myanmar	★ Central Bank of Myanmar Financial Stability	(NA)
Lao PDR	★ Bank of Lao PDR Financial Institution Supervision Department	(NA)
India	★ Reserve Bank of India	Securities and Exchange Board of India
Pakistan	★ State Bank of Pakistan	Securities and Exchange Commission of Pakistan
Sri Lanka	★ Central Bank of Sri Lanka	Securities and Exchange Commission of Sri Lanka
Bangladesh	★ Bangladesh Bank	(NA)

NA = not applicable.
Notes: ★ indicates a main financial supervisor.
Sources: Author's creation based on countries' information and Bank for International Settlements, Regulatory Authorities and Supervisory Agencies (www.bis.org/regauth.htm?m=2%7C269).

It has been debated whether monetary policy should target solely CPI inflation rate, as the typical inflation targeter should do, or whether it should prevent financial boom and bust. An asset price inflation can occur without CPI inflation. That was the case in Japan in the second half of the 1980s. Should the interest rate be used to curb asset price inflation even if it may prematurely be ending a boom or sending the CPI inflation rate into a negative territory?

One view is that the interest rate is a blunt instrument to control a financial bubble. Other financial instruments such as macroprudential measures should be employed to lower risk of financial boom and bust. Another view is that the interest rate is a powerful tool to influence the asset price. Monetary policy needs to be conducted on the balance of CPI inflation and asset price inflation. Since this has been debated thoroughly in the literature (see Cecchetti et al. 2000; Ito 2010b; Stein 2013; Svensson 2009; and White 2009 for summary), it is not repeated here. Since the Asian currency crisis of 1997–1998, no major real estate and stock price bubble has occurred in Asia, except possibly in the PRC. Since the PRC has many control measures over banks, such as the reserve requirement, while the exchange rate stability is also very important, the interest rate was not a main instrument to control a credit boom.

Conclusion

Major issues related to central banking in Asia were covered in the chapter. Since the exchange rate stability is important for some of the Asian countries, a trade-off between inflation stability and exchange rate stability may arise in some of the Asian countries. Diverse exchange rate regimes and monetary policy regimes coexist in Asia. One extreme is Hong Kong, China's currency board regime with respect to the US dollar. Another extreme is that Japan adopts free floating. Those who float relatively freely have adopted inflation targeting in an attempt to anchor inflation expectation. Institutional details of inflation targeters were described. In many developing countries, central banks are in charge of financial stability in addition to price stability, while in some higher-income countries, bank regulation and supervision has been moved to an independent agency outside the central bank. Which model works better has not been tested in Asia.

Notes

1 See Ito (2007, 2012) for the Asian financial crisis.
2 See Ito (2010a) and Ito (2017: tables 6 and 7).
3 See "foreign exchange regulations" in the homepage of the central bank of Taipei,China (www.cbc. gov.tw/ct.asp?xItem=857&CtNode=481&mp=2).
4 The Chinn-Ito (2016) openness index is not available for Taipei,China and Brunei Darussalam.
5 Eliminated samples are Hong Kong, China I, II, III, IV; PRC I, III, Malaysia I; and Bangladesh III.
6 Ito and Hayashi (2004) was an early survey of the performance of the four Asian inflation targeters. See also Morgan (2013).
7 See Ito (2004) for the reasons that the Bank of Japan was resistant to a suggestion of adopting inflation targeting. Ito (2006) also describes performance of the Bank of Japan for the period of 1998 and 2005.
8 The Letter of Intent of 3 December 1997 includes a sentence: "The inflation target reflects a very limited pass-through of the recent depreciation of the won to the aggregate price level." It appears that the IMF strongly suggested or endorsed Republic of Korea to adopt inflation targeting. However, the preparation for inflation targeting had been underway inside the Bank of Korea prior to the sudden crisis that had developed in November 1997.
9 See Kim and Park (2006).
10 www.bi.go.id/en/moneter/kerangka-kebijakan/Contents/Default.aspx.
11 See Ito (2004) for possible political economy explanations.
12 See Kawai and Morgan (2012).

References

Cecchetti, S., H. Genberg, J. Lipsky, and S. Wadhwani. 2000. Asset Prices and Central Bank Policy. Geneva Reports on the World Economy No. 2. Geneva: International Center for Monetary and Banking Studies.
Chinn, M.D., and H. Ito. 2006. What Matters for Financial Development? Capital Controls, Institutions, and Interactions. *Journal of Development Economics* 81(1): 163–192.
Chinn, M.D., and H. Ito. 2008. A New Measure of Financial Openness. *Journal of Comparative Policy Analysis* 10(3): 309–322.
Chinn, M.D., and H. Ito. 2016. The Chinn-Ito Index – A de jure Measure of Financial Openness http://web.pdx.edu/~ito/Chinn-Ito_website.htm (accessed 3 July 2016).
Fernandez, A., M. Klein, A. Rebucci, M. Schindler, and M. Uribe. 2015. Capital Control Measures: A New Dataset. IMF Working Paper No. 15/80. Washington, DC: International Monetary Fund.
Grenville, S., and T. Ito. 2010. *An Independent Evaluation of the Bank of Thailand's Monetary Policy Under the Inflation Targeting Framework, 2000–2010*. Bangkok: Bank of Thailand. www.bot.or.th/English/MonetaryPolicy/Pages/MonetaryPolicy.aspx
IMF. 2016. *Annual Report on Exchange Arrangements and Exchange Restrictions 2016*. Washington, DC: International Monetary Fund.

Ito, T. 2004. Inflation Targeting and Japan: Why Has the Bank of Japan not adopted Inflation Targeting? In *The Future of Inflation Targeting*, edited by C. Kent and S. Guttmann. www.rba.gov.au/publications/confs/2004/ito.html

Ito, H. 2006a. Financial Development in Asia: Thresholds, Institutions, and the Sequence of Liberalization. *North American Journal of Economics and Finance* 17(3): 303–327.

Ito, T. 2006b. Japanese Monetary Policy: 1998–2005 and Beyond in Bank of International Settlements. In *Monetary Policy in Asia: Approaches and Implementation*, BIS Papers No. 31. Basel: Bank of International Settlements, pp. 105–132.

Ito, T. 2007. Asian Currency Crisis and the IMF, Ten Years Later: Overview. *Asian Economic Policy Review* 2(1): 16–49.

Ito, T. 2010a. China as Number One: How about the Renminbi? *Asian Economic Policy Review* 5(2): 249–276.

Ito, T. 2010b. Monetary Policy and Financial Stability: Is Inflation Targeting Passé? ADB Working Paper No. 206. Manila: Asian Development Bank.

Ito, T. 2012. Can Asia Overcome the IMF Stigma? *American Economic Review* 102(3): 198–202.

Ito, T. 2017. A New Financial Order in Asia: Will a RMB Bloc Emerge? *Journal of International Money and Finance* 74: 232–257.

Ito, T., and T. Hayashi. 2004. Inflation Targeting in Asia. Hong Kong Institute for Monetary Research Occasional Paper No. 1. Hong Kong, China: Hong Kong Institute for Monetary Research.

Kawai, M., and P.J. Morgan. 2012. Central Banking of Financial Stability in Asia. *Public Policy Review, Policy Research Institute, Ministry of Finance, Japan* 8(3): 215–246.

Kim, S., and Y.C. Park. 2006. Inflation Targeting in Korea: A Model of Success? In *Monetary Policy in Asia: Approaches and Implementation*, BIS Papers No. 31. Basel: Bank of International Settlements, pp. 140–164.

Klein, M.W. 2012. Capital Controls: Gates versus Walls. *Brookings Papers on Economic Activity 2012* (Fall): 317–355.

Morgan, P.J. 2013. Monetary Policy Frameworks in Asia: Experience, Lessons, and Issues. ADBI Working Paper No. 435, September. Tokyo: Asian Development Bank Institute.

Stein, J. 2013. Overheating in Credit Markets: Origins, Measurement, and Policy Responses. Speech at the Restoring Household Financial Stability After the Great Recession: Why Household Balance Sheets Matter Research Symposium Sponsored by the Federal Reserve Bank of St. Louis, 7 February.

Svensson, L. 2009. Inflation Targeting and Leaning against the Wind. In *Fourteen Years of Inflation Targeting in South Africa and the Challenge of a Changing Mandate*. Pretoria: South African Reserve Bank.

White, W. 2009. Should Monetary Policy 'Lean or Clean'? Federal Reserve Bank of Dallas Globalisation and Monetary Policy Institute Working Paper No. 34. Dallas: Federal Reserve Bank.

23

MACROPRUDENTIAL REGULATION AND CAPITAL FLOW MANAGEMENT MEASURES IN ASIA

Pornpinun Chantapacdepong

Introduction

Over the 2000s and 2010s, Asian economies have been confronted with multiple challenges and shocks from the global financial crisis of 2007–2008, the European sovereign debt and banking crisis, and the subsequent unconventional monetary policy by developed economies such as the US, Europe, and Japan. The unconventional monetary policy and the ultra-low interest rates in developed economies have sent international capital flowing into Asian equities, government bonds, and housing markets to search for higher yields. The better growth prospects and improved balance sheets and policy performance in many emerging market economies are major factors attracting the inflows (Checki 2013). However, like many emerging economies, financial markets in Asia are relatively small in size. This results in artificially inflated equity prices and house prices and lower yields of government bonds, which creates external financial vulnerability and financial stability concerns. Subsequently, Asia's asset prices are influenced more strongly by developed economies' policies rather than by the countries' own monetary policies and economic fundamentals. As a result, the surge in international capital flows complicates macroeconomic management of the authorities. It also creates macroeconomic imbalances by generating local currency overvaluation, which has eroded the comparative price advantage. And due to the typically underdeveloped capital markets, companies have limited options to hedge exchange rate risks. In addition, the US dollar-denominated debt has been increasing gradually in Asia since the cost of borrowing money in developed economies became cheaper.

With tighter cross-border financial linkages, monetary policy spillovers from developed countries to Asia had considerable implications for their economies. There is a widespread co-movement in capital flows, asset prices, and credit growth across countries. This suggest that the global financial cycle in capital flows, asset prices and in credit growth has been more prominent than before (Rey 2015). The cycle has also been more sensitive to global risk sentiment such as the economic and financial system recovery of developed economies, the financial stability concern in the People's Republic of China (PRC), the political risk, the geopolitical tension, and previous concerns of pace and timing for tapering of the quantitative easing policy. These uncertainties could create systemic instability risk, volatility in international capital flows, foreign exchange rates, asset prices, and credit growth to a greater extent than before. Looking ahead, international capital flows are expected to remain volatile and to continue to be sensitive to the pace of monetary policy normalization in major advanced economies.

Conventional policy responses to challenges from sustained capital inflows and financial stability challenges were generally employed as the first line of defense. Ostry et al. (2010) listed macroeconomic and prudential tools to address the challenges from surges in capital inflows. The use of macroeconomic tools, ranging from allowing exchange rate appreciation, capital controls, foreign currency intervention, and sterilization, to tightening monetary policy and fiscal policies, is a conventional policy response. However, these tools have their own limits and side effects. Allowing a sharp local currency appreciation could hamper external price competitiveness and affect business decision. Also, if a currency is already overvalued, it could create external imbalances. The option of foreign currency intervention through reserve accumulation is ideal for precautionary perspective if the country has relatively low reserves. The resulting increase in the local money supply, after an intervention, can be sterilized to curb inflation. However, if the level of reserve were already high, the continued reserve accumulation could lead to foreign currency mismatch. The negative interest rate carry can also occur when large stocks of foreign currency reserves (developed economies' bond, lower yield) were financed with domestic currency liabilities (domestic bond, higher yield).[1] Tightening monetary and fiscal policy to dampen overheating pressure to address sector specific issues can be costly as the impact is broad based. For instance, a large and unnecessary rise in policy rate may be needed to mitigate the effects of financial distortions and to contain the asset price bubble. Raising policy interest rates could also widen interest rate spreads and induce more capital inflows, which exacerbate financial stability challenge. In addition, a monetary policy tool is broad based and lacks sectoral features, which can possibly lead to financial distortions and discourage productive investment. Lastly, price stability should remain the primary objective of monetary policy. The political considerations and implementation lags could limit the scope for fiscal tightening measure. Among these conventional tools, many Asian economies relied more on reserve accumulation due to their heavy reliance on export and less developed financial market. However, due to the limit of conventional tools, many countries used the unconventional tools to supplement their policy actions.

Macroprudential measures (MPMs) and capital flow management measures (CFMs) are unconventional tools, especially from the perspective of advanced economies, to supplement the macroeconomic policy response above. These tools are more target specific, directly respond to types and nature of capital inflows, address financial vulnerability from sources, and can be aggressively tight. The continued improvement in data monitoring systems and the better regulatory frameworks allow monetary authorities in Asia to use these unconventional tools. In the past, authorities in developing Asia could not trace the composition of capital inflows, for instance, it was difficult to accurately discriminate between bonds versus equity flows, between direct investment, commercial bank loans, and other types of investment, among others. The resulting measures were thus the broad-based traditional capital controls such as general taxes, tariffs, outright legislation, volume restrictions, and reserve requirement on capital inflows. Nowadays, the authorities can exercise CFMs to control for specific non-resident inflows into the local bond market, equity market, housing market, and balance sheet of commercial banks and/or the corporate sector. However, CFMs and MPMs are not a "silver bullet." These tools complement, but do not substitute the conventional macroeconomic policies. They need strong implementation frameworks, transparency, and good communication. They are subject to risk of evasion and circumvention. On the multilateral perspective, it can create unintended spillover effects to other countries.

This chapter explores the framework for the implementation of CFMs and MPMs in Asia. The next sections survey the definition of MPMs and CFMs and discuss country experiences from adopting these measures. A literature review follows before concluding the findings.

Definition of macroprudential measures and capital flow management measures

The IMF (2012, 2013) distinguishes between capital flow management measures (CFMs) and Macroprudential measures (MPMs) by the target and the objectives of the measure. CFMs seek to limit capital flows by targeting nonresidents, while MPMs focus on limiting systemic risk of domestic financial sector and supporting a country's financial stability. Details are as follows.

Macroprudential measures (MPMs)

MPMs are defined as measures intended primarily to contain systemic financial risks (IMF 2013). The measures are an extension of macroeconomic management tools (monetary and fiscal policies) and microprudential supervision and regulations. The former tool is to ensure over all macroeconomic stability. The latter is used to ensure safety and soundness of individual financial institutions and mitigate externalities arising from individual institutions' behavior. The objective of MPMs is to limit (the buildup of) systemic risks and to achieve greater financial stability, which ultimately reduce frequency and severity of financial crisis. The IMF (2014) defines systemic risk as "the risk of disruptions to the provision of financial services that is caused by an impairment of all or parts of the financial system, and can cause serious negative consequences for the real economy." The MPMs should address time dimension (signal the gradual build-up of imbalances and vulnerabilities) and cross-sectional dimensions (alert concentration of risk within the system) of systemic risk (IMF, FSB, and BIS 2011).

Generally, the tools for MPMs are those which impact the asset and the liability sides of the balance sheet of commercial banks, since banks are significant financial intermediaries in the economy. MPMs generally rely on the microprudential tools, which can be considered as the macro perspective of the financial regulation. An example of the microprudential policy includes the forward-looking provisioning of expected loss, caps on loan-to-value (LTV) ratios, or minimum collateral haircut, higher risk weights on specific types of exposure, leverage ratios, and Basel III standards (capital conservation buffer, minimum capital requirement, liquid asset buffer, limits on currency, and maturity mismatches, among others; Ostry et al. 2011). However, its scope is expanded by focusing on the financial system as a whole, including the interaction between the financial system and the real sectors. In addition, activities outside the banking system such as capital market activities and market-based financing are expanding. MPMs are developing to cover the systemic risks in these sectors. MPM tools from a bank's balance sheet perspective are listed in Table 23.1.

These tools are used to reduce risks in the banking system, local bonds market, and the real economy, and to curb speculative activity in the foreign exchange market. For instances, tools to curb excessive credit expansion and asset price booms, particularly in the real estate market, are dynamic capital buffers, dynamic provisions, loan-to-value, and debt-service-to-income ratios. Capital tools are employed to address systemic risk linked to leverage; liquidity-related tools are employed to tackle maturity mismatches. Additional loss-absorbing capacity tools for systemically important financial institutions (SIFIs) are employed to mitigate structural vulnerabilities in the system and limit systemic spillovers in times of stress (see IMF, FSB, and BIS (2011)).

Table 23.1 Macroprudential tools classified by bank's balance sheet perspective

Type of MPM Tools	Description and Objective	Examples of Tools
Capital-based tools	**Broad-based capital tools** to address risks from broad-based credit booms, to increase resilience, and to help maintain the supply of credit through adverse conditions	Dynamic provisioning requirements Counter-cyclical capital buffers Time-varying leverage ratio caps Comprehensive capital analysis review
	Sectoral capital tools to help maintain lender's resilience to risks arising from lending to specific sectors and a deterioration of lending standards for such loans	Sectoral capital requirements Risk weight floors Cap of share of exposures to specific sectors such as foreign currency loans to corporates
Asset side tools	**Loan restrictions** to increase resilience of borrowers to asset price and income shocks, and to increase resilience of lenders	Caps on loan-to-value (LTV) Debt service to income ratio Loan to income ratio (These tools can be targeted at mortgages, credit cards, commercial property or leveraged loans to corporate sectors.)
Liquidity-related tools	To address the buildup of liquidity and foreign exchange risk associated with lending booms, affect loan growth.	
	Build up a stock of highly liquid assets	Differentiated reserve requirement Base III liquidity coverage ratio
	Tools to contain maturity mismatch	Core funding ratios
	Price-based tools	Levy on volatile funding
	Other tools	Caps on loan-to-deposit ratio

Source: IMF, FSB, and BIS (2016).

The intermediate objectives of MPMs are to increase the resilience of the financial system to aggregate shocks, contain the build-up of systemic vulnerabilities over time, and control structural vulnerabilities within the financial system that arise through interlinkages, common exposures, and the critical role of the big financial intermediaries (IMF, FSB, and BIS 2016). From the toolkit above, Zhang and Zoli (2016) classify MPMs according to their use to address particular areas of vulnerability (Table 23.2). Tools can be used in combination to support each other. Internationally, one size does not fit all. Macroprudential policies need to be tailored to suit each country's macroeconomic framework (monetary policy, exchange rate policy, and capital account openness), financial development, environment (pressure on exchange rate), and domestic circumstances (credit growth, currency mismatch in the corporate balance sheet, and asset price conditions).

In the context of Asia, authorities have a greater widespread use of MPMs than other regions (Zhang and Zoli 2016). This is especially the case for housing-related measures such as loan-to-value ratio caps, housing tax measures, mortgage loan limits, and the limit of leverage by financial institutions.

Table 23.2 Macroprudential tools classified by use

Measures	Objective	Example of Tools
Housing-related measures	Address risk in housing markets	LTV ratios, DTI ratios, imposing higher risk weights on mortgage loans in the calculation of capital asset ratios, requiring larger loan-loss provisions on mortgage loans, and housing and land related tax
Consumer loan measures	Reduce consumer loans	Debt service limits on credit cards and personal loans
Bank credit limits	Reduce bank credit	Explicit ceilings on bank's credit growth or loan to deposit ratio
Capital-related measures	Bank stability	Counter-cyclical capital requirements, restrictions on profit distribution
Dynamic provisioning	Bank stability	Require bank to build a cushion of reserve provisions during the upswing phase of business cycles
Reserve requirements on deposits in local currency	Reduce bank credit	Reserve requirement
Other liquidity tools	Bank stability	Minimum core funding ratios, other liquidity ratio requirements
Discourage transaction in foreign currency	Reduce foreign exchange exposure	Limits on foreign currency borrowing, reserve requirement on foreign currency deposits, additional provisioning requirement on foreign exchange lending
Residency-based CFMs	Deter the capital flows into specific sectors	Unremunerated reserve requirement on non-resident deposits, withholding tax or restrictions on non-resident holdings of domestic assets

Source: Author.

Capital flow management measures (CFMs)

According to the IMF's institutional view on liberalization and management of capital flows, CFMs refer to measures that are designed to limit capital flows, by affecting the scale or composition of these flows; and discourage transactions in foreign currency. They apply exclusively to financial transaction between residents and nonresidents, and discriminate between domestic and international financial markets. *Residency-based CFMs* are measures affecting cross-border financial activities that discriminate on the basis of residency, such as tax and regulation. *Other CFMs* do not discriminate on the basis of residency but aim to limit capital flows such as prudential-type measures, measures that differentiate transactions on the basis of currency, and measures applied to non-financial sectors (Arora et al. 2012).

CFMs have been used to address concerns about economic overheating, export price competitiveness, financial stability, and the fiscal cost of reserve accumulation, which could challenge macroeconomic management and put pressures on asset markets (Pradhan et al. 2011). There are several types of CFMs in Asia, which mainly depends on the nature and the type of the flows. Many economies in Asia adopt the measures differently depending on factors such as the capacity of the conventional policy response (monetary policy and fiscal policy) to limit the challenges from the flow, the size and composition of the flows that have implication on the financial sector pressure, and the concern about the volatility of the inflows which have direct implication on the foreign exchange rates.

CFMs employed in the Asia and Pacific region can be classified into repatriation and surrender requirement; controls on capital and money market instruments (such as bond and equity); controls on derivative and other instruments; controls on credit operations; controls direct investment; controls on real estate transactions; controls on personal transactions; provisions specific to commercial banks and institutional investors. Table 23.3 presents CFMs taken by 12 Asia-Pacific economies – Australia; China; Hong Kong, China; Japan; Republic of Korea; New Zealand; Singapore; India; Indonesia; Malaysia; the Philippines; and Thailand – from 2003 to 2015. The table summarizes CFMs by type of measures, country and direction (that is, tightening or loosening, inflow or outflow).

Measures that are both CFMs and MPMs

MPMs themselves do not aim to affect capital flows and exchange rates. However, in some cases, CFMs and MPMs can overlap. MPMs can also be CFMs if the measure is designed to limit systemic financial risks associated with capital flows and exposure of financial system to exchange rate shocks. As highlighted by IMF (2014: 1), "To the extent that capital flows are the source of systemic financial risks, the tools used to address those risks can be seen as both

Table 23.3 Capital flow measures in Asia and the Pacific★

Type of Measure	AU	CN	HK	JP	KR	NZ	SG	IN	ID	MY	PH	TH
Repatriation and surrender requirement	0	4	0	0	2	0	0	3	2	0	0	0
Controls on capital and money market instruments	0	34	0	0	11	0	0	38	8	23	8	21
Controls on derivative and other instruments	0	0	0	0	0	0	0	9	2	3	2	0
Controls on credit operations	0	3	0	0	0	0	0	23	0	3	0	0
Controls on direct investment	8	19	0	0	6	2	0	22	0	6	6	5
Controls on real estate transactions	1	9	5	0	8	0	5	10	0	6	0	3
Controls on personal transactions	0	18	0	0	17	0	0	38	1	17	18	18
Provisions specific to commercial banks and institutional investors	5	35	1	0	35	0	1	56	13	21	16	22
Total	*14*	*122*	*6*	*0*	*79*	*2*	*6*	*199*	*26*	*79*	*50*	*69*
Direction												
Total tighten	*3*	*30*	*5*	*0*	*23*	*0*	*6*	*27*	*14*	*4*	*14*	*10*
– Tighten Inflow	0	29	5	0	22	0	5	19	13	4	12	9
– Tighten outflow	0	1	0	0	0	0	1	8	1	1	0	1
Total loosen	*11*	*59*	*0*	*0*	*39*	*2*	*0*	*131*	*9*	*57*	*28*	*40*
– Loosen Inflow	9	37	0	0	18	1	0	85	5	32	6	15
– Loosen outflow	1	28	0	0	21	1	0	53	6	29	20	25

★The dataset is available in Excel format, for the time period of 2003–2015, for 12 Asia-Pacific economies. It contains details of the measure, the website for the source of the measure, the date of the measure (announcement, effective, specified in AREAER, if available), type of the measure, direction of the measure (tighten/loosen, inflow/outflow), application to residence/non-residence, qualitative/quantitative type. Please visit https://sites.google.com/site/pornpinunchantapacdepong/dataset-on-capital-flow-management-measures.

Note: The table is an updated version of Chantapacdepong and Shim (2015).

AU = Australia, CN = People's Republic of China, HK = Hong Kong, China, JP = Japan, KR = Republic of Korea, NZ = New Zealand, SG = Singapore, IN = India, ID = Indonesia, MY = Malaysia, PH = Philippines, TH = Thailand.

Source: Compiled by author.

CFMs and MPMs." In response to a surge in capital flows, the measures that are both CFMs and MPMs can complement the macroeconomic policy (which may have limited room for adjustment, require times to take effects) and safeguard financial system stability. Examples of measures are summarized in Table 23.4.

Table 23.4 Examples of measures which are both MPMs and CFMs

Type of Measure	Description	Purpose of Measure	IMF Assessment
Limit	Limit on banks' *foreign exchange derivative contracts* set as a percentage of bank capital.	– Increases the cost of derivative transactions, thereby limiting banks' reliance on short-term external funding. – Introduced in the context of capital flow volatility and limits the systemic impact of large movements in capital flows. – mitigates systemic liquidity risks associated with banks' reliance on FX funding and volatile capital inflows.	– Limits banks' reliance on short-term external funding and the exposure of the financial sector to systemic liquidity risks associated with a sudden stop in capital flows (MPMs). – Designed to limit capital flows (CFMs), although there is no discrimination on the residency.
Limit	Limit on the *daily balance of banks' short-term (up to one year) liabilities to nonresidents* set as a percentage of bank capital.	– Increases the cost of banks' use of short-term funding from nonresidents beyond a set limit. – Contains systemic liquidity risk by reducing banks' reliance on short-term external funding and indirectly dampens excessive credit growth funded by capital inflows.	– Increases the cost of banks' reliance on short-term external funding, thereby limiting excessive credit growth and the exposure of the financial sector to systemic liquidity risks associated with a sudden stop in capital flows (MPMs). – Discriminates between resident and non-resident lenders (CFMs).
Tax	*Additional buyer's stamp duty* on purchases of certain categories of *residential property* levied at a higher rate *for nonresidents* than residents.	– Mitigates the build-up of systemic risk stemming from capital flows to an overheating property market. – Reduces nonresidents' housing demand by increasing the costs of purchase of residential property.	– Reduces the systemic risk associated with property price corrections when these inflows recede (MPMs). – Discriminates between resident and non-residents (CFMs).
Tax	*Bank levy on non-deposit FX liabilities* with maturities shorter than one year.	– Increases the cost of short-term non-core FX funding (in the context of capital flow volatility and limits the systemic impact of large movements in capital flows).	– Limits banks' reliance on short-term external funding and the exposure of the financial sector to systemic liquidity risk associated with a sudden stop in capital flows (MPMs).

Type of Measure	Description	Purpose of Measure	IMF Assessment
		− Mitigates systemic liquidity risk associated with banks' excessive reliance on short-term non-core FX funding and volatile capital flows.	− Designed to limit capital flows (CFMs), although there is no discrimination on the residency.
Reserve requirement	A reserve requirement on domestic banks' *foreign currency swap and forward transactions with nonresidents.*	− Increases the cost to domestic banks of foreign currency swap and forward transactions with nonresidents. − Mitigates systemic liquidity risk related to increasing currency and maturity mismatches on banks' balance sheets driven by short-term capital inflows.	− Limits systemic liquidity risks related to increasing currency and maturity mismatches on banks' balance sheets caused by short-term capital inflows (MPMs). − Discriminates between resident and nonresidents (CFMs).
Reserve requirement	A reserve requirement on banks' *credit lines and other external obligations with nonresidents of three years or less in maturities.*	− Increases the cost of banks' reliance on external funding. − Prevents the build-up of systemic risk associated with FX lending in the context of a highly dollarized economy and strong capital inflows.	− Increases the cost of banks' reliance on external funding and the exposure of the financial sector to systemic risks associated with currency mismatches on banks' balance sheets and a sudden stop in capital flows (MPMs). − Discriminates between resident and nonresident lenders (CFMs).

CFM = capital flow management measure, MPM = macroprudential measure.

Source: IMF (2015).

Experiences of Asian economies

Authorities in Asia often employed MPMs to curb house price growth, credit growth and bank leverage. The most popular tools are housing-related measures such as loan to value ratio caps (Hong Kong, China; India; Indonesia; Malaysia; Philippines; Republic of Korea; Singapore; the PRC; and Thailand), housing tax measures and stamp duties (Singapore), mortgage loan limits (the PRC, Singapore, Malaysia, and Hong Kong, China), and risk weight for housing loans (India). These also aim to reduce nonresidents' housing demand by increasing the costs of purchase of residential properties, especially in the case of Singapore and Hong Kong, China. Hence, the measure is also considered as a CFM. Singapore and Hong Kong, China experienced a surge in mortgage loans and a sharp rise in real house prices, especially after 2009. The two economies are financial centers in Asia. Given that the respective currency board (Hong Kong, China) and currency basket arrangements (Singapore) compromise monetary policy autonomy, they faced persistently low interest rates after the global financial crisis. The domestic demand for housing has thus increased due to the search for yield behavior by households, and foreign investors further boosted the demand for housing. Measures to limit credit growth are also employed in Asia, ranging from explicit ceiling on bank's loan to deposit ratio and loan to income ratio (PRC), consumer loan limit (Indonesia and Thailand), credit card loan limit (Thailand), and local currency reserve requirement (Indonesia, Philippines, India, and the PRC). Measures to discourage transactions in foreign currency are relatively less frequent in Asia since the capital account is not fully liberalized in most economies. These measures aim to reduce foreign exchange exposure such as reserve requirements on foreign currency accounts (Indonesia and India), limits on the use of foreign currency denominated loans (Republic of Korea and India), limits on banks' short-term external borrowing (Indonesia), capped foreign exchange positions relative to their equity capital (Republic of Korea, Philippines, and Thailand), reduced corporate foreign currency hedging limits (Republic of Korea), impose a bank levy on non-deposit foreign currency liabilities (Republic of Korea), and forward exchange position limits (Republic of Korea).

In general, financial markets in Asia are relatively less open and less developed than those of developed economies, hence the use of CFMs is less frequent than MPMs. Also, Zoli (2014) suggested that the use of CFMs in Asia is less frequent than other regions. Moreover, CFMs and MPMs have occasionally been used as counter-cyclical tool. They have been used to limit systemic financial stability risks mainly stemming from capital inflow surge during quantitative easing (QEs) and ultra-ease monetary policy in developed economies during 2009–2013. Hong Kong, China; the Republic of Korea; Singapore; Thailand; and Indonesia experienced large capital inflows, credit booms, and asset price booms; hence, CFMs are employed by these economies. Examples of measures are caps on LTV ratios and measures to limit foreign exchange transactions. Other residency-based capital flows measure are mainly on local bond markets, such as minimum holding periods on central bank bills (Indonesia), and withholding tax on foreign holding of government bonds and central banks securities (Republic of Korea and Thailand). The taxes increase the relative cost of short-term carry trade, and hence deter such flows. The minimum period requirement helps to lengthen the maturity of liabilities and deter the short-term speculative flows. Other tools are occasionally employed such as capital outflow liberalization (Republic of Korea, Malaysia, Philippines, Thailand, and India). The merits of the measure are to reduce the net capital inflow as some of the inflows are offset by outflows. It can help improve financial market development. However, in some circumstances, it further attracts the inflow, as it provides greater assurance that the fund can be repatriated.

In the face of capital outflows, some economies eased their residency-based CFMs to reduce disincentives for foreign investors. Indonesia is a good example. After the "taper tantrum" in May 2013, Indonesia faced large capital outflows and falling equity prices. The authorities responded by raising policy interest rates to attract funds and shortening minimum holding periods on central bank bills in September 2013. However, MPMs were tightened; such as tightening the LTV limits on second and third properties, and raising reserve requirements to curb high inflation and the continued demand pressure. In other cases, MPMs were also relaxed to ease monetary conditions during the economic slowdown. For instance, the Republic of Korea temporarily reduced the LTV ratio and debt-to-income ratio in 2014, Malaysia waived 100% of stamp duty on instruments of transfer and loan agreements for first time home buyers in Jan 2014. Indonesia raised the LTV ratio and financing-to-value ratio (FTV) for mortgage loans and cut down payments on automotive loans for two- and three-wheelers and more in June 2015, raised the LTV and FTV on housing loans/financing, relaxed financing criteria in line with construction progress as a second financing facility, raised the floor on the Reserve Requirement–Loan to Funding Ratio (RR-LFR) in June 2016, and loosened regulations on local currency reserve requirements in April 2017, among others.

There is heterogeneity in the application of MPMs and CFMs among economies in Asia (Table 23.5). Measures vary widely within Asia, depending mostly on the economy-specific

Table 23.5 Examples of MPMs and CFMs in Asia

Economy	MPM (Date)	CFM (Date)
Indonesia	• Rupiah term deposits introduced (July 2010) • Primary rupiah reserve requirement increased from 5% to 8% (Nov 2010) • Policy to limit bank's short-term external borrowing normalized (Jan 2011) • Reserve requirement on foreign currency accounts raised from 1% to 5% (Mar 2011) • loan to deposit ratio (LDR) based reserve requirement introduced (Mar 2011) • Loan-to-value cap tightened (Q2-2012, Q3-2013) • Consumer loan measures tightened (Q2-2012) • The loan-to-deposit-ratio-linked reserve requirement (LDR–RR) regulation revised, loan-to-value (LTV) ratio and financing-to-value (FTV) ratio for mortgage loans and cut down payments on automotive loans for two raised, as well as three-wheelers and more (24 Jun 2015)★ • LTV ratio and FTV ratio raised on housing loans/financing, financing criteria in line with construction progress as a second financing facility relaxed, the floor on the reserve requirement-loan to funding ratio (RR–LFR) raised from 78% to 80% (16 June 2016)★ • Regulations on local currency reserve requirements loosened (21 April 2017)★	• One-month holding period on central bank bills (Bank Sentral Republik Indonesia certificate: SBI) (June 2010) • Introduced SBI lengthening maturity profile (implemented in a number of phases) (Mar 2010–Dec 2011)
Republic of Korea	• Restrictions on lending locally in foreign exchange eliminated (2001) • LTV ratio limited (Sep 2002) • Liquidity ratio guideline strengthened (Mar 2002), and banks whose liquidity ratios were below the precautionary level, 105%, warned and ordered to submit plans for improving their financial statuses • Banks' liquidity requirements tightened (2001–2001, 2004) • Limit on insurance companies' investments in foreign currency denominated assets increased (Mar 2005) • Banks' net open foreign exchange position raised from 30% to 50% (2006) • Thin capitalization rules extended to foreign bank branches, limiting the tax deductibility of interest on borrowing from parent banks to three times the capital (Aug 2007) • Limits on the use of foreign-currency-denominated loans introduced (Jan 2008) • Foreign currency (FX) liquidity ratio regulation adjusted upward from 70% to 80% (Jun 2000), further raised to 85% (2004) • LTV ratio cap raised (Mar 2004 and 2011) and lowered★ (Jul 2009 and Jul 2014) • Debt-to-income (DTI) ratio limited (Aug 2005), expanded (Nov 2006, Sep 2009), and suspended (Aug 2010). Expanded and lower★ (Jul 2014) • FX forward positions of banks relative to their equity capital capped. Reduce corporate FX hedging limit from 125% to 100% of export receipt (Jun 2010) • Bank levy on non-deposit foreign currency liabilities introduced (Aug 2011) • Forward exchange position limit introduced (Oct 2010), and decreased (Jul 2011, Jan 2013)	• 14% withholding tax on foreign holdings of government bonds and central bank securities (Jan 2011) reintroduced • Outflow liberalization such as: limits on deposits abroad eliminated (2001), limit on lending to nonresidents increased (2001), residents' personal capital transfers liberalized (2001), ceiling on commercial credits increased (2002), limit on individuals' FDI raised to USD 3 million and on certain real estate purchases to USD 500,000 (2005), further increased and eliminated (Mar 2006), rules for the repatriation of proceeds from capital transactions further eased and all approval requirements for capital transactions changed to notification (Jan 2006), threshold for prior notification of won-establishment bank branches abroad further liberalized (2007–2008)

(*Continued*)

Table 23.5 (Continued)

Economy	MPM (Date)	CFM (Date)
Malaysia	• Maximum 70% LTV on 3rd housing loan onwards (Nov 2010) • Maximum 60% LTV on non-individuals taking loans for residential properties (Dec 2011) • Maximum tenure of 35 years for purchase of properties (Jul 2013) • Prohibit housing loans with interest capitalization (ICS) or developer interest bearing schemes (DIBS) (Nov 2013) • Abolish stamp duty on certain real estate★ (Jan 2014) and plan to further relax in 2018	• Outflow liberalization such as overseas investment limit of the Employee Provident Fund raised from 7% to 20% (Oct 2010) • Raised local property gain tax by discriminating between local and foreigner (2014)
Philippines	• LTV cap tightened (Q3–2002) • Non-financial corporations required to report monthly their purchases, sales, and daily foreign exchange positions (2000) • Liquidity reserve requirement on peso reduced (2002) and gradually increased (2003–2006) • Foreign exchange banking units of domestic banks allowed to lend under certain conditions to resident banking units in foreign exchange (2002) • Conditions for the establishment and operations of foreign currency units eased (2006–2007) • Banks' net open foreign exchange position set at the lower of 20% of their unimpaired capital or USD 50 million (Apr 2007)	• Outflow liberalization such as limits on bank's long foreign exchange position reduced (2003), increased ceilings on residents' purchase of FX and foreign assets from authorized agent banks (Nov 2010), limit on residents' FDI and portfolio investments abroad increased (2007), and further increased (2008)
Thailand	• Open position limits in accordance with Basel I introduced (2002) • Regulations on credit card loan tightened (2002, 2004, 2005) • Personal loan lending limit of five times of average monthly income introduced (2005) • Net foreign exchange position tightened (2002) • Asset classification and provisioning regulations tightened (2006) • LTV ratio tightened (2003, 2009, 2010) • Loan-loss provisioning aligned with IAS tightened (2006, 2007)	• Outflow liberalization such as raised ceilings on residents' outward direct investment, lending abroad, and foreign currency holdings (Feb and Sep 2010) • 15% withholding tax re-imposed for state bonds on foreign investors (Oct 2010)
Hong Kong, China	• LTV ratio cap tightened (Oct 2009, Aug 2010, Nov 2010, Jun 2011, Sep 2012, Feb 2013, Feb 2015) • Limit on debt service-to-income (DSTI) of mortgage tightened (Aug 2010, Sep 2012) • Banks required to stress-test the adjusted mortgage applicants' repayment ability (Aug 2010) • Maximum loan tenor of all new property mortgage loans limited (Sep 2012) • Scope of DSTI extended (Feb 2013) • Risk weight floor introduced (Feb 2013) • Maximum debt-servicing ratio (DSR) lowered for borrowers who buy a second residential property for self-use and non-self-use properties, and lowered the stressed-DSR cap (Feb 2015)	

Singapore	• Interest absorption scheme and interest-only housing loans removed (Sep 2009) • LTV cap in housing adjusted (Feb 2010, Aug 2010, Jan 2011, Jan 2013) • Seller stamp duty (SSD) implemented (Feb 2010), extended and adjusted (Aug 2010, 2011) • Additional buyer's stamp duty (ADSB) imposed (Dec 2011), adjusted (Jan 2013) • Limit on all new housing loans granted by financial institutions introduced (Oct 2012) • Mortgage servicing ratio (MSR) adjusted (Jan 2013) • LTV ceilings for motor vehicle loans adjusted (Feb 2013) • Tax measures targeting the non-owner-occupied residential properties adjusted (Feb 2013) • Total debt servicing ratio (TDSR) framework introduced (Jun 2013) • Maximum tenor reduced and MSR adjusted (Aug 2013 and Dec 2013) • Financial institutions required to review borrower's total debt and credit limits (Sep 2013)	
India	• Preemptive counter-cyclical provisioning and differentiated risk weights for certain sensitive sectors adopted (2004) • Framework for closer monitoring and supervision of large and potentially systematically important financial institutions/groups put in place (2004) • Risk weight for banks' exposure to Commercial Real Estate (CRE) increased from 100% to 125% (Jul 2005) and further to 150% (May 2006) • Risk weight on retail housing loans increased from 50% to 65% (Dec 2004) • Risk weights on smaller size housing loans reduced from 75% to 50% • Risk weights on larger loans and those with LTV ratio exceeding 75% increased to 100% • Risk weights on consumer credit and capital market exposers increased from 100% to 125% • Provisions for standard assets revised upwards (Nov 2005, May 2006, Jan 2007) • Cap on LTV ratios introduced (2010) • Higher risk weights for large housing loans and higher standard asset provisioning for "teaser" housing loans introduced (2010) • Reserve requirement on short-term foreign currency deposits gradually lowered (2002–2003) and increased (2004) • Reserve requirement on local currency deposits decreased (2003) • Maximum open position limits on individual currencies removed (2002) • Restrictions on the use of foreign exchange loans introduced (2003) and tightened (2008) • Rules on lending to purchase securities and on the operation of securities companies and investment funds tightened (Jan 2007) • Banks' total securities-related credit exposures limited (May 2007) and more widely limited (2008)	Outflow liberalization measures such as • Limit on investments in employee stock option plans increased (2001) and lifted (2004) • Banks allowed to invest in money market instruments and/or debt instruments abroad and offer foreign currency swaps (2002) • Limit on mutual funds' equity investments abroad raised to USD 1 billion (2003) • Limit on resident individuals' capital transactions increased to USD 200,000 (2004–2007) • Approval requirement on residents' transfer of shares to nonresidents removed (2004) • External borrowing for foreign direct investment (FDI) abroad allowed (2004) • Exporters allowed to open accounts abroad (2007) • Exporters allowed to use their foreign exchange proceeds for certain investments • Limits on Indian companies' FDI and portfolio investments raised (2007) • Aggregate ceiling for mutual funds' foreign investment raised to USD 5 billion (Oct 2007)

(Continued)

Table 23.5 (Continued)

Economy	MPM (Date)	CFM (Date)
PRC	• LTV limits raised to 80% for first mortgages (Sep 2008)	
	• Caps on LTV lowered from 80% to 70% for primary homes and to 50% for second homes (Apr 2010)	
	• Interest rates on mortgages for second homes raised to 1.1 times the officially administered benchmark lending rate (Apr 2010)	
	• Mortgages for third homes suspended (Oct 2010)	
	• LTV cap on second home mortgages lowered to 40% (Jan 2011)	
	• Mortgages terms eased and first residential mortgage definitions broadened (Sep 2014)	
	• LTV limit increased for second mortgages (Apr 2015)	
	• Reserve requirement raised 12 times for a total of 600 basis points (Jan 2010–Jun 2011)	
	• Reserve requirement decreased three times for a total of 150 basis points (Dec 2011–May 2012), two targeted cuts (Apr, Jun 2014), two cuts (Feb, Apr 2015)	
	• Dynamic adjustment on differentiated reserve ratio introduced for individual banks on a quarterly/monthly basis (2011)	
	• Loan-to-income ratio requirements set less than 50% (2004)	
	• Loan-to-deposit ratio adjusted basis for calculation and excluded micro/small enterprise and rural loans that are funded by bond issuance, included more types of liabilities (Jul 2014)	
	• Liquidity coverage ratio (LCR) introduced (Mar 2014). Banks required to meet the 60% LCR requirement by end-2014, with incremental 10% raise until end-2018, in line with the Basel III requirements	
	• Minimum leverage ratio set at 4% for all banks but with different transition period, SIBs required to meet standard by end-2013, Non SIBs required to meet standard by end-2016	
	• Minimum loan loss reserves coverage ratio increased to 150% (2009)	
	• Capital conservation buffer of 2.5%, counter-cyclical capital buffer of 0%–2.5% and capital surcharge of 1% for SIBs introduced (2012)	
	• Broad guidance on encouraging lending to certain sectors and restricting lending to others provided (most recently, Q1-2015)	

Note: ★ represents easing policy.

CFM = capital flow management measure, MPM = macroprudential measure, PRC = People's Republic of China.

Sources: Akinci and Olmstead-Rumsey (2015), Agung (2012), Darbar and Wu (2016), Financial Stability Board (2015), Barnett and Maino (2013), Chai-Anant (2012), Chakrabarty (2014), Habermeier, Kokenyne, and Baba (2011), Kim (2014), Lau (2015), Lee (2013), Lee (2014), Wang and Sun (2013), and Yiu (2011).

factors. The prudential instruments that have been used mostly in Hong Kong, China and Singapore are caps on LTV and DTI ratios as well as housing tax measures. The two economies have lost their monetary policy autonomy due to the opened capital account and the exchange rate targeting regime (Singapore) and currency board system (Hong Kong, China). The low interest rate that has been transmitted from the US resulted in housing price pressures. Being financial centers, other types of CFMs that limit the flows into the banking system and financial assets were not introduced. Normally, countries with relatively less open capital accounts will experience smaller inflows than a country with a more liberalized capital account. Hence the application of CFMs is less often in those countries. The Republic of Korea has relatively higher financial advancement than many economies in Asia. It has been an active user of both MPMs and CFMs. Banks in the Republic of Korea have large exposure to short-term external debt due to growing demand for foreign exchange derivative transactions. The imbalances have emerged among domestic banks as well as in foreign exchange transactions, along with the housing boom. Thus, the Republic of Korea frequently implements the housing measures, as well as a levy on bank non-deposit foreign exchange liability, and a ceiling on bank foreign exchange derivative position to deter the speculative flows. The PRC and India have relatively closed capital accounts, and have been heavy users of traditional monetary policy tools like reserve requirements and some housing measures. The Association of Southeast Asian Nations (ASEAN) economies have relied on a mixture of traditional monetary policy tools, MPMs, and CFMs. These policies complement each other. Indonesia and Thailand introduced restrictions on non-resident access to the domestic bonds market, a bond holding period, and a withholding tax on bonds. Lastly, before the global financial crisis, many economies in Asia were in the process of gradually liberalizing their capital account, this in part was to improve capital market development. As a result, in response to the capital inflow surges, the measures to liberalize capital outflow tend to be more popular than the measures to tighten inflow.

CFMs and MPMs in the literature

There are three main discussions in the literature on CFMs: (1) Can CFMs reduce capital inflows and outflows? (2) What cross-over effects are there from CFMs to other policies (such as monetary policy and fiscal policy) to safeguard financial stability, appropriate inflation rates and credit growth? (3) Are there any cross-country effects whereby the CFM policies in one country have an impact on other countries?

The literature is divided on the question of whether CFMs can reduce capital flows. Ahmed and Zlate (2013) find in a cross-country study that both portfolio and net flows are reduced when capital controls are tightened. Bruno, Shim, and Shin (2017) show that bond market CFMs reduce bond inflows and banking sector CFMs reduce banking inflows. Forbes, Fratzscher, and Straub (2015) look at Brazil's tax on capital inflows and conclude that it led to a significant reduction in both bond and equity inflows. Zhang and Zoli (2016) present more mixed evidence, finding that CFMs reduced portfolio equity inflows in non-Asian countries but not in Asia.

Another major strand of the literature contends that CFMs do not reduce net inflows but can have positive effects on financial stability. In an IMF discussion note, Ostry et al. (2011) find that CFMs can help dampen credit booms and reduce balance sheet risks, while stressing the contingency of these benefits and the existence of attendant distortions. Forbes, Fratzscher, and Straub (2015) show that CFMs reduce financial fragility in many cases but do not significantly affect the volume of flows. Qureshi et al. (2011) find that CFMs and MPMs are associated with a lower proportion of foreign currency loans in domestic bank lending and a shift away from portfolio debt flows toward portfolio equity and FDI flows. In a review of empirical studies, Magud, Reinhart, and Rogoff (2011) similarly find no reduction to net inflows but report that capital inflow controls can increase monetary policy independence and change the composition of flows. In agreement with Ostry et al. (2011), they find that the effectiveness of capital controls is strongly contingent on each country's circumstances. An emerging area of research is in the cross-country spillover effects of capital controls. In their study of Brazil's capital inflow tax, Forbes, Fratzscher, and Straub (2015) discover that the introduction of the tax led both bond and equity investors to adjust their portfolio country allocations to compensate, in accordance with their investment strategies and their expectations of similar policy decisions in other countries. Chantapacdepong and Shim (2015) demonstrate that loosening bond inflow controls in the Asia-Pacific leads to greater bond flow correlations across the region, providing further evidence for the importance of signaling in determining the effects of capital controls. For the cross-country spillover effect, Pasricha et al. (2015) find significant spillovers of capital control actions (via cross-border bank lending and exchange rate channels) from Brazil, the Russian Federation, India, the People's Republic of China, and South Africa (BRICS) to other EMEs during the 2000s. Spillovers are more pronounced after the global financial crisis than before the crisis, and from inflow tightening actions, rather than outflow easing measures. Due to greater cross-border banking and more open capital accounts in Latin America than in Asia, the spillovers seem to be more prevalent in the former countries.

Galati and Moessner (2013) provide an extensive literature review of Macroprudential policies. Shim et al. (2013) review what types of policy action were taken in many economies and assess their effectiveness. MPMs in other literature can be classified into (1) guidelines as a precondition of the measures, and (2) assessment of effectiveness of the measures. For the guidelines, a comprehensive and rigorous analysis of systemic vulnerability should be the first step prior to applying MPMs (IMF 2014). Then authorities should assess the buildup of risk over time through channels such as excessive private credit growth, exposure to the corporate sector, excessive maturity, and foreign exchange mismatches within the financial sector. The fragility from linkages within and across key classes of intermediaries and market infrastructure should also be considered. In addition, the tools can be relaxed when systemic risks dissipate or if they create negative side effects. The side effect can be tight financial conditions and adverse macroeconomic effects. Moreover, Maddalonia and Peydró (2013) find that monetary policy and prudential policy are connected and influence each other. Monetary policy rates affect bank stability, and their impact depends both on bank balance sheet strength and on banking prudential policy. Policy rates and prudential policies (time-varying and counter-cyclical LTV or capital requirements) complement each other in safeguarding financial stability.

Generally, the effectiveness of MPMs can be assessed in two ways: (1) by measuring the extent to which the measures employed have the desired impact, such as reducing the built up of debt, the cooling of asset price inflation, lowering the probability of bank default, among others; and (2) whether the measures employed reduce credit and risk indicators and improve market behavior. Claessens, Ghosh, and Mihet (2014) find that macroprudential policies that aim at borrowers (i.e., caps on debt-to-income and loan-to-value ratios) and at financial institutions (i.e., limits on credit growth and foreign currency lending) are effective in reducing a bank's asset growth and its buildup of banking system vulnerabilities. Akinci and Olmstead-Rumsey (2015) find that tightening MPMs is associated with lower bank credit growth, housing credit growth, and house price inflation. Cerutti, Claessens, and Laeven (2015) find that MPMs associate with lower growth in household credit, however, effects are less in more developed and open economies. Lee, Asuncion, and Kim (2015) find that credit-related MPMs can effectively dampen credit expansion and housing price inflation, while liquidity-related

MPMs moderate leverage growth and housing price escalation. Lim et al. (2011) find that many MPMs (caps on the LTV ratio, caps on the debt-to-income ratio, ceilings on credit or credit growth, reserve requirements, counter-cyclical capital requirements and time-varying and/or dynamic provisioning) are effective in reducing procyclicality of bank credit growth and leverage growth. However, the effectiveness is sensitive to the type of shock facing the financial sector. He (2014) finds that for Hong Kong, China the dampening effect of LTV policy on household leverage is more apparent than its effect on property prices. The effect on loan growth is likely to be state-dependent, being more effective in cases of excess credit demand in Hong Kong, China. Wong at al. (2011) find that LTV policy is effective in reducing systemic risk associated with boom-and-bust cycles in property markets in Hong Kong, China, while mortgage insurance programs can mitigate LTV's drawback of liquidity constraints without undermining the effectiveness of LTV ratios.

Conclusion

Compared with the experience during the Asian financial crisis 20 years ago, many emerging economies are now better prepared to cope with crises and financial shocks. More flexible exchange rate regimes are in place and the health of banking sectors has improved. However, the financial markets in many emerging economies remain small and shallow, hence they remain vulnerable to macroeconomic shocks and the volatile capital flows. This chapter provides a comprehensive overview of macroprudential policy and capital flow management measures and their application in the context of Asia. There is cross-country heterogeneity in the application of the measures, due to different exchange rate regimes, the nature and degree of openness of the capital markets, and the financial market development. Asian economies employ MPMs more often than CFMs. In the empirical literature, the effectiveness of MPMs is found to be pronounced in reducing credit growth and systemic risks. CFMs are found to help maintain financial stability by discouraging portfolio flows and short-term speculative flows in many cases.

Note

1 See the experience of Thailand and other Asian economies in Chantapacdepong, Chutasripanich, and Jindarak (2012).

References

Agung, J. 2012. Incorporating Macroprudential Instruments into Monetary Policy: Indonesian Experience. Presentation During Monetary Policy Workshop on Strengthening Macroprudential Frameworks. www.imf.org/external/oap/np/seminars/2012/macroprudential/pdf/II5Agung.pdf

Ahmed, S., and A. Zlate. 2013. Capital Flows to Emerging Market Economies: A Brave New World? FRB International Finance Discussion Paper No. 1081, 20 June. https://ssrn.com/abstract=2412153 or https://doi.org/10.2139/ssrn.2412153

Akinci, O., and J. Olmstead-Rumsey. 2015. How Effective are Macroprudential Policies? An Empirical Investigation. International Finance Discussion Paper No. 1136. Washington, DC: Board of Governors of the US Federal Reserve System.

Arora, V., K. Habermeier, J.D. Ostry, and R. Weeks-Brown. 2012. *The Liberalization and Management of Capital Flows: An Institutional View*. Washington, DC: International Monetary Fund.

Barnett, S., and R. Maino. 2013. *Macroprudential Frameworks in Asia*. Washington, DC: International Monetary Fund.

Bruno, V., I. Shim, and H.S. Shin. 2017. Comparative Assessment of Macroprudential Policies. *Journal of Financial Stability* 28(February): 183–202.

Cerutti E., S. Claessens, and L. Laeven. 2015. The Use and Effectiveness of Macroprudential Policies: New Evidence. IMF Working Paper No. 15/61. Washington, DC: International Monetary Fund.

Chai-Anant, C. 2012. Incorporating Macro-Prudential Instrument into Monetary Policy: Thailand's Experience. In: Barnett, S., and R. Maino (eds), *Macroprudential Frameworks in Asia*. Washington, DC: International Monetary Fund, pp. 29–33.

Chakrabarty, K.C. 2014. Framework for the Conduct of Macroprudential Policy in India: Experiences and Perspectives. *Banque de France Financial Stability Review* 18: 131–144.

Chantapacdepong P., N. Chutasripanich, and B. Jindarak. 2012. Central Bank Balance Sheet and Policy Implications. Bank of Thailand Discussion Paper No. 07/2012. Bangkok: Bank of Thailand.

Chantapacdepong, P., and I. Shim. 2015. Correlations Across Asia-Pacific Bond Markets and the Impact of Capital Flow Measures. *Pacific-Basin Finance Journal* 34(September): 71–101.

Checki, T.J. 2013. Observations on Global Financial Cycles and Recent Emerging Market Volatility. Remarks at the Thirty-Seventh Annual Jackson Hole Symposium, Jackson Hole, Wyoming, US, 24 August. www.newyorkfed.org/newsevents/speeches/2013/che130829.html

Claessens, S., S.R. Ghosh, and R. Mihet. 2014. Macro-Prudential Policies to Mitigate Financial System Vulnerabilities. IMF Working Paper No. 14/155. Washington, DC: International Monetary Fund.

Darbar, S.M., and X. Wu. 2016. Experiences with Macroprudential Policy – Five Case Studies. *Journal of International Commerce, Economics and Policy* 7(3): 1–34.

Financial Stability Board. 2015. *Peer Review of China: Review Report*, 13 August. www.fsb.org/wp-content/uploads/China-peer-review-report.pdf

Forbes, K., M. Fratzscher, and R. Straub. 2015. Capital-Flow Management Measures: What Are They Good for? *Journal of International Economics* 96(S1): S76–S97.

Galati, G., and R. Moessner. 2013. Macroprudential Policy – A Literature Review. *Journal of Economic Surveys* 27(5): 846–878.

Habermeier, K., A. Kokenyne, and C. Baba. 2011. The Effectiveness of Capital Controls and Prudential Policies in Managing Large Inflows. IMF Staff Discussion Note No. 11/14. Washington, DC: International Monetary Fund.

He, D. 2014. The Effects of Macroprudential Policies on Housing Market Risks: Evidence from Hong Kong. *Financial Stability Review. Banque de France* 18(April): 105–120.

International Monetary Fund (IMF). 2012. *The Liberalization and Management of Capital Flows: An Institutional View*, 14 November. Washington, DC: International Monetary Fund.

IMF. 2013. *Key Aspects of Macroprudential Policy 2013*. Washington, DC: International Monetary Fund.

IMF. 2014. *Staff Guidance Note on Macroprudential Policy*, December. Washington, DC: International Monetary Fund.

IMF. 2015. *Measures Which Are Both Macroprudential and Capital Flow Management Measures: IMF Approach*, May. Washington, DC: International Monetary Fund.

IMF, FSB, and BIS. 2011. *Macroprudential Policy Tools and Frameworks – Progress Report to G20*. Basel and Washington, DC: Financial Stability Board, International Monetary Fund and Bank for International Settlements, 27 October. www.imf.org/external/np/g20/pdf/102711.pdf

IMF, FSB, and BIS. 2016. *Elements of Effective Macroprudential Policies: Lessons from International Experience*. Mimeo, 31 August. www.imf.org/external/np/g20/pdf/2016/083116.pdf

Kim, C. 2014. Macroprudential Policies in Korea – Key Measures and Experiences. Financial Stability Review, Banque de France, issue 18: 121–130.

Lau, C.C. 2015. *Macroprudential Surveillance and Policy Framework – Malaysia's Experience*. CEMLA V Meeting on Financial Stability, Buenos Aires. www.cemla.org/actividades/2015/2015-07-Estabilidad Financiera/2015-07-EstabilidadFinanciera6.pdf

Lee, J.K. 2013. The Operation of Macroprudential Policy Measures: The Case of Korea in the 2000s. Bank of Korea Working Paper No. 2013-1. Seoul: Bank of Korea.

Lee, J. 2014. The Effectiveness of Korea's Capital Flow Management System and Its Implications on Exchange Rate Policy. *Journal of International Logistics and Trade* 12: 77–96.

Lee, M., R.C.O. Asuncion, and J. Kim. 2015. Effectiveness of Macroprudential Policies in Developing Asia: An Empirical Analysis, July. Asian Development Bank Economics Working Paper No. 439. Manila: Asian Development Bank.

Lim C., F. Columba, A. Costa, P. Kongsamut, A. Otani, M. Saiyid, T. Wezel, and X. Wu. 2011. Macroprudential Policy: What Instruments and How to Use Them? Lessons from Country Experiences. IMF Working Paper No. 11/238. Washington, DC: International Monetary Fund.

Maddalonia, A., and J.-L. Peydro. 2013. Monetary Policy, Macroprudential Policy, and Banking Stability: Evidence from the Euro Area. *International Journal of Central Banking* 9(1): 121–169.

Magud, N. E., C. M. Reinhart, and K. S. Rogoff. 2011. Capital Controls: Myth and Reality – A Portfolio Balance Approach. NBER Working Paper No. 16805. Washington, DC: National Bureau of Economic Research.

Ostry, J. D., A. R. Ghosh, K. Habermeier, M. Chamon, M. S. Qureshi, and D.B.S. Reinhardt. 2010. *Capital Inflows: The Role of Controls*. IMF Staff Position Note. 19, SPN/10/04, February. Washington, DC: International Monetary Fund.

Ostry, J. D., A. R. Ghosh, K. Habermeier, L. Laeven, M. Chamon, M. S. Qureshi, and A. Kokenyne. 2011. Managing Capital Inflows: What Tools to Use? IMF Staff Discussion Note, SDN/11/06, 5 April. Washington, DC: International Monetary Fund.

Pasricha, G. K., M. Falagiarda, M. Bijsterbosch, and J. Aizenman. 2015. Domestic and Multilateral Effects of Capital Controls in Emerging Markets. ECB Working Paper No. 1844. Frankfurt: European Central Bank.

Pradhan, M., R. Balakrishnan, R. Baqir, G. Heenan, S. Nowak, C. Oner, and S. Panth. 2011. *Policy Responses to Capital Flows in Emerging Markets*. IMF Staff Discussion Note, SDN/11/10, 21 April. Washington, DC: International Monetary Fund.

Qureshi, M. S., J. D. Ostry, A. R. Ghosh, and M. Chamon. 2011. Managing Capital Inflows: The Role of Capital Controls and Prudential Policies. NBER Working Paper No. w17363, August. https://ssrn.com/abstract=1919437

Rey, H. 2015. Dilemma Not Trilemma: The Global Financial Cycle and Monetary Policy Independence. NBER Working Paper No. 21162. Washington, DC: National Bureau of Economic Research.

Shim, I., B. Bogdanova, J. Shek, and A. Subelyte. 2013. Database for Policy Actions on Housing Markets. *BIS Quarterly Review* (September): 83–95.

Wang, B., and T. Sun. 2013. How Effective Are Macroprudential Policies in China? IMF Working Paper No. 13/75. Washington, DC: International Monetary Fund.

Wong, T. C., T. Fong, K.-F. Li, and H. Choi. 2011. Loan-to-Value Ratio as a Macroprudential Tool – Hong Kong's Experience and Cross-Country Evidence. In *Systemic Risk, Basel III, Financial Stability and Regulation*, February. https://doi.org/10.2139/ssrn.1768546

Yiu, M. S. 2011. The Effect of Capital Flow Management Measures in Five Asian Economies on the Foreign Exchange Market. HKIMR Working Paper No. 412011. Hong Kong, China: Hong Kong Institute for Monetary Research.

Zhang, L., and E. Zoli. 2016. Leaning Against the Wind: Macroprudential Policy in Asia. *Journal of Asian Economics* 42: 33–52.

Zoli, E. 2014. Macroprudential Policy and Capital Flow Measures in Asia: Use and Effectiveness. In *Regional E1conomic Outlook, April 2014. Asia and Pacific: Sustaining the Momentum: Vigilance and Reforms.* Washington, DC: International Monetary Fund.

24

CAPITAL FLOWS AND EXCHANGE RATE POLICIES

Joshua Aizenman and Hiro Ito

Introduction

Asian emerging market economies (EMEs) have been vulnerable to policy changes taken by advanced economies (AEs). When AEs implemented both conventional and nonconventional monetary measures in reaction to the 2008 global financial crisis (GFC), many small open EMEs, including those in Asia, experienced a rise in capital inflows and currency appreciation pressure. After the US started contracting its monetary measures in 2014, some EMEs experienced capital flight. Although most of the Asian EMEs faced this situation with higher levels of exchange rate flexibility and a much thicker buffer of international reserves (IR), it reminded policy leaders in Asia of the crisis in the late 1990s in which the influx of capital was followed by the crisis breakout.

Since the time of the Asian crisis, many Asian EMEs have become large IR holders, joining Japan. In the mid-2000s, the People's Republic of China (PRC) became the largest IR holder and its IR holding peaked at the end of 2014, amounting USD 3.86 trillion, about 32% of the world's total (Figure 24.1a).[1] Among the top 10 largest IR holders, five are East Asian economies whose amount accounts for 49% of the worlds' total IR (Figure 24.1b).[2]

While many motives have been identified to explain EMEs' IR hoarding, precautionary motive and exchange rate stability are often pointed to as major factors for Asian EMEs (e.g., Aizenman and Lee 2007). By observing the severity of the currency crisis as well as the stringency of the International Monetary Fund's conditionality for rescue loans, many economies in the region have found it better to accumulate IR on their own while maintaining intermediate levels of exchange rate stability. However, ironically, it has also been argued that massive IR holdings by EMEs have contributed to financing profligate economies – such as the US economy – with accessibility to liquidity that eventually contributed to bubbles. Furthermore, increased dollar liquidity made EMEs more vulnerable to US policy changes, thus making it appear as though economies are subject to "global financial cycles" (Rey 2013). Thus, in the post-GFC period, Asian EMEs are facing a difficult challenge in international macroeconomics, which can be observed by examining the patterns of capital flows and exchange rate arrangements pertaining to Asian EMEs.

This chapter looks into the policy configuration of Asian economies, especially Asian EMEs, from the perspective of open macro policies. In particular, we focus on both the arrangements of exchange rate regimes and cross-border capital flows. We first review the open macro policy

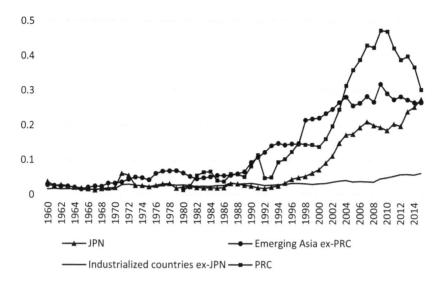

Figure 24.1a   International reserve holdings: as a ratio to GDP

GDP = gross domestic product, PRC = People's Republic of China.

Note: For the country groups, the group's aggregate IR is divided by the group's aggregated GDP. Emerging Asia ex-PRC includes Afghanistan; Bangladesh; Hong Kong, China; India; Indonesia; Republic of Korea; Malaysia; Pakistan; Philippines; Singapore; Sri Lanka; Taipei,China; Thailand, and Viet Nam.

Source: Compiled by authors.

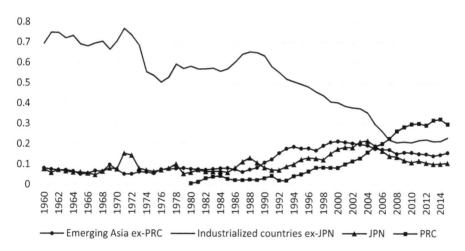

Figure 24.1b   International reserve holdings: as a ratio to the world total

Note: For the country groups, the group's aggregate IR is divided the world's total IR. PRC = People's Republic of China.

Source: Compiled by authors.

arrangements in the context of Mundell's "trilemma" hypothesis. Then we examine whether and to what extent Asian economies are vulnerable to shocks arising from advanced economies, namely the US. Next we show the risks to which Asian economies are exposed that involve the dollar as a key currency, and trade with the US, before concluding.

Review of the open macro policies among Asian EMEs in the context of the trilemma

In the process of managing open macroeconomic policies, policy-makers cannot avoid confronting the "impossible trinity," or the "trilemma" – Mundell's (1963) hypothesis that states that a country may simultaneously choose any two, but not all, of the three goals of monetary independence, exchange rate stability, and financial integration. Hence, we can evaluate the macroeconomic conditions and policies in the Asian region through the lens of this hypothesis.

The trilemma hypothesis can be explained using Figure 24.2, in which each of the three sides of the triangle – representing monetary independence, exchange rate stability, and financial integration – depicts a potentially desirable goal. Although policy-makers can implement a mix of the three either within the triangle, or on one of the three vertexes or sides, it is impossible to be on all three sides of the triangle simultaneously.[3]

Theory and empirical evidence tell us that each one of the three trilemma policy choices can be a double-edged sword. Each of the three policy goals has singular merits and shortcomings.[4] To make matters more complicated, the effect of each policy choice can differ depending on how it is paired with other policies. For example, although exchange rate stability can be more destabilizing if paired with financial openness, it can be stabilizing if paired with greater monetary autonomy. In reality, however, it is more of a rare case when a country faces the stark polarized binary choices often envisioned by the trilemma triangle. As we see in emerging Asia, countries often mix all three policy choices at intermediate levels (i.e., choosing a policy mix that can be depicted as somewhere inside the triangle).[5]

To show visually the configuration of Asian economies' open macroeconomic policies, we use a set of the "trilemma indexes" developed by Aizenman et al. (2008) that measure the degree to which each of the three policy choices is implemented by economies for more than 180 economies from 1970 through 2014. The monetary independence index is based on the correlation of a country's interest rates with the base country's interest rate. The index for exchange rate stability is an invert of exchange rate volatility, that is, standard deviations of the

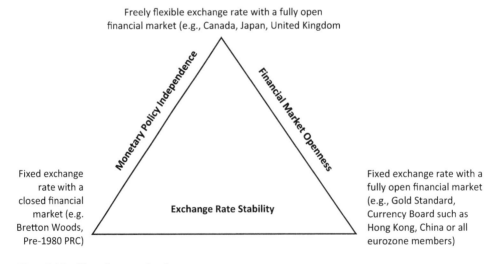

Figure 24.2 The trilemma triangle

Source: Compiled by authors.

monthly rate of depreciation for the exchange rate between the home and base economies. The degree of financial integration is measured with the Chinn and Ito (2006, 2008) capital controls index (KAOPEN).[6]

Figure 24.3 shows the trajectories of the trilemma indexes for different income-country groups. For the industrialized economies, financial openness accelerated in the 1990s while, at the same time, the extent of monetary independence started to decline and exchange rate stability began to rise significantly. All of these trends reflect the introduction of the euro in 1999. Developing economies do not present such a distinct divergence of the indexes, though their experiences differ depending on whether they are emerging or non-emerging market economies.[7] For EMEs, exchange rate stability declined rapidly from the 1970s through the mid-1980s. After some retrenchment around the early 1980s, financial openness started rising from 1990 onwards, though it started to decline again at the end of the 2000s. These trends are not discernable among the non-EME developing economies.

Interestingly, for EMEs, the indexes suggest a convergence toward the middle ground. In other words, these economies may have been maintaining moderate levels for all of the three indices. This policy trend coincides with the period of time in which some of these economies began accumulating sizeable IR to potentially buffer the trade-off arising from the trilemma.

While this is not observed among non-EME developing countries (Figure 24.3c), Asian emerging markets stand out from other geographical groups of economies in that these economies have had this sort of convergence for almost the entire sample period (Figure 24.4a).[8] However, with the exception of the Asian crisis years of 1997–1998, exchange rate stability seems to have been the most pervasive policy choice for most of the time. Although the indexes diverged in the 2000s post-crisis years, they have converged again in recent years. This characterization does not apply to non-EME Asian economies (panel b) or Latin America (panel c). For non-EME economies in Asia, convergence in the trilemma configurations occurs in the later part of the sample period. Among non-Asian developing economies, exchange rate stability is distinctly the first priority throughout the sample period and middle-ground convergence has not occurred at all.

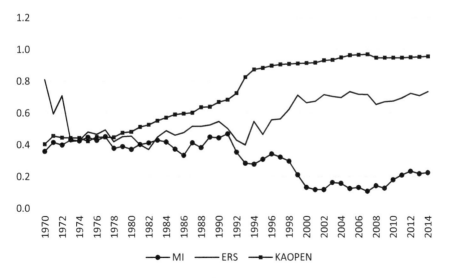

Figure 24.3a   Development of the trilemma configurations over time: industrialized countries

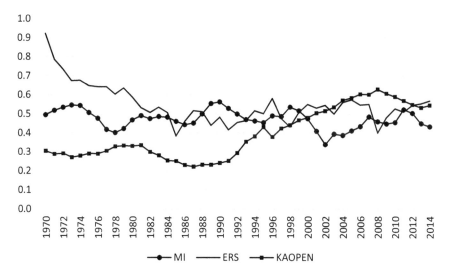

Figure 24.3b   Development of the trilemma configurations over time: emerging market economies (EMEs)

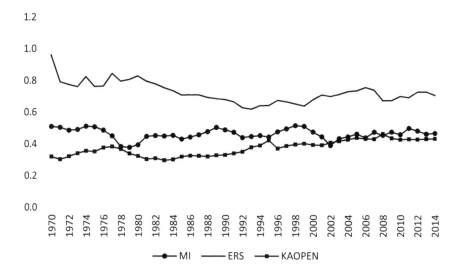

Figure 24.3c   Development of the trilemma configurations over time: non-EME developing countries

EMG = Emerging market economies, KAOPEN = capital controls index.

Source: Compiled by authors.

We now add the role of IR holding to the three-trilemma dimensions to shed further light on the open macro configuration, especially for the Asian region. As we have seen, since the Asian crisis of 1997–1998, EMEs, especially those in East Asia and the Middle East, have been rapidly increasing their amounts of IR holding. Researchers have tried to identify the causes for rapid IR accumulation among EMEs, especially those in Asia. Aizenman and Lee (2007) provide evidence that countries hold IR for both precautionary and exchange rate stability

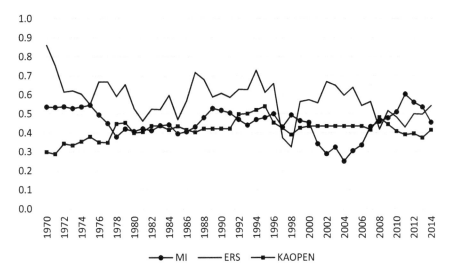

Figure 24.4a Regional comparison of the development of the trilemma configurations: emerging market economies (EMG) in Asia

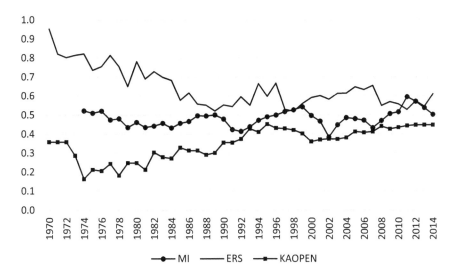

Figure 24.4b Regional comparison of the development of the trilemma configurations: non-EMG, developing Asia

motives. Many researchers have argued the benefits of self-insurance against the volatility associated with financial globalization (Aizenman and Marion 2003; Cheung and Ito 2008, 2009). As a series of crises experienced in emerging markets in the late 1990s and early 2000s led to reserve hoarding by the PRC and other EMEs in the 2000s, new factors have been added to the list of determinants of IR hoarding, including mercantilist motives (Aizenman and Lee 2007), regional competitive incentives ("keeping up with the Joneses," Cheung and Qian 2009), and

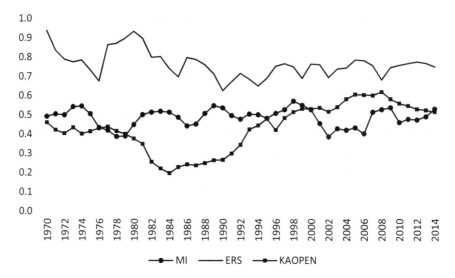

Figure 24.4c   Regional comparison of the development of the trilemma configurations: Latin American countries

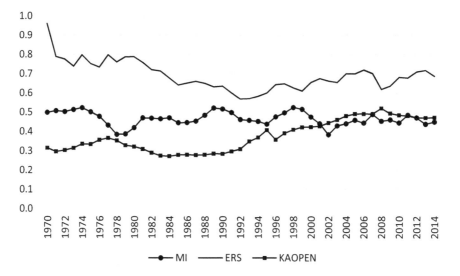

Figure 24.4d   Regional comparison of the development of the trilemma configurations: less developed countries (LDC) excluding Asia

ERS = exchange rate stability, KAOPEN = capital controls index, MI = monetary independence index.

Source: Compiled by authors

self-insurance against local residents' flight from domestic assets in the trilemma context (Obstfeld, Shambaugh, and Taylor 2010; Aizenman et al. 2011; Aizenman et al. 2015).

One might argue that economies accumulate massive IR to achieve a certain combination of exchange rate stability, monetary policy autonomy, and financial openness. For example, a country pursuing a stable exchange rate and monetary autonomy may try to liberalize cross-border financial transactions while simultaneously deciding not to give up current levels of exchange rate stability and monetary autonomy. This sort of policy combination, however, could lead the monetary authorities to hold a sizeable amount of IR so that they can stabilize the exchange rate movement while retaining monetary autonomy.[9]

The "diamond charts" in Figure 24.5 trace the changing patterns of the trilemma configurations while incorporating IR holding. In each "diamond," four vertices measure monetary independence, exchange rate stability, IR/GDP ratio, and financial integration with the origin normalized so as to represent zero monetary independence, pure float, zero international reserves, and financial autarky. We present the diamond charts for the original 12 euro countries, emerging Asian economies, the PRC, and Latin American economies.

In Figure 24.5, we see that again Asian EMEs have not experienced the divergence of the trilemma configurations over the years as has happened for industrial economies, especially for the euro member countries – that is, a move toward deeper financial integration, greater exchange rate stability, and weaker monetary independence (Figure 24.5a). Asian EMEs are distinct from the other groups of economies in having a middle-ground convergence of trilemma policy convergence; the three indexes have been clustered around the middle range. Interestingly, however, in recent years, both the extent of monetary independence and the level of IR holding has risen while financial openness and exchange rate stability have been inching down. Also, while the extent of monetary independence has been cyclically changing over years, the levels of IR holding has been steadily increasing, making one suspect the potential implications of such holdings on trilemma policy choices and macroeconomic performances. These characterizations are not applicable to Latin American economies (and other country groups though not reported).

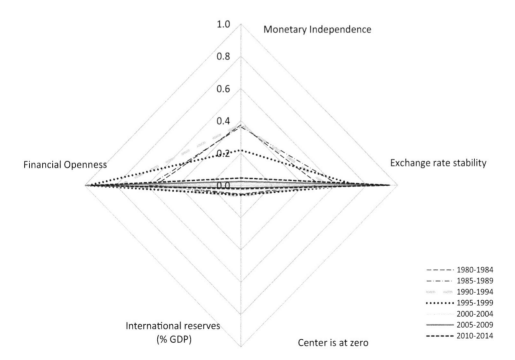

Figure 24.5a The diamond charts: variation of the trilemma and IR configurations across different country groups: Euro 12 countries

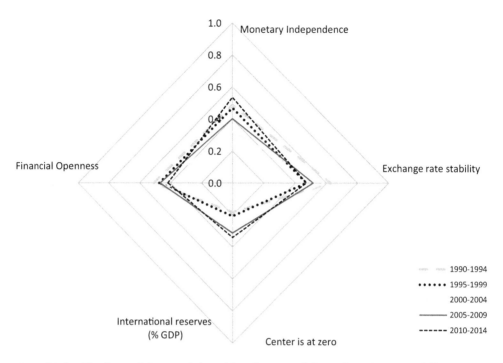

Figure 24.5b   The diamond charts: variation of the trilemma and IR configurations across different country groups: emerging Asia

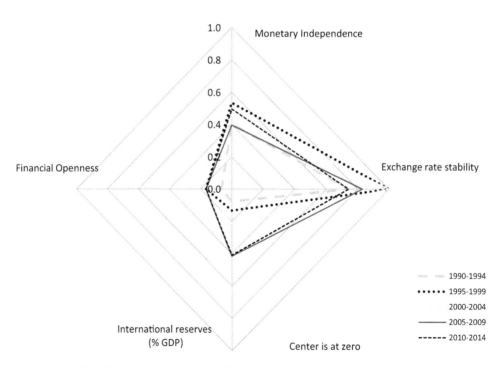

Figure 24.5c   The diamond charts: variation of the trilemma and IR configurations across different country groups: PRC

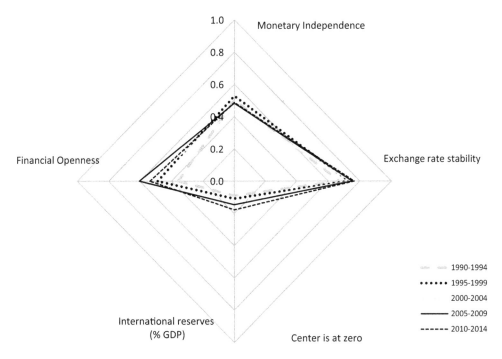

Figure 24.5d The diamond charts: variation of the trilemma and IR configurations across different country groups: Latin America

PRC = People's Republic of China, GDP = gross domestic product, IR = international reserves.

Source: Compiled by authors.

Vulnerability to the center

Connectivity with the center economies

Recently, a number of researchers have argued that financial globalization has made domestic asset prices and interest rates more vulnerable to developments in capital markets abroad. The most representative work of this view is the paper by Rey (2013), who argues that financial globalization has made countries' macroeconomic conditions more sensitive to the "global financial cycle" in capital flows, asset prices, and credit growth. In the markets where capital is freely mobile, Rey continues, the center country's monetary policy influences other countries' national monetary policies through capital flows, credit growth, and bank leverages, thus determining the global financial cycle.

Let us see if global shocks or monetary shocks of the center country (i.e., the US) affect the ebb and flow of cross-border capital movements, especially in small open economies. Figure 24.6 displays the development of the "VIX index" that measures the implied volatility of S&P 500 Index options as well as the development of net capital flows to EMEs. The VIX index is a measure of uncertainty or risk aversion of the markets, thus its scale (on the right-hand side) is reversed so to be seen as a measure of investor risk appetite. From the figure, we can see that the volumes of capital flows to EMEs tend to rise when the risk appetite is higher. We can also see that prior to the 2008 GFC, a large volume of capital flowed into emerging markets, though this was followed by massive capital outflows once the crisis broke out. However, the capital flow

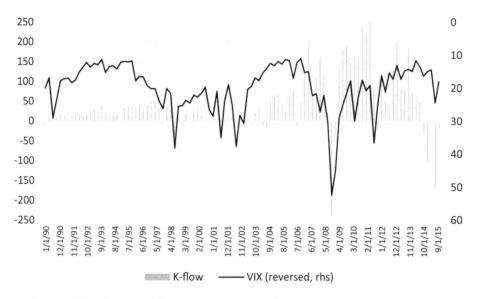

Figure 24.6a   VIX and net capital flows to EMEs: EME total

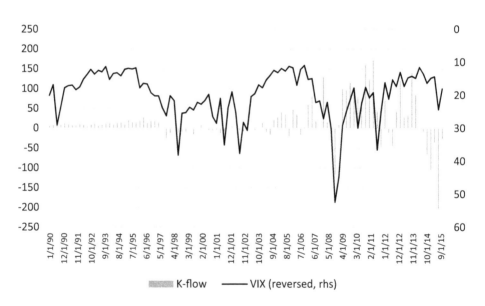

Figure 24.6b   VIX and net capital flows to EMEs: Asian EMEs

became reversed with massive capital flowing back to EMEs again once advanced economies implemented zero, or extremely low, interest policies to fight recessionary situations.

This generalization applies well to the group of Asian EMEs in terms of ebb-and-flow volumes and patterns. Although Latin American EMEs also experienced an influx of capital in the post-GFC period, not as much capital flowed to these economies before the crisis. In contrast, Eastern or Central European EMEs experienced massive capital inflows before the crisis, but capital inflows did not resume to the pre-crisis level in the post-crisis period. Furthermore, both

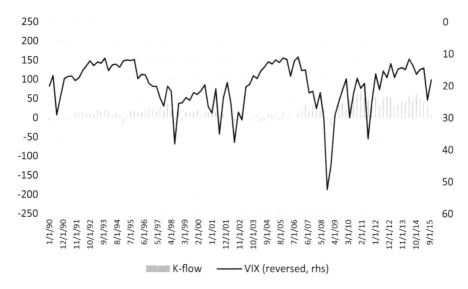

Figure 24.6c VIX and net capital flows to EMEs: Latin American EMEs

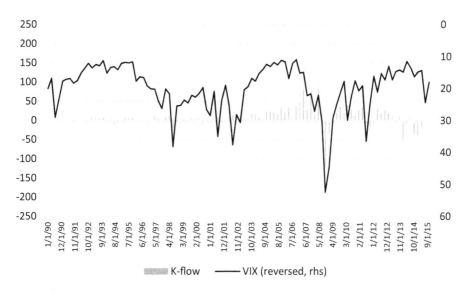

Figure 24.6d VIX and net capital flows to EMEs: Eastern/Central European EMEs

EME = emerging market economy.

Notes: VIX is a measure of the implied volatility of S&P 500 index options. Both VIX and net capital flows are shown as four-months moving averages. The scale for the VIX index (on the right-hand side) is reversed to express the degree of risk appetite. The data for private capital flow are extracted from the IMF's International Financial Statistics. The VIX index is from the Chicago Board Options Exchange.

Source: Compiled by authors.

the full EME sample and the subsample of Asian EMEs show massive capital outflows once the US started downsizing its unconventional monetary policy in 2014.

Figure 24.7a illustrates the 36-month rolling correlations of domestic money market rates with the US money market rate for different country groups, including Asian EMEs, and the

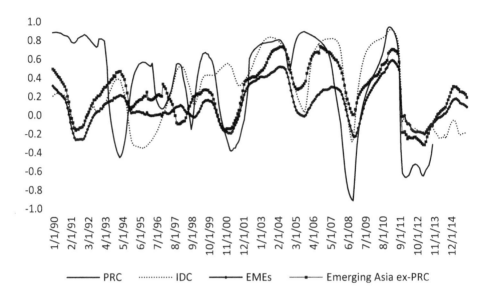

Figure 24.7a　Connectivity with the US: short-term interest rate

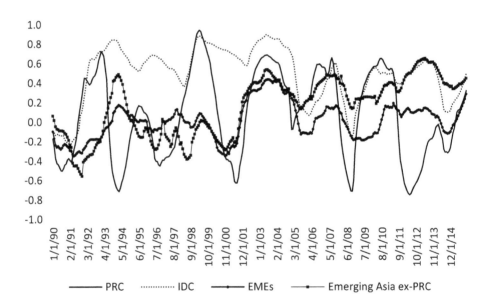

Figure 24.7b　Connectivity with the US: long-term interest rate

PRC. The figure shows that from 2003 through 2012, in Asian EMEs and the PRC, the correlation between domestic and the US interest rates oscillates at relatively high levels except in 2005 and 2008.[10] In the last few years, however, the correlations have been negative, mainly reflecting the unconventional monetary policies taken by the US.

Figure 24.7b recreates the long-term interest rates. The long-term interest rates of the Asian EMEs are highly correlated with that of the US for much of the last decade and a half. Since 2005, the correlation has been on a rising trend despite the GFC and the rapid decline in the

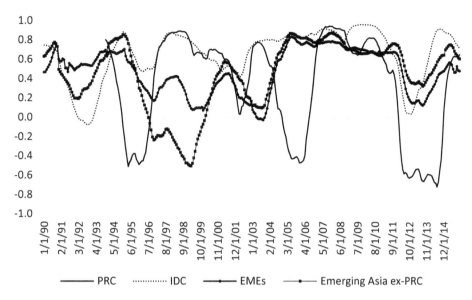

Figure 24.7c Connectivity with the US: stock market price

PRC = People's Republic of China, EME = emerging market economy, IDC = industrialized economies.

Source: Compiled by authors.

correlations of the short-term interest rates we saw in panel (a). In the last few years of the sample period, short- and long-term interest rates have been decoupled, which may suggest that policy-makers find it difficult to control macroeconomic and financial conditions through maneuvering short-term interest rates.

Figure 24.7c illustrates the correlations of stock market price indexes with the US index for the same subsamples and the PRC. Since the early 2000s up until 2012 or so, all of the country groups had maintained high levels of correlations of stock market price indexes with the US stock market. Since the GFC, the correlation has been declining for all of the groups, but only to a lesser extent for emerging Asian economies.

In the last few figures, we saw that in the last decade or so, the correlations of the long-term interest rates or stock market price indexes with those of the US are higher than correlations of the short-term interest rates. Considering that the extent of risk exposure is greater for stock market prices, the long-term interest rates, and the short-term interest rates in the descending order, the more risk a financial asset is exposed to, the more tendency there is for that particular asset's price to follow that of the center economy (i.e., the US). This is consistent with the "global financial cycle" view of Rey (2013).

Does Asia continue to be vulnerable as it was in the 1990s?

In the aftermath of the EME crises in the late 1990s and the early 2000s, many of the EMEs, whether they experienced the crisis or not, started rapidly increasing their IR holdings. However, ironically, this active IR accumulation, in retrospect, sowed the seeds for the world economy to provide ample liquidity for advanced and profligate economies that eventually led to those economies' bubbles and bust in the late 2000s. In other words, it was a self-fulfilling prophecy that EMEs' efforts to hold IR to ensure self-insurance or protection ended up creating an environment for which these economies needed insurance or protection.

Asian EMEs may face challenges from increasing connectivity. As we saw previously, they are still on their way to further financial opening, although they are already exposed to risks from the center economies. Borensztein and Loungani (2011) and Genberg (this volume) show that Asian economies are considerably integrated with major economies outside rather than inside their regions. Hence, intra-Asia trade of financial assets is also expected to expand, which would inevitably lead to further financial openings by the economies in the region.

With this undeniable trend for further financial openings, the trilemma hypothesis suggests that economies in the region will have to decide whether to retain monetary autonomy but give up pursuing exchange rate stability, or to pursue exchange rate stability but subject their monetary policies to those of the center economies. Either way, these economies will become more exposed to external shocks.

Now, the question is, are the economies in the Asian region facing a situation that is vulnerable to external shocks as they were before the Asian financial crisis of 1997–1998? Figure 24.8 can help us answer this question as it presents the development of the key economic variables that illustrate different aspects of vulnerability, namely, (a) the index for exchange rate stability; (b) IR holding as a share of GDP; (c) international debt securities as a ratio to gross national income (GNI); (d) short-term liability to foreign banks as a ratio to GNI; (e) "credit gap" as a measure of credit excesses or "credit booms"; and (f) the exchange market pressure (EMP) index.[11]

We note several interesting observations. First, all of the economies in the region, with the exception of the PRC, are now pursuing higher levels of exchange rate *flexibility* unlike the time right before the breakout of the Asian crisis. In particular, the Republic of Korea, Indonesia, and Thailand, all of which experienced currency crises in 1997–1998, aborted pegged exchange rate policies. Thus, major Asian EMEs, except for the PRC, are not constrained by exchange rate rigidities at this moment. Second, mainly because of the harsh experience of the crisis economies in the 1990s, all of the economies shown in Figure 24.10b, with the exception of Indonesia, increased their levels of IR holdings. Apparently, these economies believe that holding IR will provide a buffer to external financial shocks.

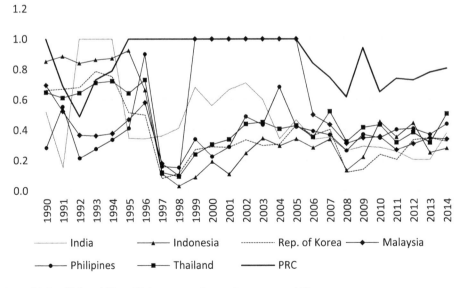

Figure 24.8a Vulnerability of Asian economies: exchange rate stability

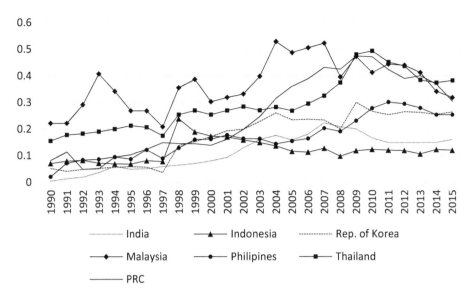

Figure 24.8b   Vulnerability of Asian economies: international reserve holdings

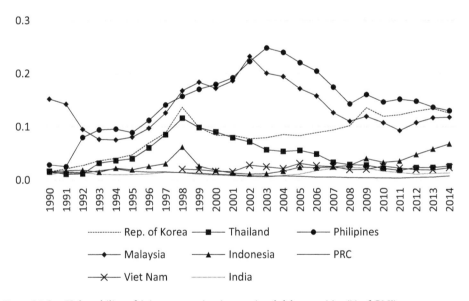

Figure 24.8c   Vulnerability of Asian economies: international debt securities (% of GNI)

Third, many major Asian economies experienced a rapid increase in external debt around the end of the 1990s, but the debt level of these economies is lower at present. The only exception is Republic of Korea. Panel (c) illustrates that the size of outstanding international debt securities for the Philippines and Malaysia was almost as high as 25% of their GNI in the late 1990s, but it is now around 13%–14%. The size of short-term liability to foreign banks (as a share of GNI) was almost 30% of GNI for Thailand and Indonesia at that time, but it is now as low as 7%–8% (panel (d)). The only concern is Republic of Korea. Both outstanding

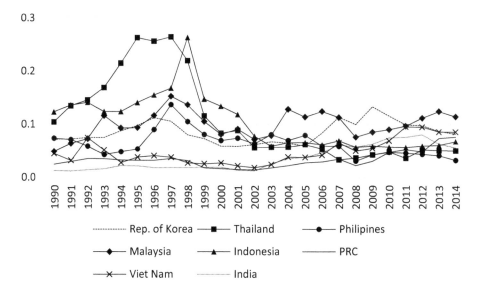

Figure 24.8d   Vulnerability of Asian economies: short-term liability to banks (% of GNI)

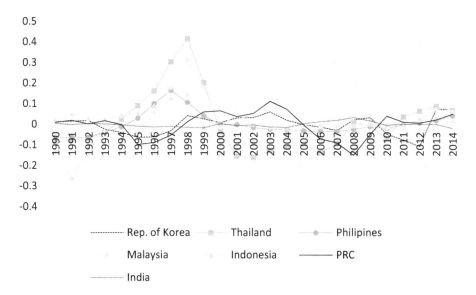

Figure 24.8e   Vulnerability of Asian economies: credit gap

international debt securities and short-term liability to foreign banks declined in most of the 2000s. However, they went up at the end of the 2000s, hovering around the same level as during the Asian crisis period.

Last, Asian economies are not facing both internal and external pressure in the financial sector. Panel (e) of Figure 24.8 illustrates the development of "credit gap" or "credit excesses," which is the deviation of private credit creation from its long-term trend. When the gap is in positive territory, we can think of that as a sign of overheating in the financial sector. Although

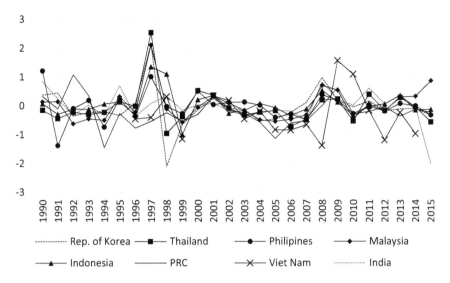

Figure 24.8f Vulnerability of Asian economies: exchange market pressure

GNI = gross national income, PRC = People's Republic of China.

Source: Compiled by authors.

we observed an influx of capital once advanced economies implemented zero, or extremely low, interest rate policies in the aftermath of the GFC, we do not observe large-scale positive credit gaps in the 2010s. Around the same time period, the EMP index, a proxy for stress levels in the foreign exchange market, does not appear high, except in Malaysia. Exchange rate flexibility seems to be absorbing stress in the foreign exchange market. Thus, major Asian economies are not exposed to high levels of internal or external financial pressure.

Exposure to the dollar

Although we have shown that major Asian economies are not vulnerable to financial shocks internally or externally, as we have shown, these economies continue to be exposed to financial risks emanating from the center economy (i.e., the US).

More strictly speaking, however, it is not just the US that has so much significant influence on the economies in the region, it is the dollar that has been overwhelmingly important for these economies. Since the beginning of the new millennium, there have been webs of extensive and intensive supply chain networks in the Asian region. Most of these networks are aimed at the US as the final export destination. That is reflected as high levels of reliance on the dollar as a trade invoicing or settlement currency. In Thailand and Indonesia, 80% or more of the countries' exports are invoiced or settled in dollar (Figure 24.9 (a)). India, the third-largest Asian economy after the PRC and Japan, has more than 88% of its exports invoiced in the dollar; in Republic of Korea, the fourth-largest Asian economy, the dollar share is about 85%. Even Japan has half of its exports invoiced in the dollar despite its long time efforts to make the yen one of the major international currencies.[12]

The high reliance on the dollar for trade invoicing or settlement is also reflected in the weight of the currencies included in the implicit currency basket on which policy-makers base their exchange rate or monetary policy decisions. Using the methodology popularized

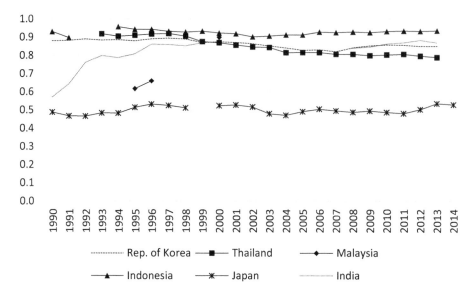

Figure 24.9a   Heavy reliance on the dollar: dollar share in export invoicing

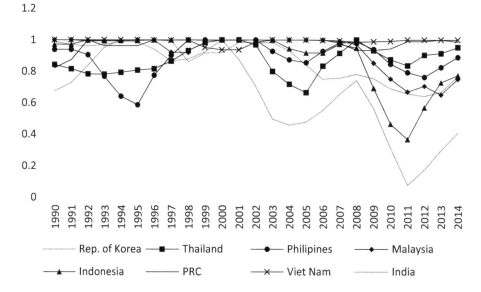

Figure 24.9b   Heavy reliance on the dollar: dollar weight in currency baskets

by Frankel and Wei (1996), Ito and Kawai (2016) estimate the weights of the dollar, the euro (or the German deutsche mark and the French franc before the introduction of the euro in 1999), the yen, and the British sterling with a rolling window of 36 months.[13] Figure 24.9b illustrates the development of the estimated dollar weights for the major EMEs in Asia. In the figure, we can see that, with the exception of Republic of Korea and Malaysia in recent years, Asian EMEs have had high weights in their implicit currency baskets. In other words, these economies can be categorized as economies in the "dollar zone" to which the monetary and

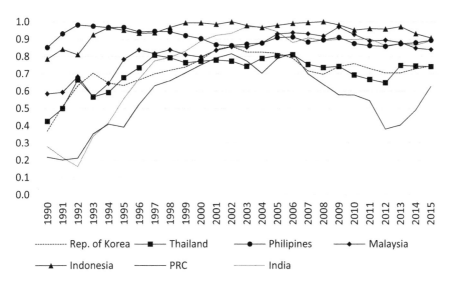

Figure 24.9c   Heavy reliance on the dollar: dollar share in international debt denomination

PRC = People's Republic of China.

Source: Compiled by authors.

financial conditions of the dollar matter the most. For such economies, higher dollar weights facilitate dollar invoicing, though causality can go the other way around.

Another dimension that can be added is that these economies are also reliant on the dollar to issue international debt securities. According to Figure 24.9 (c), in all of the major Asian EMEs, with the exception of the PRC, the dollar share as the currency for debt denomination is high, greater than 75%.[14] In other words, the "original sin" phenomenon – developing countries often cannot issue debt in international markets unless they issue debt in a major hard currency such as the dollar – still applies to Asian EMEs. Interestingly, although currency mismatches were one of the biggest problems faced by the economies that experienced the currency crisis in 1997–1998, the extent of the reliance on the dollar for debt issuance has not changed much since the late 1990s.

Despite this constant reliance, Figure 24.10a shows that the share of the US as an export destination has been in a declining trend for most of the major Asian emerging market economies (with the notable except of Viet Nam, whose trade with the US dramatically increased after a trade relationship with the US was normalized in 2001). In contrast, and not surprisingly, the share of the PRC as an export destination has been a rising trend. Again, this does not mean that the US is becoming less influential on Asian economies; it is the dollar that continues to have great influence on the economies in the Asian region.

We can interpret the estimated weights of the four major currencies in the currency basket that we estimated previously as the extent of belonging to each of the four currency zones. Using the four currency weights as well as the data on the volume of trade with each of the four currency issuers, we can estimate the share of trade (i.e., exports plus imports) for each of the four currency zones. Figure 24.10c illustrates the shares of trade with the economies that belong to the dollar zone for Japan and Asian EMEs. Interestingly, for most of the economies, the share of trade with the dollar-zone economies has been quite stable over time, ranging from 50% to 70% across countries. The share of dollar-zone trade for Japan has been quite high,

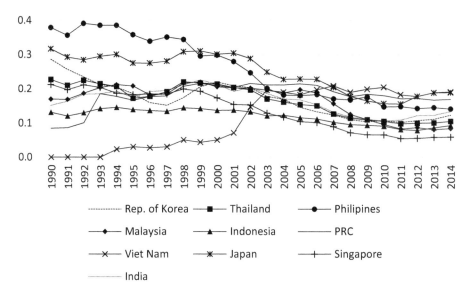

Figure 24.10a Changing trade structure and stable reliance on the dollar: share of the US as an export destination

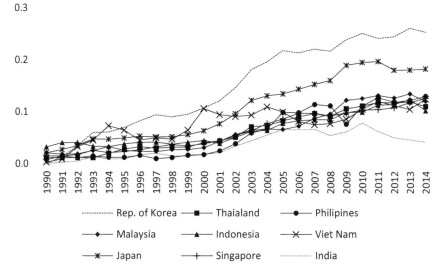

Figure 24.10b Changing trade structure and stable reliance on the dollar: share of the PRC as an export destination

ranging from 62% to almost 80%, though the country is an issuer of one of the four major currencies. Although we have seen that Asian EMEs have managed to achieve intermediate levels of exchange rate stability, we can now see that they have maintained stable ties with the dollar. While many Asian economies are experiencing a declining share of trade with the US, the figure shows that the dollar continues to be influential for the economies in the region. This is probably the reason why Asian EMEs are susceptible to shocks arising in the US financial markets even though their levels of financial openness are still intermediate.

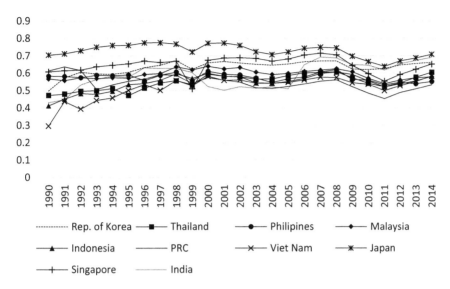

Figure 24.10c Changing trade structure and stable reliance on the dollar: share of trade with dollar-zone economies

PRC = People's Republic of China, US = United States.

Source: Compiled by authors.

The continuing importance of the dollar is partly driven by the fact that the PRC is quite a dollar-oriented economy. We saw in Figure 24.10a and Figure 24.10b that the PRC's increasing presence as a trading partner for Asian economies has replaced some of the US presence. Thus, if the PRC succeeded in "internationalizing" the yuan and forming its own currency zone, the picture in Figure 24.10c would change significantly.

Now that the PRC has replaced the US as the largest trading partner in the Asian region, will it also succeed the US as the issuer of the most dominant currency in the region?

The rising PRC income level and the country's role as a major global trading country will help the yuan to become more widely used as an international currency.[15] However, two uncertainties warrant attention regarding the future of the yuan as a dominant, key international currency.

First, it is uncertain whether the PRC will proceed with a smooth financial liberalization and deregulation, although economists agree that financial development and liberalization are necessary conditions for a currency to become a major international currency (Ito and Chinn 2015; Ito and Kawai 2016). The fact that the PRC economy started slowing down in 2014 has made policy-makers in Beijing more cautious about further liberalization. Further, as we have seen since the summer of 2015, the slump of the PRC's financial markets, following the economic slowdown, has led PRC financial authorities to become more active to intervene in financial markets, making the future of the liberalization efforts unknown.

Second, as we have seen, countries that belong to the dollar block surround the PRC. Ito and Kawai (2016) find that the extent to which a country belongs to one of the major currency zones affects its decision to use that currency for trade invoicing. This explains why the Japanese yen has not been used as a trade invoicing currency not just by Japan but also by neighboring economies: almost all of Japan's neighboring countries belong to the dollar zone.[16] The PRC will face the same challenge. The number of the PRC's neighboring Asian countries that will break away from the dollar block and start using the yuan for international trade and financial activity is an important key to the yuan's further internationalization.

Ito and McCauley (2017) show that capital flows to the dollar zone would change if the PRC becomes less of a dollar-zone country. Hence, the map of capital flows and exchange rate arrangements in Asia could very much depend on how much yuan internationalization proceeds. For now, the Asian region's international finance continues to be dollar-centric.

Concluding remarks

Asian economies continue to face challenges as they continue to open their financial markets toward international investment. In this chapter, we reviewed the economies' macroeconomic situations, with the main focus on emerging market economies in the region.

We first evaluated the situation of openness to capital flow and exchange rate regimes from the perspective of the "trilemma" hypothesis. Using the "trilemma indexes" developed by Aizenman et al. (2008, 2010, 2011), we find many emerging markets manage exchange rate flexibility while maintaining medium levels of monetary independence and financial integration. Interestingly, for Asian EMEs, we find such a "middle-ground" convergence is not a recent phenomenon in these economies, but a trend that can trace back to early 1980s, though exchange rate stability has been the most pervasive policy choice. Another recent, distinct characteristic of Asian EMEs is the high level of IR holdings.

Furthermore, financial globalization seems to have made asset prices and interest rates in Asian EMEs more vulnerable to global movements of capital. The level of risk appetite and US monetary policy influences the capital flowing into and out of Asian EMEs.

The US presence in trade ties with Asian economies has been declining over the last two decades, whereas the PRC's has been on a rising trend. However, we found that the share of trade among Asian economies with the dollar-zone economies has been quite stable. That means that it the dominant position of the dollar that has been influential in the Asian region. One big dollar-zone economy that has been increasing its presence in Asia is the PRC. However, the PRC has been making efforts to internationalize the yuan. Hence, if the PRC succeeds in its internationalization efforts and creates a yuan zone, the dynamics between the US and Asia will most likely change; it is, however, uncertain to what extent the yuan will become an international currency. Recently, PRC authorities have become more interventionist because of the slowdown of the economy and financial markets. For now, the Asian region's international finance continues to be dollar-centric.

Notes

1 In 2015 and 2016, the PRC experienced capital outflow and currency depreciation pressure, which led the amount of IR holding to go down to USD 3.03 as of the end of 2016, though still accounting for 28% of the world's total.
2 They are the PRC, Japan, Republic of Korea, Hong Kong, China, and Singapore. Additionally, India is ranked as the ninth-largest IR holder.
3 See Aizenman, Chinn, and Ito (2010, 2011, 2013, 2016), Aizenman and Ito (2013), Klein and Shambaugh (2015), Obstfeld (2014), Obstfeld, Shambaugh, and Taylor (2005), and Shambaugh (2004) for further discussion and references dealing with the trilemma.
4 For monetary independence, refer to Obstfeld, Shambaugh, and Taylor (2005), Shambaugh (2004), and Frankel, Schmukler, and Serven (2004). On the impact of the exchange rate regime, refer to Ghosh, Gulde, and Ostry (1997), Levy-Yeyati and Sturzenegger (2003), and Eichengreen and Leblang (2003). The empirical literature on the effect of financial liberalization is surveyed by Henry (2007), Kose et al. (2009), and Prasad et al. (2003).

5 For the determinants of trilemma policy configurations, refer to Ito and Kawai (2014). For the macroeconomic impacts of different types of trilemma configurations, refer to Aizenman, Chinn, and Ito (2010, 2011).

6 More details on the construction of the indexes can be found in Aizenman, Chinn, and Ito (2008, 2010, 2011), and the indexes are available at http://web.pdx.edu/~ito/trilemma_indexes.htm.

7 The emerging market economies are defined as the economies classified as either emerging or frontier during 1980–1997 by the International Financial Corporation.

8 The sample of "Asian Emerging Market Economies" include Bangladesh; the PRC; Hong Kong, China; India; Indonesia; Republic of Korea; Malaysia; Pakistan; Philippines; Singapore; Sri Lanka; Taiwan; Thailand; and Viet Nam.

9 Aizenman, Chinn, and Ito (2010, 2011) show the macroeconomic impact of trilemma policy configurations can depend upon the level of IR holding.

10 The two dips in the correlations correspond to the time when the US Federal Reserve changed its policy rate rapidly. The Federal Reserve started raising the federal fund rate target from 1.00% in June 2004 to 5.25% in June 2006. It started lowering the target from 5.25% in September 2007 all the way essentially to the 0.00–0.25 by December 2008.

11 For exchange rate stability, we use the index from the trilemma indexes (Aizenman, Chinn, and Ito 2008, 2010, and updates). The data for international debt securities are extracted from the Bank for International Settlements (BIS) website. The data for short-term liability to banks are from the Joint External Debt Hub (JEDH). We define "credit gap" as the gap between private credit creation (as a share of GDP) and its long-term trend measured by HP-filtered series. The EMP index is constructed following the oft-used methodology introduced by Eichengreen, Rose, and Wyplosz (1995, 1996). For more details, refer to Aizenman and Ito (2013).

12 For comparison, refer to Ito and Kawai (2016).

13 The basic assumption of this exercise is that monetary authorities use an implicit basket of currencies as the portfolio of official foreign exchange reserves, but that the extent of response to the change in the value of the entire basket should vary over time and across countries. If the authorities want to maintain a certain level of exchange rate stability, whether against a single currency or a basket of several currencies, they should allow the currency value to adjust only in accordance with the change in the *entire* value of the basket of major currencies.

14 The volume of international debt securities the PRC issues is small, however.

15 For more details on the issue of yuan internationalization, refer to Eichengreen and Kawai (2015), Frankel (2011), Ito (2011), and Ito and Kawai (2016).

16 As of 2014, the share of Japan's exports invoiced in the yen is less than 40%, while that of exports in US dollars is more than 50%. In imports, these shares are 20% and 75%, respectively. See Ito and Kawai (2016).

References

Aizenman, J., Y.-W. Cheung, and H. Ito. 2015. International Reserves Before and After the Global Crisis: Is There No End to Hoarding? *Journal of International Money and Finance* 52(April): 102–126.

Aizenman, J., M.D. Chinn, and H. Ito. 2008. Assessing the Emerging Global Financial Architecture: Measuring the Trilemma's Configurations over Time. NBER Working Paper No. 14533. Cambridge, MA: National Bureau of Economic Research.

Aizenman, J., M.D. Chinn, and H. Ito. 2010. The Emerging Global Financial Architecture: Tracing and Evaluating New Patterns of the Trilemma Configuration. *Journal of International Money and Finance* 29(2010): 615–641.

Aizenman, J., M.D. Chinn, and H. Ito. 2011. Surfing the Waves of Globalization: Asia and Financial Globalization in the Context of the Trilemma. *Journal of the Japanese and International Economies* 25(3): 290–320.

Aizenman, J., M.D. Chinn, and H. Ito. 2013. The 'Impossible Trinity' Hypothesis in an Era of Global Imbalances: Measurement and Testing. *Review of International Economics* 21(3): 447–458.

Aizenman, J., M.D. Chinn, and H. Ito. 2016. Monetary Policy Spillovers and the Trilemma in the New Normal: Periphery Country Sensitivity to Core Country Conditions. *Journal of International Money and Finance* 68(November): 298–330.

Aizenman, J., and J. Lee. 2007. International Reserves: Precautionary versus Mercantilist Views, Theory and Evidence. *Open Economies Review* 18(2): 191–214.

Aizenman, J., and N. Marion. 2003. The High Demand for International Reserves in the Far East: What's Going On? *Journal of the Japanese and International Economies* 17: 370–400.

Aizenman, J., and H. Ito. 2013. Living with the Trilemma Constraint: Relative Trilemma Policy Divergence, Crises, and Output Losses for Developing Countries. *Journal of International Money and Finance* 49: 28–51.

Borensztein, E., and P. Loungani. 2011. Asian Financial Integration: Trends and Interruptions. IMF Working Paper WP/11/4. Washington, DC: International Monetary Fund.

Cheung, Y.-W., and H. Ito. 2008. Hoarding of International Reserves: A Comparison of the Asian and Latin American Experiences. In *Exchange Rate, Monetary and Financial Issues and Policies in Asia*, edited by S. Ramkishen, S. Rajan, and R.A. Parinduri. Singapore: World Scientific Publishing.

Cheung, Y.-W., and H. Ito. 2009. Cross-Sectional Analysis on the Determinants of International Reserves Accumulation. *International Economic Journal* 23(4): 447–481.

Cheung, Y.-W., and Q. Xingwang. 2009. Hoarding of International Reserves: Mrs. Machlup's Wardrobe and the Joneses. *Review of International Economics* 17(4): 824–843.

Chinn, M.D., and H. Ito. 2006. What Matters for Financial Development? Capital Controls, Institutions, and Interactions, *Journal of Development Economics* 81(1): 163–192.

Chinn, M.D., and H. Ito. 2007. Current Account Balances, Financial Development and Institutions: Assaying the World 'Savings Glut'. *Journal of International Money and Finance* 26(4): 546–569.

Chinn, M.D., and H. Ito. 2008. A New Measure of Financial Openness. *Journal of Comparative Policy Analysis* 10(3): 309–322.

Eichengreen, B., and M. Kawai. 2015. *Renminbi Internationalization: Achievements, Prospects, and Challenges*. Washington, DC: Brookings Institution Press.

Eichengreen, B., and D. Leblang. 2003. Exchange Rates and Cohesion: Historical Perspectives and Political-Economy Considerations. *Journal of Common Market Studies* 41(5): 797–822.

Eichengreen, B., A. Rose, and C. Wyplosz. 1995. Exchange Market Mayhem: The Antecedents and Aftermaths of Speculative Attacks. *Economic Policy* 21: 249–312.

Eichengreen, B., A. Rose, and C. Wyplosz. 1996. Contagious Currency Crises: First Tests. *Scandinavian Journal of Economics* 98(4): 463–484.

Frankel, J. 2011. Historical Precedents for Internationalization of the RMB. A CGS/IIGG Working Paper. Washington, DC: Council on Foreign Relations.

Frankel, J.A., S.L. Schmukler, and L. Serven. 2004. Global Transmission of Interest Rates: Monetary Independence and Currency Regime. *Journal of International Money and Finance* 23(5): 701–733.

Frankel, J., and S.J. Wei. 1996. Yen Bloc or Dollar Bloc? Exchange Rate Policies in East Asian Economies. In *Macroeconomic Linkage: Savings, Exchange Rates, and Capital Flows*, edited by T. Ito and A. Krueger. Chicago: University of Chicago Press.

Ghosh, A., A. Gulde, and J. Ostry. 1997. Does the Nominal Exchange rate Regime Matter? NBER Working Paper No. 5874. Cambridge, MA: National Bureau of Economic Research.

Henry, P.B. 2007. Capital Account Liberalization: Theory, Evidence, and Speculation. *Journal of Economic Literature* 45(4): 887–935.

Ito, T. 2011. The Internationalization of the RMB: Opportunities and Pitfalls. CGS/IIGG Working Paper. Washington, DC: Council on Foreign Relations.

Ito, H., and M. Chinn. 2015. The Rise of the 'Redback' and China's Capital Account Liberalization: An Empirical Analysis on the Determinants of Invoicing Currencies. In *Renminbi Internationalization: Achievements, Prospects, and Challenges*, edited by B. Eichengreen and M. Kawai. Washington, DC: Brookings Institution Press.

Ito, H., and M. Kawai. 2014. Determinants of the Trilemma Policy Combination. ADBI Working Paper No. 456. Tokyo: Asian Development Bank Institute.

Ito, H., and M. Kawai. 2016. Trade Invoicing in Major Currencies in the 1970s–1990s: Lessons for Renminbi Internationalization. *Journal of the Japanese and International Economies* 42: 123–145.

Ito, H., and R. McCauley. 2017. *A Key Currency View of Global Imbalances. Mimeo*. Basel: Bank for International Settlements.

Klein, M., and J. Shambaugh. 2015. Rounding the Corners of the Policy Trilemma: Sources of Monetary Policy Autonomy. *American Economic Journal: Macroeconomics* 7(4) (October): 33–66.

Kose, M.A., E. Prasad, K. Rogoff, and S.J. Wei. 2009. Financial Globalization: A Reappraisal. IMF Staff Papers No. 56(1). Washington, DC: International Monetary Fund.

Levy-Yeyati, E., and F. Sturzenegger. 2003. To Float or to Fix: Evidence on the Impact of Exchange Rate Regimes on Growth. *The American Economic Review* 93(4): 1173–1193.

Mundell, R. A. 1963. Capital Mobility and Stabilization Policy under Fixed and Flexible Exchange Rates. *Canadian Journal of Economic and Political Science* 29(4): 475–485.

Obstfeld, M. 2014. *Trilemmas and Tradeoffs: Living with Financial Globalization. Mimeo.* Berkeley: University of California.

Obstfeld, M., J. C. Shambaugh, and A. M. Taylor. 2005. The Trilemma in History: Tradeoffs among Exchange rates, Monetary Policies, and Capital Mobility. *Review of Economics and Statistics* 87(August): 423–438.

Obstfeld, M., J. C. Shambaugh, and A. M. Taylor. 2010. Financial Instability, Reserves, and Central Bank Swap Lines in the Panic of 2008. *American Economic Review* 99(2): 480–486.

Prasad, E. S., K. Rogoff, S. J. Wei, and M. A. Kose. 2003. Effects of Financial Globalization on Developing Countries: Some Empirical Evidence. Occasional Paper No. 220. Washington, DC: International Monetary Fund.

Rey, H. 2013. Dilemma Not Trilemma: The Global Financial Cycle and Monetary Policy Independence. Prepared for the 2013 Jackson Hole Meeting.

Shambaugh, J. C. 2004. The Effects of Fixed Exchange Rates on Monetary Policy. *Quarterly Journal of Economics* 119(1): 301–352.

25

FINANCIAL INTEGRATION IN ASIA

Hans Genberg

Introduction

This chapter provides a review and appraisal of financial integration initiatives and outcomes in Asia. For the purposes of the chapter, the term "Asia" refers to economies in a geographical area stretching from Mongolia in the northwest to Pakistan in the southwest, Japan in the northeast, and New Zealand in the southeast. This covers jurisdictions with a wide variety of economic and financial structures, from financial centers such as Hong Kong, China and Singapore, with highly developed financial markets fully integrated with the global financial system, to economies such as Myanmar, with only nascent financial markets. As a result, and because of the purposely brief nature of the chapter, the discussion will necessarily be quite general, touching on the main features of debates and outcomes rather than attempting to provide details of the financial integration process and achievements in each jurisdiction.

The next section of the chapter provides a synopsis of the principal integration initiatives that have been undertaken in the region since the Asian financial crisis in the late 1990s. These include discussions about exchange-rate cooperation and the formation of an Asian Monetary Fund, the establishment of an Asian Bond Fund, and the creation of a multilateral foreign exchange swap agreement under the Chiang Mai Initiative Multilateralization. The section also notes particular initiatives undertaken in regional groupings such as the ASEAN economies and debates in the People's Republic of China (PRC) regarding the sequencing of capital account liberalization in relation to liberalization of domestic financial markets.

In the two subsequent sections the chapter reviews attempt to measure the evolution of financial integration in the region, relying in turn on so-called de jure measures that codify regulations on international financial transactions on the one hand and on de facto measures that rely on actual international investment positions and asset price co-movements to assess the degree of integration on the other. Attempts to interpret the sometimes contradictory results of these measurements are given. In the case of de jure measures, it is noted that these do not typically take into account the intensity of enforcement of formal regulations and could therefore understate the openness of the economy to international financial transactions. In the case of de facto measures, a distinction is made between co-movements of asset prices due to the effects of common external shocks and those that are due to arbitrage between financial markets in the region.

The final section of the chapter briefly discusses the potential consequences of closer financial integration for the effectiveness of monetary policy and introduces two topics that warrant further study: regional versus global financial integration, and whether the end goal of a financial integration process should necessarily be the elimination of all restrictions to cross-border financial transactions.

Integration initiatives

Monetary and financial integration in Asia has many facets, and differing views on how rapidly to proceed and what the ultimate goal should be have evolved over time. The evolution mirrors more general views about the trade-offs between benefits and costs of integration of financial markets. At the individual country level, the desire to integrate is driven by the perceived benefits of being part of the global financial system. Among these benefits are greater opportunities for portfolio diversification and risk sharing, enhanced competition in the domestic market for financial services, and increased ability to smooth consumption amid fluctuations in domestic economic activity. Initiatives to liberalize international capital movements may also have been driven by peer pressures associated with the so-called Washington Consensus according to which free mobility of capital was to be encouraged by institutions such as the International Monetary Fund (IMF).

In the years since the Asian financial crisis, views on the desirability of capital account liberalization have evolved. Potential costs associated with the volatility of capital flows, and consequent implications for macroeconomic instability more generally, are now routinely invoked as reasons why a completely open capital account may not be desirable, at least before domestic financial markets are sufficiently developed to intermediate smoothly potentially large shifts in international investors' risk aversion and the resulting large in- or outflows of capital from emerging market economies. A similar argument holds that opening the economy to larger capital flows should wait until instruments for hedging risks associated with exchange-rate fluctuations are readily available and routinely used by domestic economic agents.

Current debates in many Asian jurisdictions reflect these trade-offs between the costs and benefits of capital account liberalization. This debate is particularly significant in the PRC, where proponents of external liberalization as a way to foster competition in the domestic market for financial services and to increase the role of the yuan as an international currency are pitted against those who warn about the potential instability associated with international capital flows in the context of still not fully developed domestic financial system. The debate and the pace of opening up the PRC financial market is significant because of the consequences they carry for other economies in the region and indeed for the international financial system as a whole. A PRC economy that is more open to the global financial system is likely to lead to greater fluctuation of the yuan relative to the US dollar and the euro which in turn could have significant impacts on smaller regional economies which engage in trade in goods and services with each of these three regions. A more open PRC economy is also significant for the international monetary system as a whole, because it is likely to lead to a greater role of the yuan in international finance and trade alongside the US dollar. Whether a bi-polar or multi-polar international financial system is more or less stable than the current system dominated by the US currency is an open question.

At the regional level, the most significant development is arguably the efforts of ASEAN countries to integrate their financial markets.[1] These efforts are part of a more ambitious initiative to create an ASEAN Economic Community (AEC) to promote economic, political, social and cultural cooperation across the region. The goal is for the AEC to be "highly integrated and cohesive; competitive, innovative, and dynamic; with enhanced connectivity and sectoral cooperation; and a more resilient, inclusive, and people-oriented, people-centred community, integrated with the global economy [by 2025]."[2] The financial aspects of the ASEAN integration process cover many areas such as banking integration, capital market development – involving efforts to facilitate cross-border securities offerings, common disclosure standards, transparent corporate governance frameworks, and cross-border settlement services – bond market development (on which more is said below), and cross-border payment simplification. A recent notable example of cross-border payment simplification involves an agreement between the central banks of Malaysia and Thailand to promote bilateral trade settlement in the local currencies rather than through a vehicle currency.

These financial integration efforts are underpinned by capacity-building initiatives undertaken bilaterally by ASEAN-5 central banks and multilaterally through such institutions as the SEACEN Centre in Kuala Lumpur and the Asian Development Bank. The objective of these initiatives is to promote greater understanding and readiness in the less financially developed BCLMV economies in the group for the challenges associated with greater financial integration in ASEAN as a whole.

At the multilateral level, a number of significant developments are noteworthy. The experience with large intra-regional exchange-rate fluctuations resulting from the Asian financial crisis combined with the early positive assessment of the monetary unification process in Europe led to an interest in exploring the usefulness of some form of coordinated exchange rate policy and even monetary union in Asia.[3] This author argued that a strategy of pursuing greater financial integration, on the one hand, and coordinated exchange rate policy on the other, would be destabilizing in the absence of a much more developed institutional framework, and proposed an alternative framework for collaboration among central banks focusing on policy objectives rather than on outcomes (Genberg 2006). Other papers were written to explore which countries could plausibly be considered to constitute a stable (if not fully optimal) currency area based on the optimal currency (Genberg and Siklos 2010). As it happened, policy-makers were not persuaded and there is currently little remaining enthusiasm for the idea of Asian monetary unification in the foreseeable future, particularly in view of the recent difficulties in the euro area.

While formal exchange rate coordination has not been embraced, actual exchange rate movements do reflect a different reality now compared to the pre-July 2015 period when the yuan was effectively pegged to the US dollar. Since the loosening of this peg, movements in the currencies of several of the smaller Asian economies are more sensitive to the CNY/USD exchange rate than previously.[4] This may be due in part to conscious policy decisions, but it may also simply reflect market reactions to the reality of increasing economic relations and competition with the PRC.

More progress has been achieved in the promotion of a local currency bond market. The Asian Bond Market Initiative (ABMI) signed by ASEAN+3 finance ministers in 2003 led to the launch of the Asian Bond Fund by the governors of 11 central banks in Asia and the Pacific region.[5] An important achievement of ABMI has been to foster harmonization of regulations on cross-border bond transactions in the region. Nevertheless, the size of emerging economy bond markets in the region, particularly corporate bond markets, is still small (Genberg 2015).[6]

At the time of the Annual Meeting of the IMF and World Bank in Hong Kong, China in September 1997, the Japanese authorities proposed the establishment of an Asian Monetary Fund (AMF) that would assist Asian countries in future economic crises. In particular, the AMF was supposed to provide liquidity support for countries with balance of payments difficulties. The proposal met with strong resistance from the IMF and the US Treasury, and the AMF never saw the light of day. However, the idea of a regionally funded safety net was born and led in 2000 to an agreement among the ASEAN+3 central bank governors to establish a bilateral network of foreign reserve swaps, the Chiang Mai Initiative, that could be used by members in the event of a crisis. The bilateral nature of the agreement was cumbersome, and it was expanded to a multilateral arrangement, the Chiang Mai Initiative Multilateralization, in 2010. It currently has a size of USD 240 billion (Kawai 2015).

Measuring financial integration 1: de jure and (quantity-based) de facto measures

In this section, we review attempts to measure the degree of financial integration by documenting formal restrictions placed on international financial transactions in an economy, and by measuring the degree to which domestic (foreign) residents hold foreign (domestic) assets. The former measures are conventionally referred to as de jure measures, whereas the latter are intended to capture de facto financial integration.

De jure measures

De jure measures are typically based on the IMF publication Annual Report of Exchange Arrangements and Exchange Restrictions, which provides descriptive accounts of measures taken by members to restrict capital account transactions. A number of authors have converted these descriptions into numerical measures of financial openness.[7] One example is the Chinn–Ito index described in Chinn and Ito (2006). The Chinn–Ito index is calculated as the first principal component of indices indicating the presence of multiple exchange rates, restrictions on current account transactions, restrictions on capital account transactions, and requirements to surrender export proceeds. It is available for 182 countries for the period 1970 to 2013.

A more granular index has just been constructed and described in Fernandez et al. (2015) and also made available online. It focuses only on capital account transactions, but takes into account 10 different types of assets and distinguishes between capital inflows and outflows. It has been tabulated for 100 countries over the period 1995 to 2013.

Figure 25.1 shows the Chinn–Ito openness index in the form of an average for 24 economies in East Asia and the Pacific region.[8] For ease of comparison with openness indices presented

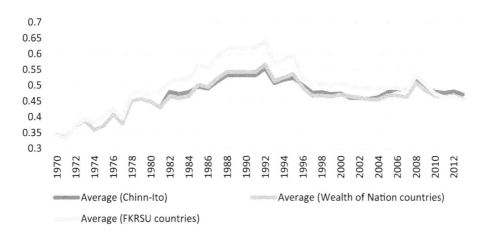

Figure 25.1   Degree of financial openness based on the Chinn-Ito index

FKRSU = Fernandez, Klein, Rebucci, Schindler, and Uribe index.

Source: Own calculations using the Chinn-Ito database.

later, the figure also shows the Chinn-Ito average for those countries that are also included in the Fernandez et al. database,[9] and those for which we have quantity-based openness indices.[10] For all three groups, there is a clear trend increase in financial openness from the start of the sample until the early 1990s, after which there is a small but still noticeable gradual decrease.

Figure 25.2 is based on the Fernandez et al. database.[11] As already noted, this database started only in 1995, but allows for a distinction between controls on outflows and inflows and between different types of assets. For bond flows as well as equity flows, there is a notable decrease in the degree of de jure financial openness in Asia based also on this index. For direct investment flows, there is a difference between outflow and inflow restrictions. The regime for outflows has become slightly more open over time whereas the opposite is the case for inflows. For total flows, which also include commercial credit, financial credit, money market, residential assets, derivatives, collective investments, and guarantees, sureties and financial backup facilities, there is also a difference between openness to inflows and outflows: on average, the economies in the sample have become slightly more open with respect to inflows, whereas they have become less so with respect to outflows.

On balance, the message from these two indices of de jure financial openness seems to be that while Asian economies on average became more open during the 1970s and 1980s, the trend since then has if anything been the reverse. It bears repeating, however, that these indices are based on measures of statutory restrictions on international financial transactions reported to the IMF. The degree to which the restrictions are enforced is not recorded.

Quantity-based measures

Quantity-based indices of financial openness are intended to record the extent to which domestic residents hold foreign financial assets in their portfolios and correspondingly what proportion of domestic financial instruments are held by nonresidents. There are two difficulties associated with constructing and interpreting these indices. First, while balance of payments statistics provide reasonably comprehensive data on the cross-border flow of financial assets, there is much less information about international investment positions which are the results of these flows but which are also affected to an important extent by valuation changes. In addition, cumulating flows to obtain stock figures require accurate starting values if they are to be reliable.

The second problem associated with quantity-based measures of financial openness relates to interpretation. What would be the extent of international portfolio diversification in the absence of statutory restrictions on such diversification? Calculating the benchmark so defined would require a model of optimal international diversification rendering the interpretation of the index dependent on the appropriateness of the model.

The problem associated with measuring international investment positions has been addressed in the meticulous work by Lane and Milesi-Ferreti (2007). The latest database available contains data on stocks of assets and liabilities related to portfolio equity investments, foreign direct investments, debt, financial derivatives, and foreign exchange reserves for the period 1970 to 2011 for 189 jurisdictions/regions.[12] These data make it possible to trace the evolution of the international asset and liability position of an economy over time. In lieu of a model of optimal international portfolio diversification, a common metric used to interpret this evolution is to relate foreign asset holdings to the size of the economy (i.e., to its GDP). However, one difficulty of interpreting this metric is that financial deepening may lead to an increase in this index without there being any increase in international diversification as such. For this reason, this chapter considers an alternative measure which can be thought of as the degree of de facto integration of economy *i relative* to the average integration of all other economies in the world

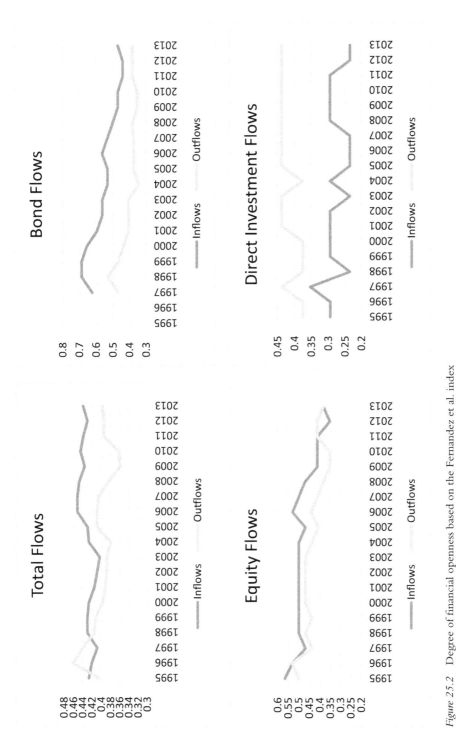

Figure 25.2 Degree of financial openness based on the Fernandez et al. index

Source: Author's calculations using the Fernandez et al. database.

(W), that is, $\dfrac{\dfrac{FA^i}{GDP^i}}{\dfrac{FA^w}{GDP^w}}$. While this measure does control for generalized financial deepening, it is

not perfect, since such deepening does not necessarily proceed at equal speed in all economies and regions. Nevertheless, we believe that it is a more informative measure of a region's de facto integration into the global financial market.

The index is presented in Figure 25.3 together with the more traditional index that measures the foreign asset position only in relation to domestic GDP. The index is calculated as the average of those 22 countries that overlap with the Chinn-Ito sample.[13] Two versions are presented, one with and one without Hong Kong, China and Singapore, two economies that are large international financial centers, which may distort the results.

The left-hand panel is consistent with the hypothesis that the ratio of foreign assets to GDP increases over time as a result of financial deepening. It also shows that Hong Kong, China and Singapore are special cases due to their status as financial centers, and that averages including them need to be interpreted with care. The right-hand panel adjusts for financial deepening using an index that measures the financial openness of Asia relative to the financial opening of the world as a whole. It shows that since at least the early 1990s and possibly even the mid-1970s the integration of Asian economies into the global financial system has declined over time in comparison with the integration of other regions.

Figure 25.4 provides another perspective on the de facto integration of a subset of Asian economies for which the corresponding data are available in the IMF's Coordinated Portfolio Investment Survey.[14] These data record portfolio holdings of residents of an economy of liabilities issued by residents of another economy. In the figure, the issuing countries have been aggregated into Asia, ASEAN, and the World. Thus, in the left-hand panel the entries for Malaysia, for example, show the ratio of holdings in Malaysia of liabilities issued by all other Asian economies relative to the holdings of liabilities issued by all reporting economies. As an average for the period from 2001 to 2006 prior to the global financial crisis (GFC) this ratio stood at 24%. It rose to 36% after the GFC suggesting that Malaysia became relatively more integrated with its Asian neighbors. The same panel shows that this is the case also for the other ASEAN-5 economies. The right-hand panel contains a similar message: intra-Asian financial integration has increases from before the GFC in four of the six economies represented, with a decline only in the case of India and an unchanged level in New Zealand.

Remolona and Shim (2015) contains similar information for cross-border banking relationships. Using the BIS locational banking statistics, the authors show that cross-border bank lending to emerging economies in Asia by Asia and the Pacific region banks has increased substantially subsequent to the GFC, outpacing considerably lending conducted by European and US banks. They also suggest that while much of the cross-border lending is currently intermediated by banks residents in the two financial centers, Hong Kong, China and Singapore, the Qualified ASEAN Bank initiative adopted by members of ASEAN is likely to have an impact on cross-border banking relationships more generally. Under this initiative, ASEAN banks meeting specific criteria will be given enhanced access to other ASEAN markets. This is likely to foster increased banking integration in ASEAN economies much like the "single passport" for banks operating in the European Economic Area did in Europe. For the time being, the Qualified ASEAN Bank initiative is being implemented on a bilateral reciprocal basis until all members are ready to open their banking sector to external competition.

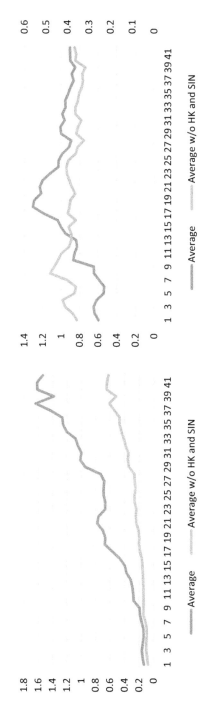

Figure 25.3 Degree of financial openness based on actual holdings of foreign assets

HK = Hong Kong, China, SIN = Singapore.

Source: Author's calculations based on an updated and extended version of dataset constructed by Lane and Milesi-Ferretti (2007).

Figure 25.4　Holdings of liabilities issued by residents of countries in Asia (ASEAN) relative to holdings of liabilities issued by all reporting economies, "World"

ASEAN = Association of Southeast Asian Nations.

Source: Author's calculations based on the International Monetary Fund's Coordinated Portfolio Investment Survey.

Provisional conclusion

The measures shown in this section do not present a clear trend in the degree of integration of financial markets neither within Asia and the Pacific region nor between Asia and the Pacific region and global financial markets. While some measures do suggest that integration both within the region and externally has increased, others are less equivocal. The lack of a clear-cut assessment is likely a reflection of the difficulty in measuring financial integration. As already noted, there are reasons why the conventional measures proposed in the literature and used here may not give an accurate picture of the actual degree of integration. In particular, de jure measures do not take into account the level of enforcement of statutory regulations on capital flows, and the quantity-based de facto measures may be contaminated by financial deepening. In addition, it should be stressed that the measures presented represent averages; results for individual countries may tell different stories, but to uncover them is beyond the scope of this chapter.

Measuring financial integration 2: price-based measures

As noted, de jure and quantity-based de facto measures of financial integration are not without drawbacks. For this reason, researchers have turned to price-based measures. The underlying principle is simple: in the absence of restrictions on arbitrage, prices of two assets with identical attributes should be the same, even if they are traded in different locations. In practice, it is difficult to identify assets with identical attributes, so tests for integration in this spirit are typically concerned with co-movements over time in asset prices and returns across jurisdictions.

A very large number of studies have been undertaken to assess financial integration using price-based measures applied to equity markets, bond markets, and to a lesser extent money markets. For equity markets, the emphasis has been on correlations between market indices across jurisdictions. Four main results emerge. First, although the correlations fluctuate, there is a tendency for them to increase over time. Second, correlations between Asian markets and world markets, often represented by the US market, are typically larger than the correlations between markets within Asia. Third, although it is not generally emphasized, it appears that correlations with the world market tend to increase during turbulent periods. Fourth, correlations involving the PRC stock market are generally lower than correlations that do not.

How to interpret these results? The last seems the easiest to explain. Controls on capital account transactions in the PRC prevent significant arbitrage activities between the domestic market and foreign markets thus limiting co-movements of prices. A particularly vivid example of this lack of arbitrage is the large price differences between prices of shares of the same company listed in the PRC (so-called A shares) on the one hand and on the Hong Kong, China market (H shares) on the other. The former have typically traded at a considerable premium without the possibility of traders to benefit from the price difference.

What about the result that correlations have tended to increase over time? One likely reason is that financial integration has effectively increased tying markets together more closely as fund managers are increasingly able to diversify their portfolios across jurisdictions without being encumbered by legal restrictions. But such diversification would not necessarily lead to greater co-movement of prices unless there are fundamental reasons why share prices in different economies should move together, at least partially. Increased trade integration, and increased use of cross-border production chains – so-called global value chains – provide such a reason however. If trade integration leads to increased real linkages between companies across borders, then the share prices of those companies will show certain co-movements whether or not there is actual cross-border trading in such shares. Of course, if there is such cross-border trading, the co-movements will tend to be correspondingly larger.

The preceding paragraph illustrates a general point, namely that co-movements of equity markets across jurisdictions may not necessarily be the result of transmission from one market to another, but rather of the reaction of several markets to common shocks. This could then explain the third result mentioned above, that correlations between stock markets tend to increase during turbulent periods in financial markets such as during the Asian financial crisis, the dot-com bubble, and the recent GFC originating in the US and Europe. In the last of these, when global stock market correlations seem to have increased particularly significantly, the common external shock was particularly large in Asia compared with the idiosyncratic shocks affecting each Asian economy separately. It is easy to show that in such a situation, the correlation with the global (read: US) market will increase.

The common-shock hypothesis is also consistent with the second result in the literature, that correlations between each Asian market separately and the world market are larger than the correlations between two Asian markets. This result does not necessarily mean that Asian markets are not integrated, but that they are driven in part by country-specific idiosyncratic shocks. In addition, if the structure of Asian economies differs, they may react differently to common external shocks so that bilateral correlations will be lower than the correlation with the world market. A particularly vivid illustration of this is the reaction of equity markets in different countries to commodity price shocks. The market in a commodity-exporting country could be expected to react very differently from that in a commodity-importing country.

Results from comparisons of sovereign bond yields across Asian economies share some characteristics of those for equities, but they also display some noteworthy differences. First, interest rate spreads on sovereign bonds over comparable US treasury securities have declined since the Asian financial crisis with a notable exception of a large increase during the GFC. The declining spread over time is consistent with the idea that Asian bond markets have become increasingly integrated with global bond markets, just like the increased correlation of equity indices with their global counterparts could be interpreted as increased integration of equity markets. The increasing bond spreads during crisis periods is, however, contrary to the increasing correlation in equity markets during such periods. The likely explanation is a "flight to safety" in bond markets in crisis times leading to sharply increased spreads in emerging markets.

Second, cross-country differences in bond spreads have also declined over time, again with breaks during periods of market turbulence. The first part of this finding is again consistent with the hypothesis of increased regional integration of bond markets, whereas the second part suggests that global investors' flight to safety is differentiated according to country specifics, and that regional investors do not counter this tendency.

Third, just like in equity markets, global factors play an important role in the evolution of bond spreads in Asia, although domestic factors are also significant.

Overall, the results are consistent with the hypothesis of increasing bond market integration in the region. However, an alternative explanation of the results is also possible. According to this, the reason for declining Asian bond spreads over US treasuries and for declining cross-country differences of these spreads is that the risk of Asian sovereigns has declined over time and has also become more similar across countries. In part, this would be a reflection of increasingly prudent fiscal policies and more transparent monetary policy regimes pursued by central banks with increased independence from their political masters (Filardo and Genberg 2010).

Policy implications and issues for further analysis

Monetary policy

As already noted, financial integration influences the impact of monetary policy, a point that has been appreciated in the literature at least since the work of Robert Mundell and Marcus Fleming in the 1950s which has since been incorporated in standard international macroeconomics as the Mundell-Fleming model. It says that when exchange rates are fixed, monetary policy will gradually lose its effectiveness as financial integration (capital mobility) increases. With floating exchange rates, on the contrary, monetary policy will gain effectiveness as financial integration proceeds. An important part of the transmission takes place through the exchange channel.

Recently a body of literature exemplified by Rey (2013) and Turner (2015) argues that monetary policy has become less effective as financial integration has increased even in economies with flexible exchange rates.[15] The argument is based on empirical results indicating that interest rates in such economies co-move with conditions of the global financial markets, particularly during turbulent periods. But as already noted the *relatively* less strong influence of domestic monetary policy during such periods could simply be the result of external shocks being larger as noted in the previous section. Central bank policy can still influence monetary conditions even with increased financial integration. This is even more so when the exchange rate channel is taken into account (Georgiadis and Mehl 2015).

It should also be remembered that co-movement of domestic and international interest rates which are interpreted as a sign of reduced monetary policy effectiveness may instead be the result either of central banks reacting in similar ways to common external shocks or not pursuing output and inflation stabilization objectives as vigorously as previously, because they are concerned with other objectives, in particular, exchange-rate fluctuations. Such fluctuations may have become larger as a consequence of increased international integration of financial markets. The implication here is not that monetary policy has become less effective, but rather that central banks have chosen to use it less aggressively for demand management purposes.

Regional versus global integration

Monetary and financial integration in Asia is an evolving project. As we have seen, in some cases it involves purely regional initiatives, but in others it involves integration with global financial markets. Indeed, financial centers like Hong Kong, China and Singapore are essentially fully integrated with global markets. This raises issues related to the benefits from regional integration among a set of countries as distinct from each one separately integrating with the global financial system.[16] Pursuing capital account openness on a regional level has been offered as a way to modify the terms of the trade-off between efficiency gains from an open capital account and the associated risk of instability. While foregoing full integration with global financial markets would constitute a cost, this would be more than compensated for, the argument goes, by having a larger regional capital market that would be better able to absorb swings in international investor sentiment. The threat of financial stability would be reduced.

This of course presumes that financial shocks originate primarily in the global financial system rather than within the integrating region. This may be a reasonable assumption at present, but policy-makers should not lose sight of the possibility that when a region becomes more financially integrated, disparate economic developments and country-specific shocks will more easily spill over and threaten financial stability in neighboring countries. Recent developments in the euro area offer a vivid example. To guard against this possibility, regional integration initiatives should be accompanied by enhanced surveillance of financial markets and coordinated supervision of institutions that have substantial cross-border activities.[17]

Another aspect of the regional-versus-global integration question relates to the benefits from international portfolio diversification. Information from the IMF's Coordinated Portfolio Investment Survey on cross-border asset holdings used in Figure 25.4 above to show that while intra-Asian cross-border holdings of assets have increased since before the GFC relative to holdings of assets issued in other jurisdictions the intra-Asia holdings are still smaller.[18] This echoes results in Park (2013) which showed that advanced economies still account for a major share of international asset portfolios of economies in Asia. One interpretation of these results would be that there are still obstacles to diversification across regional markets and that integration efforts should be strengthened so that the share of regional investors' portfolios held with the region will increase at the expense of the share held outside the regions. This, however, overlooks the possibility that gains from diversification within a region have limitations due to similarities of the economic structures and the intra-regional co-movements of business cycles. What optimally diversified portfolios should consist of in "typical" Asian emerging economies, and how this compares with actual portfolio allocations would be an interesting topic to investigate.

What should be the goal of Asian financial integration?

A thoughtful study sponsored and published by the Asian Development Bank in 2013 contains two statements that illustrate the complexity of the issue of financial integration. On the one hand, it states that "ASEAN does not envision the complete elimination of all restrictions, prudential or otherwise, on cross-border capital flows, even by 2020 or 2025" (p. 26), thus reflecting the increasingly common view that removal of all controls on cross-border financial transactions may not be desirable because of the heightened risk of financial instability originating in volatile capital flows. On the other hand, the online summary of the study also states that "Full and complete capital account and financial services liberalization is ultimately key to the success of the AEC."[19]

To reconcile the two statements, it is necessary to think of the full liberalization process as taking a long time because of the need to build the institutional and policy infrastructure that can support completely integrated financial markets. The recently coined term "financial trilemma" contends that financial stability, financial integration, and national financial policies are incompatible (Schoenmaker 2011). Any two of the three can prevail, but not all three. As giving up financial stability is clearly not an option, some coordination of national financial policies will thus be necessary if full financial integration is the goal. It is perhaps for this reason that ASEAN does not envision that full capital account liberalization can be achieved before 2020 according to the ADB study.

In fact, the most recent blueprint for the ASEAN economic community does not mention full capital account liberalization as an objective even for 2025. Instead, its vision for financial market integration in 2025 mentions financial inclusion and financial stability as important complements to integration as such. It explicitly recognizes the dangers associated with increased financial integration by noting the necessity of adopting "adequate safeguards measures against potential macroeconomic instability and systemic risks that may arise from the liberalization process, including the right to adopt the necessary measures to ensure macroeconomic and financial stability" (ASEAN Secretariat 2017: 10).

But if dismantling restrictions on capital account transactions is pursued, even gradually, might the region not arrive at a tipping point where the remaining controls become ineffective? And if so, what will be the consequences for financial stability? The answer may be that building a robust framework for domestic and cross-border financial regulation must come prior to capital account liberalization between integrating economies. While this is recognized by ASEAN policy-makers, its implementation faces both conceptual and practical hurdles discussed elsewhere in this volume.

Notes

1 The ASEAN members are frequently divided into two groups distinguished by their degree of economic and financial development: the ASEAN-5, which includes Indonesia, Malaysia, Philippines, Singapore, and Thailand, and the BCLMV members: Brunei Darussalam, Cambodia, Lao PDR, Myanmar, and Viet Nam.

2 ASEAN Community Vision 2025. p. 15 (www.asean.org/wp-content/uploads/images/2015/November/aec-page/ASEAN-Community-Vision-2025.pdf (accessed 10 April 2017). For a recent review, see Volz (2016).

3 See Volz (2010) for a comprehensive review and analysis.

4 See Kawai and Pontines (2016) and references therein.

5 The 11 central banks are the Reserve Bank of Australia, People's Bank of China, Hong Kong Monetary Authority, Bank Indonesia, Bank of Japan, the Bank of Korea, Bank Negara Malaysia, Reserve Bank of New Zealand, Bangko Sentral ng Pilipinas, Monetary Authority of Singapore, and Bank of Thailand. They go under the acronym EMEAP (Executives' Meeting of East Asia Pacific Central Banks) and their work has evolved to constitute an important foundation for central bank cooperation on a number of issues of common concern. See https://aric.adb.org/initiative/executives-meeting-of-east-asia-pacific-central-banks-initiative for descriptions of the initial Fund as well as the subsequent Asian Bond Fund 2.

6 The corporate bond market in Malaysia is an exception, as is the size of the overall bond market in the PRC.

7 It should be noted that while the indices measure whether or not restrictions are in place, they do not capture the extent to which they are enforced.

8 Australia; Bangladesh; Bhutan; Cambodia; the PRC; Hong Kong, China; India; Indonesia; Japan; Republic of Korea; Lao PDR; Malaysia; Maldives; Mongolia; Myanmar; Nepal; New Zealand; Pakistan; Philippines; Papua New Guinea; Singapore; Sri Lanka; Thailand; and Viet Nam.

9 Australia; Bangladesh; the PRC; Hong Kong, China; India; Indonesia; Japan; Republic of Korea; Malaysia; Myanmar; New Zealand; Pakistan; Philippines; Singapore; Sri Lanka; Thailand; and Viet Nam.

10 The latter are referred to in the figure as Wealth of Nation Countries. See below for details.

11 The Fernandez et al. index measures restrictions on capital flows on a scale from 0 (no restrictions) to 1 (completely closed capital account). To ease visual comparison with the Chinn-Ito index, the numbers in Figure 25.2 show 1 minus the Fernandez et. al. index.

12 www.philiplane.org/EWN.html.

13 The two countries missing are Bhutan and Cambodia.

14 I am grateful to Ulrich Volz for drawing my attention to this survey.

15 Much the same argument had been made a decade earlier in Frankel, Schmukler, and Serven (2004).

16 On this topic, see Martin (2011).

17 Indeed, the establishment in 2011 of the ASEAN+3 Macroeconomic Research Office (AMRO) by the ASEAN+3 governments goes some way toward addressing this need for regional surveillance. According to the agreement establishing the office, "the purpose of AMRO is to contribute to securing the economic and financial stability of the region through conducting regional economic surveillance and supporting the implementation of the regional financial arrangement."

18 In view of the efforts made by ASEAN economies to promote financial integration, a somewhat surprising result in Figure 25.4 is the middle panel which shows that intra-ASEAN cross-border holdings have declined in four of the five reporting ASEAN economies relative to their holdings of assets issued by non-ASEAN Asian economies.

19 www.adb.org/publications/road-asean-financial-integration (accessed 10 April 2017).

References

ASEAN Secretariat. 2017. *ASEAN Economic Community Blueprint 2025*. Jakarta: ASEAN Secretariat.

Asian Development Bank. 2013. *The Road to ASEAN Financial Integration*. Manila: Asian Development Bank.

Chinn, M.D., and H. Ito. 2006. What Matters for Financial Development? Capital Controls, Institutions, and Interactions. *Journal of Development Economics* 81(1): 163–192.

Fernandez, A., M. Klein, A. Rebucci, M. Schindler, and M. Uribe. 2015. Capital Control Measures: A New Dataset. NBER Working Paper No. 20970. Cambridge, MA: National Bureau of Economic Research.

Filardo, A., and H. Genberg. 2010. Targeting Inflation in Asia and the Pacific: Lessons from the Recent Past. In *Inflation Targeting Twenty Years On: Past Lessons and Future Prospects*, edited by David Cobham, Oyvind Eitrheim, Stefan Gerlach, and Jan F. Qvigstand. Cambridge, MA: Cambridge University Press.

Frankel, J., S. Schmukler, and L. Serven. 2004. Global Transmission of Interest Rates: Monetary Independence and Currency Regime. *Journal of International Money and Finance* 23: 701–733.

Genberg, H. 2006. Exchange-Rate Arrangements and Financial Integration in East Asia: On a Collision Course? *International Economics and Economic Policy* 3(3): 359–377.

Genberg, H. 2015. Capital Market Development and Emergence of Institutional Investors in the Asia-Pacific Region. *Asia-Pacific Development Journal* 22(2): 1–26.

Genberg, H., and P.L. Siklos. 2010. Revisiting the Shocking Aspects of Asian Monetary Unification. *Journal of Asian Economics* 21(5): 445–455.

Georgiadis, G., and A. Mehl. 2015. Trilemma, Not Dilemma: Financial Globalisation and Monetary Policy Effectiveness. http://dallasfed.org/assets/documents/institute/wpapers/2015/0222.pdf

Kawai, M. 2015. From the Chiang Mai Initiative to an Asian Monetary Fund. ADBI Working Paper No. 527. Tokyo: Asian Development Bank Institute.

Kawai, M., and V. Pontines. 2016. Is there Really a Renminbi Block in Asia? A Modified Frankel-Wei Approach. *Journal of International Money and Finance* 62: 72–97.

Lane, P., and G.M. Milesi-Ferretti. 2007. The External Wealth of Nations Mark II: Revised and Extended Estimates of Foreign Assets and Liabilities, 1970–2004. *Journal of International Economics* 73: 223–250.

Martin, P. 2011. Regional and Global Financial Integration: An Analytical Framework. In *The Dynamics of Asian Financial Integration Facts and Analytics*, edited by M. Devereux, P. Lane, C. Park, and S. Wei. London and New York: Routledge.

Park, C. 2013. Asian Capital Market Integration: Theory and Evidence. ADB Economics Working Paper No. 351. Manila: Asian Development Bank.

Remolona, E., and I. Shim. 2015. The Rise of Regional Banking in Asia and the Pacific. *BIS Quarterly Review* (September): 119–134.

Rey, H. 2013. Dilemma Not Trilemma: The Global Financial Cycle and Monetary Policy Independence. Federal Reserve Bank of Kansas City Economic Policy Symposium.

Schoenmaker, D. 2011. The Financial Trilemma. *Economics Letters* 111: 57–59.

Turner, P. 2015. Global Monetary Policies and Markets: Policy Dilemmas in the Emerging Markets. *Comparative Economic Studies* 57: 276–299.

Volz, U. 2010. *Prospects for Monetary Cooperation and Integration in East Asia*. Cambridge, MA: The MIT Press.

Volz, U. 2016. Regional Financial Integration in East Asia against the Backdrop of Recent European Experiences. *International Economic Journal* 30(2): 272–293.

26

BANKING REGULATION AND SUPERVISION IN ASIA

Michael J. Zamorski[1]

Introduction

Asian economies are very diverse in terms of the size, complexity, and stage of development of their financial systems. While there are some advanced economies in Asia, such as Japan; Republic of Korea; Hong Kong, China; and Singapore, most of the region consists of emerging market economies (EMEs). One common feature of Asian economies is that their banking systems play an important role in facilitating economic growth.

Access to capital markets to finance business activity is generally available only to larger, well-established companies with a track record of stable financial performance. Small and medium-sized enterprises (SMEs), fledgling entrepreneurs, and consumers rely significantly on banks and non-bank lenders, such as finance companies, to obtain credit.[2] SMEs are a major contributor to gross domestic product (GDP) in EMEs. Therefore, to achieve sustainable economic growth and development, it is important that Asia's banking systems consist of sound, stable, and resilient banks positioned to meet the productive credit needs of their customers.

A sound banking system is one where problems are manageable and, while there might be some bank failures, they are not large or systemic,[3] and their overall impact is small. Effective bank regulation and supervision are key factors in maintaining banking system soundness.

This chapter provides a background on banking regulation and supervision in Asia and highlights major issues in establishing effective bank regulatory and supervision programs. Information is also provided on the relative strength of bank regulation and supervision programs for selected Asian jurisdictions.

Financial stability, systemic risk, and banking system "safety nets"

The concept of financial stability does not have a universally accepted definition. One description of financial stability that captures common elements cited by many observers is

> a condition where (a jurisdiction's) financial system – comprising institutions, markets and infrastructure – is able to: allocate savings to investment opportunities efficiently; ensure the rapid settlement of payments; effectively manage potential risks that may harm its performance; and absorb shocks without impairing its operations.[4]

Responsibility for promoting financial stability is frequently included in central banks' (CBs) legal mandates. However, one or more other domestic authorities may also be involved, including non-CB bank supervisors and regulators; financial market regulators; deposit insurers; and finance ministries. These same authorities usually also constitute a jurisdiction's banking system "safety net," which consists of national authorities who have differing legal mandates, but work together to ensure banking system stability during times of stress or crisis:

- CBs frequently have direct responsibility for the chartering/licensing, regulation and supervision of banks – this is by far the predominant arrangement adopted by Asian jurisdictions. Under their lender of last resort function, CBs have discretionary authority to provide short-term loans to banks to assist them in a temporary liquidity emergency;
- Non-CB bank regulators have primary responsibility for the licensing, regulation and supervision of banks in some Asian jurisdictions (e.g., People's Republic of China [PRC], Japan, Indonesia, Republic of Korea);
- Financial market regulators are typically charged with maintaining fair and orderly financial markets, such as stock and commodities exchanges, and may oversee exchange-traded companies' financial reporting;
- Deposit insurers promote public confidence in a banking system by protecting the safety of depositors' funds in the event of bank failures. They may also be responsible for arranging orderly resolutions of failing banks. Some deposit insurers may have secondary bank examination authority and/or a role in bank license/charter revocations;
- Finance ministries are mainly involved in providing government funds (i.e., taxpayers' funds), when crises pose systemic risk and governmental intervention is deemed warranted to preserve public confidence in the banking system.

A 2001 Group of Ten report describes "systemic financial risk" as

> the risk that an event will trigger a loss of economic value or confidence in, and attendant increases in uncertainty about, a substantial portion of the financial system that is serious enough to quite probably have significant adverse effects on the real economy.[5]

Individual banks can also pose risks to jurisdictions' financial stability – these are referred to as systemically important banks (SIBs) – if they encounter financial difficulties severe enough to threaten their viability or solvency. The regulatory and supervisory implications of SIBs are discussed later in this chapter.

Overview of the banking business

Credit intermediation

Banks' specific business models vary. However, their primary business activity is making loans which are funded by accepting deposits from individuals and corporations – referred to as the banks' credit intermediation function. Banks are chartered and licensed by governmental authorities in large part based on their commitment to provide reliable access to credit products and other essential financial services in their local communities.

Effective corporate governance: the first "line of defense" in protecting bank soundness

Why do some banks succeed while others underperform or encounter problems that can jeopardize their stability or even viability? Banks' corporate governance, risk management capabilities, and risk culture are the main differentiating factors in bank performance and soundness. For this reason, bank supervisors focus on these areas during bank examinations.

Corporate governance has various definitions. The Organisation for Economic Co-operation and Development (OECD) describes corporate governance as "the structure through which the objectives of (a) company are set, and the means of attaining those objectives and monitoring performance are determined" (OECD 2015: 9).

An active, interested, and vigilant bank board of directors serves as an effective "check and balance" on excessive risk-taking, and monitoring the performance of a bank's senior executive management. Members of a bank's board of directors have individual and collective legal duties to ensure that a bank's business is conducted prudently and risk tolerance is within reasonable limits.

The nature of bank regulation and supervision

Bank regulation and supervision are closely related and are frequently the responsibility of the same national authority. While the terms "regulation" and "supervision" tend to be used interchangeably, they are not the same.

Bank regulation

Bank regulation encompasses the body of laws, rules, and implementing regulations specifying minimum licensing and operational requirements to ensure prudent operation and proper conduct of business. Prudential laws, rules, and regulations impose restrictions and limitations on banks' business activities are designed to ensure that they operate in a safe and sound manner and maintain a safe and sound condition.

Banks are also typically subject to laws, rules and regulations on how they conduct business, including consumer protection obligations. Bank regulators and supervisors also issue regulatory guidance to explain or clarify regulatory/supervisory expectations as to how banks should comply with specific laws, rules, and regulations.

Bank supervision

Bank supervision encompasses both prudential supervision, sometimes referred to as microprudential supervision, and macroprudential supervision. Prudential supervision has historically focused on assessing individual banks' safety and soundness, primarily through on-site bank examinations. Macroprudential supervision refers to the imposition of rules, regulations, or policies intended to control risk to the banking system more broadly, for example, bank minimum capital requirements and limits on the amount banks can lend on various types of collateral.

On-site bank supervision activities are supplemented by offsite surveillance of banks' financial performance. Offsite surveillance is a useful tool in detecting "red flags" and "outliers" in prioritizing finite examiner resources. However, it is not a substitute for on-site examinations or inspections conducted at reasonable intervals by experienced professionals, with an appropriate level of transaction testing.[6]

471

Regulatory and supervisory architecture

Designing effective regulatory and supervisory oversight structures for the financial services industry (banks, insurers, wealth management, securities brokerage services, etc.) is a public policy determination based on national circumstances that can change over time. Political considerations can also significantly influence such decisions. Traditionally, the predominant arrangement globally and in Asia is for central banks to oversee banking industry regulation and supervision.

Over the last 20 years, competition, achieving business efficiency and customer convenience have driven cross-sectoral mergers among financial services providers, such as banks, securities brokers and insurance firms. This trend toward conglomeratization has caused a reassessment of the efficacy of jurisdictions' traditional regulatory arrangements.

Receiving timely information is essential to ensure that large financial services firms, which are frequently systemically important, are effectively regulated, as close to "real time" as possible. This consideration seemed to be the main driver in Republic of Korea's decision to establish the Financial Supervisory Service in 1999, and a factor in Indonesia's decision to establish its Financial Services Authority (Otoritas Jasa Keuangan, OJK) in 2011. A regulator with cross-sectoral oversight responsibilities may be able to avoid delays in sharing information that may be experienced when dealing with multiple regulators. However, most Asian jurisdictions have kept bank regulation and supervision as a central bank mandate, without any apparent problems. Table 26.1 summarizes current regional arrangements.

Table 26.1 Authorities with primary responsibility for bank supervision in selected Asian jurisdictions

Jurisdiction	*Bank Supervision Authority*
Brunei Darussalam	Autoriti Monetari Brunei Darussalam
Cambodia	National Bank of Cambodia
PRC	China Banking Regulatory Commission★
Hong Kong, China	Hong Kong Monetary Authority
India	Reserve Bank of India
Indonesia	Otoritas Jasa Keuangan (OJK)/Financial Services Authority★
Japan	Financial Services Agency★
Lao PDR	National Bank of Laos
Malaysia	Bank Negara Malaysia
Mongolia	Central Bank of Mongolia
Myanmar	Central Bank of Myanmar
Nepal	Nepal Rastra Bank
Pakistan	State Bank of Pakistan
Philippines	Bangko Sentral ng Pilipinas
Singapore	Monetary Authority of Singapore
Republic of Korea	Financial Supervisory Service★
Sri Lanka	Central Bank of Sri Lanka
Thailand	Bank of Thailand
Viet Nam	State Bank of Viet Nam

PRC = People's Republic of China, Lao PDR = Lao People's Democratic Republic.

Note: ★indicates non-CB prudential supervisory authority.

Source: Authors.

Macroprudential policy actions

The historical focus of banking system stability monitoring on individual institution risk may not detect the build-up of macroeconomic risks and vulnerabilities that can adversely affect many financial institutions simultaneously. Financial institutions that appear sound can be adversely impacted by common behavior and mutual interaction. For example, asset price bubbles may arise in certain asset classes in an economy, such as commercial and residential real estate, that serve as collateral for bank loans. Sharp price declines in these asset classes could have a destabilizing effect on many banks simultaneously.

Timely identification of emerging macroeconomic risks and imbalances can serve as the basis to activate macroprudential policy measures, alone or in concert with other policy actions, to avert, dampen or mitigate periods of instability or crisis. Macroprudential surveillance is undertaken by national authorities, usually central banks, to detect and control risks that may adversely affect the financial performance and stability of the banking industry more broadly.

Responsibility for implementing macroprudential measures may reside in different national authorities, and not necessarily be a central bank mandate. Policy actions necessitate close cooperation and coordination among domestic authorities to ensure they do not have contradictory goals or offset each other. Monetary, fiscal, and tax policies can also influence systemic risk.

Singapore has been a very active user of macroprudential policy measures, particularly to control banking system lending risks arising from sharp price escalations in property markets that seem to be unsustainable and driven by speculation. Macroprudential policy measures to dampen speculative rises in property prices implemented by the Monetary Authority of Singapore have included an introduction of stamp duties for buyers and sellers; a capital gains tax to sales of property within three years of purchase to discourage speculative activity; the imposition of limits for loan-to-value and total debt servicing ratios; restrictions on foreigners from taking on Singapore dollar loans for property purchases; and requirements for minimum cash down payments (Wong, Lim, and Wong 2015).

Table 26.2 provides an overview of the use of macroprudential policies across Asian economies. Besides the Monetary Authority of Singapore, the financial authorities of the PRC, Pakistan, Mongolia, Bangladesh, Nepal, and Republic of Korea have been among the most active users of macroprudential policies.

Considerations in regulating and supervising systemically important banks

Periods of banking system instability or crisis, regardless of their root cause, frequently manifest themselves as funding pressures on banks, caused by public concerns over their financial soundness. This was the case during the global financial crisis of 2007–2008 (GFC). In September 2008, a liquidity crisis erupted in the interbank funding market when large bank participants, many of whom were global and domestic systemically important banks (G-SIBs and D-SIBs), began to restrict and eventually withdraw credit, even to long-term trusted counterparties. Central banks then had to intervene and provide emergency replacement funding to avert a wider crisis and preserve public confidence in banks and markets. Subsequently, there were a number of large banks that received extraordinary governmental (taxpayer-backed) interventions in order to prevent potential systemic impacts that could threaten the stability of the banking system.

In the aftermath of this episode, in 2011 the Basel Committee saw the need for "adopting additional policy measures for G-SIBs based on the "negative externalities" (i.e., adverse

Table 26.2 Macroprudential index for Asian economies

Economy	2000	2001	2002	2003	2004	2005	2006	2007	2008	2009	2010	2011	2012	2013	CB
Bangladesh	2	2	2	2	4	4	4	4	4	4	4	4	4	4	0.8
Bhutan	1	1	1	1	1	1	1	1	1	1	1	1	1	1	1
Brunei Darussalam	0	0	0	0	0	1	1	1	1	1	1	1	3	3	1
Cambodia	2	2	2	2	2	2	2	2	2	2	2	2	2	2	1
PRC	1	1	1	2	4	4	4	4	5	5	5	7	7	8	0.3
Hong Kong, China	3	3	3	3	3	3	3	3	3	3	3	3	3	3	1
India	1	1	1	1	1	1	1	2	2	2	2	2	2	2	0
Indonesia	0	0	0	0	0	1	1	1	1	1	1	1	2	2	0.5
Japan	1	1	1	1	1	1	1	1	1	1	1	1	1	1	0
Lao PDR	2	2	2	2	2	2	2	2	2	2	2	2	2	2	1
Malaysia	2	2	2	2	2	2	2	2	2	2	2	2	2	2	1
Mongolia	3	3	3	3	3	3	3	3	3	3	3	3	4	7	0.9
Nepal	2	2	2	2	2	2	2	2	2	3	3	3	4	4	1
Pakistan	4	4	5	5	5	6	6	6	8	8	8	8	8	8	0.9
Philippines	1	1	2	2	2	2	2	2	2	2	2	2	2	2	0.5
Singapore	1	1	2	2	2	2	2	2	2	2	2	2	2	5	0.8
Republic of Korea	0	0	1	1	1	2	2	3	3	3	3	4	4	4	0.5
Sri Lanka	1	1	1	1	1	1	1	1	1	1	1	1	1	1	1
Thailand	0	0	0	1	1	1	1	1	1	1	1	2	2	2	1

PRC = People's Republic of China, Lao PDR = Lao People's Democratic Republic.

Note: The macroprudential index ranges from 0 to 12. The higher the index, the more of the following macroprudential tools are employed: Loan-to-Value Ratio Caps, Debt-to-Income Ratio, Time-Varying/ Dynamic Loan-Loss Provisioning, General Counter-cyclical Capital Buffer/Requirement, Leverage Ratio, Capital Surcharges on Systemically Important Financial Institutions, Limits on Interbank Exposures, Concentration Limits, Limits on Foreign Currency Loans, FX and/or Counter-cyclical Reserve Requirements, Limits on Domestic Currency Loans, Levy/Tax on Financial Institutions. CB stands for fraction of macroprudential instruments that are controlled by the central bank as of 2013 and ranges from 0 to 1.

Source: Compiled with data from Cerutti, Claessens, and Puy (2017).

side effects) created by systemically important banks which current regulatory policies do not address" (BCBS 2011: 1). As a consequence, those banks designated as G-SIBs or D-SIBs are required to hold supplemental loss-absorbing capital. The list of G-SIBs is updated annually in November as of the prior year-end. As of November 2016, there were 30 G-SIBs. Table 26.3 lists the seven G-SIBs headquartered in Asia. Individual national authorities also designate D-SIBs which, similar to G-SIBs, may be subject to capital surcharges.

International standards for bank regulation and supervision

The Bank for International Settlements (BIS) hosts various standard–setting committees that prescribe minimum regulatory and supervisory standards for the international financial services industry. The oldest of these committees is the Basel Committee on Banking Supervision (BCBS) which covers the banking industry.[7] The BCBS promotes good and sound bank supervisory practices and standards, focused mainly on internationally active banks. While the Basel

Table 26.3 Global systemically important banks headquartered in Asia (end 2016)

Bank	Country	Total Assets (in USD trillion) through 31 December 2016
Industrial and Commercial Bank of China Limited	PRC	3.473
China Construction Bank Corp.	PRC	3.017
Agricultural Bank of China Limited	PRC	2.816
Bank of China Limited	PRC	2.604
Mitsubishi UFG Financial Group Inc.	Japan	1.649
Mizuho Financial Group Inc.	Japan	1.752
Sumitomo Mitsui Financial Group Inc.	Japan	1.649

PRC = People's Republic of China.

Source: Compiled by author with data from Financial Stability Board (2016) and SNL Financial.

Committee has no supranational authority, member jurisdictions usually adopt agreed upon standards, sometimes for all their banks.

Harmonization of supervisory practices and regulatory requirements helps to avoid "regulatory arbitrage," which refers to conscious and deliberate strategies by banks to evade or circumvent legal requirements, or take advantage of less stringent (or no) legal requirements, or perceived less stringent supervision, or even the absence of supervisory oversight of certain activities. This can occur, for example, by conducting business in jurisdictions where regulation and supervision of banks is less developed or less stringent.

The BCBS has identified 29 essential preconditions necessary for regulatory jurisdictions to have effective bank supervision programs in "Core Principles for Effective Supervision," known as the Basel Core Principles (BCP).[8] The BCP were originally issued in 1997, and revised in 2006 and 2012. The current version of the BCP states that "The revised Core Principles will continue to provide a comprehensive standard for establishing a sound foundation for the regulation, supervision, governance, and risk management of the banking sector" (BCBS (2012: 3). Each core principle is intended to apply to the prudential supervision of all banks, ranging from large, complex internationally active banks to small, non-complex deposit-taking institutions.

Lessons learned from prior banking crises and periods of financial instability

There have been many episodes of financial instability in recent decades, including systemic banking crises. Laeven and Valencia (2012), who produced a database of all systemic banking, currency, and sovereign debt crises, identified 147 banking crises for the period 1970–2011.[9] Many of these crisis events mostly involved individual countries, though some had cross-border spillover effects. Table 26.4 shows an overview of banking crises in Asia. Apart from Mongolia, crisis events occurred at least two decades ago, with the greatest cluster being around 1997. These episodes of instability and crisis, and the displacements they caused, typically resulted in costly governmental interventions to contain the crises. Lengthy post-crisis recovery periods also resulted in substantial economic output losses.

The GFC, which was centered in the US and Eurozone, was the most significant period of global financial instability since the Great Depression. Pre-crisis, many countries most directly and

Table 26.4 Banking crises in Asia

Country	Years of crisis
PRC	1998
India	1993
Japan	1997
Republic of Korea	1997
Malaysia	1997
Mongolia	2008
Nepal	1988
Philippines	1983, 1997
Sri Lanka	1989
Thailand	1983, 1997
Viet Nam	1997

PRC = People's Republic of China.

Source: Data from Laeven and Valencia (2012).

substantially affected by the GFC were reputed to have sophisticated monitoring systems to track financial system stability. Yet, those systems and attendant analytical methods almost universally failed to predict the onset, severity, and spillover effects of the GFC. Many financial stability assessments published by those jurisdictions reflected no material systemic risk concerns prior to crisis onset. Asian jurisdictions were impacted by the GFC, but more indirectly. It is important that bank regulatory and supervisory authorities remain vigilant in their surveillance of banks and the industry to be alert for any trends or conditions that could lead to instability or crisis. Lending problems are frequently the root cause of problem banks and banking industry problems.

Cross-border banking conglomerates and consolidated supervision

The structures of companies providing banking and other financial services continue to evolve as they seek to expand their geographic reach, and achieve economies of scale and scope as restrictions on banks' affiliations and permissible activities are relaxed or removed in many countries.

Banks are increasingly owned by holding companies or other parent companies that operate in multiple countries. The size and geographic reach of some financial conglomerates and/or their interlinkages may make them systemically important in multiple jurisdictions, thus practicing effective consolidated supervision is essential in promoting financial stability. Timely and effective regulatory examinations and information-sharing is essential to understanding the risks in these entities and controlling cross-border spillovers, contagion effects, and regulatory arbitrage.

Complex structures may be driven by legitimate business reasons such as legal or tax considerations. It is important for a bank supervisor to understand the business reason(s) behind the chosen corporate architecture and whether the chosen corporate structure can be adequately supervised.

Asian jurisdictions are both home and host supervisors for large, geographically dispersed banking organizations that are part of financial conglomerates operating across the region. Also, global banking organizations operate extensive regional banking networks. Countries' effective implementation of consolidated supervision is, therefore, an important part of promoting regional financial stability.

There are five large regional banking conglomerates in Asia, each with consolidated total assets exceeding USD 100 billion, which operate in multiple jurisdictions:

- DBS Bank, Singapore
- OCBC Bank, Singapore
- United Overseas Bank, Singapore
- Maybank, Malaysia
- CIMB Bank, Malaysia.

Consolidated supervision is a long-standing, fundamental principle and essential element of effective bank supervision, which seeks to determine the financial soundness of a bank, considering the financial soundness and risks posed by affiliate relationships. Bank supervisors need to answer the following questions in understanding the risks within a corporate banking conglomerate: What is the financial condition of affiliated organizations and what effect could they have – positive, negative, or neutral – on the financial condition and stability of an affiliated bank? Is there a potential for excessive risk arising from financial transactions with affiliated organizations?

Supervisory colleges

The Basel Committee has promoted the implementation of supervisory colleges as a mechanism for home and host country supervisors to collaborate and share supervisory information on cross-border banking groups. An October 2010 Basel Committee Report titled "Good Practice Principles on Supervisory Colleges" describes supervisory colleges as "multilateral working groups of relevant (bank) supervisors that are formed for the collective purpose of enhancing effective consolidated supervision of an international banking group on an ongoing basis" (BCBS 2010: 1). The report further states that "Despite not being decision-making bodies, supervisory colleges have developed a key role over time as a forum for broader issues such as discussion and planning of supervisory assessments and sharing information about the overall risk of . . . international banking group(s)" (BCBS 2010: 2).

The supervisory college concept has also been used by regional bank supervisors, including Asia, to help achieve consolidated supervision of regional banking conglomerates operating in multiple jurisdictions.

How do Asian jurisdictions' bank regulation and supervision regimes compare?

Sources of information

Respected multilateral organizations, such as the Basel Committee, the Financial Stability Board and International Monetary Fund (IMF), perform independent expert assessments that provide insights on the relative strength of Asian jurisdictions' bank regulation and supervision programs. These assessments are typically published and readily accessible on the internet.

The most in-depth publicly available reviews are the IMF's BCP assessments, usually conducted during their on-site Financial Sector Assessment Program (FSAP) missions.[10] Commentary on the adequacy of bank regulation and supervision performance and infrastructure is also typically included in the IMF's annual Article IV Consultations (Article IV reports) of member jurisdictions.[11]

BCP reviews are based on information provided, and discussions with, senior officials from a jurisdiction's bank regulatory and supervisory authorities. While a jurisdiction may be in apparent conformity with BCP standards, independent assessors seek to judge whether the relevant jurisdictional authorities are implementing the standards in practice.

The following excerpt from the 2012 Japan FSAP summarizes the BCP assessment scale for compliance with individual core principles (CP):

> To determine the level of compliance of each CP the FSAP assessment has made use of five rating categories: compliant; largely compliant; materially noncompliant; non-compliant; and non-applicable. An assessment of *"compliant"* is given when all essential criteria are met without any significant deficiencies, including instances where the relevant CP has been achieved by other means. A *"largely compliant"* assessment is given when there are only minor shortcomings, which do not raise serious concerns about the authorities' ability to achieve the objective of the CP and there is clear intent to achieve full compliance with the CP within a prescribed period of time. A CP is considered to be *"materially noncompliant"* in case of severe shortcomings, despite the existence of formal rules and procedures and there is evidence that supervision has clearly not been effective, the practical implementation is weak or that the shortcomings are sufficient to raise doubts about the authority's ability to achieve compliance. A CP is assessed *"noncompliant"* if it is not substantially implemented, several essential criteria are not complied with, or supervision is manifestly ineffective. Finally, a category of *"non-applicable"* is reserved . . . for those cases where the criteria would not be relevant for the (jurisdiction's) situation. [Emphasis added]

Bank regulations and supervisory infrastructure sometimes "look good on paper," but the real test of effectiveness is whether the bank supervisory authorities have sufficient technical expertise and judgment, independence, and the will to act when confronted with situations posing safety and soundness concerns. Sometimes bank supervisors are inhibited by a lack of legal authority, political interference or a lack of legal protections (the latter meaning that they have no legal shield or indemnification against lawsuits, personal liability or other sanctions even for taking justified action in good faith).

Rating criteria

There is no universally accepted methodology for rating jurisdictions' relative level of bank supervisory performance. The commentary that follows in this section represents the author's judgment of the relative strength and stage of development of selected Asian jurisdictions' bank regulation and supervision regimes. The categorizations, while based partly on information contained in IMF FSAP and Article IV reports, primarily reflects the author's first-hand experience in working with central banks and other bank supervisory authorities in the Asia and the Pacific region. The opinions expressed are solely those of the author.

The quality of Asian bank regulation and supervision is a wide continuum. I have chosen to delineate four categories of development and effectiveness: Very Strong, Strong, Sound, and Foundational. Certainly there are differences between jurisdictions in the same category, but they are similar in overall performance relative to the total population of Asian jurisdictions. Following is a brief description of each rating category:

- Very Strong: Jurisdictions with bank regulation and supervision programs that are among the best globally, which is a very limited number of jurisdictions.

- Strong: Programs of bank regulation and supervision which have substantially implemented the BCP with few exceptions.
- Basic: Programs of bank regulation and supervision which generally meet the BCP but need to build supervisory capacity and enhance examination methodologies consistent with international standards.
- Foundational: Programs in an early stage of development which may not meet a substantial portion of the BCP and are frequently focused on rules compliance rather than judgmental analyses of risk.

Asian jurisdictions with very strong bank regulation and supervision programs

Hong Kong, China: very strong

Hong Kong, China's bank regulation and supervision regime, carried out by the Hong Kong Monetary Authority (HKMA), is regarded as *very strong*. The IMF conducted a BCP assessment during a 2014 FSAP that disclosed an outstanding level of compliance with the 29 BCP, with the following ratings assigned: Compliant: 26; Largely Compliant: 3; Materially Non-Compliant: 0; and Non-compliant: 0. The FSAP report stated:

> HKSAR has a very high level of compliance with the Basel Core Principles for Effective Banking Supervision." "The HKMA is maintaining its commitment to the international regulatory reform agenda and is an early adopter of many standards. Supervisory practices, standards and approaches are well integrated, risk based and of very high quality. A number of the HKMA practices around corporate governance issues, including close and continuing attention to fit and proper standards and to the role played by the Board of an authorized institution . . . deserve particular commendation.[12]

The highly favorable view of the jurisdiction's bank regulation and supervision capabilities was reaffirmed in an Article IV report issued in January 2017.[13]

Singapore: very strong

Singapore's bank regulation and supervision regime, carried out by the Monetary Authority of Singapore (MAS) is regarded as *very strong*. The IMF conducted a BCP assessment during a 2013 FSAP that disclosed an outstanding level of compliance with the 29 BCP, with the following ratings assigned: Compliant: 25; Largely Compliant: 4; Materially Non-Compliant: 0; and Non-compliant: 0. The IMF FSAP documents state:

> The assessment of the Monetary Authority of Singapore (MAS) represents a very high level of compliance with the Basel Core Principles for Effective Banking Supervision and demonstrates a strong commitment by MAS to their implementation.[14]
>
> The Singapore financial system is highly developed, and well-regulated and supervised . . . and Singapore's current regulation and supervision are among the best globally.[15]

The highly favorable view of the jurisdiction's bank regulation and supervision capabilities was reaffirmed in an Article IV report issued in May 2017.[16]

Asian jurisdictions with strong bank regulation and supervision programs

Republic of Korea: strong

Republic of Korea's bank regulation and supervision regime, carried out by the Financial Supervisory Service, is regarded as *strong*. An Article IV report published in August 2016 states:

> The financial system remains resilient. Financial soundness indicators – capital adequacy, liquidity, and asset quality of both banks and NBFIs (non-bank financial institutions) are relatively strong on a point-in-time basis. . . . The government recently implemented the Basel Committee's recommendations on additional capital requirements for domestic systemically important banks (D-SIBs) and countercyclical capital buffers (which were set at zero initially).[17]

Malaysia: strong

Malaysia's bank regulation and supervision regime, carried out by Bank Negara Malaysia (BNM), the central bank, is regarded as *strong*. An FSAP report published in issued in August 2016 states:

> The regulatory and supervisory regime for banks, insurance firms, securities markets, and market infrastructure exhibits a high degree of compliance with international standards. Areas for improvement include enhancing the framework of consolidated supervision and addressing legal provisions that could potentially compromise supervisory independence.[18]

An Article IV report issued in April 2017 reaffirmed the FSAP assessment:

> Risks of a severe downturn in the financial cycle appear to be low, largely due to a resilient banking system, supported by BNM's prudential policies and oversight.
> Progress toward adopting remaining recommendations of the Financial Sector Assessment Program (FSAP) in the area of financial oversight continued. Following the change in legislation that extended its legal powers over finance holding companies (FHC), BNM has completed the process of identifying and designating the appropriate holding companies as FHCs for all financial groups.[19]

Japan: strong

Japan's bank regulation and supervision regime, carried out by the Financial Services Agency is regarded as *strong* based on the FSAP conducted in 2003 and an FSAP update in 2012. The latest FSAP report issued in July 2017 states:

> Further developing internal processes is key to supporting full risk-based prudential supervision to keep pace with the more sophisticated activities emerging across banks, insurers, and securities firms. Corporate governance needs to be strengthened across the whole banking and insurance sectors. Capital requirements need to be more tailored to individual bank risk profiles, and a stronger principles-based approach to related party exposures is required to prevent risks from building up as banks form

alliances with other banks and other types of financial services firms. . . . The macro-prudential framework could be further strengthened by clarifying the mandate of the Council for Cooperation on Financial Stability and proactively expanding the macro-prudential toolkit.

It is therefore important to continue engaging with financial institutions on the implications of macroeconomic and demographic trends, and take actions on a timely basis when viability concerns are identified. The authorities are encouraged to further engage with bank boards and senior management to ensure that banks fully understand the implications of underlying trends for the future viability of their institutions and act promptly to facilitate the exit of firms when they are no longer viable. Regional banks should be encouraged to consider increasing fee-based income. Consolidation among regional banks may bring valuable economies of scale and scope and smoothen the transition to smaller financial systems at the regional level, although consolidation alone is unlikely to be sufficient to address the challenges. The supply of financial services by the industry should continue to adapt to the demands of an aging population.

These long-term challenges for business models of many banks, combined with the existence of large systemic institutions, highlight the need for a strong crisis management and resolution framework. Despite important advances in the design of the framework and in recovery and resolution planning, there remains room for improvement. The complexity of the framework, and ambiguities regarding the circumstances under which different components of the framework would be used, could prove challenging for implementation and may thereby contribute to expectations of public support. Further steps to ensure that supervisory powers are deployed without delay should be embedded more firmly in the authorities' framework for early intervention. Expansion of the resolution toolkit, enhancements and clarifications in the legal framework – including its extension to central counterparties – and improvements in operational aspects would help authorities' readiness and steer market expectations and incentives.[20]

India: strong

India's bank regulation and supervision regime, carried out by Reserve Bank of India, the central bank, is regarded as *strong*. An FSAP review was published in August 2013 that contained the following comments:

> The Reserve Bank of India (RBI) is to be commended for its tightly controlled regulatory and supervisory regime, consisting of higher than minimum capital requirements, frequent, hands-on and comprehensive onsite inspections, a conservative liquidity risk policy and restrictions on banks' capacity to take on more volatile exposures.
>
> Despite this strong performance, several gaps and constraints in the implementation of the regulatory and supervision framework remain. The most significant gaps are in the area of international and, to a lesser extent, domestic supervisory information sharing and cooperation. In addition, some previously observed weaknesses in the financial architecture, particularly with regard to the independence of RBI and the inherent conflict of interest when supervising state owned banks, remain. Also, the assessors identified a number of opportunities to better align current supervisory policies and procedures to international best practice.

The independence of the RBI is not enshrined in the law and there are some legal provisions that could seriously undermine the independence from the government. In practice, however, the assessors have not come across evidence of government or industry interference.[21]

An Article IV report issued in February 2017 states:

The successful implementation of the AQR (asset quality review) process, the new bankruptcy code, and additional debt recovery mechanisms will bridge critical gaps in the resolution of bank asset quality distress and enhance financial stability.[22]

Philippines: strong

The Philippines' bank regulation and supervision regime, carried out by Bangko Sentral ng Pilipinas (BSP), the central bank, is regarded as *strong*. The jurisdiction underwent an FSAP review in 2002, with an FSAP Update published in 2010 stating:

Major progress has been made since the 2002 FSAP in strengthening the legal and regulatory framework and improving supervisory practices.[23]

An Article IV report issued in February 2017 states:

Systemic risks appear contained but merit continued monitoring. While most indicators suggest that credit growth remains below typical cutoffs for credit booms, the mixed signals provided by available indicators and the composition of credit growth across sectors warrant careful monitoring to continue assessing the need for macroprudential measures, including countercyclical capital buffers, supported by strong microprudential supervision. Firm-level stress tests show that overall debt-at-risk is still low in nonfinancial corporates but there are pockets of vulnerability, where leverage has increased and is concentrated. . . . When credit growth becomes excessive for some sectors, the BSP would consider targeted macroprudential policy responses.[24]

People's Republic of China: strong

The PRC's bank regulation and supervision regime, carried out by the China Banking Regulatory Commission, regarded as *strong*. A June 2017 Article IV report states:

Important supervisory and regulatory action is being taken against financial sector risks. Corporate debt is growing more slowly, reflecting restructuring initiatives and overcapacity reduction. The house price boom is being gradually contained and excess inventory reduced. Local government borrowing frameworks are being improved and a blueprint for reforming central-local fiscal relations has been published.

The critically important recent focus on tackling financial sector risks should continue, even if it entails some financial tensions and slower growth. We will have more detailed analysis and recommendations on the financial sector in our five-yearly Financial Sector Assessment Program (FSAP) review, which we expect to be completed by the end of the year.[25]

Indonesia: strong

Indonesia's bank regulation and supervision regime, carried out by the Otoritas Jasa Keuangan (OJK), translated Financial Services Authority, is regarded as *strong*. A June 2017 FSAP report states:

> Systemic risk is low and the banking system appears generally resilient to severe shocks. Market based indicators point to relatively low levels of systemic risk. Under severe stress-test scenarios, banks experience sizable credit losses, particularly from corporate exposures, but high capital levels and strong profitability help to absorb most of these losses and the resulting capital shortfalls are modest. Many banks face relatively small shortfalls in liquidity stress tests, including in foreign currency, and these appear manageable for Bank Indonesia (BI) (the central bank). The authorities have been pursuing an ambitious agenda to strengthen financial oversight and crisis management. Since the last FSAP, the authorities have implemented the Basel III capital framework . . . and improved supervisory practices across sectors. Importantly, in 2011, the Financial Services Authority (OJK) was established as an integrated regulator to oversee the entire financial sector. In addition, BI has developed analytical tools to assess systemic risk and has introduced several macroprudential instruments. The framework for crisis management and resolution, and safety nets was revamped in 2016. . . .
>
> The FSAP took stock of the progress that has been made and identified areas where further progress will be needed. Notably, the mandates for OJK supervision and BI's macroprudential policy do not give clear primacy to financial stability over developmental objectives and this can undermine timely actions. Further, although legal protection for staff and agencies involved in oversight and crisis management has been strengthened with recent reforms, it is not in line with best international practice and risks causing inaction bias. On supervision, the main remaining challenges to effective supervision stem from the complex structure and weak governance practices of financial conglomerates and OJK's capacity to supervise them, silos in OJK's internal structure, and an insufficiently intrusive supervisory approach across sectors.[26]

Thailand: strong

Thailand's bank regulation and supervision regime, carried out by the Bank of Thailand (BOT), the central bank, is regarded as *strong*. The May 2017 Article IV report states:

> The BOT made significant strides in strengthening the financial stability framework. . . . Building on the Financial Stability Unit, macrofinancial surveillance capacity should be further upgraded by enhancing cooperation among regulators. This should focus on identifying and correcting any mispricing of systemic risk, including from newer forms of finance. Financial regulators for banks, NBFIs, and cooperatives should have explicit financial stability mandates with formal roles and responsibilities, under the BOT's coordination. This can proceed separately from establishing the resolution authority over SFIs and contingency plans for systemic crisis, which remain critical.[27]

Asian jurisdictions with basic bank regulation and supervision programs

Viet Nam: basic

Viet Nam's bank regulation and supervision regime, carried out by the State Bank of Viet Nam, the central bank, is regarded as *basic*. The July 2017 Article IV report states:

> (IMF) Directors welcomed progress made in banking sector reforms to address impaired assets and increase provisioning. They stressed that the pace of reforms should be accelerated and their scope broadened to include development of a legal framework for bank resolution . . . and implementation of further reforms to strengthen debt enforcement and market discipline. Enhancing the AML/CFT framework and its effective implementation will also support financial stability.[28]

Sri Lanka: basic

Banking regulation and supervision is the responsibility of the Central Bank of Sri Lanka and is regarded as *basic* based on some of the developmental needs specified in the June 2016 Article IV report:

> (IMF) Staff welcomed steps toward supervision on a consolidated basis and shifting to Basel III. The preliminary draft on the amendments to the Banking Act to bring the single borrower limit (SBL) and related party lending definitions in line with international best practices, are welcome.[29]

Asian jurisdictions with foundational bank regulation and supervision programs

Brunei Darussalam, Cambodia, Lao People's Democratic Republic, Mongolia, Myanmar, and Nepal are deemed to have *foundational* bank regulation and supervision programs. Most have regulations that fall significantly short of compliance with international standards, and examination and supervision tend to be based on rules compliance, rather than judgmental assessments of risk. These jurisdictions typically need to add experienced staff with the technical knowledge to help capacity building efforts and train and mentor less experienced staff. Some of the jurisdictions lack the necessary legal authority to implement elements of the BCP. Due to space constraints it is not possible to provide details here on these jurisdictions; detailed information on the state of these jurisdictions' financial regulatory system can be found in the most recent IMF Article IV reports that can be sourced from the IMF website.[30]

Regulatory consistency assessments

The Basel Committee established a Regulatory Consistency Assessment Programme (RCAP)[31] in 2012, which provides periodic public disclosures of the progress jurisdictions are making in implementing key standards. Table 26.5 shows that all four Asian jurisdictions that are Basel Committee members have been verified by a BCBS-sponsored independent assessment team as having implemented the risk-based capital standards of Basel III.

Table 26.5 Basel committee's "Regulatory Consistency Assessment Programme": Asian BCBS member jurisdictions' implementation of risk-based capital standards

Regulatory Standard Area	Jurisdiction	Publication Date of Assessment	Overall Assessment Grade
Risk-based capital standards	Japan	October 2012/December 2016	Compliant
	Singapore	March 2013	Compliant
	PRC	September 2013	Compliant
	Hong Kong, China	March 2015	Compliant

BCBS = Basel Committee on Banking Supervision, PRC = People's Republic of China.

Source: Author.

Conclusion

Asian economies will continue to experience periodic structural shifts and volatility that will provide future challenges to financial stability. Strong systems of bank regulation and supervision are necessary to help meet those challenges and help to avoid, dampen, or mitigate future periods of financial instability or crisis. A key lesson learned from the GFC and other crises is that the cost of developing a strong system of bank regulation and supervision is a small fraction of the direct and indirect costs of periods of financial instability or crisis.

As noted earlier, the more-developed Asian economies have generally established sound bank regulation and supervision programs. They seem to be satisfactorily implementing the extensive post-GFC regulatory reforms that have been promulgated by the Basel Committee and the FSB. This will enhance the strength and resiliency of individual banks and banking systems to withstand future periods of adversity and instability. Less developed Asian economies need to devote the resources to building sound bank regulation and supervision regimes to achieve sound banking systems that will help achieve sustainable long-term economic growth.

Notes

1 The comments, conclusions, and opinions expressed by the author are his own and do not represent the opinions of the SEACEN Centre or the author's current or former employers. Use of the term "country" or "jurisdiction" in this chapter is not intended to make or imply any judgments as to the legal or other status of any territory or area.

2 SMEs and consumers in EMEs who do not have sufficient creditworthiness to obtain loans from banks rely on non-bank lenders for credit, such as finance companies, which may be unregulated or lightly regulated. Banks' lending activities are usually subject to detailed regulations regarding loan terms and conditions, which seek to reduce the possibility of unfair and deceptive lending practices. Bank credit also typically costs less. Therefore, borrowers attempt to attain a financial standing that allows them to access bank credit.

3 Systemic risk in this context means that the failure of a bank, particularly if it is large or has many interconnections with other banks (such as granting or receiving loans from them), or offers some unique functions for many banks, such as operating a securities market clearing and settlement system, could have negative impacts that jeopardize the stability of those other banks.

4 Michael C. Bonello, governor of the Central Bank of Malta, 23 May 2011.

5 Group of Ten (2001), p. 163.

6 Transaction testing refers to sampling techniques employed by bank examiners in reviewing a bank's books and records. For example, the focal point of most examinations is a review of loan portfolio quality. Examiners will typically select a sample of loans to review in detail.

7 The Basel Committee on Banking Supervision ("BCBS") consists of senior representatives of bank supervisory authorities and central banks. Member jurisdictions are Argentina, Australia, Belgium,

Brazil, Canada, the PRC, the European Union, France, Germany, Hong Kong, India, Indonesia, Italy, Japan, Korea, Luxembourg, Mexico, the Netherlands, Russia, Saudi Arabia, Singapore, South Africa, Spain, Sweden, Switzerland, Turkey, the UK, and the US. Source: BCBS website accessed 31 July 2017 (www.bis.org/bcbs/membership.htm).

8   For a high-level summary of the 29 BCP, see BCBS (2012), Paragraph 41, pp. 10–13.

9   Thirteen of the 147 identified systemic banking crises were characterized as "borderline" events, meaning that while they met the crisis definition, they were less-severe events.

10 An index of FSAP Reports from 2001 to the present, including stand-alone BCP assessment reports and BCP assessments embedded in FSAP reports, is available online at www.imf.org/external/np/fsap/fssa.aspx with links available to electronic versions of the indexed documents. IMF Article IV Consultation reports can also be retrieved from the search function on the IMF website at www.imf.org.

11 High-level assessments of the adequacy of a jurisdiction's bank regulation and supervision are also covered in annual IMF Article IV Consultations, though in a more summary fashion. The IMF's Article IV Consultation Reports contain the following standard description of the consultation process: "Under Article IV of the IMF's Articles of Agreement, the IMF holds bilateral discussions with members, usually every year. A staff team visits the country, collects economic and financial information, and discusses with officials the country's economic developments and policies. On return to headquarters, the staff prepares a report, which forms the basis for discussion by the Executive Board."

12 IMF Country Report No. 14/207, July 2014/FSAP-BCP for Effective Banking Supervision, accessible at www.imf.org/external/pubs/ft/scr/2014/cr14207.pdf.

13 IMF Article IV Consultation Staff Report, IMF Country Report No. 17/11, January 2017, accessible at www.imf.org/external/pubs/ft/scr/2017/cr1711.pdf.

14 IMF Country Report No. 13/342, December 2013/Detailed Assessment of Compliance – BCP for Effective Banking Supervision, accessible at www.imf.org/en/Publications/CR/Issues/2016/12/31/Singapore-Detailed-Assessment-of-Compliance-on-the-Basel-Core-Principles-for-Effective-41083.

15 IMF Financial Stability System Assessment, IMF Country Report No. 13/325, November 2013, accessible at www.imf.org/external/pubs/ft/scr/2013/cr13325.pdf.

16 IMF Staff Article IV Mission to Singapore, Mission Concluding Statement, 9 May 2017, accessible at www.imf.org/en/news/articles/2017/05/09/pr17156-singapore-imf-staff-completes-2017-article-iv-mission.

17 IMF Article IV Consultation Staff Report, IMF Country Report No. 16/278, August 2016, www.imf.org/external/pubs/ft/scr/2016/cr16278.pdf.

18 IMF Financial System Stability Assessment, IMF Country Report No. 13/52, February 2013, accessible at www.imf.org/external/pubs/ft/scr/2013/cr1352.pdf.

19 IMF Article IV Consultation Staff Report, IMF Country Report No. 17/101, April 2017, accessible at www.imf.org/external/pubs/ft/scr/2017/cr17101.pdf.

20 IMF Financial System Stability Assessment, IMF Country Report No. 17/244, July 2017, accessible at www.imf.org/~/media/files/publications/cr/2017/cr17244.ashx.

21 IMF Country Report No. 13/267, August 2013/Detailed Assessment of Compliance – BCP for Effective Banking Supervision accessible at www.imf.org/external/pubs/ft/scr/2013/cr13267.pdf.

22 IMF Article IV Consultation Staff Report, IMF Country Report No. 17/54, February 2017, accessible at www.imf.org/external/pubs/ft/scr/2017/cr1754.pdf.

23 IMF Country Report No. 10/90, April 2010, Financial Stability Assessment Update, accessible at www.imf.org/external/pubs/ft/scr/2010/cr1090.pdf.

24 IMF Article IV Consultation Staff Report, IMF Country Report No. 16/309, September 2016, accessible at www.imf.org/external/pubs/ft/scr/2016/cr16309.pdf.

25 IMF Staff Completes 2017 Article IV Mission to China, 14 June 2017, accessible at www.imf.org/en/news/articles/2017/06/07/pr17219-china-imf-staff-completes-2017-article-iv-mission.

26 IMF Financial System Stability Assessment, IMF Country Report No. 17/152, June 2017, accessible at www.imf.org/external/pubs/ft/scr/2017/cr17152.pdf.

27 IMF Article IV Consultation Staff Report, IMF Country Report No. 17/136, May 2017, accessible at www.imf.org/external/pubs/ft/scr/2017/cr17136.pdf.

28 IMF Article IV Consultation Staff Report, IMF Country Report No. 17/190, July 2017, accessible at. www.imf.org/external/pubs/ft/scr/2017/cr17190pdf.

29 IMF Article IV Consultation Staff Report, IMF Country Report No. 16/150, June 2016, accessible at www.imf.org/external/pubs/ft/scr/2016/cr16150.pdf.

30 www.imf.org/external/np/sec/aiv/index.aspx.
31 Information regarding the RCAP program is available at www.bis.org/bcbs/publ/d361.pdf.

References

Basel Committee on Banking Supervision (BCBS). 2010. Good Practice Principles on Supervisory Colleges – Final Document. Basel: Bank for International Settlements. www.bis.org/publ/bcbs177.htm

BCBS. 2011. *Global Systemically Important Banks: Assessment Methodology and the Additional Loss Absorbency Requirement – Rules Text*. Basel: Bank for International Settlements. www.bis.org/publ/bcbs207.htm

BCBS. 2012. *Core Principles for Effective Banking Supervision*. Basel: Bank for International Settlements. www.bis.org/publ/bcbs230.htm

Bonello, M. 2011. Introductory Remarks at the Launch of the Forum for Financial Stability, Valetta, Malta, 23 May.

Cerutti, E., S. Claessens, and L. Laeven. 2017. The Use and Effectiveness of Macroprudential Policies: New Evidence. *Journal of Financial Stability* 28: 203–224.

Financial Stability Board (FSB). 2016. *2016 List of Globally Systemically Important Banks (G-SIBs)*. Basel: Financial Stability Board. www.fsb.org/wp-content/uploads/2016-list-of-global-systemically-important-banks-G-SIBs.pdf (accessed 21 November 2016).

Laeven, L., and F. Valencia. 2012. Systemic Banking Crises Database: An Update. IMF Working Paper No. 12/163. Washington, DC: International Monetary Fund.

OECD. 2015. *G20/OECD Principles of Corporate Governance*. Paris: OECD. http://dx.di.org/10.1787/9789264236882-en

OECD/IMF/BIS. 2001. *Group of Ten Report on Consolidation in the Financial Sector*. https://www.imf.org/external/np/g10/2001/01/Eng/pdf/file1.pdf

Viñals, J., and J. Fiechter, et al. 2010. The Making of Good Supervision: Learning to Say 'No'. IMF Staff Discussion Note SPN/10/08.

Wong, N., Lim, A., and Wong, S. 2015. Using Macroprudential Tools to Address Systemic Risks in the Property Sector in Singapore. *SEACEN Financial Stability Journal* 4(May).

27

FOSTERING GREEN FINANCE FOR SUSTAINABLE DEVELOPMENT IN ASIA

Ulrich Volz

Introduction: green finance for sustainable development

To place the Asian economies onto a sustainable development pathway requires an unprecedented shift in investment away from greenhouse gas, fossil fuel and natural resource intensive industries toward more resource efficient technologies and business models. The financial sector will have to play a central role in this green transformation. Green finance is defined as comprising "all forms of investment or lending that consider environmental effect and enhance environmental sustainability" (Volz et al. 2015: 2). Important aspects of green finance are sustainable investment and banking, where investment and lending decisions are taken based on environmental screening and risk assessment to meet sustainability standards, as well as insurance services that cover environmental and climate risk.

Aligning economic growth with sustainable development is a universal challenge. Yet the challenge is vast for most developing Asian economies given that their growth models have been very resource and carbon intensive. Although the carbon intensity of economic output has declined substantially in most developing Asian economies over the last decades – with Bangladesh, Lao People's Democratic Republic (Lao PDR), Nepal, Thailand, and Viet Nam being notable exceptions – it is still much higher than in advanced economies inside or outside of the region.

Moreover, many Asian countries are also extremely vulnerable to climate risk. Bangladesh, Myanmar, the Philippines, and Thailand, and Viet Nam have been among the countries worldwide that have been most affected by climate change over the last two decades (Kreft et al. 2016). According to the University of Notre Dame's (2017) Global Adaptation Index, many South and Southeast Asian countries are highly vulnerable to climate change while economic, social, and governance readiness to improve resilience is lacking.

Against the backdrop of climate change vulnerability and the need for a reduction of carbon emissions, huge investments in green and climate-resilient infrastructure are needed across the region. The infrastructure gap in developing Asia has been assessed by the Asian Development Bank (ADB) to amount to USD 26.2 trillion between 2016 and 2030 or USD 1.7 trillion annually (ADB 2017). Of the USD 26.2 trillion that need to be invested by the ADB's 45 developing member countries, USD 3.6 trillion are specifically required for climate change mitigation and adaption costs. Fifty-six percent of the investment is needed for power, 32%

for transportation, 9% for telecommunications and 3% for sanitation. For Southeast Asia alone, the *ASEAN Investment Report 2015* estimates that USD 110 billion a year will be needed for infrastructure investment in power, transport, information, and communication technology, and water and sanitation in the Association of Southeast Asian Nations (ASEAN) through 2025 (ASEAN Secretariat and UNCTAD 2015).

All of this investment will have to be sensitive to environmental, climate, and associated policy risks. Funds for this investment will need to come from both the private and public sectors, including both domestic and international sources. The financing of sustainable infrastructure requires new approaches for mobilizing and intermediating long-term finance in the region. Integrating environmental and social considerations into lending decisions and product design is only a first step in making the financial systems instrumental in funding the required transformation toward a green economy in the region. The funding of energy efficiency, renewable energy and sustainable infrastructure requires new concepts and new financial instruments which are adapted to local circumstances. Green banks, green bonds, and appropriate regulatory frameworks are to be introduced in a coordinated framework. Last but not least, there is also a need for developing the insurance of climate risk, including risk mitigation instruments for agriculture, which for many countries in developing Asia remains a major economic sector.

As pointed out in a study by ADB and ADBI (2012), "[d]ecoupling emissions from economic growth requires a fundamental and wide-ranging response encompassing the public and private sector, targets and regulations as well as deep investment" (6). There is no question about the importance of implementing an adequate environmental policy and regulation and for the need of targeted industrial policies for creating the conditions for sustainable investment and thereby enhancing green, low-carbon growth. But there has been a growing recognition that for achieving a green transformation it is also crucial to align the financial system with sustainability goals, given that the financial system is the place where investment decisions are taken or influenced. The need for financial institutions to "incorporate climate-proofing and climate resilience measures" (UNFCCC 2015: §44) has also been recognized in the Paris Agreement. Accounting for climate and other environmental risk is not least important with respect to safeguarding the stability of financial systems (Volz 2016b). A failure to address systemic sustainability challenges will in the longer-term impinge on the growth and returns of individual firms and economies at large, with repercussions for the financial institutions that have financed non-sustainable investments. There is hence a strong case for financial institutions as well as for financial regulators to take account of environmental, social, and governance (ESG) risks.

Against this backdrop, this chapter reviews the state of green lending and investment in Asia and provides an overview of green financial governance initiatives across Asia. It also identifies market innovations to increase green finance in Asia as well as barriers to green investments and financial policy.

What are Asian banks and institutional investors currently doing?

For the time being, only relatively few financial institutions in Asia systematically integrate ESG factors into their lending or investment decision-making processes. Green banking and sustainable investment are still a niche market, and few staff in the industry have been trained in ESG issues.

A relatively small number of Asian financial institutions have signed up to global sustainable finance initiatives. Only 122 out of 1,874 signatories to the Principles for Responsible Investment (6.5%) are from Asia. Signatories include asset owners, investment managers and professional service partner. Of the 214 global signatories of the UNEP Statement of Commitment by Financial Institutions on Sustainable Development, 38 or 17.8% are from the Asia, while 12 out of 91 Equator Principles Financial Institutions (13%) are from the region. Of the 66 partner exchanges of the Sustainable Stock Exchanges (SSE) initiative, 14 are from Asia (21%).[1] Like all SSE partner exchanges they have made voluntary public commitments to promote improved ESG disclosure and performance among listed companies. Of the 57 insurance companies that have globally signed the UNEP FI Principles for Sustainable Insurance, eight are from Asia (14%).

The relatively low scale of involvement of Asian financial institutions in international sustainability initiatives is reflected in the low level of green lending and investment. According to the *2016 Global Sustainable Investment Review*, the total amount of sustainable investment assets under management in Asia (excluding Japan) reached USD 52 billion in 2016 (Global Sustainable Investment Association [GSIA] 2017; Table 27.1). The most widely adopted sustainable investment strategies in Asia, according to ASrIA (2015: 8), are ESG integration and exclusion/negative screening. Singapore; Hong Kong, China; Seoul; and Kuala Lumpur have emerged as the main Asian (excluding Japan) financial centers in which sustainable assets are managed. However, the fastest growing market for sustainable investments in the region between 2014 and 2016 was in Japan where sustainable investment assets increased from USD 7 billion to USD 473.6 billion (GSIA 2017: 4). This surge in sustainable assets can be explained by changes in the sustainable investment market in Japan as well as greater reporting and sustainable investment activity by institutional asset owners (cf. GSIA 2017: 18).

Overall, sustainability-themed investment strategies are becoming more prominent in Asia with rising awareness of challenges such as climate change, energy and water security. However, while the sustainable market segment has grown rapidly in absolute terms over recent years, it has grown from a very small base and still constitutes only a small percentage of the funds under management in Asia. Indeed, with USD 52 billion the proportion of socially responsible investments (SRI) relative to total managed assets in Asia (excluding Japan) stood at only 0.8%

Table 27.1 Sustainable investment assets under management by market (USD million)

	2011	*2013*	*2016*
Bangladesh		14	
People's Republic of China	1,535	1,729	7,290
Hong Kong, China	7,328	11,329	13,538
India	153	115	
Indonesia	595	1,142	
Japan	10,000	6,507	473,570
Republic of Korea	6,288	8,426	7,290
Malaysia	9,956	15,087	15,621
Pakistan	427	505	
Singapore	2,967	5,660	
Taipei,China	724	714	
Thailand	14	20	
Viet Nam		195	
Asia (including Japan)	39,987	51,443	525,640
Asia (excluding Japan)	29,987	44,936	52,070

Source: Compiled with data from ASrIA (2015: 11), GSIA (2017: 16, 27), and Japan Sustainable Investment Forum (2013a: 4, 2013b).

in 2016, much lower than in other world regions (Table 27.2).[2] In Japan, SRI accounted for 3.4% of total assets under management. Including Japan, Asia reached a global share of SRI assets of only 2.3% in 2016; Japan alone accounted for 2.1% of global SRI assets (GSIA 2017: 8).

A common problem complicating sustainable investment across the region has been the lack of or insufficient disclosure requirements that address environmental or long-term systemic risk factors. A good example for insufficient disclosure practices are palm oil, timber, and pulp and paper companies in Indonesia, Malaysia, and Singapore. Even though there is a strong business rationale for improved ESG performance of these firms, WWFN (2015: 11) points out that "the leading companies from these sectors listed in Singapore, Indonesia and Malaysia provide insufficient relevant disclosure for investors to assess their management of material ESG issues." WWFN (2015) also highlights that domestic investors have undertaken little efforts to address the disclosure gaps – in contrast to international investors for whom ESG scrutiny has already become standard practice. A survey among institutional investors in Indonesia confirmed this general picture (Volz 2015a): with the exemption of general insurance firms, hardly any institutional investors in Indonesia integrate ESG factors into their decision-making processes, and very few professional investment staff in the industry have been trained in ESG issues. Only recently, ESG disclosure and reporting requirements have been enhanced across the region (see Section 27.3).

The case of Malaysian palm oil firm IOI, whose sustainability certification was temporarily suspended by the Roundtable on Sustainable Palm Oil (RSPO) in March 2016 because of serious non-compliance with RSPO standards, causing major international customers to cancel their contracts with IOI (Taufik 2016), shows clearly how non-sustainable business practices can adversely affect a firm's cash flow, and diminish its market value. Given the importance of the palm oil and other extractive sectors in many of the region's countries, there is a strong case for both investors and financial authorities to take sustainability challenges more seriously.

At the same time, however, there are examples of green financial innovation across Asian markets, even if the market for sustainable investment is still nascent. In the PRC, for instance, the Shanghai Stock Exchange (SSE) launched the SSE Sustainable Development Index in 2013. In Malaysia, Bursa Malaysia Bhd launched an ESG index, FTSE4Good Bursa Malaysia (F4GBM) Index in December 2014, including listed companies demonstrating strong ESG practices. In neighboring Indonesia, the Indonesian Stock Exchange (IDX) and KEHATI launched a Social and Responsible Investment (SRI) index in June 2009.[3] The stocks of 25 companies listed at

Table 27.2 Percentage of SRI relative to total managed assets

	2012	2014	2016
Europe	49.0	58.8	52.6
Canada	20.2	31.3	37.8
United States	11.2	17.9	21.6
Australia/New Zealand	12.5	16.6	50.6
Asia	0.6	0.8	0.8
Japan			3.4
Global	21.5	30.2	26.3

SRI = socially responsible investments.

Note: Asia figures for 2012 and 2014 include Japan.

Source: GSIA (2015: 7), GSIA (2017: 7).

IDX are selected based on both negative (excluded sectors) and positive (enhanced social and environmental management) criteria. IDX and KEHATI consider the SRI KEHATI Index as the "first green index in ASEAN," even though the criteria for "green" are rather low. In 2014, an exchange-traded fund tracking the SRI KEHATI index was listed on the IDX. Yet, despite such positive developments, the sustainable investment market in Indonesia is still embryonic, and "investors continue to channel funds towards assets that maximize short-term risk-adjusted investment returns, with environmental, social or governance considerations of less concern" (ASrIA 2014: 34).

Local currency bond markets as a source of long-term finance have developed quite well in a number of Asian countries, although governments and enterprises still rely to a large extent on bank finance and forex lending, which entails considerable macroeconomic and stability risks. The reasons for the relative underdevelopment of bond markets differ between countries, but regulatory and corporate governance issues are at the core. It will be important to further develop local currency bond markets as a source for financing long-term infrastructure, while at the same time enhancing ESG disclosure requirements through bond exchanges and financial regulation.

The Asian green bond market has started to develop only recently, but current developments are encouraging. In an attempt to quantify bonds used to finance low-carbon and climate-resilient infrastructure, the Climate Bond Initiative (CBI) is looking at "labeled green bonds" that fund strictly defined and labeled green projects, as well as at "climate-aligned" bonds that do not carry a strict green label. The total amount of outstanding climate-aligned bonds reached USD 895 billion in September 2017 (up from USD 174 billion in 2012), out of which USD 221 billion were labeled green bonds (CBI 2017). While Asia accounted for only 4.1% of all global climate-aligned bonds outstanding in 2012, its share rose to 42.2% in September 2017 – a development that is very much related to the rapid growth of the Chinese green bond market over the last two years.

China's first corporate green bond was issued offshore in Hong Kong, China by Xinjiang Goldwind Science and Technology in August 2015 (Kidney 2016). This was followed by the first green bond issue by a Chinese bank by Agricultural Bank of China in London in October 2015. According to Reuters (2015), 94% of the USD 1 billion issue was sold to Asian investors, showing that demand for such assets is there. Following the release of the Green Financial Bond Guidelines by the People's Bank of China in December 2015, the PRC has seen the launch of its first two domestic green bonds (by China Industrial Bank and the Shanghai Pudong Development Bank) in January 2016. Since then, the Chinese green bond market has grown rapidly, reflecting the government's ambitions to make it a cornerstone of its plan to meet annual investment needs in clean energy, energy efficiency and environmental protection which are estimated to amount to about CNY 2 trillion (Zhang et al. 2015). In 2016, the total issuance of labeled green bonds amounted to CNY 238 billion (USD 36.2 billion); with 39% of global issuance, China was the biggest issuer of green bonds in 2016 (CBI and China Central Depository and Clearing Company [CCDC] 2017). Total green bond issuance rose slightly to CNY 248.6 billion (USD 37.1 billion) in 2017 (CBI and CCDC 2018). The total amount of outstanding climate-aligned bonds in China is estimated at USD 246 billion and USD 310 billion for 2016 and 2017, respectively. China therefore accounts now for about four-fifth of climate-aligned bonds in Asia and the Pacific region (CBI 2017).

The first Asian green bond was issued in 2013 by Export-Import Bank of Korea, raising USD 500 million (AllensLinklaters 2015). Indonesia saw its first green bond launch in April 2014. Supported by a partial credit guarantee from the International Finance Corporation (IFC), PT Ciputra Residence, a residential property developer, issued an IDR 500 billion (USD 44 million) bond based on green building standards on the IDX. In July 2014, the firm

Advanced Semiconductor Engineering in Taipei,China issued the first Asian corporate green bond without public support (Münzer-Jones and Johnson 2016).

India saw its first green bond issuance by Yes Bank in February 2015, with further issuances over the year by Yes Bank, Export-Import Bank of India, CLP Wind Farms and IDBI that brought the total green bond issuance to USD 1.1 billion for 2015 (Kidney 2016). The September 2015 issuance of Yes Bank was purchased by the IFC which financed this through the issue of the first green "Masala" bond, the first green bond issued in the offshore rupee markets (IFC 2015). The Indian green bond market is expected to expand after the Securities and Exchange Board of India (SEBI) published official green bond requirements in January 2016. In February 2016, Hero Future Energies issued India's first certified climate bond with proceeds being used to fund wind energy (Münzer-Jones and Johnson 2016). India has since seen various green bond issuances, with labeled green bond issuances of USD 4.3 billion in 2017.

Efforts to develop green bond markets are also underway elsewhere in the region. In March 2017, the Monetary Authority of Singapore (MAS) launched a Green Bond Grant Scheme which covers the costs up to SGD 100,000 per issuance of obtaining an external review for qualifying green bond issuances (Tan 2017). In September 2017, the ASEAN Capital Markets Forum, which brings together the capital market regulators of the 10 member countries of the ASEAN, launched the ASEAN Green Bond Standards, which are based on the International Capital Markets Association' Green Bond Principles.

The green bond market has been developed not least by public development banks and international financial institutions which also helped to develop standards such as the Green Bond Principles. In Asia, the IFC has helped several green bond issuances. The Development Bank of Japan placed the first Japanese green bond issuance of EUR 250 million in October 2014 (AllensLinklaters 2015). The ADB, which has issued USD 2.2 billion of water and clean-energy bonds since 2010, issued its first green bond over USD 500 million in March 2015. The ADB raised USD 1.3 billion and USD 1.25 billion in further green bond issuances in August 2016 and August 2017, respectively.

A crucial step in opening up demand for green bonds to institutional investors, such as pension funds and insurance companies lies in rating and labeling these bonds as benchmark-eligible securities in order to allow these institutions to add them to their portfolios. Initial steps into this direction are uniform standards for bonds that carry the label "green," through standards for what constitutes green projects and activities. Another measure implemented to attract institutional investors has been the creation of green bond indices in 2014 by banks and rating agencies (OECD 2017).

A more recent development in Asia and the Pacific region has been the interest in a market for the issuance of catastrophe bonds, or so-called cat bonds that pay out in the event of a natural disaster. So far, cat bonds have been mainly used in the US to mitigate storm-related risks and are one of the fastest growing parts of the global insurance market with bonds worth USD 11 billion issued in the first six months of 2017 (Ralph 2017). Most recently in Asia, Singapore has entered the cat bond market for insurance-linked securities (ILS) with the announcement that the MAS is to fund 100% of the upfront issuance costs for cat bonds out of Singapore starting January 2018 (Ralph 2017). Singapore is the first Asian country to roll out an incentive scheme of this scale in order to encourage the ILS market. The MAS has also discussed the creation of special purpose reinsurance vehicle legislation in order to further encourage the ILS and catastrophe business (MAS 2008) and has recently introduced an application process for the prior approval by the MAS for the establishment of special purpose reinsurance vehicles (MAS 2017).

While bond markets have become more important as a source of long-term finance across Asia, Asian financial systems continue to be dominated by banking. Reliable data on green banking is scarce, given that only few Asian countries have introduced green lending frameworks and therefore for most part banks had no definition of what constitutes green or sustainable lending. In most Asian economies, the concept of green banking is rather new, and most banks have little or no experience in environmental risk analysis. Overall, lending for sustainable consumption and production constitutes only a small share of total commercial lending and is sold at a premium compared to conventional finance (e.g., SWITCH-Asia and ASrIA 2015a, 2015b). There are, however, also positive developments as increased efforts at green financial governance (which will be discussed in a later section) have raised awareness in the banking industry. Two notable pioneers in green banking in Asia are the PRC and Bangladesh.

In the PRC, green lending has increased substantially over recent years as a result of the efforts of the financial authorities of the PRC to boost green finance.[4] While green credit stood at CNY 341 billion in 2007, it has increased to CNY 7.5 trillion (USD 1.14 trillion) at the end of 2016 – an increase from 0.6% of total banking assets to 3.2% (Figure 27.1). According to the China Banking Association, 21 major banks from the PRC reported more that CNY 8.2 trillion in lending to green projects by 2017, about 10% of their total outstanding loans.

In Bangladesh, the central bank's efforts at greening the banking system have had considerable effect. In the fiscal year 2016, Bangladeshi banks extended a total of BDT 503.2 billion in green finance (Figure 27.2) (a share of 7.5% of total credit); moreover, all banks have conducted environmental risk rating of new projects financed (BB 2017).

Lastly, turning to the insurance sector, even though efforts have been made for several years to establish weather and climate insurance products across Asian countries, the share of uninsured households is still large. Green insurance can be defined in narrow terms as environmental pollution liability insurance and in broader terms as insurance that covers schemes related

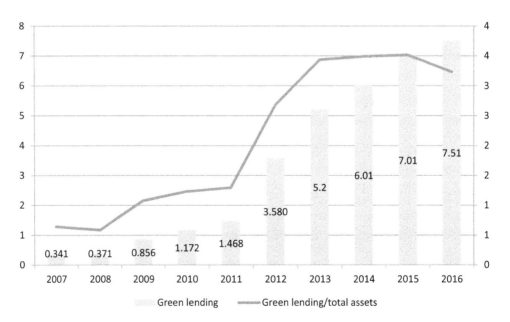

Figure 27.1   Green lending by banks in the People's Republic of China (in CNY trillion and as a share of total banking assets)

Note: Scale for green lending/total assets is on the right axis.

Source: Compiled with data from Zadek and Zhang (2014: 17), UNEP (2017), China Banking Regulatory Commission (2016: 192), China Daily (2015), and the China Banking Regulatory Commission.

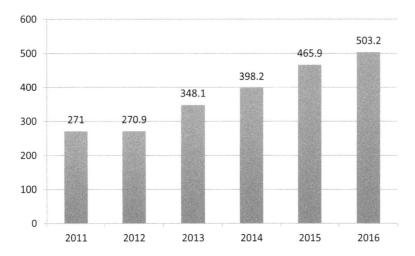

Figure 27.2 Total green finance extended in Bangladesh (BDT billion)

Note: "Total green finance" includes loans disbursed to key green sectors and loans disbursed to industrial facilities with effluent treatment ("indirect green financing").

Source: Compiled with data from Bank Bangladesh (various publications).

to environmental risk management and resilience as well as innovative products safeguarding low-carbon solutions (UNEP 2017). For instance, according to World Bank FINDEX data for 2011, only 5.7% of people working in agriculture in South Asia are insured against climate-related risks (Deutsche Gesellschaft für Internationale Zusammenarbeit 2015). Traditional, publicly subsidized agricultural insurance schemes such as the ones provided by the Agricultural Insurance Company of India have already been in place for a while. However, the success of such traditional indemnity based weather insurance schemes has been viewed critically by some (Sirimanne and Srivastava 2015), and there is clearly a need to further develop innovative insurance products such as index-based insurance programs for farmers or flooding risk insurance and extend their outreach in Asia (e.g., Schanz and Wang 2015).

Green finance policies in Asia

Several Asian countries have been at the forefront of introducing sustainable finance guidelines and regulation. As can be seen in Figure 27.3, 13 out of the 32 countries represented in the Sustainable Banking Network – a knowledge-sharing network of banking regulators and banking associations established in 2012 that supports the development of environmental and social risk management by financial institutions and promotes green and inclusive lending – are from Asia.[5]

The MAS and the People's Bank of China were two of the eight founding members of the Central Banks and Supervisors Network for Greening the Financial System, which was launched at the One Planet Summit in Paris in December 2017 (CBSNGFS 2017). Four Asian cities – Astana; Hong Kong, China; Qatar; and Shanghai – were among the 11 founding members of the International Network of Financial Centres for Sustainability, which was launched in September 2017. Members of the network have committed to utilize their financial expertise to drive action on climate change and sustainable development. In December 2017, five other financial centers joined the network, including Shenzhen, so that five of the 16 financial centers of the network are Asian.

MEXICO
The Mexican Banking Association launched the Sustainability Protocol in 2016.

COLOMBIA
Through the Colombian banking association Asobancaria, major Colombian banks adopted the Colombia Green Protocol in 2012.

PERU
The Superintendency of Banking, Insurance and Private Pension Fund Administrators of Peru (SBS) launched the Regulation for Social and Environmental Risk Management in 2015.

BRAZIL
The Central Bank of Brazil issued a regulation on Environmental and Social Risk Management for Banks in 2014.

TURKEY
The Banks Association of Turkey issued voluntary Sustainability Guidelines for the banking sector in 2014.

NIGERIA
The Central Bank of Nigeria required all banks to implement the Nigerian Sustainable Banking Principles in 2012.

KENYA
Through the Kenya Bankers Association, Kenya banks adopted the Sustainable Finance Initiative (SFI) Guiding Principles in 2015.

MONGOLIA
Through the Mongolian Bankers Association, Mongolian banks adopted the Mongolian Sustainable Finance Principles in 2014.

CHINA
The China Banking Regulatory Commission issued the Green Credit Guidelines in 2012 and the Green Credit Statistics Systems and Key Performance Indicators in 2014.

VIETNAM
The State Bank of Vietnam issued the Directive on Promoting Green Credit and Managing Environmental and Social Risk in Lending Activities in 2015.

BANGLADESH
The Bangladesh Bank issued the Environmental Risk Management Guidelines in 2011.

INDONESIA
The Indonesian Financial Services Authority (OJK) launched the Roadmap for Sustainability Finance in 2014.

Existing guidance: Bangladesh, Brazil, China, Colombia, Ecuador, Indonesia, Kenya, Mexico, Mongolia, Morocco, Nigeria, Peru, South Africa, Turkey, Vietnam

In dialogue: Argentina, Cambodia, Chile, Egypt, Fiji, Ghana, Honduras, India, Jordan, Laos, Nepal, Pakistan, Panama, Paraguay, Philippines, Sri Lanka, Thailand

Figure 27.3   Sustainable banking network members and countries having introduced green finance guidelines and regulations

Source: Created with information from the Sustainable Banking Network website (accessed on 6 December 2017) (www.ifc.org/wps/wcm/connect/topics_ext_content/ifc_external_corporate_site/sustainability-at-ifc/company-resources/sustainable-finance/sbn).

As can be seen in Table 27.3, financial authorities in Bangladesh; the PRC, Hong Kong, China; India; Indonesia; Japan; Mongolia; Singapore; and Viet Nam have already started to take concrete steps to align the financial system or parts of it with sustainable development. Financial authorities in Cambodia; Lao PDR; Nepal; Pakistan; the Philippines; Sri Lanka; and Thailand are currently working on green finance policies.[6]

Table 27.3 Sustainable finance policies across Asia

Bangladesh	
2008	Bangladesh Bank: Circular on "Mainstreaming Corporate Social Responsibility in Banks and Financial Institutions in Bangladesh"
2011	Bangladesh Bank: "Policy Guidelines for Green Banking" and "Guidelines on Environmental Risk Management"
2015	Bangladesh Bank: Mandatory Green Finance Credit Targets l
2016	Bangladesh Bank: "Integrated Risk Management Guidelines for Financial Institutions"
2017	Bangladesh Bank: Guidelines on Environmental and Social Risk Management for Banks and Financial Institutions
People's Republic of China	
2007	China Banking Regulatory Commission (CBRC), People's Bank of China (PBOC), and Ministry of Environmental Protection (MEP): Green Credit Policy ("Opinions on Enforcing Policies and Regulations on Environmental Protection to Prevent Credit Risk") MEP and China Insurance Regulatory Commission (CIRC): Green Insurance Policy ("Guiding Opinions on Environmental Pollution Liability Insurance")
2008	China Securities Regulatory Commission (CSRC) and MEP: Green Securities Policy ("Guidance Opinions on Strengthening the Oversight of Public Companies") Shanghai Stock Exchange: Shanghai CSR Notice and Shanghai Environmental Disclosure Guidelines
2009	Shenzhen Stock Exchange: Social Responsibility Instructions to Listed Companies
2012	CBRC: Green Credit Guidelines
2013	MEP and CIRC: "Guiding Opinions on Implementing the Pilot Programs of Compulsory Environmental Pollution Liability"
2014	CBRC: Green Credit Monitoring and Evaluation mechanism and Key Performance Indicators Checklist PBOC: Green Finance Task Force MEP and CIRC: "Guiding Opinions on Pilot Scheme for Compulsory Environmental Pollution Liability Insurance"
2015	PBOC: Green Financial Bond Directive and Green Bond-Endorsed Project Catalogue for Bonds Issued by Financial Institutions and Corporations PBOC: Green Finance Committee
2016	PBOC: Guidelines for Establishing the Green Financial System NDRC and Shanghai Stock Exchange: Green Bond Guidelines China Bond Green and Climate-Aligned Bond Index
2017	State Council: Establishment of five green finance pilot zones in Zhejiang, Jiangxi, Guangdong, Guizhou and Xinjiang MEP and CSRC: Environmental Disclosure for Listed Companies CSRC: Guidelines for Green Bond Issuance by Listed Companies MEP and CIRC: Draft Guideline on Environmental Pollution Liability Insurance Shanghai's Lujiazui Financial City: Lujiazui Standard of Green Finance
2018	CSRC and MEP: Mandatory ESG disclosures for listed companies and bond issuers by 2020

(Continued)

Table 27.3 (Continued)

Hong Kong, China

2016	Securities and Futures Commission: Principles of Responsible Ownership
	Financial Services Development Council: Report on "Hong Kong as a Regional Green Finance Hub"
2018	Hong Kong Quality Assurance Agency: Green Finance Certification Scheme

India

2007	Corporate Social Responsibility, Sustainable Development and Non-Financial Reporting – Role of Banks
2011	Ministry of Corporate Affairs: National Voluntary Guidelines on Social, Environmental and Economic Responsibilities of Business
2012	Securities and Exchange Board of India (SEBI): Annual Business Responsibility Reporting
2014	SEBI: Infrastructure Investment Trusts (InvIT) Regulations
2015	Reserve Bank of India: Priority Sector Lending – Targets and Classification
	Indian Banks Association: National Voluntary Guidelines for Responsible Financing
2016	SEBI: Guidelines for the Issuance and Listing of Green Bonds
2017	SEBI: Disclosure Requirements for Issuance and Listing of Green Bonds

Indonesia

2012	Bank Indonesia: Green Lending Model Guidelines for Mini Hydro Power Plant Projects
	Government Regulation on Social and Environmental Responsibility of Limited Liability Companies
2014	Otoritas Jasa Keuangan (OJK)/ Financial Services Authority: Roadmap for Sustainable Finance in Indonesia 2015–2019
2015	IFC, USAID, OJK: Clean Energy Handbook for Financial Service Institutions
2017	OJK: Framework and regulation for green bond issuance in Indonesia
	OJK: Regulation on the Application of Sustainable Finance for Financial Services Companies, Issuers and Publicly Listed Companies

Japan

2012	Ministry of the Environment: Principles for financial action toward a sustainable society
2014	Financial Services Agency: Japan Stewardship Code
2015	Tokyo Stock Exchange: Corporate Governance Code and Infrastructure Fund Market
2017	Ministry of the Environment: Green Bond Guidelines

Mongolia

2014	Bank of Mongolia and Mongolia Banking Association: Mongolia Sustainable Finance Principles and Sector Guidelines

Philippines

2008	Government of Philippines: National Disaster Risk Reduction and Management Law
2011	Securities and Exchange Commission: Corporate Governance Guidelines for Companies Corporate Responsibility Act updated
2015	Government of Philippines: Joint Catastrophe Risk Insurance Facility for Governments (Local Government Units Pool)

Singapore

2010	Singapore Stock Exchange (SGX): "Guide to Sustainability Reporting for Listed Companies"
2015	Association of Banks in Singapore: Guidelines on Responsible Financing
2017	Monetary Authority of Singapore: Green Bond Grant Scheme

---

Thailand

2008   Stock Exchange Thailand and Securities and Exchange Commission of Thailand: Guidelines for Sustainability Reporting

2014   Stock Exchange Thailand: CSR Reporting Requirements

Securities and Exchange Commission of Thailand: Sustainability Development Roadmap for Listed Companies

Viet Nam

2015   State Bank of Viet Nam (SBV): Directive on Promoting Green Credit Growth and Managing Environmental and Social Risks in Credit Extension

SBV: Action Plan of Banking Sector to Implement the National Green Growth Strategy until 2020

2016   SBV: Circular on lending transactions of credit institutions and/or foreign bank branches with customers

2017   SBV: Renewed commitment to implementing the Green Growth program and the program of preventing climate change

---

Source: Compiled by author.

In its global survey of sustainable finance approaches, the UNEP Inquiry (2015) identified five areas of emerging practice in embedding sustainable development into the financial system. Examples for each of these areas can be found across Asia and are given in the following.

(i) Enhancing market practice: disclosure, analysis, risk management

(a) Sustainability disclosure: The Shanghai Stock Exchange introduced Guidelines on Listed Companies' Environmental Information Disclosure already in 2008. In 2010 the Singapore Stock Exchange (SGX) released a "Guide to Sustainability Reporting for Listed Companies." In June 2016, SGX made it mandatory for all listed companies to publish sustainability reports from December 2017 onwards. In 2012, the Hong Kong Exchanges and Clearing Limited introduced voluntary ESG Reporting Guidelines. Since 2012, the SEBI requires the 100 largest listed enterprises to publish annual Business Responsibility Reports, while the Indian Ministry of Corporate Affairs' imposed CSR reporting requirements under the Companies Act 2013. In 2015, SEBI established a "comply or explain" reporting system for corporate governance under which the top 500 companies were asked to report, among other issues their E&S risk assessment standards and how climate change and global warming are addressed. Philippines Securities Exchange Commission (SEC) requests an Annual Corporate Governance Report from listed firms since 2013. In Viet Nam, the State Securities Commission introduced a Sustainability Reporting Handbook for Vietnamese Companies in 2013.

(b) Integrating environmental risks into financial regulation: Bank Bangladesh requires environmental risk management from bank and nonbank financial institutions. The State Bank of Viet Nam issued the "Directive on Promoting Green Credit Growth and Environmental Social Risks Management in Credit Granting Activities" (State Bank of Viet Nam 2015), requiring financial institutions to take environmental factors into account in their lending decisions.

(c) Industry guidelines for sustainable market practice: The Association of Banks in Singapore released Guidelines on Responsible Financing in October 2015. The same year the Indian Banking Association introduced the National Voluntary Guidelines for Responsible Finance.

(ii) Upgrading governance architectures: internalizing sustainable development into financial decision-making of financial regulators and central banks

    (a) Inclusion of environmental risk to secure financial and monetary stability: The Bangladesh Bank considers its green finance policies as integral part of its mandate to maintain monetary and financial stability. The Reserve Bank of India pays close attention to agricultural prices as these have a significant impact on consumer price inflation. Bank Indonesia is considering to include environmental and climate risk into its macroprudential framework. In China, the PBOC is considering to include the green credit performance of banks into the central banks' assessment of macroprudential risk (Yao and Borsuk 2017).

    (b) Multi-stakeholder dialogue between financial authorities and the financial industry: In 2015, the PBOC established the Green Finance Committee to develop green finance practices, environmental stress testing for the banking sector, and guidelines on greening China's overseas investment. Also in 2015, the Indonesian financial services regulator OJK has established a multi-stakeholder task force to promote and further develop its Roadmap for Sustainable Finance through dialogue.

(iii) Encouraging cultural transformation: capacity building, behavior, market structure

    (a) Action to enhance the current skill set of financial professionals and regulators: Indonesia's Sustainable Finance Roadmap seeks to develop the sustainability skills of professionals. In Viet Nam, the central bank has also voiced its intent to organize training workshops for bank personnel.

    (b) Mainstreaming CSR and ESG considerations: Bangladesh Bank has been mainstreaming CSR in banks and financial institutions.

    (c) Market development: With the new Green Financial Bond Directive, the PBOC has taken a first step to develop a new market segment for sustainable investment in the Chinese capital market.

(iv) Harnessing the public balance sheets: fiscal incentives, public financial institutions, and central banks

    (a) Fiscal incentives for investors: Thailand introduced a feed-in premium programme in 2010 which has helped to more than doubled its installed clean energy capacity.

    (b) Preferential central bank refinancing: Banks in Bangladesh extending loans for green projects can access the Bangladesh Bank's refinancing arrangements and pass on preferential interest rates to their clients.

    (c) Green credit and bond guarantees: Development banks such as the ADB have offered risk-sharing facilities in various Asian countries where partial credit guarantees were provided to partner banks sharing the payment risk of underlying borrowers, for example for energy efficiency projects. USAID's Development Credit Authority has extended bond guarantees to support Asian municipalities in raising funds for constructing urban resilient infrastructure.

    (d) Public pension funds: In Japan, the Government Pension Investment Fund (GPIF) and the Pension Fund Association for Local Government Officials endorsed the Principles for Responsible Institutional Investors along with 160 other institutions within six months of its launch in February 2014 by Japan's Financial Services Agency (GSIA 2014: 25). In 2017, GPIF adopted an ESG investment strategy. In 2014, the Korean

National Assembly requested from the National Pension Service, the world's fourth largest pension fund, to enhance its ESG standards.

(v) Directing finance through policy: requirements and prohibitions, enhanced liability

   (a) Green lending requirements: Since 2015, Bangladesh Bank requires banks to allocate 5% of bank lending into green projects, including renewable energy, energy efficiency, and waste management. It also uses differentiated capital requirements and preferential refinancing to incentivise green financing.

   (b) Priority sector lending programmes: In April 2015, the Reserve Bank of India included lending to small renewable energy projects and drinking water facilities within the Priority Sector Lending (PSL) targets. The PSL scheme requires banks to allocate 40% of lending to key sectors such as agriculture and small and medium-sized enterprises.

   (c) Quotas for priority areas: Since 2002, the Obligations of Insurers to Rural Social Sectors issued by the Insurance Regulatory and Development Authority of India require Indian insurance firms to satisfy quotas for the extension of insurance coverage to low-income and rural clients.

While the first three areas of emerging green finance practice are straightforward and fairly uncontroversial, this cannot be said about (iv) and (v). For instance, using the central bank balance sheet to incentivize green lending or even invest directly is considered a taboo in orthodox central banking circles (Volz 2016b). Likewise, directed credit allocation has earned a bad reputation in the 1960s and 1970s (e.g., Krueger 1990), although there certainly have been successful cases too. The initiatives referred to above are mostly too recent to provide a conclusive assessment of their efficacy, and in the case of Bangladesh, where the central bank's targeted refinancing policies have been in place since 2009, a comprehensive evaluation is still outstanding. In each specific country context, policy options have to be considered cautiously and instruments and policies have to be designed carefully to avoid potential adverse effects. The respective policy frameworks also have to take account of differences in financial market structure which are likely to impact on policy outcomes (Volz 2015b). To counter the danger that green finance policies may result in politicized or crony lending, it will be crucial to strengthen corporate governance of the involved institutions, including through tighter internal and external auditing, and improved accounting practices and risk management. Moreover, once implemented, green finance policies need to be reviewed regularly and adjusted, or abolished, if needed.

Conclusion

While green finance and investment is currently still a niche market in Asian financial systems, growth rates have been high, and different Asian markets have already seen various green financial innovations. Moreover, the financial authorities of several Asian countries have been developing green finance frameworks, while other countries are in the process of doing so. The challenges for achieving a green transformation to a low-carbon economy are high; aligning the financial sector with sustainable development will be a key element for Asian economies to succeed.

To this end, a dialogue among all relevant domestic stakeholders is needed. Public financial institutions, including central banks, development banks, and public pension funds, can play an important role in developing and promoting the adaption of new green financial products.

International initiatives and networks such as the UNEP Finance Initiative, the Sustainable Banking Network, the Sustainable Stock Exchanges Initiative, the G7 Initiative on Climate Risk Insurance ("InsuResilience"), and the G20 Sustainable Finance Study Group can help countries to leverage on international experiences.

Moreover, to enhance green finance and investment, it is imperative to address "real economy" barriers and bottlenecks. Gaps in the enforcement of environmental regulation and the non-pricing of negative production and consumption externalities such as carbon emissions clearly reduce the demand for green investment. Addressing such real economy barriers through binding environmental regulation, emissions trading schemes or other policies that help to internalize negative externalities, is critical to mobilizing green investment.

Acknowledgments

This study builds on Volz (2016a). A longer version is published as Volz (2018). I would like to thank Simon Dikau for excellent research assistance.

Notes

1 These are: BSE India Limited, National Stock Exchange of India (NSE), Kazakhstan Stock Exchange, Korea Exchange, Bursa Malaysia, Colombo Stock Exchange, Stock Exchange of Thailand, Hanoi Stock Exchange, and Ho Chi Minh Stock Exchange.
2 Sustainable investment is defined by GSIA (2015) as encompassing the following activities and strategies: (1) negative/exclusionary screening; (2) positive/best-in-class screening; (3) norms-based screening; (4) integration of ESG factors; (5) sustainability-themed investing; (6) impact/community investing; and (7) corporate engagement and shareholder action. GSIA (2015) includes data for 13 Asian markets: Bangladesh; PRC; Hong Kong, China; India; Indonesia; Japan; Republic of Korea; Malaysia; Pakistan; Singapore; Taipei, China; Thailand, and Viet Nam.
3 For a survey of sustainable finance in Indonesia, see Volz (2015a).
4 According to CBRC's definition, green credit comprises loans to green agriculture; green forestry; energy/water saving in industrial sector; nature protection, biological restoring and disaster prevention; recycling projects; garbage treatment and pollution prevention; renewable energy and clean energy; water projects in urban and rural areas; green buildings; green transportation; energy efficiency and environmental services; overseas green projects.
5 The Asian SBN members are Bangko Sentral ng Pilipinas (Central Bank of the Philippines), Bank of Bangladesh, Bank of Lao PDR, Bank of Mongolia, China Banking Association, China Banking Regulatory Commission, China Ministry of Environmental Protection, Department of Environmental and Natural Resources of the Philippines, Mongolia Bankers Association, Mongolia Ministry of Environment and Green Development, Nepal Rastra Bank, Otoritas Jasa Keuangan (Indonesia Financial Services Authority), State Bank of Pakistan, State Bank of Viet Nam, Thai Bankers Association, and Viet Nam Ministry of Natural Resources and Environment.
6 For a discussion of green finance policies in the PRC and Bangladesh, see Volz (2018).

References

AllensLinklaters. 2015. *Green Bonds: Emergence of the Australian and Asian Markets*. Melbourne and Hong Kong: AllensLinklaters.
ASEAN Secretariat and UNCTAD. 2015. *ASEAN Investment Report 2015. Infrastructure Investment and Connectivity*. Jakarta: ASEAN Secretariat and United Nations Conference on Trade and Development.
ADB. 2017. *Meeting Asia's Infrastructure Needs*. Manila: Asian Development Bank.
ADB and Asian Development Bank Institute (ADBI). 2012. *Policies and Practices for Low-Carbon Green Growth in Asia. ADB-ADBI Study on Climate Change and Green Asia*. Manila and Tokyo: Asian Development Bank and Asian Development Bank Institute.

Asian News Network (ANN). 2016. *BB Lines up $200m Green Fund for Textile, Leather Makers*. ANN, 13 January. www.asianews.network/content/bangladesh's-central-bank-lines-200m-green-fund-textile-leather-makers-7351.

ASrIA. 2014. *2014 Asia Sustainable Investment Review*. Hong Kong: Association for Sustainable and Responsible Investment in Asia.

ASrIA. 2015. *2015 Asia Sustainable Investment Review*. Hong Kong: Association for Sustainable and Responsible Investment in Asia.

Bangladesh Bank. 2017. *Annual Report 2015–2016*. Dhaka: Bangladesh Bank.

Central Banks and Supervisors Network for Greening the Financial System. 2017. Joint Statement by the Founding Members of the Central Banks and Supervisors Network for Greening the Financial System, Paris, 12 December. www.mas.gov.sg/News-and-Publications/Media-Releases/2017/Joint-statement-by-the-Founding-Members-of-the-Central-Banks-and-Supervisors-Network.aspx

China Banking Regulatory Commission. 2016. *2015 Annual Report*. Beijing: China Banking Regulatory Commission.

China Daily. 2015. Green Finance Booming among Chinese Banks. *China Daily*, 26 August. http://europe.chinadaily.com.cn/business/2015-08/26/content_21709856.htm

Climate Bonds Initiative (CBI). 2017. *Bonds and Climate Change. The State of the Market 2017*. London: CBI.

CBI and China Central Depository and Clearing Company (CCDC). 2017. *China Green Bond Market 2016*. London and Beijing: CBI and CCDC.

CBI and CCDC. 2018. *China Green Bond Market 2017*. London and Beijing: CBI and CCDC.

Deutsche Gesellschaft für Internationale Zusammenarbeit. 2015. *Climate Risk Insurance for Strengthening Climate Resilience of Poor People in Vulnerable Countries. A Background Paper on Challenges, Ambitions and Perspectives*. Bonn and Eschborn: Deutsche Gesellschaft für Internationale Zusammenarbeit.

Global Sustainable Investment Alliance (GSIA). 2015. 2014 *Global Sustainable Investment Review*. Brussels, Sydney, London, Washington, and Utrecht: GSIA.

GSIA. 2017. 2016 *Global Sustainable Investment Review*. Brussels, Sydney, London, Washington, and Utrecht: GSIA.

International Finance Corporation. 2015. IFC Issues First Green Masala Bond, August. www.ifc.org/wps/wcm/connect/news-ext-content/ifc-external-corporate-site/news+and+events/news/ifc+issues+first+green+masala+bond+on+london+stock+exchange.

Japan Sustainable Investment Forum (JSIF). 2013a. *2013 Review of Socially Responsible Investment in Japan*. Tokyo: JSIF.

JSIF. 2013b. *Pension Funds and ESG Investment in Japan 2013: From a Survey by JSIF*. Tokyo: JSIF.

Kidney, S. 2016. 2015 Year End Review – From Tall Trees to Many Green Shoots: The Evolution of the Green Bond Market Continues with 2015 Seeing $41.8bn Green Bonds Issued – That's the Biggest Ever! 11 January. www.climatebonds.net/2016/01/2015-year-end-review-tall-trees-many-green-shoots-evolution-green-bond-market-continues-2015

Kreft, S., D. Eckstein, L. Dorsch, and L. Fischer. 2016. Global Climate Risk Index 2016. Who Suffers Most from Extreme Weather Events? Weather-Related Loss Events in 2014 and 1995 to 2014. Briefing Paper. Bonn: Germanwatch.

Krueger, A. O. 1990. Government Failures in Development. *Journal of Economic Perspectives* 4(3): 9–23.

Monetary Authority of Singapore (MAS). 2008. *Proposed Regulatory Framework Governing Special Purpose Reinsurance Vehicles. P003–2008*. Singapore: MAS.

MAS. 2017. *Application to Establish a Special Purpose Reinsurance Vehicle*. Singapore: MAS.

Münzer-Jones, V., and D. Johnson. 2016. Recent Developments in the Asian Green Bond Markets, February. www.nortonrosefulbright.com/knowledge/publications/137413/recent-developments-in-the-asian-green-bond-markets

Organisation for Economic Co-operation and Development (OECD). 2017. *Green Bonds – Mobilising the Debt Capital Markets for a Low-Carbon Transition*. Paris: Organisation for Economic Co-operation and Development.

Ralph, O. 2017. Singapore Seeks to Muscle in on Market for Catastrophe Bonds. *Financial Times*, 1 November. www.ft.com/content/55229b4c-befd-11e7-b8a3-38a6e068f464

Reuters. 2015. China Agricultural Bank Sells $1 Billion Debut "Green Bond" in London, 14 October. uk.reuters.com/article/uk-china-bonds-offshore-idUKKCN0S807Q20151014

Schanz, K.-U., and S. Wang. 2015. *Insuring Flood Risk in Asia's High-Growth Markets*. Geneva: The Geneva Association.

Sirimanne, S., and S. Srivastava. 2015. *Weather Insurance for Adaptation to Climate Risk: Emerging Trends from Asia and the Pacific Region. Information and Communications Technology and Disaster Risk Reduction Division Information Note.* Bangkok: United Nations Economic and Social Commission for Asia and the Pacific.

State Bank of Viet Nam. 2015. *Directive on Promoting Green Credit Growth and Environmental-Social Risk Management in Credit Granting Activities.* Hanoi: State Bank of Viet Nam.

SWITCH-Asia and ASrIA. 2015a. Enabling SME Access to Finance for Sustainable Consumption and Production in Asia. An Overview of Finance Trends and Barriers in Indonesia, Malaysia, and Thailand. www.switch-asia.eu/fileadmin/user_upload/Publications/2015/SWITCH-Asia-and-ASrIA-Study-Green-Finance.pdf

SWITCH-Asia and ASrIA. 2015b. Enabling SME Access to Finance for Sustainable Consumption and Production in Asia. An Overview of Finance Trends and Barriers in Sri Lanka and the Philippines. www.switch-asia.eu/fileadmin/user_upload/Publications/2015/SWITCH-Asia-and-ADFIAP-Study-Green-Finance.pdf.

Tan, M. 2017. Singapore, Are You Ready to Invest in Green Bonds? *Asia Finance*, 18 November. www.asia.finance/singapore-ready-invest-green-bonds

Taufik, K. 2016. Unilever Palm Oil Supplier Must Suspend All Plantation Expansion to Save Reputation. *The Guardian*, 9 April. www.theguardian.com/sustainable-business/2016/apr/09/ioi-malaysian-palm-oil-company-unilever-mars-kellogg-rspo-deforestation

UNEP Inquiry. 2015. *The Financial System We Need. Aligning the Financial System with Sustainable Development.* Geneva: UNEP Inquiry into the Design of a Sustainable Financial System.

UNEP Inquiry. 2017. *Establishing China's Green Financial System: Progress Report 2017.* Geneva: UNEP Inquiry into the Design of a Sustainable Financial System.

UNFCCC. 2015. *Adoption of the Paris Agreement, 21st Conference of the Parties.* Paris: United Nations/ Framework Convention on Climate Change.

University of Notre Dame. 2017. Notre Dame Global Adaptation Index. http://index.gain.org/ranking

Volz, U. 2015a. *Towards a Sustainable Financial System in Indonesia.* Geneva and Washington, DC: UNEP Inquiry into the Design of a Sustainable Financial System and International Finance Corporation.

Volz, U. 2015b. *Effects of Financial System Size and Structure on the Real Economy. What Do We Know and What Do We Not Know?* Geneva: UNEP Inquiry into the Design of a Sustainable Financial System.

Volz, U. 2016a. Fostering Green Finance in Asia. Report Prepared for the 2016 ADB Annual Meeting. Bonn: German Development Institute/Deutsches Institut für Entwicklungspolitik.

Volz, U. 2016b. *On the Role of Central Banks in Enhancing Green Finance.* Geneva: UNEP Inquiry into the Design of a Sustainable Financial System.

Volz, U. 2018. Fostering Green Finance for Sustainable Development in Asia. ADBI Working Paper No. 814. Tokyo: Asian Development Bank Institute.

Volz, U., J. Böhnke, V. Eidt, L. Knierim, K. Richert, and G.-M. Roeber. 2015. *Financing the Green Transformation – How to Make Green Finance Work in Indonesia.* Houndmills, Basingstoke: Palgrave Macmillan.

World Wide Fund for Nature (WWFN). 2015. *Sustainable Finance Report 2015. Sustainable Finance in Singapore, Indonesia and Malaysia: A Review of Financiers' ESG Practices, Disclosure Standards and Regulations.* Gland: World Wide Fund for Nature.

Yao, K., and R. Borsuk. 2017. *China Central Bank Plans Fresh Incentives to Support Green Financing.* Reuters, 16 June. www.reuters.com/article/us-china-banking-greenfinance/china-central-bank-plans-fresh-incentives-to-support-green-financing-idUSKBN1970R1

Zadek, S., and C. Zhang. 2014. *Greening China's Financial System. An Initial Exploration.* Winnipeg and Beijing: Institute for Sustainable Development and Development Research Center of the State Council.

Zhang C., S. Zadek, C. Ning, and M. Halle. 2015. *Greening China's Financial System: Synthesis Report.* Winnipeg and Beijing: Institute for Sustainable Development and Development Research Center of the State Council.

28

AN OVERVIEW OF ISLAMIC BANKING AND FINANCE IN ASIA

Akbar Komijani and Farhad Taghizadeh-Hesary

Introduction

The concept of Islamic banking and finance takes its origin from the aspiration of removing *riba* (usury) from the Islamic community. The Quran prohibits *riba*. Despite differing views on the concept of *riba* in the pre-Islamic era and the present time, Islamic scholars have sought to design and implement *riba*-free (usury-free) banking since the early 1950s. The first Islamic institutions which offered widespread Islamic banking services date back to the 1960s when Islamic banks started to appear in countries with large Muslim population.

Muslim thinkers and bankers have made substantial progress in both theoretical and practical aspects in the fields of Islamic money, banking, and insurance in the five decades after the emergence of the first Islamic financial institutions. They have discussed theoretical issues concerning the principles that should guide Islamic financial systems and their distinction with those of other financial systems. Such discussions rotate around the main differences between economic systems due to their views on the universe, the purpose of creation, and the mission of humankind. Islam places high significance for the position of humankind and views it as the axis of creation and as the proxy of Allah on earth.[1] The difference between an Islamic economic system and secular economics lies in the former's emphasis upon social justice from an economic domain. All values governing the Islamic economic and banking system are extracted from the Quran.

Significant attempts made by Muslim economists in the last half century include designing a *Shariah*[2]-based financial and banking system while maintaining the standards of efficiency and stability.

In this chapter, the first section provides an overview of Islamic banking and finance by presenting the principles, characteristics, and the features of an Islamic financial system. The following section, which is the core of this chapter, describes the growing Islamic banking and finance sector in Asia by highlighting the current status, challenges in capital market, regulatory environments, and recent developments in the issuance of infrastructure *Sukuk*.

Overview of Islamic banking and finance

A transformation of Islamic economic and financial systems started in the late 19th century when protests against the payment of interest gained momentum. In the 1890s, Barclays Bank opened a branch in Cairo in order to finance the construction of the Suez Canal (Kettell 2010).

The establishment of an interest-based bank in a majority-Muslim country led to some opposition and led to some jurists declaring in 1903 that the interest paid to depositors in the post office contradicted Islamic rules and values.

Islamic scholars designed alternatives to conventional banking by extracting *Shariah*-compliant contracts. Due to a high demand for *Shariah*-compliant banking services, many Islamic banks were established in the Middle East and parts of Asia, including Malaysia in 1963, Bangladesh in 1983, and Indonesia in 1991. The Islamic Development Bank (IDB) was founded in 1975 as a regional development institution with the goal of promoting economic development of Muslim countries and providing *Shariah*-compliant finance.

The Islamic Financial Services Board (IFSB) is an international institution which designs and publishes *Shariah*-compliant standards aiming at enhancement of health and stability of the Islamic financial service industry, including guidelines for banking, insurance, and capital markets. The activities of the IFSB complement the measures and activities of the Basel Committee on Banking Supervision, the International Organization of Securities Commissions and the International Association of Insurance Supervisors. The IFSB, which is based in Kuala Lumpur, was officially inaugurated in November 2002 and started operations in March 2003.

Islamic capital markets have experienced substantial growth. Securities backed by Islamic assets are known as *Sukuk*. These securities have appeared in various structures in Malaysia, Indonesia, Iran, and other Islamic financial centers. Private corporations, international organizations such as the IDB, the World Bank, and governments are among the issuers of *Sukuk*, including the governments of Indonesia, Iran, and Malaysia. A number of high-profile non-Muslim Asian jurisdictions including Singapore and Hong Kong, China have also now issued sovereign *Sukuk* (ADB and IFSB 2015). Several funds based on *Shariah*-compliant shares were established during the boom years of the 1990s (Iqbal and Mirakhor 2007).

Since the early 2000s, the global Islamic capital market has been growing in depth and size across jurisdictions, with numerous entities across sectors raising capital in ways that comply with Islamic principles. As of today, the global Islamic capital market is a multisector segment that includes holistic financial instruments including *Sukuk* Islamic equities, Islamic funds, and other Islamic structured products, including real estate and investment trusts and exchange-traded funds. The Islamic equity sector has firmly established itself in key global bourses and jurisdictions, and the world's major financial index providers, such as Dow Jones, Standard & Poor's, and FTSE, all have *Shariah*-compliant equity listings which have allowed the *Shariah*-compliant equity and funds market to blossom. As an example, the Dow Jones Islamic Market indices cover more than USD 10 trillion market capitalization in over 40 countries. These developments have enhanced the attractiveness of Islamic financial markets as an asset class for investment (ADB and IFSB 2015).

In the following, we will briefly discuss the principles, characteristics, and the features of Islamic banking and finance in order to clarify the differences with conventional banking and finance practices.

The principles of Islamic financial systems

An Islamic economy is supposed to reflect the principles of Islamic worldview and morality. Islamic jurists and scholars extract *Shariah* laws and the values of an Islamic economic system from the Quran and performance of the Holy Prophet and Imams. The main *Shariah* rules with regard to banking and finance include the following (Moosavian 2007):

1   Money does not have any intrinsic value and is used merely as a medium of exchange and a tool for preserving and assessing the value of goods, services, and properties.

2   Emphasis should be on activities in the real economy and on the sharing of risks and rewards.
3   Socially destructive activities such as trading alcoholic drinks, betting, and gambling are prohibited.
4   *Riba* (interest) is prohibited.
5   *Gharar* (ambiguous and risky transactions) is prohibited.

Characteristics of an Islamic financial system

Prohibition of *riba* results in immediate disappearance of bonds and the debt market in an Islamic economic system. Most jurists believe that debt instruments such as bonds whose nominal value is guaranteed by the issuer are not tradable in an Islamic market even though interest may be absent. The main reason behind the prohibition of conventional debt and bond markets in Islam is the notion behind *ownership* in conventional bonds. Bonds are securities in form of debt; however, *Sukuk* indicates ownership of an asset (i.e., an infrastructural project). A *Sukuk* can increase in value when the assets increase in value, and also there is a possibility of a decrease in value; when you sell a *Sukuk*, you are selling ownership in the assets backing them, whereas the sale of bonds is the sale of debt.

Except participation contracts (see endnote and the next subsection for more information), the assets of an Islamic financial intermediary are connected to other assets.[3] This basket of assets has interesting features. First, it includes a vast range of maturities from short-term business finance to mid-term rent contracts. Second, these assets have low risks since their yields are directly related to pre-determined cash flows. Finally, pre-determined cash flows and fixed maturities make these securities suitable alternatives for conventional fixed-return bonds. Such securities will also be attractive in conventional financial systems. Recent developments in mortgage-based securities in conventional financial markets show that a dynamic and efficient market can develop on the basis of real assets. In essence, the debt market has been replaced by an asset-based security market in an Islamic financial system. This market assumes a vital role by providing liquidity for the financial system.

Financial derivatives construct the second important market. Muslim jurists have so far been of the opinion that conventional derivatives include the element of *gharar* and, therefore, are prohibited in *Shariah*. *Gharar* means the ambiguity and ignorance which prevails with regard to the price and delivery time of the assets which back derivatives such as forwards, futures, options, and swaps. However, some financial derivatives such as futures and options for subordinate sale of shares – which insure shares against price reductions – have gained permission from jurists to be traded in the Iranian capital market (TSE 2010, 2012).

In asset pricing, the representation of lender payoffs under put-call parity permits the identification and exact valuation of all constituent components of asset-based Islamic finance as balance sheet identities within the standard Black-Scholes-Merton framework of capital structure based option pricing theory (Black and Scholes 1973; Merton, 1973, 1974). Jobst (2007) shows how to derive the fair market price of Islamic lending transactions if the underlying collateral conforms to a lognormal asset process. In particular, Jobst (2007) characterizes the implicit interest rate of Islamic lending as a result of the premium payments (i.e., periodic rental payments) received by the lender in return for the call position on assets held by the borrower in Islamic finance.

The role of financial intermediation and the dependency of an Islamic financial system on Islamic banks is clear. It is also in line with the empirical evidence that highlights the role of financial intermediaries in less developed capital markets. In a nutshell, an Islamic financial system will be similar to a bank-based one for the following reasons:

1   Due to the prohibition of *riba* and debt papers, the debt-based capital market will be non-existent. Therefore, financial intermediation will take the form of direct financing via *mudarabah*[4] and participation contracts.
2   In the absence of a debt market, there will be demand for the development of asset-based security markets in order to increase the liquidity of bank assets. Financial intermediation can play a vital role in this development via introduction and accumulation of financial instruments through securitization and enhancement of credit during the life cycle of assets.
3   Since risk-shifting violates basic principles of *Shariah* law, derivatives, however, remain controversial in Islamic finance. In particular, derivatives trading is still not readily accepted by *Shariah* scholars due to its often speculative and unfunded nature (Jobst and Solé 2009). Unavailability or restriction of the derivative market will increase pressure on financial intermediaries to offer sharing and mitigation of risks.

Features of Islamic banks and Islamic banking contracts

The features of Islamic banking include:

1   The relationship between the bank and its customer is not the one between a debtor and a creditor; rather, it means sharing risks and rewards.
2   An Islamic bank keeps separate accounts for its own capital and deposits so as to avoid mixing of its own share of profits with those belonging to depositors and distribute proportionate according to the profit-and-loss-sharing agreement.
3   Unlike conventional banks, Islamic banks do not offer cash loans; rather, facilities are granted based on either Islamic contracts with uncertain return such as *musharakah* (participation), *mudarabah, muzaraah,*[5] and *musaghat*[6] or contracts with certain return such as *murabahah,*[7] sale on installments, and *ijarah.*[8] Deals in the real economy form the lion's share of Islamic banking activities, with the bank purchasing the merchandise for customers and selling it to them against cash or gradual payments with an agreed profit.
4   Islamic banks are multi-purpose institutions. They perform the roles of commercial, investment, and development banks. Based on its resources, an Islamic bank involves in short-term operations just as a commercial bank does, or participates in mid- and long-term investments just like development banks and non-bank financial institutions.
5   Islamic banks are supposed to contribute to the development of the whole society. Although making profit is important, it is not the main objective of finance in Islamic banking. An Islamic bank shall stress realization of socio-economic goals without any violation of *Shariah* law.
6   Islamic banking is based on shares. In order to mobilize funds, Islamic banks receive term deposits with uncertain interest rates and then, on behalf of depositors, consolidate these funds with their own resources to offer facilities to applicants based on contracts with either certain or uncertain profits. Eventually, the realized profits are shared in accordance with the agreement between the bank and depositors.
7   An Islamic banking system is supposed to comply with high moral values.
8   In addition to existing audits conducted in conventional banks, Islamic banks are usually being audited by an Islamic supervisory board so as to ensure their compliance with *Shariah* while absorbing funds and making investments; however, this may differ across countries.

Islamic banks are financial intermediaries that receive deposits and act like conventional banks in offering interest-free services including opening current accounts, issuing letters of credit, holding valuable objects, transfer of funds, issuing letters of guarantee, deposit boxes, and other services which are offered against payment of fees (Khan 2000).

Islamic bank contracts can be divided into two groups: (1) liabilities side contracts and (2) asset side contracts. Liability side contracts are divided into two subgroups: (1) *qarz* (zero interest loans) and (2) *wakala* (agency contracts). In the *Shariah* legal framework, a *qarz* is defined as a temporary transfer of ownership to the borrower and must not incur any interest burden stated by the terms of the contract. However, non-stipulated compensation of the lender is accepted and expected. In *wakala* contracts, the bank acts as an agent of the depositor against a certain fee. To avoid the principle-agent problem, capital is pooled with depositors' savings. It is important to mention that depositors in Islamic banks are like shareholders that are legally entitled to withdraw their money capital out of an account.

On the assets side, Islamic contracts are structured around the notion of profits and in reference to the financing of real assets. Islamic credit facilities are statutorily classified into two categories: participatory modes which are based on profit and loss sharing; and debt-creating modes which are based on fixed charges. The revenue of an Islamic bank is generally made up of "fees and commissions" and "trade income." No "interest income" is recognized in Islamic banking activities. Participatory mode contracts are:

1   *Musharaka* (sharing)
2   Civil partnership (involving a joint enterprise)
3   Legal partnership (buying equities)
4   *Mudaraba* (bank provides the capital and the other side provides labor)
5   *Muzaria* (bank provides the land and the farmer provides cultivation)
6   *Musaqat* (bank provides orchard and the farmer provides labor).

Participatory activities are "high-risk" ventures. While the loss is divided in accordance with the ratio of the capital invested.

Debt-creating modes belong to a "low-risk" category and normally create debt when applied by Islamic banks. Once debt is created through a lawful permitted transaction, there can be no stipulated increase in the amount of debt. However, it can be discounted at spot market rates. These contracts include:

1   *Murabaha* (a cost-plus sale with a spot or deferred payment)
2   Installment sale (a *murabaha* of goods on installment)
3   *Joa'la* (a *murabaha* of services with a deferred payment)
4   *Salam* (forward purchase)
5   *Istisna'a* (the order to manufacture)
6   Hire purchase (buying and leasing with the final transfer of the property to the lessee)
7   *Bay' al-Dayn* (sale and purchase of an outstanding debt)
8   *Qarz al-Hasan* (zero-interest loan).

Islamic banking and finance in Asia

Asia is an important part of the global economy as well as the Islamic financial system. Asia is the home to the largest Muslim population in the world. A majority of the population in many Asian countries are Muslim, including Pakistan (96.4%), Bangladesh (86.3%), Indonesia (87.2%), and Malaysia (61.4%). In some other Asian countries, the Muslim population is a minority, but still sizeable. In India, 14.2% of the population, or 172 million people, are Muslim.

Presently, the Islamic finance market in Asia is dominated by Islamic banking and *Sukuk*. According to IFSB (2015), the total size of Islamic finance sector in Asia amounted in 2014 to more than USD 419 billion or an estimated 22.4% of global Islamic financial assets, out of which 48.6% (USD 203.8 billion) is for Islamic banking assets, 44.93% (USD 188.4 billion) is for outstanding *Sukuk*, 5.5% (USD 23.2 billion) is for Islamic funds and 0.93% (USD 3.9 billion) for takaful (Islamic insurance) are small but growing.

In Asia, Islamic banking and finance have seen rapid growth and development. Table 28.1 shows a breakdown of Islamic finance segments by region and compares the size of Islamic banking assets in Asia with other parts of the world.

The size of Islamic banking assets and financial products in Asia is much larger when comparing to Europe and North America, largely spearheaded by the Malaysian Islamic finance marketplace. Malaysia is one of the global leaders for Islamic financial services and held an estimated 10.0% share of the global Islamic banking assets as at the end of 2013. Comparatively, Brunei Darussalam, Indonesia, and Pakistan have smaller shares, but their growth and regulatory developments in recent years have enabled them to expand their volume of *Shariah*-compliant banking assets. As at the end of 2013, Malaysia contributed 70.5% of the regional Islamic banking assets (USD 135.5 billion), followed by Indonesia (9.5%, USD 20.2 billion), and Pakistan (5.3%, USD 10.2 billion) (ADB and IFSB 2015).

Figure 28.1 shows share of global Islamic banking assets by country, which are including Asian countries.

Among majority-Muslim countries, numerous securities have been designed over the last two decades to finance governments, provide the required capital for manufacturing firms, and enforce monetary policies introduced by central banks. *Shariah*-compliant securities that usually receive their licenses from *Shariah* councils are recognized as *Sukuk*. The Malaysian Government Investment Issue as well as *ijarah* papers issued in Brunei Darussalam, Indonesia, and Pakistan are all among securities that lie in this category (Ghazavi and Bazmohammadi 2011). The first Brunei Darussalam government *Sukuk-Ijarah* was issued in 2006. In 2008, the Indonesian government started to raise funding using a *Shariah*-compliant *Sukuk-Ijarah* for the first time, which is called *Sukuk Negara*. In 2002, Malaysia achieved a further significant milestone

Table 28.1 Breakdown of Islamic financial segments by region (USD billion, 2014 YTD★)

Region	Banking Assets	Sukuk Outstanding	Islamic Funds AuM	Takaful Contributions
Asia	203.8	188.4	23.2	3.9
GCC	564.2	95.5	33.5	9.0
MENA (exc. GCC)	633.7	0.1	0.3	7.7
Sub-Saharan Africa	20.1	1.3	1.8	0.6
Others	54.4	9.4	17.0	0.3
Total	1476.2	294.7	75.8	21.4

AuM = assets under management, GCC = Gulf Cooperation Council, MENA = Middle East and North Africa.

★Data for banking and takaful as of 1H2014, while for *Sukuk* and funds as of 3Q2014.

Note: Takaful contributions are used as a basis to reflect the growth in the takaful industry. The breakdown of Islamic funds' AuM is by domicile of the funds.

Source: IFSB (2015).

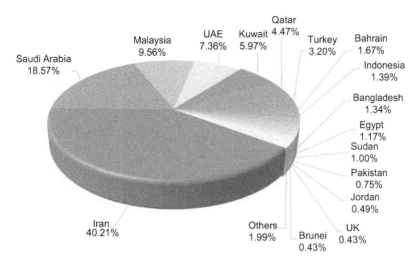

Figure 28.1　Share of global Islamic banking assets (2014)

UAE = United Arab Emirates, UK = United Kingdom.

Source: IFSB (2015).

when the Malaysian government issued the first global sovereign *Sukuk*, raising USD 600 million. With this issuance, it became an international benchmark for the issuance of global *Sukuk*. The *Sukuk* issue was listed on the Luxembourg Stock Exchange and the Labuan International Financial Stock Exchange in Malaysia. There have since been further sovereign issues in the global capital market (Aziz 2007).

Like Malaysia, several other Asian countries, including Bangladesh, Brunei Darussalam, Indonesia, and Pakistan, have both Islamic and conventional banking systems. Both approaches have contributed significantly to the deepening and widening of the financial sector through the use of innovative financial instruments that offer new ways of mobilizing resources for both public and corporate sectors.

As of 2013, 66% of the globally outstanding *Sukuk* were issued in Asia (ADB and IFSB 2015). Malaysia has maintained its dominance in *Sukuk* issuances over the years globally, and continues to be the leader in global *Sukuk* issuance. Malaysian new *Sukuk* issuances accounted for 68.8% of the global primary *Sukuk* market share as at the end of 2013 followed by Indonesia (4.68%), Pakistan (0.37%), and Brunei Darussalam (0.33%). Among other economies that have issued *Sukuk* in Asia are Singapore, Kazakhstan, and Hong Kong, China that are looking to diversify their funding options following liquidity constraints in international markets (Figure 28.2).

For instance, on 28 May 2015, the government of Hong Kong, China issued a USD 1 billion five-year *Sukuk* which was priced at a rate of 1.894%. This was the second *Sukuk* issued by the government, with the first taking place in September 2014. The government said that the *Sukuk* is based on the *wakala* structure, in which one-third of the assets are based on units in a Hong Kong, China building and the remainder are in *Shariah*-compliant commodities (ADB 2015). In 2012, the Development Bank of Kazakhstan issued a Malaysian ringgit (MYR)-denominated *Sukuk* program in Malaysia worth MYR 1.5 billion. This transaction represents the first-ever *Sukuk* issue out of the Commonwealth of Independent States (CIS). The transaction also represents the first issuer from the CIS region to tap the Malaysian market. The Kazakh parliament approved changes allowing the ministry of finance to issue its first sovereign

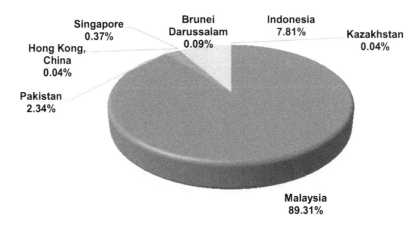

Figure 28.2 Sukuk outstanding in Asia (2013)

Note: Asia in above figure is limited to Asian members of the Asian Development Bank (ADB).

Source: ADB and IFSB (2015).

Sukuk amounting to USD 500 million to finance road construction in 2011. Kazakhstan stands as the second CIS major oil producer and requires significant investment for exploration activities and constructions of infrastructure projects (KFHR 2013).

As for the finance side, Islamic financial instruments such as *Sukuk* have been utilized to finance a wide range of social and physical infrastructure as well as corporate investments, and are becoming increasingly important for driving growth in the region. The growing market of Islamic finance in Asia could be an appropriate source for different sectors including (1) infrastructure financing, (2) government fiscal and revenue expenditure financing, (3) corporate and retail financing, (4) ethical investment solutions to corporate and retail investors, (5) trade financing for international trade, and (6) Islamic insurance services.

Challenges of the Islamic capital market

The development of secondary financial markets is vital for an expansion of primary markets. Savers have different preferences with regard to liquidity and risk of their portfolios. The faster and with fewer risks the savers can liquidate or transform their assets, the more likely they are to hold long-term securities. When Islamic banks are able to issue various securities with either certain or uncertain returns to finance real economic activities, investors will show a greater interest in Islamic financial products when security markets are sound and well developed.

Islamic bonds traded along with conventional papers such as stocks and options in financial markets help Islamic banks to diversify and distribute risk and manage the liquidity of portfolios. Moreover, as Islamic banks are necessarily involved in financing and investment in real economy, the existence of commodity markets may assist the transparency and reduction of costs for Islamic banks and may improve the efficiency of Islamic financing systems (Mirakhor 1992).

A pressing challenge is the lack of liquid and active secondary *Sukuk* markets in key Islamic finance domiciles, which limits investors' ability to trade *Sukuk* instruments. To date, in Asia only Malaysia and Iran have a fully functioning Islamic money market with an active secondary market that is very effective in addressing the domestic Islamic financial market's liquidity management issues (IFSB 2015).

Regulatory environment for Islamic banking and finance in Asia

An IMF survey on the legal, regulatory, and supervisory frameworks for Islamic banking and finance shows that some Asian countries like Kazakhstan use a single integrated regulatory framework applied to all banks with references identifying provisions applying only to Islamic banks. In some other Asian countries like Indonesia and Malaysia, there is existence of a mixed approach, that is, a similar regulatory framework is adopted for areas that are applicable to Islamic and conventional banks, but separate guidelines and regulations are issued for areas that are specific to Islamic banks (Kammer et al. 2015).

Specific *Shariah*-based standards have been developed by specialized standard-setting bodies in different Asian countries. Here we provide some of the regulatory frameworks from the selective Asian economies:

> The Islamic Financial Services Act 2013 (IFSA) is a Malaysian law which has been in effect since 30 June 2014. IFSA lays out the regulation and supervision of Islamic financial institutions, payment systems and other relevant entities and the oversight of the Islamic money market and Islamic foreign exchange market to promote financial stability and compliance with *Shariah* and for related consequential or incidental matters. In supporting the aspirations of the Act, Malaysia's central bank, Bank Negara Malaysia, is currently developing several standards for key Islamic contracts that set out the *Shariah* and operational requirements of a particular contract. Among other things, the Act also distinguishes investment accounts from Islamic deposits, and prohibits principal and profit guarantees on investment accounts.
>
> *(IFSB 2015)*

IFSA offers a new dimension to the regulatory framework for Islamic finance as it accords greater prominence to the *Shariah* contracts in Islamic finance transactions. The statutory foundation for a contract-based regulatory framework in IFSA has enabled the issuance of *Shariah* standards that define the underlying *Shariah* principles adopted by Islamic financial institutions and support the effective application of *Shariah* contracts in the offering of Islamic financial products and services. This represents a significant step forward in aligning legal and regulatory principles with *Shariah* precepts, and can serve as a useful benchmark for evolving more comprehensive regulatory frameworks globally that promote greater legal and operational certainty in Islamic finance. More importantly, the contract-based regulatory framework is developed in a manner that facilitates the next level of Islamic banking business, transcending financial intermediation to include real economic sector participation. Such a distinctive regulatory approach seeks to realize further the value proposition of Islamic finance as the industry advances toward a new level of maturity and sophistication (IFSB 2015).

In India, the world's second-most populated country, the Reserve Bank of India, the country's central bank, has begun a review of regulations on Islamic banking. The Reserve Bank of India has established an internal committee consisting of senior central bank officials amid calls for a re-evaluation of Islamic banking regulations in the country (ADB and IFSB 2015).

Hong Kong, China's Legislative Council passed the Loans (Amendments) Bill 2014 in March 2014 which enables the government to raise money through alternative bonds such as *Sukuk.* (ADB and IFSB 2015). The Philippines is expected to debut in the global takaful industry in the near future, as the Insurance Commission of the Philippines is formulating takaful regulations to enable takaful services in the country (IFSB 2015).

In January 2014, the State Bank of Pakistan (SBP) prepared a Strategic Plan for the Islamic Banking Industry of Pakistan 2014–2018. The plan focuses on initiatives necessary for improving public perception of Islamic banking and promoting it as a distinct and viable system to address the financial services need of the public in general and business community in particular. Acting to this plan, SBP in collaboration with stakeholders would keep its focus on the following key areas/objectives to facilitate and catalyze stable and distinct growth of Islamic banking in Pakistan: (1) Enabling Policy Environment; (2) *Shariah* Governance and Compliance; (3) Awareness and Capacity Building; and (4) Market Development. The functional strategies and action plan for achieving objectives in each area have been developed in consultation with the Islamic banking institutions and their *Shariah* advisors, SBP Shariah Board members, academics, internal SBP departments, the Securities and Exchange Commission of Pakistan and the Institute of Chartered Accountants of Pakistan. It is expected that with the implementation of this strategic plan, Pakistan's Islamic banking industry will grow prudently and distinctly with enhanced acceptance and confidence of the general masses contributing in the economic development of the country (SBP 2014).

Although the Islamic banking and finance regulatory framework is well developed in some Asian countries, regulatory and supervisory frameworks in many jurisdictions do not yet cater to the unique risks of the industry. Although Islamic banks appear well capitalized, there will be challenges with the implementation of the Basel III Accord. For example, further clarification will be needed from national regulators regarding the instruments that are eligible for treatment as additional Tier 1 and Tier 2 capital. Also, the scarcity of Shariah-compliant high-quality liquid assets will make it difficult for Islamic banks to satisfy the Basel III liquidity coverage ratio requirement. Therefore, it is important that national authorities use the leeway given by the Basel standards to grant highly rated and tradable *Sukuk* high-quality liquid assets status, and take steps to deepen local *Sukuk* and money markets. Safety nets and resolution frameworks remain underdeveloped. Very few countries with Islamic banking have a full-fledged Islamic deposit insurance scheme with premiums invested in *Shariah*-compliant.

Recent developments in issuance of the infrastructure Sukuk

An important and growing segment in Islamic finance in Asia has been the market for infrastructure *Sukuk*. Recent ADB (2017) estimates put the infrastructure financing needs of developing Asian economies at USD 26 trillion for the 25 years from 2016 to 2030, which equates to USD 1.7 trillion per year. In many less developed countries in Asia, lack of proper infrastructure is one of the major obstacles to development. The use of cross-border financing and investment through Islamic finance (i.e., Infra-*Sukuk*) can help to widen the investor base and lower the cost of financing for the development of infrastructure in Asia.

Sukuk have played an important role in infrastructure financing for public and private projects. USD 73.1 billion of infrastructure *Sukuk* have been issued by more than 10 different countries between 2002 and 3Q2015. The global infrastructure *Sukuk* market is dominated by issuances from Malaysia (61%), followed by Saudi Arabia (30%) and the United Arab Emirates (7%) (Figure 28.3). Malaysia's Economic Transformation Program will accelerate spending plans by issuance of Infra-*Sukuk* to meet its economic and socio-economic targets by 2020 (Nik-Musa 2015).

In the following, we briefly highlight two examples of *Sukuk* issued in Malaysia for financing infrastructure projects. The first example is the financing of the PLUS highway project, shown in Table 28.2, which was the single largest ringgit-denominated *Sukuk* issuance and also the single largest *Sukuk* issuance globally, in any currency (Nik-Musa 2015).

The second example, shown in Table 28.3, relates to the financing of a Malaysian Mass-Rapid Transit project through the first *Sukuk* with fixed income asset listed on Bursa Malaysia

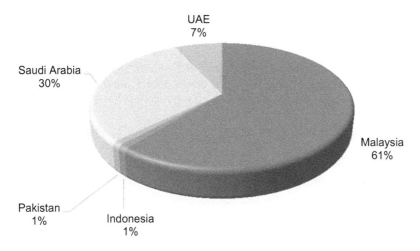

Figure 28.3   Infra-*Sukuk* issued by domicile of issuer (2012Q1–2015Q3)

UAE = United Arab Emirates.

Source: Nik-Musa (2015).

Table 28.2 Example 1: PLUS highway in Malaysia financed by Infra-*Sukuk*

Issuer	Projek Lebuhraya Utara-Selatan Berhad (PLUS)
Issue Size	MYR 30.4 billion
Sector	Transportation
Profit rate	3.9%–5.75%
Tenure	5–25 years
Structure	Musharaka
Governing Law	Laws of Malaysia
Purpose of Issuance	The proceeds of the issuance are to finance the construction of highways.

PLUS = Projek Lebuhraya Utara-Selatan Berhad, MYR = Malaysian ringgit.

Source: Zawya, IFIS, KFH Research.

Table 28.3 Example 2: mass-rapid transit project in Malaysia financed by exchange-traded bonds and *Sukuk*

Issuer	DanaInfra Nasional Berhad
Program Size	MYR 8 billion
Program Tenure	50 years
Issuance	Exchange-traded bonds and *Sukuk*
Issue Size	MYR 300 million
Issue tenure	10 years
Purpose of Issuance	To finance the capital expenditure and operating expenses for the MRT project

MRT = Mass-Rapid Transit, MYR = Malaysian ringgit.

Source: Nik-Musa (2015).

for retail investors. The debut issuance of the exchange-traded bonds and Sukuk was oversubscribed by 1.61 times (1,424 applications representing MYR 484 million in value). The public was able to purchase this *Sukuk* via application forms or the ATMs of participating banks. The landmark transaction was part of the initiatives under the Capital Market Masterplan 2 to facilitate greater retail participation in the bond and *Sukuk* market and intend to make available a wider range of investment products to retail segment (Nik-Musa 2015).

Outlook

The Islamic finance industry has grown substantially in Asia over the two last decades. The growth of Islamic banking and finance can be expected to continue underpinned by the following factors:

1   Muslim populations in different Asian countries, especially in Southeast Asia, are rising. Rapid Muslim population growth and improving living standards may enhance the popularity of Islamic finance as a keen alternative to conventional financing mechanisms. In addition, investors from the Middle East and Asia are increasingly seeking to invest in products that are in sync with their religious beliefs. Surveys suggest that half of the Muslims worldwide would opt for Islamic finance if given reliable alternative to conventional services (KFHR 2013).
2   The governments and financial authorities in several Asian countries have played active roles in promoting the development of Islamic financial markets in line with the efforts to boost investments and achieve sustainable funding to enhance economic growth by tapping huge liquidity from oil and commodity producing countries.
3   The ethical character and financial stability of Islamic financial products may increase its attraction. Islamic financial products have an ethical focus (notably excluding investment in alcohol and gambling) with a risk profile that appeals to wider ethically conscious investors. Islamic finance has been put forward as a viable alternative financial system (KFHR 2013).
4   Given that in Islamic banking returns on investments are based on underlying economic activities and/or assets on which the contractual relationship between transacting parties is structured, the asset-based nature and risk-sharing aspects of Islamic finance can be utilized for greater integration with the real economy and improve the overall economic balance between real and finance sectors.

Overall, the outlook for Islamic banking and finance in Asia is bright, given the region is home to more than 60% of the world's Muslim population, its strong economic and financial fundamentals as well as Asia's growing middle class. In addition, a combination of strong political support, large investor base and generous tax incentives are enticements to further Islamic finance in Asia.

Notes

1 The Holy Quran, Albagharah, verses 29–30.
2 Shariah, Islamic Shariah, or Islamic law is the religious legal system governing the members of the Islamic faith. It is derived from the religious precepts of Islam, particularly the Quran and the Hadith.
3 Islamic banks' asset sides contract divided into two groups: Participatory contracts which are based on profit and loss sharing. Debt-creating modes which are based on fixed charges.
4 A partnership contract between the capital provider (*Rabb-Al-Mal*) and an entrepreneur (*Muḍarib*) whereby the capital provider would contribute capital to an enterprise or activity that is to be managed

by the entrepreneur. Profits generated by that enterprise or activity are shared in accordance with the percentage specified in the contract, while losses are to be borne solely by the capital provider unless the losses are due to the entrepreneur's misconduct, negligence, or breach of contracted terms.

5 It is another Shariah-compliant contract based on which one party (*muzare*) delegates a piece of land to the other party (*zare*, or agent) to cultivate it and later, share the crops in agreed upon proportions. *muzaraah* is a financing instrument in agriculture and the bank always takes the role of a *muzare*. Therefore, a bank can enter a *muzaraah* contract only when it possesses the land or production factors or a combination of the two. A *muzaraah* contract terminates when the crops are divided and the bank takes its share.

6 It is a contract between the owner of an orchard and an agent who grows and harvests the products against a certain share. The bank is always the owner and can make an agreement with legal or real entities to work as the agent in their orchard. The agent takes the responsibility to grow, take care of, and harvest the products which will later be shared between the bank and the agent based on the *musaghat* contract.

7 It is similar to sale on installment contract, but with a wider range of applicability. Based on *murabahah*, the bank informs the applicant about the full price of properties and services and then adds a certain percentage as the profit. The applicant should make either bullet or balloon payments upon maturities. In accordance with the application, the banks may purchase raw materials, spare parts, tools, machinery, installations, land, and other goods or services required by firms or residence, durable goods and services for households. These items shall be transferred to the applicant via a *murabahah* contract. In order to ensure repayment, the banks are required to take sufficient collateral.

8 An agreement made by an institution offering Islamic financial services to lease to a customer an asset specified by the customer for an agreed period against specified rental. An *ijarah* contract commences with a promise to lease that is binding on the part of the potential lessee prior to entering the *ijarah* contract.

References

Asian Development Bank (ADB). 2015. *Asia Bond Monitor*, September 2015. Manila: Asian Development Bank.

ADB. 2017. *Meeting Asia's Infrastructure Needs*. Manila: Asian Development Bank.

ADB and IFSB. 2015. *Islamic Finance for Asia: Development, Prospects, and Inclusive Growth*. Manila: Asian Development Bank.

Aziz, Z. A. 2007. The Challenge for a Global Islamic Capital Market: Strategic Developments in Malaysia. Keynote Address at the Sukuk Summit 2007, London, 20 June.

Black, F., and M. Scholes 1973. The Pricing of Options and Corporate Liabilities. *Journal of Political Economy* 813: 637–654.

Ghazavi, H., and H. Bazmohammadi. 2011. *Open Market Operation in the Framework of Riba-Free Banking, Case Study of Islamic Treasury Bonds in Farsi*. Tehran: Central Bank of Iran.

Iqbal, Z., and A. Mirakhor. 2007. *An Introduction to Islamic Finance: Theory and Practice*. Hoboken, NJ: John Wiley & Sons.

Islamic Financial Services Act (IFSA). 2013. *Islamic Financial Services Act 2013. Laws of Malaysia Act 759*. Kuala Lumpur: Bank Negara Malaysia.

Islamic Financial Services Board (IFSB). 2015. *Islamic Financial Services Industry Stability Report 2015*. Kuala Lumpur: Islamic Financial Services Board.

Jobst, A. A. 2007. The Economics of Islamic Finance and Securitization. IMF Working Paper WP/07/117. Washington, DC: International Monetary Fund.

Jobst, A. A., and J. Solé. 2009. The Governance of Derivatives in Islamic Finance. *Journal of International Banking Law and Regulation* 241: 556–564.

Kammer, A., M. Norat, M. Piñón, A. Prasad, C. Towe, Z. Zeidane, and an IMF Staff Team 2015. Islamic Finance: Opportunities, Challenges, and Policy Options. IMF Staff Discussion Note No. 15/05. Washington, DC: International Monetary Fund.

Khan, Z. A. 2000. *Islamic Banking and its Operations*. London: Institute of Islamic Banking and Insurance.

Kettell, B. 2010. *Frequently Asked Questions in Islamic Finance*. West Sussex: Wiley.

Kuwait Finance House Research. 2013. *Islamic Finance in Asia: Development, Growth and Opportunities*. Kuala Lumpur: Kuwait Finance House Research Ltd.

Merton, R. 1973. Theory of Rational Option Pricing. *Bell Journal of Economics and Management Science* 4: 141–183.

Merton, R. 1974. On the Pricing of Corporate Debt; the Risk Structure of Interest Rates. *Journal of Finance* 29: 449–470.

Mirakhor, A. 1992. The Theory of Islamic Finance. In *Articles about Islamic Economics*, edited by A. Mirakhor and H. Bagheralhasani, translated by H. Golriz. Tehran: Iran Banking Institute.

Moosavian, S. A. 2007. *Islamic Banking* (in Farsi). Tehran: Monetary and Banking Research Institute.

Nik-Musa, N.M.D. 2015. *Role of Islamic Finance in Infrastructure Financing: Financing Sources for Public-Private Partnerships (PPP) Sub-Regional Expert Group Meeting (EGM) for South-East Asian Countries.* Kuala Lumpur: Bank Negara Malaysia.

State Bank of Pakistan (SPB). 2014. *Strategic Plan Islamic Banking Industry of Pakistan 2014–2018.* Karachi: State Bank of Pakistan.

Tehran Stock Exchange (TSE). 2010. *Guideline for Future Trading in the Stock Market* (in Farsi). Tehran: Tehran Stock Exchange Organization.

TSE. 2012. *Guideline for Options for Subordinate Sale of Shares of Listed Companies in the Stock Market* (in Farsi). Tehran: Tehran Stock Exchange Organization.

INDEX

Note: Page numbers in italics indicate figures, and page numbers in bold indicate tables on the corresponding page.

For Product Safety Concerns and Information please contact our EU
representative GPSR@taylorandfrancis.com
Taylor & Francis Verlag GmbH, Kaufingerstraße 24, 80331 München, Germany